Herb Schildt's Java
Programming Cookbook

About the Author

Herbert Schildt is a leading authority on Java, C, C++, and C#, and is a master Windows programmer. His programming books have sold more than 3.5 million copies worldwide and have been translated into all major foreign languages. He is the author of numerous bestsellers on Java, including *Java: The Complete Reference, Java: A Beginner's Guide, Swing: A Beginner's Guide,* and *The Art of Java* (co-authored with James Holmes). His other bestsellers include *C: The Complete Reference, C++: The Complete Reference,* and *C#: The Complete Reference.* Schildt holds both graduate and undergraduate degrees from the University of Illinois. He can be reached at his consulting office at (217) 586-4683. His web site is **www.HerbSchildt.com**.

Herb Schildt's Java Programming Cookbook

Herb Schildt

New York   Chicago   San Francisco
Lisbon   London   Madrid   Mexico City
Milan   New Delhi   San Juan
Seoul   Singapore   Sydney   Toronto

The **McGraw·Hill** Companies

Cataloging-in-Publication Data is on file with the Library of Congress

McGraw-Hill books are available at special quantity discounts to use as premiums and sales promotions, or for use in corporate training programs. For more information, please write to the Director of Special Sales, Professional Publishing, McGraw-Hill, Two Penn Plaza, New York, NY 10121-2298. Or contact your local bookstore.

Herb Schildt's Java Programming Cookbook

1234567890 FGR FGR 01987

ISBN: 978-0-07-226315-2
MHID: 0-07-226315-6

Sponsoring Editor	**Technical Editor**	**Production Supervisor**
Wendy Rinaldi	Hale Pringle	Jim Kussow
Editorial Supervisor	**Copy Editor**	**Composition**
Patty Mon	Robert Campbell	International Typesetting and Composition
Project Management	**Proofreading**	
Sam RC, International Typesetting and Composition	Megha RC	**Illustration** International Typesetting and Composition
	Indexer	
	Sheryl Schildt	
Acquisitions Coordinator		**Art Director, Cover**
Mandy Canales		Jeff Weeks

Contents

Preface   xix

1 **Overview**   1
   What's Inside   1
   How the Recipes Are Organized   2
   A Few Words of Caution   3
   Java Experience Required   3
   What Version of Java?   4

2 **Working with Strings and Regular Expressions**   5
   An Overview of Java's String Classes   6
   Java's Regular Expression API   8
   An Introduction to Regular Expressions   8
      Normal Characters   9
      Character Classes   9
      The Wildcard Character   10
      Quantifiers   10
      Greedy, Reluctant, and Possessive Quantifiers   11
      Boundary Matchers   11
      The OR Operator   11
      Groups   12
      Flag Sequences   13
      Remember to Escape the \ in Java Strings   13
   Sort an Array of Strings in Reverse Order   14
      Step-by-Step   14
      Discussion   14
      Example   16
      Options and Alternatives   17
   Ignore Case Differences when Sorting an Array of Strings   18
      Step-by-Step   18
      Discussion   19
      Example   19
      Options and Alternatives   21
   Ignore Case Differences when Searching for or Replacing Substrings   22
      Step-by-Step   22
      Discussion   22
      Example   23
      Options and Alternatives   24
   Split a String into Pieces by Using split( )   25
      Step-by-Step   25

v

Discussion 26
Example 26
Options and Alternatives 28
Retrieve Key/Value Pairs from a String 28
Step-by-Step 29
Discussion 29
Example 29
Options and Alternatives 32
Match and Extract Substrings Using the Regular Expression API 32
Step-by-Step 33
Discussion 33
Example 33
Options and Alternatives 34
Tokenize a String Using the Regular Expression API 35
Step-by-Step 36
Discussion 37
Example 38
Bonus Example 40
Options and Alternatives 47

3   File Handling **49**
An Overview of File Handling 50
Streams 50
The RandomAccessFile Class 53
The File Class 54
The I/O Interfaces 55
The Compressed File Streams 57
Tips for Handling Errors 57
Read Bytes from a File 59
Step-by-Step 59
Discussion 59
Example 60
Options and Alternatives 61
Write Bytes to a File 62
Step-by-Step 63
Discussion 63
Example 63
Options and Alternatives 64
Buffer Byte-Based File I/O 65
Step-by-Step 66
Discussion 66
Example 66
Options and Alternatives 68
Read Characters from a File 69
Step-by-Step 69

Discussion 69
Example 70
Options and Alternatives 71
Write Characters to a File 72
Step-by-Step 72
Discussion 73
Example 73
Options and Alternatives 74
Buffer Character-Based File I/O 75
Step-by-Step 76
Discussion 76
Example 77
Options and Alternatives 79
Read and Write Random-Access Files 80
Step-by-Step 80
Discussion 80
Example 81
Options and Alternatives 83
Obtain File Attributes 83
Step-by-Step 84
Discussion 84
Example 84
Options and Alternatives 86
Set File Attributes 86
Step-by-Step 87
Discussion 87
Example 87
Options and Alternatives 89
List a Directory 90
Step-by-Step 90
Discussion 90
Example 91
Bonus Example 93
Options and Alternatives 94
Compress and Decompress Data 95
Step-by-Step 95
Discussion 96
Example 96
Options and Alternatives 99
Create a ZIP File 100
Step-by-Step 100
Discussion 101
Example 102
Options and Alternatives 105

Decompress a ZIP File 105
    Step-by-Step 105
    Discussion 106
    Example 107
    Options and Alternatives 109
Serialize Objects 110
    Step-by-Step 111
    Discussion 111
    Example 112
    Options and Alternatives 115

4 Formatting Data **117**
An Overview of Formatter 118
    Formatting Basics 119
    Specifying a Minimum Field Width 121
    Specifying Precision 121
    Using the Format Flags 122
    The Uppercase Option 122
    Using an Argument Index 123
Overview of NumberFormat and DateFormat 123
Four Simple Numeric Formatting Techniques Using Formatter 124
    Step-by-Step 124
    Discussion 124
    Example 125
    Options and Alternatives 126
Vertically Align Numeric Data Using Formatter 126
    Step-by-Step 126
    Discussion 127
    Example 127
    Bonus Example: Center Data 128
    Options and Alternatives 131
Left-Justify Output Using Formatter 131
    Step-by-Step 131
    Discussion 131
    Example 132
    Options and Alternatives 133
Format Time and Date Using Formatter 133
    Step-by-Step 134
    Discussion 134
    Example 136
    Options and Alternatives 137
Specify a Locale with Formatter 138
    Step-by-Step 138
    Discussion 138
    Example 139
    Options and Alternatives 140

Use Streams with Formatter 140
    Step-by-Step 140
    Discussion 140
    Example 141
    Options and Alternatives 142
Use printf( ) to Display Formatted Data 143
    Step-by-Step 143
    Discussion 143
    Example 144
    Bonus Example 145
    Options and Alternatives 146
Format Time and Date with DateFormat 147
    Step-by-Step 147
    Discussion 148
    Example 148
    Options and Alternatives 149
Format Time and Date with Patterns Using SimpleDateFormat 150
    Step-by-Step 151
    Discussion 151
    Example 152
    Options and Alternatives 153
Format Numeric Values with NumberFormat 153
    Step-by-Step 154
    Discussion 154
    Example 155
    Options and Alternatives 156
Format Currency Values Using NumberFormat 156
    Step-by-Step 157
    Discussion 157
    Example 157
    Options and Alternatives 157
Format Numeric Values with Patterns Using DecimalFormat 158
    Step-by-Step 158
    Discussion 158
    Example 159
    Options and Alternatives 160

5 **Working with Collections** **161**
Collections Overview 162
    Three Recent Changes 163
    The Collection Interfaces 164
    The Collection Classes 173
    The ArrayList Class 173
    The LinkedList Class 174
    The HashSet Class 175
    The LinkedHashSet Class 175

The TreeSet Class 176
The PriorityQueue Class 176
The ArrayDeque Class 177
The EnumSet Class 178
An Overview of Maps 178
The Map Interfaces 178
The Map Classes 183
Algorithms 185
Basic Collection Techniques 186
Step-by-Step 187
Discussion 187
Example 188
Options and Alternatives 190
Work with Lists 191
Step-by-Step 191
Discussion 192
Example 192
Options and Alternatives 195
Work with Sets 195
Step-by-Step 196
Discussion 196
Example 197
Bonus Example 198
Options and Alternatives 201
Use Comparable to Store Objects in a Sorted Collection 201
Step-by-Step 202
Discussion 202
Example 203
Options and Alternatives 204
Use a Comparator with a Collection 205
Step-by-Step 205
Discussion 205
Example 206
Options and Alternatives 209
Iterate a Collection 209
Step-by-Step 210
Discussion 210
Example 211
Options and Alternatives 213
Create a Queue or a Stack Using Deque 214
Step-by-Step 214
Discussion 215
Example 216
Options and Alternatives 217

Reverse, Rotate, and Shuffle a List 218
    Step-by-Step 219
    Discussion 219
    Example 219
    Options and Alternatives 220
Sort and Search a List 221
    Step-by-Step 221
    Discussion 221
    Example 222
    Options and Alternatives 223
Create a Checked Collection 224
    Step-by-Step 224
    Discussion 224
    Example 225
    Options and Alternatives 227
Create a Synchronized Collection 227
    Step-by-Step 228
    Discussion 228
    Example 228
    Options and Alternatives 231
Create an Immutable Collection 231
    Step-by-Step 231
    Discussion 232
    Example 232
    Options and Alternatives 233
Basic Map Techniques 233
    Step-by-Step 234
    Discussion 235
    Example 235
    Options and Alternatives 238
Convert a Properties List into a HashMap 238
    Step-by-Step 239
    Discussion 239
    Example 239
    Options and Alternatives 240

6 Applets and Servlets **241**
Applet Overview 241
    The Applet Class 242
    Applet Architecture 244
    The Applet Life Cycle 245
    The AppletContext, AudioClip, and AppletStub Interfaces 246
Servlet Overview 246
    The javax.servlet Package 246
    The javax.servlet.http Package 249

The HttpServlet Class 251
The Cookie Class 251
The Servlet Life Cycle 253
Using Tomcat for Servlet Development 254
Create an AWT-Based Applet Skeleton 255
Step-by-Step 256
Discussion 256
Example 256
Options and Alternatives 257
Create a Swing-Based Applet Skeleton 257
Step-by-Step 258
Discussion 258
Example 259
Options and Alternatives 260
Create a GUI and Handle Events in a Swing Applet 260
Step-by-Step 261
Discussion 261
Historical Note: getContentPane( ) 263
Example 263
Bonus Example 266
Options and Alternatives 268
Paint Directly to the Surface of an Applet 269
Step-by-Step 269
Discussion 270
Example 271
Options and Alternatives 273
Pass Parameters to Applets 275
Step-by-Step 275
Discussion 275
Example 276
Options and Alternatives 277
Use AppletContext to Display a Web Page 278
Step-by-Step 278
Discussion 278
Example 278
Options and Alternatives 281
Create a Simple Servlet Using GenericServlet 282
Step-by-Step 282
Discussion 282
Example 283
Options and Alternatives 284
Handle HTTP Requests in a Servlet 285
Step-by-Step 285
Discussion 285
Example 286

Bonus Example 287
Options and Alternatives 290
Use a Cookie with a Servlet 290
Step-by-Step 290
Discussion 290
Example 291
Options and Alternatives 293

7   Multithreading **295**
Multithreading Fundamentals 296
The Runnable Interface 297
The Thread Class 298
Create a Thread by Implementing Runnable 299
Step-by-Step 300
Discussion 300
Example 300
Options and Alternatives 303
Create a Thread by Extending Thread 304
Step-by-Step 305
Discussion 305
Example 305
Options and Alternatives 306
Use a Thread's Name and ID 307
Step-by-Step 307
Discussion 308
Example 308
Options and Alternatives 310
Wait for a Thread to End 311
Step-by-Step 311
Discussion 311
Example 312
Options and Alternatives 313
Synchronize Threads 314
Step-by-Step 315
Discussion 315
Example 316
Options and Alternatives 318
Communicate Between Threads 318
Step-by-Step 319
Discussion 319
Example 320
Options and Alternatives 322
Suspend, Resume, and Stop a Thread 323
Step-by-Step 323
Discussion 324

        Example   325
        Options and Alternatives   327
    Use a Daemon Thread   328
        Step-by-Step   329
        Discussion   329
        Example   329
        Bonus Example: A Simple Reminder Class   331
        Options and Alternatives   336
    Interrupt a Thread   336
        Step-by-Step   337
        Discussion   337
        Example   337
        Options and Alternatives   339
    Set and Obtain a Thread's Priority   341
        Step-by-Step   341
        Discussion   342
        Example   342
        Options and Alternatives   344
    Monitor a Thread's State   344
        Step-by-Step   345
        Discussion   345
        Example   346
        Bonus Example: A Real-Time Thread Monitor   349
        Options and Alternatives   353
    Use a Thread Group   353
        Step-by-Step   354
        Discussion   354
        Example   355
        Options and Alternatives   357

8   Swing **359**
    Overview of Swing   360
    Components and Containers   361
        Components   362
        Containers   362
        The Top-Level Container Panes   363
    Layout Manager Overview   363
    Event Handling   364
        Events   365
        Event Sources   365
        Event Listeners   365
    Create a Simple Swing Application   366
        Step-by-Step   366
        Discussion   367
        Historical Note: getContentPane( )   369

Example 369
Options and Alternatives 371
Set the Content Pane's Layout Manager 372
Step-by-Step 372
Discussion 372
Example 373
Options and Alternatives 375
Work with JLabel 376
Step-by-Step 376
Discussion 377
Example 379
Options and Alternatives 382
Create a Simple Push Button 383
Step-by-Step 384
Discussion 384
Example 385
Options and Alternatives 387
Use Icons, HTML, and Mnemonics with JButton 390
Step-by-Step 391
Discussion 391
Example 393
Options and Alternatives 395
Create a Toggle Button 396
Step-by-Step 397
Discussion 397
Example 398
Options and Alternatives 400
Create Check Boxes 400
Step-by-Step 401
Discussion 401
Example 401
Options and Alternatives 405
Create Radio Buttons 405
Step-by-Step 406
Discussion 406
Example 407
Options and Alternatives 410
Input Text with JTextField 411
Step-by-Step 411
Discussion 412
Example 413
Bonus Example: Cut, Copy, and Paste 416
Options and Alternatives 419
Work with JList 420
Step-by-Step 420

Discussion 420
Example 422
Options and Alternatives 424
Use a Scroll Bar 426
Step-by-Step 427
Discussion 427
Example 429
Options and Alternatives 431
Use JScrollPane to Handle Scrolling 433
Step-by-Step 433
Discussion 433
Example 433
Options and Alternatives 436
Display Data in a JTable 438
Step-by-Step 439
Discussion 440
Example 441
Options and Alternatives 444
Handle JTable Events 446
Step-by-Step 447
Discussion 447
Example 450
Options and Alternatives 455
Display Data in a JTree 456
Step-by-Step 458
Discussion 458
Example 461
Options and Alternatives 464
Create a Main Menu 466
Step-by-Step 467
Discussion 467
Example 469
Options and Alternatives 471

9 Potpourri 473
Access a Resource via an HTTP Connection 474
Step-by-Step 474
Discussion 475
Example 476
Options and Alternatives 479
Use a Semaphore 480
Step-by-Step 481
Discussion 482
Example 482
Options and Alternatives 485

Return a Value from a Thread 486

Step-by-Step 487

Discussion 487

Example 488

Options and Alternatives 491

Use Reflection to Obtain Information about a Class at Runtime 491

Step-by-Step 492

Discussion 492

Example 493

Bonus Example: A Reflection Utility 494

Options and Alternatives 496

Use Reflection to Dynamically Create an Object and Call Methods 496

Step-by-Step 497

Discussion 497

Example 498

Options and Alternatives 501

Create a Custom Exception Class 501

Step-by-Step 502

Discussion 502

Example 504

Options and Alternatives 505

Schedule a Task for Future Execution 506

Step-by-Step 507

Discussion 507

Example 508

Options and Alternatives 510

Index **511**

Preface

For many years, friends and readers have asked me to write a cookbook for Java, sharing some of the techniques and approaches that I use when I program. From the start I liked the idea, but was unable to make time for it in my very busy writing schedule. As many readers know, I write extensively about many facets of programming, with a special focus on Java, C/C++, and C#. Because of the rapid revision cycles of those languages, I spend nearly all of my available time updating my books to cover the latest versions of those languages. Fortunately, early in 2007 a window of opportunity opened and I was finally able to devote time to writing this Java cookbook. I must admit that it quickly became one of my most enjoyable projects.

Based on the format of a traditional food cookbook, this book distills the essence of many general-purpose techniques into a set of step-by-step *recipes*. Each recipe describes a set of key ingredients, such as classes, interfaces, and methods. It then shows the steps needed to assemble those ingredients into a code sequence that achieves the desired result. This organization makes it easy to find the technique in which you are interested and then put that technique *into action*.

Actually, "into action" is an important part of this book. I believe that good programming books contain two elements: solid theory and practical application. In the recipes, the step-by-step instructions and discussions supply the theory. To put that theory into practice, each recipe includes a complete code example. The examples demonstrate in a concrete, unambiguous way how the recipes can be applied. In other words, the examples eliminate the "guesswork" and save you time.

Although no cookbook can include every recipe that one might desire (there is a nearly unbounded number of possible recipes), I tried to span a wide range of topics. My criteria for including a recipe are discussed in detail in Chapter 1, but briefly, I included recipes that would be useful to many programmers and that answered frequently asked questions. Even with these criteria, it was difficult to decide what to include and what to leave out. This was the most challenging part of writing this book. Ultimately, it came down to experience, judgment, and intuition. Hopefully, I have included something to satisfy every programmer's taste!

HS

Example Code on the Web

The source code for all of the examples in this book is available free of charge on the Web at **www.osborne.com.**

More from Herbert Schildt

Herb Schildt's Java Programming Cookbook is just one of Herb's many programming books. Here are some others that you will find of interest.

To learn more about Java, we recommend

Java: The Complete Reference

Java: A Beginner's Guide

The Art of Java

Swing: A Beginner's Guide

To learn about C++, you will find these books especially helpful.

C++: The Complete Reference

C++: A Beginner's Guide

C++ From the Ground Up

STL Programming From the Ground Up

The Art of C++

To learn about C#, we suggest the following Schildt books:

C#: The Complete Reference

C#: A Beginner's Guide

If you want to learn about the C language, then the following title will be of interest.

C: The Complete Reference

When you need solid answers, fast, turn to Herbert Schildt, the recognized authority on programming.

CHAPTER

Overview

This book is a collection of techniques that show how to perform various programming tasks in Java. As the title implies, it uses the well-known "cookbook" format. Each "recipe" illustrates how to accomplish a specific operation. For example, there are recipes that read bytes from a file, iterate a collection, format numeric data, construct Swing components, create a servlet, and so on. In the same way that a recipe in a food cookbook describes a set of ingredients and a sequence of instructions necessary to prepare a dish, each technique in this book describes a set of key program elements and the sequence of steps necessary to use them to accomplish a programming task.

Ultimately, the goal of this book is to save you time and effort during program development. Many programming tasks consist of a set of API classes, interfaces, and methods that must be applied in a specific sequence. The trouble is that sometimes you don't know which API classes to use or in what order to call the methods. Instead of having to wade through reams of API documentation and online tutorials to determine how to approach some task, you can look up its recipe. Each recipe shows one way to craft a solution, describing the necessary elements and the order in which they must be used. With this information, you can design a solution that fits your specific need.

What's Inside

No cookbook is exhaustive. The author of a cookbook must make choices about what is and isn't included. The same is true for this cookbook. In choosing the recipes for this book, I focused on the following categories:

- String processing (including regular expressions)
- File handling
- Formatting data
- Applets and servlets
- Swing
- The Collections Framework
- Multithreading

1

I chose these categories because they relate to a wide range of programmers. (I purposely avoided specialized topics that apply to only a narrow subset of cases.) Each of the categories became the basis for a chapter. In addition to the recipes related to the foregoing topics, I had several others that I wanted to include but for which an entire chapter was not feasible. I grouped those recipes into the final chapter.

Of course, choosing the topics was only the beginning of the selection process. Within each category, I had to decide what to include and what not to include. In general, I included a recipe if it met the following two criteria.

1. The technique is useful to a wide range of programmers.

2. It provides an answer to a frequently asked programming question.

The first criterion is largely self-explanatory and is based on my experience. I included recipes that describe how to accomplish a set of tasks that would commonly be encountered when creating Java applications. Some of the recipes illustrate a general concept that can be adapted to solve several different types of problems. For example, Chapter 2 shows a recipe that uses the Regular Expression API to search for and extract substrings from a string. This general procedure is useful in several contexts, such as finding an e-mail address or a telephone number within a sentence, or extracting a keyword from a database query. Other recipes describe more specific, yet widely used techniques. For example, Chapter 4 shows how to format the time and date by using **SimpleDateFormat**.

The second criterion is based on my experience as the author of programming books. Over the many years that I have been writing, I have been asked hundreds and hundreds of "how to" questions by readers. These questions come from all areas of Java programming and range from the very easy to the quite difficult. I have found, however, that a central core of questions occurs again and again. Here is one example: "How do I format output?" Here is another: "How do I compress a file?" There are many others. These same types of questions also occur frequently on various programmer forums on the Web. I used these commonly asked "how to" questions to guide my selection of recipes.

The recipes in this book span various skill levels. Some illustrate basic techniques, such as reading bytes from a file or creating a Swing **JTable**. Others are more advanced, such as creating a servlet or using reflection to instantiate an object at runtime. Thus, the level of difficulty of an individual recipe can range from relatively easy to significantly advanced. Of course, most things in programming are easy once you know how to do them, but difficult when you don't. Therefore, don't be surprised if some recipe seems obvious. It just means that you already know how to accomplish that task.

How the Recipes Are Organized

Each recipe in this book follows the same format, which has the following parts:

- A description of the problem that the recipe solves.
- A table of key ingredients used by the recipe.
- The steps necessary to complete the recipe.
- An in-depth discussion of the steps.
- A code example that puts the recipe into action.
- Options and alternatives that suggest other ways to craft a solution.

A recipe begins by describing the task to accomplish. The key ingredients used by the recipe are shown in a table. These include the API classes, interfaces, and methods required to create a solution. Of course, putting a recipe into practice may imply the use of additional elements, but the key ingredients are those that are fundamental to the task at hand.

Each recipe then presents step-by-step instructions that summarize the procedure. These are followed by an in-depth discussion of the steps. In many cases the summary will be sufficient, but the details are there if you need them.

Next, a code example is presented that shows the recipe in action. All code examples are presented in their entirety. This avoids ambiguity and lets you clearly see precisely what is happening without having to fill in additional details yourself. Occasionally, a bonus example is included that further illustrates how a recipe can be applied.

Each recipe concludes with a discussion of various options and alternatives. This section is especially important because it suggests different ways to implement a solution or other ways to think about the problem.

A Few Words of Caution

There are a few important points that you should keep in mind when you use this book. First, a recipe shows *one way* to craft a solution. Other ways may (and often do) exist. Your specific application may require an approach that is different from the one shown. The recipes in this book can serve as starting points, they can help you choose a general approach to a solution, and they can spur your imagination. However, in all cases, you must determine what is and what isn't appropriate for your application.

Second, it is important to understand that the code examples are *not* optimized for performance. They are optimized for *clarity and ease of understanding.* Their purpose is to clearly illustrate the steps of recipe. In many cases you will have little trouble writing tighter, more efficient code. Furthermore, the examples are exactly that: examples. They are simple uses that do not necessarily reflect the way that you will write code for your own application. In all circumstances, you must create your own solution that fits the needs of your application.

Third, each code example contains error handling that is appropriate for that specific example, but may not be appropriate in other situations. In all cases, you must properly handle the various errors and exceptions that can result when adapting a recipe for use in your own code. Let me state this important point again: when implementing a solution, you must provide error handling appropriate to your application. You cannot simply assume that the way that errors or exceptions are handled (or not handled) by an example is sufficient or adequate for your use. Typically, additional error handling will be required in real-world applications.

Java Experience Required

This book is for every Java programmer, whether beginner or experienced pro. However, it does assume that you know the fundamentals of Java programming, including Java's keywords, syntax, and basic API classes. You should also be able to create, compile, and run Java programs. None of these things are taught by this book. (As explained, this book is about applying Java to a variety of real-world programming problems. It is not about teaching the fundamentals of the Java language.) If you need to improve your Java skills, I recommend my books *Java: The Complete Reference* and *Java: A Beginner's Guide.* Both are published by McGraw-Hill, Inc.

What Version of Java?

As most readers know, Java has been in a state of constant evolution since its creation. With each new release, features are added. In many cases a new release will also deprecate (render obsolete) several older features. As a result, not all modern Java code can be compiled by an older Java compiler. This is important because the code in this book is based on Java SE 6, which (at the time of this writing) is the current version of Java. The developer's kit for Java SE 6 is JDK 6. This is also the JDK used to test all of the code examples.

As you may know, beginning with JDK 5, several important new features were added to Java. These include generics, enumerations, and autoboxing. Some of the techniques in this book employ these features. If you are using a version of Java prior to JDK 5, then you will not be able to compile the examples that use these newer features. Therefore, it is strongly recommended that you use a modern version of Java.

CHAPTER 2

Working with Strings and Regular Expressions

One of the most common programming tasks is string handling. Nearly all programs deal with strings in one form or another because they are often the conduit through which we humans interact with digital information. Because of the important part that string handling plays, Java provides extensive support for it.

As all Java programmers know, the primary string class is **String**. It supplies a wide array of string handling methods. Many of these methods provide the basic string operations with which most Java programmers are quite familiar. These include methods that compare two strings, search one string for an occurrence of another, and so on. However, **String** also contains a number of less well-known methods that offer a substantial increase in power because they operate on *regular expressions*. A regular expression defines a general pattern, not a specific character sequence. This pattern can then be used to search a string for substrings that match the pattern. This is a powerful concept that is revolutionizing the way that Java programmers think about string handling.

Java began providing support for regular expressions in version 1.4. Regular expressions are supported by the regular expression API, which is packaged in **java.util.regex**. As just explained, regular expressions are also supported by several methods in **String**. With the addition of regular expressions, several otherwise difficult string handling chores are made easy.

This chapter contains recipes that illustrate various string handling techniques that go beyond the basic search, compare, and replace operations found in **String**. Several also make use of regular expressions. In some cases, the regular expression capabilities of **String** are employed. Others use the regular expression API itself.

Here are the recipes contained in this chapter:

- Sort an Array of Strings in Reverse Order
- Ignore Case Differences When Sorting an Array of Strings
- Ignore Case Differences When Searching for or Replacing Substrings
- Split a String into Pieces by Using **split( )**
- Retrieve Key/Value Pairs from a String

- Match and Extract Substrings Using the Regular Expression API
- Tokenize a String Using the Regular Expression API

An Overview of Java's String Classes

A string is a sequence of characters. Unlike some other programming languages, Java does not implement strings as arrays of characters. Rather, it implements strings as objects. This enables Java to define a rich assortment of methods that act on strings. Although strings are familiar territory to most Java programmers, it is still useful to review their key attributes and capabilities.

Most strings that you will use in a program are objects of type **String**. **String** is part of **java.lang**. Therefore, it is automatically available to all Java programs. One of the most interesting aspects of **String** is that it creates *immutable strings*. This means that once a **String** is created, its contents cannot be altered. While this may seem like a serious restriction, it is not. If you need to change a string, you simply create a new one that contains the modification. The original string remains unchanged. If the original string is no longer needed, discard it. The unused string will be recycled the next time the garbage collector runs. By using immutable strings, **String** can be implemented more efficiently than it could be if it used modifiable ones.

Strings can be created in a variety of ways. You can explicitly construct a string by using one of **String**'s constructors. For example, there are constructors that create a **String** instance from a character array, a byte array, or another string. However, the easiest way to make a string is to use a string literal, which is a quoted string. All string literals are automatically objects of type **String**. Thus, a string literal can be assigned to a **String** reference, as shown here:

```
String str = "Test";
```

This line creates a **String** object that contains the word "Test" and then assigns to **str** a reference to that object.

String supports only one operator: **+**. It concatenates two strings. For example,

```
String strA = "Hello";
String strB = " There";
String strC = strA + strB;
```

This sequence results in **strC** containing the sequence "Hello There".

String defines several methods that operate on strings. Since most readers have at least passing familiarity with **String**, there is no need for a detailed description of all its methods. Furthermore, the recipes in this chapter fully describe the **String** methods that they employ. However, it is helpful to review **String**'s core string-handling capabilities by grouping them into categories.

String defines the following methods that search the contents of one string for another:

contains	Returns **true** if one string contains another.
endsWith	Returns **true** if a string ends with a specified string.
indexOf	Returns the index within a string at which the first occurrence of another string is found. Returns –1 if the string is not found.
lastIndexOf	Returns the index within the invoking string at which the last occurrence of the specified string is found. Returns –1 if the string is not found.
startsWith	Returns **true** if a string starts with a specified string.

The following methods compare one string to another:

compareTo	Compares one string to another.
compareToIgnoreCase	Compares one string to another. Case differences are ignored.
contentEquals	Compares a string to a specified character sequence.
equals	Returns **true** if two strings contain the same character sequence.
equalsIgnoreCase	Returns **true** if two strings contain the same character sequence. Case differences are ignored.
matches	Returns **true** if a string matches a specified regular expression.
regionMatches	Returns **true** if the specified region of one string matches the specified region of another.

Each of the methods within the following group replaces a portion of a string with another:

replace	Replaces all occurrences of one character or substring with another.
replaceFirst	Replaces the first character sequence that matches a specified regular expression.
replaceAll	Replaces all character sequences that match a specified regular expression.

The following methods extract substrings from a string:

split	Splits a string into substrings based on a sequence of delimiters specified by a regular expression.
substring	Returns the specified portion of a string.
trim	Returns a string in which the leading and trailing spaces have been removed.

The following two methods change the case of the letters within a string:

toLowerCase	Converts a string to lowercase.
toUpperCase	Converts a string to uppercase.

In addition to the core string handling methods just described, **String** defines several other methods. Two that are quite commonly used are **length( )**, which returns the number of characters in a string, and **charAt( )**, which returns the character at a specified index.

For the most part, the recipes in this chapter use **String**, and it is usually your best choice when working with strings. However, in those few cases in which you need a string that can be modified, Java offers two choices. The first is **StringBuffer**, which has been a part of Java since the start. It is similar to **String** except that it allows the contents of a string to be changed. Thus, it provides methods, such as **setCharAt( )** and **insert( )**, that modify the string. The second option is the newer **StringBuilder**, which was added to Java in version 1.5. It is similar to **StringBuffer** except that it is not thread-safe. Thus, it is more efficient when multithreading is not used. (In multithreaded applications, you must use **StringBuffer** because it *is* thread-safe.) Both **StringBuffer** and **StringBuilder** are packaged in **java.lang**.

Java's Regular Expression API

Regular expressions are supported in Java by the **Matcher** and **Pattern** classes, which are packaged in **java.util.regex**. These classes work together. You will use **Pattern** to define a regular expression. You will match the pattern against another sequence using **Matcher**. The precise procedures are described in the recipes that use them.

Regular expressions are also used by other parts of the Java API. Perhaps most importantly, various methods in **String**, such as **split( )** and **matches( )**, accept a regular expression as an argument. Thus, often you will use a regular expression without explicitly using **Pattern** or **Matcher**.

Several of the recipes in this chapter make use of regular expressions. Most do so through **String** methods, but three explicitly use **Pattern** and **Matcher**. For detailed control over the matching process, it is often easier to use **Pattern** and **Matcher**. In many cases, however, the regular expression functionality provided by **String** is both sufficient and more convenient.

Several methods that use regular expressions will throw a **PatternSyntaxException** when an attempt is made to use a syntactically incorrect regular expression. This exception is defined by the regular expression API and is packaged in **java.util.regex**. You will need to handle this exception in a manner appropriate to your application.

An Introduction to Regular Expressions

Before you can use regular expressions, you must understand how they are constructed. If you are new to regular expressions, then this overview will help you get started. Before continuing it is important to state that the topic of regular expressions is quite large. In fact, entire books have been written about them. It is well beyond the scope of this book to describe them in detail. Instead, a brief introduction is given here that includes sufficient information for you to understand the examples in the recipes. It will also let you begin experimenting with regular expressions of your own. However, if you will be making extensive use of regular expressions, then you will need to study them in significantly more detail.

As the term is used here, a *regular expression* is a string of characters that describes a *pattern*. A pattern will match *any* character sequence that fits the pattern. Thus, a pattern constitutes a general form that will match a variety of specific sequences. In conjunction with a regular expression engine (such as that provided by Java's regular expression API), a pattern can be used to search for matches in another character sequence. It is this ability that gives regular expressions their power when manipulating strings.

A regular expression consists of one or more of the following: normal characters, character classes (sets of characters), the wildcard character, quantifiers, boundary matchers, operators, and groups. Each is examined briefly here.

NOTE *There is some variation in the way that regular expressions are handled by different regular expression engines. This discussion describes Java's implementation.*

Normal Characters

A normal character (i.e., a character literal) is matched as-is. Thus, if a pattern consists of xy, then the only input sequence that will match it is "xy". Characters such as newline and tab are specified using the standard escape sequences, which begin with a \. For example, a newline is specified by \n.

Character Classes

A character class is a set of characters. A character class is specified by putting the characters in the class between brackets. A class will match any character that is part of the class. For example, the class [wxyz] matches w, x, y, or z. To specify an inverted set, precede the characters with a ^. For example, [^wxyz] matches any character *except* w, x, y, or z. You can specify a range of characters using a hyphen. For example, to specify a character class that will match the digits 1 through 9, use [1-9]. A class can contain two or more ranges by simply specifying them. For example, the class [0-9A-Z] matches all digits and the uppercase letters A through Z.

The Java regular expression API provides several predefined classes. Here are some that are commonly used:

Predefined Class	Matches
\d	The digits 0 through 9
\D	All non-digits
\s	Whitespace
\S	All non-whitespace
\w	Characters that can be part of a word. In Java, these are the upper- and lowercase letters, the digits 0 through 9, and the underscore. These are commonly referred to as *word characters*.
\W	All non-word characters

In addition to these classes, Java supplies a large number of other character classes which have the following general form:

\p{*name*}

Here, *name* specifies the name of the class. Here are some examples:

\p{Lower}	Contains the lowercase letters.
\p{Upper}	Contains the uppercase letters.
\p{Punct}	Contains all punctuation.

There are several more. You should consult the API documentation for the character classes supported by your JDK.

A class can contain another class. For example, [[abc][012]] defines a class that will match the characters a, b, or c, or the digits 0, 1, or 2. Thus, it contains the union of the two sets. Of course, this example can be more conveniently written as [abc012]. However, nested classes are very useful in other contexts, such as when working with predefined sets or when you want to create the intersection of two sets.

To create a class that contains the intersection of two or more sets of characters, use the && operator. For example, this creates a set that matches all word characters except for uppercase letters: [\w && [^A-Z]].

Two other points: Outside a character class, - is treated as a normal character. Also, outside a class, the ^ is used to specify the start of a line, as described shortly.

The Wildcard Character

The wildcard character is the . (dot), and it matches any character. Thus, a pattern that consists of . will match these (and other) input sequences: "A", "a", "x", and "!". In essence, the dot is a predefined class that matches all characters.

To create a pattern that matches a period, precede the period with a \. For example, given this input string:

Game over.

this expression

```
over\.
```

matches the sequence "over."

Quantifiers

A quantifier determines how many times an expression is matched. The quantifiers are shown here:

+	Match one or more.
*	Match zero or more.
?	Match zero or one.

For example, x+ will match one or more x's, such as "x", "xx", "xxx", and so on. The pattern . * will match any character zero or more times. The pattern , ? will match zero or one comma.

You can also specify a quantifier that will match a pattern a specified number of times. Here is the general form:

{*num*}

Therefore, x{2} will match "xx", but not "x" or "xxx". You can specify that a pattern be matched at least a minimum number of times by using this quantifier:

{*min,* }

For example, x[2,] matches xx, xxx, xxxx, and so on.

You can specify that a pattern will be matched at least a minimum number of times but not more than some maximum by using this quantifier:

{*min, max*}

Greedy, Reluctant, and Possessive Quantifiers

Actually, there are three varieties of quantifiers: *greedy, reluctant,* and *possessive.* The quantifier examples just shown are examples of the greedy variety. They match the longest matching sequence. A reluctant quantifier (also called a *lazy quantifier*) matches the shortest matching sequence. To create a reluctant quantifier, follow it with a ?. A possessive quantifier matches the longest matching sequence and will not match a shorter sequence even if it would enable the entire expression to succeed. To create a possessive quantifier, follow it with a +.

Let's work through examples of each type of quantifier that attempt to find a match in the string "simple sample". The pattern s.+e will match the longest sequence, which is the entire string "simple sample" because the greedy quantifier .+ will match all characters after the first *s*, up to the final *e*.

The pattern s.+?e will match "simple", which is the shortest match. This is because the reluctant quantifier .+? will stop after finding the first matching sequence.

The patttern s.++e will fail, because the possessive quantifier .++ will match all characters after the initial s. Because it is possessive, it will not release the final *e* to enable the overall pattern to match. Thus, the final *e* will not be found and the match fails.

Boundary Matchers

Sometimes you will want to specify a pattern that begins or ends at some boundary, such as at the end of a word or the start of a line. To do this, you will use a *boundary matcher*. Perhaps the most widely used boundary matchers are ^ and $. They match the start and end of the line being searched, which by default are the start and end of the input string. For example, given the string "test1 test2", the pattern test.?$ will match "test2", but the pattern ^test.? matches "test1". If you want to match one of these characters as itself, you will need to use an escape sequence: \^ or \$.

The other boundary matchers are shown here:

Matcher	Matches
\A	Start of string
\b	Word boundary
\B	Non-word boundary
\G	End of prior match
\Z	End of string (Does not include line terminator.)
\z	End of string (Includes the line terminator.)

The OR Operator

When creating a pattern, you can specify one or more alternatives by using the OR operator, which is |. For example, the expression may|might will match either the word "may" or the word "might". Often the OR operator is used within a parenthesized group. To understand why, imagine that you want to find all uses of either "may" or "might" along with any words that surround them. Here is one way to compose an expression that does this:

```
\w+\s+(may|might)\s+\w+\b
```

Given the string

I might go. I may not.

this regular expression finds these two matches:

I might go
I may not

If the parentheses around the | are removed, as in

`\w+\s+may|might\s+\w+\b`

the expression will find these two matches:

might go
I may

The reason is that the | now separates the entire subexpression `\w+\s+may` from the subexpression `might\s+\w+\b`. Therefore, the entire expression will match phrases that begin with some word followed by "may", or phrases that begin with "might" followed by some word.

Groups

A group is created by enclosing a pattern within parentheses. For example, the parenthesized expression `(may|might)` in the preceding section forms a group. In addition to linking the elements of a subexpression, groups have a second purpose. Once you have defined a group, another part of a regular expression can refer to the sequence captured by that group. Each set of parentheses defines a group. The leftmost opening parenthesis defines group one, the next opening parenthesis defines group two, and so on. Within a regular expression, groups are referred to by number. The first group is `\1`, the second is `\2`, and so forth.

Let's work through an example. Assume that you want to find phrases within the same sentence in which both singular and plural forms of a word are used. For the sake of simplicity, also assume that you only want to find plurals that end in *s*. (In other words, assume that you want to find plurals such as dogs, cats, and computers, and not special-case plurals such as oxen.) For instance, given these sentences

I had one dog, but he had two dogs.
She had a cat, but did she want more cats?
She also has a dog. But his dogs were bigger.

you want to find the phrase "dog, but he had two dogs" because it contains both a singular form and a plural form of dog within the same sentence and the phrase "cat, but did she want more cats" because it contains both "cat" and "cats" within the same sentence. You don't want to find instances that span two or more sentences, so you don't want to find the "dog" and "dogs" contained in the last two sentences. Here is one way to write a regular expression that does this:

`\b(\w+)\b[^.?!]*?\1s`

Here, the parenthesized expression `(\w+)` creates a group that contains a word. This group is then used to match subsequent input when it is referred to by `\1`. Any number of characters can come between the word and its plural as long as they are not the sentence terminators (.?!). Therefore, the remainder of the expression succeeds only when a subsequent word is found within the same sentence that is the plural of the word contained in \1. For example, when applied to the first example sentence, (\w+) will match words, putting the word into group \1. For the entire expression to succeed, a subsequent word in the sentence must match the word contained in \1 and be immediately followed by an *s*. This occurs only when \1 contains the word "dog" because "dogs" is found later in the same sentence.

One other point: You can create a *non-capturing group* by following the opening parenthesis with ?:, as in (?:\s*). Other types of groups that use positive or negative look-ahead or look-behind are possible, but these are beyond the scope of this book.

Flag Sequences

The Java regular expression engine supports a number of options that control how a pattern is matched. These options are set or cleared by using the following construct: (?*f*), where *f* specifies a flag to set. There are six flags, which are shown here:

d	Turns on Unix line mode.
i	Ignores case differences.
m	Enables multiline mode, in which ^ and $ match the beginning and ending of lines, rather than the entire input string.
s	Turns on "dotall" mode, which causes the dot (.) to match all characters, including the line terminator.
u	In conjunction with **i**, causes case-insensitive matches to be done according to the Unicode standard rather than assuming only ASCII characters.
x	Ignores whitespace and # comments in a regular expression.

You can turn off a mode by preceding its flag with a minus sign. For example, (?-i) turns off case-insensitive matching.

Remember to Escape the \ in Java Strings

One short reminder before moving on to the recipes. When creating Java strings that contain regular expressions, remember that you must use the escape sequence \\ to specify a \. Therefore, the following regular expression

```
\b\w+\b
```

Must be written like this when specified as a string literal in a Java program:

```
"\\b\\w+\\b"
```

Forgetting to escape the \ is a common source of problems because it doesn't always result in compile-time or runtime errors. Instead, your regular expression just doesn't match what you thought it would. For example, using \b rather than \\b in the preceding string results in an expression that attempts to match the backspace character, not a word boundary.

Sort an Array of Strings in Reverse Order

Key Ingredients	
Classes and Interfaces	**Methods**
java.lang.String	int compareTo(String *str*)
java.util.Arrays	static <T> void sort(T[ ] *array*, Comparator<? super T> *comp*)
java.util.Comparator<T>	int compare(T *objA*, T *objB*)

Sorting is a common task in programming, and sorting arrays of strings is no exception. For example, you might want to sort a list of the items sold by an online store or a list of customer names and e-mail addresses. Fortunately, Java makes sorting arrays of strings easy because it provides the **sort( )** utility method, which is defined by the **Arrays** class in **java.util**. In its default form, **sort( )** orders strings in case-sensitive, alphabetical order, and this is fine for many situations. However, sometimes you want to sort an array of strings in reverse alphabetical order. This requires a bit more work.

There are a number of ways to approach the problem of sorting in reverse. For example, one naive solution is to sort the array and then copy it back to front into another array. Besides lacking elegance, this technique is also inefficient. Fortunately, Java provides a simple, yet effective way to reverse-sort an array of strings. This approach uses a custom **Comparator** to specify how the sort should be conducted and a version of **sort( )** that takes the **Comparator** as an argument.

Step-by-Step

Sorting an array of strings in reverse involves these three steps:

1. Create a **Comparator** that reverses the outcome of a comparison between two strings.
2. Create an object of that **Comparator**.
3. Pass both the array to be sorted and the **Comparator** to a version of **java.util.Arrays.sort( )** that takes a comparator as an argument. When **sort( )** returns, the array will be sorted in reverse.

Discussion

Comparator is a generic interface that is declared as shown here:

Comparator<T>

The type parameter **T** specifies the type of data that will be compared. In this case, **String** will be passed to **T**.

Comparator defines the following two methods:

int compare(T *objA*, T *objB*)
boolean equals(Object *obj*)

Of these, only **compare( )** must be implemented. The **equals( )** method simply specifies an override of **equals( )** in **Object**. Implementing **equals( )** enables you to determine if two **Comparator**s are equal. However, this capability is not always needed. When it is not needed (as it is not in the examples in this chapter), there is no need to override **Object**'s implementation.

The method in which we are interested is **compare( )**. It determines how one object compares to another. Normally, it must return less than zero if *objA* is less than *objB*, greater than zero if *objA* is greater than *objB*, and zero if the two objects are equal. Implementing **compare( )** in this way causes it to operate according to the natural ordering of the data. For strings, this means alphabetical order. However, you are free to implement **compare( )** to suit the needs of your task. To reverse-sort an array of strings, you will need to create a version of **compare( )** that reverses the outcome of the comparison.

Here is one way to implement a reverse comparator for **String**s.

```
// Create a Comparator that returns the outcome
// of a reverse string comparison.
class RevStrComp implements Comparator<String> {

  // Implement the compare() method so that it
  // reverses the order of the string comparison.
  public int compare(String strA, String strB) {
    // Compare strB to strA, rather than strA to strB.
    return strB.compareTo(strA);
  }
}
```

Let's look at **RevStrComp** closely. First, notice that **RevStrComp** implements **Comparator**. This means that an object of type **RevStrComp** can be used any place that a **Comparator** is needed. Also notice that it implements a **String**-specific version of **Comparator**. Thus, **RevStrComp** is not, itself, generic. It works only with strings.

Now, notice that the **compare( )** method calls **String**'s **compareTo( )** method to compare two strings. **compareTo( )** is specified by the **Comparable** interface, which is implemented by **String** (and many other classes). A class that implements **Comparable** guarantees that objects of the class can be ordered. The general form of **compareTo( )** as implemented by **String** is shown here:

int compareTo(String *str*)

It returns less than zero if the invoking string is less than *str*, greater than zero if the invoking string is greater than *str*, and zero if they are equal. One string is less than another if it comes before the other in alphabetical order. One string is greater than another if it comes after the other in alphabetical order.

The **compare( )** method of **RevStrComp** returns the result of the call to **compareTo( )**. However, notice that **compare( )** calls **compareTo( )** in reverse order. That is, **compareTo( )** is called on **strB** with **strA** passed as an argument. For a normal comparison, **strA** would invoke **compareTo( )**, passing **strB**. However, because **strB** invokes **compareTo( )**, the outcome of the comparison is reversed. Therefore, the ordering of the two strings is reversed.

Once you have created a reverse comparator, create an object of that comparator and pass it to this version of **sort( )** defined by **java.util.Arrays**:

static <T> void sort(T[ ] *array*, Comparator<? super T> *comp*)

Notice the **super** clause. It ensures that the array passed to **sort( )** is compatible with the type of **Comparator**. After the call to **sort( )**, the array will be in reverse alphabetical order.

Example

The following example reverse-sorts an array of strings. For demonstration purposes, it also sorts them in natural, alphabetical order using the default version of **sort( )**.

```java
// Sort an array of strings in reverse order.

import java.util.*;

// Create a Comparator that returns the outcome
// of a reverse string comparison.
class RevStrComp implements Comparator<String> {

  // Implement the compare() method so that it
  // reverses the order of the string comparison.
  public int compare(String strA, String strB) {
    // Compare strB to strA, rather than strA to strB.
    return strB.compareTo(strA);
  }
}

// Demonstrate the reverse string comparator.
class RevStrSort {
  public static void main(String args[]) {

    // Create a sample array of strings.
    String strs[] = { "dog", "horse",  "zebra", "cow", "cat" };

    // Show the initial order.
    System.out.print("Initial order: ");
    for(String s : strs)
      System.out.print(s + " ");
    System.out.println("\n");

    // Sort the array in reverse order.
    // Begin by creating a reverse string comparator.
    RevStrComp rsc = new RevStrComp();
```

```
// Now, sort the strings using the reverse comparator.
Arrays.sort(strs, rsc);

// Show the reverse sorted order.
System.out.print("Sorted in reverse order: ");
for(String s : strs)
  System.out.print(s + " ");
System.out.println("\n");

// For comparison, sort the strings in natural order.
Arrays.sort(strs);

// Show the natural sorted order.
System.out.print("Sorted in natural order: ");
for(String s : strs)
  System.out.print(s + " ");
System.out.println("\n");

  }
}
```

The output from this program is shown here.

```
Initial order: dog horse zebra cow cat

Sorted in reverse order: zebra horse dog cow cat

Sorted in natural order: cat cow dog horse zebra
```

Options and Alternatives

Although this recipe sorts strings in reverse alphabetical order, the same basic technique can be generalized to other situations. For example, you can reverse-sort other types of data by creating the appropriate **Comparator**. Simply adapt the approach shown in the example.

The **compareTo( )** method defined by **String** is case-sensitive. This means that uppercase and lowercase letters will be sorted separately. You can sort data independent of case differences by using **compareToIgnoreCase( )**. (See *Ignore Case Differences When Sorting an Array of Strings*).

You can sort strings based on some specific substring. For example, if each string contains a name and an e-mail address, then you could create a comparator that sorts on the e-mail address portion of each string. One way to approach this is to use the **regionMatches( )** method. You can also sort by some criteria other than a strict alphabetic relationship. For example, strings representing pending tasks could be sorted in order of priority.

Ignore Case Differences when Sorting an Array of Strings

Key Ingredients	
Classes and Interfaces	**Methods**
java.lang.String	int compareToIgnoreCase(String *str*)
java.util.Arrays	static <T> void sort(T[ ] *array*, Comparator<? super T> *comp*)
java.util.Comparator<T>	int compare(T *objA*, T *objB*)

In Java, the natural ordering for strings is case-sensitive. This means that uppercase letters are separate and distinct from lowercase letters. As a result, when you sort an array of strings, some unwelcome surprises might occur. For example, if you sort a **String** array that contains the following words:

    alpha beta Gamma Zeta

The resulting order will be as shown here:

    Gamma Zeta alpha beta

    As you can see, even though Gamma and Zeta would normally come after alpha and beta, they are at the start of the sorted array. The reason is that in Unicode, the uppercase letters are represented by values that are less than the values used by the lowercase letters. Therefore, even though Zeta would normally fall at the end of the list when sorting in alphabetical order, it comes before alpha when case differences are significant. This can lead to sorts that produce technically accurate, but undesirable results!

NOTE *As a point of interest, an uppercase letter is exactly 32 less than its lowercase equivalent. For example, the Unicode value for A is 65. For a, it is 97.*

    Fortunately, it is quite easy to sort an array of strings based on true alphabetical order by creating a **Comparator** that ignores the case of a letter during the sort process. The technique is similar to that described in *Sort an Array of Strings in Reverse Order*. The specifics are described here.

Step-by-Step

To ignore case differences when sorting an array of strings involves these three steps:

1. Create a **Comparator** that ignores the case differences between two strings.
2. Create an object of that **Comparator**.

3. Pass both the array to be sorted and the **Comparator** to the comparator version of **java.util.Arrays.sort( )**. When **sort( )** returns, the array will be sorted without regard to case differences.

Discussion

To ignore case differences when sorting an array of strings, you will need to implement a case-insensitive **Comparator** for strings. To do this, define a version of **compare( )** that ignores case differences when comparing **String** objects. You can use an approach similar to that used to sort an array of strings in reverse order, shown earlier. (See *Sort an Array of Strings in Reverse Order* for details about **Comparator**.)

Here is one way to implement a comparator for **String**s that ignores case differences.

```
// Create a Comparator that returns the outcome
// of a case-insensitive string comparison.
class IgnoreCaseComp implements Comparator<String> {

  // Implement the compare() method so that it
  // ignores case differences when comparing strings.
  public int compare(String strA, String strB) {
    return strA.compareToIgnoreCase(strB);
  }
}
```

Notice that **compare( )** calls **String**'s **compareToIgnoreCase( )** method to compare two strings. The **compareToIgnoreCase( )** ignores case differences when comparing two strings. The general form of **compareToIgnoreCase( )** is shown here:

   int compareToIgnoreCase(String *str*)

It returns less than zero if the invoking string is less than *str*, greater than zero if the invoking string is greater than *str*, and zero if they are equal. The **compare( )** method returns the result of the call to **compareToIgnoreCase( )**. Thus, case differences between the two strings being compared are ignored.

Once you have created a case-insensitive comparator, create an object of that comparator and pass it to this version of **sort( )** defined by **java.util.Arrays**:

   static <T> void sort(T[ ] *array*, Comparator<? super T> *comp*)

After calling **sort( )**, the array will be in true alphabetical order, with case differences ignored.

Example

The following example ignores case differences when it sorts an array of strings. For demonstration purposes, it also sorts them using the default ordering.

```
// Sort an array of strings, ignore case difference.

import java.util.*;

// Create a Comparator that returns the outcome
// of a case-insensitive string comparison.
class IgnoreCaseComp implements Comparator<String> {
```

```java
    // Implement the compare() method so that it
    // ignores case differences when comparing strings.
    public int compare(String strA, String strB) {
      return strA.compareToIgnoreCase(strB);
    }
}

// Demonstrate the case-insensitive string comparator.
class IgnoreCaseSort {
  public static void main(String args[]) {

    // Create a sample array of strings.
    String strs[] = { "alpha", "Gamma", "Zeta", "beta", };

    // Show the initial order.
    System.out.print("Initial order: ");
    for(String s : strs)
      System.out.print(s + " ");
    System.out.println("\n");

    // Sort the array, but ignore case differences.
    // Create a case-insensitive string comparator.
    IgnoreCaseComp icc = new IgnoreCaseComp();

    // Sort the strings using the comparator.
    Arrays.sort(strs, icc);

    // Show the case-insensitive sorted order.
    System.out.print("Case-insensitive sorted order: ");
    for(String s : strs)
      System.out.print(s + " ");
    System.out.println("\n");

    // For comparison, sort the strings using the default order,
    // which is case-sensitive.
    Arrays.sort(strs);

    // Show the case-sensitive sorted order.
    System.out.print("Default, case-sensitive sorted order: ");
    for(String s : strs)
      System.out.print(s + " ");
    System.out.println("\n");

  }
}
```

The output from this program is shown here. Notice that the default sort puts uppercase letters before lowercase ones, which often results in an unsatisfactory sort. Using the **IgnoreCaseComp** comparator corrects this problem.

```
Initial order: alpha Gamma Zeta beta

Case-insensitive sorted order: alpha beta Gamma Zeta

Default, case-sensitive sorted order: Gamma Zeta alpha beta
```

Options and Alternatives

Although the **compareToIgnoreCase( )** method works well in many cases (such as when comparing strings in English), it will not work for all languages and locales. To ensure full internationalization support, you should use the **compare( )** method specified by **java.text.Collator**. It is shown here:

> int compare(String *strA*, String *strB*)

It returns less than zero if the invoking string is less than *str*, greater than zero if the invoking string is greater than *str*, and zero if they are equal. It uses the standard collating order defined by the locale. You can obtain a **Collator** for the default locale by calling its factory method **getInstance( )**. Next, set the strength level of the collator so that only primary differences between characters are used. This is done by calling **setStrength( )**, passing **Collator.PRIMARY** as an argument. Using this approach, **IgnoreCaseComp** can be rewritten as shown here:

```
// This Comparator uses a Collator to determine the
// proper, case-insensitive lexicographical ordering
// of two strings.
class IgnoreCaseComp implements Comparator<String> {
  Collator col;

  IgnoreCaseComp() {
    // Get a Collator for this locale.
    col = Collator.getInstance();

    // Have it consider only primary differences.
    col.setStrength(Collator.PRIMARY);
  }

  // Uses Collator's compare() method to compare strings.
  public int compare(String strA, String strB) {
    return col.compare(strA, strB);
  }
}
```

If you substitute this version into the example, it will produce the same results as before. However, now it will work in a locale-independent manner.

NOTE   *In some situations when using* **Collator**, *you may find the* **java.text.CollationKey** *class helpful.*

Ignore Case Differences when Searching for or Replacing Substrings

Key Ingredients	
Classes	**Methods**
java.lang.String	boolean matches(String *regExpr*)
	String replaceAll(String *regExpr*, String *repStr*)

String contains several methods that enable you to search a string for a specific substring. For example, you can use **contains( )**, **indexOf( )**, **lastIndexOf( )**, **startsWith( )**, or **endsWith( )**, depending on your needs. However, in all of these, the search is performed in a case-sensitive manner. Therefore, if you are searching for the substring "the" in the string "The sky is blue", the search will fail. This can be a problem in many search situations. Fortunately, **String** gives you an easy way to perform searches in a case-insensitive manner through the use of the **matches( )** method and regular expressions.

Related to case-insensitive searching is case-insensitive substring replacement. **String** supplies two methods that replace one substring with another. The first is the **replace( )** method. It can be used to replace one character with another, or one substring with another. However, it works in a case-sensitive manner. To perform a case-insensitive search, you can use the **replaceAll( )** method. It replaces all occurrences of strings that match a regular expression. Thus, it can be used to perform search and replace operations that ignore case.

Step-by-Step

To search for or replace a substring in a case-insensitive manner involves these two steps:

1. Construct a regular expression that specifies the character sequence that you are looking for. Precede the sequence with the ignore-case flag **(?i)**. This causes matches to be found independently of case differences.

2. To search for the pattern, call **matches( )**, specifying the regular expression. Alternatively, to replace all occurrences of one substring with another, call **replaceAll( )**, specifying the regular expression and the replacement.

Discussion

It is quite easy to create a regular expression that will match a specific substring, but ignore case differences. Just precede the desired character sequence with the ignore-case flag: **(?i)**. For example, to search for the sequence "here" in a case-insensitive manner, you can use this pattern: `(?i)here`. This will match "here", "Here", and "HERE", for example. It will also match "there" because there is no requirement that the "here" being searched for be a separate word. To find only whole words, use this expression: `\b(?i)here\b`.

Once you have defined the case-insensitive pattern, you can call **matches( )** to determine if any character sequence matches that pattern. Its general form is shown here:

boolean matches(String *regExpr*)

If returns **true** if a sequence that matches *regExpr* is found in the invoking string and false otherwise. For example, this call to **matches( )** returns true:

```
"The River Runs Deep".matches(".*(?i)runs.*");
```

Because the literal "runs" is preceded by **(?i)**, it will match the "Runs" in the invoking string. Case differences are ignored. Without the use of **(?i)**, the search would fail because of the case differences between "runs" and "Runs". The **matches( )** method will throw a **PatternSyntaxException** if *regExpr* is invalid.

You can replace all occurrences of one substring with another by calling **replaceAll( )**. Its general form is shown here:

String replaceAll(String *regExpr*, String *repStr*)

It returns a new string in which all occurrences of the pattern specified by *regExpr* in the invoking string have been replaced by *repStr*. If you specify the ignore-case flag when constructing *regExpr,* then case differences are ignored. For example, assume that *str* contains the following string:

What is today? Is it Friday?

Then the following call replaces all occurrences of "is" with "was":

```
str.replaceAll("(?i)is", "was");
```

The resulting string is:

What was today? was it Friday?

The **replaceAll( )** method will also throw **PatternSyntaxException** if *regExpr* is invalid.

Example

The following example shows how to search and replace in a case-insensitive manner.

```
// Ignore case differences when searching for
// or replacing substrings.

class IgnoreCaseDemo {

  public static void main(String args[]) {
    String str = "This is a TEST.";

    System.out.println("Ignore case when searching.\n" +
                       "Looking for 'test' in: " + str);

    // Use matches() to find any version of test.
    if(str.matches("(?i).*test.*"))
      System.out.println("test is in the string.");

    System.out.println();

    str = "alpha beta, Alpha beta, alPHa beta, ALPHA beta";
```

```
        // Use replaceAll() to ignore case when replacing one
        // substring with another.
        // In this example, replace all versions of alpha with zeta.
        System.out.println("Ignore case when replacing.\n" +
                           "Replace any version of 'alpha' " +
                           "with 'zeta' in:\n" + "    " + str);

        String result = str.replaceAll("(?i)alpha", "zeta");

        System.out.println("After replacement:\n" +
                           "    " + result);
    }
}
```

The output is shown here:

```
Ignore case when searching.
Looking for 'test' in: This is a TEST.
test is in the string.

Ignore case when replacing.
Replace any version of 'alpha' with 'zeta' in:
    alpha beta, Alpha beta, alPHa beta, ALPHA beta
After replacement:
    zeta beta, zeta beta, zeta beta, zeta beta
```

As a point of interest: Because the regular expressions are hard-coded in this example and known to be syntactically valid, there is no need to catch a **PatternSyntaxException**, because one will not occur. (This is also the case with several other examples in this chapter.) However, in your own code, you may need to handle this potential error. This is especially true if the regular expressions are constructed at runtime, such as from user input.

Options and Alternatives

Although **matches( )** offers the power and elegance of using a regular expression, it is not the only way to search a string in a case-insensitive manner. In some situations you might be able to use this version of the **regionMatches( )** method:

> boolean regionMatches(boolean *ignCase*, int *start*,
> String *str2*, int *start2*, int *numChars*)

If *ignCase* is true, then the search ignores case differences. The starting point for the search in the invoking string is specified by *start*. The starting point for the search in the second string is passed in *start2*. The second string is specified by *str2*, and the number of characters to compare is specified by *numChars*. Of course, **regionMatches( )** only compares the specified portions of the two strings, but this will be sufficient for some needs.

Another way to ignore case differences when searching for a substring is to first convert both strings to lowercase (or uppercase, as you so choose). Then, call **contains( )** to determine if the string contains the substring. In general, this approach is less appealing than using a case-insensitive pattern with **matches( )**. However, it might be a good choice if you have another reason for converting the strings to a single case. For example, if the string to be searched contains a series of database commands, then normalizing the commands to a single case may simplify other parts of your program.

If you only want to replace the first occurrence of a pattern, use **replaceFirst( )** rather than **replaceAll( )**. It is shown here:

String replaceFirst(String *regExpr*, String *repStr*)

The first sequence in the invoking string that matches *regExpr* will be replaced by *repStr*. A **PatternSyntaxException** will be thrown if *regExpr* is invalid.

Its also possible to use the Java regular expression API to achieve a case-insensitive search and replacement.

Split a String into Pieces by Using split( )

Key Ingredients	
Classes	**Methods**
java.lang.String	String[ ] split(String *regExpr*)

Sometimes you will want to decompose a string into a set of substrings based on some criteria. For example, given an e-mail address, you might want to obtain two substrings. The first is the name of the addressee; the second is the URL. In this case, the separator is the @. In the past, you would have had to manually search for the @ using a method such as **indexOf( )** and then use **substring( )** to retrieve each part of the address. However, beginning with Java 1.4, a more convenient option became available: **split( )**.

The **split( )** method employs a regular expression to provide a very convenient way to decompose a string into a set of substrings in a single step. Because the characters that form the delimiters between substrings are specified by a pattern, you can use **split( )** to handle some very complicated decomposition problems. For example, using **split( )**, it is easy to obtain a list of the words contained within a string. Simply specify a regular expression that matches all non-word characters. Many other types of splits are also easy. For example, to split a string containing a list of comma-separated values, such as 10, 20, 30, and so on, simply specify a comma as the delimiting expression. Whatever your use, **split( )** is one of **String**'s most important regular-expression-based methods. Once you master it, you will be surprised at how often you use it.

Step-by-Step

Splitting a string into pieces involves these two steps:

1. Create a regular expression that defines the delimiter that will be used to split the string.
2. Call **split( )** on the string, passing in the regular expression. An array of strings containing the pieces is returned.

Discussion

The **split( )** method defined by **String** decomposes the invoking string into pieces. Where one substring ends and the next begins is determined by a regular expression. Thus, the regular expression specifies the delimiters that terminate a substring. (The first substring is bounded by the beginning of the string. The final substring is bounded by the end of the string.) There are two forms of **split( )**. The one used in the recipe is shown here:

String[ ] split(String *regExpr*)

The delimiting expression is specified by *regExpr*. The method returns an array that contains the pieces of the string. If no matches with *regExpr* are found, then the entire string is returned. The **split( )** method will throw a **PatternSyntaxException** if *regExpr* does not contain a valid regular expression.

When constructing a regular expression for use in **split( )** keep in mind that you are defining the pattern that separates one substring from another. You are *not* specifying a pattern that matches the pieces you want. For example, given the string—

This is a test.

to split this string into words that are separated by spaces, pass the following regular expression to *regExpr*.

"\\s+"

This results in an array that contains the following substrings:

This
is
a
test.

The final substring "test." includes the period because only spaces match the regular expression. However, as explained, the last substring terminates with the end of the input string and does not need to end in a match with the regular expression.

Example

The following example shows several examples that split a string into parts based on various regular expressions.

```
// Use split() to extract substrings from a string.

class SplitDemo {
  static void showSplit(String[] strs) {
    for(String str : strs)
      System.out.print(str + "|");

    System.out.println("\n");
  }

  // Demonstrate split().
  public static void main(String args[]) {
    String result[];

    // Split at spaces.
```

```
    String testStr = "This is   a test.";
    System.out.println("Original string: " + testStr);
    result = testStr.split("\\s+");
    System.out.print("Split at spaces: ");
    showSplit(result);


    // Split on word boundaries.
    testStr = "One, Two, and Three.";
    System.out.println("Original string: " + testStr);
    result = testStr.split("\\W+");
    System.out.print("Split at word boundaries: ");
    showSplit(result);


    // Split same string on commas and zero or more spaces.
    System.out.println("Original string: " + testStr);
    result = testStr.split(",\\s*");
    System.out.print("Split at commas: ");
    showSplit(result);


    // Split on word boundaries, but allow embedded
    // periods and @.
    testStr = "Jerry Jerry@HerbSchildt.com";
    System.out.println("Original string: " + testStr);
    result = testStr.split("[\\W && [^.@]]+");
    System.out.print("Allow . and @ to be part of a word: ");
    showSplit(result);

    // Split on various punctuation and zero or more trailing spaces.
    testStr = "This, is. a!:; test?";
    System.out.println("Original string: " + testStr);
    result = testStr.split("[.,!?:;]+\\s*");
    System.out.print("Split on various punctuation: ");
    showSplit(result);
  }
}
```

The output is shown here:

```
Original string: This is   a test.
Split at spaces: This|is|a|test.|

Original string: One, Two, and Three.
Split at word boundaries: One|Two|and|Three|

Original string: One, Two, and Three.
Split at commas: One|Two|and Three.|

Original string: Jerry Jerry@HerbSchildt.com
Allow . and @ to be part of a word: Jerry|Jerry@HerbSchildt.com|

Original string: This, is. a!:; test?
Split on various punctuation: This|is|a|test|
```

Options and Alternatives

Although the **split( )** method is quite powerful, it is a bit lacking in flexibility. For example, it is difficult to use **split( )** to decompose a string based on delimiters that change relative to the context. Although it is possible to devise very complex regular expressions that can handle quite sophisticated matching operations, this is not always the best approach. Furthermore, there may be times when you want to fully *tokenize* a string, in which all parts of the string (including delimiters) are obtained. In these situations, you can use the **Pattern** and **Matcher** classes supplied by Java's regular expression API to gain more convenient, detailed control. This approach is shown in *Tokenize a String Using the Regular Expression API*.

You can limit the number of matches that **split( )** will find, and thus the number of substrings that will be returned, by using this form of **split( )**:

    String[ ] split(String *regExpr*, int *num*)

Here, *regExpr* specifies the delimiting expression. The number of times that it will be matched is passed in *num*. It will throw a **PatternSyntaxException** if *regExpr* does not contain a valid regular expression.

Retrieve Key/Value Pairs from a String

Key Ingredients	
Classes	**Methods**
java.lang.String	String[ ] split(String *regExpr*)
	String trim( )

One especially good use for **split( )** is found when retrieving key/value pairs from a string. Key/value pairs are quite common in programming, especially Web-based programming. For this reason Java provides significant support for them. For example, the **Properties** class and the various implementations of the **Map** interface operate on pairs of keys and values. Unfortunately, we are not always given key/value pairs in a form as convenient to use as a **HashMap**, for example. Often, key/value pairs are received in the form of a string and we are left with the job of extracting them. The recipe shown here illustrates one approach to performing this common task.

Key/value pairs can be represented in a string in a variety of ways. The recipe shown here assumes the following organization:

    key = value, key = value, key = value, ...

Each key/value pair is separated from the next by a comma. Each key is linked with its value by an equal sign. Spaces are allowed, but not necessary. The technique shown here can be easily adapted to handle other formats.

Step-by-Step

Extracting key/value pairs from a string involves these steps:

1. Remove any leading or trailing whitespace from the string containing the key/value pairs by calling **trim( )**.

2. Split the string containing the key/value pairs into individual substrings that contain a single key and value by using a comma (with optional whitespace) as a delimiter in a call to **split( )**. Here is one way to specify the delimiter expression: \s*,\s*. Each element in the resulting array contains a key/value pair.

3. Split each individual key/value substring into its key and value by calling **split( )** with the = being the delimiter. Allow, but do not require, whitespace. Here is one way to specify the delimiter: \s*=\s*. The resulting array contains an individual key and its value.

Discussion

The operation of **split( )** is described by the preceding recipe.

To remove leading and trailing spaces from the input string, **String**'s **trim( )** method is used. It is shown here:

String trim( )

It removes leading and trailing spaces from the invoking string and returns the result.

The way that the input string is formatted determines how the delimiter expressions are constructed. As explained, this recipe assumes a fairly common format. However, if your input string differs, then you must adjust the delimiters appropriately.

Example

The following example creates a general-purpose method called **getKVPairs( )** that reduces a string containing one or more key/value pairs into its constituent parts. Each key/value pair is stored in an object of type **KVPair**, which is defined by the program. An array of **KVPair** is returned by **getKVPairs( )**.

The **getKVPairs( )** method lets you specify the regular expressions that define the delimiters that separate each key/value pair from the next, and that separate an individual key from its value. Thus, **getKVPairs( )** can be used to dissect a wide variety of key/value formats. If the input string is not in the expected format, **getKVPairs( )** throws a **KVSplitException**, which is an exception defined by the program. If either delimiter expression is invalid, a **PatternSyntaxException** is thrown.

```
// Use split() to extract key/value pairs from a string.

import java.util.regex.PatternSyntaxException;

// A class that holds key/value pairs as Strings.
class KVPair {
  String key;
  String value;
```

```java
  KVPair(String k, String v) {
    key = k;
    value = v;
  }
}

// An exception class for getKVPairs() errors.
class KVSplitException extends Exception {
  // Fill in details as needed.
}

// This class encapsulates the static getKVPairs() method.
class KVSplit {

  // This method extracts the key/value pairs stored
  // within a string and returns an array that contains
  // each key and value encapsulated within a KVPair object.
  //
  // It is passed the string that contains the key/value pairs
  // and two regular expressions that describe the delimiters
  // used to extract the key/value pairs. The pairSep parameter
  // specifies the pattern that separates one key/value pair
  // from the next within the string. The kvSep parameter
  // specifies the pattern that separates a key from a value.
  //
  // It throws a PatternSyntaxException if a separator
  // expression is invalid and a KVSplitException if
  // the incoming string does not contain key/value pairs
  // in the expected format.
  public static KVPair[] getKVPairs(String str,
                                    String pairSep,
                                    String kvSep)
    throws PatternSyntaxException, KVSplitException {

    // First, trim incoming string to remove leading and
    // trailing spaces.
    str = str.trim();

    // Next, split the incoming string into individual strings
    // that each contain one key/value pair. The expression
    // in pairSep determines the character sequence that separates
    // one key/value pair from the next.
    String[] kvStrs = str.split(pairSep);

    // Now, construct a KVPair array that will hold
    // each key and value as individual strings.
    KVPair[] kvps = new KVPair[kvStrs.length];

    // Extract each key and value.
    String[] tmp;
    for(int i = 0; i < kvStrs.length; i++) {
      tmp = kvStrs[i].split(kvSep); //
```

```
        // If an array returned by split() has more
        // or less than 2 elements, then the input
        // string contains something other than
        // key/value pairs, or it is in an invalid
        // format. In this case, an exception is thrown.
        if(tmp.length != 2) throw new KVSplitException();

        // Otherwise, store the next key and value.
        kvps[i] = new KVPair(tmp[0], tmp[1]);
      }

    return kvps;
  }
}

// Demonstrate getKVPairs().
class KVPairsDemo {
  public static void main(String args[]) {
    String testStr =
      "Name = Tom, Age = 27, IDNum = 1432, Wage = 37.25";

    System.out.println("Key/value string: " + testStr);

    // Get an array that contains the keys and values.
    KVPair kvpairs[];
    try {

      // This call to getKVPairs() specifies that
      // key/value pairs are separated by a comma (and
      // any number of spaces) and that a key is separated
      // from its value by an = (and any number of spaces).
      kvpairs =
        KVSplit.getKVPairs(testStr, "\\s*,\\s*", "\\s*=\\s*");

    } catch(PatternSyntaxException exc) {
      System.out.println("Invalid separator expression.");
      return;
    } catch(KVSplitException exc) {
      System.out.println("Error obtaining keys and values.");
      return;
    }

    // Display each key and its value.
    for(KVPair kvp : kvpairs)
      System.out.println("Key: " + kvp.key +
                          "\tValue: " + kvp.value);

  }
}
```

The output is shown here:

```
Key/value string: Name = Tom, Age = 27, IDNum = 1432, Wage = 37.25
Key: Name    Value: Tom
Key: Age     Value: 27
Key: IDNum   Value: 1432
Key: Wage    Value: 37.25
```

Options and Alternatives

Although using **split( )** is usually the far easier approach, you can extract key/value pairs by employing a combination of other **String** methods, such as **indexOf( )** and **substring( )**. Such an implementation might be appropriate when the string containing the key/value pairs does not use a uniform format.

Extracting key/value pairs is a special case of a more general concept: tokenizing. In some cases, it might be easier (or more convenient) to tokenize the input stream into all of its constituent parts and then determine what constitutes a key/value pair using other program logic. Such an approach would be especially useful if the input string contains more than just key/value pairs. See *Tokenize a String Using the Regular Expression API* for details on tokenizing.

Match and Extract Substrings Using the Regular Expression API

Key Ingredients	
Classes	**Methods**
java.util.regex.Pattern	Pattern.compile(String *regExpr*)
	Matcher matcher(CharSequence *str*)
java.util.regex.Matcher	boolean find( )
	String group( )

Although **String**'s support for regular expressions is certainly very useful, it does not provide access to all of the features supported by the regular expression API. There are times when you will need to use the regular expression API directly. One such time is when you want to obtain a substring that matches a general pattern. For example, assume that you have a string that contains a list of contact information for the employees of a company that includes telephone numbers and e-mail addresses. Further assume that you want to extract the e-mail addresses from this string. How do you accomplish this? Although Java's API offers a number of ways to solve this problem, the most straightforward is to use the **Pattern** and **Matcher** classes defined by the regular expression API. This recipe shows how to accomplish this task.

Step-by-Step

To obtain a substring that matches a regular expression involves the following steps:

1. Create a **Pattern** instance by calling its **compile( )** factory method. Pass to **compile( )** the regular expression that describes the pattern that you are seeking.

2. Create a **Matcher** that contains the input string by calling **matcher( )** on the **Pattern** object.

3. Call **find( )** on the **Matcher** to search for a match. It returns **true** if a matching sequence is found and false otherwise.

4. If **find( )** succeeds, call **group( )** on the **Matcher** to obtain the matching sequence.

Discussion

The **Pattern** class defines no constructors. Instead, a pattern is created by calling the **compile( )** factory method. The form used this recipe is shown here:

    static Pattern compile(String *regExpr*)

Here, *regExpr* is the regular expression that you want to find. The **compile( )** method transforms *regExpr* into a pattern that can be used for pattern matching by the **Matcher** class. It returns a **Pattern** object that contains the pattern. If *regExpr* specifies an invalid expression, a **PatternSyntaxException** is thrown.

Once you have created a **Pattern** object, you will use it to create a **Matcher** object. **Matcher** has no constructors. Instead, a **Matcher** is created by calling the **matcher( )** factory method defined by **Pattern**. It is shown here:

    Matcher matcher(CharSequence *str*)

Here *str* is the character sequence that the pattern will be matched against. **CharSequence** is an interface that defines a read-only set of characters. It is implemented by the **String** class, among others. Thus, you can pass a string to **matcher( )**.

To determine if a subsequence of the input sequence matches the pattern, call **find( )** on the **Matcher**. It has two versions; the one used here is:

    boolean find( )

It returns **true** if there is a matching sequence and false otherwise. This method can be called repeatedly, allowing it to find all matching sequences. Each call to **find( )** begins where the previous one left off.

To obtain the string containing the current match, call **group( )**. The form used here is:

    String group( )

The matching string is returned. If no match exists, then an **IllegalStateException** is thrown.

Example

The following program shows an example that extracts an e-mail address of the form *name*@XYZ.com from a string that contains contact information for employees of an imaginary company called XYZ.

```
// Extract a substring by matching a regular expression.
import java.util.regex.*;
```

```
class UseRegExpr {

  public static void main(String args[]) {

    // Create a Pattern instance whose regular expression
    // matches e-mail addresses of anyone at XYZ.com.
    Pattern pat = Pattern.compile("\\b\\w+@XYZ\\.com\\b");

    // Create a Matcher for the pattern.
    Matcher mat = pat.matcher("Company Contact Info\n" +
                        "Tom 555-1111 tom@XYZ.com\n" +
                        "Mary 555-2222 Mary@XYZ.com\n" +
                        "Don 555-3333 Don@XYZ.com");

    // Find and display all e-mail addresses.
    while(mat.find())
      System.out.println("Match: " + mat.group());
  }
}
```

The output is shown here:

```
Match: tom@XYZ.com
Match: Mary@XYZ.com
Match: Don@XYZ.com
```

Options and Alternatives

You can enable case-insensitive matches by using this form of **compile( )**.

static Pattern compile(String *regExpr*, int *options*)

Here, *regExpr* is the regular expression that describes the pattern and *options* contains one or more of the following values (defined by **Pattern**):

CASE_INSENSITIVE	CANON_EQ	COMMENTS
DOTALL	LITERAL	MULTILINE
UNICODE_CASE	UNIX_LINES	

Except for **CANON_EQ**, these options have the same effect as the corresponding regular expression flags, such as **(?i)**, described earlier in this chapter. (There is no corresponding regular expression flag for **CANON_EQ**.) For case-insensitive matching, pass **CASE_INSENSITIVE** to *options*.

You can obtain the index of the current match within the input string by calling **start( )**. The index one past the end of the current match is obtained by calling **end( )**. These methods are shown here:

int start( )
int end( )

Both throw an **IllegalStateException** if no match has yet been made. This information is helpful if you want to remove the match from the string, for example.

Tokenize a String Using the Regular Expression API

Key Ingredients	
Classes	**Methods**
java.util.regex.Pattern	Pattern.compile(String *regExpr*)
	Matcher matcher(CharSequence *str*)
java.util.regex.Matcher	boolean find( )
	String group( )
	Matcher usePattern(Pattern *pattern*)

Tokenizing a string is one programming task that just about every programmer will face at one time or another. *Tokenizing* is the process of reducing a string into its individual parts, which are called *tokens*. Thus, a token represents the smallest indivisible element that can be meaningfully extracted from a string.

Of course, what constitutes a token depends on what type of input is being processed, and for what purpose. For example, when tokenizing a string containing text, the individual parts are words, punctuation, and numbers. When tokenizing program elements, the parts include keywords, identifiers, operators, separators, and so on. When tokenizing a data stream that contains stock market information, the tokens might be the company name, its current stock price, and its P/E ratio. The key point is that what constitutes a token will change, depending on the circumstance.

There are two basic approaches that can be used to tokenize a string. The first is based on defining the delimiters that separate one token from another. This approach is often useful when tokenizing a stream of data that uses a fixed format. For example, real-time stock market data might be available in the following form:

name, price, P/E ratio | name, price, P/E ratio | ...

Here, the data is in a fixed format in which each company's information is separated from the next by a vertical bar, and the values associated with each company are separated from each other by commas. In this case, you could use the **split( )** method defined by **String** to reduce such a string into its individual tokens by specifying ",|" as the set of delimiters.

However, such a delimiter-based approach is not always appropriate or convenient. In some cases what constitutes a delimiter will vary from case to case within the same string. Computer programs are a prime example of this. For example, given this fragment

```
done = len <= (12/port23);
```

What set of delimiters will divide this string into its individual tokens? Clearly, you can't use whitespace, since 12 is not separated from the / even though both constitute individual tokens. Also, the identifier **port23** contains both letters and digits, so it's not valid to specify digits as a delimiter. Furthermore, the operators =, <=, and / must be returned as tokens, meaning that they cannot be used as delimiters. In general, what separates one token from another is based on the syntax and semantics of the program, not on a fixed format. When faced with this type of tokenization, the second approach to tokenizing must be used.

Instead of tokenizing based on delimiters, the second approach extracts each token based on the *pattern that it matches.* For example, when tokenizing a program, a typical identifier will match a pattern that starts with a letter or underscore and is followed by other letters, digits, or underscores. A comment will match a pattern that starts with a // and terminates with the end of the line, or that starts with a /* and ends with a */. An operator will match an operator pattern, which can be defined to include single-character operators (such as +) and multicharacter operators (such as +=). The advantage to this technique is that the tokens do not need to occur in any predefined order or be separated by a fixed set of delimiters. Instead, the tokens are identified by the pattern that they match. This is the approach used by this recipe. As you will see, it is both flexible and readily adaptable.

Tokenizing is such an important task that Java provides extensive built-in support for it. For example, it supplies three classes specifically designed for this purpose:

StreamTokenizer, **Scanner**, and the obsolete **StringTokenizer**. Furthermore (as mentioned), the **String** class contains the **split( )** method, which can also be used to tokenize in certain simple situations. As helpful as these classes are, they are most useful for tokenizing a string that is defined in terms of delimiters.

To tokenize based on patterns, you will usually find Java's regular expression API a better choice. This is the approach used by the recipe in this section. By using the regular expression API, you gain direct and detailed control over the tokenization processes. Also, implementing a tokenizer by using the **Pattern** and **Matcher** classes provides an elegant solution that is clear and easy to understand.

Step-by-Step

To tokenize a string based on patterns by using the regular expression API requires the following steps:

1. Create the set of regular expressions that define the patterns that you will be matching. Each type of token that you want to obtain must be represented by a pattern. To enable the regular expression engine to move progressively through the string, begin each pattern with the \G boundary specifier. This requires the next match to begin at the point at which the previous match ended.

2. Compile the patterns into **Pattern** objects by using **Pattern.compile( )**.

3. Create a **Matcher** that contains the string to be tokenized.

4. Obtain the next token by adapting the following algorithm:

   while(still patterns to try) {
       Specify pattern to match by calling **usePattern( )** on the **Matcher**.
       Search for the pattern by calling **find( )** on the **Matcher**.
       If a match is found, obtain token.
       Otherwise try next pattern.
   }

   Often, the patterns must be tried in a specific order. Therefore, when you implement this algorithm, you must try each pattern in the correct order.

5. Once a token has been found, obtain the token by calling **group( )** on the **Matcher**.

6. Repeat Steps 4 and 5 until the end of the string is reached.

Discussion

The basic procedure used to create a **Pattern** and a **Matcher** and to use **find( )** and **group( )** to search a string is described in the preceding recipe (*Match and Extract Substrings Using the Regular Expression API*), and those discussions are not repeated here. Instead, we will focus on the two key elements that enable a string to be tokenized. The first is the definition of the set of patterns that describe the tokens. The second is **usePattern( )**, which changes the pattern being matched.

The key to using the regular expression API to tokenize a string is the **\G** boundary matcher. By starting each pattern with **\G**, each match must begin precisely where the previous match left off. (In the first match, the **\G** will match the start of the string.) Using this mechanism, the **find( )** method can be called repeatedly on a **Matcher**. Each subsequent match will begin where the previous one ended. This enables the regular expression engine to move through the string, but not skip any tokens in the process.

Here are some examples of regular expressions that match words, punctuation, whitespace, and numbers:

Matches	Pattern
Words	\G\p{Alpha}+
Punctuation	\G\p{Punct}
Whitespace	\G\s+
Numbers	\G\d+\.?\d*

In each case, the token being matched must begin immediately after the previous match. For example, given this string:

Jump one, not 2, times.

first, "Jump" is matched by the word pattern. The next pattern that will match is whitespace because it is the only pattern that can follow the previous match. Next, "one" is matched by the word pattern, again because it is the only pattern that can follow the previous match. The punctuation pattern will then match the comma, the word pattern will match "not", the number pattern will match "2", and so on. A key point is that because each pattern must start at the end of the previous match, no tokens are skipped when the regular expression engine attempts to find a match. For example, after "Jump" is found, an attempt to find a number will fail because "2" does not immediately follow "Jump".

To enable one **Matcher** to use different patterns, you will use the **usePattern( )** method. This method changes the pattern without resetting the entire **Matcher**. It is shown here:

Matcher usePattern(Pattern *regExpr*)

The pattern to use is specified by *regExpr.*

When attempting to obtain the next token, the order in which the patterns are tried is important. For example, consider these two patterns:

```
\G[<>=!]
\G((<=)|(>=)|(==)|(!=))
```

The first pattern matches the <, >, =, and ! as single-character operators. The second pattern matches <=, >=, ==, and !=, which are two-character operators. To correctly tokenize a string that contains both types of operators, you must first search for the two-character operators, then for the single-character operators. If you reverse this order, then given <=, the < and the = will be retrieved as two individual tokens, rather than as the single token <=.

Example

The following program puts into practice the preceding discussion. It tokenizes a string into its textual components: words, numbers, or punctuation. Although it is a simple example, it illustrates the basic techniques used to tokenize any type of input.

```java
// A simple tokenizer for text.
import java.util.regex.*;

class SimpleTextTokenizer {

  // Create patterns that match simple text.
  static Pattern end = Pattern.compile("\\G\\z");
  static Pattern word = Pattern.compile("\\G\\w+");
  static Pattern punct = Pattern.compile("\\G\\p{Punct}");
  static Pattern space = Pattern.compile("\\G\\s");
  static Pattern number = Pattern.compile("\\G\\d+\\.?\\d*");

  // This method returns the next token retrieved from
  // the Matcher passed to mat.
  static String getTextToken(Matcher mat) {

    // First, skip leading spaces.
    mat.usePattern(space);
    mat.find();

    // Next, obtain the next token in the string
    // by attempting to match each pattern.
    // The token found by the first matching pattern
    // is returned. The order in which the patterns
    // are tried matters. Checking for a word
    // before checking for a number can change the results.

    // First, check for a number.
    mat.usePattern(number);
    if(mat.find()) return mat.group();

    // If not a number, check for a word.
    mat.usePattern(word);
    if(mat.find()) return mat.group();

    // If not a word, check for punctuation.
    mat.usePattern(punct);
    if(mat.find()) return mat.group();

    // Finally, check for end of string.
    mat.usePattern(end);
    if(mat.find()) return "";
```

```
      // Token is not recognized.
      return null; // invalid token
  }


  // Demonstrate tokenizing.
  public static void main(String args[]) {
    String token;

    // Create a Matcher.
    Matcher mat = end.matcher("The first item is a hammer," +
                              " with a cost of $132.99.");

    // Display the tokens in the string.
    do {
      token = getTextToken(mat);

      if(token == null) {
        System.out.println("Invalid Token");
        break;
      }

      if(token.length() != 0)
        System.out.println("Token: " + token);
      else
        System.out.println("End of String");

    } while(token.length() != 0);
  }
}
```

This program produces the following output:

```
Token: The
Token: first
Token: item
Token: is
Token: a
Token: hammer
Token: ,
Token: with
Token: a
Token: cost
Token: of
Token: $
Token: 132.99
Token: .
End of String
```

SimpleTextTokenizer begins by defining several patterns that can be used to tokenize English text into either words, numbers, or punctuation. Notice that each pattern starts with \G. This forces each pattern to begin where the previous match left off. Also, notice that the word pattern is specified using \w. Thus, it can match both letters and digits. In a moment you will see why this is significant.

Next is the **getTextToken( )** method. This is where the work of tokenizing takes place. To **getTextToken( )**'s **mat** parameter is passed a **Matcher** that contains the string to be tokenized. Using this **Matcher**, it tries to match the next token in the string. It does this by first skipping any leading whitespace. Then, it tries each of the other patterns in sequence. This is accomplished by first setting the pattern used by **mat** by calling **usePattern( )**. Then **find( )** is called on **mat**. Recall that **find( )** returns **true** when it finds a match, and false otherwise. Therefore, if the first pattern fails, the next pattern is tried, and so on. The token found by the first pattern to match is returned. If the end of the string is found, then a zero-length string is returned. If no pattern matches, then some character sequence was encountered that is not part of normal English text and **null** is returned.

It is important to understand that the order in which the patterns are attempted can affect how tokens are found. In this example, the tokenizer first attempts to match the number pattern before it attempts the word pattern. This is necessary because, for the sake of illustration, the **\w** pattern was used to define the **word** pattern. As you know, the **\w** class matches both letters and digits. Therefore, in the example, if you search for words before numbers, then the number 132.99 is tokenized incorrectly as three tokens: 132 (word), a period (punctuation), and 99 (word). This is why it's necessary to first search for numbers. Of course, in this example it would have been possible to define the **word** pattern so that it excludes digits and prevent this, but such easy solutions are not always available. Usually, you will need to carefully select the order in which the patterns are tried.

One other point: In the interest of clarity, **getTextToken( )** calls **usePattern( )** and **find( )** in two separate statements. For example:

```
mat.usePattern(number);
if(mat.find()) return mat.group();
```

However, this sequence can be more compactly written like this:

```
if(mat.usePattern(number).find()) return mat.group();
```

This works because **usePattern( )** returns the **Matcher** upon which it operates. This more compact form is common in professionally written code.

Bonus Example

Although the preceding example shows the basic mechanism to tokenize a string, it does not illustrate the real power and flexibility of the approach. For this reason a substantially more sophisticated example is included that creates a general-purpose tokenizer. This tokenizer can be adapted to tokenize nearly any type of input string based on nearly any type of tokens.

The general-purpose tokenizer is fully contained within a class called **Tokenizer**. **Tokenizer** defines several built-in patterns. Four are general-purpose patterns that tokenize a string into words, numbers, punctuation, and whitespace, which are similar to those used by the preceding example. The second set defines tokens that represent a subset of the Java language. (You can easily add other patterns if you desire.)

An enumeration is included that represents the type of each token. The type describes the basic pattern that the token matches, such as word, punctuation, operator, and so on. Both the token and its type are returned each time a new token is obtained. Linking a token with its type is common in all but the simplest tokenizing situations.

The default constructor creates an object that can tokenize normal English text. The parameterized constructor lets you specify an array of token types that you want the tokenizer to use, in the order in which they are to be applied. Thus, this constructor lets you precisely tailor a tokenizer to handle nearly any type of input string.

The following program demonstrates tokenizing both normal text and program fragments.

```
// A general-purpose tokenizer class.
// It uses the \G boundary matcher to enable the tokenizer
// to move through the input string from beginning to end.
// It can be adapted to tokenize different types of input sequences.

import java.util.regex.*;

class Tokenizer {
  // This is the Matcher used by the tokenizer.
  private Matcher mat;

  // Several token patterns are defined here.  You
  // can add others of your own, if desired.

  // EOS is the pattern that describes the end
  // of the input string.
  private static Pattern EOS = Pattern.compile("\\G\\z");

  // The unknown pattern matches one character
  // to allow tokenization to move forward. Of course,
  // users of Tokenizer are free to stop tokenization if
  // an unknown token is found.
  private static Pattern unknown = Pattern.compile("\\G.");

  // Some general token patterns.
  private static Pattern word = Pattern.compile("\\G\\p{Alpha}+");
  private static Pattern punct = Pattern.compile("\\G\\p{Punct}");
  private static Pattern space = Pattern.compile("\\G\\s+");
  private static Pattern number = Pattern.compile("\\G\\d+\\.?\\d*");

  // Some Java-like program-related patterns.

  // This matches a keyword or an identifier, which
  // must not begin with a digit.
  private static Pattern kwOrIdent =
    Pattern.compile("\\G[\\w&&\\D]\\w*");

  // Specify the various separators.
  private static Pattern separator =
    Pattern.compile("\\G[(){}\\[\\];,.]");

  // These match the various operators.
  private static Pattern singleOp =
    Pattern.compile("\\G[=><!~?:+\\-*/&|\\^%@]");
  private static Pattern doubleOp =
    Pattern.compile("\\G((<=)|(>=)|(==)|(!=)|(\\|\\|)|" +
                    "(\\&\\&)|(<<)|(>>)|(--)|(\\+\\+))");
```

```java
private static Pattern assignOp =
  Pattern.compile("\\G((\\+=)|(-=)|(/=)|(\\*=)|(<<=)|" +
                  "(>>=)|(\\|=)|(&=)|(\\^=)|(>>>=))");
private static Pattern tripleOp = Pattern.compile("\\G>>>");

// This matches a string literal.
private static Pattern strLiteral = Pattern.compile("\\G\".*?\"");

// This matches a comment.
private static Pattern comment =
  Pattern.compile("\\G((//.*(?m)$)|(/\\*(?s).*?\\*/))");

// This enumeration defines the token types
// and associates a pattern to each type.
// If you define another token type, then
// add it to the enumeration.
enum TokType {
  // Initialize the enumeration values with their
  // corresponding patterns.
  WORD(word), PUNCT(punct), SPACE(space), NUMBER(number),
  KW_OR_IDENT(kwOrIdent), SEPARATOR(separator),
  SINGLE_OP(singleOp), DOUBLE_OP(doubleOp),
  TRIPLE_OP(tripleOp), ASSIGN_OP(assignOp),
  STR_LITERAL(strLiteral), COMMENT(comment), END(EOS),
  UNKNOWN(unknown);

  // This holds the pattern associated with each token type.
  Pattern pat;

  TokType(Pattern p) {
    pat = p;
  }
}

// This array holds the list of tokens that this
// tokenizer will search for, in the order in
// which the search will be conducted. Therefore,
// the order of the elements in this array matters
// because it determines the order in which matches
// will be attempted.
TokType patterns[];

// Each time a new token is obtained, the
// token and its type are returned in an
// object of type Token.
class Token {
  String token; // string containing the token
  TokType type; // the token's type
}

// This contains the current token.
Token curTok;
```

```
// Create a default Tokenizer. It tokenizes text.
Tokenizer(String str) {
  mat = unknown.matcher(str);

  // This describes the tokens for the simple
  // tokenization of text.
  TokType textTokens[] = {
    TokType.NUMBER,
    TokType.WORD,
    TokType.PUNCT,
    TokType.END,
    TokType.UNKNOWN
  };
  patterns = textTokens;
  curTok = new Token();
}

// Create a custom Tokenizer that matches the
// list of tokens given the types passed to ptns.
Tokenizer(String str, TokType ptns[]) {
  mat = unknown.matcher(str);

  // Always add END and UNKNOWN to the end
  // of the patterns array.
  TokType tmp[] = new TokType[ptns.length+2];
  System.arraycopy(ptns, 0, tmp, 0, ptns.length);
  tmp[ptns.length] = TokType.END;
  tmp[ptns.length+1] = TokType.UNKNOWN;

  patterns = tmp;
  curTok = new Token();
}

// This method returns the next token from the
// input string. What constitutes a token is
// determined by the contents of the patterns
// array.  Therefore, changing the array
// changes what type of tokens are obtained.
Token getToken() {

  // First, skip any leading whitespace.
  mat.usePattern(space).find();

  for(int i=0; i<patterns.length; i++) {
    // Select the next token pattern to use.
    mat.usePattern(patterns[i].pat);

    // Now, try to find a match.
    if(mat.find()) {
      curTok.type = patterns[i];
      curTok.token = mat.group();
      break;
    }
  }
}
```

```
      return curTok; // return the token and its type
  }
}


// Demonstrate Tokenizer.
class TokenizerDemo {

  public static void main(String args[]) {

    Tokenizer.Token t;

    // Demonstrate tokenizing text.
    Tokenizer tok =
      new Tokenizer("This is some sample text. Is today Monday, " +
                    "February 28, 2008?");

    // Read and display text tokens until
    // the END token is read.
    System.out.println("Tokenizing text.");
    do {
      // Get the next token.
      t = tok.getToken();

      // Display the token and its type.
      System.out.println("Token: " + t.token +
                         "\tType: " + t.type);

    } while(t.type != Tokenizer.TokType.END);


    // Now, create a tokenizer for a subset of Java.
    // Remember, order matters.  For example, an
    // attempt to match a double operator, such as <=
    // must occur before there is an attempt to match
    // a single operator, such as <.
    Tokenizer.TokType progToks[] = {
      Tokenizer.TokType.NUMBER,
      Tokenizer.TokType.KW_OR_IDENT,
      Tokenizer.TokType.STR_LITERAL,
      Tokenizer.TokType.COMMENT,
      Tokenizer.TokType.ASSIGN_OP,
      Tokenizer.TokType.TRIPLE_OP,
      Tokenizer.TokType.DOUBLE_OP,
      Tokenizer.TokType.SINGLE_OP,
      Tokenizer.TokType.SEPARATOR,
    };

    // Demonstrate tokenizing a program.
    tok = new Tokenizer("// comment\n int count=10; if(a<=b) count--;"+
                        "a = b >>> c; a = b >> d; result = meth(3);" +
                        "w = a<0 ? b*4 : c/2; done = !done;" +
                        "for(int i=0; i<10; i++) sum += i;" +
                        "String str = \"a string literal\"" +
                        "class Test { /* ... */ }", progToks);
```

```
    // Display each token and its type.
    System.out.println("\nTokenizing program fragments.");
    do {
      t = tok.getToken();
      System.out.println("Token: " + t.token +
                          "\tType: " + t.type);
    } while(t.type != Tokenizer.TokType.END);
  }
}
```

A portion of the output is shown here:

```
Tokenizing text.
Token: This      Type: WORD
Token: is        Type: WORD
Token: some      Type: WORD
Token: sample    Type: WORD
Token: text      Type: WORD
Token: .         Type: PUNCT
Token: Is        Type: WORD
Token: today     Type: WORD
Token: Monday    Type: WORD
Token: ,         Type: PUNCT
Token: February  Type: WORD
Token: 28        Type: NUMBER
Token: ,         Type: PUNCT
Token: 2008      Type: NUMBER
Token: ?         Type: PUNCT
Token:   Type: END

Tokenizing program fragments.
Token: // comment      Type: COMMENT
Token: int       Type: KW_OR_IDENT
Token: count     Type: KW_OR_IDENT
Token: =         Type: SINGLE_OP
Token: 10        Type: NUMBER
Token: ;         Type: SEPARATOR
Token: if        Type: KW_OR_IDENT
Token: (         Type: SEPARATOR
Token: a         Type: KW_OR_IDENT
Token: <=        Type: DOUBLE_OP
Token: b         Type: KW_OR_IDENT
Token: )         Type: SEPARATOR
Token: count     Type: KW_OR_IDENT
Token: --        Type: DOUBLE_OP
Token: ;         Type: SEPARATOR
Token: a         Type: KW_OR_IDENT
Token: =         Type: SINGLE_OP
Token: b         Type: KW_OR_IDENT
Token: >>>       Type: TRIPLE_OP
  .
  .
  .
```

This is a fairly sophisticated example and it warrants an in-depth examination of its operation. The **Tokenizer** class defines these key elements:

Element	Description
The **mat** instance variable	Holds a reference to the **Matcher** that will be used by **Tokenizer** instance.
Several precompiled token patterns	These are the patterns that describe the various types of tokens.
The **TokType** enumeration	This enumeration represents the type of each token. It also links a token type with its pattern.
The **patterns** array	This array holds an ordered set of **TokType** objects which specify the types of tokens to be obtained. The order of the array elements is the order in which **Tokenizer** tries the patterns, looking for a match.
The **Token** class	This convenience class links the current token with its type. It is nested within **Tokenizer**. Therefore, to refer to it outside **Tokenizer**, you must qualify it with **Tokenizer**, as in **Tokenizer** **.Token**.
The **curTok** instance variable	Holds a reference to the current token, which is the one obtained by the most recent call to **getToken( )**. It is returned by **getToken( )**.
The **Tokenizer** constructors	Constructs a tokenizer. The one-parameter constructor tokenizes normal English text. The two-parameter constructor allows the tokenizer to be configured to tokenize other types of input.
The **getToken( )** method	Returns the next token from the string.

Let's look more closely at each part. First, each instance of **Tokenizer** has its own **Matcher**, which is referred to via **mat**. This means that two or more **Tokenizers** can be used within the same program, each operating independently Next, notice the various patterns. The regular expressions all begin with **\G**, which means that a matching sequence must begin at the end of the previous match. As explained, this enables the regular expression engine to advance through the string. (If you don't include the **\G** boundary matcher, then the regular expression engine will find a matching sequence anywhere in the string, possibly skipping several tokens in the process.) If you add additional patterns, then you must be sure to begin each with **\G**.

Notice the patterns that tokenize a subset of Java. The **kwOrIdent** pattern matches either keywords or identifiers. (It's not often practical to distinguish between the two during tokenization. Other parts of a compiler or interpreter usually handle that chore.) Other patterns match the various separators and operators. Notice that four different patterns are required to handle the operators, each matching a different type of operator, including those composed of single characters, double characters, or triple characters. The assignment operators could have been handled as double-character operators, but for clarity, they are given a pattern of their own. Patterns that match comments and string literals are also provided.

After the patterns have been compiled, the **TokType** enumeration is created. It defines the token types that correspond to the patterns and links each pattern to its type. This linkage of pattern with type shows the power of Java enumerations, which are class types rather than simple lists of named integers (as they are in several other computer languages).

The **patterns** array holds a list of **TokType** objects that specify what types of tokens will be obtained by the tokenizer. The order of the types in the array specifies the order in which **Tokenizer** searches for a token. Because the order in which the search is conducted can matter (for example, you must look for <= before you look for <), you must take care to order this array properly. In all cases, the last two entries in the array must be **END** and **UNKNOWN**.

Next, the **Token** class is defined. This nested class is not technically necessary, but it allows a token and its type to be encapsulated within a single object. The **curTok** variable, which is an instance of **Token**, holds the most recently obtained token. A reference to it is returned by **getToken( )**. Technically, **curTok** is not necessary because it would be possible to simply construct a new **Token** object for each token obtained, and have **getToken( )** return the new object. However, when tokenizing a very large string, a large number of objects would be created and then discarded. This would result in additional garbage collection cycles. By using only one **Token** object, this potential inefficiency is eliminated.

The one-parameter **Tokenizer** constructor creates a tokenizer that handles regular English text by reducing it to words, punctuation, and numbers. The string to be tokenized is passed to the constructor. It assigns to **patterns** an array that handles these simple text elements.

The two-parameter constructor allows you to specify an array of **TokType** that will be assigned to **patterns**. This enables you to configure a tokenizer that will handle different types of input. In **TokenizerDemo**, the **progToks** array is constructed in such a way that a subset of the Java language can be tokenized. Other types of tokenizers can be created by specifying a different **TokType** array. One other point: Notice that this constructor always adds **END** and **UNKNOWN** on to the list of token types. This is necessary to ensure that **getToken( )** finds the end of the string and that it returns **UNKNOWN** when it can't find any of the patterns.

The **getToken( )** method obtains the next token in the string. It will always succeed because the token will be **END** when the end of the string has been reached and **UNKNOWN** if no matching token is found. Notice that **getToken( )** skips any leading whitespace. Normally, tokens don't include whitespace, so **getToken( )** simply discards it.

To use the tokenizer, first create a **Tokenizer** that searches for the tokens that you desire. Next, set up a loop that calls **getToken( )** on the tokenizer until the end of the string is reached. When this occurs, the type of the token returned will be **EOS**. In the program, this procedure is demonstrated by the **TokenizerDemo** class. An unknown token can either be ignored (as it is in the example) or treated as an error condition.

Options and Alternatives

As mentioned, when tokenizing based on delimiters you can use **StringTokenizer** (now deprecated), **StreamTokenizer**, **Scanner**, or the **split( )** method. If your input can be tokenized based on delimiters, then these offer effective solutions that are easy to implement.

As the preceding examples have shown, pattern-based tokenizing can be efficiently implemented by employing the **Pattern** and **Matcher** classes defined by the regular expression API. This is the approach that I prefer. However, other approaches are possible.

One alternative is based on the **Scanner** class. **Scanner** can be used for pattern-based tokenizing by employing its **findWithinHorizon( )** method to obtain a token. As mentioned earlier, **Scanner** normally tokenizes based on delimiters. However, the **findWithinHorizon( )** method ignores the delimiters and attempts to find a match to the regular expression that you pass as an argument. The match is attempted within a specified portion of the input string, which can be the entire string if necessary. Although this approach works, **Matcher** offers a cleaner, more direct approach. (Of course, if you want to alternate between tokenizing based on delimiters and tokenizing based on patterns, then using **Scanner** might be the perfect solution.)

Pattern-based tokenizing can also be implemented by hand, in which the string is scanned character by character, and the tokens are constructed one character at a time. This was the approach often used prior to the availability of the regular expression API. For some cases, it still might be the most efficient approach. However, regular expressions offer substantially more compact, maintainable code.

Be default, the entire string passed to **Matcher** will be searched for a match. However, you can restrict the search to a smaller region by calling **region( )**, shown here:

Matcher region(int *begin*, int *end*)

The index to begin searching is passed via *begin*. The search stops at *end*–1. You can obtain the current search limits by calling **regionStart( )** and **regionEnd( )**.

File Handling

File handling is an integral part of nearly all programming projects. Files provide the means by which a program stores data, accesses stored data, or shares data. As a result, there are very few applications that don't interact with a file in one form or another. Although no aspect of file handling is particularly difficult, a great many classes, interfaces, and methods are involved. Being able to effectively apply them to your projects is the mark of a professional.

It is important to understand that file I/O is a subset of Java's overall I/O system. Furthermore, Java's I/O system is quite large. This is not surprising given that it supports two distinct I/O class hierarchies: one for bytes and one for characters. It contains classes that enable a byte array, a character array, or a string to be used as source or target of I/O operations. It also provides the ability to set or obtain various attributes associated with a file, itself, such as its read/write status, whether the file is a directory, or if it is hidden. You even obtain a list of files within a directory.

Despite is size, Java's I/O system is surprisingly easy to use. One reason for this is its well-thought-out design. By structuring the I/O system around a carefully crafted set of classes, this very large API is made manageable. Once you understand how to use the core classes, it's easy to learn its more advanced capabilities. The I/O system's consistency makes it easy to maintain or adapt code, and its rich functionality provides solutions to most file handling tasks.

The core of Java's I/O system is packaged in **java.io**. It has been included with Java since version 1.0, and it contains the classes and interfaces that you will most often use when performing I/O operations, including those that operate on files. Simply put, when you need to read or write files, **java.io** is the package that you will normally turn to. As a result, all of the recipes in this chapter use its capabilities in one form or another.

Another package that includes file handling classes is **java.util.zip**. The classes in **java.util.zip** can create a compressed file, or decompress a file. These classes build on the functionality provided by the I/O classes defined in **java.io**. Thus, they are integrated in to Java's overall I/O strategy. Three recipes demonstrate the use of data compression when handling files.

This chapter provides several recipes that demonstrate file handling. It begins by describing several fundamental operations, such as reading and writing bytes or characters. It then shows various techniques that help you utilize and manage files.

Here are the recipes contained in this chapter:

- Read Bytes from a File
- Write Bytes to a File
- Buffer Byte-Based File I/O
- Read Characters from a File
- Write Characters to a File
- Buffer Character-Based File I/O
- Read and Write Random-Access Files
- Obtain File Attributes
- Set File Attributes
- List a Directory
- Compress and Decompress Data
- Create a ZIP file
- Decompress a ZIP file
- Serialize Objects

NOTE *Beginning with version 1.4, Java began providing an additional approach to I/O called NIO (which stands for New I/O). It creates a channel-based approach to I/O and is packaged in* **java.nio**. *The NIO system is not intended to replace the stream-based I/O classes found in* **java.io**. *Instead, NIO supplements them. Because the focus of this chapter is stream-based I/O, no NIO-based recipes are included. The interested reader will find a discussion of NIO (and of I/O in general) in my book* Java: The Complete Reference.

An Overview of File Handling

In Java, file handling is simply a special case aspect of a larger concept because file I/O is tightly integrated into Java's overall I/O system. In general, if you understand one part of the I/O system, it's easy to apply that knowledge to another situation. There are two aspects of the I/O system that make this feature possible. The first is that Java's I/O system is build on a cohesive set of class hierarchies, at the top of which are abstract classes that define much of the basic functionality shared by all specific concrete subclasses. The second is the *stream*. The stream ties together the file system because all I/O operations occur through one. Because of the importance of the stream, we will begin this overview of Java's file handling capabilities there.

Streams

A *stream* is an abstraction that either produces or consumes information. A stream is linked to a physical device by the I/O system. All streams behave in the same manner, even if the actual physical devices they are linked to differ. Thus, the same I/O classes and methods can be applied to different types of devices. For example, the same methods that you use to write to the console can also be used to write to a disk file or to a network connection. The core Java streams are implemented within class hierarchies defined in the **java.io** package. These are the streams that you will usually use when handling files. However, some other packages also define streams. For example, **java.util.zip** supplies streams that create and operate on compressed data.

Modern versions of Java define two types of streams: byte and character. (The original 1.0 version of Java defined only byte streams, but character streams were quickly added.) Byte streams provide a convenient means for handling input and output of bytes. They are used, for example, when reading or writing binary data. They are especially helpful when working with files. Character streams are designed for handling the input and output of characters, which streamlines internationalization.

The fact that Java defines two different types of streams makes the I/O system quite large because two separate class hierarchies (one for bytes, one for characters) are needed. The sheer number of I/O classes can make the I/O system appear more intimidating that it actually is. For the most part, the functionality of byte streams is paralleled by that of the character streams.

One other point: at the lowest level, all I/O is still byte-oriented. The character-based streams simply provide a convenient and efficient means for handling characters.

The Byte Stream Classes

Byte streams are defined by two class hierarchies: one for input and one for output. At the top of these are two abstract classes: **InputStream** and **OutputStream**. **InputStream** defines the characteristics common to byte input streams, and **OutputStream** describes the behavior of byte output streams. The methods specified by **InputStream** and **OutputStream** are shown in Tables 3-1 and 3-2. From **InputStream** and **OutputStream** are created several subclasses, which offer varying functionality. These classes are shown in Table 3-3.

Of the byte-stream classes, two are directly related to files: **FileInputStream** and **FileOutputStream**. Because these are concrete implementations of **InputStream** and **OutputStream**, they can be used any place an **InputStream** or an **OutputStream** is needed. For example, an instance of **FileInputStream** can be wrapped in another byte stream class, such as a **BufferedInputStream**. This is one reason why Java's stream-based approach to I/O is so powerful: it enables the creation of a fully integrated class hierarchy.

The Character Stream Classes

Character streams are defined by using class hierarchies that are different from the byte streams. The character stream hierarchies are topped by these two abstract classes: **Reader** and **Writer**. **Reader** is used for input, and **Writer** is used for output. Tables 3-4 and 3-5 show the methods defined by these classes. Concrete classes derived from **Reader** and **Writer** operate on Unicode character streams. In general, the character-based classes parallel the byte-based classes. The character stream classes are shown in Table 3-6.

Of the character-stream classes, two are directly related to files: **FileReader** and **FileWriter**. Because these are concrete implementations of **Reader** and **Writer**, they can be used any place a **Reader** or **Writer** is needed. For example, an instance of **FileReader** can be wrapped in a **BufferedReader** to buffer input operations.

Method	Description
int available( ) throws IOException	Returns the number of bytes of input currently available for reading.
void close( ) throws IOException	Closes the input source.
void mark(int *numBytes*)	Places a mark at the current point in the input stream that will remain valid until *numBytes* bytes are read. Not all streams implement **mark( )**.
boolean markSupported( )	Returns **true** if **mark( )/reset( )** are supported by the invoking stream.
abstract int read( ) throws IOException	Returns an integer representation of the next available byte of input. −1 is returned when the end of the file is encountered.
int read(byte *buffer*[ ]) throws IOException	Attempts to read up to *buffer.length* bytes into *buffer* and returns the actual number of bytes that were successfully read. −1 is returned when the end of the file is encountered.
int read(byte *buffer*[ ], int *offset*, int *numBytes*) throws IOException	Attempts to read up to *numBytes* bytes into *buffer* starting at *buffer*[*offset*], returning the number of bytes successfully read. −1 is returned when the end of the file is encountered.
void reset( ) throws IOException	Resets the input pointer to the previously set mark. Not all streams support **reset( )**.
long skip(long *numBytes*) throws IOException	Ignores (that is, skips) *numBytes* bytes of input, returning the number of bytes actually ignored.

TABLE 3-1 The Methods Defined by **InputStream**

Method	Description
void close( ) throws IOException	Closes the output stream.
void flush( ) throws IOException	Finalizes the output state so that any buffers are cleared. That is, it flushes the output buffers.
abstract void write(int *b*) throws IOException	Writes the low-order byte of *b* to the output stream.
void write(byte *buffer*[ ]) throws IOException	Writes a complete array of bytes to the output stream.
void write(byte *buffer*[ ], int *offset*, int *numBytes*) throws IOException	Writes a subrange of *numBytes* bytes from the array *buffer*, beginning at *buffer*[*offset*].

TABLE 3-2 The Methods Specified by **OutputStream**

Byte Stream Class	Description
BufferedInputStream	Buffered input stream.
BufferedOutputStream	Buffered output stream.
ByteArrayInputStream	Input stream that reads from a byte array.
ByteArrayOutputStream	Output stream that writes to a byte array.
DataInputStream	An input stream that contains methods for reading Java's standard data types.
DataOutputStream	An output stream that contains methods for writing Java's standard data types.
FileInputStream	Input stream that reads from a file.
FileOutputStream	Output stream that writes to a file.
FilterInputStream	Implements **InputStream** and allows the contents of another stream to be altered (filtered).
FilterOutputStream	Implements **OutputStream** and allows the contents of another stream to be altered (filtered).
InputStream	Abstract class that describes stream input.
OutputStream	Abstract class that describes stream output.
PipedInputStream	Input pipe.
PipedOutputStream	Output pipe.
PrintStream	Output stream that contains **print( )** and **println( )**.
PushbackInputStream	Input stream that allows bytes to be returned to the stream.
RandomAccessFile	Supports random-access file I/O.
SequenceInputStream	Input stream that is a combination of two or more input streams that will be read sequentially, one after the other.

TABLE 3-3   The Byte Stream Classes

A superclass of **FileReader** is **InputStreamReader**. It translates bytes into characters. A superclass of **FileWriter** is **OutputStreamWriter**. It translates characters into bytes. These classes are necessary because all files are, at their foundation, byte-oriented.

The RandomAccessFile Class

The stream classes just described operate on files in a strictly sequential fashion. However, Java also allows you to access the contents of a file in non-sequential order. To do this, you will use **RandomAccessFile**, which encapsulates a random-access file. **RandomAccessFile** is not derived from **InputStream** or **OutputStream**. Instead, it implements the interfaces

Method	Description
abstract void close( ) throws IOException	Closes the input source.
void mark(int *numChars*) throws IOException	Places a mark at the current point in the input stream that will remain valid until *numChars* characters are read. Not all streams support **mark( )**.
boolean markSupported( )	Returns **true** if **mark( )**/**reset( )** are supported on this stream.
int read( ) throws IOException	Returns an integer representation of the next available character from the input stream. −1 is returned when the end of the file is encountered.
int read(char *buffer*[ ]) throws IOException	Attempts to read up to *buffer.length* characters into *buffer* and returns the actual number of characters that were successfully read. −1 is returned when the end of the file is encountered.

abstract int read(char *buffer*[ ],
        int *offset*,
        int *numChars*)
    throws IOException
	Attempts to read up to *numChars* characters into *buffer* starting at *buffer*[*offset*], returning the number of characters successfully read. −1 is returned when the end of the file is encountered.

boolean ready( ) throws IOException	Returns **true** if input is pending. Otherwise, it returns **false**.
void reset( ) throws IOException	Resets the input pointer to the previously set mark. Not all streams support **reset( )**.
long skip(long *numChars*) throws IOException	Skips over *numChars* characters of input, returning the number of characters actually skipped.

TABLE 3-4   The Methods Defined by **Reader**

DataInput and **DataOutput** (which are described shortly). **RandomAccessFile** supports random access because it lets you change the location in the file at which the next read or write operation will occur. This is done by calling its **seek( )** method.

The File Class

In addition to the classes that support file I/O, Java provides the **File** class, which encapsulates information about a file. This class is extremely useful when manipulating a file itself (rather than its contents) or the file system of the computer. For example, using **File** you can determine if a file is hidden, set a file's date, set a file to read-only, list the contents of a directory, or create a new directory, among many other things. Thus, **File** puts the file system under your control. This makes **File** one of the most important classes in Java's I/O system.

Method	Description
Writer append(char *ch*) throws IOException	Appends *ch* to the end of the invoking output stream. Returns a reference to the stream.
Writer append(CharSequence *chars*) throws IOException	Appends *chars* to the end of the invoking output stream. Returns a reference to the stream.
Writer append(CharSequence *chars*, int *begin*, int *end*) throws IOException	Appends a subrange of *chars*, specified by *begin* and *end*, to the end of the output stream. Returns a reference to the stream.
abstract void close( ) throws IOException	Closes the output stream.
abstract void flush( ) throws IOException	Finalizes the output state so that any buffers are cleared. That is, it flushes the output buffers.
void write(int *ch*) throws IOException	Writes the character in the low-order 16 bits of *ch* to the output stream.
void write(char *buffer*[ ]) throws IOException	Writes a complete array of characters to the output stream.
abstract void write(char *buffer*[ ], int *offset*, int *numChars*) throws IOException	Writes a subrange of *numChars* characters from the array *buffer*, beginning at *buffer*[*offset*] to the output stream.
void write(String *str*) throws IOException	Writes *str* to the output stream.
void write(String *str*, int *offset*, int *numChars*)	Writes a subrange of *numChars* characters from the string *str*, beginning at the specified *offset*.

TABLE 3-5   The Methods Defined by **Writer**

The I/O Interfaces

Java's I/O system includes the following interfaces (which are packaged in **java.io**):

Closeable	DataInput	DataOutput
Externalizable	FileFilter	FilenameFilter
Flushable	ObjectInput	ObjectInputValidation
ObjectOutput	ObjectStreamConstants	Serializable

Those used either directly or indirectly by the recipes in this chapter are **DataInput**, **DataOutput**, **Closeable**, **Flushable**, **FileFilter**, **FilenameFilter**, **ObjectInput**, and **ObjectOutput**.

The **DataInput** and **DataOutput** interfaces define a variety of read and write methods, such as **readInt( )** and **writeDouble( )**, that can read and write Java's primitive data types. They also specify **read( )** and **write( )** methods that parallel those specified by **InputStream** and **OutputStream**. All operations are byte-oriented. **RandomAccessFile** implements the **DataInput** and the **DataOutput** interfaces. Thus, random-access file operations in Java are byte-oriented.

Character Stream Class	Meaning
BufferedReader	Buffered input character stream.
BufferedWriter	Buffered output character stream.
CharArrayReader	Input stream that reads from a character array.
CharArrayWriter	Output stream that writes to a character array.
FileReader	Input stream that reads from a file.
FileWriter	Output stream that writes to a file.
FilterReader	Filtered reader.
FilterWriter	Filtered writer.
InputStreamReader	Input stream that translates bytes to characters.
LineNumberReader	Input stream that counts lines.
OutputStreamWriter	Output stream that translates characters to bytes.
PipedReader	Input pipe.
PipedWriter	Output pipe.
PrintWriter	Output stream that contains **print( )** and **println( )**.
PushbackReader	Input stream that allows characters to be returned to the input stream.
Reader	Abstract class that describes character stream input.
StringReader	Input stream that reads from a string.
StringWriter	Output stream that writes to a string.
Writer	Abstract class that describes character stream output.

TABLE 3-6   The Character Stream Classes

The **Closeable** and **Flushable** interfaces are implemented by several of the I/O classes. They provide a uniform way of specifying that a stream can be closed or flushed. The **Closeable** interface defines only one method, **close( )**, which is shown here:

    void close( ) throws IOException

This method closes an open stream. Once closed, the stream cannot be used again. All I/O classes that open a stream implement **Closeable**.

The **Flushable** interface also specifies only one method, **flush( )**, which is shown here:

    void flush( ) throws IOException

Calling **flush( )** causes any buffered output to be physically written to the underlying device. This interface is implemented by the I/O classes that write to a stream.

FileFilter and **FilenameFilter** are used to filter directory listings.

The **ObjectInput** and **ObjectOutput** interfaces are used when serializing (saving and restoring) objects.

The Compressed File Streams

In **java.util.zip**, Java provides a very powerful set of specialized file streams that handle the compression and decompression of data. All are subclasses of either **InputStream** or **OutputStream**, described earlier. The compressed file streams are shown here:

DeflaterInputStream	Reads data, compressing the data in the process.
DeflaterOutputStream	Writes data, compressing the data in the process.
GZIPInputStream	Reads a GZIP file.
GZIPOutputStream	Writes a GZIP file.
InflaterInputStream	Reads data, decompressing the data in the process.
InflaterOutputStream	Writes data, decompressing the data in the process.
ZipInputStream	Reads a ZIP file.
ZipOutputStream	Writes a ZIP file.

Using the compressed file streams, it is possible to automatically compress data while writing to a file or to automatically decompress data when reading from a file. You can also create compressed files that are compatible with the standard ZIP or GZIP formats, and you can decompress files in those formats.

The actual compression is provided by the **Inflater** and **Deflater** classes, also packaged in **java.util.zip**. They use the ZLIB compression library. You won't usually need to deal with these classes directly when compressing or decompressing files because their default operation is sufficient.

Tips for Handling Errors

File I/O poses a special challenge when it comes to error handling. There are two reasons for this. First, I/O failures are a very real possibility when reading or writing files. Despite the fact that computer hardware (and the Internet) is much more reliable than in the past, it still fails at a fairly high rate, and any such failure must be handled in a manner consistent with the needs of your application. The second reason that error handling presents a challenge when working with files is that nearly all file operations can generate one or more exceptions. This means that nearly all file handling code must take place within a **try** block.

The most common I/O exception is **IOException**. This exception can be thrown by many of the constructors and methods in the I/O system. As a general rule, it is generated when something goes wrong when reading or writing data, or when opening a file. Other common I/O-related exceptions, such as **FileNotFoundException** and **ZipException**, are subclasses of **IOException**.

There is another common exception related to file handling: **SecurityException**. Many constructors or methods will throw a **SecurityException** if the invoking application does not have permission to access a file or perform a specific operation. You will need to handle this exception in a manner appropriate to your application. For simplicity, the examples in this chapter *do not* handle security exceptions, but it may be necessary for your applications to do so.

Because so many constructors and methods can generate an **IOException**, it is not uncommon to see code that simply wraps all I/O operations within a single **try** block and then catches any **IOException** that may occur. While adequate for experimenting with file I/O or possibly for simple utility programs that are for your own personal use, this approach is not usually suitable for commercial code. This is because it does not let you easily deal individually with each potential error. Instead, for detailed control, it is better to put each operation within its own **try** block. This way, you can precisely report and respond to the error that occurred. This is the approach demonstrated by the examples in this chapter.

Another way that **IOException**s are sometimes handled is by throwing them out of the method in which they occur. To do this you must include a **throws IOException** clause in the method's declaration. This approach is fine in some cases, because it reports an I/O failure back to the caller. However, in other situations it is a dissatisfying shortcut because it causes all users of the method to handle the exception. The examples in this chapter do not use this approach. Rather, they handle all **IOException**s explicitly. This allows each error handler to report precisely the error that occurred.

If you do handle **IOException**s by throwing them out of the method in which they occur, you must take extra care to close any files that have been opened by the method. The easiest way to do this is to wrap your method's code in a **try** block and then use a **finally** clause to close the files(s) prior to the method returning.

In the examples in this chapter, any I/O exceptions that do occur are handled by simply displaying a message. While this approach is acceptable for the example programs, real applications will usually need to provide a more sophisticated response to an I/O error. For example, you might want to give the user the ability to retry the operation, specify an alternative operation, or otherwise gracefully handle the problem. Preventing the loss or corruption of data is a primary goal. Part of being a great programmer is knowing how to effectively manage the things that might go wrong when an I/O operation fails.

One final point: a common mistake that occurs when handling files is forgetting to close a file when you are done with it. Open files use system resources. Thus, there are limits to the number of files that can be open at any one time. Closing a file also ensures that any data written to the file is actually written to the physical device. Therefore, the rule is very simple: if you open a file, close the file. Although files are typically closed automatically when an application ends, it's best not to rely on this because it can lead to sloppy programming and bad habits. It is better to explicitly close each file, properly handling any exceptions that might occur. For this reason, all files are explicitly closed by the examples in this chapter, even when the program is ending.

Read Bytes from a File

Key Ingredients	
Classes	**Methods**
java.io.FileInputStream	int read( )
	void close( )

The two most fundamental file operations are reading bytes from a file and writing bytes to a file. This recipe shows how to accomplish the first. (The following recipe shows how to handle the second.) Although Java offers the ability to read other types of data, such as characters, floating-point values, or lines of text, byte-based I/O is at the foundation of file handling because all file operations are, at their core, byte-oriented. Furthermore, byte-based file operations can be used with any type of file, no matter what the file contains. For example, if you want to write a file utility that displays the hexadecimal representation of the bytes within a file, then you will need to use the byte-based I/O classes. This allows the program to create a "hex dump" for any type of file, including those that contain text, graphics, executable code, and so on.

One way to read bytes from a file is to use **FileInputStream**. It is derived from **InputStream**, which defines the basic functionality of all byte input streams. It implements the **Closeable** interface.

Step-by-Step

To read bytes from a file using **FileInputStream** involves these steps:

1. Open the file by creating a **FileInputStream** instance.
2. Read from the file by using the **read( )** method.
3. Close the file by calling **close( )**.

Discussion

To open a file for input, create a **FileInputStream** object. **FileInputStream** defines three constructors. The one we will use is:

FileInputStream(String *fileName*) throws FileNotFoundException

Here, *fileName* specifies the name of the file that you want to open. If the file does not exist, then **FileNotFoundException** is thrown.

To read from the file, you can use any version of the **read( )** method (which is inherited from **InputStream**). The one that we will use is shown here:

int read( ) throws IOException

It reads a single byte from the file and returns the byte as an integer value. **read( )** returns –1 when the end of the file is encountered. It will throw an **IOException** if an I/O error occurs. Other versions of **read( )** can input multiple bytes at a time and put them into an array.

When you are done with the file, you must close it by calling **close( )**. It is shown here:

void close( ) throws IOException

An **IOException** is thrown if an error occurs when closing the file.

Example

The following program uses **FileInputStream** to display the contents of a file, byte by byte, in hexadecimal format.

```
// Display a file in hex.
//
// To use this program, specify the name
// of the file that you want to see.
// For example, to see a file called test.exe,
// use the following command line:
//
// java HexDump test.exe
//

import java.io.*;

class HexDump {
  public static void main(String args[])
  {
    FileInputStream fin;

    // First make sure that a file has been specified
    // on the command line.
    if(args.length != 1) {
      System.out.println("Usage: java HexDump File");
      return;
    }

    // Now, open the file.
    try {
      fin = new FileInputStream(args[0]);
    } catch(FileNotFoundException exc) {
      System.out.println("File Not Found");
      return;
    }

    // Read bytes and display their hexadecimal values.
    try {
      int i;
      int count = 0;

      // Read bytes until EOF is encountered.
      do {
        i = fin.read();
        if(i != -1) System.out.printf("%02X ", i);
        count++;
```

```
            if(count == 16) {
              System.out.println();
              count = 0;
            }
        } while(i != -1);
    } catch(IOException exc) {
      System.out.println("Error Reading File");
    }

    // Close the file.
    try {
      fin.close();
    } catch(IOException exc) {
      System.out.println("Error Closing File");
    }
  }
}
```

Here is a portion of the output produced when this program is run on its own class file.

```
CA FE BA BE 00 00 00 31 00 40 0A 00 0B 00 1C 09
00 1D 00 1E 08 00 1F 0A 00 20 00 21 07 00 22 0A
00 05 00 23 07 00 24 08 00 25 0A 00 05 00 26 08
00 27 07 00 28 0A 00 29 00 2A 0A 00 20 00 2B 0A
00 20 00 2C 07 00 2D 08 00 2E 0A 00 05 00 2F 08
00 30 07 00 31 01 00 06 3C 69 6E 69 74 3E 01 00
03 28 29 56 01 00 04 43 6F 64 65 01 00 0F 4C 69
6E 65 4E 75 6D 62 65 72 54 61 62 6C 65 01 00 04
```

Options and Alternatives

There are two other forms of **read( )** that you can use to read bytes from a file. First, you can read a block of bytes from the file by using this form of **read( )**:

  int read(byte *buf*[ ]) throws IOException

It fills the array referred to by *buf* with bytes read from the file. It returns the number of bytes actually read, which might be less than **buf.length** if the end of the file is encountered. Attempting to read at end-of-file causes **read( )** to return –1. For example, in the preceding program, here is another way to write the sequence that reads and displays the bytes in the file:

```
// Read bytes and display their hexadecimal values.
try {
  int len;
  byte data[] = new byte[16];

  // Read bytes until EOF is encountered.
  do {
    len = fin.read(data);
    for(int j=0; j<len; j++)
      System.out.printf("%02X ", data[j]);
```

```
    System.out.println();
  } while(len != -1);
} catch(IOException exc) {
  System.out.println("Error Reading File");
}
```

This approach creates a 16-byte array and uses it to read up to 16 bytes of data with each call to **read( )**. This is more efficient than performing 16 separate read operations, as the example does.

The last form of **read( )** is shown here:

int read(byte buf[ ], int *startIdx*, int *num*) throws IOException

This version reads *num* bytes from the file and stores them in *buf,* beginning at the index specified by *startIdx*. It returns the number of bytes actually read, which might be less than *num* if the end of the file is encountered. Attempting to read at end-of-file causes **read( )** to return –1.

FileInputStream supplies additional constructors that enable you to create an object by passing a **File** object or by passing a **FileDescriptor**. These constructors may offer a convenient alternative in some situations.

To read characters (i.e., objects of type **char**) rather than bytes, use **FileReader**. (See *Read Characters from a File.*)

You can buffer input from a file by wrapping a **FileInputStream** within a **BufferedInputStream**. This can make file operations more efficient. (See *Buffer Byte-Based File I/O.*)

Write Bytes to a File

Key Ingredients	
Classes	**Methods**
java.io.FileOutputStream	int write(int *byteval*)
	void close( )

As the preceding recipe stated, there are two fundamental file operations: reading bytes from a file and writing bytes to a file. The preceding recipe showed how to read bytes. This recipe shows how to write bytes. Although Java gives you the ability to write other types of data, byte-based output is useful in circumstances in which raw data (that is, unformatted data) needs to be written to a file. For example, if you want to save the contents of a screen buffer to disk, then byte-based output is the right choice. It is also the right choice when creating various file utilities, such as those that copy, split, merge, or search files, because byte-based file operations can be used with any type of file, no matter what that file contains or the format of its data.

To write bytes to a file, you can use **FileOutputStream**. It is derived from **OutputStream**, which defines the basic functionality of all byte output streams. It implements the **Closeable** and **Flushable** interfaces.

Step-by-Step

To write to a file using **FileOutputStream** involves these steps:

1. Open the file by creating a **FileOutputStream** object.
2. Write to the file using the **write( )** method.
3. Close the file by calling **close( )**.

Discussion

To open a file for output, create a **FileOutputStream** object. **FileOutputStream** defines several constructors. The one we will use is

FileOutputStream(String *fileName*) throws FileNotFoundException

Here, *fileName* specifies the name of the file that you want to open. If the file cannot be created, then **FileNotFoundException** is thrown. Any preexisting file by the same name will be destroyed.

To write to a file, you can use any version of the **write( )** method (which is inherited from **OutputStream**). Its simplest form is shown here:

void write(int *byteval*) throws IOException

This method writes the byte specified by *byteval* to the file. Although *byteval* is declared as an integer, only the low-order eight bits are written to the file. If an error occurs during writing, an **IOException** is thrown. Other versions of **write( )** can output an array of bytes. When you are done with the file, you must close it by calling **close( )**. It is shown here:

void close( ) throws IOException

An **IOException** is thrown if an error occurs while closing the file.

Example

The following example uses **FileOutputStream** to write bytes to a file. It first creates a file called **Test.dat**. It then writes every other byte in the **vals** array to the file. The **vals** array contains the ASCII codes for the letters A through J. Therefore, after the program runs, **Test.dat** will contain the ASCII characters ACEGI.

```
// Use FileOutputStream to write the bytes to a file.

import java.io.*;

class WriteBytes {
  public static void main(String args[])
  {
    // This array contains the ASCII code for the
    // letters A through J.
    byte[] vals = { 65, 66, 67, 68, 69, 70, 71, 72, 73, 74 };
```

```
FileOutputStream fout;

try {
  // Open output file.
  fout = new FileOutputStream("Test.dat");
} catch(FileNotFoundException exc) {
  System.out.println("Error Opening Output File");
  return;
}

try {
  // Write every other value in the vals array to the file.
  for(int i=0; i<vals.length; i+=2)
    fout.write(vals[i]);
} catch(IOException exc) {
  System.out.println("Error Writing File");
}

try {
  fout.close();
} catch(IOException exc) {
  System.out.println("Error Closing File");
}
  }
}
```

Options and Alternatives

There are two other forms of **write( )** that you can use to write bytes to a file. First, you can write a block of bytes by using this form of **write( )**:

void write(byte *buf*[ ]) throws IOException

The contents of the array referred to by *buf* are written to the file. For example, in the preceding program, if you wanted to write the entire contents of the **vals** array to the file, you could use this single call to **write( )**:

```
fout.write(vals);
```

This would be more efficient than writing one byte at a time.
    You can write a portion of an array to a file by using this form of **write( )**:

void write(byte *buf*[ ], int *startIdx*, int *num*) throws IOException

This version writes *num* bytes from *buf* to a file, beginning at the index specified by *startIdx*.
    FileOutputStream supplies several additional constructors. First, you can specify the file to open by passing a **File** object or by passing a **FileDescriptor**. You can also specify whether output is to be appended to the end of the file by using one of these constructors:

FileOutputStream(String *fileName*, boolean *apnd*)
        throws FileNotFoundException

FileOutputStream(File *fileObj*, boolean *apnd*)
        throws FileNotFoundException

In the first version, *fileName* specifies the name of the file that you want to open. In the second version, *fileObj* specifies the **File** object that describes the file you want to open. If *apnd* is true, then the contents of a preexisting file will be preserved and all output will be written to the end of the file. This is useful when you want to add to an existing file. Otherwise, when *apnd* is false, the contents of any preexisting file by the same name will be destroyed. In both cases, if the file cannot be opened, then **FileNotFoundException** is thrown. You can see the effects of opening a file using append mode by substituting this line into the example:

```
fout = new FileOutputStream("Test.dat", true);
```

Now, each time that you run the program, the characters will be added to the end of the previous contents of **Test.dat**.

You can buffer output to a file by wrapping a **FileOutputStream** within a **BufferedOutputStream**. (See *Buffer Byte-Based File I/O*.)

To write characters (i.e., objects of type **char**) rather than bytes, use **FileWriter**. (See *Write Characters to a File*.)

Buffer Byte-Based File I/O

Key Ingredients	
Classes	**Methods**
java.io.BufferedInputStream	int read( )
	void close( )
java.io.BufferedOutputStream	void write(int *byteval*)
	void close( )

The preceding two recipes showed the general procedure to read bytes from and write bytes to a file by using **FileInputStream** and **FileOutputStream**. Although there is nothing wrong with this, neither class provides automatic buffering. This means that every read or write operation ultimately interacts with various system-level I/O drivers (which provide access to the physical file). This is often not an efficient approach. In many cases, a better way is to provide a buffer for the data. In the case of output, data is stored in a buffer until the buffer is full. Then the entire buffer is written to the underlying file in a single operation. For input, an entire buffer is read from the underlying file and then each input operation obtains its data from the buffer. When the buffer is exhausted, the next buffer is obtained from the file. This mechanism causes the number of individual file operations to be greatly reduced.

Although it is possible to manually buffer the I/O operations by reading and writing arrays of bytes (rather than individual bytes), this is neither a convenient nor appropriate solution in many cases. Instead, to achieve the performance benefits of buffered file I/O operations, you will usually want to wrap a file stream within one of Java's buffered stream classes. Doing so will often dramatically increase the speed of your I/O operations without any extra effort on your part.

To create a buffered input stream, use **BufferedInputStream**. It is derived from **InputStream** and from **FilterInputStream**. It implements the **Closeable** interface.

To create a buffered output stream, use **BufferedOutputStream**. It is derived from **OutputStream** and from **FilterOutputStream**. It implements the **Closeable** and **Flushable** interfaces.

Step-by-Step

Buffering a file stream involves these steps:

1. Create the underlying file stream. For input, this will be an instance of **FileInputStream**. For output, this will be an instance of **FileOutputStream**.

2. Wrap the file stream in the appropriate buffered stream. For input, wrap the file stream in a **BufferedInputStream**. For output, wrap the file stream in a **BufferedOutputStream**.

3. Perform all I/O operations through the buffered stream.

4. Close the buffered stream. Closing the buffered stream automatically causes the underlying file stream to be closed.

Discussion

To create a buffered input stream, use **BufferedInputStream**. It defines two constructors. The one we will use is:

    BufferedInputStream(InputStream *strm*)

This creates a buffered input stream that buffers the input stream specified by *strm*. It uses the default buffer size.

To create a buffered output stream, use **BufferedOutputStream**. It defines two constructors. The one we will use is:

    BufferedOutputStream(OutputStream *strm*)

This creates a buffered output stream that buffers the output stream specified by *strm*. It uses the default buffer size.

To read from a buffered stream, you can use **read( )**. To write to a buffered stream, you can use **write( )**. (See *Read Bytes From a File* and *Write Bytes to a File* for details.)

When you are done with the buffered stream, you must close it by calling **close( )**. It is shown here:

    void close( ) throws IOException

Closing a buffered stream also causes the underlying stream to be closed automatically. An **IOException** will be thrown if an error occurs.

Example

The following example shows both **BufferedInputStream** and **BufferedOutputStream** in action. It creates a program that copies a file. Because byte streams are used, any type of file can be copied, including those that contain text, data, or programs.

```
// Use buffered streams to copy a file.
//
// To use this program, specify the name
// of the source file and the destination file.
// For example, to copy a file called sample.dat
// to a file called sample.bak, use the following
// command line:
//
//    java BufferedFileCopy sample.dat sample.bak
//

import java.io.*;

class BufferedFileCopy {

  public static void main(String args[])
  {
    BufferedInputStream fin;
    BufferedOutputStream fout;

    // First make sure that both files have been specified.
    if(args.length != 2) {
      System.out.println("Usage: BufferedFileCopy From To");
      return;
    }

    // Open an input file that is wrapped in a BufferedInputStream.
    try {
      fin = new BufferedInputStream(new FileInputStream(args[0]));
    } catch(FileNotFoundException exc) {
      System.out.println("Input File Not Found");
      return;
    }

    // Open an output file that is wrapped in a BufferedOutputStream.
    try {
      fout = new BufferedOutputStream(new FileOutputStream(args[1]));
    } catch(FileNotFoundException exc) {
      System.out.println("Error Opening Output File");

      // Close the open input file.
      try {
        fin.close();
      } catch(IOException exc2) {
        System.out.println("Error Closing Input File");
      }
      return;
    }

    // Copy the file.
    // Because buffered streams are used, the
    // read and write operations are automatically
    // buffered, which results in higher performance.
    try {
      int i;
```

```
     do {
       i = fin.read();
       if(i != -1) fout.write(i);
     } while(i != -1);
   } catch(IOException exc) {
     System.out.println("File Error");
   }

   try {
     fin.close();
   } catch(IOException exc) {
     System.out.println("Error Closing Input File");
   }

   try {
     fout.close();
   } catch(IOException exc) {
     System.out.println("Error Closing Output File");
   }
  }
}
```

Options and Alternatives

The increase in performance that is generated by the use of buffered streams can be quite dramatic. In fact, you don't have to resort to nanosecond timing to see the difference. It is often readily apparent just by observation. This is true of the file copy program just shown. To see the difference that buffering makes, first use the example program as shown to copy a very large file and notice how long it takes to run. Then, modify the program so that it uses **FileInputStream** and **FileOutputStream** directly. In other words, do not wrap either file within a buffered input stream. Then, rerun the program, copying the same large file. If the file you are copying is sufficiently large, you will easily notice that the unbuffered version takes longer.

Although the size of the buffers automatically provided by **BufferedInputStream** and **BufferedOutputStream** are normally sufficient, it is possible to specify the buffer size. You might want to do this if your data is organized into fixed-size blocks and you will be operating on it a block at a time. To specify the buffer size for buffered input, use the following constructor:

BufferedInputStream(InputStream *strm*, int *len*)

This creates a buffered input stream that buffers the stream specified by *strm*. The length of the buffer is passed via *len*, which must be greater than zero. To specify the buffer size for buffered output, use the following constructor:

BufferedOutputStream(OutputStream *strm*, int *len*)

This creates a buffered output stream that buffers the stream specified by *strm*. The length of the buffer is specified by *len*, which must be greater than zero.

BufferedInputStream overrides the **mark( )** and **reset( )** methods specified by **InputStream**. This is important because in **InputStream**, **mark( )** does nothing and **reset( )** throws an **IOException**. By overriding these methods, **BufferedInputStream** enables you to move within a buffer. You might find this capability useful in certain situations.

Read Characters from a File

Key Ingredients	
Classes	**Methods**
java.io.FileReader	int read( )
	void close( )

Although byte streams are technically sufficient to handle all file input tasks (because all files can be treated as a stream of bytes), Java offers a better approach when operating on character data: the character streams. The character-based streams operate directly on objects of type **char** (rather than bytes). Therefore, when operating on files that contain text, the character-based streams are often the best choice.

To read characters from a file, you can use **FileReader**. **FileReader** is derived from **InputStreamReader** and **Reader**. (**InputStreamReader** provides the mechanism that translates bytes into characters.) **FileReader** implements the **Closeable** and **Readable** interfaces. (**Readable** is packaged in **java.lang** and defines an object that supplies characters via the **read( )** method.) When reading a file via **FileReader**, the translation of bytes into characters is handled automatically.

Step-by-Step

To read a file using **FileReader** involves three main steps:

1. Open the file using **FileReader**.
2. Read from the file using the **read( )** method.
3. Close the file by calling **close( )**.

Discussion

To open a file, you simply create a **FileReader** object. **FileReader** defines three constructors. The one we will use is

FileReader(String *fileName*) throws FileNotFoundException

Here, *fileName* is the name of a file. It throws a **FileNotFoundException** if the file does not exist. To read a character from the file, you can use this version of **read( )** (inherited from **Reader**):

int read( ) throws IOException

Each time that it is called, it reads a single character from the file and returns the character as an integer value. **read( )** returns –1 when the end of the file is encountered. It will throw an **IOException** if an I/O error occurs. Other versions of **read( )** can input multiple characters at a time and put them into an array.

When you are done with the file, you must close it by calling **close( )**. It is shown here:

void close( ) throws IOException

If an error occurs when attempting to close the file, an **IOException** is thrown.

Example

The following program uses **FileReader** to input and display the contents of a text file, one character at a time.

```java
// Use a FileReader to display a text file.
//
// To use this program, specify the name
// of the file that you want to see.
// For example, to see a file called Test.txt,
// use the following command line.
//
//    java ShowFile Test.txt
//

import java.io.*;

class ShowFile {
  public static void main(String args[])
  {
    FileReader fr;

    // First make sure that a file has been specified.
    if(args.length != 1) {
      System.out.println("Usage: ShowFile file");
      return;
    }

    try {

      // Open the file.
      fr = new FileReader(args[0]);

    } catch(FileNotFoundException exc) {
      System.out.println("File Not Found");
      return;
    }

    // At this point, the file is open and
    // its contents can be read.
    try {

      int ch;

      // Read the file one character at a time.
      do {
        ch = fr.read();
        if(ch != -1) System.out.print((char)ch);
      } while(ch != -1);

    } catch(IOException exc) {
      System.out.println("Error Reading File");
    }
```

```
      try {
        fr.close();
      } catch(IOException exc) {
        System.out.println("Error closing File");
      }
    }
}
```

Options and Alternatives

There are three other forms of **read( )** available to **FileReader**. The first is

>   int read(char *buf*[ ]) throws IOException

This method fills the array referred to by *buf* with characters read from the file. It returns the number of characters actually read, which might be less than **buf.length** if the end of the file is encountered. Attempting to read at end-of-file causes **read( )** to return –1. For example, in the preceding program, here is another way to write the portion of code that reads and displays the characters in the file:

```
try {

  int count;
  char chrs[] = new char[80];

  // Read the file one buffer at a time.
  do {
    count = fr.read(chrs);
    for(int i=0; i < count; i++)
      System.out.print(chrs[i]);
  } while(count != -1);

} catch(IOException exc) {
  System.out.println("Error Reading File");
}
```

This approach creates a 80-character array and uses it to read up to 80 characters with each call to **read( )**. This is more efficient than performing 80 separate read operations, as the example does.

The next form of **read( )** is shown here:

>   int read(char *buf*[ ], int *startIdx*, int *num*) throws IOException

This version reads *num* characters from the file and stores them in *buf*, beginning at the index specified by *startIdx*. It returns the number of characters actually read, which might be less than *num* if the end of the file is encountered. Attempting to read at end-of-file causes **read( )** to return –1.

The final version of **read( )** is shown here:

>   int read(CharBuffer *buf*) throws IOException

This version of **read( )** is specified by the **Readable** interface. It reads characters into the buffer referred to by *buf*. It returns the number of characters actually read, which might be less than the size of the buffer if the end of the file is encountered. Attempting to read at end-of-file causes **read( )** to return –1. **CharBuffer** is packaged in **java.nio** and used by the NIO system.

FileReader supplies two additional constructors that enable you to create an object by passing a **File** object or by passing in a **FileDescriptor**. These constructors may offer a convenient alternative in some situations.

To read the bytes contained in a file rather than characters, use **FileInputStream**. (See *Read Bytes from a File*.)

You can buffer input from a file by wrapping a **FileReader** in a **BufferedReader**. (See *Buffer Character-Based File I/O*.)

Write Characters to a File

Key Ingredients	
Classes	**Methods**
java.io.FileWriter	void write(String *str*)
	void close( )

Although a byte stream can be used to write characters to a file, it is not the best choice. In cases in which you are dealing exclusively with text, Java's character-based file streams are the far better solution because they automatically handle the translation of characters into bytes. Not only can this be more efficient, it can also simplify internationalization.

To write characters to a file, you can use **FileWriter**. **FileWriter** is derived from **OutputStreamWriter** and **Writer**. (**OutputStreamWriter** provides the mechanism that translates characters into bytes.) **FileWriter** implements the **Closeable, Flushable,** and **Appendable** interfaces. (**Appendable** is packaged in **java.lang**. It defines an object to which characters can be added via the **append( )** method.) When writing to a file via **FileWriter**, the translation of characters into bytes is handled automatically.

Step-by-Step

To write to a file using **FileWriter** involves these steps:

1. Open the file using **FileWriter**.
2. Write to the file using the **write( )** method.
3. Close the file by calling **close( )**.

Discussion

To open a file, simply create a **FileWriter** object. **FileWriter** defines several constructors. The one we will use is

FileWriter(String *fileName*) throws IOException

Here, *fileName* is the name of a file. It throws an **IOException** on failure.
To write to the file, use the **write( )** method (which is inherited from **Writer**). One version is shown here:

void write(String *str*) throws IOException

This version of **write( )** writes *str* to the file. It throws an **IOException** if an error occurs while writing. Several other versions of **write( )** are available that write individual characters, portions of a string, or the contents of a **char** array.
When you are done with the file, you must close it by calling **close( )**. It is shown here:

void close( ) throws IOException

Example

This example uses a **FileWriter** to write an array of strings (each containing a five-digit employee ID number and an e-mail address) to a file called **Employees.dat**. Notice that after each string in the array is written, a newline is written. This causes each string to be on its own line. Without the newline, the next string would begin on the same line, immediately after the previous one. Of course, the addition of the newline is not something that all applications will need.

```java
// Use FileWriter to write an array of strings to a file.

import java.io.*;

class WriteChars {

  public static void main(String args[])
  {
    String str;
    FileWriter fw;
    String strs[] = { "32435 Tom@HerbSchildt.com",
                      "86754 Mary@HerbSchildt.com",
                      "35789 TC@HerbSchildt.com" };
    try {

      // Open the output file.
      fw = new FileWriter("Employees.dat");

    } catch(IOException exc) {
      System.out.println("Error Opening File");
      return ;
    }
```

```
    try {

      // Write the strings in strs to the file.
      for(int i=0; i < strs.length; i++) {
        fw.write(strs[i]); // write line to file
        fw.write("\n"); // output a newline
      }

    } catch(IOException exc) {
      System.out.println("Error Writing File");
    }

    try {
      fw.close();
    } catch(IOException exc) {
      System.out.println("Error Closing File");
    }
  }
}
```

After this program runs, **Employees.dat** will contain the following output:

```
32435 Tom@HerbSchildt.com
86754 Mary@HerbSchildt.com
35789 TC@HerbSchildt.com
```

Options and Alternatives

There are several other forms of **write( )** that you can use. They are shown here:

void write(int *ch*) throws IOException

void write(char *buf*[ ]) throws IOException

void write(char *buf*[ ], int *startIdx*, int *num*) throws IOException

void write(String *str*, int *startIdx*, int *num*) throws IOException

The first form writes the low-order 16 bits of *ch*. The second form writes the contents of *buf*. The third form writes *num* characters from *buf*, beginning at the index specified by *startIdx*. The final form writes *num* characters from *str*, beginning at the index specified by *startIdx*.

The last form of **write( )** can sometimes be especially useful. For example, assuming the employee strings used in the example (a 5-digit employee ID number, followed by a space, followed by the employee's e-mail address), the following call to **write( )** will write only the e-mail addresses to a file:

```
fw.write(strs[i], 6, strs[i].length()-6);
```

If this line is substituted into the example, then the **Employees.dat** file will contain the following:

```
Tom@HerbSchildt.com
Mary@HerbSchildt.com
TC@HerbSchildt.com
```

As is evident, the employee ID portion of each string is not stored in the file.

FileWriter supplies several additional constructors. First, you can create an object by passing a **File** object or by passing in a **FileDescriptor**. You can also specify whether output is to be appended to the end of the file by using one of these constructors:

FileWriter(String *fileName*, boolean *apnd*) throws IOException

FileWriter(File *fileObj*, boolean *apnd*) throws IOException

In the first version, *fileName* specifies the name of the file that you want to open. In the second version, *fileObj* specifies the **File** object that describes the file. In both cases, if *apnd* is true, then the contents of a preexisting file will be preserved and all output will be written to the end of the file. This is useful when you want to add to an existing file. Otherwise, when *apnd* is false, the contents of any preexisting file by the same name will be destroyed. If the file cannot be opened, then both constructors throw **IOException**. You can see the effects of opening a file using append mode by substituting this line into the example:

```
fw = new FileWriter("Employees.dat", true);
```

Now, each time that you run the program, the employee data will be added to the end of the existing file.

To write bytes rather than characters, use **FileOutputStream**. (See *Write Bytes to a File.*)

You can buffer output to a file by wrapping a **FileWriter** in a **BufferedWriter**. (See *Buffer Character-Based File I/O.*)

Buffer Character-Based File I/O

Key Ingredients	
Classes	**Methods**
java.io.BufferedReader	int read( )
	void close( )
java.io.BufferedWriter	void write(int *byteval*)
	void close( )

Although **FileReader** and **FileWriter** provide the capabilities to read from and write to a text file, using them alone may not always be the most efficient approach. The reason is that each individual read or write operation translates into an operation (directly or indirectly) on the underlying file, and file accesses are time-consuming. Often, a better approach is to provide a buffer for the data. In this approach, each input operation reads from a block of data and each output operation writes to a block of data. Thus, the number of file operations is reduced, resulting in improved performance.

Although it is possible to manually buffer the I/O operations by reading and writing arrays of characters (rather than individual characters), this approach will not be optimal in all cases. Instead, to achieve the performance benefits of buffering file I/O operations, you will usually want to wrap a character stream within one of Java's buffered reader or writer classes. Doing so will often dramatically increase the speed of your I/O operations without any extra effort on your part.

To create a buffered input stream reader, use **BufferedReader**. It is derived from **Reader**, and it implements the **Closeable** and **Readable** interfaces. (**Readable** is packaged in **java.lang** and defines an object that supplies characters via the **read( )** method.)

To create a buffered output stream reader, use **BufferedWriter**. It is derived from **Writer**, and it implements the **Closeable, Flushable**, and **Appendable** interfaces. (**Appendable** is packaged in **java.lang**. It defines an object to which characters can be added via the **append( )** method.)

Step-by-Step

Buffering a character-based file stream involves these steps:

1. Create the underlying stream. For input, this will be an instance of **FileReader**. For output, this will be an instance of **FileWriter**.

2. Wrap the file stream in the appropriate buffered reader or writer. For input, use **BufferedReader**. For output, use **BufferedWriter**.

3. Perform all I/O operations through the buffered reader or writer.

4. Close the buffered stream. Closing the buffered stream automatically causes the underlying file stream to be closed.

Discussion

To create a buffered reader, use **BufferedReader**. It defines two constructors. The one we will use is

    BufferedReader(Reader *rdr*)

This creates a reader that buffers the input stream specified by *rdr*. It uses the default buffer size. To buffer file input operations, you will pass a **FileReader** to *rdr*.

To create a buffered writer, use **BufferedWriter**. It defines two constructors. The one we will use is

    BufferedWriter(OutputStream *wtr*)

This creates a writer that buffers the output stream specified by *wtr*. It uses the default buffer size. Therefore, to buffer file operations, you will pass a **FileWriter** to *wtr*.

For example, assuming a file called **Test.dat**, the following lines show how to create a **BufferedReader** and a **BufferedWriter** linked to that file.

```
BufferedReader br = new BufferedReader(new FileReader("Test.dat"));
BufferedWriter bw = new BufferedWriter(new FileWriter("Test.dat"));
```

To read from a **BufferedReader**, you can use any of the **read( )** methods, which are inherited from **Reader**. The one we will use is shown here:

    int read( ) throws IOException

It returns the next character in the stream (in the low-order 16 bits of an integer) or −1 if the end of the stream has been reached. If an error occurs during reading, an **IOException** is thrown.

To write to a buffered stream, you can use any version of the **write( )** method, which is inherited from **Writer**. The one we will use is shown here:

void write(int *ch*) throws IOException

This method writes the character specified by *ch* to the file. Although *byteval* is declared as an integer, only the low-order 16 bits are written to the stream. If an error occurs during writing, an **IOException** is thrown. Other versions of **write( )** can output an array of characters.

When you are done with a buffered reader or writer, you must close it by calling **close( )**. It is shown here:

void close( ) throws IOException

Closing a **BufferedReader** or **BufferedWriter** also causes the underlying stream to be closed automatically.

Example

The following example uses a **BufferedReader** and a **BufferedWriter** to copy a file. In the process, it inverts the case of letters. In other words, lowercase letters become uppercase, uppercase letters become lowercase. All other characters are unchanged.

```
// Use a BufferedReader and a BufferedWriter to
// copy a text file, inverting the case of letters
// in the process.
//
// To use this program, specify the name of the
// source file and the destination file. For example,
// to copy a file called test.txt to a file called
// test.inv, use the following command line:
//
//   java InvertCopy test.txt test.inv
//

import java.io.*;

class InvertCopy {

  public static void main(String args[])
  {
    BufferedReader br;
    BufferedWriter bw;

    // First make sure that both files have been specified.
    if(args.length != 2) {
      System.out.println("Usage: InvertCopy From To");
      return;
    }
```

```java
// Open a FileReader that is wrapped in a BufferedReader.
try {
  br = new BufferedReader(new FileReader(args[0]));
} catch(FileNotFoundException exc) {
  System.out.println("Input File Not Found");
  return;
}

// Open a FileWriter that is wrapped in a BufferedWriter.
try {
  bw = new BufferedWriter(new FileWriter(args[1]));
} catch(IOException exc) {
  System.out.println("Error Opening Output File");

  // Close the open input reader.
  try {
    br.close();
  } catch(IOException exc2) {
    System.out.println("Error Closing Input File");
  }
  return;
}

// Copy the file, inverting case in the process.
// Because buffered streams are used, the
// read and write operations are automatically
// buffered, which results in higher performance.
try {
  int i;
  char ch;

  do {
    i = br.read();
    if(i != -1) {
      if(Character.isLowerCase((char) i))
        bw.write(Character.toUpperCase((char) i));
      else if(Character.isUpperCase((char) i))
        bw.write(Character.toLowerCase((char) i));
      else
        bw.write((char) i);
    }
  } while(i != -1);
} catch(IOException exc) {
  System.out.println("File Error");
}

try {
  br.close();
} catch(IOException exc) {
  System.out.println("Error Closing Input File");
}
```

```
     try {
       bw.close();
     } catch(IOException exc) {
       System.out.println("Error Closing Output File");
     }
   }
}
```

Options and Alternatives

It is easy to see firsthand the performance improvement that results from wrapping a file stream inside a buffered stream, by trying the following experiment. First, run the example program as shown on a very large text file. Notice how long it takes to run. Then, modify the program so that it uses the **FileReader** and the **FileWriter** directly. In other words, do not wrap either within a buffered class. Then, rerun the program on the same large text file. If the file you are operating on is sufficiently large, you will easily notice that the unbuffered version takes longer.

As a general rule, the default buffer size provided by **BufferedReader** and **BufferedWriter** is sufficient, but it is possible to specify a buffer size of your own choosing. However, setting the buffer size is most applicable to situations in which a file is organized into blocks of characters, with each block being a fixed size. Frankly, when working with text files, this situation is not common. Therefore, the default buffer size is often the proper choice. To specify the buffer size for a **BufferedReader**, use this constructor:

BufferedReader(Reader *rdr*, int *len*)

This creates a buffered reader based on *rdr* that has a buffer length of *len,* which must be greater than zero. To specify the buffer size for a **BufferedWriter**, use this constructor:

BufferedWriter(OutputStream *wtr*, int *len*)

This creates a buffered writer based on *wtr* that has a buffer length of *len,* which must be greater than zero.

BufferedReader overrides the **mark( )** and **reset( )** methods specified by **Reader**. This is important because the default implementations provided by **Reader** (which are inherited by **FileReader**) simply throw an **IOException**. By overriding these methods, **BufferedReader** enables you to move within a buffer. You might find this capability useful in certain situations.

BufferedReader provides a method that you will find especially useful in some cases: **readLine( )**. This method reads an entire line of text. It is shown here:

String readLine( ) throws IOException

It returns a string that contains the characters read. It returns null if an attempt is made to read at the end of the stream. The string returned by **readLine( )** is not terminated by the end-of-line characters, such as carriage-return or linefeed. These characters are consumed by the read operation, however.

Read and Write Random-Access Files

Key Ingredients	
Classes	**Methods**
java.io.RandomAccessFile	void seek(long *newPos*)
	long length( )
	int read( )
	void write(int *val*)
	void close( )

The preceding recipes have shown how to read and write files in a linear fashion, one byte or character after another. However, Java also allows you to access the contents of a file in random order. To do this, you will use **RandomAccessFile**, which encapsulates a random-access file. **RandomAccessFile** supports positioning requests, which means that you can read or write anywhere within the file.

RandomAccessFile is byte-oriented, but it is not derived from **InputStream** or **OutputStream**. Instead, it implements the interfaces **DataInput** and **DataOutput**, which define the basic I/O methods, such as **readInt( )** and **writeDouble( )**, that read and write Java's primitive types. It also provides several byte-based **read( )** and **write( )** methods. The **Closeable** interface is also implemented.

Step-by-Step

To read and write bytes in non-sequential order involves the following steps:

1. Open a random-access file by creating an instance of **RandomAccessFile**.
2. Use the **seek( )** method to position the file pointer to the location at which you want to read or write.
3. Use one of **RandomAccessFile**'s methods to read or write data.
4. Close the file.

Discussion

RandomAccessFile supplies two constructors. The one we will be using is shown here:

RandomAccessFile(String *fileName*, String *access*)
          throws FileNotFoundException

The name of the file is passed in *fileName* and *access* determines what type of file access is permitted. If *access* is "r", the file can be read but not written. If it is "rw", the file is opened in read-write mode. Other valid access values are described under *Options and Alternatives*. A **FileNotFoundException** is thrown if the file cannot be opened for "r" access or the file cannot be opened or created for "rw" access.

The location within the file at which the next I/O operation will occur is determined by the position of the *file pointer*. This is essentially an index into the file. The position of the file pointer is set by calling the method **seek( )**, shown here:

void seek(long *newPos*) throws IOException

Here, *newPos* specifies the new position, in bytes, of the file pointer from the beginning of the file. After a call to **seek( )**, the next read or write operation will occur at the new file position. The value of *newPos* must be greater than zero. Attempting to use a value less than zero will cause an **IOException**. Thus, it is not possible to seek before the beginning of a file. It is possible to seek past the end, however.

RandomAccessFile supports several **read( )** and **write( )** methods, of which many are specified by the **DataInput** and **DataOutput** interfaces. The ones used by the example are shown here:

int read( ) throws IOException

void write(int *val*) throws IOException

The **read( )** method returns the byte at the current file pointer location; **write( )** writes *val* to the current file pointer location.

When working with random-access files, it is sometimes useful to know the length of the file in bytes. One reason is so that you can seek to the end of the file. You can obtain the current length of the file by calling **length( )**, shown here:

long length( ) throws IOException

It returns the size of the file.

Example

The following example illustrates random-access file operations. It reverses the contents of a file by exchanging the position of bytes, front to back. For example, given a file that contains

ABCDE

after running **ReverseFile** on it, the file will contain

EDCBA

```
// Use RandomAccessFile to reverse a file.
//
// To use this program, specify the name of the file.
// For example, to reverse a file called test.txt use the
// following command line:
//
//    java ReverseFile test.txt
//

import java.io.*;

class ReverseFile {

  public static void main(String args[])
```

```
{
  // First make sure that a file has been specified.
  if(args.length != 1) {
    System.out.println("Usage: ReverseFile name");
    return;
  }

  RandomAccessFile raf;

  try {

    // Open the file.
    raf = new RandomAccessFile(args[0], "rw");

  } catch(FileNotFoundException exc) {
    System.out.println("Cannot Open File");
    return ;
  }

  try {
    int x, y;

    // Reverse the file.
    for(long i=0, j=raf.length()-1; i < j; i++, j--) {

      // Read the next set of bytes.
      raf.seek(i);
      x = raf.read();
      raf.seek(j);
      y = raf.read();

      // Swap the bytes.
      raf.seek(j);
      raf.write(x);
      raf.seek(i);
      raf.write(y);

    }
  } catch(IOException exc) {
    System.out.println("Error Writing File");
  }

  try {
    raf.close();
  } catch(IOException exc) {
    System.out.println("Error Closing File");
  }
}
}
```

Options and Alternatives

There is a second form of **RandomAccessFile** that opens the file specified by a **File** instance. This form is shown here:

RandomAccessFile(File *fileObj*, String *access*)
        throws FileNotFoundException

It opens the file specified by *fileObj* with the access mode passed in *access*.

    RandomAccessFile supports two additional access modes. The first is "rws", and it causes every change to a file's data or metadata to immediately affect the physical device. The second is "rwd", and it causes every change to a file's data to immediately affect the physical device.

Obtain File Attributes

Key Ingredients	
Classes	**Methods**
java.io.File	boolean canRead( )
	boolean canWrite( )
	boolean exists( )
	boolean isDirectory( )
	boolean isFile( )
	boolean isHidden( )
	long lastModified( )
	long length( )

The foregoing recipes illustrate techniques used to read and write files. However, there is another aspect of file handling that does not relate to manipulating the contents of a file, but rather deals with the attributes of the file itself, such as its length, the time it was last modified, whether it is read-only, and so on. The file attributes can be very useful when managing files. For example, you might want to confirm that a file is not read-only before attempting to write to it. Or, you might want to know the length of a file before copying it so that you can confirm that it will fit on the destination device.

    To obtain and set the attributes associated with a file, you will use the **File** class. This recipe describes the procedure used to obtain file attributes. The following recipe shows how several can be set.

Step-by-Step

To obtain the attributes associated with a file involves these steps:

1. Create a **File** object that represents the file.
2. If necessary, confirm that the file exists by calling **exists( )** on the **File** instance.
3. Obtain the attribute or attributes in which you are interested by calling one or more **File** methods.

Discussion

File defines four constructors. The one we will use is shown here:

File(String *name*)

The name of the file is specified by *name*, which can include a full pathname. Keep in mind two important points. First, creating a **File** object does not cause a file to be opened, nor does it imply that a file by that name actually exists. Instead, it creates an object that represents a pathname. Second, *name* can also specify a directory. As far as **File** is concerned, a directory is simply a special type of file. For the ease of discussion, the following descriptions use the term "file" to refer to both cases, unless otherwise indicated.

Often you will want to confirm that the file represented by a **File** object actually exists before you attempt to obtain information about it. To do this, use the **exists( )** method, shown here:

boolean exists( )

It returns **true** if the file exists and false otherwise.

To obtain a file's attributes, you will use one or more of the following methods:

boolean canRead( )	Returns **true** if the file exists and can be read.
boolean canWrite( )	Returns **true** if the file exists and can be written.
boolean isDirectory( )	Returns **true** if the file exists and is a directory.
boolean isFile( )	Returns **true** if the file exists and *is a file* rather than a directory or some other object supported by the file system.
boolean isHidden( )	Returns **true** if the file is hidden.
long lastModified( )	Returns the date and time at which the file was last modified in terms of milliseconds from January 1, 1970. This value can be used to construct a **Date** object, for example. Zero is returned if the file doesn't exist.
long length( )	Returns the size of the file, or zero if the file does not exist.

Example

The following example creates a method called **showAttribs( )**, which displays the attributes associated with a file. To use the program, specify the file on the command line.

```
// Display the attributes associated with a file.
//
// To use the program, specify the name of the file on the
```

```
// command line.  For example, to display the attributes
// of a file called test.tst, use the following command line:
//
//     java ShowFileAttributes test.tst
//

import java.io.*;
import java.util.*;

class ShowFileAttributes {

  // Display a file's attributes.
  public static void showAttribs(String name) {
    File f;

    // Create a File object for the file.
    f = new File(name);

    // First, confirm that the file exists.
    if(!f.exists()) {
      System.out.println("File not found.");
      return;
    }

    // Display various file attributes.
    System.out.println("File Attributes: ");

    if(f.canRead()) System.out.println("  Readable");
    if(f.canWrite()) System.out.println("  Writeable");
    if(f.isDirectory()) System.out.println("  Is a Directory");
    if(f.isFile()) System.out.println("  Is a File");
    if(f.isHidden()) System.out.println("  Is Hidden");

    System.out.println("  Last modified on " +
                       new Date(f.lastModified()));

    System.out.println("  Length: " + f.length());
  }

  // Demonstrate the showAttribs() method.
  public static void main(String args[])
  {

    // First make sure that a file has been specified.
    if(args.length != 1) {
      System.out.println("Usage: ShowFileAttributes filename");
      return;
    }

    showAttribs(args[0]);
  }
}
```

When run on its own source file, **ShowFileAttributes** produces the following output:

```
File Attributes:
  Readable
  Writeable
  Is a File
  Last modified on Mon Jan 22 10:36:02 CST 2007
  Length: 1506
```

Options and Alternatives

If you are using Java 6 or later, and if your platform supports it, you can determine if a file can be executed by your application by calling **canExecute( )**, shown here:

    boolean canExecute( )

It returns **true** if the file can be executed by the invoking program and false otherwise.

In addition to the **File** constructor used by the recipe, **File** provides three others. They are shown here:

    File(String *dir*, String *name*)

    File(File *dir*, String *name*)

    File(URI *uri*)

In the first two forms, *dir* specifies a parent directory and *name* specifies the name of a file or subdirectory. In the last form, *uri* specifies a **URI** object that describes the file.

Set File Attributes

Key Ingredients	
Classes	**Methods**
java.io.File	boolean exists( )
	boolean setLastModified(long *newTime*)
	boolean setReadOnly( )
	boolean setWritable(boolean *canWrite*, boolean *who*)

The preceding recipe showed how to obtain various attributes about a file by using the **File** class. **File** also gives you the ability to set attributes. This recipe shows the procedure.

Step-by-Step

To set the attributes associated with a file involves these steps:

1. Create the **File** object that represents the file.
2. If necessary, confirm that the file exists by calling **exists( )** on the **File** instance.
3. Set the attribute or attributes in which you are interested by calling one or more **File** methods.

Discussion

File's constructors and the **exists( )** method are described in detail by the preceding recipe. (See *Obtain File Attributes* for details.) As mentioned, often you will want to confirm that the file represented by a **File** object actually exists before you attempt to obtain information about it. This is done by calling **exists( )**.

To set a file's attributes, you will use one or more of the following methods. Notice that **setWritable( )** requires Java 6 or later to use.

boolean setLastModified(long *newTime*)	Sets the file's time stamp to *newTime*. Returns **true** if successful. The time is represented as the number of milliseconds from January 1, 1970. You can obtain a time in this form by using the **Calendar** class.
boolean setReadOnly( )	Makes the file read-only. Returns **true** if successful.
boolean setWritable(boolean *canWrite*, boolean *who*)	Sets a file's write-permission attribute. If *canWrite* is true, then write operations are enabled. Otherwise, write-operations are denied. If *who* is true, then the change applies only to the file's owner. Otherwise, the change applies generally. (Requires Java 6 or later.)

Example

The following example shows how to set a file's attributes.

```
// Set file attributes.
//
// To use the program, specify the name of the file
// on the command line.  For example, to set the attributes
// for a file called test.tst, use the following command line:
//
//     java SetFileAttributes test.tst
//
import java.io.*;
import java.util.*;

class SetFileAttributes {

  // Show a file's read/write status.
  static void rwStatus(File f) {
```

```java
    if(f.canRead()) System.out.println("  Readable");
    else System.out.println("  Not Readable");

    if(f.canWrite()) System.out.println("  Writable");
    else System.out.println("  Not Writable");
  }

  public static void main(String args[])
  {

    // First make sure that a file has been specified.
    if(args.length != 1) {
      System.out.println("Usage: SetFileAttributes filename");
      return;
    }

    File f = new File(args[0]);

    // Confirm that the file exists.
    if(!f.exists()) {
      System.out.println("File not found.");
      return;
    }

    // Display original read/write status and time stamp.
    System.out.println("Original read/write permission and time:");
    rwStatus(f);
    System.out.println("  Last modified on " +
                        new Date(f.lastModified()));
    System.out.println();

    // Update the time stamp.
    long t = Calendar.getInstance().getTimeInMillis();
    if(!f.setLastModified(t))
      System.out.println("Can't set time.");

    // Set the file to read-only.
    if(!f.setReadOnly())
      System.out.println("Can't set to read-only.");

    System.out.println("Modified read/write permission and time:");
    rwStatus(f);
    System.out.println("  Last modified on " +
                        new Date(f.lastModified()));
    System.out.println();

    // Return to read/write status.
    if(!f.setWritable(true, false))
      System.out.println("Can't return to read/write.");

    System.out.println("Read/Write permissions are now: ");
    rwStatus(f);
  }
}
```

The output is shown here:

```
Original read/write permission and time:
  Readable
  Writable
  Last modified on Fri Jan 12 12:15:20 CST 2007

Modified read/write permission and time:
  Readable
  Not Writable
  Last modified on Tue Jan 16 12:16:10 CST 2007

Read/Write permissions are now:
  Readable
  Writable
```

Options and Alternatives

In addition to the constructor used by this recipe, **File** defines three others. See *Obtain File Attributes* for a description.

If you are using Java 6 or later and if your platform supports it, you can set or clear a file's executable-permission attribute by calling **setExecutable( )**. It has two forms, which are shown here:

   boolean setExecutable(boolean *canExec*)

   boolean setExecutable(boolean *canExec*, boolean *who*)

If *canExec* is true, then execute operations are enabled. Otherwise, execute operations are denied. The first form affects only the file's owner. In the second form, if *who* is true, then the change applies only to the file's owner. If *who* is false, the change applies generally.

If you are using Java 6 or later and if your platform supports it, you can set or clear a file's read-only attribute by calling **setReadable( )**. It has two forms, which are shown here:

   boolean setReadable(boolean *canRead*)

   boolean setReadable(boolean *canRead*, boolean *who*)

If *canRead* is true, then read operations are enabled. Otherwise, read operations are denied. The first form affects only the file's owner. In the second form, if *who* is true, then the change applies only to the file's owner. If *who* is false, the change applies generally.

In addition to setting a file's attributes, **File** also lets you delete a file, rename a file, and create a directory. The methods that do this are shown here:

boolean delete( )	Deletes a file (or an empty directory). Returns **true** if successful.
boolean mkdir( )	Creates a directory. Returns **true** if successful.
boolean mkdirs( )	Creates an entire directory path (which includes all necessary parent directories). It returns **true** if successful.
boolean renameTo(File *newName*)	Renames the file to *newName*. Returns **true** if successful.

List a Directory

Key Ingredients	
Classes and Interfaces	**Methods**
java.io.File	File[ ] listFiles( )
	File[ ] listFiles(FileFilter *ff*)
	String getName( )
	boolean isDirectory( )
java.io.FileFilter	boolean accept(File *name*)

Another common file-related task is obtaining a list of the files within a directory. For example, you might want to obtain a list of all files in a directory so that they can be transmitted to a back up site or so that you can confirm that all files for an application have been properly installed. Whatever the purpose, obtaining a directory listing can be conveniently accomplished using the **File** class.

Step-by-Step

Java provides a variety of ways to obtain a directory listing. The approach used by this recipe involves these steps:

1. Create a **File** object that represents the directory.
2. Confirm that the **File** object exists and actually represents a valid directory. (In cases in which the **File** object is known to represent an existent directory, this step can be skipped.)
3. If you want to obtain a filtered list of files (such as those with a specified file extension), create a **FileFilter** object that describes the pattern that the files must match.
4. To obtain a directory listing, call **listFiles( )** on the **File** object. It returns an array of **File** objects that represent the files in the directory. There are three versions of **listFiles( )**. One gives you all files; the other two let you filter the files.
5. To obtain the name of the file, call **File**'s **getName( )** method.
6. If you are only interested in normal files and not directories, use the **isDirectory( )** method to determine which files represent directories.

Discussion

See *Obtain File Attributes* for a description of **File**'s constructors, and the **exists( )** and **isDirectory( )** methods. It is important to understand that a directory listing can only be obtained if the **File** object represents a directory. Therefore, it is often necessary to confirm that the object is, indeed, a valid directory before attempting to obtain the file list.

File defines three versions of **listFiles( )**. The first returns an array of strings that contains all files (including those that represent subdirectories). Thus, it obtains an unfiltered list of files. It is shown here:

File[ ] listFiles( )

To obtain a filtered file list, you can use one of the other two forms. The one used by this recipe is shown here:

File[ ] listFiles(FileFilter *ff*)

It obtains a list of only those files (and directories) that meet the criteria specified by *ff*.

Given the array containing the directory listing, you can obtain the name of each file by calling **getName( )**, which is defined by **File**. It is shown here:

String getName( )

The string representation of the file (or directory) name is returned.

To restrict the list of files to only those that fit a certain criteria, implement a **FileFilter**. **FileFilter** is an interface that specifies only one method: **accept( )**. It is shown here:

boolean accept(File *name*)

This method must return **true** for files that you want to be part of the directory listing and false for those that are to be excluded. Depending upon how you implement **accept( )**, it can be used to include all files whose names fit a general pattern. For example, here is a simple implementation that accepts all Java source files:

```
// A simple file filter for Java source files.
class JavaFiles implements FileFilter {
  public boolean accept(File f) {
    if(f.getName().endsWith(".java")) return true;
    return false;
  }
}
```

For more sophisticated filtering, you can use regular expressions. With this approach, you can easily create filters that handle wildcards, match alternatives, ignore case differences, and so on. (An overview of regular expressions is found in Chapter 2.)

Example

The following example illustrates both the filtered and unfiltered forms of **listFiles( )**. To use the program, specify the name of the directory to list on the command line. The program first displays all files in the specified directory. Then, it uses a filter to display only Java source files.

```
// Display a list of the files and subdirectories
// in the directory specified on the command line.
// For example, to list the contents of a directory
// called \MyPrograms, use
//
//    java ListFiles \MyPrograms
//

import java.io.*;
```

```java
// A simple file filter for Java source files.
class JavaFiles implements FileFilter {
  public boolean accept(File f) {
    if(f.getName().endsWith(".java")) return true;
    return false;
  }
}

class ListFiles {
  public static void main(String args[]) {

    // First make sure that a file has been specified.
    if(args.length != 1) {
      System.out.println("Usage: ListFiles dirname");
      return;
    }

    File dir = new File(args[0]);

    // Confirm existence.
    if(!dir.exists()) {
      System.out.println(args[0] + " not found.");
      return;
    }

    // Confirm that it is a directory.
    if(!dir.isDirectory()) {
      System.out.println(args[0] + " is not a directory.");
      return;
    }

    File[] filelist;

    // Obtain a list of all files.
    filelist = dir.listFiles();

    // Display the files.
    System.out.println("All Files:");
    for(File f : filelist)
      if(!f.isDirectory()) System.out.println(f.getName());


    // Obtain a list of just Java source files.
    //
    // Begin by creating a filter for .java files.
    JavaFiles jf = new JavaFiles();

    // Now, pass that filter to list().
    filelist = dir.listFiles(jf);

    // Display the filtered files.
    System.out.println("\nJava Source Files:");
```

```
    for(File f : filelist)
      if(!f.isDirectory()) System.out.println(f.getName());

  }
}
```

Sample output is shown here:

```
All Files:
HexDump.java
WriteBytes.java
BufferedFileCopy.java
ShowFile.java
InvertCopy.java
WriteChars.java
HexDump.class
WriteBytes.class
BufferedFileCopy.class
WriteChars.class
InvertCopy.class
ShowFile.class

Java Source Files:
HexDump.java
WriteBytes.java
BufferedFileCopy.java
ShowFile.java
InvertCopy.java
WriteChars.java
```

Bonus Example

Java's regular expression capabilities enable you to create very powerful file filters that use sophisticated wildcard filters. Regular expressions also let you implement filters that accept one or more alternatives. For example, you can create a file filter that accepts files that end in ".class" or ".java". Here is another example. Using regular expressions, you can create a file filter that accepts files that contain either of these two substrings: "bytes" or "chars". Such a filter would then accept both of these filenames:

WriteBytes.java

WriteChars.java

Through the use of regular expressions, the capabilities of a file filter are nearly unlimited.

One of the easiest ways to use a regular expression in a file filter is to use **String**'s **matches( )** method. Recall from Chapter 2 that it has this general form:

boolean matches(String *regExpr*)

It returns **true** if the regular expression finds a match in the invoking string and false otherwise.

Here is a file filter that uses a regular expression to match all files whose name contains either the sequence "chars" or the sequence "bytes". Notice that it ignores the case of the letters.

```
// A file filter that accepts names that include
// either "bytes" or "chars".
class MyFF implements FileFilter {
  public boolean accept(File f) {
    if(f.getName().matches(".*(?i)(bytes|chars).*"))
      return true;

    return false;
  }
}
```

If this filter is applied to the same directory as that used by the preceding example, the following files are accepted:

```
WriteBytes.java
WriteChars.java
WriteBytes.class
WriteChars.class
```

You can try this file filter by substituting it into the previous example program. You might want to experiment with it a bit, trying different patterns. You will find that regular expressions offer a tremendous amount of power and control over the filtering process.

Options and Alternatives

As just described, **listFiles( )** returns the file list as an array of **File** objects. This is often the form that you want. However, you can obtain a list that contains just the names of the files in an array of **String** objects. This is done by using the **list( )** method, which is also defined by **File**. There are two versions of **list( )**. The first obtains all files. Thus, it obtains an unfiltered list of files. It is shown here:

String[ ] list( )

To obtain a filtered file list, use this second form of **list( )**:

String[ ] list(FilenameFilter *fnf*)

It obtains a list of only those files that meet the criteria specified by *fnf.*
Notice that the filtered form of **list( )** uses a **FilenameFilter** rather than a **FileFilter**. **FilenameFilter** is an interface that offers an alternative way to construct a filter. It specifies only one method, **accept( )**, shown here:

boolean accept(File *dir*, String *name*)

In this method, the directory is passed to *dir* and the filename is passed to *name*. It must return **true** for files that match the filename specified by *name*. Otherwise, it must return false.
You can also use **FilenameFilter** with **listFiles( )** to obtain a filtered file list. This form of **listFiles( )** is shown here:

File[ ] listFiles(FilenameFilter *fnf*)

Compress and Decompress Data

Key Ingredients	
Classes	**Methods**
java.util.zip.DeflaterOutputStream	void write(int *byteVal*)
	void close( )
java.util.zip.InflaterInputStream	int read( )
	void close( )

As mentioned near the start of this chapter, Java provides stream classes that automatically compress and decompress data. These classes are packaged in **java.util.zip**. Four of the classes are used to read and write standard GZIP and ZIP files. However, it is also possible to use the compression algorithms directly, without creating one of these standard files. There is one very good reason why you might want to do this: it enables your application to operate directly on compressed data. This may be especially valuable when using very large data files.

For example, a database that contains the inventory of a large online retailer might contain several thousand entries. By storing that database in compressed form, its size can be significantly reduced. Because Java's compressed file streams give you the ability to read and write a compressed file directly, all file operations can take place on the compressed file, without the need to create a decompressed copy. This recipe shows one way to implement such a scheme. As you will see, using compressed data is very easy because it involves a nearly transparent overlay to the basic file handling required by the application.

At the foundation of the compression library are the classes **Deflater** and **Inflater**. They provide the algorithms that compress and decompress data. As mentioned near the start of this chapter, the default implementation of these classes uses the ZLIB compression library. Default implementations of these classes are used by the compressed data streams defined by **java.util.zip**. These default implementations are adequate for most compression tasks, and you normally will not need to interact with **Deflater** or **Inflater** directly.

This recipe uses **DeflaterOutputStream** to write to a compressed data file and **InflaterInputStream** to read from a compressed data file. **DeflaterOutputStream** is derived from **OutputStream** and **FilterOutputStream** and implements the **Closeable** and **Flushable** interfaces. **InflaterInputStream** is derived from **InputStream** and **FilterInputStream** and implements the **Closeable** interface.

Step-by-Step

To compress data and write it to a file involves these steps:

1. Create a file stream that uses **DeflaterOutputStream**.

2. Write output to the **DeflaterOutputStream** instance. You can use one of the standard **write( )** methods to write the data. Often, however, a **DeflaterOutputStream** is wrapped in a **DataOutputStream**, which lets you conveniently write primitive data types, such as **int** or **double**. In either case, the data will automatically be compressed.

3. Close the output stream when done writing.

To read data from a compressed file involves these steps:

1. Create a file stream that uses **InflaterInputStream**.
2. Read from the **InflaterInputStream** instance. You can use one of the standard **read( )** methods to read the data. Often, however, an **InflaterInputStream** is wrapped in a **DataInputStream**, which lets you conveniently read primitive data types, such as **int** or **double**. In either case, the data will automatically be decompressed.
3. Close the input stream when done writing.

Discussion

The **DeflaterOutputStream** and **InflaterInputStream** are at the core of Java's file compression capabilities. They can be used explicitly (as this recipe does), or implicitly when you create a GZIP or ZIP file. **DeflaterOutputStream** writes data to a file, compressing it in the process. **InflaterInputStream** reads data from a file, decompressing it in the process.

DeflaterOutputStream and **InflaterInputStream** define three constructors each. Here are the ones used by this recipe:

DeflaterOutputStream(OutputStream *outStrm*)

InflaterInputStream(InputStream *inStrm*)

Here, *outStrm* specifies the output stream and *inStrm* specifies the input stream. These constructors use the default inflater and deflater. As mentioned, these are objects of type **Inflater** and **Deflater**. They provide the algorithms that perform the actual compression and decompression of the data. The other constructors allow you to specify an inflater or deflater, and a buffer size. However, the default inflater, deflater, and buffer size are adequate for most tasks.

Once the compression-based streams are open, compression or decompression occurs automatically each time a write or a read operation takes place. Therefore, the data contained in a file written by **DeflaterOutputStream** will be in a compressed format. The data read from a compressed file through an **InflaterInputStream** will be in its decompressed (i.e., plain) format. This means that you can store data in a compressed form, but your program will have transparent access to it (as if it were stored in a non-compressed file). This is one reason why Java's compression library is so powerful.

To write data, you can use any of the standard **write( )** methods defined by **OutputStream**. To read data, you can use any of the standard **read( )** methods defined by **InputStream**. (These are described in *Write Bytes to a File* and *Read Bytes from a File*.) However, often it is better to wrap **DeflaterOutputStream** in a **DataOutputStream** and to wrap **InflaterInputStream** in a **DataInputStream**. Doing so gives you access to methods such as **writeInt( )**, **writeDouble( )**, **readInt( )**, and **readDouble( )**, which let you conveniently read and write primitive data.

Example

The following example shows how to create a compressed data file and then read the data in the file. The data file is a collection of **double** values. However, the file begins with an integer that contains a count of the **double**s in the file. Notice that **DeflaterOutputStream** is wrapped in a **DataOutputStream**. **InflaterInputStream** is wrapped in a **DataInputStream**.

This enables values of the primitive types, such as **int** or **double**, to be conveniently written in a compressed form and then read back.

The program creates the data file by writing an array of six **double** values to a file called **data.cmprs**. First, it writes a count of the number of values that will follow by calling **writeInt( )**. The count is six in this example. Then it writes the **double** values by calling **writeDouble( )**. Because a **DeflaterOutputStream** is used, the data is automatically compressed before being stored in the file.

The program then reads the values. It does this by first obtaining the count by calling **readInt( )**. It then reads that number of values by calling **readDouble( )**. In the process, it averages the values. The point to understand is that the file is compressed and decompressed "on the fly." At no time does a decompressed version of the file exist.

As a point of interest, the compressed file created by this program is 36 bytes long. Without compression, the file would be 52 bytes long.

```
// Create a compressed data file by using a
// DeflaterOutputStream and then read that data
// through an InflaterInputStream.
//
// This program uses Java's default compression
// library, which is ZLIB.  The compressed file
// created by this program is not in a specific
// format, such as ZIP or GZIP.  It simply contains
// a compressed version of the data.

import java.io.*;
import java.util.zip.*;

class DemoCompression {

  public static void main(String args[])
  {
    DataOutputStream fout;
    DataInputStream fin;

    double data[] = { 1.1, 2.2, 3.3, 4.4, 5.5, 6.6 };

    // Open the output file.
    try {
      fout = new DataOutputStream(
                new DeflaterOutputStream(
                  new FileOutputStream("data.cmprs")));
    } catch(FileNotFoundException exc) {
      System.out.println("Error Opening Output File");
      return;
    }

    // Compress the data using ZLIB.
    try {
      // Just write the data normally.  The
      // DeflaterOutputStream will compress it
      // automatically.
```

```java
      // First, write the size of the data.
      fout.writeInt(data.length);

      // Now, write the data.
      for(double d : data)
        fout.writeDouble(d);

    } catch(IOException exc) {
      System.out.println("Compressed File Error");
    }

    try {
      fout.close();
    } catch(IOException exc) {
      System.out.println("Error Closing Output File");
    }

    // Now, open data.cmprs for input.  There is no need
    // to create a decompressed copy of the file because
    // decompression is handled on the fly, by InflaterInputStream.
    // Thus, decompression is automatic and transparent.
    try {
      fin = new DataInputStream(
               new InflaterInputStream(
                   new FileInputStream("data.cmprs")));
    } catch(FileNotFoundException exc) {
      System.out.println("Input File Not Found");
      return;
    }

    // Decompress the file on the fly.
    try {
      // First, retrieve the amount of data
      // contained in the file.
      int num = fin.readInt();

      double avg = 0.0;
      double d;

      System.out.print("Data: ");

      // Now, read the data.  Decompression is automatic.
      for(int i=0; i < num; i++) {
        d = fin.readDouble();
        avg += d;
        System.out.print(d + " ");
      }

      System.out.println("\nAverage is " + avg / num);
```

```
  } catch(IOException exc) {
    System.out.println("Error Reading Input File");
  }

  try {
    fin.close();
  } catch(IOException exc) {
    System.out.println("Error Closing Input File");
  }

  }
}
```

The output is shown here:

```
Data: 1.1 2.2 3.3 4.4 5.5 6.6
Average is 3.85
```

Options and Alternatives

As mentioned, both **DeflaterOutputStream** and **InflaterInputStream** offer constructors that
let you specify the inflater or deflater, or the buffer size.

The compression library also supports checksums through the following classes:
Alder32 and **CRC32**. You can create streams that use a checksum with these classes:
CheckedInputStream and **CheckedOutputStream**.

Although using **DeflaterOutputStream** and **InflaterInputStream** directly is perfectly
acceptable, often you will want to use their subclasses:

GZIPInputStream

GZIPOutputStream

ZipInputStream

ZipOutputStream

These classes create compressed files in either the GZIP or ZIP format. The advantage is that
your data files will be in a format that standard tools can understand. However, if that is not
a benefit to your application, then using **DeflaterOutputStream** and **InflaterInputStream**
directly is a bit more efficient. (The following recipes show how to create, compress, and
decompress a ZIP file.)

Create a ZIP File

Key Ingredients	
Classes	**Methods**
java.util.zip.ZipInputStream	void closeEntry( ) ZipEntry getNextEntry( )
java.util.zip.ZipOutputStream	void closeEntry( ) void putNextEntry(ZipEntry ze) void write(int val)
java.util.zip.ZipEntry	long getCompressedSize( ) long getSize( )

There are two highly popular compressed file formats: GZIP and ZIP. Java provides support for both. Creating a GZIP file is easy: Simply create a **GZIPOutputStream** and then write to it. To read a GZIP file is equally easy: Just create a **GZIPInputStream** and then read from it. However, the situation is a bit more complicated if you want to create a ZIP file. This recipe shows the basic procedure.

Before we begin, it is important to note that ZIP files can be fairly complex. This recipe shows how to create a basic skeleton. If you will be working extensively with ZIP files, you will need to study both **java.util.zip** and the ZIP file specification closely.

In general, a ZIP file can contain one or more compressed files. Each file has associated with it an entry that describes the file. This is an object of type **ZipEntry**. The **ZipEntry**s identify each file within the ZIP file. Therefore, to compress a file, you will first write its **ZipEntry** and then its data.

Step-by-Step

Creating a ZIP file that contains one or more compressed files involves these steps:

1. Create the ZIP file by opening a **ZipOutputStream**. Any data written to this stream will automatically be compressed.

2. Open the file to be compressed. You can use any appropriate file stream, such as a **FileInputStream** wrapped in a **BufferedInputStream**.

3. Create a **ZipEntry** to represent the file being compressed. Often the name of the file being compressed becomes the name of the entry. Write the entry to the **ZipOutputStream** instance by calling **putNextEntry( )**.

4. Write the contents of the input file to the **ZipOutputStream**. The data will automatically be compressed.

5. Close the **ZipEntry** for the input file by calling **closeEntry( )**.

6. Typically, you will want to report the progress of the compression, including the size reduction of the file. To help you do this, **ZipEntry** provides **getSize( )**, which

obtains the uncompressed size of the file, and **getCompressedSize( )**, which obtains the compressed size.

7. Repeat Steps 3 through 5 until all the files that you want to store in the ZIP file have been written.

8. Close the files.

Discussion

To create a ZIP file, you will use an instance of **ZipOutputStream**. Data written to a **ZipOutputStream** is automatically compressed into a ZIP file. **ZipOutputStream** is derived from **DeflaterOutputStream**, and it implements the **Closeable** and **Flushable** interfaces. It defines only one constructor, shown here:

ZipOutputStream(OutputStream *strm*)

The stream that will receive the compressed data is specified by *strm*. This will normally be an instance of **FileOutputStream**.

Before you can compress a file, you must create a **ZipEntry** instance that represents the file and write the entry to the ZIP file. Thus, each file stored in a ZIP file is associated with a **ZipEntry** instance. **ZipEntry** defines two constructors. The one we will use is

ZipEntry(String *entryName*)

Here, *entryName* specifies the name of the entry. Typically this will be the name of the file being stored.

To write the **ZipEntry** to the file, call **putNextEntry( )** on the **ZipOutputStream** instance. It is shown here:

void putNextEntry(ZipEntry *ze*) throws IOException

The entry to be written is passed in *ze*. It throws an **IOException** if an I/O error occurs. It will also throw a **ZipException** in the case of a format error. Because **ZipException** is a subclass of **IOException**, handling an **IOException** is often sufficient. However, you will want to handle both exceptions individually when greater control is needed.

After the **ZipEntry** has been written, you can write the compressed data to the file. This is accomplished by simply calling one of the **write( )** methods supported by **ZipOutputStream**. The one used here is

void write(int *val*) throws IOException

This is, of course, simply an override of the same method defined by **OutputStream**. This version throws an **IOException** if an I/O error occurs. When you write data to the **ZipOutputStream** instance, it is automatically compressed.

After the file has been written, you must close its entry by calling **closeEntry( )**, shown here:

void closeEntry( ) throws IOException

It throws an **IOException** if an I/O error occurs. It will also throw a **ZipException** in the case of a format error.

You determine the effectiveness of the compression by calling **getSize( )** and **getCompressedSize( )** on the **ZipEntry** associated with a file. They are shown here:

long getSize( )

long getCompressedSize( )

The uncompressed size is returned by **getSize( )**. The compressed size is returned by **getCompressedSize( )**. Both methods return –1 if the size is not available. The **ZipEntry** associated with the file must be closed before these methods are called.

When you are done compressing all of the files that will be stored in the ZIP file, close all of the streams. This includes the **ZipOutputStream**. Keep in mind that the version of **close( )** implemented by **ZipOutputStream** will throw an **IOException** if an I/O error occurs and a **ZipException** in the case of a format error.

Example

The following example puts the recipe into action. It can be used to create a ZIP file that contains the compressed form of one or more files. To use the program, specify the name of the ZIP file, then the list of files to be compressed. For example, to compress the files **sampleA.dat** and **sampleB.dat** into a file called **samples.zip**, use the following command line:

```
java Zip samples.zip sampleA.dat sampleB.dat
```

As the program runs, progress is reported. This includes the name of the file being compressed, its original size, and its compressed size.

As is normally the case, the program uses the names of the files as the names for the **ZipEntry**s. However, there is one important point to understand about this program. It does not store any directory path information for the files. If a filename has a path associated with it, it is removed when the **ZipEntry** is created. (Notice that **File.separator** is used to specify the separator character. This is because it differs between Unix and Windows.) As most readers know, most popular ZIP tools give you the option of including pathnames or ignoring them. However, this is left to you as an exercise.

```
// Create a simple ZIP File.
//
// To use this program, specify the name of the
// file that will receive the compressed data and
// one or more source files that contain the data
// to be compressed.
//
// This program does not retain any directory path
// information about the files being compressed.
//
// For example, to compress the files sampleA.dat
// and sampleB.dat into a file called samples.zip,
// use the following command line:
//
//    java Zip samples.zip sampleA.dat sampleB.dat
//
```

```java
import java.io.*;
import java.util.zip.*;

class Zip {

  // Remove any path information from a filename.
  static String rmPath(String fName) {
    int pos = fName.lastIndexOf(File.separatorChar);
    if(pos > -1)
      fName = fName.substring(pos+1);
    return fName;
  }

  public static void main(String args[])
  {
    BufferedInputStream fin;
    ZipOutputStream fout;

    // First make sure that files have been specified.
    if(args.length < 2) {
      System.out.println("Usage: Zip To <filelist>");
      return;
    }

    // Open the output file.
    try {
      fout = new ZipOutputStream(
                new BufferedOutputStream(
                    new FileOutputStream(args[0])));
    } catch(FileNotFoundException exc) {
      System.out.println("Error Opening Output File");
      return;
    }

    for(int n=1; n < args.length; n++) {

      // Open an input file.
      try {
        fin = new BufferedInputStream(
                new FileInputStream(args[n]));
      } catch(FileNotFoundException exc) {
        System.out.println("Input File Not Found");

        // Close the open output file.
        try {
          fout.close();
        } catch(ZipException exc2) {
          System.out.println("ZIP File Invalid");
        } catch(IOException exc2) {
          System.out.println("Error Closing Output File");
        }
        return;
      }
```

```
      // Create the next ZipEntry. In this program,
      // no directory path information is retained, so
      // any path associated with the filename is
      // first removed by a call to rmPath().
      ZipEntry ze = new ZipEntry(rmPath(args[n]));

      // Compress the next file.
      try {
        fout.putNextEntry(ze);

        int i;
        do {
          i = fin.read();
          if(i != -1) fout.write(i);
        } while(i != -1);

        fout.closeEntry();
      } catch(ZipException exc) {
        System.out.println("ZIP File Invalid");
      } catch(IOException exc) {
        System.out.println("Output File Error");
      }

      try {
        fin.close();

        // Report progress and size reduction.
        System.out.println("Compressing " + args[n]);
        System.out.println(" Original Size: " +
                          ze.getSize() +
                          " Compressed Size: " +
                          ze.getCompressedSize() + "\n");
      } catch(IOException exc) {
        System.out.println("Error Closing Input File");
      }
    }

    try {
      fout.close();
    } catch(ZipException exc2) {
      System.out.println("ZIP File Invalid");
    } catch(IOException exc) {
      System.out.println("Error Closing ZIP File");
    }
  }
}
```

Here is a sample run:

```
Compressing HexDump.java
 Original Size: 1384 Compressed Size: 612

Compressing WriteBytes.java
 Original Size: 895 Compressed Size: 428
```

Options and Alternatives

The **ZipEntry** class gives you the ability to set or obtain the value of several attributes associated with a ZIP file entry. Here are a few. You can obtain the entry name by calling **getName( )**. You can set the name by calling **setName( )**. You can set the entry's creation time by calling **setTime( )**. You can get its creation time by calling **getTime( )**. By default, the current system time is used.

There is one method that is potentially very useful: **isDirectory( )**. It returns **true** if the entry represents a directory. However, there is a bit of a problem with this method because it returns **true** only if the entry's name ends with /. (This is in keeping with the ZIP file specification.) As most readers know, however, Windows environments use \ as the path separator. Thus, **isDirectory( )** will not work properly when given a Windows path. There are obvious ways around this limitation, such as substituting each \ with a / when the entry name is created. You can experiment with this and other solutions if you want to store directory information.

Decompress a ZIP File

Key Ingredients	
Classes	**Methods**
java.util.zip.ZipEntry	long getCompressedSize( )
	long getSize( )
	String getName( )
java.util.zip.ZipFile	void close( )
	Enumeration<? extends ZipEntry> entries( )
	InputStream getInputStream(ZipEntry ze)

The preceding recipe shows the steps necessary to create a ZIP file. This recipe describes how to decompress a ZIP file. There are two general approaches that you can use to decompress a ZIP file. The first approach uses **ZipInputStream** to obtain each entry in the ZIP file. Although there is nothing wrong with this, it requires that you manually handle the process. The second approach uses **ZipFile** to streamline the process. This is the method used by this recipe.

Step-by-Step

Decompressing a ZIP file involves the following steps:

1. Open the ZIP file by creating a **ZipFile** instance.

2. Obtain an enumeration of the entries in the ZIP file by calling **entries( )** on the **ZipFile** instance.

3. Cycle through the enumeration of entries, decompressing each entry, in turn, as described by the following steps.

4. Obtain an input stream to an entry by calling **getInputStream( )** on the current entry.

5. Obtain the name of the entry by calling **getName( )** and use it as the name of the output stream that will receive the decompressed file.

6. To decompress the entry, copy bytes from the input stream to the output stream. Decompression is automatic.

7. Typically, you will want to report the progress of the decompression, including the size of both the compressed and expanded file. To do this you can use methods provided by **ZipEntry**. To obtain the uncompressed size of the file call **getSize( )**. To obtain the file's compressed size, call **getCompressedSize( )**.

8. Close both the input and output streams.

9. Repeat Steps 4 through 7 until all entries have been decompressed.

10. Close the **ZipFile** instance.

Discussion

The easiest way to decompress a ZIP file is to use **ZipFile** because it streamlines the process of finding and reading each entry in the file. It provides three constructors. The one used here is:

ZipFile(String *zipFileName*) throws IOException

The name of the ZIP file to decompress is specified by *zipFileName*. It throws an **IOException** if an I/O error occurs. A **ZipException** is thrown if the specified file is not a valid ZIP file. **ZipException** is a subclass of **IOException**. Therefore, catching an **IOException** will handle both exceptions. However, for more precise error handling, both exceptions need to be handled individually.

An enumeration of the entries in the ZIP file can be obtained by calling **entries( )** on the **ZipFile** instance. It is shown here:

Enumeration<? extends ZipEntry> entries( )

Using the enumeration returned by **entries( )**, you can cycle through the entries in the file, decompressing each in turn. (You can also skip an entry, if desired. There is no rule that says that you must decompress every entry in a ZIP file.)

To obtain an input stream to the entry, call **getInputStream( )** on the **ZipFile** instance. It is shown here:

InputStream getInputStream(ZipEntry *ze*) throws IOException

The stream will read input from the entry passed in *ze*. It throws an **IOException** if an I/O error occurs. A **ZipException** is thrown if the entry is improperly formatted.

You can obtain the name of an entry by calling **getName( )** on the **ZipEntry** instance. It is shown here:

String getName( )

You can then use the entry name as the name of the restored (i.e., decompressed) output file.

Once you have decompressed all entries in the file, you must close the **ZipFile** instance by calling **close( )**, shown here:

void close( ) throws IOException

In addition to closing the ZIP file, it will also close any streams opened by calls to **getInputStream( )**. (However, I prefer not to rely on this. Instead, I like to close each input stream separately, as the decompression proceeds, to avoid having several unused, but open streams still allocating resources.)

The sizes of the compressed and decompressed entry can be obtained by calling **getCompressedSize( )** and **getSize( )**, respectively. These methods are described by the preceding recipe. You can use this information to provide feedback about the progress of the decompression.

Example

The following example decompresses a ZIP file. It will recognize a full pathname for the entry, but it will not create the directory path if it does not exist. This is a capability that you can add, if desired.

```
// Decompress a ZIP file.
//
// To use this program, specify the name of the
// compressed file. For example, to decompress
// a file called sample.zip use the following
// command line:
//
//   java Unzip sample.zip
//
// Note: This program will decompress an entry
// that includes directory path information,
// but it will not create the directory path
// if it does not already exist.
//

import java.io.*;
import java.util.zip.*;
import java.util.*;

class Unzip {

  public static void main(String args[])
  {
    BufferedInputStream fin;
    BufferedOutputStream fout;
    ZipFile zf;

    // First make sure that an input file has been specified.
    if(args.length != 1) {
      System.out.println("Usage: Unzip name");
      return;
    }
```

```
// Open the zip file.
try {
  zf = new ZipFile(args[0]);
} catch(ZipException exc) {
  System.out.println("Invalid ZIP File");
  return;
} catch(IOException exc) {
  System.out.println("Error Opening ZIP File");
  return;
}

// Obtain an enumeration of the entries in the file.
Enumeration<? extends ZipEntry> files = zf.entries();

// Decompress each entry.
while(files.hasMoreElements()) {
  ZipEntry ze = files.nextElement();

  System.out.println("Decompressing " + ze.getName());
  System.out.println("  Compressed Size: " +
                       ze.getCompressedSize() +
                       "  Expanded Size: " +
                       ze.getSize() + "\n");

  // Open an input stream to the specified entry.
  try {
    fin = new BufferedInputStream(zf.getInputStream(ze));
  } catch(ZipException exc) {
    System.out.println("Invalid ZIP File");
    break;
  } catch(IOException exc) {
    System.out.println("Error Opening Entry");
    break;
  }

  // Open the output file. Use the name provided
  // by the entry.
  try {
    fout = new BufferedOutputStream(
              new FileOutputStream(ze.getName()));
  } catch(FileNotFoundException exc) {
    System.out.println("Can't Create Output File");

    // Close the open input stream.
    try {
      fin.close();
    } catch(IOException exc2) {
      System.out.println("Error Closing ZIP Input File");
    }
    break;
  }
```

```
      // Decompress the entry.
      try {
        int i;
        do {
          i = fin.read();
          if(i != -1) fout.write(i);
        } while(i != -1);

      } catch(IOException exc) {
        System.out.println("File Error While Decompressing");
      }

      // Close the output file for the current entry.
      try {
        fout.close();
      } catch(IOException exc) {
        System.out.println("Error Closing Output File");
      }

      // Close the input stream for the current entry.
      try {
        fin.close();
      } catch(IOException exc) {
        System.out.println("Error Closing Entry");
      }
    }

    // Close the ZipFile.
    try {
      zf.close();
    } catch(IOException exc) {
      System.out.println("Error Closing ZipFile");
    }
  }
}
```

Sample output is shown here:

```
Decompressing HexDump.java
  Compressed Size: 612   Expanded Size: 1384

Decompressing WriteBytes.java
  Compressed Size: 428   Expanded Size: 895
```

Options and Alternatives

ZipFile provides two additional constructors, shown here:

ZipFile(File *f*) throws ZipException, IOException

ZipFile(File *f*, int *how*) throws IOException

Each opens the ZIP file specified by *f*. The value of *how* must be either

ZipFile.OPEN_READ

or

ZipFile.OPEN_READ | ZipFile.OPEN_DELETE

When **OPEN_DELETE** is specified, the ZIP file will be deleted. However, you will still be able to read the file through the open **ZipFile** instance. This option lets you automatically erase a ZIP file after it has been decompressed. For example, if you substitute this line in the example, it will delete the ZIP file after decompressing it:

```
zf = new ZipFile(new File(args[0]),
                 ZipFile.OPEN_READ | ZipFile.OPEN_DELETE);
```

Of course, you must use this option with caution because it erases the ZIP file, which means that it cannot be reused later. One other point: the second constructor may also throw a **ZipException**.

If you want to extract a specific entry from a ZIP file, you can call **getEntry( )** on the **ZipFile** instance. It is shown here:

ZipEntry getEntry(String *ename*)

The name of the entry is passed in *ename*. A **ZipEntry** for the entry is returned. If the entry cannot be found, null is returned.

Serialize Objects

Key Ingredients	
Classes and Interfaces	**Methods**
java.io.ObjectInputStream	void close( ) Object readObject( )
java.io.ObjectOutputStream	void close( ) void writeObject(Object *obj*)
Serializable	

In addition to bytes, characters, and Java's primitive types, you can also write objects to a file. Once stored, these objects can be read and restored. This process is called *serialization*. Serialization is used for a variety of purposes, including the storing of data that consists of objects and Remote Method Invocation (RMI). Because one object may contain references to other objects, the serialization of objects may involve a fairly sophisticated process. Fortunately, **java.io** supplies the **ObjectOutputStream** and **ObjectInputStream** classes to handle this task for you. This recipe describes the basic procedures needed to save and restore an object.

ObjectOutputStream extends **OutputStream** and implements the **ObjectOutput** interface, which extends the **DataOutput** Interface. **ObjectOutput** adds the **writeObject( )** method, which writes objects to a stream. **ObjectOutputStream** also implements the **Closeable** and **Flushable** interfaces, along with **ObjectStreamConstants**.

ObjectInputStream extends **InputStream** and implements the **ObjectInput** interface, which extends the **DataInput** interface. **ObjectInput** adds the **readObject( )** method, which reads objects from a stream. **ObjectInputStream** also implements the **Closeable** and **ObjectStreamConstants** interface.

In order for an object to be serialized, its class must implement the **Serializable** interface. The **Serializable** interface defines no members. It is simply used to indicate that a class may be serialized. If a class is serializable, all of its subclasses are also serializable. However, variables that are declared as **transient** are not saved by the serialization facilities. Also, **static** variables are not saved. Thus, serialization saves the current state of the object.

One other point: The recipe shown here serializes an object using the default mechanism supplied by **ObjectInputStream** and **ObjectOutputStream**. It is possible to take manual control of this process, but such techniques are beyond the scope of this book.

Step-by-Step

To save an object to a file involves these steps:

1. Ensure that the object that you want to save implements the **Serializable** interface.
2. Open the file by creating an **ObjectOutputStream** object.
3. Write the object to the file by calling **writeObject( )**.
4. Close the stream when done.

To read an object from a file involves these steps:

1. Open the file by creating an **ObjectInputStream** object.
2. Read the object from the file by calling **readObject( )**. You must cast the object to the type of object being read.
3. Close the stream when done.

Discussion

The **ObjectOutputStream** class is used to write objects to a stream. The public constructor for this class is shown here:

ObjectOutputStream(OutputStream *strm*) throws IOException

The argument *strm* is the output stream to which serialized objects will be written. It throws an **IOException** if the file cannot be opened.

Once the output stream is open, you can write an object to it by calling **writeObject( )**, shown here:

final void writeObject(Object *obj*) throws IOException

The object to be written is passed to *obj*. An **IOException** is thrown if an error occurs while writing the object. If you attempt to write an object that does not implement **Serializable**, a **NotSerializableException** is thrown. An **InvalidClassException** is also possible.

The **ObjectInputStream** class is used to read objects from a stream. Its public constructor is shown here:

ObjectInputStream(InputStream *strm*) throws IOException

The stream from which objects will be read is specified by *strm*. It throws an **IOException** if the file cannot be opened.

Once the input stream is open, you can write an object to it by calling **readObject( )**, shown here:

final Object readObject(Object *obj*)
            throws IOException, ClassNotFoundException

It returns the next object from the file. An **IOException** is thrown if an error occurs while reading the object. If the class of the object cannot be found, a **ClassNotFoundException** is thrown. Other exceptions are also possible.

When you are done with an **ObjectInputStream** or an **ObjectOutputStream**, you must close it by calling **close( )**. It is the same for both classes and is shown here:

void close( ) throws IOException

An **IOException** is thrown if an error occurs while closing the file.

Example

The following example shows a simple example of serialization. It creates a class called **MyClass** that contains three fields: a string, an array, and a **File** object. It then creates two **MyClass** objects, displays their contents, and saves them to a file called **obj.dat**. It then reads the objects back and displays their contents. As the output shows, the contents of the reconstructed objects are the same as the original ones.

```java
// Demonstrate object serialization.

import java.io.*;

// A simple serializable class.
class MyClass implements Serializable {
  String str;
  double[] vals;
  File fn;

  public MyClass(String s, double[] nums, String fname) {
    str = s;
    vals = nums;
    fn = new File(fname);
  }

  public String toString() {
    String data = "  str: " + str + "\n  vals: ";

    for(double d : vals)  data += d + " ";
```

```
      data += "\n  fn: " + fn.getName();

      return data;
    }
}

public class SerialDemo {
  public static void main(String args[]) {
    double v[] = { 1.1, 2.2, 3.3 };
    double v2[] = { 9.0, 8.0, 7.7 };

    // Create two MyClass objects.
    MyClass obj1 = new MyClass("This is a test",
                               v, "Test.txt");

    MyClass obj2 = new MyClass("Alpha Beta Gamma",
                               v2, "Sample.dat");

    // Open the output file.
    ObjectOutputStream fout;
    try {
      fout = new ObjectOutputStream(new FileOutputStream("obj.dat"));
    } catch(IOException exc) {
      System.out.println("Error opening Output File");
      return;
    }

    // Write objects to a file.
    try {
      System.out.println("Writing objects to the file.");

      System.out.println("obj1:\n" + obj1);
      fout.writeObject(obj1);

      System.out.println("obj2:\n" + obj2);
      fout.writeObject(obj2);

    } catch(IOException exc) {
      System.out.println("Error Writing Object");
    }

    try {
      fout.close();
    } catch(IOException exc) {
      System.out.println("Error Closing Output File");
      return;
    }

    // Read the object from the file.
    ObjectInputStream fin;

    // Open the input file.
    try {
```

```
      fin = new ObjectInputStream(new FileInputStream("obj.dat"));
    } catch(IOException exc) {
      System.out.println("Error opening Input File");
      return;
    }


    System.out.println("\nReading objects from the file.");

    try {
      MyClass inputObj;

      inputObj = (MyClass) fin.readObject();
      System.out.println("First object:\n" + inputObj);

      inputObj = (MyClass) fin.readObject();
      System.out.println("Second object:\n" + inputObj);
    }
    catch(IOException exc) {
      System.out.println("Error Reading Object Data");
    }
    catch(ClassNotFoundException exc) {
      System.out.println("Class Definition Not Found");
    }

    try {
      fin.close();
    } catch(IOException exc) {
      System.out.println("Error Closing Input File");
      return;
    }
  }
}
```

The output is shown here:

```
Writing objects to the file.
obj1:
  str: This is a test
  vals: 1.1 2.2 3.3
  fn: Test.txt
obj2:
  str: Alpha Beta Gamma
  vals: 9.0 8.0 7.7
  fn: Sample.dat

Reading objects from the file.
First object:
  str: This is a test
  vals: 1.1 2.2 3.3
  fn: Test.txt
Second object:
  str: Alpha Beta Gamma
```

```
vals: 9.0 8.0 7.7
fn: Sample.dat
```

Options and Alternatives

Members of a class that you don't want stored can be modified by the **transient** specifier. This is useful when an instance variable contains a value that is not important to the state of the object. By not saving fields unnecessarily, the size of the file is reduced. You can confirm this for yourself by making **fn** transient in the example. After this is done, **fn** will not be saved when a **MyClass** object is saved. Thus, it won't be reconstructed and its value will be null after the call to **readObject( )**. This will result in a **NullPointerException** being thrown when **toString( )** attempts to access it.

Several of the input methods provided by **ObjectInputStream** throw an **EOFException** when the end of the file is encountered while reading an object. **EOFException** is a subclass of **IOException**. Therefore, if your code needs to discern between an EOF condition and other types of I/O errors, then you will want to catch **EOFException** explicitly when reading objects.

You can take a degree of manual control over the serialization of objects by implementing the **Externalizable** interface. It specifies the methods **readExternal( )** and **writeExternal( )**, which you will implement to read and write objects.

4

CHAPTER

Formatting Data

Whether you are displaying the time and date, working with monetary values, or simply wanting to limit the number of decimal digits, formatting data in a specific, human-readable form is an important part of many programs. It's also an area of programming that raises many "How to" questions. One reason for this is the size and complexity of the problem: there are many different types of data, formats, and options. Another reason is the richness of Java's formatting capabilities. In many cases, Java offers more than one way to format data. For example, you can format a date using either **java.util.Formatter** or **java.text.DateFormat**. This chapter examines the topic of formatting and presents recipes that show various ways to solve several common formatting tasks.

The primary focus of this chapter is **java.util.Formatter**, which is Java's general-purpose, full-featured formatting class. **Formatter** is also used by **printf( )**, which is supported by **PrintStream** and **PrintWriter**. The **printf( )** method is essentially a shortcut for using **Formatter**-style formatting when outputting information directly to a stream. As a result, the majority of the recipes use **Formatter**, either directly or indirectly.

Java includes several alternative formatting classes that predate **Formatter** (which was added by Java 5). Two are **java.text.DateFormat** and **java.text.NumberFormat**. They offer a different approach to formatting date, time, and numeric data that might be helpful in some cases. (**NumberFormat** is especially useful when formatting currency values in a locale-sensitive manner.) Two other formatting classes are **java.text.SimpleDateFormat** and **java.text.DecimalFormat**, which are subclasses of **DateFormat** and **NumberFormat**, respectively. They enable you to format dates, times, and numbers based on patterns. Although the main focus of this chapter is **Formatter**, several recipes utilize these alternatives, mostly in the interest of completeness, but also because they offer simple, yet elegant solutions to some types of formatting tasks.

Here are the recipes in this chapter:

- Four Simple Numeric Formatting Techniques Using **Formatter**
- Vertically Align Numeric Data Using **Formatter**
- Left-Justify Output Using **Formatter**
- Format Time and Date Using **Formatter**
- Specify a Locale with **Formatter**
- Use Streams with **Formatter**

- Use **printf( )** to Display Formatted Data
- Format Time and Date with **DateFormat**
- Format Time and Date with Patterns Using **SimpleDateFormat**
- Format Numeric Values with **NumberFormat**
- Format Currency Values Using **NumberFormat**
- Format Numeric Values with Patterns Using **DecimalFormat**

An Overview of Formatter

Formatter is Java's general-purpose formatting class, and most of the recipes in this chapter rely on it. It is packaged in **java.util**, and it implements the **Closeable** and **Flushable** interfaces. Although the individual recipes discuss its features in detail, it is useful to present an overview of its capabilities and basic mode of operation. It is important to state at the outset that **Formatter** is a relatively new class, added by Java 5. Therefore, you will need to be using a modern version of Java to use its capabilities.

Formatter works by converting the binary form of data used by a program into formatted, human-readable text. It outputs the formatted text to a target object, which can be a buffer or a stream (including a file stream). If the target is a buffer, then the contents of the buffer can be obtained by your program whenever they are needed. It is possible to let **Formatter** supply this buffer automatically, or you can specify the buffer explicitly when a **Formatter** object is created. If the target is a stream, then the output is written to the stream and is not otherwise available to your program.

The **Formatter** class defines many constructors, which enable you to construct a **Formatter** in a variety of ways. Perhaps the most widely used is the default constructor:

Formatter( )

It automatically uses the default locale and allocates a **StringBuilder** as a buffer to hold the formatted output. Other constructors let you specify the target and/or the locale. You can also specify a file or another type of **OutputStream** as the repository of formatted output. Here is a sampling of **Formatter**'s constructors:

```
Formatter(Locale loc)
Formatter(Appendable target)
Formatter(Appendable target, Locale loc)
Formatter(String filename)
    throws FileNotFoundException
Formatter(OutputStream outStrm)
Formatter(PrintStream outStrm)
```

The *loc* parameter specifies a locale. If no locale is specified, the default locale is used. By specifying a locale, you can format data relative to a country and/or language. The *target* parameter specifies a destination for the formatted output. This target must implement the **Appendable** interface, which describes objects to which data can be added at the end. (**Appendable** is implemented by **StringBuilder**, **PrintStream**, and **PrintWriter**, among several others.) If *target* is null, then **Formatter** automatically allocates a **StringBuilder** to use as a buffer for the formatted output. The *filename* parameter specifies the name of a file

Method	Description
void close( )	Closes the invoking **Formatter**. This causes any resources used by the object to be released. After a **Formatter** has been closed, it cannot be reused.
void flush( )	Flushes the format buffer. This causes any output currently in the buffer to be written to the destination.
Formatter format(String *fmtStr*, Object ... *args*)	Formats the arguments passed via *args* according to the format specifiers contained in *fmtStr*. Returns the invoking object.
Formatter format(Locale *loc*, String *fmtStr*, Object ... *args*)	Formats the arguments passed via *args* according to the format specifiers contained in *fmtStr*. The locale specified by *loc* is used for this format. Returns the invoking object.
IOException ioException( )	If the underlying object that is the destination for output throws an **IOException**, then this exception is returned. Otherwise, null is returned.
Locale locale( )	Returns the invoking object's locale.
Appendable out( )	Returns a reference to the underlying object that is the destination for output.
String toString( )	Returns the string obtained by calling **toString( )** on the target object. If this is a buffer, then the formatted output will be returned.

TABLE 4-1   The Methods Defined by **Formatter**

that will receive the formatted output. The *outStrm* parameter specifies a reference to an output stream that will receive output.

   Formatter defines the methods shown in Table 4-1. Except for **ioException( )**, any attempt to use one of these methods after the **Formatter** instance has been closed will result in a **FormatterClosedException**.

Formatting Basics

After you have created a **Formatter**, you can use its **format( )** method to create a formatted string. Its two forms are shown here:

   Formatter format(Locale *loc*, String *fmtStr*, Object ... *args*)
   Formatter format(String *fmtStr*, Object ... *args*)

In the first form, the *loc* parameter specifies the locale. In the second form, the locale of the **Formatter** instance is used. For this reason, the second form is probably the more common. For both forms, the *fmtStr* consists of two types of items. The first type is composed of characters that are simply copied to the target. The second type contains *format specifiers* that define the way the subsequent arguments passed via *args* are formatted.

   In its simplest form, a format specifier begins with a percent sign followed by the *format conversion specifier*. All format conversion specifiers consist of a single character. For example, the format specifier for floating-point data is **%f**. In general, there must be the same number of arguments as there are format specifiers, and the format specifiers and the arguments are matched in order from left to right. For example, consider this fragment:

```
Formatter fmt = new Formatter();
fmt.format("Formatter is %s powerful %d %f", "very", 88, 3.1416);
```

This sequence creates a **Formatter** that contains the following string:

```
Formatter is very powerful 88 3.141600
```

In this example, the format specifiers, **%s**, **%d**, and **%f**, are replaced with the arguments that follow the format string. Thus, **%s** is replaced by "very", **%d** is replaced by 88, and **%f** is replaced by 3.1416. All other characters are simply used as-is. As you might guess, the format specifier **%s** specifies a string, and **%d** specifies an integer value. As mentioned earlier, the **%f** specifies a floating-point value.

It is important to understand that for any given **Formatter** instance, each call to **format( )** adds output to the end of the previous output. Therefore, if the target of the **Formatter** is a buffer, then each call to **format( )** appends output to the end of the buffer. In other words, a call to **format( )** *does not* reset the buffer. For example, these two calls to **format( )**

```
fmt.format("%s %s", "this", "is");
fmt.format("%s", " a test.");
```

create a string that contains "This is a test." Thus, a sequence of calls can be made to **format( )** to construct the desired string.

The **format( )** method accepts a wide variety of format specifiers, which are shown in Table 4-2. Notice that many specifiers have both upper- and lowercase forms. When an uppercase specifier is used, then letters are shown in uppercase. Otherwise, the upper- and lowercase specifiers perform the same conversion. It is important to understand that Java type-checks each format specifier against its corresponding argument. If the argument doesn't match, an **IllegalFormatException** is thrown. An **IllegalFormatException** is also thrown if a format specifier is malformed or if no corresponding argument is supplied to match a format specifier. There are several subclasses of **IllegalFormatException** that describe specific errors. (Consult the Java API documentation for details.)

If you are using a buffer-based version of **Formatter**, then after calling **format( )**, you can obtain the formatted string by calling **toString( )** on the **Formatter**. It returns the result of calling **toString( )** on the buffer. For example, continuing with the preceding example, the following statement obtains the formatted string contained in **fmt**:

```
String str = fmt.toString();
```

Of course, if you simply want to display the formatted string, there is no reason to first assign it to a **String** object. When a **Formatter** object is passed to **println( )**, for example, its **toString( )** method is automatically called, which (in this case) returns the result of calling **toString( )** on the buffer.

One other point: You can obtain a reference to the underlying target by calling **out( )**. It returns a reference to the **Appendable** object to which the formatted output was written. In the case of a buffer-based **Formatter**, this will be a reference to the buffer, which is a **StringBuilder** by default.

Format Specifier	Conversion Applied
%a %A	Floating-point hexadecimal
%b %B	Boolean
%c	Character
%d	Decimal integer
%h %H	Hash code of the argument
%e %E	Scientific notation
%f	Decimal floating-point
%g %G	Uses **%e** or **%f**, whichever is shorter
%o	Octal integer
%n	Inserts a newline character
%s %S	String
%t %T	Time and date
%x %X	Integer hexadecimal
%%	Inserts a % sign

TABLE 4-2   The Format Specifiers

Specifying a Minimum Field Width

An integer placed between the % sign and the format conversion specifier acts as a *minimum field-width specifier*. This pads the output with spaces to ensure that it reaches a certain minimum length. If the string or number is longer than that minimum, it will still be printed in full. The default padding is done with spaces. If you want to pad with 0's, place a 0 before the field-width specifier. For example, **%05d** will pad a number of less than five digits with 0's so that its total length is five. The field-width specifier can be used with all format specifiers except **%n**.

Specifying Precision

A *precision specifier* can be applied to the **%f**, **%e**, **%g**, and **%s** format specifiers. It follows the minimum field-width specifier (if there is one) and consists of a period followed by an integer. Its exact meaning depends upon the type of data to which it is applied.

When the precision specifier is applied to floating-point data formatted by **%f** or **%e**, it determines the number of decimal places displayed. For example, **%10.4f** displays a number at least ten characters wide with four decimal places. When using **%g**, the precision specifier determines the number of significant digits. The default precision is 6.

Applied to strings, the precision specifier specifies the maximum field length. For example, **%5.7s** displays a string at least five and not exceeding seven characters long. If the string is longer than the maximum field width, the end characters will be truncated.

Using the Format Flags

Formatter recognizes a set of format *flags* that lets you control various aspects of a conversion. All format flags are single characters, and a format flag follows the % in a format specification. The flags are shown here:

Flag	Effect
–	Left justification
#	Alternate conversion format
0	Output is padded with zeros rather than spaces
space	Positive numeric output is preceded by a space
+	Positive numeric output is preceded by a + sign
,	Numeric values include group separators
(	Negative numeric values are enclosed within parentheses

Of these, the **#** requires some explanation. The **#** can be applied to **%o**, **%x**, **%a**, **%e**, and **%f**. For **%a**, **%e**, and **%f**, the **#** ensures that there will be a decimal point even if there are no decimal digits. If you precede the **%x** format specifier with a **#**, the hexadecimal number will be printed with a **0x** prefix. Preceding the **%o** specifier with **#** causes the number to be printed with a leading zero.

The Uppercase Option

As mentioned earlier, several of the format specifiers have uppercase versions that cause the conversion to use uppercase where appropriate. The following table describes the effect:

Specifier	Effect
%A	Causes the hexadecimal digits *a* through *f* to be displayed in uppercase as *A* through *F*. Also, the prefix **0x** is displayed as **0X**, and the **p** will be displayed as **P**.
%B	Uppercases the values **true** and **false**.
%E	Causes the *e* symbol that indicates the exponent to be displayed in uppercase.
%G	Causes the *e* symbol that indicates the exponent to be displayed in uppercase.
%H	Causes the hexadecimal digits *a* through *f* to be displayed in uppercase as *A* through *F*.
%S	Uppercases the corresponding string.
%T	Causes all alphabetical output related to the date or time (such as the names of months or the AM/PM indicator) to be displayed in uppercase.
%X	Causes the hexadecimal digits *a* through *f* to be displayed in uppercase as *A* through *F*. Also, the optional prefix **0x** is displayed as **0X**, if present.

Using an Argument Index

Formatter includes a very useful feature that lets you specify the argument to which a format specifier applies. Normally, format specifiers and arguments are matched in order, from left to right. That is, the first format specifier matches the first argument, the second format specifier matches the second argument, and so on. However, by using an *argument index*, you can explicitly control which argument matches which format specifier.

An argument index immediately follows the % in a format specifier. It has the following format:

n$

where *n* is the index of the desired argument, beginning with 1. For example, consider this example:

```
fmt.format("%3$s %1$s %2$s", "alpha", "beta", "gamma");
```

It produces this string:

```
gamma alpha beta
```

In this example, the first format specifier matches "gamma", the second matches "alpha", and the third matches "beta". Thus, the arguments are used in an order other than strictly left to right.

One advantage of argument indexes is that they enable you to reuse an argument without having to specify it twice. For example, consider this line:

```
fmt.format("%s in uppercase is %1$S", "Testing");
```

It produces the following string:

```
Testing in uppercase is TESTING
```

As you can see, the argument "Testing" is used by both format specifiers.

There is a convenient shorthand called a *relative index* that enables you to reuse the argument matched by the preceding format specifier. Simply specify < for the argument index. For example, the following call to **format( )** produces the same results as the previous example:

```
fmt.format("%s in uppercase is %<S", "Testing");
```

Overview of NumberFormat and DateFormat

NumberFormat and **DateFormat** are abstract classes that are part of **java.text**. **NumberFormat** is used to format numeric values. **DateFormat** is used to format the time and date. They both also provide support for parsing data, and both work in a locale-sensitive manner. These classes predate **Formatter** and provide another way to format information. A concrete subclass of **NumberFormat** is **DecimalFormat**. It supports a pattern-based approach to formatting numeric values. A concrete subclass of **DateFormat** is **SimpleDateFormat**, which also supports a pattern-based approach to formatting. The operation of these classes is described in the recipes that use them.

Four Simple Numeric Formatting Techniques Using Formatter

Key Ingredients	
Classes	**Methods**
java.util.Formatter	Formatter format(String *fmtStr*, Object ... *args*)

Some of the most frequently asked questions by beginners relate to the formatting of numeric values. Here are four:

- How do I control the number of decimal places displayed when I output a floating-point value? For example, how do I display only two decimal places?

- How do I include group separators in a number? For example, in English, commas are used to separate groups of three digits, as in 1,234,709. How are such groupings created?

- Is there a simple way to include a + at the start of a positive value? If so, how?

- Can I display negative values inside parentheses? If so, how?

Fortunately, all of these questions are easy to answer because **Formatter** offers very simple solutions to these types of formatting tasks. This recipe shows how.

Step-by-Step

To format a numeric value using **Formatter** involves the following steps:

1. Construct a **Formatter**.
2. Create a format specifier for the desired format as described in the following steps.
3. To specify the number of decimal places displayed, use a precision specifier with the **%f** or **%e** formats.
4. To include group separators, use the **,** flag with **%f**, **%g**, or **%d**.
5. To display a + at the start of a positive value, specify the **+** flag.
6. To display negative values inside parentheses, use the **(** flag.
7. Pass the format specifier and value to **format( )** to create a formatted value.

Discussion

For a description of **Formatter**'s constructors and the **format( )** method, refer to *An Overview of Formatter*, presented near the start of this chapter.

To specify the number of decimal places (in other words, the number of fractional digits) that will be displayed, use a precision specifier with either the **%f** or **%g** format. The precision specifier consists of a period following by the precision. It immediately precedes the conversion specifier. For example, **%.3f** causes three decimal digits to be displayed.

To include group separators (which are commas in English), use the , flag. For example, **%,d** inserts the group separator into an integer value.

To precede positive values with a + sign, use the + flag. For example, **%+f** causes a positive, floating-point value to be preceded by a +.

In some cases, such as when creating profit and loss statements, it is customary to display negative values inside parentheses. This is easily accomplished by use of the **(** flag. For example, **%(.2f** displays a value using two decimal digits. If the value is negative, it is enclosed within parentheses.

Example

The following program puts the recipe into action.

```
// Use Formatter to:
//
//    . Specify the number of decimal digits.
//    . Use a group separator.
//    . Precede a positive value with a + sign.
//    . Show negative values within parentheses.

import java.util.*;

class NumericFormats {
  public static void main(String args[]) {
    Formatter fmt = new Formatter();

    // Limit the number of decimal digits
    // by specifying the precision.
    fmt.format("Default precision: %f\n", 10.0/3.0);
    fmt.format("Two decimal digits: %.2f\n\n", 10.0/3.0);

    // Using group separators.
    fmt.format("No group separators: %d\n", 123456789);
    fmt.format("With group separators: %,d\n\n", 123456789);

    // Show positive values with a leading +
    // and negative values within parentheses.
    fmt.format("Default positive and negative format: %.2f %.2f\n",
              423.78, -505.09);

    fmt.format("With + and parentheses: %+.2f %(.2f\n",
              423.78, -505.09);

    // Display the formatted output.
    System.out.println(fmt);
  }
}
```

The output is shown here:

```
Default precision: 3.333333
Two decimal digits: 3.33
```

```
No group separators: 123456789
With group separators: 123,456,789

Default positive and negative format: 423.78 -505.09
With + and parentheses: +423.78 (505.09)
```

Options and Alternatives

The **java.text.NumberFormat** class can also be used to format numeric values. It does not support all of the options available through **Formatter**, but it does allow you to specify the minimum and maximum number of fractional digits to display. It can also format values in the currency format of the locale. You can also use **DecimalFormat** to format numeric values. (See the **NumberFormat** and **DecimalFormat** recipes near the end of this chapter for details.)

You can use the # flag with **%e** and **%f** to ensure that there will be a decimal point even if no decimal digits are shown. For example, **%#.0f** causes the value 100.0 to be displayed as **100.**.

You can use more than one flag at a time. For example, to show negative numbers with group separators inside parentheses, use this format specifier: **%,(f**.

Vertically Align Numeric Data Using Formatter

Key Ingredients	
Classes	**Methods**
java.util.Formatter	Formatter format(String *fmtStr*, Object ... *args*)

One common formatting task involves the creation of tables in which the numeric values in a column line up. For example, you might want financial data in a profit-and-loss statement to line up. As a general rule, aligning numeric values in a column implies that the decimal points line up. In the case of integer values, the one's digits must align.

The easiest way to vertically align numeric data involves the use of a minimum field-width specifier. Often, you will also want to specify the precision to enhance the presentation. This is the approach used by this recipe.

Step-by-Step

To vertically align numeric values involves these steps:

1. Construct a **Formatter**.
2. Create a format specifier that defines the width of the field in which the values will be displayed. The width must be equal to or greater than the width of the largest value (including the decimal point, sign, and group separators).

3. Pass the format specifier and the data to **format( )** to create a formatted value.

4. Arrange the formatted values vertically, one over the other.

Discussion

For a description of **Formatter**'s constructors and the **format( )** method, refer to *An Overview of Formatter*, presented near the start of this chapter.

In general, aligning numeric values in a table requires that you specify a minimum field width. When a minimum field width is used, output is padded with spaces to ensure that it reaches a certain minimum length. Understand, however, that if the string or number being formatted is longer than that minimum, it will still be printed in full. This means that you must make the minimum width at least as long as the longest value if you want the values to line up. By default, spaces are used to pad the output.

When aligning floating-point data, you will often want the values aligned such that the decimal points are over each other. For integer data, the one's digits align vertically.

Example

The following example shows how to use a minimum field width to vertically align data. It displays several values and their cube roots. It uses a width of 12 and shows four decimal places.

```java
// Use Formatter to vertically align numeric values.

import java.util.*;

class AlignVertical {
  public static void main(String args[]) {
    double data[] = { 12.3, 45.5764, -0.09, -18.0, 1232.01 };

    Formatter fmt = new Formatter();

    // Create a table that contains values and the
    // the cube roots of those values.
    fmt.format("%12s %12s\n", "Value", "Cube Root");

    for(double v : data) {
      fmt.format("%12.4f %12.4f\n", v, Math.cbrt(v));
    }

    // Display the formatted data.
    System.out.println(fmt);
  }
}
```

The output is shown here:

```
       Value   Cube Root
     12.3000      2.3084
     45.5764      3.5720
     -0.0900     -0.4481
    -18.0000     -2.6207
   1232.0100     10.7202
```

Bonus Example: Center Data

Sometimes you will want to vertically align data by centering it rather than left- or right-justifying it. This example shows one way to do this. It creates a static method called **center( )** that centers an item within a specified field width. The method is passed a reference to the **Formatter**, the format specifier that determines the format of the data, the data to be formatted (in the form of an **Object** reference), and the field width. The **center( )** method has one important restriction that must be pointed out: it works only for the default locale. However, you can easily enhance it to work with a specified locale.

```
// Center data within a field.

import java.util.*;

class CenterDemo {

  // Center data within a specified field width.
  // The format of the data is passed to fmtStr,
  // the Formatter is passed to fmt, the data to format
  // is passed to obj, and the field width is passed to width.
  static void center(String fmtStr, Formatter fmt,
                     Object obj, int width) {

    String str;
    try {
      // First, format the data so that its length can
      // be determined. Use a temporary Formatter for
      // this purpose.
      Formatter tmp = new Formatter();
      tmp.format(fmtStr, obj);
      str = tmp.toString();
    } catch(IllegalFormatException exc) {
      System.out.println("Invalid Format Request");
      fmt.format("");
      return;
    }

    // Obtain the difference between the length of the
    // data and the length of the field.
    int dif = width - str.length();

    // If data is longer than the field width, then just
    // use it as-is.
    if(dif < 0) {
      fmt.format(str);
      return;
    }

    // Add padding to the start of the field.
    char[] pad = new char[dif/2];
    Arrays.fill(pad, ' ');
    fmt.format(new String(pad));
```

```
    // Add the data.
    fmt.format(str);

    // Add padding to the end of the field.
    pad = new char[width-dif/2-str.length()];
    Arrays.fill(pad, ' ');
    fmt.format(new String(pad));
  }

  // Demonstrate center().
  public static void main(String args[]) {
    Formatter fmt = new Formatter();

    fmt.format("|");
    center("%s", fmt, "Source", 12);
    fmt.format("|");
    center("%10s", fmt, "Profit/Loss", 14);
    fmt.format("|\n\n");

    fmt.format("|");
    center("%s", fmt, "Retail", 12);
    fmt.format("|");
    center("%,10d", fmt, 1232675, 14);
    fmt.format("|\n");

    fmt.format("|");
    center("%s", fmt, "Wholesale", 12);
    fmt.format("|");
    center("%,10d", fmt, 23232482, 14);
    fmt.format("|\n");

    fmt.format("|");
    center("%s", fmt, "Rents", 12);
    fmt.format("|");
    center("%,10d", fmt, 3052238, 14);
    fmt.format("|\n");

    fmt.format("|");
    center("%s", fmt, "Royalties", 12);
    fmt.format("|");
    center("%,10d", fmt, 329845, 14);
    fmt.format("|\n");

    fmt.format("|");
    center("%s", fmt, "Interest", 12);
    fmt.format("|");
    center("%,10d", fmt, 8657, 14);
    fmt.format("|\n");

    fmt.format("|");
    center("%s", fmt, "Investments", 12);
```

```
    fmt.format("|");
    center("%,10d", fmt, 1675832, 14);
    fmt.format("|\n");

    fmt.format("|");
    center("%s", fmt, "Patents", 12);
    fmt.format("|");
    center("%,10d", fmt, -2011, 14);
    fmt.format("|\n");

    // Display the formatted data.
    System.out.println(fmt);
  }
}
```

Sample output is shown here. Notice that the data in both columns is centered within the field width. The field-width extents are indicated by the vertical bars.

```
|    Source    | Profit/Loss  |

|    Retail    |   1,232,675  |
|  Wholesale   |  23,232,482  |
|    Rents     |   3,052,238  |
|  Royalties   |     329,845  |
|   Interest   |       8,657  |
|Investments   |   1,675,832  |
|   Patents    |      -2,011  |
```

In the program, pay special attention to this sequence inside **center( )**:

```
// First, format the data so that its length can
// be determined. Use a temporary Formatter for
// this purpose.
Formatter tmp = new Formatter();
tmp.format(fmtStr, obj);
String str = tmp.toString();
```

Although the data being formatted is passed as an **Object** reference via **obj**, it can still be formatted because **format( )** automatically attempts to format the data based on the format specifier. In general, all **format( )** arguments are **Object** references anyway because all arguments are passed via a var-args parameter of type **Object**. Again, it is the type of the format specifier that determines how the argument is interpreted. If the argument's type does not match the data, then an **IllegalFormatException** will be thrown.

One other point: notice that many of the calls to **format( )** specify a format string that does not contain any format specifiers or any arguments to format. This is perfectly legal. As explained, the format string can contain two types of items: regular characters that are simply output as-is, and format specifiers. However, neither are required. Therefore, when no format specifiers are included, no additional arguments are needed.

Options and Alternatives

By default, spaces are used as padding to achieve a minimum field width, but you can pad with 0's, by placing a 0 before the field-width specifier. For example, if you substitute this format string **"%012.4f %012.4f\n"** into the first example, the output will look like this:

```
      Value     Cube Root
0000012.3000 0000002.3084
0000045.5764 0000003.5720
-000000.0900 -000000.4481
-000018.0000 -000002.6207
0001232.0100 0000010.7202
```

In some cases, you can use left justification to align values vertically. This technique is demonstrated by the next recipe.

Left-Justify Output Using Formatter

Key Ingredients	
Classes	**Methods**
java.util.Formatter	Formatter format(String *fmtStr*, Object ... *args*)

When a minimum field width is used, output is right-justified by default. However, this is not always what is needed. For example, when formatting strings within a fixed-width field, often the strings need to be left-justified. This is easy to achieve when using **Formatter** because it requires only the use of the left-justification flag: –.

Step-by-Step

To left-justify data involves these steps:

1. Construct a **Formatter**.
2. Create a format specifier that defines the width of the field in which the data will be displayed. Use the left-justification flag – to cause the formatted data to be left-justified within that field.
3. Pass the format specifier and the data to **format( )** to create left-justified output.

Discussion

For a description of **Formatter**'s constructors and the **format( )** method, refer to *An Overview of Formatter*, presented near the start of this chapter.

The left-justification flag can only be used in a format specifier that includes a minimum field-width specification. Although left justification works with numeric values, it is frequently applied to strings when data is presented in a table. This allows the strings to be vertically aligned, flush left over one another.

Example

The following example shows how left justification can be used to improve the appearance of a table. The table presents a very simple profit and loss statement in which the left column describes an income category and the right column shows the profit (or loss) from the category. The strings in the first column are left-justified. This causes them to displayed flush left within a 12-column field. Notice that the values in the second column are right-justified (which allows them to align vertically).

```java
// Use Formatter to left-justify strings within a table.

import java.util.*;

class Table {
  public static void main(String args[]) {
    Formatter fmt = new Formatter();

    fmt.format("%-12s %12s\n\n", "Source", "Profit/Loss");

    fmt.format("%-12s %,12d\n", "Retail", 1232675);
    fmt.format("%-12s %,12d\n", "Wholesale", 23232482);
    fmt.format("%-12s %,12d\n", "Rents", 3052238);
    fmt.format("%-12s %,12d\n", "Royalties", 329845);
    fmt.format("%-12s %,12d\n", "Interest", 8657);
    fmt.format("%-12s %,12d\n", "Investments", 1675832);
    fmt.format("%-12s %,12d\n", "Patents", -2011);

    // Display the formatted table.
    System.out.println(fmt);
  }
}
```

The output is shown here:

```
Source       Profit/Loss

Retail         1,232,675
Wholesale     23,232,482
Rents          3,052,238
Royalties        329,845
Interest           8,657
Investments    1,675,832
Patents           -2,011
```

Options and Alternatives

To understand the usefulness of left justification, try this experiment: remove the left-justification flags from the string specifiers. In other words, change the following calls to **format( )** as shown here:

```
fmt.format("%12s %12s\n\n", "Source", "Profit/Loss");

fmt.format("%12s %,12d\n", "Retail", 1232675);
fmt.format("%12s %,12d\n", "Wholesale", 23232482);
fmt.format("%12s %,12d\n", "Rents", 3052238);
fmt.format("%12s %,12d\n", "Royalties", 329845);
fmt.format("%12s %,12d\n", "Interest", 8657);
fmt.format("%12s %,12d\n", "Investments", 1675832);
fmt.format("%12s %,12d\n", "Patents", -2011);
```

After making these changes, the output will now look like this:

```
     Source  Profit/Loss

     Retail   1,232,675
  Wholesale  23,232,482
      Rents   3,052,238
  Royalties     329,845
   Interest       8,657
Investments   1,675,832
    Patents      -2,011
```

As you can see, the results are not as pleasing.

Format Time and Date Using Formatter

Key Ingredients	
Classes	**Methods**
java.util.Formatter	Formatter format(String *fmtStr*, Object ... *args*)
java.util.Calendar	static Calendar getInstance( )
java.util.Date	

One of the more powerful conversion specifiers provided by **Formatter** is **%t**, which formats time and date information. Because of the wide variety of formats in which the time and date can be represented, the **%t** specifier supports many options. For example, the time can be represented using a 12-hour or a 24-hour clock. The date can be shown using short forms, such as 10/15/2008, or longer forms, such as Wednesday, Oct 15, 2008. The time and date options are specified by using one or more suffixes that follow the **t** format. This recipe describes the process.

Step-by-Step

To format the time and/or date, follow these steps.

1. Create a **Formatter** object.
2. Using the suffixes shown in Table 4-3 to indicate the precise format, create a **%t** format specifier that describes the way in which you want to display the time and/or date.
3. Obtain an instance that contains the time and date that you want to format. This must be an object of type **Calendar**, **Date**, **Long**, or **long**.
4. Pass the format specifier and the time to **format( )** to create a formatted value.

Discussion

For a description of **Formatter**'s constructors and the **format( )** method, refer to *An Overview of Formatter*, presented near the start of this chapter.

The **%t** specifier works a bit differently than the others because it requires the use of a suffix to describe the portion and precise format of the time or date desired. The suffixes are shown in Table 4-3. For example, to display minutes, you would use **%tM**, where **M** indicates minutes in a two-character field. The argument corresponding to the **%t** specifier must be of type **Calendar**, **Date**, **Long**, or **long**.

The **%t** specifier causes any alphabetical information associated with the date and time, such as the names of days or the AM/PM indicator, to be displayed in lowercase. If you want to display these items in uppercase, use **%T** instead.

As explained, the argument that corresponds to **%t** must be an instance of **Calendar**, **Date**, **Long**, or **long**. However, most often you will use either a **Calendar** or **Date** instance (which will often contain the current system time and date). Both **Calendar** and **Date** are packaged in **java.util**.

To obtain the current date and time using **Calendar**, call the factory method **getInstance( )**. It is shown here:

    static Calendar getInstance( )

It returns a **Calendar** instance that contains the date and time at which the object was created.

To obtain the current date and time using **Date**, simply create a **Date** object by using this constructor:

    Date( )

This instantiates a **Date** that contains the current time and date of the system.

As Table 4-3 shows, **Formatter** gives you very detailed control of the formatting of time and date information. The best way to understand the effect of each suffix is to experiment.

Suffix	Replaced By
a	Abbreviated weekday name
A	Full weekday name
b	Abbreviated month name
B	Full month name
c	Standard date and time string formatted as *day month date hh::mm:ss tzone year*
C	First two digits of year
d	Day of month as a decimal (01–31)
D	month/day/year
e	Day of month as a decimal (1–31)
F	year-month-day
h	Abbreviated month name
H	Hour (00 to 23)
I	Hour (01 to 12)
j	Day of year as a decimal (001 to 366)
k	Hour (0 to 23)
l	Hour (1 to 12)
L	Millisecond (000 to 999)
m	Month as decimal (01 to 13)
M	Minute as decimal (00 to 59)
N	Nanosecond (000000000 to 999999999)
p	Locale's equivalent of AM or PM in lowercase
Q	Milliseconds from 1/1/1970
r	*hh:mm:ss* (12-hour format)
R	*hh:mm* (24-hour format)
S	Seconds (00 to 60)
s	Seconds from 1/1/1970 UTC
T	*hh:mm:ss* (24-hour format)
y	Year in decimal without century (00 to 99)
Y	Year in decimal including century (0001 to 9999)
z	Offset from UTC
Z	Time zone name

TABLE 4-3   The Time and Date Format Suffixes

Example

Here is a program that demonstrates a variety of time and date formats. Notice one other thing in this program: the last call to **format( )** uses relative indexing to enable the same date value to be used by three format specifiers. This line is shown here:

```
fmt.format("Hour and Minute: %tl:%1$tM %1$Tp", cal);
```

Because of relative indexing, the argument **cal** need only be passed once, rather than three times.

```java
// Display several time and date formats
// using the %t specifier with Formatter.

import java.util.*;

class TimeAndDate {

  public static void main(String args[]) {
    Formatter fmt = new Formatter();

    // Get the current time and date.
    Calendar cal = Calendar.getInstance();

    // Display 12-hour time format.
    fmt.format("Time using 12-hour clock: %tr\n", cal);

    // Display 24-hour time format.
    fmt.format("Time using 24-hour clock: %tT\n", cal);

    // Display short date format.
    fmt.format("Short date format: %tD\n", cal);

    // Display date using full names.
    fmt.format("Long date format: ");
    fmt.format("%tA %1$tB %1$td, %1$tY\n", cal);

    // Display complete time and date information.
    // The first version uses lowercase.
    // The second version uses uppercase.
    // As explained, uppercase is selected by
    // using %T rather than %t.
    fmt.format("Time and date in lowercase: %tc\n", cal);
    fmt.format("Time and date in uppercase: %Tc\n", cal);

    // Display hour and minute, and include
    // AM or PM indicator. Note use of uppercase %T.
    // This causes AM or PM to be in uppercase.
    fmt.format("Hour and Minute: %tl:%1$tM %1$Tp\n", cal);
```

```
        // Display the formatted times and dates.
        System.out.println(fmt);
    }
}
```

The output is shown here:

```
Time using 12-hour clock: 02:04:06 PM
Time using 24-hour clock: 14:04:06
Short date format: 02/05/07
Long date format: Monday February 05, 2007
Time and date in lowercase: Mon Feb 05 14:04:06 CST 2007
Time and date in uppercase: MON FEB 05 14:04:06 CST 2007
Hour and Minute: 2:04 PM
```

Options and Alternatives

As mentioned, the time and/or date can be contained in a **Calendar**, **Date**, **Long**, or **long** object. The example uses a **Calendar** object, but you can use one of the other objects if they are more convenient. For example, here is one way to rewrite the first call to **format( )**:

```
fmt.format("Time using 12-hour clock: %tr\n", new Date());
```

It passes a **Date**, rather than a **Calendar**, instance.

A **long** version of the date and time can be obtained from **Calendar** by calling **getTimeInMillis( )**. A **long** version of the date and time can be obtained from **Date** by calling **getTime( )**.

If you want to use something other than the current system time and date, you can use the **set( )** method defined by **Calendar** to set the time and date. Alternatively, you can use **GregorianCalendar**, which is a subclass of **Calendar**. It supplies constructors that let you specify the date and time explicitly. For example, here the date and time is constructed using a **GregorianCalendar**:

```
fmt.format("Time and date in lowercase: %tc\n",
           new GregorianCalendar(2007, 1, 28, 14, 30, 0));
```

The date is set to February 28, 2007. The time is set to 2:30:00 pm.

An important alternative for time and date formatting is **java.text.DateFormat**. It offers a different way to create time and date formats that might be easier to use in some cases. Of special interest is its subclass **SimpleDateFormat**, which lets you specify the time and date by using a pattern. (See *Format Time and Date with* **DateFormat** and *Format Time and Date with Patterns Using* **SimpleDateFormat**.)

Specify a Locale with Formatter

Key Ingredients	
Classes	**Methods and Fields**
java.util.Formatter	Formatter format(Locale *loc*, String *fmtStr*, Object ... *args*)
java.util.Locale	Locale.FRANCE Locale.GERMAN Locale.ITALY

Although **Formatter** uses the current locale by default, it is possible to specify the locale explicitly. Doing so lets you format data in a form compatible with other countries or languages. Locale information is encapsulated within the **Locale** class, which is packaged in **java.util**.

There are two basic ways to specify a locale when formatting. First, you can pass a **Locale** instance to one of **Formatter**'s locale-enabled constructors. (Several are shown in the **Formatter** overview at the start of this chapter.) Second, you can use the locale-aware form of **format( )**. This is the approach used by this recipe.

Step-by-Step

To format data relative to a specific locale, follow these steps:

1. Create or obtain a **Locale** object that represents the desired locale.

2. Create a **Formatter** object.

3. Use the **format( )** method to format the data, specifying the **Locale** object. This causes the format to automatically incorporate locale-sensitive attributes.

Discussion

For a description of **Formatter**'s constructors and the **format( )** method, refer to *An Overview of Formatter*, presented near the start of this chapter.

Locales are represented by **Locale** objects, which describe a geographical or cultural region. **Locale** is one of the classes that helps internationalize a program. It contains information that determines, for example, the formats used to display dates, times, and numbers in different countries and languages. Internationalization is a large topic that is beyond the scope of this chapter. However, it is easy to use **Locale** to tailor the formats produced by **Formatter**.

The constructors for **Locale** are

Locale(String *language*)
Locale(String *language*, String *country*)
Locale(String *language*, String *country*, String *data*)

These constructors build a **Locale** object to represent a specific *language* and, in the case of the last two, *country*. These values must contain ISO-standard language and country codes. (See the API documentation for **Locale** for information on country and language codes.) Auxiliary browser- and vendor-specific information can be provided in *data*.

Instead of constructing a **Locale** instance yourself, often you can use one of the predefined locales defined by **Locale**. They are shown here:

CANADA	GERMAN	KOREAN
CANADA_FRENCH	GERMANY	PRC
CHINA	ITALIAN	SIMPLIFIED_CHINESE
CHINESE	ITALY	TAIWAN
ENGLISH	JAPAN	TRADITIONAL_CHINESE
FRANCE	JAPANESE	UK
FRENCH	KOREA	US

These fields are all static objects of type **Locale** that have been initialized to the indicated language or country. For example, the field **Locale.CANADA** represents the **Locale** object for Canada. The field **Locale.JAPANESE** represents the **Locale** object for the Japanese language.

Example

The following example illustrates the use of locales when formatting the date and time. It first shows the default time and date format (which is US English in the sample output). It then shows the formats for Italy, German, and France.

```
// Demonstrate locale-specific formatting.

import java.util.*;

class LocaleFormatDemo {

  public static void main(String args[]) {
    Formatter fmt = new Formatter();

    // Get the current time and date.
    Calendar cal = Calendar.getInstance();

    // Display complete time and date information
    // for various locales.
    fmt = new Formatter();
    fmt.format("Default locale: %tc\n", cal);

    fmt.format(Locale.GERMAN, "For Locale.GERMAN: %tc\n", cal);

    fmt.format(Locale.ITALY, "For Locale.ITALY: %tc\n", cal);

    fmt.format(Locale.FRANCE, "For Locale.FRANCE: %tc\n", cal);

    System.out.println(fmt);
  }
}
```

The output is shown here:

```
Default locale: Thu Feb 01 16:15:45 CST 2007
For Locale.GERMAN: Do Feb 01 16:15:45 CST 2007
For Locale.ITALY: gio feb 01 16:15:45 CST 2007
For Locale.FRANCE: jeu. févr. 01 16:15:45 CST 2007
```

Options and Alternatives

As mentioned, you can create a locale-specific **Formatter** by using one of its locale-enabled constructors. Subsequent calls to **format( )** will then automatically target that locale.

You can obtain locale-specific information about currencies by using the **java.util.Currency** class. For example, its **getSymbol( )** method returns a string that contains the currency symbol for the locale (which is $ for US). The **getDefaultFractionDigits( )** method returns the number of decimal places (i.e., fractional digits) that are normally displayed (which is 2 in English).

Use Streams with Formatter

Key Ingredients	
Classes	**Methods**
java.util.Formatter	Formatter format(String *fmtStr*, Object ... *args*)

Although often the target for formatted data will be a buffer (typically of type **StringBuilder**), you can also create **Formatter**s that output to a stream. This capability lets you write formatted output directly to a file, for example. You can also use this feature to write formatted output directly to the console. This recipe shows the process.

Step-by-Step

To write formatted data directly to a stream involves these steps:

1. Create a **Formatter** that is linked to a stream.
2. Create the desired format specifier.
3. Pass the format specifier and the data to **format( )**. Because the **Formatter** is linked to a stream, the formatted output is automatically written to the stream.

Discussion

To link a **Formatter** with a stream, you must use one of **Formatter**'s stream-enabled constructors. The ones used here are

Formatter(OutputStream *outStrm*)
Formatter(PrintStream *outStrm*)

The *outStrm* parameter specifies a reference to an output stream that will receive output. The first version works with any **OutputStream**, including **FileOutputStream**. The second version works with **PrintStream**s. The **PrintStream** class provides the **print( )** and **println( )** methods that are used to output Java's basic data types (such as **int**, **String**, and **double**) in a human-readable form. As you may know, **System.out** is an instance of **PrintStream**. Thus, a **Formatter** linked to **System.out** will write directly to the console.

For a description of the **format( )** method defined by **Formatter**, refer to *An Overview of Formatter*, presented near the start of this chapter.

Example

The following example shows how to use **Formatter** to write to the console and to a file.

```
// Write formatted output directly to the console
// and to a file.

import java.io.*;

import java.util.*;

class FormatterStreams {
  public static void main(String args[]) {
    // Create a Formatter linked to the console.
    Formatter fmtCon = new Formatter(System.out);

    // Create a Formatter linked to a file.
    Formatter fmtFile;
    try {
     fmtFile = new Formatter(new FileOutputStream("test.fmt"));
    } catch(FileNotFoundException exc) {
      System.out.println("Cannot Open File");
      return;
    }

    // First, write to the console.
    fmtCon.format("This is a negative number: %(.2f\n\n",
                 -123.34);

    fmtCon.format("%8s %8s\n", "Value", "Square");

    for(int i=1; i < 20; i++)
      fmtCon.format("%8d %8d\n", i, i*i);


    // Now, write to the file.
    fmtFile.format("This is a negative number: %(.2f\n\n",
                 -123.34);

    fmtFile.format("%8s %8s\n", "Value", "Square");
```

```
    for(int i=1; i < 20; i++)
      fmtFile.format("%8d %8d\n", i, i*i);


    fmtFile.close();

    // Use ioException() to check for file errors.
    if(fmtFile.ioException() != null) {
      System.out.println("File I/O Error Occurred");
    }
  }
}
```

The output that is displayed on the console and written to the file is shown here:

```
This is a negative number: (123.34)

    Value    Square
        1         1
        2         4
        3         9
        4        16
        5        25
        6        36
        7        49
        8        64
        9        81
       10       100
       11       121
       12       144
       13       169
       14       196
       15       225
       16       256
       17       289
       18       324
       19       361
```

Options and Alternatives

When writing formatted data to the console, it is often easier to use the **printf( )** method defined by **PrintStream**. (See *Use printf( ) to Display Formatted Data*.)

When creating a **Formatter** linked to an **OutputStream**, there are additional constructors that enable you to specify the locale and a charset that defines the mapping between characters and bytes.

Use printf( ) to Display Formatted Data

Key Ingredients	
Classes	**Methods**
java.io.PrintStream	PrintStream printf(String *fmtStr*, Object ... *args*)
java.io.PrintWriter	PrintWriter printf(String fmtStr, Object ... *args*)

Although using a **Formatter** linked to **System.out** is an easy way to display formatted data on the console, it still involves two steps. First, a **Formatter** must be created, and second, **format( )** must be called. While there is certainly nothing wrong with this approach, Java provides a more convenient alternative: the **printf( )** method. The **printf( )** method is defined by both **PrintStream** and **PrintWriter**.

The **printf( )** method automatically uses **Formatter** to create a formatted string. It then outputs that string to the invoking stream. Because **System.out** is an instance of **PrintStream**, **printf( )** can be called on it. Thus, by calling **printf( )** on **System.out**, formatted output can be displayed on the console in one step. Of course, **printf( )** can be called on any **PrintStream** or **PrintWriter** instance. Thus, it can also be used to write formatted output to a file.

NOTE *The printf( ) method is based on, and very similar to, the C/C++ printf( ) function. This makes it easy to convert C/C++ code into Java.*

Step-by-Step

Using **printf( )** involves these steps:

1. Obtain a reference to a **PrintStream** or a **PrintWriter**.
2. Construct the format string that contains the format specifiers that you will be using.
3. Pass the format string and the corresponding data to **printf( )**. The formatted data will be written to the invoking stream.

Discussion

The **printf( )** method is defined by both **PrintStream** and **PrintWriter**. Here are its two forms for **PrintStream**:

```
PrintStream printf(String fmtStr, Object ... args)
PrintStream printf(Locale loc, String fmtStr, Object ... args)
```

The first version writes *args* to the invoking stream in the format specified by *fmtStr,* using the default locale. The second lets you specify a locale. Both return the invoking **PrintStream.**

Here are its two forms for **PrintWriter:**

PrintWriter printf(String *fmtStr,* Object ... *args*)
PrintWriter printf(Locale *loc,* String *fmtStr,* Object ... *args*)

The first version writes *args* to the invoking stream in the format specified by *fmtStr,* using the default locale. The second lets you specify a locale. Both return the invoking **PrintWriter.**

In general, **printf( )** works in a manner similar to the **format( )** method defined by **Formatter.** The *fmtStr* consists of two types of items. The first type is composed of characters that are simply written to the stream. The second type contains format specifiers that define the way the subsequent arguments, specified by *args,* are formatted. (See the overview of **Formatter** at the start of this chapter for details.) An **IllegalFormatException** will be thrown if a format specifier is malformed, if it does not match its corresponding argument, or if there are more format specifiers than there are arguments.

Because **System.out** is a **PrintStream,** you can call **printf( )** on **System.out.** Thus, **printf( )** can be used in place of **println( )** when writing to the console whenever formatted output is desired. This makes it very easy to display formatted output.

Another very good use of **printf( )** is to write formatted output to a file. Just wrap a **FileOutputStream** in a **PrintStream,** or a **FileWriter** in a **PrintWriter,** and then call **printf( )** on that stream.

Example

The following example uses **printf( )** to write several different types of formatted data to the console.

```
// Use printf() to display various types of formatted data.

import java.util.*;

class PrintfDemo {
  public static void main(String args[]) {

    // First use PrintStream's printf() method.
    System.out.printf("Two decimal digits: %.2f\n", 10.0/3.0);

    System.out.printf("Use group separators: %,.2f\n\n",
                      1546456.87);

    System.out.printf("%10s %10s %10s\n",
                      "Value", "Root", "Square");

    for(double i=1.0; i < 20.0; i++)
      System.out.printf("%10.2f %10.2f %10.2f\n",
                        i, Math.sqrt(i), i*i);

    System.out.println();
```

```
      Calendar cal = Calendar.getInstance();
      System.out.printf("Current time and date: %tc\n", cal);
   }
}
```

The output is shown here:

```
Two decimal digits: 3.33
Use group separators: 1,546,456.87
```

Value	Root	Square
1.00	1.00	1.00
2.00	1.41	4.00
3.00	1.73	9.00
4.00	2.00	16.00
5.00	2.24	25.00
6.00	2.45	36.00
7.00	2.65	49.00
8.00	2.83	64.00
9.00	3.00	81.00
10.00	3.16	100.00
11.00	3.32	121.00
12.00	3.46	144.00
13.00	3.61	169.00
14.00	3.74	196.00
15.00	3.87	225.00
16.00	4.00	256.00
17.00	4.12	289.00
18.00	4.24	324.00
19.00	4.36	361.00

```
Current time and date: Sat Feb 03 12:07:07 CST 2007
```

Bonus Example

One very good use for **printf( )** is to create a time stamp. Time stamps are needed in many programming situations. For example, you might want to print the date and time that a report was generated, or you might want to maintain a log file that records the times at which events occur. Whatever the reason, creating a time stamp by using **printf( )** is an easy matter. The following example shows one approach.

The program defines a method called **timeStamp( )** that outputs the current time and date (plus an optional message) to the **PrintWriter** that it is passed. Notice how little code is needed to create and output the time stamp. The program demonstrates its use by writing time stamps to a file called **logfile.txt**. One time stamp is written when the file is opened, and another is written when it is closed.

```
// Use printf() to create a time stamp.

import java.io.*;
import java.util.*;

class TimeStamp {
```

```
// Output a time stamp to the specified PrintWriter.
// You can precede the time stamp with a message
// by passing a string to msg. If no message is
// desired, pass an empty string.
static void timeStamp(String msg, PrintWriter pw) {
  Calendar cal = Calendar.getInstance();
  pw.printf("%s %tc\n", msg, cal);
}

public static void main(String args[]) {

  // Create a PrintWriter that is linked to a file.
  PrintWriter pw;
  try {
    pw = new PrintWriter(new FileWriter("logfile.txt", true));
  } catch(IOException exc) {
    System.out.println("Cannot Open logfile.txt");
    return;
  }

  timeStamp("File opened", pw);

  try {
    Thread.sleep(1000); // sleep for 1 second
  } catch(InterruptedException exc) {
    pw.printf("Sleep Interrupted");
  }

  timeStamp("File closed", pw);

  pw.close();

  // When using a PrintWriter, check for errors by
  // calling checkError().
  if(pw.checkError())
    System.out.println("I/O error occurred.");
  }
}
```

After you run this program, **logfile.txt** will contain the time and date at which the file was opened and closed. Here is a sample:

```
File opened Mon Feb 05 15:05:24 CST 2007
File closed Mon Feb 05 15:05:25 CST 2007
```

Options and Alternatives

PrintStream defines the **format( )** method, which is an alternative to **printf( )**. It has these general forms:

PrintStream format(String *fmtStr*, Object ... *args*)
PrintStream format(Locale *loc*, String *fmtStr*, Object ... *args*)

It works exactly like **printf( )**.

PrintWriter also defines the **format( )** method, as shown here:

PrintWriter format(String *fmtStr*, Object ... *args*)
PrintWriter format(Locale *loc*, String *fmtStr*, Object ... *args*)

It too works exactly like **printf( )**.

Format Time and Date with DateFormat

Key Ingredients	
Classes	**Methods**
java.text.DateFormat	static final DateFormat getDateInstance(int *fmt*)
	static final DateFormat getTimeInstance(int *fmt*)
	final String format(Date *d*)
java.util.Date	

The **DateFormat** class offers an alternative to the capabilities provided by **Formatter** when formatting the time and date. **DateFormat** is locale-sensitive, which means that you can format date and time information for various languages and countries. **DateFormat** is packaged in **java.text**. It is an abstract class. However, it provides several factory methods that return **DateFormat** objects. **DateFormat** extends **Format** (which is an abstract class that defines the basic formatting methods). It is a superclass of **SimpleDateFormat**.

NOTE *DateFormat also gives you the ability to parse strings containing date and time information into Date objects. Thus, it has capabilities beyond just formatting.*

Step-by-Step

There are various ways to format the date by using **DateFormat**. This recipe uses the following steps:

1. Obtain a **DateFormat** instance by calling the static method **getDateInstance( )**, specifying the desired date format.
2. Obtain a **Date** instance that contains the date to be formatted.
3. Produce a string containing a formatted date value by calling the **format( )** method, specifying the **Date** object.

There are also various ways to format the time by using **DateFormat**. This recipe uses the following steps:

1. Obtain a **DateFormat** instance by calling the static method **getTimeInstance( )**, specifying the desired time format.

2. Obtain a **Date** instance that contains the time to be formatted.

3. Produce a string containing a formatted time value by calling the **format( )** method, specifying the **Date** object.

Discussion

To obtain a **DateFormat** object suitable for formatting the date, call the static method **getDateInstance( )**. It is available in several forms. The one used by this recipe is

> static final DateFormat getDateInstance(int *fmt*)

To obtain a **DateFormat** object suitable for formatting the time, use **getTimeInstance( )**. It is also available in several versions. The one used by the recipe is

> static final DateFormat getTimeInstance(int *fmt*)

For both methods, the *fmt* argument must be one of the following values: **DEFAULT**, **SHORT**, **MEDIUM**, **LONG**, or **FULL**. These are **int** constants defined by **DateFormat**. They cause different details about the date or time to be presented when formatted. The date and time formats are sensitive to language and country conventions. The versions of **getDateInstance( )** and **getTimeInstance( )** just shown use the current (i.e., default) locale. Other versions enable you to explicitly specify the locale.

Next, obtain a **java.util.Date** object that contains the date and/or time to be formatted. One way is to create a **Date** object by using this constructor:

> Date( )

This creates a **Date** object that contains the current time and date of the system.

Once you have obtained both **DateFormat** and **Date** instances, you can format a date or time by calling **format( )**. There are various forms of this method. The one we will use is shown here:

> final String format(Date *d*)

The argument is a **Date** object that is to be displayed. The method returns a string containing the formatted information.

Example

The following example shows how to format date and time information. It begins by creating a **Date** object. This captures the current date and time information. Then it outputs the short and long forms of the date and time for the default locale (which is the United States in the sample output).

```
// Display short and long date and time formats.

import java.text.*;
import java.util.*;
```

```
class DateFormatDemo {
  public static void main(String args[]) {
    Date date = new Date();
    DateFormat df;

    df = DateFormat.getDateInstance(DateFormat.SHORT);
    System.out.println("Short form: " + df.format(date));

    df = DateFormat.getDateInstance(DateFormat.LONG);
    System.out.println("Long form: " + df.format(date));

    System.out.println();

    df = DateFormat.getTimeInstance(DateFormat.SHORT);
    System.out.println("Short form: " + df.format(date));

    df = DateFormat.getTimeInstance(DateFormat.LONG);
    System.out.println("Long form: " + df.format(date));
  }
}
```

Sample output is shown here.

```
Short form: 2/1/07
Long form: February 1, 2007

Short form: 4:45 PM
Long form: 4:45:13 PM CST
```

Options and Alternatives

There are additional forms of **getDateInstance( )** and **getTimeInstance( )**. You can use the default format and locale by calling these versions:

>   static final DateFormat getDateInstance( )
>   static final DateFormat getTimeInstance( )

You can specify the format and the locale by calling these versions:

>   static final DateFormat getTimeInstance(int *fmt*, Locale *locale*)
>   static final DateFormat getDateInstance(int *fmt*, Locale *locale*)

The *fmt* parameter is as described earlier. The *locale* parameter is used to specify a locale that will govern the conversion. In the example program, you can explicitly specify that the date be formatted for the United States by substituting this call to **getDateInstance( )**:

```
df = DateFormat.getDateInstance(DateFormat.SHORT, Locale.US);
```

To format the date for Japan, you can use

```
df = DateFormat.getDateInstance(DateFormat.SHORT, Locale.JAPAN);
```

For a discussion of creating **Locale** objects see *Specify a Locale with **Formatter***.

If you will be formatting both the time and date, you can use **getDateTimeInstance( )** to obtain a **DateFormat** object that can be used for both. It has these three versions:

static final DateFormat getDateTimeInstance( )
static final DateFormat getDateTimeInstance(int *dateFmt*, int *timeFmt*)
static final DateFormat getDateTimeInstance(int *dateFmt*, int *timeFmt*, Locale *locale*)

Here, *dateFmt* specifies the date format and *timeFmt* specifies the time format. The locale is specified by *locale*. If no arguments are used, then the system defaults are applied. For example, inserting the following sequence into the example program causes the current date and time to be displayed in the default formats:

```
df = DateFormat.getDateTimeInstance();
System.out.println("Date and Time default form: " + df.format(date));
```

Here is sample output:

```
Date and Time default form: Feb 1, 2007 2:48:39 PM
```

Another way to format date and time is to use the **java.text.SimpleDateFormat** class. This is a concrete subclass of **DateFormat**. One advantage to this class is that it lets you create a pattern that describes which pieces of the date or time you want to display. This enables you to easily create custom time and date formats. (See *Format Time and Date with Patterns Using SimpleDateFormat*.)

Of course, you can also format the time and date by using **Formatter**, or by calling the **printf( )** method. (See *Format Time and Date Using Formatter* and *Use printf( ) to Format Data*.)

Format Time and Date with Patterns Using SimpleDateFormat

Key Ingredients	
Classes	**Methods**
java.text.SimpleDateFormat	final String format(Date *d*)
java.util.Date	

java.text.SimpleDateFormat is a concrete subclass of **DateFormat**. It allows you to define your own formatting patterns that are used to display date and time information. As such, it offers an interesting alternative to both **DateFormat** and **Formatter**.

Step-by-Step

To format the date and time using **SimpleDateFormat** involves the following steps:

1. Create a pattern that describes the desired date and/or time format.
2. Create a **SimpleDateFormat** instance, specifying the pattern.
3. Obtain a **Date** instance that contains the date to be formatted.
4. Produce a string containing a formatted date value by calling the **format( )** method, specifying the **Date** object.

Discussion

SimpleDateFormat defines several constructors. The one we will use is shown here:

SimpleDateFormat(String *fmtStr*)

The argument *fmtStr* describes a pattern that depicts how date and time information is displayed. A pattern consists of a set of symbols that determine the information that is displayed. Table 4-4 shows these symbols and gives a description of each.

Symbol	Description
a	AM or PM
d	Day of month (1–31)
h	Hour in AM/PM (1–12)
k	Hour in day (1–24)
m	Minute in hour (0–59)
s	Second in minute (0–59)
w	Week of year (1–52)
y	Year
z	Time zone
D	Day of year (1–366)
E	Day of week (for example, Thursday)
F	Day of week in month
G	Era (that is, AD or BC)
H	Hour in day (0–23)
K	Hour in AM/PM (0–11)
M	Month
S	Millisecond in second
W	Week of month (1–5)
Z	Time zone in RFC822 format

TABLE 4-4 Formatting Symbols for **SimpleDateFormat**

In most cases, the number of times a symbol is repeated determines how that data is presented. Text information is displayed in an abbreviated form if the pattern letter is repeated less than four times. Otherwise, the unabbreviated form is used. For example, a zzzz pattern can display Pacific Daylight Time, and a zzz pattern can display PDT.

For numbers, the number of times a pattern letter is repeated determines how many digits are presented. For example, hh:mm:ss can present 01:51:15, but h:m:s displays the same time value as 1:51:15.

M or MM causes the month to be displayed as one or two digits. However, three or more repetitions of M cause the month to be displayed as a text string.

Here is an example pattern:

```
"dd MMM yyyy hh:mm:ss"
```

This pattern incorporates the day of the month, the name of the month, the year, and the time (using a 12-hour clock). Here is an example of the output it will produce:

08 Feb 2007 10:12:33

Notice how two digits are used for the day of the month and four are used for the year. Also notice the short form of the name of the month.

Once you have constructed a **SimpleDateFormat** with the desired pattern, obtain a **Date** instance that contains the desired date and then use **format( )** to create the formatted output. (See *Format Time and Date with **DateFormat*** for details on creating a **Date** and using **format( )**.)

Example

The following program shows several time and date patterns.

```java
// Demonstrate SimpleDateFormat.
import java.text.*;
import java.util.*;

public class SDFDemo {

  public static void main(String args[]) {
    Date date = new Date();
    SimpleDateFormat simpDate;

    // Time in 12-hour format.
    simpDate = new SimpleDateFormat("hh:mm:ss a");
    System.out.println(simpDate.format(date));

    // Time in 24-hour format.
    simpDate = new SimpleDateFormat("kk:mm:ss");
    System.out.println(simpDate.format(date));

    // Date and time with month.
    simpDate = new SimpleDateFormat("dd MMM yyyy hh:mm:ss a");
    System.out.println(simpDate.format(date));
```

```
      // Date and time with day and month fully spelled-out.
      simpDate = new SimpleDateFormat("EEEE MMMMM dd yyyy kk:mm:ss");
      System.out.println(simpDate.format(date));
   }
}
```

The output is shown here:

```
01:10:53 PM
13:10:53
07 Feb 2007 01:10:53 PM
Wednesday February 07 2007 13:10:53
```

Options and Alternatives

Although **SimpleDateFormat**'s ability to use patterns is an excellent feature, often
Formatter is a better choice because it enables a formatted date or time to be easily
integrated into a larger formatted string.

You can localize the time and date format by using this **SimpleDateFormat** constructor:

SimpleDateFormat(String *fmtStr*, Locale *loc*)

Here, *loc* specifies the desired locale. (See *Specify a Locale with* **Formatter** for details on
Locale.)

Format Numeric Values with NumberFormat

Key Ingredients	
Classes	**Methods**
java.text.NumberFormat	static final NumberFormat getInstance( )
	void setMaximumFractionDigits(int *numDigits*)
	void setMinimumFractionDigits(int *numDigits*)
	void setGroupingUsed(boolean *useGrouping*)
	final String format(double *val*)

As mentioned earlier, some of the questions most commonly asked by beginners relate to
the formatting of numeric values. The reason is easy to understand: the default numeric
format is quite plain. There are no group separators, and you have no control over the
number of decimal places displayed or the way that negative values are represented.

Also, in many cases you will want to represent currency values in a currency format, which is, of course, sensitive to the current locale.

Fortunately, Java provides a number of different ways to format numeric values, including the **Formatter** class described earlier. However, in some situations, especially those involving currency, **java.text.NumberFormat** offers a helpful alternative. This recipe shows the basic procedure required to use it.

NumberFormat is an abstract class. However, it provides several factory methods that return **NumberFormat** objects. **NumberFormat** extends **Format** (which is an abstract class that defines the basic formatting methods). It is a superclass of both **ChoiceFormat** and **DecimalFormat**.

NOTE *NumberFormat also gives you the ability to parse numeric strings into numeric values. Thus, it has capabilities beyond just formatting.*

Step-by-Step

To format a numeric value by using **NumberFormat** involves these steps:

1. Obtain a **NumberFormat** instance by calling **getInstance( )**.
2. Adjust the format by calling various methods defined by **NumberFormat**.
3. Produce a string containing the formatted value by calling the **format( )** method defined by **NumberFormat**.

Discussion

To obtain a **NumberFormat** object, call the static method **getInstance( )**. There are two forms defined by **NumberFormat**. The simplest one (and the one we will use) is shown here:

    static final NumberFormat getInstance( )

It returns a **NumberFormat** instance for the current locale.

NumberFormat defines several methods that let you determine how a numeric value is formatted. The ones we will use are shown here:

    void setMaximumFractionDigits(int numDigits)
    void setMinimumFractionDigits(int numDigits)
    void setGroupingUsed(boolean useGrouping)

To set the maximum number of digits displayed to the right of the decimal point, call **setMaximumFractionDigits( )**, passing the number of digits to *numDigits*. To set the minimum number of digits displayed to the right of the decimal point, call **setMinimumFractionDigits( )**, passing the number of digits to *numDigits*. For example, to ensure that two decimal places are always displayed, you would use this sequence of calls (where **nf** is a reference to a **NumberFormat** object):

    nf.setMinimumFractionDigits(2);
    nf.setMaximumFractionDigits(2);

When the number of fractional digits is less than those contained in the value, the result is rounded.

By default, the group separator (which is a comma in English) is inserted every three digits to the left of the decimal point. You can remove the group separator by calling **setGroupingUsed( )**, shown here, with a false argument:

   void setGroupingUsed(boolean *useGroups*)

Once you have configured the **NumberFormat** instance, you can format a value by calling **format( )**. There are various forms of this method. The one we will use is shown here:

   final String format(double *val*)

It returns a human-readable version of the value passed to *val* in the format that you have specified.

Example

The following example demonstrates formatting numeric values via the **NumberFormat** class.

```
// Use java.text.NumberFormat to format some numeric values.

import java.text.NumberFormat;

class NumberFormatDemo {
  public static void main(String args[]) {
    NumberFormat nf = NumberFormat.getInstance();

    System.out.println("Default format: " +
                       nf.format(1234567.678));

    // Set format to two decimal places.
    nf.setMinimumFractionDigits(2);
    nf.setMaximumFractionDigits(2);


    System.out.println("Format with two decimal places: " +
                       nf.format(1234567.678));

    nf.setGroupingUsed(false);

    System.out.println("Format without groupings: "   +
                       nf.format(1234567.678));

    // Notice that two decimal places are
    // provided, even though not all digits are
    // present in these cases.
    System.out.println("Notice two decimal places: " +
                       nf.format(10.0) + ", " +
                       nf.format(-1.8));
  }
}
```

The output from this program is shown here:

```
Default format: 1,234,567.678
Format with two decimal places: 1,234,567.68
Format without groupings: 1234567.68
Notice two decimal places: 10.00, -1.80
```

Options and Alternatives

To gain more detailed control over formatting, including the ability to specify a format pattern, try the **DecimalFormat** class, which is a subclass of **NumberFormat**. (See *Format Numeric Values with Patterns Using DecimalFormat*.)

The **format( )** method used by the recipe formats floating-point values. You can format integer values by using this version of **format( )**:

final String format(long *val*)

Here, *val* is the value to be formatted. Other versions of **format( )** are provided that let you specify a **StringBuffer** to write the output to and a field position.

You can format relative to a specific locale by using this version of **getInstance( )**:

static NumberFormat getInstance(Locale *loc*)

The locale is passed via *loc*. (**Locale** is described in *Specify a Locale with Formatter*.)

You can format values in their standard currency format by using **getCurrencyInstance( )**. (See *Format Currency Values Using NumberFormat*.)

You can format values as percentages by using **getPercentInstance( )**.

Format Currency Values Using NumberFormat

Key Ingredients	
Classes	**Methods**
java.text.NumberFormat	static final NumberFormat getCurrencyInstance( )
	final String format(double *val*)

One of the especially useful features of **NumberFormat** is its ability to format currency values. To format currency, simply obtain a **NumberFormat** object by calling **getCurrencyInstance( )** rather than **getInstance( )**. Subsequent calls to **format( )** will result in the value being formatted using the currency conventions of the current (or specified) locale.

Step-by-Step

To format a currency value by using **NumberFormat** involves these steps:

1. Obtain a **NumberFormat** instance by calling **getCurrencyInstance( )**.
2. Produce a string containing the formatted value by calling the **format( )** method.

Discussion

To format a value as currency, use **getCurrencyInstance( )** to obtain a **NumberFormat** object. It has two forms. The one used here is

    static final NumberFormat getCurrencyInstance( )

It returns an object that represents the currency of the current locale. When formatting currencies, the fractional digits, grouping, and currency symbol are automatically supplied. (It really is that easy!)

Once you have configured the **NumberFormat** instance, you can format a value by calling **format( )**, which is described by the preceding recipe.

Example

The following example shows how to format values as currency by using the **NumberFormat** class.

```
// Use java.text.NumberFormat to format a currency value.

import java.text.NumberFormat;
import java.util.*;

class CurrencyFormatDemo {

  public static void main(String args[]) {
    NumberFormat nf = NumberFormat.getCurrencyInstance();

    System.out.println("1989.99 and -210.5 in currency format: " +
                 nf.format(1989.99) + " " +
                 nf.format(-210.5));
  }
}
```

The output from this program is shown here.

```
1989.99 and -210.5 in currency format: $1,989.99 ($210.50)
```

Options and Alternatives

You can format relative to a specific locale by using this version of **getCurrencyInstance( )**:

    static NumberFormat getCurrencyInstance(Locale *loc*)

The locale is passed via *loc*. (**Locale** is described in *Specify a Locale When Formatting*.)

Format Numeric Values with Patterns Using DecimalFormat

Key Ingredients	
Classes	**Methods**
java.text.DecimalFormat	final String format(double *val*)

java.text.DecimalFormat is a concrete subclass of **NumberFormat**. It allows you to define your own formatting patterns that are used to display numeric information, including integer and floating-point values. As such, it offers an interesting alternative to both **NumberFormat** and **Formatter**.

Step-by-Step

To format a numeric value using **DecimalFormat** involves the following steps:

1. Create a pattern that describes the desired numeric format.
2. Create a **DecimalFormat** instance, specifying the pattern.
3. Produce a string containing a formatted value by calling the **format( )** method, specifying the value to be formatted.

Discussion

DecimalFormat defines three constructors. The one we will use is shown here:

   DecimalFormat(String *fmtStr*)

The argument *fmtStr* describes a pattern that depicts how a numeric value is displayed. A pattern consists of symbols that determine how the value is displayed. Table 4-5 shows the symbols and gives a description of each.

Symbol	Description
.	Decimal point
,	Group separator
#	Digit, trailing zeros are not shown
0	Digit, trailing zeros are shown
–	Minus
%	Show the value as a percentage. (In other words, multiply the value by 100.)
E	The E in scientific notation
'	Quote a symbol so as to use it as a normal character
\u00a4	Currency symbol appropriate for locale
/u2030	Show the value in terms of milles. (In other words, multiply the value by 1000.)

TABLE 4-5 A Sampling of Formatting Symbols for **DecimalFormat**

All **DecimalFormat** patterns consist of two subpatterns: one for positive values and one for negative values. However, the negative subpattern need not be explicitly specified. If it is not present, then the negative pattern consists of the positive pattern prefixed with a minus sign. The two subpatterns are separated by a semicolon (;). Once a pattern has been specified, all numeric output will be formatted to match the pattern. Here is an example:

```
"#,###.00;(#,###.00)"
```

This creates a pattern that uses group separators every three digits and shows trailing zeros. It also shows negative values inside parentheses.

Once you have constructed a **DecimalFormat** with the desired pattern, use **format( )** (inherited from **NumberFormat**) to create the formatted output. (See *Format Numeric Values with NumberFormat* for details.)

Example

The following example demonstrates **DecimalFormat**.

```java
// Demonstrate DecimalFormat.
import java.text.*;

public class DFDemo {

  public static void main(String args[]) {
    DecimalFormat df;

    // Use group separators and show trailing zeros.
    // Negative values are shown inside parentheses.
    df = new DecimalFormat("#,###.00;(#,###.00)");
    System.out.println(df.format(7123.00));
    System.out.println(df.format(-7123.00));

    // Don't show trailing zeros.
    df = new DecimalFormat("#,###.##;(#,###.##)");
    System.out.println(df.format(7123.00));
    System.out.println(df.format(-7123.00));

    // Display a percentage.
    df = new DecimalFormat("#%");
    System.out.println(df.format(0.19));
    System.out.println(df.format(-0.19));

    // Display a currency value.
    df = new DecimalFormat("\u00a4#,##0.00");
    System.out.println(df.format(4232.19));
    System.out.println(df.format(-4232.19));
  }
}
```

The output is shown here:

```
7,123.00
(7,123.00)
7,123
(7,123)
19%
-19%
$4,232.19
-$4,232.19
```

Options and Alternatives

Although **DecimalFormat**'s ability to use patterns can make some types of formatting easy, often **Formatter** is a better choice because it enables a formatted value to be easily integrated into a larger formatted string.

NumberFormat, which is the superclass of **DecimalFormat**, offers several standard formats that work well for many applications and can be automatically configured for specific locales. In many cases, these will be more convenient than constructing patterns manually. (See *Format Numeric Values with* **NumberFormat**.)

5
CHAPTER

Working with Collections

The Collections Framework is arguably the most powerful subsystem in the Java API because it supplies ready-to-use versions of programming's most widely used data structures. For example, it provides support for stacks, queues, dynamic arrays, and linked lists. It also defines trees, hash tables, and maps. These "data engines" make it easy to work with groups (i.e., collections) of data. It is not necessary, for example, to write your own linked-list routines. You can simply use the **LinkedList** class provided by the Collections Framework.

The Collections Framework has had a profound effect on the way that Java programs are written. Because of the ease with which one of the collection classes can be employed, there is seldom the need to create your own custom solution. By using a standard collection, you gain three major advantages:

1. Development time is reduced because the collections are thoroughly tested and ready to use. You don't need to spend time developing your own custom implementations.

2. The standard collections are efficiently implemented. As a general rule, there is little (if any) benefit in creating a custom implementation.

3. Your code is easier to maintain. Because the standard collections are part of the Java API, most programmers are familiar with them, and with the way that they operate. Thus, anyone working on your code will understand a collection-based approach.

Because of these advantages, collections have become an integral part of many Java programs.

Collections are a large topic. No single chapter can demonstrate all of their features or explore all of their nuances. As a result, the focus of this chapter is on recipes that demonstrate several key techniques, such as using a comparator, iterating a collection, creating a synchronized collection, and so on. The chapter begins with an overview of the classes and interfaces that comprise the core of the Collections Framework.

Here are the recipes in this chapter:

- Basic Collection Techniques
- Work with Lists
- Work with Sets

- Use **Comparable** to Store Objects in a Sorted Collection
- Use a **Comparator** with a Collection
- Iterate a Collection
- Create a Queue or a Stack Using **Deque**
- Reverse, Rotate, and Shuffle a **List**
- Sort and Search a **List**
- Create a Checked Collection
- Create a Synchronized Collection
- Create an Immutable Collection
- Basic **Map** Techniques
- Convert a **Properties** List into a **HashMap**

NOTE *Although this chapter presents an overview of the Collections Framework that is sufficient for the recipes in this chapter, it does not discuss the Collections Framework in detail. Additional coverage of the Collections Framework can be found in my book* Java: The Complete Reference.

Collections Overview

Collections have not always been a part of Java. Originally, Java relied on classes such as **Dictionary**, **HashTable**, **Vector**, **Stack**, and **Properties** to provide the basic data structures. Although these classes were quite useful, they were not part of a unified whole. To remedy this situation, Java 1.2 added the Collections Framework, which standardized the way in which groups of objects are handled by your programs. Each subsequent Java release has added to and improved this important API.

The core of the Collections Framework is packaged in **java.util**. It contains the interfaces that define collections and provides several concrete implementations of these interfaces. These are the collections that programmers normally think of when they use the term "Collections Framework," and they are the focus of this chapter.

In addition to the collections defined in **java.util**, several other collections are contained in **java.util.concurrent**. These collections are relatively new, being added by Java 5. They support concurrent programming, but otherwise operate like the other collections. Because concurrent programming is a topic unto itself, the concurrent collections are not included in this chapter. (See Chapter 7 for recipes that use **java.util.concurrent**.)

The Collections Framework is defined by three main features:

- A set of standard interfaces that define the functionality of a collection
- Concrete implementations of the interfaces
- Algorithms that operate on collections

The collection interfaces determine the characteristics of a collection. At the top of the interface hierarchy is **Collection**, which defines the features common to all collections. Subinterfaces add the attributes related to specific types of collections. For example, the **Set** interface specifies the functionality of a set, which is a collection of unique (i.e., non-duplicate) elements. Several classes, such as **ArrayList**, **HashSet**, and **LinkedList**, provide concrete implementations of the collection interfaces. These concrete implementations provide "off-the-shelf" solutions to most data storage and retrieval tasks. *Algorithms* are static methods defined within the **Collections** class that operate on collections. For example, there are algorithms that search, sort, or reverse a collection. In essence, algorithms provide a standard means of manipulating collections.

When working with a collection, you will often want to cycle through its elements. One way to do this is with an *iterator,* which is defined by the **Iterator** interface. An iterator offers a general-purpose, standardized way of accessing the elements within a collection, one at a time. In other words, an iterator provides a means of enumerating the contents of a collection. Because each collection implements **Iterator**, an iterator can be used to cycle through the elements of any collection class.

Another feature defined by the Collections Framework is the *map.* A map stores key/value pairs. Although maps *are* part of the Collections Framework, they *are not* "collections" in the strict use of the term because they do not implement the **Collection** interface. You can, however, obtain a *collection-view* of a map. Such a view contains the elements from the map stored in a collection. Thus, you can process the contents of a map as a collection, if you choose.

Three Recent Changes

As you may know, the Java language underwent a substantial change when several new features were added by Java 5. Three of these features had a profound effect on the Collections Framework: generics, autoboxing, and the for-each style **for** loop. Although these features are now a well-established part of Java programming, not all programmers are aware of how much they have impacted collections. Because the recipes in this chapter make use of these features, a brief discussion is warranted.

With the release of Java 5, the entire Java API, including the Collections Framework, was reengineered for generics. As a result, today all collections are generic, and many of the methods that operate on collections take generic type parameters. Generics improve collections by adding type safety. Prior to generics, all collections stored **Object** references, which meant that any collection could store any type of object. Thus, it was possible to accidentally store incompatible types in a collection. Doing so could result in runtime type mismatch errors. With generics, the type of data being stored is explicitly specified, and runtime type mismatches can be avoided.

Autoboxing/unboxing facilitates the storing of primitive types in collections. A collection can store only references, not primitive types. In the past, if you wanted to store a primitive type in a collection, you had to manually box it into its type wrapper. For example, to store an **int** value, you needed to create an **Integer** object that contained that value. When the value was retrieved, it needed to be manually unboxed (by using an explicit cast) into its proper primitive type. Because of autoboxing/unboxing, Java can now automatically perform the proper boxing and unboxing needed when storing or retrieving primitive types. There is no need to manually perform these operations. This makes it much easier to store primitive types in a collection.

All collection classes now implement the **Iterable** interface. This enables a collection to be cycled through by use of the for-each style **for** loop. In the past, cycling through a collection required the use of an iterator. Although iterators are still needed for some uses, in many cases, iterator-based loops can be replaced by **for** loops.

REMEMBER *Because the code examples in this chapter make extensive use of these newer features, you must use JDK 5 or later to compile and run them.*

The Collection Interfaces

The Collections Framework is defined by a set of interfaces, which are shown in Table 5-1. At the top of the interface hierarchy is **Collection**. It must be implemented by all collections. From **Collection** are derived several subinterfaces, such as **List** and **Set**, which define specific types of collections, such as lists and sets.

In addition to the collection interfaces, collections also use the **Comparator**, **RandomAccess**, **Iterator**, and **ListIterator** interfaces. **Comparator** defines how two objects are compared. **Iterator** and **ListIterator** enumerate the objects within a collection. By implementing **RandomAccess**, a list indicates that it supports efficient, random access to its elements.

The Collections Framework supports both modifiable and unmodifiable collections. To enable this, the collection interfaces allow methods that modify a collection to be optional. If an attempt is made to use one of these methods on an unmodifiable collection, an **UnsupportedOperationException** is thrown. All the built-in collections are modifiable, but it is possible to obtain an immutable view of a collection. (Obtaining an immutable collection is described in *Create an Immutable Collection*.)

The Collection Interface

The **Collection** interface specifies the functionality common to all collections, and it must be implemented by any class that defines a collection. **Collection** is a generic interface that has this declaration:

```
interface Collection<E>
```

Interface	Description
Collection	Enables you to work with groups of objects. **Collection** is at the top of the collections hierarchy, and all collection classes must implement it.
Deque	Extends **Queue** to handle a double-ended queue.
List	Extends **Collection** to handle sequences (lists of objects).
NavigableSet	Extends **SortedSet** to handle retrieval of elements based on closest-match searches.
Queue	Extends **Collection** to handle special types of lists in which elements are removed only from the head.
Set	Extends **Collection** to handle sets, which must contain unique elements.
SortedSet	Extends **Set** to handle sorted sets.

TABLE 5-1   The **Collection** Interfaces

Here, **E** specifies the type of objects that the collection will hold. **Collection** extends the **Iterable** interface. This means that all collections can be cycled through by use of the for-each style **for** loop. (Only classes that implement **Iterable** can be cycled through by **for**.)

The methods declared by **Collection** are summarized in Table 5-2. Several exceptions are possible. An **UnsupportedOperationException** is thrown if an attempt is made to modify an immutable collection. A **ClassCastException** is generated when one object is incompatible with another, such as when an attempt is made to add an incompatible object to a collection. A **NullPointerException** is thrown if an attempt is made to store a **null** object and **null** elements are not allowed in the collection. An **IllegalArgumentException** is thrown if an invalid argument is used. An **IllegalStateException** is thrown if an attempt is made to add an element to a fixed-length collection that is full.

Method	Description
boolean add(E *obj*)	Adds *obj* to the invoking collection. Returns **true** if *obj* was added to the collection. Returns **false** if *obj* is already a member of the collection and the collection does not allow duplicates.
boolean addAll(Collection<? extends E> *col*)	Adds all the elements of *col* to the invoking collection. Returns **true** if the operation succeeded (i.e., the elements were added). Otherwise, returns **false**.
void clear( )	Removes all elements from the invoking collection.
boolean contains(Object *obj*)	Returns **true** if *obj* is an element of the invoking collection. Otherwise, returns **false**.
boolean containsAll(Collection<?> *col*)	Returns **true** if the invoking collection contains all elements of *col*. Otherwise, returns **false**.
boolean equals(Object *obj*)	Returns **true** if the invoking collection and *obj* are equal. Otherwise, returns **false**. The precise meaning of "equality" may differ from collection to collection. For example, **equals( )** could be implemented so that it compares the values of elements stored in the collection. Alternatively, **equals( )** could compare references to those elements.
int hashCode( )	Returns the hash code for the invoking collection.
boolean isEmpty( )	Returns **true** if the invoking collection is empty. Otherwise, returns **false**.
Iterator<E> iterator( )	Returns an iterator for the invoking collection.
boolean remove(Object *obj*)	Removes an element that matches *obj* from the invoking collection. Returns **true** if the element was removed. Otherwise, returns **false**.
boolean removeAll(Collection<?> *col*)	Removes all elements of *col* from the invoking collection. Returns **true** if the collection changed (i.e., elements were removed). Otherwise, returns **false**.

TABLE 5-2   The Methods Defined by **Collection**

Method	Description
boolean retainAll(Collection<?> *col*)	Removes all elements from the invoking collection except those in *col*. Returns **true** if the collection changed (i.e., elements were removed). Otherwise, returns **false**.
int size( )	Returns the number of elements held in the invoking collection.
Object[ ] toArray( )	Returns an array that contains all the elements stored in the invoking collection. The array elements are copies of the collection elements.
<T> T[ ] toArray(T *array*[ ])	Returns an array that contains the elements of the invoking collection. The array elements are copies of the collection elements. If the size of *array* equals the number of elements, these are returned in *array*. If the size of *array* is less than the number of elements, a new array of the necessary size is allocated and returned. If the size of *array* is greater than the number of elements, the array element following the last collection element is set to **null**. An **ArrayStoreException** is thrown if any collection element has a type that is not a subtype of *array*.

TABLE 5-2   The Methods Defined by **Collection** *(continued)*

The List Interface

The **List** interface extends **Collection** and declares the behavior of a collection that stores a sequence of elements. Elements can be inserted or accessed by their position in the list, using a zero-based index. A list may contain duplicate elements. **List** is a generic interface that has this declaration:

interface List<E>

Here, **E** specifies the type of objects that the list will hold.

In addition to the methods defined by **Collection**, **List** defines some of its own, which are summarized in Table 5-3. Pay special attention to the **get( )** and **set( )** methods. They provide access to the elements in the list through an index. The **get( )** method obtains the object stored at a specific location, and **set( )** assigns a value to the specified element in the list.

List specifies that the **equals( )** method must compare the contents of two lists, returning true only if they are exactly the same. (In other words, they must contain the same elements, in the same sequence.) If not, then **equals( )** returns **false**. Therefore, any collection that implements **List**, implements **equals( )** in this way.

Several of these methods will throw an **UnsupportedOperationException** if an attempt is made to modify an immutable collection, and a **ClassCastException** is generated when one object is incompatible with another, such as when an attempt is made to add an incompatible object to a collection. A **NullPointerException** is thrown if an attempt is made to store a **null** object and **null** elements are not allowed in the list. An **IllegalArgumentException** is thrown if an invalid argument is used.

Method	Description
void add(int *idx*, E *obj*)	Inserts *obj* into the invoking list at the index passed in *idx*. Any preexisting elements at or beyond the point of insertion are shifted up. Thus, no elements are overwritten.
boolean addAll(int *idx*, Collection<? extends E> c)	Inserts all elements of *c* into the invoking list at the index passed in *idx*. Any preexisting elements at or beyond the point of insertion are shifted up. Thus, no elements are overwritten. Returns **true** if the invoking list changes and returns **false** otherwise.
E get(int *idx*)	Returns the object stored at the specified index within the invoking collection.
int indexOf(Object *obj*)	Returns the index of the first instance of *obj* in the invoking list. If *obj* is not an element of the list, −1 is returned.
int lastIndexOf(Object *obj*)	Returns the index of the last instance of *obj* in the invoking list. If *obj* is not an element of the list, −1 is returned.
ListIterator<E> listIterator( )	Returns an iterator to the start of the invoking list.
ListIterator<E> listIterator(int *idx*)	Returns an iterator to the invoking list that begins at the specified index.
E remove(int *idx*)	Removes the element at position *idx* from the invoking list and returns the deleted element. The resulting list is compacted. That is, the indexes of subsequent elements are decremented by one.
E set(int *idx*, E *obj*)	Assigns *obj* to the location specified by *idx* within the invoking list.
List<E> subList(int *start*, int *end*)	Returns a list that includes elements from *start* to *end*–1 in the invoking list. Elements in the returned list are also referenced by the invoking object.

TABLE 5-3 The Methods Defined by **List**

The Set Interface

The **Set** interface defines a set. It extends **Collection** and declares the behavior of a collection that does not allow duplicate elements. Therefore, the **add( )** method returns **false** if an attempt is made to add duplicate elements to a set. It does not define any additional methods of its own. **Set** is a generic interface that has this declaration:

    interface Set<E>

Here, **E** specifies the type of objects that the set will hold.

    Set specifies that the **equals( )** method must compare the contents of two sets, returning **true** only if they contain the same elements. If not, then **equals( )** returns **false**. Therefore, any collection that implements **Set**, implements **equals( )** in this manner.

The SortedSet Interface

The **SortedSet** interface extends **Set** and declares the behavior of a set sorted in ascending order. **SortedSet** is a generic interface that has this declaration:

interface SortedSet<E>

Here, **E** specifies the type of objects that the set will hold.

In addition to those methods defined by **Set**, the **SortedSet** interface declares the methods summarized in Table 5-4. These methods make set processing more convenient. Several methods throw a **NoSuchElementException** when no items are contained in the invoking set. A **ClassCastException** is thrown when an object is incompatible with the elements in a set. A **NullPointerException** is thrown if an attempt is made to use a **null** object and **null** is not allowed in the set. An **IllegalArgumentException** is thrown if an invalid argument is used.

The NavigableSet Interface

A recent addition to the Collections Framework is **NavigableSet**. It was added by Java 6 and extends **SortedSet**. **NavigableSet** declares the behavior of a collection that supports the retrieval of elements based on the closest match to a given value or values. **NavigableSet** is a generic interface that has this declaration:

interface NavigableSet<E>

Here, **E** specifies the type of objects that the set will hold. In addition to the methods that it inherits from **SortedSet**, **NavigableSet** adds those summarized in Table 5-5. A **ClassCastException** is thrown when an object is incompatible with the elements in the set. A **NullPointerException** is thrown if an attempt is made to use a **null** object and **null** is not allowed in the set. An **IllegalArgumentException** is thrown if an invalid argument is used.

Method	Description
Comparator<? super E> comparator( )	Returns the invoking sorted set's comparator. If natural ordering is used for this set, **null** is returned.
E first( )	Returns the first element in the invoking sorted set.
SortedSet<E> headSet(E end)	Returns a **SortedSet** containing those elements less than end that are contained in the invoking sorted set. Elements in the returned sorted set are also referenced by the invoking sorted set.
E last( )	Returns the last element in the invoking sorted set.
SortedSet<E> subSet(E start, E end)	Returns a **SortedSet** that includes those elements between start and end–1. Elements in the returned collection are also referenced by the invoking object.
SortedSet<E> tailSet(E start)	Returns a **SortedSet** that contains those elements greater than or equal to start that are contained in the sorted set. Elements in the returned set are also referenced by the invoking object.

TABLE 5-4 The Methods Defined by **SortedSet**

Method	Description
E ceiling(E *obj*)	Searches the set for the smallest element e such that e >= *obj*. If such an element is found, it is returned. Otherwise, **null** is returned.
Iterator<E> descendingIterator( )	Returns an iterator that moves from the greatest to least. In other words, it returns a reverse iterator.
NavigableSet<E> descendingSet( )	Returns a **NavigableSet** that is the reverse of the invoking set. The resulting set is backed by the invoking set.
E floor(E *obj*)	Searches the set for the largest element e such that e <= *obj*. If such an element is found, it is returned. Otherwise, **null** is returned.
NavigableSet<E> headSet(E *upperBound*, boolean *incl*)	Returns a **NavigableSet** that includes all elements from the invoking set that are less than *upperBound*. If *incl* is **true**, then an element equal to *upperBound* is included. The resulting set is backed by the invoking set.
E higher(E *obj*)	Searches the set for the smallest element e such that e > *obj*. If such an element is found, it is returned. Otherwise, **null** is returned.
E lower(E *obj*)	Searches the set for the largest element e such that e < *obj*. If such an element is found, it is returned. Otherwise, **null** is returned.
E pollFirst( )	Returns the first element, removing the element in the process. Because the set is sorted, this is the element with the least value. **null** is returned if the set is empty.
E pollLast( )	Returns the last element, removing the element in the process. Because the set is sorted, this is the element with the greatest value. **null** is returned if the set is empty.

NavigableSet<E>
   subSet(E *lowerBound*,
       boolean *lowIncl*,
       E *upperBound*,
       boolean *highIncl*)
	Returns a **NavigableSet** that includes all elements from the invoking set that are greater than *lowerBound* and less than *upperBound*. If *lowIncl* is **true**, then an element equal to *lowerBound* is included. If *highIncl* is **true**, then an element equal to *upperBound* is included. The resulting set is backed by the invoking set.

NavigableSet<E> tailSet(E *lowerBound*, boolean *incl*)	Returns a **NavigableSet** that includes all elements from the invoking set that are greater than *lowerBound*. If *incl* is **true**, then an element equal to *lowerBound* is included. The resulting set is backed by the invoking set.

TABLE 5-5 The Methods Defined by **NavigableSet**

The Queue Interface

The **Queue** interface extends **Collection** and declares the behavior of a queue. Queues are often first-in, first-out lists, but there are types of queues in which the ordering is based upon other criteria. **Queue** is a generic interface that has this declaration:

interface Queue<E>

Here, **E** specifies the type of objects that the set will hold.

In addition to the methods that **Queue** inherits from **Collection**, it defines several of its own. They are shown in Table 5-6. Several methods throw a **ClassCastException** when an object is incompatible with the elements in the queue. A **NullPointerException** is thrown if an attempt is made to store a **null** object and **null** elements are not allowed in the queue. An **IllegalArgumentException** is thrown if an invalid argument is used. An **IllegalStateException** is thrown if an attempt is made to add an element to a fixed-length queue that is full. Some methods throw a **NoSuchElementException** if an attempt is made to remove an element from an empty queue.

Queue has several interesting features. First, elements can be removed only from the head of the queue. Second, there are two methods that obtain and remove elements: **poll( )** and **remove( )**. The difference between them is that **poll( )** returns **null** if the queue is empty, but **remove( )** throws a **NoSuchElementException** exception. Third, there are two methods, **element( )** and **peek( )**, that obtain but don't remove the element at the head of the queue. They differ only in that **element( )** throws a **NoSuchElementException** exception if the queue is empty, but **peek( )** returns **null**. Finally, notice that **offer( )** only attempts to add an element to a queue. Because fixed-length queues are permitted and such a queue might be full, **offer( )** can fail. If it does fail, **offer( )** returns **false**. This differs from **add( )** (inherited from **Collection**), which will throw an **IllegalStateException** if an attempt is made to add an element to a full, fixed-length queue. Therefore, **Queue** gives you two ways to handle queue-full and queue-empty states when performing queue operations: by handling exceptions or by monitoring return values. You should choose the approach most appropriate for your application.

Method	Description
E element( )	Returns the element at the head of the queue. The element is not removed. It throws **NoSuchElementException** if the queue is empty.
boolean offer(E *obj*)	Attempts to add *obj* to the queue. Returns **true** if *obj* was added and **false** otherwise.
E peek( )	Returns the element at the head of the queue. It returns **null** if the queue is empty. The element is not removed.
E poll( )	Returns the element at the head of the queue, removing the element in the process. It returns **null** if the queue is empty.
E remove( )	Removes the element at the head of the queue, returning the element in the process. It throws **NoSuchElementException** if the queue is empty.

TABLE 5-6   The Methods Defined by **Queue**

The Deque Interface

Another recent addition to the Collections Framework is **Deque**. It was added by Java 6 and it extends **Queue**. **Deque** declares the behavior of a double-ended queue. Double-ended queues can function as standard, first-in, first-out queues or as last-in, first-out stacks. **Deque** is a generic interface that has this declaration:

    interface Deque<E>

Here, **E** specifies the type of objects that the deque will hold.

In addition to the methods that it inherits from **Queue**, **Deque** adds those methods summarized in Table 5-7. Several methods throw a **ClassCastException** when an object is incompatible with the elements in the deque. A **NullPointerException** is thrown if an attempt is made to store a **null** object and **null** elements are not allowed in the deque. An **IllegalArgumentException** is thrown if an invalid argument is used. An **IllegalStateException** is thrown if an attempt is made to add an element to a fixed-length deque that is full. A **NoSuchElementException** is thrown if an attempt is made to remove an element from an empty deque.

Perhaps the most important features of **Deque** are **push( )** and **pop( )**. These methods are commonly used to enable a **Deque** to function as a stack. To put an element on the top of the stack, call **push( )**. To remove the top element, call **pop( )**. Also, notice the

Method	Description
void addFirst(E *obj*)	Adds *obj* to the head of the deque. Throws an **IllegalStateException** if a capacity-restricted deque is out of space.
void addLast(E *obj*)	Adds *obj* to the tail of the deque. Throws an **IllegalStateException** if a capacity-restricted deque is out of space.
Iterator<E> descendingIterator( )	Returns an iterator that moves from the tail to the head of the deque. In other words, it returns a reverse iterator.
E getFirst( )	Returns the first element in the deque. The object is not removed from the deque. It throws **NoSuchElementException** if the deque is empty.
E getLast( )	Returns the last element in the deque. The object is not removed from the deque. It throws **NoSuchElementException** if the deque is empty.
boolean offerFirst(E *obj*)	Attempts to add *obj* to the head of the deque. Returns **true** if *obj* was added and **false** otherwise. Therefore, this method returns **false** when an attempt is made to add *obj* to full, capacity-restricted deque.
boolean offerLast(E *obj*)	Attempts to add *obj* to the tail of the deque. Returns **true** if *obj* was added and **false** otherwise.

TABLE 5-7 The Methods Defined by **Deque**

Method	Description
E peekFirst( )	Returns the element at the head of the deque. It returns **null** if the deque is empty. The object is not removed.
E peekLast( )	Returns the element at the tail of the deque. It returns **null** if the deque is empty. The object is not removed.
E pollFirst( )	Returns the element at the head of the deque, removing the element in the process. It returns **null** if the deque is empty.
E pollLast( )	Returns the element at the tail of the deque, removing the element in the process. It returns **null** if the deque is empty.
E pop( )	Returns the element at the head of the deque, removing it in the process. It throws **NoSuchElementException** if the deque is empty.
void push(E *obj*)	Adds *obj* to the head of the deque. Throws an **IllegalStateException** if a capacity-restricted deque is out of space.
E removeFirst( )	Returns the element at the head of the deque, removing the element in the process. It throws **NoSuchElementException** if the deque is empty.
boolean removeFirstOccurrence(Object *obj*)	Removes the first occurrence of *obj* from the deque. Returns **true** if successful and **false** if the deque did not contain *obj.*
E removeLast( )	Returns the element at the tail of the deque, removing the element in the process. It throws **NoSuchElementException** if the deque is empty.
boolean removeLastOccurrence(Object *obj*)	Removes the last occurrence of *obj* from the deque. Returns **true** if successful and **false** if the deque did not contain *obj.*

TABLE 5-7   The Methods Defined by **Deque** *(continued)*

descendingIterator( ) method. It returns an iterator that returns elements in reverse order. In other words, it returns an iterator that moves from the end of the collection to the start.

A **Deque** implementation can be *capacity-restricted*, which means that only a limited number of elements can be added to the deque. When this is the case, an attempt to add an element to the deque can fail. **Deque** allows you to handle such a failure in two ways. First, methods such as **push( )**, **addFirst( )**, and **addLast( )** throw an **IllegalStateException** if a capacity-restricted deque is full. Second, other methods, such as **offerFirst( )** and **offerLast( )**, return **false** if the element could not be added. You can select the approach most suited to your application.

A similar situation occurs relative to removing elements from a **Deque**. Methods such as **pop( )** and **removeFirst( )** throw a **NoSuchElementException** if they are called on an empty collection. Methods such as **pollFirst( )** or **pollLast( )** return **null** if the collection is empty. Again, choose the approach most compatible with your application.

The Collection Classes

The collection classes implement the collection interfaces. Some of the classes provide full implementations that can be used as-is. Others are abstract, providing skeletal implementations that are used as starting points for creating concrete collections. The collection classes defined in **java.util** are summarized in the following table. The recipes in this chapter make use of several of these classes. A brief overview of each concrete collection class follows.

Class	Description
AbstractCollection	Implements most of the **Collection** interface. It is a superclass for all of the concrete collection classes.
AbstractList	Extends **AbstractCollection** and implements most of the **List** interface.
AbstractQueue	Extends **AbstractCollection** and implements parts of the **Queue** interface.
AbstractSequentialList	Extends **AbstractList** for use by a collection that uses sequential rather than random access of its elements.
AbstractSet	Extends **AbstractCollection** and implements most of the **Set** interface.
ArrayDeque	Implements a dynamic double-ended queue by extending **AbstractCollection** and implementing the **Deque** interface.
ArrayList	Implements a dynamic array by extending **AbstractList**.
EnumSet	Extends **AbstractSet** for use with **enum** elements.
HashSet	Extends **AbstractSet** for use with a hash table.
LinkedHashSet	Extends **HashSet** to allow insertion-order iterations.
LinkedList	Implements a linked list by extending **AbstractSequentialList**. It also implements the **Deque** interface.
PriorityQueue	Extends **AbstractQueue** to support a priority-based queue.
TreeSet	Implements a set stored in a tree. Extends **AbstractSet** and implements the **SortedSet** interface.

The ArrayList Class

ArrayList supports dynamic arrays that can grow or shrink as needed. In other words, an **ArrayList** can increase or decrease in size at runtime. An **ArrayList** is created with an initial size. When this size is exceeded, the collection is automatically enlarged. When objects are removed, the array can be shrunk.

ArrayList extends **AbstractList** and implements the **List** interface. (It also implements **RandomAccess** to indicate that it supports fast random access to its elements.) It is a generic class that has this declaration:

class ArrayList<E>

Here, **E** specifies the type of objects that the list will hold.

ArrayList defines these constructors:

ArrayList( )
ArrayList(Collection<? extends E> *col*)
ArrayList(int *capacity*)

The first constructor builds an empty array list. The second constructor builds an array list that is initialized with the elements of the collection *col*. The third constructor builds an array list that has the specified initial *capacity*. The capacity is the size of the underlying array that is used to store the elements. The capacity grows automatically as elements are added to an array list. In cases in which you know that a certain minimum number of elements will be stored, you can set the initial capacity in advance. This prevents subsequent reallocations, which are costly in terms of time.

ArrayList offers a useful alternative to Java's normal arrays. In Java, arrays are of a fixed length. After an array has been created, it cannot grow or shrink, which means that you must know in advance how many elements an array will hold. However, sometimes this is not possible. For example, you might want use an array to hold a list of values (such as product ID numbers) received via an Internet connection in which the list is terminated by a special value. Thus, the number of values is not known until the terminator is received. In such a case, how large do you make the array that will receive the values? **ArrayList** offers a solution to this type of problem.

In addition to the methods defined by the interfaces that it implements, **ArrayList** defines two methods of its own: **ensureCapacity( )** and **trimToSize( )**. They are shown here:

void ensureCapacity(int *cap*)
void trimToSize( )

The **ensureCapacity( )** method lets you manually increase the capacity of an **ArrayList**, which is the number of elements that it can hold before the list will need to be enlarged. The new capacity is specified by *cap*. Alternatively, **trimToSize( )** lets you reduce the size of an **ArrayList** so that it precisely fits the number of elements that it holds.

The LinkedList Class

LinkedList provides a linked-list data structure. It extends **AbstractSequentialList** and implements the **List** and **Deque** interfaces. Because it uses a doubly-linked list, a **LinkedList** will automatically grow when an element is added to the list and shrink when an element is removed. Linked lists are especially useful in situations in which items are inserted or removed from the middle of the list. New items are simply linked in. When an item is removed, the links to old items are replaced by links to the items that preceded and followed the deleted item. Rearranging links is often more efficient than physically compacting or expanding an array, for example.

LinkedList is a generic class that has this declaration:

class LinkedList<E>

Here, **E** specifies the type of objects that the list will hold. **LinkedList** has the two constructors shown here:

    LinkedList( )
    LinkedList(Collection<? extends E> *col*)

The first constructor builds an empty linked list. The second constructor builds a linked list that is initialized with the elements of the collection *col*.

The HashSet Class

HashSet creates a collection that uses a hash table for storage. A hash table stores information by using a mechanism called *hashing*. In hashing, the informational content of a key is used to determine a unique value, called its *hash code*. The hash code is then used as the index at which the data associated with the key is stored. The transformation of the key into its hash code is performed automatically—you never see the hash code itself. Also, your code can't directly index the hash table. The advantage of hashing is that it allows the execution time of **add( )**, **contains( )**, **remove( )**, and **size( )** to remain constant even for large sets. Duplicate elements are not allowed in a **HashSet**.

    HashSet extends **AbstractSet** and implements the **Set** interface. It is a generic class that has this declaration:

    class HashSet<E>

Here, **E** specifies the type of objects that the set will hold.
    HashSet defines the following constructors:

    HashSet( )
    HashSet(Collection<? extends E> *col*)
    HashSet(int *capacity*)
    HashSet(int *capacity*, float *fillRatio*)

    The first form constructs a default hash set. The second form initializes the hash set by using the elements of *col*. The third form initializes the capacity of the hash set to *capacity*. The fourth form initializes both the capacity and the fill ratio (also called *load capacity*) of the hash set. The fill ratio must be between 0.0 and 1.0, and it determines how full the hash set can be before it is resized upward. Specifically, when the number of elements is greater than the capacity of the hash set multiplied by its fill ratio, the hash set is expanded. For constructors that do not take a fill ratio, 0.75 is used.
    Here is a key point about **HashSet**: the elements are not in any particular order. For example, they are neither sorted, nor are they stored in insertion order. This is because the process of hashing does not lend itself to the creation of ordered sets. Therefore, the order in which elements are obtained when the collection is enumerated via an iterator or a for-each style **for** loop is unspecified.

The LinkedHashSet Class

LinkedHashSet uses a hash table for storage, but also maintains a double-linked list of the elements in the collection. The list is in the order in which elements are inserted into the collection. This allows insertion-order iteration over the set. That is, when cycling through a **LinkedHashSet** using an iterator or a for-each style **for** loop, the elements will be returned in the order in which they were inserted. However, the benefits of hashing's fast look-ups are still achieved.

LinkedHashSet extends **HashSet** and adds no members of its own. It is a generic class that has this declaration:

    class LinkedHashSet<E>

Here, **E** specifies the type of objects that the set will hold.

LinkedHashSet defines the following constructors:

    LinkedHashSet( )
    LinkedHashSet(Collection<? extends E> col)
    LinkedHashSet(int capacity)
    LinkedHashSet(int capacity, float fillRatio)

They work the same as their corresponding equivalents in **HashSet**.

The TreeSet Class

TreeSet creates a sorted collection that uses a tree for storage. Objects are stored in sorted, ascending order. Because of the tree structure, access and retrieval times are quite fast. This makes **TreeSet** an excellent choice for quick access to large amounts of sorted information. The only restriction is that no duplicate elements are allowed in the tree.

TreeSet extends **AbstractSet** and implements the **NavigableSet** interface. It is a generic class that has this declaration:

    class TreeSet<E>

Here, **E** specifies the type of objects that the set will hold.

TreeSet has the following constructors:

    TreeSet( )
    TreeSet(Collection<? extends E> col)
    TreeSet(Comparator<? super E> comp)
    TreeSet(SortedSet<E> ss)

The first form constructs an empty tree set that will be sorted in ascending order according to the natural order of its elements. The second form builds a tree set that contains the elements of *col*. The third form constructs an empty tree set that will be sorted according to the comparator specified by *comp*. The fourth form builds a tree set that contains the elements of *ss*.

The PriorityQueue Class

PriorityQueue creates a queue that is prioritized. The elements in a **PriorityQueue** are stored in order of their priority. By default, the priority is based on the natural order of the elements. However, you can alter this behavior by specifying a comparator when the **PriorityQueue** is constructed.

PriorityQueue extends **AbstractQueue** and implements the **Queue** interface. It is a generic class that has this declaration:

    class PriorityQueue<E>

Here, **E** specifies the type of objects stored in the queue. **PriorityQueue**s are dynamic, growing as necessary.

PriorityQueue defines the six constructors shown here:

PriorityQueue( )
PriorityQueue(int *capacity*)
PriorityQueue(int *capacity*, Comparator<? super E> *comp*)
PriorityQueue(Collection<? extends E> *col*)
PriorityQueue(PriorityQueue<? extends E> *col*)
PriorityQueue(SortedSet<? extends E> *col*)

The first constructor builds an empty queue. Its starting capacity is 11. The second constructor builds a queue that has the specified initial capacity. The third constructor builds a queue with the specified capacity and comparator. The last three constructors create queues that are initialized with the elements of the collection passed in *col*. In all cases, the capacity grows automatically as elements are added.

If no comparator is specified when a **PriorityQueue** is constructed, then the default comparator for the type of data stored in the queue is used. The default comparator will order the queue in ascending order. Thus, the head of the queue will be the smallest value. However, by providing a custom comparator, you can specify a different ordering scheme. For example, when storing items that include a time stamp, you could prioritize the queue such that the oldest items are first in the queue. See *Use a **Comparator** with a Collection* for an example.

In addition to the methods specified by the interfaces that it implements, **PriorityQueue** defines one additional method: **comparator( )**. It returns a reference to the comparator used by a **PriorityQueue**. It is shown here:

Comparator<? super E> comparator( )

If natural ordering is used for the invoking queue, **null** is returned.

One last point: the order of the elements returned by iterating through a **PriorityQueue** (using either an iterator or a for-each **for** loop) is undefined. To cycle through a **PriorityQueue** in order of priority, you must call **poll( )** or **remove( )**.

The ArrayDeque Class

ArrayDeque was added by Java 6, which makes it a recent addition to the Collections Framework. It creates a dynamic array based on the **Deque** interface. This makes **ArrayDeque** especially useful for implementing stacks and queues whose sizes are not known in advance. In addition to implementing **Deque**, **ArrayDeque** extends **AbstractCollection**.

ArrayDeque is a generic class that has this declaration:

class ArrayDeque<E>

Here, **E** specifies the type of objects stored in the collection.

ArrayDeque defines the following constructors:

ArrayDeque( )
ArrayDeque(int *size*)
ArrayDeque(Collection<? extends E> *col*)

The first constructor builds an empty deque. Its starting capacity is 16. The second constructor builds a deque that has the specified initial capacity. The third constructor creates a deque that is initialized with the elements of the collection passed in *col*. In all cases, the capacity grows as needed to handle the elements added to the collection.

The EnumSet Class

EnumSet is a collection specifically designed for use with values of an **enum** type. It extends **AbstractSet** and implements **Set**. It is a generic class that has this declaration:

    class EnumSet<E extends Enum<E>>

Here, **E** specifies the elements. Notice that **E** must extend **Enum<E>**, which enforces the requirement that the elements must be of the specified **enum** type. **EnumSet** defines no constructors. Instead, it uses factory methods, such as **allOf( )** or **range( )**, to obtain an **EnumSet** instance.

An Overview of Maps

Maps are part of the Collections Framework but are not, themselves, collections because they do not implement the **Collection** interface. Instead of storing groups of objects, maps store key/value pairs. A defining characteristic of a map is its ability to retrieve a value given its key. In other words, given a key, you can find its value. This makes a map an excellent choice in many look-up-based applications. For example, you might use a map to store names and telephone numbers. The names are the keys and the numbers are values. You could then find a number given a person's name.

In a map, both keys and values must be objects. They cannot be primitive types. Furthermore, all keys must be unique. This makes sense because a key is used to find a value. Thus, you can't have the same key map to two different values. However, two different keys can map to the same value. Thus, keys must be unique, but values may be duplicated.

Maps don't implement the **Iterable** interface. This means that you cannot cycle through a map using a for-each style **for** loop. You also can't obtain an iterator to a map. However, you can obtain a collection-view of a map, which does allow the use of either the **for** loop or an iterator.

The Map Interfaces

Maps are defined by the set of interfaces shown here:

Interface	Description
Map	Maps unique keys to values.
Map.Entry	Describes an element (a key/value pair) in a map. This is an inner class of **Map**.
NavigableMap	Extends **SortedMap** to handle the retrieval of entries based on closest-match searches.
SortedMap	Extends **Map** so that the keys are maintained in ascending order.

Each interface is examined next, in turn.

The Map Interface

The **Map** interface links unique keys to values. Each key/value pair constitutes an entry in the map. Therefore, given a key and a value, you can store an entry in a **Map**. After the entry is stored, you can retrieve its value by using its key.

Map is generic and is declared as shown here:

interface Map<K, V>

Here, **K** specifies the type of keys, and **V** specifies the type of values.

The methods declared by **Map** are summarized in Table 5-8. Pay special attention to **get( )** and **put( )**. To store a value in a map, use **put( )**, specifying the key and the value. To obtain a value, call **get( )**, passing the key as an argument. The value is returned. Thus, **get( )** and **put( )** define the fundamental storage and retrieval methods used by all **Map** implementations.

Method	Description
void clear( )	Removes all key/value pairs from the invoking map.
boolean containsKey(Object *k*)	Returns **true** if the invoking map contains *k* as a key. Otherwise, returns **false**.
boolean containsValue(Object *v*)	Returns **true** if the map contains *v* as a value. Otherwise, returns **false**.
Set<Map.Entry<K, V>> entrySet( )	Returns a **Set** that contains the entries in the map. The set contains objects of type **Map.Entry**. Thus, this method provides a set-view of the invoking map.
boolean equals(Object *obj*)	Returns **true** if *obj* is a **Map** and contains the same entries. Otherwise, returns **false**.
V get(Object *k*)	Returns the value associated with the key *k*. Returns **null** if the key is not found.
int hashCode( )	Returns the hash code for the invoking map.
boolean isEmpty( )	Returns **true** if the invoking map is empty. Otherwise, returns **false**.
Set<K> keySet( )	Returns a **Set** that contains the keys in the invoking map. This method provides a set-view of the keys in the invoking map.
V put(K *k*, V *v*)	Puts an entry in the invoking map, overwriting any previous value associated with the key. The key and value are *k* and *v*, respectively. Returns **null** if the key did not already exist. Otherwise, the previous value linked to the key is returned.
void putAll(Map<? extends K, ? extends V> *m*)	Puts all the entries from *m* into this map.
V remove(Object *k*)	Removes the entry whose key equals *k*. It returns the value removed, or **null** if the key is not in the map.
int size( )	Returns the number of key/value pairs in the map.
Collection<V> values( )	Returns a collection containing the values in the map. This method provides a collection-view of the values in the map.

TABLE 5-8   The Methods Defined by **Map**

Several methods throw a **ClassCastException** when an object is incompatible with the elements in a map. A **NullPointerException** is thrown if an attempt is made to use a **null** object and **null** is not allowed in the map. An **UnsupportedOperationException** is thrown when an attempt is made to change an unmodifiable map. An **IllegalArgumentException** is thrown if an invalid argument is used.

The SortedMap Interface

The **SortedMap** interface extends **Map**. The entries in the map are maintained in sorted order based on the keys. Sorted maps allow very efficient manipulations of *submaps* (in other words, subsets of a map). **SortedMap** is generic and is declared as shown here:

> interface SortedMap<K, V>

Here, **K** specifies the type of keys, and **V** specifies the type of values.

In addition to the methods specified by **Map**, **SortedMap** adds several of its own. They are summarized in Table 5-9. Several methods throw a **NoSuchElementException** when no items are in the invoking map. A **ClassCastException** is thrown when an object is incompatible with the elements in a map. A **NullPointerException** is thrown if an attempt is made to use a **null** object when **null** is not allowed in the map. An **IllegalArgumentException** is thrown if an invalid argument is used.

The NavigableMap Interface

The **NavigableMap** interface is a recent addition to the Collections Framework (it was added by Java 6). It extends **SortedMap** and declares the behavior of a map that supports the retrieval of entries based on the closest match to a given key or keys. **NavigableMap** is a generic interface that has this declaration:

> interface NavigableMap<K,V>

Here, **K** specifies the type of the keys, and **V** specifies the type of the values associated with the keys.

Method	Description
Comparator<? super K> comparator( )	Returns the sorted map's comparator. If natural ordering is used for the invoking map, **null** is returned.
K firstKey( )	Returns the first key in the invoking map.
SortedMap<K, V> headMap(K *end*)	Returns a sorted map for those map entries with keys that are less than *end*.
K lastKey( )	Returns the last key in the invoking map.
SortedMap<K, V> subMap(K *start*, K *end*)	Returns a map containing those entries with keys that are greater than or equal to *start* and less than *end*.
SortedMap<K, V> tailMap(K *start*)	Returns a map containing those entries with keys that are greater than or equal to *start*.

TABLE 5-9   The Methods Defined by **SortedMap**

In addition to the methods that it inherits from **SortedMap**, **NavigableMap** adds those summarized in Table 5-10. Several methods throw a **ClassCastException** when an object is incompatible with the keys in the map. A **NullPointerException** is thrown if an attempt is made to use a **null** object and **null** keys are not allowed in the map. An **IllegalArgumentException** is thrown if an invalid argument is used.

Method	Description
Map.Entry<K,V> ceilingEntry(K *obj*)	Searches the map for the smallest key *k* such that *k* >= *obj*. If such a key is found, its entry is returned. Otherwise, **null** is returned.
K ceilingKey(K *obj*)	Searches the map for the smallest key *k* such that *k* >= *obj*. If such a key is found, it is returned. Otherwise, **null** is returned.
NavigableSet<K> descendingKeySet( )	Returns a **NavigableSet** that contains the keys in the invoking map in reverse order. Thus, it returns a reverse set-view of the keys. The resulting set is backed by the map.
NavigableMap<K,V> descendingMap( )	Returns a **NavigableMap** that is the reverse of the invoking map. The resulting map is backed by the invoking map.
Map.Entry<K,V> firstEntry( )	Returns the first entry in the map. This is the entry with the least key.
Map.Entry<K,V> floorEntry(K *obj*)	Searches the map for the largest key *k* such that *k* <= *obj*. If such a key is found, its entry is returned. Otherwise, **null** is returned.
K floorKey(K *obj*)	Searches the map for the largest key *k* such that *k* <= *obj*. If such a key is found, it is returned. Otherwise, **null** is returned.
NavigableMap<K,V> headMap(K *upperBound*, boolean *incl*)	Returns a **NavigableMap** that includes all entries from the invoking map that have keys that are less than *upperBound*. If *incl* is **true**, then an element equal to *upperBound* is included. The resulting map is backed by the invoking map.
Map.Entry<K,V> higherEntry(K *obj*)	Searches the set for the largest key *k* such that *k* > *obj*. If such a key is found, its entry is returned. Otherwise, **null** is returned.
K higherKey(K *obj*)	Searches the set for the largest key *k* such that *k* > *obj*. If such a key is found, it is returned. Otherwise, **null** is returned.

TABLE 5-10   The Methods Defined by **NavigableMap**

Method	Description
Map.Entry<K,V> lastEntry( )	Returns the last entry in the map. This is the entry with the largest key.
Map.Entry<K,V> lowerEntry(K *obj*)	Searches the set for the largest key *k* such that *k* < *obj*. If such a key is found, its entry is returned. Otherwise, **null** is returned.
K lowerKey(K *obj*)	Searches the set for the largest key *k* such that *k* < *obj*. If such a key is found, it is returned. Otherwise, **null** is returned.
NavigableSet<K> navigableKeySet( )	Returns a **NavigableSet** that contains the keys in the invoking map. The resulting set is backed by the invoking map.
Map.Entry<K,V> pollFirstEntry( )	Returns the first entry, removing the entry in the process. Because the map is sorted, this is the entry with the least key value. **null** is returned if the map is empty.
Map.Entry<K,V> pollLastEntry( )	Returns the last entry, removing the entry in the process. Because the map is sorted, this is the entry with the greatest key value. **null** is returned if the map is empty.
NavigableMap<K,V> subMap(K *lowerBound*, boolean *lowIncl*, K *upperBound* boolean *highIncl*)	Returns a **NavigableMap** that includes all entries from the invoking map that have keys that are greater than *lowerBound* and less than *upperBound*. If *lowIncl* is **true**, then an element equal to *lowerBound* is included. If *highIncl* is **true**, then an element equal to *upperBound* is included. The resulting map is backed by the invoking map.
NavigableMap<K,V> tailMap(K *lowerBound*, boolean *incl*)	Returns a **NavigableMap** that includes all entries from the invoking map that have keys that are greater than *lowerBound*. If *incl* is **true**, then an element equal to *lowerBound* is included. The resulting map is backed by the invoking map.

TABLE 5-10   The Methods Defined by **NavigableMap** (*continued*)

The Map.Entry Interface

The **Map.Entry** interface enables you to work with a map entry. The **entrySet( )** method declared by the **Map** interface returns a **Set** containing the map entries. Each of these set elements is a **Map.Entry** object. **Map.Entry** is generic and is declared like this:

```
interface Map.Entry<K, V>
```

Method	Description
boolean equals(Object *obj*)	Returns **true** if *obj* is a **Map.Entry** whose key and value are equal to that of the invoking object.
K getKey( )	Returns the key for this map entry.
V getValue( )	Returns the value for this map entry.
int hashCode( )	Returns the hash code for this map entry.
V setValue(V *v*)	Sets the value for this map entry to *v*. A **ClassCastException** is thrown if *v* is not the correct type for the map. An **IllegalArgumentException** is thrown if there is a problem with *v*. A **NullPointerException** is thrown if *v* is **null** and the map does not permit **null** keys. An **UnsupportedOperationException** is thrown if the map cannot be changed.

TABLE 5-11   The Methods Defined by **Map.Entry**

Here, **K** specifies the type of keys, and **V** specifies the type of values. Table 5-11 summarizes the methods declared by **Map.Entry**.

The Map Classes

Several classes provide implementations of the map interfaces. The ones defined in **java.util** are shown here:

Class	Description
AbstractMap	Implements most of the **Map** interface. It is a superclass for all concrete map implementations.
EnumMap	Extends **AbstractMap** for use with **enum** keys.
HashMap	Extends **AbstractMap** to use a hash table.
TreeMap	Extends **AbstractMap** to use a tree. It also implements **NavigableMap**.
WeakHashMap	Extends **AbstractMap** to use a hash table with weak keys. Weak keys allow an element in a map to be garbage-collected when its key is otherwise unused.
LinkedHashMap	Extends **HashMap** to allow insertion-order iterations.
IdentityHashMap	Extends **AbstractMap** and uses reference equality when comparing entries. This class is not for general use.

   WeakHashMap and **IdentityHashMap** are special-use maps and are not discussed further here. The other map classes are described by the following sections.

The HashMap Class

HashMap uses a hash table to store the map. It extends **AbstractMap** and implements the **Map** interface. **HashMap** is a generic class that has this declaration:

    class HashMap<K, V>

Here, **K** specifies the type of keys, and **V** specifies the type of values.

The following constructors are defined:

    HashMap( )
    HashMap(Map<? extends K, ? extends V> m)
    HashMap(int capacity)
    HashMap(int capacity, float fillRatio)

The first form constructs a default hash map. The second form initializes the hash map by using the elements of m. The third form initializes the capacity of the hash map to capacity. The fourth form initializes both the capacity and fill ratio of the hash map by using its arguments. The meaning of capacity and fill ratio is the same as for **HashSet**, described earlier.

Because **HashMap** uses a hash table, its elements are not in any particular order. Therefore, the order in which elements are added to a hash map is not necessarily the order in which they are read by an iterator, nor are they sorted.

The TreeMap Class

TreeMap uses a tree to hold a map. A **TreeMap** provides an efficient means of storing key/ value pairs in sorted order and allows rapid retrieval. **TreeMap** extends **AbstractMap** and implements the **NavigableMap** interface. It is a generic class that has this declaration:

    class TreeMap<K, V>

Here, **K** specifies the type of keys, and **V** specifies the type of values.

The following **TreeMap** constructors are defined:

    TreeMap( )
    TreeMap(Comparator<? super K> comp)
    TreeMap(Map<? extends K, ? extends V> m)
    TreeMap(SortedMap<K, ? extends V> sm)

The first form constructs an empty tree map that will be sorted by using the natural order of its keys. The second form constructs an empty tree-based map that will be sorted by using the **Comparator** comp. The third form initializes a tree map with the entries from m, which will be sorted by using the natural order of the keys. The fourth form initializes a tree map with the entries from sm, which will be sorted in the same order as sm.

The LinkedHashMap Class

LinkedHashMap maintains a linked list of the entries in the map, in the order in which they were inserted. This allows insertion-order iteration over the map. That is, when iterating through a collection-view of a **LinkedHashMap**, the elements will be returned in the order in which they were inserted. You can also create a **LinkedHashMap** that returns its elements in the order in which they were last accessed.

LinkedHashMap extends **HashMap**. It is a generic class that has this declaration:

class LinkedHashMap<K, V>

Here, **K** specifies the type of keys, and **V** specifies the type of values.

LinkedHashMap defines the following constructors:

LinkedHashMap( )
LinkedHashMap(Map<? extends K, ? extends V> *m*)
LinkedHashMap(int *capacity*)
LinkedHashMap(int *capacity*, float *fillRatio*)
LinkedHashMap(int *capacity*, float *fillRatio*, boolean *Order*)

The first form constructs a default **LinkedHashMap**. The second form initializes the **LinkedHashMap** with the elements from *m*. The third form initializes the capacity. The fourth form initializes both the capacity and fill ratio. The meaning of capacity and fill ratio are the same as for **HashMap**. The last form allows you to specify whether the elements will be stored in the linked list by insertion order, or by order of last access. If *Order* is **true**, then access order is used. If *Order* is **false**, then insertion order is used.

The EnumMap Class

EnumMap is specifically for use with keys of an **enum** type. It extends **AbstractMap** and implements **Map**.

EnumMap is a generic class that has this declaration:

class EnumMap<K extends Enum<K>, V>

Here, **K** specifies the type of key, and **V** specifies the type of value. Notice that **K** must extend **Enum<K>**, which enforces the requirement that the keys must be of an **enum** type.

EnumMap defines the following constructors:

EnumMap(Class<K> *kType*)
EnumMap(Map<K, ? extends V> *m*)
EnumMap(EnumMap<K, ? extends V> *em*)

The first constructor creates an empty **EnumMap** of type *kType*. The second creates an **EnumMap** map that contains the same entries as *m*. The third creates an **EnumMap** initialized with the values in *em*.

Algorithms

The Collections Framework provides many algorithms that operate on collections and maps. These algorithms are declared as static methods within the **Collections** class. It is outside the scope of this book to describe them all. However, several are used by the recipes, and they are described by the recipes in which they are used.

Basic Collection Techniques

Key Ingredients	
Classes and Interfaces	**Methods**
java.util.Collection<E>	boolean add(E *obj*)
	boolean addAll(Collection<? extends E> *col*)
	void clear( )
	boolean contains(Object *obj*)
	boolean containsAll(Collection<?> *col*)
	boolean isEmpty( )
	boolean remove(Object *obj*)
	boolean removeAll(Collection<?> *col*)
	boolean retainAll(Collection<?> *col*)
	int size( )
	<T> T[ ] toArray(T *array*[ ])
java.util.ArrayList<E>	

Because all collection classes implement the **Collection** interface, all collections share a common functionality. For example, all collections allow you to add elements to the collection, determine if some object is part of the collection, or obtain the size of the collection. This recipe demonstrates this common functionality by showing how to

- Create a collection
- Add elements to a collection
- Determine the size of a collection
- Determine if a collection contains a specific element
- Cycle through a collection with a for-each style **for** loop
- Remove elements
- Determine if a collection is empty
- Create an array that contains the collection.

This recipe uses the **ArrayList** collection, but only those methods defined by **Collection** are used, so the same general principles can be applied to any collection class.

NOTE *Iterators are also supported by all collections, but they are described separately. See* Iterate a Collection.

Step-by-Step

To create and use a collection involves these steps:

1. Create an instance of the desired collection. In this recipe, **ArrayList** is used, but any other collection (except for **EnumSet**, which is specifically designed for use with **enum** types) could have been selected.

2. Perform various operations on the collection by using the methods defined by **Collection** as described by the following steps.

3. Add elements to the collection by calling **add( )** or **addAll( )**.

4. Obtain the number of elements in the collection by calling **size( )**.

5. Determine if a collection contains one or more specific elements by calling **contains( )** or **containsAll( )**.

6. Determine if the collection is empty (i.e., contains no elements) by calling **isEmpty( )**.

7. Remove elements from the collection by calling **remove( )**, **removeAll( )**, or **retainAll( )**.

8. Remove all elements from a collection by calling **clear( )**.

9. Cycle through the elements in the collection by using a for-each style **for** loop.

10. Obtain an array that contains the elements in the collection by calling **toArray( )**.

Discussion

The methods defined by **Collection** are shown in Table 5-1, which is in *Collections Overview* earlier in this chapter. Here is a brief description of their operation.

Objects are added to a collection by calling **add( )**. Notice that **add( )** takes an argument of type **E**, which means that objects added to a collection must be compatible with the type of data expected by the collection. You can add the entire contents of one collection to another by calling **addAll( )**. Of course, both must contain compatible elements.

You can remove an object by using **remove( )**. To remove a group of objects, call **removeAll( )**. You can remove all elements except those of a specified group by calling **retainAll( )**. To empty a collection, call **clear( )**.

You can determine whether a collection contains a specific object by calling **contains( )**. To determine whether one collection contains all the members of another, call **containsAll( )**. You can determine when a collection is empty by calling **isEmpty( )**. The number of elements currently held in a collection can be determined by calling **size( )**.

The **toArray( )** method returns an array that contains the elements in the invoking collection. There are two versions of **toArray( )**. The first returns an array of **Object**. The second returns an array of elements that have the same type as the array specified as a parameter. Normally, the second form is more convenient because it returns the desired array type, and this is the version used in this recipe. The **toArray( )** method is useful because it provides a pathway between collections and arrays. This enables you to process a collection using the standard array syntax.

The example that follows uses an **ArrayList** to hold the collection. The *Collections Overview* presented near the start of this chapter describes its constructors. The one used by the recipe is its default constructor, which creates an empty collection.

Example

The following example demonstrates the basic collection techniques just described.

```java
// Demonstrate basic collection techniques.

import java.util.*;

class CollectionBasics {

  public static void main(String args[]) {

    // Create a collection.
    ArrayList<Integer> col = new ArrayList<Integer>();

    // Show initial size.
    System.out.println("Initial size: " + col.size());

    // Store some objects in the collection.
    for(int i=0; i<10; i++)
      col.add(i + 10);

    // Show size after additions.
    System.out.println("Size after additions: " + col.size());

    // Use a for-each loop to show the collection.
    System.out.println("Contents of col: ");
    for(int x : col)
      System.out.print(x + " ");

    System.out.println("\n");

    // See if the collection contains a value.
    if(col.contains(12))
      System.out.println("col contains the value 12");

    if(col.contains(-9))
      System.out.println("col contains the value -9");

    System.out.println();

    // Create another collection and then add it to the first.
    ArrayList<Integer> col2 = new ArrayList<Integer>();
    col2.add(100);
    col2.add(200);
    col2.add(8);
    col2.add(-10);

    // Show col2.
    System.out.println("Contents of col2: ");
    for(int x : col2)
      System.out.print(x + " ");

    System.out.println("\n");
```

```
// Add col2 to col.
col.addAll(col2);

// Show the resulting collection.
System.out.println("Contents of col after adding col2: ");
for(int x : col)
  System.out.print(x + " ");

System.out.println("\n");

// Use containsAll() to confirm that col now contains
// all of col2.
if(col.containsAll(col2))
  System.out.println("col now contains all of col2.");

System.out.println();

// Now remove objects from the collection.
col.remove((Integer)10);
col.remove((Integer)200);

// Show the resulting collection.
System.out.println("Contents of col after removing elements: ");
for(int x : col)
  System.out.print(x + " ");

System.out.println("\n");

// Now remove the entire col2 collection.
col.removeAll(col2);

// Show the resulting collection.
System.out.println("Contents of col after removing col2: ");
for(int x : col)
  System.out.print(x + " ");

System.out.println("\n");

// Add col2 to col again, and call retainAll().
col.addAll(col2); // add col2 to col

// Remove all elements except those in col2.
col.retainAll(col2);

// Show the resulting collection.
System.out.println("Contents of col after retaining col2: ");
for(int x : col)
  System.out.print(x + " ");

System.out.println("\n");

// Obtain an array from a collection.
Integer[] iarray = new Integer[col.size()];
```

```
    iarray = col.toArray(iarray);

    // Display the contents of the array.
    System.out.println("Contents of iarray: ");
    for(int i=0; i<iarray.length; i++)
      System.out.print(iarray[i] + " ");

    System.out.println("\n");

    // Remove all elements from the collection.
    System.out.println("Removing all elements from col.");
    col.clear();

    if(col.isEmpty())
      System.out.println("col is now empty.");
  }
}
```

The output is shown here:

```
Initial size: 0
Size after additions: 10
Contents of col:
10 11 12 13 14 15 16 17 18 19

col contains the value 12

Contents of col2:
100 200 8 -10

Contents of col after adding col2:
10 11 12 13 14 15 16 17 18 19 100 200 8 -10

col now contains all of col2.

Contents of col after removing elements:
11 12 13 14 15 16 17 18 19 100 8 -10

Contents of col after removing col2:
11 12 13 14 15 16 17 18 19

Contents of col after retaining col2:
100 200 8 -10

Contents of iarray:
100 200 8 -10

Removing all elements from col.
col is now empty.
```

Options and Alternatives

Although **ArrayList** was used to demonstrate the basic collection techniques, any of the collection classes could have been used (except for **EnumSet**, which is specifically for

enum types). For example, try substituting **LinkedList** for **ArrayList** in the example. The program will compile and run properly. The reason is, of course, that all collections implement the **Collection** interface, and only the methods defined by **Collection** are used by the example. Furthermore, because all collections implement **Iterable**, all collections can be cycled through using the for-each version of **for**, as the example shows.

Although a for-each **for** is often the most convenient approach to cycling through the elements of a collection, an iterator can also be employed. This technique is described in *Iterate a Collection.*

Work with Lists

Key Ingredients	
Classes and Interfaces	**Methods**
java.util.List<E>	void add(int *idx*, E *obj*)
	E get(int *idx*)
	int indexOf(Object *obj*)
	int lastIndexOf(Object *obj*)
	E remove(int *idx*)
	E set(int *idx*, E *obj*)
java.util.ArrayList<E>	void ensureCapacity(int *capacity*)
java.util.LinkedList<E>	

Perhaps the most commonly used collections are those based on the **List** interface. **List** extends **Collection** and defines a general-purpose collection that stores a sequence. In most cases, a list can hold duplicate elements. A list also allows elements to be accessed by index position.

The **java.util** package defines several concrete implementations of **List**. The first two are **ArrayList** and **LinkedList**. **ArrayList** implements the **List** and **RandomAccess** interfaces and adds two methods of its own. **LinkedList** implements both the **List** and the **Deque** interfaces. **List** is also implemented by the legacy classes **Vector** and **Stack**, but their use in new code is not recommended. This recipe demonstrates lists. It uses both **ArrayList** and **LinkedList**.

Step-by-Step

Using a list involves the following steps:

1. Create a concrete implementation of **List**. For array-like operation, use **ArrayList**. For a general-purpose implementation, use **LinkedList.**

2. Add elements to the list. Elements can be added to the end or inserted at a specified index by calling **add( )**.

3. The elements of the list can be accessed via the methods defined by **Collection** and **List**. For example, you can obtain the element at a specific index by calling **get( )** or set the value of an element by calling **set( )**.

Discussion

The basic collection operations defined by **Collection** (which are inherited by **List**) are described by the preceding recipe. The **List** interface also specifies several methods of its own. They are shown in Table 5-3 in the *Collections Overview*. The ones used by this recipe are shown here:

```
void add(int idx, E obj)
E get(int idx)
int indexOf(Object obj)
int lastIndexOf(Object obj)
E remove(int idx)
E set(int idx, E obj)
```

This version of **add( )** inserts *obj* into the collection at the index specified by *idx*. The **get( )** method returns the element at *idx*. The index of the first occurrence of *obj* is returned by **indexOf( )**. The index of last occurrence of *obj* is returned by **lastIndexOf( )**. Both return –1 if the object is not in the list. The **remove( )** method removes the element at *idx* and returns the deleted element. To set the element at a specified index, call **set( )**. The index is passed via *idx*, and the new object is passed in *obj*. It returns the previous element at that index.

When using an **ArrayList**, you can specify an initial capacity by calling **ensureCapacity( )**, shown here:

```
void ensureCapacity(int cap)
```

The capacity is the number of elements that an **ArrayList** can hold before it will need to be enlarged. The capacity is specified by *cap*. In cases in which you know that a certain minimum number of elements will be stored, you can set the initial capacity in advance. This prevents subsequent reallocations, which are costly in terms of time.

With the exception of **ensureCapacity( )** (and **trimToSize( )** described at the end of this recipe), a **LinkedList** has the same capabilities as an **ArrayList**. The difference is implementation. Although a **LinkedList** does allow access to an element via an index (as the example will show), such index-based accesses will be less efficient than they are for an **ArrayList**. However, insertions into and deletions from a **LinkedList** are very efficient because the links are simply rearranged. There is no need to compact or expand an underlying array. In general, a **LinkedList** should be used for applications in which arbitrarily long lists are needed and elements will be frequently inserted or removed. An **ArrayList** should be used when a dynamic array is required.

Example

The following demonstrates **List**, using both **ArrayList** and **LinkedList**.

```
// Demonstrate List.

import java.util.*;
```

```
class ListDemo {

  public static void main(String args[]) {

    System.out.println("Creating an ArrayList called al.");
    ArrayList<Character> al = new ArrayList<Character>();

    // Add elements.
    al.add('A');
    al.add('B');
    al.add('D');

    System.out.println("al in index order: ");
    for(int i=0; i < al.size(); i++)
      System.out.print(al.get(i) + " ");

    System.out.println("\n");

    // Now, insert an element at index 2.
    al.add(2, 'C');

    System.out.println("al after adding C: ");
    for(int i=0; i < al.size(); i++)
      System.out.print(al.get(i) + " ");

    System.out.println("\n");

    // Remove B.
    al.remove(1);

    System.out.println("al after removing B: ");
    for(int i=0; i < al.size(); i++)
      System.out.print(al.get(i) + " ");

    System.out.println("\n");

    // Set the value of the last element.
    al.set(al.size()-1, 'X');

    System.out.println("al after setting last element: ");
    for(int i=0; i < al.size(); i++)
      System.out.print(al.get(i) + " ");

    System.out.println("\n");

    // Add another C.
    al.add('C');

    System.out.println("al after adding another C: ");
    for(int i=0; i < al.size(); i++)
      System.out.print(al.get(i) + " ");

    System.out.println("\n");
```

```
        System.out.println("Index of first C: " +
                         al.indexOf('C'));
        System.out.println("Index of last C: " +
                         al.lastIndexOf('C'));

        System.out.println("");

        // Clear the list.
        al.clear();

        // Ensure a capacity of at least 26.
        al.ensureCapacity(26);

        // Add the letters a through z.
        for(int i=0; i < 26; i++)
          al.add(i, (char) ('a' + i));

        System.out.println("al after clearing, " +
                         "ensuring capacity,\n" +
                         "and then adding a through z: ");
        for(int i=0; i < al.size(); i++)
          System.out.print(al.get(i) + " ");

        System.out.println("\n");

        // Now create a linked list from al.
        System.out.println("Creating a LinkedList called ll.");
        LinkedList<Character> ll = new LinkedList<Character>(al);

        // LinkedList supports the same operations, except for
        // ensureCapacity() and trimToSize(), as ArrayList.
        // For example, you can cycle through the contents of
        // a LinkedList using the get() method:
        System.out.println("Contents of ll:");
        for(int i=0; i < ll.size(); i++)
          System.out.print(ll.get(i) + " ");

        System.out.println();

    }
}
```

The output is shown here:

```
Creating an ArrayList called al.
al in index order:
A B D

al after adding C:
A B C D

al after removing B:
A C D
```

```
al after setting last element:
A C X

al after adding another C:
A C X C

Index of first C: 1
Index of last C: 3

al after clearing, ensuring capacity,
and then adding a through z:
a b c d e f g h i j k l m n o p q r s t u v w x y z

Creating a LinkedList called ll.
Contents of ll:
a b c d e f g h i j k l m n o p q r s t u v w x y z
```

Options and Alternatives

The example uses explicit indexing to cycle through the contents of a list. However, all **List** implementations can be iterated by a for-each style **for** loop, as shown in the preceding recipe, or by an iterator. The use of an iterator is described in *Iterate a Collection*.

LinkedList implements the **Deque** interface, which gives **LinkedList** access to all of the methods defined by **Deque**. See *Create a Queue or a Stack Using Deque* for an example.

ArrayList lets you reduce the size of a collection to the minimum necessary to hold the number of elements currently stored. This is done by calling **trimToSize( )**. It is shown here:

    void trimToSize( )

Work with Sets

Key Ingredients	
Classes and Interfaces	**Methods**
java.util.Set<E>	boolean add(E *obj*)
java.util.SortedSet<E>	E first( )
	E last( )
java.util.NavigableSet<E>	E higher(E *obj*)
	E lower(E *obj*)
java.util.HashSet<E>	
java.util.TreeSet<E>	

Like **List**, **Set** is a subinterface of **Collection**. The **Set** interface differs from **List** in one very important way: a **Set** implementation does not allow duplicate elements. **Set** does not add any methods to those inherited from **Collection**. However, it does require that **add( )** return **false** if an attempt is made to add a duplicate element.

The **Set** interface does not require that the collection be maintained in sorted order. However, **SortedSet**, which extends **Set**, does. Therefore, if you want a sorted set, then you will use a collection that implements the **SortedSet** interface. Beginning with Java 6, **Set** is also extended by **NavigableSet**. The **java.util** package defines two concrete implementations of **Set**: **HashSet** and **LinkedHashSet**. It also provides **TreeSet**, which is a concrete implementation of **SortedSet** and **NavigableSet**. This recipe demonstrates sets. It uses **HashSet** and **TreeSet**.

Step-by-Step

Using a set involves the following steps:

1. Create a concrete implementation of **Set**. For basic set operations, use either **HashSet** or **LinkedHashSet**. For a sorted set, use **TreeSet**. For a navigable set, use **TreeSet**.

2. Add elements to the set. Remember that duplicates are not allowed.

3. All Set instances can be accessed via the methods defined by **Collection**. When using a **TreeSet**, you can also use the methods defined by **SortedSet** and **NavigableSet**.

Discussion

The basic collection operations defined by **Collection** (which are inherited by **Set**) are described in *Basic Collection Techniques*.

When working with a **SortedSet** (such as a **TreeSet**), you can use the methods defined by **Set**, but you can also use the methods provided by **SortedSet**. The ones used by this recipe are **first( )**, which returns a reference to the first element in the set, and **last( )**, which returns a reference to the last element. These methods are shown here:

```
E first( )
E last( )
```

Each obtains the indicated element.

NavigableSet, which is implemented by **TreeSet**, defines several methods that let you search the set for closest matches. This recipe uses two of these methods. The first is **higher( )**, which obtains the first element that is greater than a specified value. The second is **lower( )**, which obtains the first element that is less than a specified value. They are shown here:

```
E higher(E obj)
E lower(E obj)
```

Each obtains the indicated element.

NOTE *NavigableSet was added by Java 6. Therefore, a modern version of Java is required to use it.*

Example

The following example demonstrates collections based on **Set**, **SortedSet**, and **NavigableSet**. It uses the default conversion provided by **toString( )** to convert a set into a string for output.

```
// Demonstrate Set.

import java.util.*;

class SetDemo {

  public static void main(String args[]) {
    HashSet<String> hs = new HashSet<String>();

    // Add elements.
    hs.add("one");
    hs.add("two");
    hs.add("three");

    // Display the set using the default toString( ) conversion.
    System.out.println("Here is the HashSet: " + hs);

    // Try to add three again.
    if(!hs.add("three"))
      System.out.println("Attempt to add duplicate. " +
                         "Set is unchanged: " + hs);

    // Now use a TreeSet, which implements both
    // SortedSet and NavigableSet.
    TreeSet<Integer> ts = new TreeSet<Integer>();

    // Add elements.
    ts.add(8);
    ts.add(19);
    ts.add(-2);
    ts.add(3);

    // Notice that this set is sorted.
    System.out.println("\nHere is the TreeSet: " + ts);

    // Use first() and last() from SortedSet.
    System.out.println("First element in ts: " + ts.first());
    System.out.println("Last element in ts: " + ts.last());

    // Use higher() and lower() from NavigableSet.
    System.out.println("First element > 15: " + ts.higher(15));
    System.out.println("First element < 15: " + ts.lower(15));
  }
}
```

The output is shown here:

```
Here is the HashSet: [two, one, three]
Attempt to add duplicate. Set is unchanged: [two, one, three]

Here is the TreeSet: [-2, 3, 8, 19]
First element in ts: -2
Last element in ts: 19
First element > 15: 19
First element < 15: 8
```

Notice how the contents of the sets are shown using their default, **toString( )** conversions. When a collection is converted to a string by using **toString( )**, the elements are shown inside square brackets, with each element separated from the next by a comma.

Bonus Example

Because a **Set** does not allow duplicate elements, it can be used to define the basic set operations defined by Set Theory. These are

- Union
- Intersection
- Difference
- Symmetric difference
- Is subset
- Is superset

The meaning of each operation is described here. For the sake of this discussion, assume the following sets:

Set1: A, B, C, D
Set2: C, D, E, F

The union of two sets produces a new set that contains all of the elements of both sets. For example, the union of Set1 and Set2 is

A, B, C, D, E, F

Notice that C and D are included only once because duplicates are not allowed in a set.

The intersection of two sets produces a new set that contains only those elements that both of the original sets have in common. For example, the intersection of Set1 and Set2 produces the following set:

C, D

Because C and D are the only elements that both sets share, they are the only elements in the intersection.

The difference between two sets produces a new set that contains those elements of the first set that do not occur in the second set. For example, Set1 – Set2 produces the following set:

A, B

Because C and D are members of Set2, they are subtracted from Set1 and are, therefore, not part of the resulting set.

The symmetric difference between two sets is composed of those elements that occur in one set or the other, but not in both. For example, the symmetric difference of Set1 and Set2 is

A, B, E, F

C and D are not part of the result because they are members of both Set1 and Set2.

Given two sets SetX and SetY, SetX is a subset of SetY only if all of the elements of SetX are also elements of SetY. SetX is a superset of SetY only if all elements of SetY are also elements of SetX.

The following program implements the set operations just defined.

```
// This program creates a class called SetOps that defines
// methods that perform the following set operations:
//
//    union
//    intersection
//    difference
//    symmetric difference
//    is subset
//    is superset

import java.util.*;

// A class that supports various set operations.
class SetOps {

  // Union
  public static <T> Set<T> union(Set<T> setA, Set<T> setB) {
    Set<T> tmp = new TreeSet<T>(setA);
    tmp.addAll(setB);
    return tmp;
  }

  // Intersection
  public static <T> Set<T> intersection(Set<T> setA, Set<T> setB) {
    Set<T> tmp = new TreeSet<T>();
    for(T x : setA)
      if(setB.contains(x)) tmp.add(x);
    return tmp;
  }

  // Difference
  public static <T> Set<T> difference(Set<T> setA, Set<T> setB) {
    Set<T> tmp = new TreeSet<T>(setA);
    tmp.removeAll(setB);
    return tmp;
  }

  // Symmetric Difference
  public static <T> Set<T> symDifference(Set<T> setA, Set<T> setB) {
```

```
    Set<T> tmpA;
    Set<T> tmpB;

    tmpA = union(setA, setB);
    tmpB = intersection(setA, setB);
    return difference(tmpA, tmpB);
  }

  // Return true if setA is a subset of setB.
  public static <T> boolean isSubset(Set<T> setA, Set<T> setB) {
    return setB.containsAll(setA);
  }

  // Return true if setA is a superset of setB.
  public static <T> boolean isSuperset(Set<T> setA, Set<T> setB) {
    return setA.containsAll(setB);
  }
}

// Demonstrate the set operations.
class SetOpsDemo {

  public static void main(String args[]) {
    TreeSet<Character> set1 = new TreeSet<Character>();
    TreeSet<Character> set2 = new TreeSet<Character>();

    set1.add('A');
    set1.add('B');
    set1.add('C');
    set1.add('D');

    set2.add('C');
    set2.add('D');
    set2.add('E');
    set2.add('F');

    System.out.println("set1: " + set1);
    System.out.println("set2: " + set2);

    System.out.println();

    System.out.println("Union: " +
                       SetOps.union(set1, set2));
    System.out.println("Intersection: " +
                       SetOps.intersection(set1, set2));
    System.out.println("Difference (set1 - set2): " +
                       SetOps.difference(set1, set2));
    System.out.println("Symmetric Difference: " +
                       SetOps.symDifference(set1, set2));

    System.out.println();

    // Now, demonstrate isSubset() and isSuperset().
    TreeSet<Character> set3 = new TreeSet<Character>(set1);
```

```
        set3.remove('D');
        System.out.println("set3: " + set3);

        System.out.println("Is set1 a subset of set2? " +
                           SetOps.isSubset(set1, set3));
        System.out.println("Is set1 a superset of set2? " +
                           SetOps.isSuperset(set1, set3));
        System.out.println("Is set3 a subset of set1? " +
                           SetOps.isSubset(set3, set1));
        System.out.println("Is set3 a superset of set1? " +
                           SetOps.isSuperset(set3, set1));

    }
}
```

The output is shown here:

```
set1: [A, B, C, D]
set2: [C, D, E, F]

Union: [A, B, C, D, E, F]
Intersection: [C, D]
Difference (set1 - set2): [A, B]
Symmetric Difference: [A, B, E, F]

set3: [A, B, C]
Is set1 a subset of set2? false
Is set1 a superset of set2? true
Is set3 a subset of set1? true
Is set3 a superset of set1? false
```

Options and Alternatives

Another **Set** implementation provided by the Collections Framework is **LinkedHashSet**. It uses a hash table to store the elements in the set, but it also maintains a linked list of the elements in the order in which they were added to the set. An iterator for a **LinkedHashSet** will cycle through the elements by following the links. This means that the iterator will return elements in order of their insertion into the set. See *Iterate a Collection* for details.

Use Comparable to Store Objects in a Sorted Collection

Key Ingredients	
Classes and Interfaces	**Methods**
java.lang.Comparable<T>	int compareTo (T *obj2*)
java.util.TreeSet<E>	

In general, a collection can store any type of object. However, sorted collections, such as **PriorityQueue** or **TreeSet,** place one condition on those objects: they must implement the **Comparable** interface. Here's why: The **Comparable** interface defines the **compareTo( )** method, which determines the "natural order" for objects of the class. As it is used here, natural order means the ordering that one would normally expect. For example, the natural order of strings is alphabetical. For numeric values, it's numeric order. (In other words, A before B, 1 before 2, and so on.) The sorted collections use the natural order defined by a class to determine the order of objects. Therefore, if you want to store objects in a sorted collection, their class must implement **Comparable**. This recipe shows the general procedure. (The same general approach also applies to sorted maps.)

Step-by-Step

To store objects of classes that you create in a sorted collection involves the following steps:

1. Create the class whose objects will be stored in the sorted collection. The class must implement the **Comparable** interface.

2. Implement the **compareTo( )** method specified by the **Comparable** interface to define the natural order for the class.

3. If necessary, override **equals( )** so that it is consistent with the results produced by **compareTo( )**.

4. Construct a sorted collection, specifying your class as a type argument.

5. Add objects of your class to the collection. The **compareTo( )** method determines the order in which the elements will be stored.

Discussion

If an object will be stored in a sorted collection or map, its class must implement the **Comparable** interface. **Comparable** defines a standard way in which two objects of the same class will be compared. It is implemented by many of Java's API classes, including **Byte, Character, Double, Float, Long, Short, String,** and **Integer**.

Comparable is generic and is declared like this:

    interface Comparable<T>

Here, **T** represents the type of objects being compared.

Comparable specifies only one method: **compareTo( )**. It compares two objects and returns the result. The outcome of this comparison determines the *natural ordering* of instances of a class. The **compareTo( )** method is shown here:

    int compareTo(T *obj*)

This method compares the invoking object with *obj*. It returns 0 if the values are equal. A negative value is returned if the invoking object has a lower value. Otherwise, a positive value is returned. Of course, you determine how the comparison takes place when you implement **compareTo( )**. It will throw a **ClassCastException** if the two objects are not compatible.

There is one rule that you should normally follow when implementing **Comparable** for a class—especially if objects of that class will be stored in a **SortedSet** (or a **SortedMap**). The outcome of **compareTo( )** should be consistent with the outcome of **equals( )**. In other words, for every case in which **equals( )** returns true, **compareTo( )** should return 0. This is important because **SortedSet** does not allow duplicate elements. Because the default implementation of **equals( )** provided by **Object** uses reference equality, you will often want to override **equals( )** so that its results are consistent with your implementation of **compareTo( )**.

Example

The following example shows how **Comparable** can be used to define the natural ordering of an object so that it can be stored in a sorted collection. It uses a **TreeSet** to store objects of type **Product**, which encapsulates information about a product, including its name and ID. The **compareTo( )** method sorts **Product** instances based on the name. Thus, the collection will be sorted based on the name of the product.

```java
// Demonstrate Comparable with a sorted collection.
//
// If an object will be stored in a sorted collection
// or map, then its class must implement the
// Comparable interface. Comparable defines the
// "natural ordering" for the class.

import java.util.*;

// This class encapsulates a product's name
// and ID number. It implements Comparable
// such that the natural order is determined
// by the name of the products.
class Product implements Comparable<Product> {
  String prodName;
  int prodID;

  Product(String str, int id) {
    prodName = str;
    prodID = id;
  }

  // Compare two products based on their names.
  public int compareTo(Product p2) {
    return prodName.compareToIgnoreCase(p2.prodName);
  }

  // Override equals() so that it is consistent with compareTo().
  public boolean equals(Object p2) {
    return prodName.compareToIgnoreCase(((Product)p2).prodName)==0;
  }
}

// Demonstrate Comparable interface.
class CompDemo {

  public static void main(String args[]) {
```

```
      // Create a TreeSet that uses natural order.
      TreeSet<Product> prodList = new TreeSet<Product>();

      // Add some products to prodList.
      prodList.add(new Product("Shelf", 13546));
      prodList.add(new Product("Keyboard Tray", 04762));
      prodList.add(new Product("Desk", 12221));
      prodList.add(new Product("File Cabinet", 44387));

      // Display the products, sorted by name.
      System.out.println("Products sorted by name:\n");
      for(Product p : prodList)
        System.out.printf("%-14s ID: %d\n", p.prodName,
                          p.prodID);
    }
}
```

The output is shown here:

```
Products sorted by name:

Desk          ID: 12221
File Cabinet  ID: 44387
Keyboard Tray ID: 2546
Shelf         ID: 13546
```

Options and Alternatives

Implementing **Comparable** is the best way to specify the ordering that will be used for objects of a class, but there is an alternative that is useful in some cases. You can create a custom comparator that determines how objects are compared. This comparator is passed to the collection's constructor when it is created. The comparator is then used to compare two objects. See the following recipe for an example.

Your implementation of **compareTo( )** does not need to arrange elements in ascending order. By reversing the outcome of the comparison, elements can be arranged in reverse order. For example, try changing the **compareTo( )** method in the example as shown here. It calls **compareToIgnoreCase( )** on **p2** rather than on the invoking object. Thus, the outcome of the comparison is reversed.

```
// Reverse the outcome of a comparison between two products.
public int compareTo(Product p2) {
  return p2.prodName.compareToIgnoreCase(prodName);
}
```

After making this change, the collection will be sorted in reverse order. By the way, notice that the reverse comparison is still consistent with the override of **equals( )**. Only the ordering has changed.

Any objects that you will be using as keys in a sorted map (such as **TreeMap**) must also implement **Comparable**. Use the same basic procedure as just described.

Use a Comparator with a Collection

Key Ingredients	
Classes and Interfaces	**Methods**
java.util.Comparator<T>	int compare(T *obj1*, T *obj2*)
java.util.PriorityQueue<E>	boolean add(E *obj*)
	E poll( )

As explained by the preceding recipe, objects stored in an ordered collection (such as a **TreeSet** or a **PriorityQueue**) are arranged in their natural order by default. This ordering is determined by the outcome of the **compareTo( )** method defined by the **Comparable** interface. If you want to order elements in a way that differs from the object's natural ordering, you have two choices. First, you can change the implementation of **compareTo( )**. However, doing so changes the natural ordering of your class, which affects all uses of your class. Also, you might want to change the ordering of classes for which you do not have access to the source code.

For these reasons, the second choice is often a better choice. You can create a comparator that defines the desired ordering. A *comparator* is an object that implements the **Comparator** interface. The comparator can be passed to an ordered collection when the collection is created, and it is used to determine the order of elements within the collection. This recipe shows how to create and use a custom comparator. In the process, it demonstrates **PriorityQueue**.

Step-by-Step

To use a custom comparator to control the order of objects within a collection involves these steps:

1. Create a class that implements **Comparator** for the type of data that will be stored in the collection.
2. Code the **compare( )** method so that it orders the data in the desired manner. If necessary, it should be consistent with the outcome of **equals( )** when used on the same objects.
3. Create an ordered collection (such as **TreeSet** or **PriorityQueue**), specifying the comparator to the constructor. This causes the collection to use the comparator to order the elements of the collection, rather than using the natural ordering.

Discussion

Comparator is packaged in **java.util** and is a generic interface that has this declaration:

    interface Comparator<T>

Here, **T** specifies the type of objects being compared.

The **Comparator** interface defines two methods: **compare( )** and **equals( )**. The **compare( )** method, shown here, compares two elements for order:

int compare(T *obj1*, T *obj2*)

Here, *obj1* and *obj2* are the objects to be compared. This method returns zero if the objects are equal. It returns a positive value if *obj1* is greater than *obj2*. Otherwise, a negative value is returned. The method can throw a **ClassCastException** if the types of the objects are not compatible for comparison. Your implementation of **compare( )** determines the way that objects are ordered. For example, to sort in reverse order, you can create a comparator that reverses the outcome of a comparison.

The **equals( )** method, shown here, tests whether an object equals the invoking comparator:

boolean equals(Object *obj*)

Here, *obj* is the object to be tested for equality. The method returns **true** if *obj* and the invoking object are both **Comparator** objects and use the same ordering. Otherwise, it returns **false**. Overriding **equals( )** is usually unnecessary, and most simple comparators will not do so. (Note: this version of **equals( )** *does not* compare two objects of type **T**. It compares two comparators.)

When you create a comparator for use with a **SortedSet** (or any collection that requires unique elements), the outcome of **compare( )** should be consistent with the result of **equals( )** when used on the same two objects. In other words, given a class **X**, then **X**'s implementation of **equals( )** should return the same result as **compare( )** defined by **Comparator<X>** when two **X** objects are equal. The reason for this requirement is that a **SortedSet** cannot contain duplicate elements.

After you have created a comparator, you can pass it to the constructor of one of the ordered collections. The example that follows uses a **PriorityQueue**. Here is the constructor that is used:

PriorityQueue(int *capacity*, Comparator<? super E> *comp*)

Here, *capacity* specifies the initial capacity of the queue and *comp* specifies the comparator.

When using a **PriorityQueue**, you will add elements to the queue using either **add( )** or **offer( )**. Either will insert the element in the order determined by the element's natural order, or by the comparator specified when the **PriorityQueue** is constructed (which is the case with this recipe).

To obtain elements from a **PriorityQueue** in order of their priority, you must use **poll( )**. (You cannot use an iterator for this purpose because the elements will not be returned in priority order.) The **poll( )** method is shown here:

E poll( )

It removes and returns the next element from the queue in order of priority. It returns **null** if the queue is empty.

Example

The following example uses a comparator to create a list of prioritized messages. Each message is an object of type **Message**, which is a class that encapsulates a string and a priority code. The priority levels are specified by an **enum** called **PLevel**, which defines three priorities: **Low**, **Medium**, and **High**. **Message** implements **Comparable**, which defines the natural ordering of the elements. This is the ordering defined by **PLevel**, which is from high to low. The class **RevMsgComparer** creates a comparator for **Message** objects that reverses the natural order. Therefore, when using **RevMsgComparer**, messages are arranged from low to high. Two **PriorityQueue**s are then created. The first uses the natural order of **Message** to order the messages. The second uses **RevMsgComparer** to order the messages. As the output shows, the order of messages in the second queue is the reverse of that in the first queue.

One other point: Because **Message** is designed for use by **PriorityQueue**, it is not necessary to override **equals( )** so that it is consistent with **compare( )** in **Message** or **compareTo( )** in **RevMsgComparer**. The default implementation provided by **Object** is sufficient. In fact, attempting to make **equals( )** consistent with **compare( )** or **compareTo( )** would actually be wrong in this case, since the comparisons are based on the priority of a message, not on its contents.

NOTE *PriorityQueue was added by Java 5. Therefore, you must be using a modern version of Java to compile and run the following example.*

```java
// Use a Comparator to create a PriorityQueue for messages.

import java.util.*;

// This class encapsulates a prioritized message.
// It implements Comparable, which defines its
// "natural ordering".
class Message implements Comparable<Message> {
  String msg;

  // This enumeration defines the priority levels.
  enum PLevel {
    High, Medium, Low
  }

  PLevel priority;

  Message(String str, PLevel pri) {
    msg = str;
    priority = pri;
  }

  // Compare two messages based on their priorities.
  public int compareTo(Message msg2) {
    return priority.compareTo(msg2.priority);
  }
}

// A reverse Comparator for Message.
class RevMsgComparer implements Comparator<Message> {
  public int compare(Message msg1, Message msg2) {
    return msg2.priority.compareTo(msg1.priority);
  }
}
```

```java
// Demonstrate Comparators with PriorityQueue.
class PriMsgQDemo {

  public static void main(String args[]) {
    Message m;

    // Create a priority queue that uses natural order.
    PriorityQueue<Message> pq =
      new PriorityQueue<Message>(3);

    // Add some message to pq.
    pq.add(new Message("Meeting at main office at 3pm",
                       Message.PLevel.Low));
    pq.add(new Message("Fire in warehouse!",
                       Message.PLevel.High));
    pq.add(new Message("Report due Tuesday",
                       Message.PLevel.Medium));

    // Display the messages in natural-order priority.
    System.out.println("Messages in natural-order priority: ");
    while((m = pq.poll()) != null)
      System.out.println(m.msg + " Priority: " +
                         m.priority);

    System.out.println();

    // Now, create a priority queue that stores
    // messages in reverse order.
    PriorityQueue<Message> pqRev =
      new PriorityQueue<Message>(3, new RevMsgComparer());

    // Add the same messages to pqRev.
    pqRev.add(new Message("Meeting at main office at 3pm",
                          Message.PLevel.Low));
    pqRev.add(new Message("Fire in warehouse!",
                          Message.PLevel.High));
    pqRev.add(new Message("Report due Tuesday",
                          Message.PLevel.Medium));

    // Display the message in reverse-order priority.
    System.out.println("Messages in reverse-order priority: ");
    while((m = pqRev.poll()) != null)
      System.out.println(m.msg + " Priority: " +
                         m.priority);
  }
}
```

The output is shown here:

```
Messages in natural-order priority:
Fire in warehouse! Priority: High
Report due Tuesday Priority: Medium
Meeting at main office at 3pm Priority: Low
```

```
Messages in reverse-order priority:
Meeting at main office at 3pm Priority: Low
Report due Tuesday Priority: Medium
Fire in warehouse! Priority: High
```

Options and Alternatives

One of the main advantages of **Comparator** is that you can define a comparator for a class to which you don't have source code. For example, you can store strings in reverse order by using the following comparator:

```
// A reverse Comparator for String.
class RevStrComparer implements Comparator<String> {
  public int compare(String str1, String str2) {
    return str2.compareTo(str1);
  }
}
```

As a point of interest, this comparator is also consistent with **equals( )** as defined by **String**.

There is a very easy way to obtain a reverse comparator for a specified data type: call the **reverseOrder( )** algorithm defined by **Collections**. It returns a **Comparator** that performs a reverse comparison. It is shown here:

static <T> Comparator<T> reverseOrder( )

Among other things, a reverse comparator can be used to sort a collection in descending order.

The same basic procedure used to create a comparator for a collection also applies to using one with a sorted map, such as **TreeMap**. When a map is sorted, its ordering is based on its keys.

Iterate a Collection

Key Ingredients	
Interfaces	**Methods**
java.util.Iterator<E>	boolean hasNext( ) E next( ) void remove( )
java.util.ListIterator<E>	boolean hasNext( ) boolean hasPrevious( ) E next( ) E previous( ) void remove( )
java.util.Collection<E>	Iterator<E> iterator( )
java.util.List<E>	ListIterator<E> listIterator( )

One of the most common operations performed on a collection is to cycle through its elements. For example, you might want to display each element or perform some transformation on each element. One way to cycle through the elements of a collection is to employ an *iterator,* which is an object that implements either the **Iterator** or the **ListIterator** interface. **Iterator** enables you to cycle through a collection, obtaining or removing elements. **ListIterator** extends **Iterator** to allow bidirectional traversal of a list, and the modification of elements. This recipe shows the general procedure for using both types of iterators.

Step-by-Step

To cycle through a collection using an iterator, follow these steps:

1. Obtain an iterator for the collection by calling the collection's **iterator( )** method.
2. Set up a loop that makes a call to **hasNext( )**.
3. Within the loop, obtain each element by calling **next( )**.
4. Have the loop iterate as long as **hasNext( )** returns **true**.

For collections that implement **List**, you can use **ListIterator** to cycle through the list. To do so, follow these steps:

1. Obtain an iterator for the collection by calling the collection's **listIterator( )** method.
2. Inside a loop, use **hasNext( )** to determine if the collection has a subsequent element. Use **hasPrevious( )** to determine if the collection has a prior element.
3. Within the loop, obtain the next element by calling **next( )** or obtain the previous element by calling **previous( ).**
4. Stop iterating when there is no next or previous element available.

Discussion

Iterator and **ListIterator** are generic interfaces which are declared as shown here:

```
interface Iterator<E>
interface ListIterator<E>
```

Here, **E** specifies the type of objects being iterated. The **Iterator** interface declares the following methods:

Method	Description
boolean hasNext( )	Returns **true** if there are more elements. Otherwise, returns **false**.
E next( )	Returns the next element. Throws **NoSuchElementException** if there is not a next element.
void remove( )	Removes the current element. Throws **IllegalStateException** if an attempt is made to call **remove( )** that is not preceded by a call to **next( )**. An **UnsupportedOperationException** is thrown if the collection is immutable.

The methods defined by **Iterator** enable a collection to be cycled through in strictly sequential fashion, from start to end. An **Iterator** cannot move backward.

ListIterator extends **Iterator** and adds several methods of its own. The ones used by this recipe are shown here:

Method	Description
boolean hasPrevious( )	Returns **true** if there is a previous element. Otherwise, returns **false**.
E previous( )	Returns the previous element. A **NoSuchElementException** is thrown if there is not a previous element.

As you can see, **ListIterator** adds the ability to move backward. Thus, a **ListIterator** can obtain either the next element in the collection or the previous one.

Before you can access a collection through an iterator, you must obtain one. This is done by calling the **iterator( )** method, which returns an iterator to the start of the collection. This method is specified by the **Iterable** interface, which is inherited by **Collection**. Thus, all collections provide the **iterator( )** method. It is shown here:

Iterator<E> iterator( )

By using the iterator returned by **iterator( )**, you can access each element in the collection, front to back, one element at a time.

For collections that implement **List**, you can also obtain an iterator by calling **listIterator( )**, which is specified by **List**. There are two versions of **listIterator( )**, which are shown here:

ListIterator<E> listIterator( )
ListIterator<E> listIterator(int *idx*)

The first version returns a list iterator to the start of the list. The second returns a list iterator that starts at the specified index. The index passed via *idx* must be within the range of the list. Otherwise, an **IndexOutOfBoundsException** will be thrown. As explained, a list iterator gives you the ability to access the collection in either the forward or backward direction and lets you modify an element.

Example

The following example demonstrates both an iterator and a list iterator. It creates a simple phone list that is stored in a **LinkedList**. It displays the list in the forward direction via an **Iterator**. Then, it displays the list in reverse using a **ListIterator**.

```
// Use an Iterator to cycle through a collection
// in the forward direction.
//
// Use a ListIterator to cycle through a collection
// in the reverse direction.

import java.util.*;
```

```java
// This class encapsulates a name and a telephone number.
class PhoneEntry {
  String name;
  String number;

  PhoneEntry(String n, String num) {
    name = n;
    number = num;
  }
}

// Demonstrate Iterator and ListIterator.
class ItrDemo {

  public static void main(String args[]) {
    LinkedList<PhoneEntry> phonelist =
      new LinkedList<PhoneEntry>();

    phonelist.add(new PhoneEntry("Eric", "555-3456"));
    phonelist.add(new PhoneEntry("Cliff", "555-3976"));
    phonelist.add(new PhoneEntry("Ken", "555-1010"));

    // Use an Iterator to show the list.
    Iterator<PhoneEntry> itr = phonelist.iterator();

    PhoneEntry pe;
    System.out.println("Iterate through the list in " +
                       "the forward direction:");
    while(itr.hasNext()) {
      pe = itr.next();
      System.out.println(pe.name + ": " + pe.number);
    }

    System.out.println();

    // Use a ListIterator to show the list in reverse.
    ListIterator<PhoneEntry> litr =
      phonelist.listIterator(phonelist.size());

    System.out.println("Iterate through the list in " +
                       "the reverse direction:");
    while(litr.hasPrevious()) {
      pe = litr.previous();
      System.out.println(pe.name + ": " + pe.number);
    }
  }
}
```

The output is shown here:

```
Iterate through the list in the forward direction:
Eric: 555-3456
Cliff: 555-3976
Ken: 555-1010

Iterate through the list in the reverse direction:
Ken: 555-1010
Cliff: 555-3976
Eric: 555-3456
```

Options and Alternatives

The for-each style **for** loop offers an alternative to an iterator in situations in which you won't be modifying the contents of a collection or obtaining elements in reverse order. The for-each **for** works with any collection because the **for** can cycle through any object that implements the **Iterable** interface. Because all of the collection classes implement this interface, they can all be iterated by the **for**.

Although the preceding example used an **Iterator** to cycle through the phone list in the forward direction, this was only for the sake of illustration. When using a **Linkedlist** (or any collection that implements the **List** interface), you can use a **ListIterator** to cycle through the collection in either direction. For example, the portion of the preceding program that displays the list in the forward direction can be rewritten as shown here to use **ListIterator**.

```
// Use a ListIterator to cycle through the list in the forward direction.
ListIterator<PhoneEntry> itr = phonelist.listIterator();

PhoneEntry pe;
System.out.println("Iterate through the list in " +
                   "the forward direction:");
while(itr.hasNext()) {
  pe = itr.next();
  System.out.println(pe.name + ": " + pe.number);
}
```

This code is functionally equivalent to the same sequence in the example. The only difference is that a **ListIterator** rather than an **Iterator** is used.

ListIterator also specifies the **set( )** method, which can be used to change the value of an item obtained by calling **next( )** or **previous( )**. It is shown here:

void set(E *obj*)

Here, *obj* replaces the element last iterated. The **set( )** method makes it possible to update the value of a list while it is being iterated.

Create a Queue or a Stack Using Deque

Key Ingredients	
Classes and Interfaces	**Methods**
java.util.Collection	boolean isEmpty( )
java.util.Deque<E>	boolean add(E *obj*)
	E pop( )
	void push(E *obj*)
	E remove( )
java.util.ArrayDeque<E>	

Beginning with Java 6, the Collections Framework has provided the **Deque** interface, which defines the characteristics of a double-ended queue. It inherits the **Queue** interface, which specifies the methods for a single-ended queue (which is a queue in which elements are added to or removed from only one end). To **Queue**, **Deque** adds methods that enable elements to be added to or removed from either end. This enables implementations of **Deque** to be used as either first-in, first-out (FIFO) queues or last-in, first-out (LIFO) stacks. This recipe shows the process.

    Deque is implemented by **LinkedList** and **ArrayDeque**. This recipe uses **ArrayDeque** to demonstrate the creation of queues and stacks, but the general procedure applies to any implementation of **Deque**.

NOTE   *Although **java.util.Stack** is still provided by Java, it is a legacy class that has been superceded by implementations of **Deque**. Its use in new code should be avoided. Instead, **ArrayDeque** or **LinkedList** should be used when a stack is needed.*

Step-by-Step

Here is one way to implement a FIFO queue based on **ArrayDeque**:

1. Create an **ArrayDeque,** specifying the type of objects that will be stored.
2. Add objects to the tail of the queue by calling **add( )**.
3. Remove objects from the head of the queue by calling **remove( )**.
4. You can determine if the queue is empty by calling **isEmpty( )**. This is useful when removing objects from the queue.

Here is one way to implement a LIFO stack based on **ArrayDeque**:

1. Create an **ArrayDeque**, specifying the type of objects that will be stored.
2. Add objects to the top of the stack by calling **push( )**.

3. Remove objects from the top of the stack by calling **pop( )**.

4. You can determine if the stack is empty by calling **isEmpty( )**. This is useful when popping objects from the stack.

Discussion

ArrayDeque is a concrete implementation of **Deque** that supports a dynamic array. Thus, it grows as needed as elements are added. **ArrayDeque** supports three constructors. The one used by the recipes is shown here:

ArrayDeque( )

It creates an **ArrayDeque** with an initial capacity of 16. Of course, this collection will grow as needed as elements are added. A description of **ArrayDeque**'s other constructors is found in the *Collections Overview* presented near the start of this chapter.

Using a **Deque**, there are various ways in which you can implement a queue. The approach used by this recipe relies on **add( )** and **remove( )**. They are shown here:

boolean add(E *obj*)
E remove( )

The **add( )** method adds *obj* to the end of the queue. It returns true if the element has been added and false if it cannot be added for some reason. It will throw an **IllegalSateException** if an attempt is made to add an element to a full, capacity-restricted queue. (**ArrayDeque** creates a dynamic array and *is not* capacity-restricted.) The **remove( )** method returns the element that is at the head of the queue. It also removes the element from the queue. It throws **NoSuchElementException** if the queue is empty.

There are also a number of ways to implement a stack using **Deque**. The approach used by this recipe employs **push( )** and **pop( )**. They are shown here:

void push(E *obj*)
E pop( )

The **push( )** method adds an element to the top of the stack. It will throw an **IllegalSateException** if an attempt is made to add an element to a full, capacity-restricted stack. The **pop( )** method removes and returns the element on the top of the stack. It will throw a **NoSuchElementException** if the stack is empty.

An easy way to avoid generating a **NoSuchElementException** when removing objects from a stack or queue is to call the **isEmpty( )** method. This method is specified by **Collection** and therefore is available to all collections.

NOTE *Capacity-restricted implementations of **Deque** are allowed. In a capacity-restricted **Deque**, the **add( )** and **push( )** methods will throw an **IllegalStateException** if the collection is full. Neither of the two **Deque** implementations provided by **java.util**, **ArrayDeque** or **LinkedList**, are capacity-restricted.*

Example

The following example shows how to implement a stack and a queue by using **Deque**. It uses the **ArrayDeque** collection, but the program will also work if you substitute a **LinkedList** because both implement the **Deque** interface.

```java
// Create a Stack and Queue using ArrayDeque.

import java.util.*;

class SQDemo {
  public static void main(String args[]) {

    // Create two ArrayDeques. One for the stack
    // and one for the queue.
    ArrayDeque<String> stack = new ArrayDeque<String>();
    ArrayDeque<String> queue = new ArrayDeque<String>();

    // Demonstrate the stack.
    System.out.println("Pushing A");
    stack.push("A");
    System.out.println("Pushing B");
    stack.push("B");
    System.out.println("Pushing C");
    stack.push("C");
    System.out.println("Pushing D");
    stack.push("D");

    System.out.print("Popping the stack: ");

    while(!stack.isEmpty())
      System.out.print(stack.pop() + " ");

    System.out.println("\n");

    // Demonstrate the queue.
    System.out.println("Adding A");
    queue.add("A");
    System.out.println("Adding B");
    queue.add("B");
    System.out.println("Adding C");
    queue.add("C");
    System.out.println("Adding D");
    queue.add("D");

    System.out.print("Consuming the queue: ");

    while(!queue.isEmpty())
      System.out.print(queue.remove() + " ");

    System.out.println();
  }
}
```

The output is shown here:

```
Pushing A
Pushing B
Pushing C
Pushing D
Popping the stack: D C B A

Adding A
Adding B
Adding C
Adding D
Consuming the queue: A B C D
```

Options and Alternatives

As mentioned, there are many ways to implement a stack or a queue when using **Deque**. One alternative utilizes a second set of methods that add or remove elements from a queue or stack. Unlike **add( )** and **push( )**, which will throw an exception when an element can't be added to a capacity-restricted **Deque**, or **remove( )** and **pop( )**, which throw an exception when an attempt is made to obtain an element from an empty **Deque**, the alternative methods do not. Instead, they return values that indicate their success or failure. The alternative methods for queue-like behavior are shown here:

boolean offerLast(E *obj*)	Adds *obj* to the end of the queue. Returns **true** if successful and **false** otherwise.
E poll( )	Returns the next element in the queue or **null** if the queue is empty.

The alternative methods for stack-like behavior are

boolean offerFirst(E *obj*)	Adds *obj* to the head of the stack. Returns **true** if successful and **false** otherwise.
E poll( )	Returns the next element in the stack or **null** if the stack is empty.

Notice that **poll( )** can be used with both stacks and queues because both remove the next element from the head of the queue. The difference between a stack and a queue is where elements are added.

For example, here is another way to write the portion of the example that puts items on the stack and then removes them:

```
System.out.println("Pushing A");
stack.offerFirst("A");
System.out.println("Pushing B");
stack.offerFirst("B");
```

```
System.out.println("Pushing C");
stack.offerFirst("C");
System.out.println("Pushing D");
stack.offerFirst("D");

System.out.print("Popping the stack: ");
String tmp;
while((tmp = stack.poll()) != null)
  System.out.print(tmp + " ");
```

Notice the loop that pops elements from the stack. Because **poll( )** returns **null** when there are no more elements, its return value can be used to control the **while** loop. (Personally, I prefer using **push( )** and **pop( )** because they are the traditional names for stack operations and use **isEmpty( )** to prevent a stack underrun. Of course, some situations will benefit from **poll( )** because it does not throw an exception when the stack is empty.)

Another way to avoid generating a **NoSuchElementException** when calling **remove( )** or **pop( )** is to use **peek( )**. It is shown here:

E peek( )

This method returns *but does not remove* the element at the head of the queue, which is the next element that will be returned by **remove( )** or **pop( )**. (Remember, the difference between a stack and queue is where elements are added, not where they are removed.) The **peek ( )** method will return **null** if the collection is empty. Thus, you can use **peek( )** to determine if the queue or stack is empty.

Reverse, Rotate, and Shuffle a List

Key Ingredients	
Classes and Interfaces	**Methods**
java.util.Collections	static void reverse(List<?> *col*)
	static void rotate(List<?> *col*, int *n*)
	static void shuffle(List<?> *col*)

This recipe demonstrates the use of three related algorithms defined by the **Collections** class: **reverse( )**, **rotate( )**, and **shuffle( )**. They relate to each other because each changes the order of the collection to which it is applied. The **reverse( )** algorithm reverses a list, **rotate( )** rotates a list (that is, it takes an element off one end of a list and puts it on the other), and **shuffle( )** randomizes the order of the elements. They can be applied only to collections that implement the **List** interface.

Step-by-Step

To reverse, rotate, or shuffle a collection, follow these steps:

1. The collection being affected must implement the **List** interface.
2. After all objects have been stored in the list, call **Collections.reverse( )** to reverse the collection, **Collections.rotate( )** to rotate the collection, or **Collections.shuffle( )** to randomize the collection.

Discussion

To reverse a list, use the **reverse( )** algorithm. It is shown here:

static void reverse(List<?> *col*)

It reverses the collection passed to *col*.
    To rotate a list, use the **rotate( )** algorithm. It is shown here:

static void rotate(List<?> *col*, int *n*)

It rotates the collection passed to *col* by *n* places to the right. To rotate left, use a negative value for *n*.
    To randomize the order of the elements within a list, use **shuffle( )**. It has two forms. The one used here is

static void shuffle(List<?> *col*)

It randomizes the order of the collection passed to *col*.

Example

The following example shows the effects of **reverse( )**, **rotate( )**, and **shuffle( )**.

```
// Use reverse(), rotate(), and shuffle().

import java.util.*;

class RRSDemo {

  public static void main(String args[]) {

    LinkedList<Character> ll = new LinkedList<Character>();

    // Add A through F to the list.
    for(char n='A'; n <= 'F'; n++)
      ll.add(n);

    // Display the list before shuffling.
    System.out.println("Here is the original list: ");
    for(Character x : ll)
      System.out.print(x + " ");
    System.out.println("\n");
```

```
    // Reverse the list.
    Collections.reverse(ll);

    // Display the reversed list.
    System.out.println("Here is the reversed list: ");
    for(Character x : ll)
      System.out.print(x + " ");
    System.out.println("\n");

    // Rotate the list.
    Collections.rotate(ll, 2);

    // Display the rotated list.
    System.out.println("Here is the list after rotating " +
                       "right 2 places: ");
    for(Character x : ll)
      System.out.print(x + " ");
    System.out.println("\n");

    // Randomize the list.
    Collections.shuffle(ll);

    // Display the randomized list.
    System.out.println("Here is the randomized list:");
    for(Character x : ll)
      System.out.print(x + " ");
    System.out.println("\n");
  }
}
```

The output is shown here:

```
Here is the original list:
A B C D E F

Here is the reversed list:
F E D C B A

Here is the list after rotating right 2 places:
B A F E D C

Here is the randomized list:
F C B E D A
```

Options and Alternatives

There is a second form of **shuffle( )** that lets you specify a random number generator. This version is shown here:

```
static void shuffle(List<?> col, Random randGen)
```

Here, *randGen* is the random number generator that will be used to randomize the list. It must be an instance of **Random**, which is defined in **java.lang**.

Sort and Search a List

Key Ingredients	
Classes and Interfaces	**Methods**

java.util.Collections	static <T>
	    int binarySearch(List<? extends
	        Comparable<? super T>> *col*, T *val*)
	static <T extends Comparable<? super T>>
	    void sort(List<T> *col*)

java.util.List<E>	E get(int *idx*)

Most of the collections provided by **java.util** do not store elements in sorted order. The exception to this is **TreeSet**, which maintains a sorted tree. However, by using the **sort( )** algorithm provided by **Collections**, you can sort any collection that implements the **List** interface. Once you have sorted the collection, you can perform very fast searches on it by calling **binarySearch( )**, which is another algorithm defined by **Collections**. This recipe shows the basic procedure.

Step-by-Step

To sort a collection, follow these steps:

1. The collection being sorted must implement the **List** interface. Furthermore, the type of objects stored in the collection must implement the **Comparable** interface.
2. After all objects have been stored in the list, call **Collections.sort( )** to sort the collection.

To perform a fast search of a sorted collection, follow these steps:

1. The collection being searched must implement the **List** interface and be sorted as described.
2. Call **Collections.binarySearch( )** to find an element.
3. Using the index returned by **binarySearch( )**, you can obtain the element by calling **get( )**, which is specified by **List**.

Discussion

To sort a list, use the **sort( )** algorithm defined by **Collections**. It has two versions. The one used by the recipe is shown here:

    static <T extends Comparable<? super T>> void sort(List<T> *col*)

It sorts the collection passed to *col*. The collection must implement the **List** interface and its elements must implement the **Comparable** interface. When this method returns, *col* is in sorted order. It is important to understand that the collection remains sorted only until it is modified in some way that affects the ordering. For example, adding an element to the end of a sorted collection will usually cause the collection to become unsorted (unless that element actually is the last element in sorted order). Therefore, sorting a collection does not mean that it remains sorted.

Once a list has been sorted, it can be searched by calling **binarySearch( )**, also defined by **Collections**. It has two versions. The one used by the recipe is shown here:

static <T> int binarySearch(List<? extends Comparable<? super T>> *col*, T *val*)

The list to search is passed via *col*. The object to search for is passed to *val*. The method returns the index at which the first occurrence of the item is found, or a negative value if *val* is not in the list. (The absolute value of a negative return value is the index at which the item should be inserted into the list to keep the list sorted.)

You can obtain the object at the index returned by **binarySearch( )** by calling **get( )**. It is shown here:

E get(int *idx*)

It returns a reference to the specified element.

Example

The following example shows how to sort a list and then search the sorted list.

```
// Sort and Search a LinkedList.

import java.util.*;

class SortAndSearchDemo {

  public static void main(String args[]) {
    LinkedList<Character> ll = new LinkedList<Character>();

    // Add A through Z to the list.
    for(char n='A'; n <= 'Z'; n++)
      ll.add(n);

    // Randomize the list.
    Collections.shuffle(ll);

    // Display the randomized list.
    System.out.println("Here is the unsorted list:");

    for(Character x : ll)
      System.out.print(x + " ");
    System.out.println("\n");

    // Sort the list.
    Collections.sort(ll);
```

```
   // Display the sorted list.
   System.out.println("Here is the sorted list:");

   for(Character x : ll)
     System.out.print(x + " ");
   System.out.println("\n");

   // Search for an element.
   System.out.println("Searching for F.");
   int i = Collections.binarySearch(ll, 'F');

   if(i >= 0) {
     System.out.println("Found at index " + i);
     System.out.println("Object is " + ll.get(i));
   }
  }
}
```

The output is shown here:

```
Here is the unsorted list:
Y U O F P I X D R B Z V C G L S N K M E W J H Q T A

Here is the sorted list:
A B C D E F G H I J K L M N O P Q R S T U V W X Y Z

Searching for F.
Found at index 5
Object is F
```

Options and Alternatives

As a general rule, if your application requires a sorted collection, the **TreeSet** class is a better choice than sorting a list. As elements are added to a **TreeSet**, they are automatically inserted into the tree in order. Thus, a **TreeSet** always contains a sorted collection. By contrast, after a list is sorted, it will remain sorted only until the next out-of-order element is added. However, a **TreeSet** does not allow duplicate elements. Therefore, for applications that require a sorted collection that contains duplicates, using **Collections.sort( )** may be your best option.

You can specify a comparator when calling **sort( )** or **binarySearch( )** that determines how the elements in the list are compared. This enables you to sort or search in a manner other than natural order. It also lets you sort or search lists that store objects that don't implement **Comparable**. These versions are shown here:

static <T> int binarySearch(List<? extends T>> *col*, T *val*,
                            Comparator<? super T> *comp*)
static<T> void sort(List<T> *col*, Comparator<? super T> *comp*)

For a description of using a comparator see *Use a **Comparator** with a Collection*.

Create a Checked Collection

Key Ingredients	
Classes	**Methods**

java.util.Collections	static <E> Collection<E>
	    checkedCollection(Collection<E> *col*,
	        Class<E> *t*)

The entire Collections Framework was converted to generics with the release of Java 5. Thus, it provides a type-safe means of storing and retrieving objects. However, it is possible to bypass this type safety in a variety of ways. For example, legacy code that uses a collection declared as a raw type (one that does not specify a type argument) can add any type of object to the collection. If your modern, generic code must interface to such legacy code, then it is possible that an invalid object might be contained in the collection because the legacy code will not prevent it. Unfortunately, eventually (perhaps long after the invalid element was added) your code will operate on that invalid element and this will cause a **ClassCastException**.

To prevent this possibility, the **Collections** class offers several methods that enable you to create *checked collections.* These collections create what Java's API documentation refers to as a "dynamically typesafe view" of a collection. This view is a reference to the collection that monitors insertions into the collection for type compatibility *at runtime.* An attempt to insert an incompatible element will cause a **ClassCastException**. Therefore, the error will occur immediately, at the time of insertion, and not later on in the program. This means that the rest of your program can assume that the collection is uncorrupted.

To create a checked collection, you will use one of the **checked...** methods supplied by **Collections**. This recipe uses **checkedCollection( )**, but the same basic procedure applies to the other **checked...** methods.

Step-by-Step

To create a checked collection, follow these steps:

1. Create the collection that you want to be monitored for the insertion of invalid elements.

2. Create a type-safe view of the collection by calling **checkedCollection( )**.

3. Perform all operations that add an element to the collection through the type-safe reference.

Discussion

The **Collections** class defines four methods that return checked views of a collection. The one used by this recipe is **checkedCollection( )**. It is shown here:

```
static <E> Collection<E>
    checkedCollection(Collection<E> col, Class<E> t)
```

To create a checked collection, pass a reference to the collection to *col* and specify the type of elements in *t*. For example, if **Integer** is the type of elements stored in the collection, then pass *t* the class literal **Integer.class**. The method returns a runtime type-safe view of *col*. Any attempt to insert an incompatible element into the checked collection will cause a **ClassCastException**.

Example

The following example demonstrates how a checked collection prevents an invalid element from being added to a collection.

```
// Create and demonstrate a checked collection.
//
// Note: This example intentionally mixes generic and raw
// types to demonstrate the value of checked collections.
// Normally, you should avoid the use of raw types.

import java.util.*;

class CheckedDemo {

  public static void main(String args[]) {
    // Create a LinkedList for strings.
    LinkedList<String> llStr = new LinkedList<String>();

    // Create a checked List reference and assign llStr to it.
    Collection<String> chkCol =
        Collections.checkedCollection(llStr, String.class);

    // To see the difference that a checked list makes,
    // comment-out the preceding line and un-comment
    // the following line. It assigns llStr to chkCol
    // without first wrapping it in a checked collection.
//     Collection<String> chkCol = llStr;

    // Add some strings to the list.
    chkCol.add("Alpha");
    chkCol.add("Beta");
    chkCol.add("Gamma");

    System.out.println("Here is the list:");

    for(String x : chkCol)
      System.out.print(x + " ");
    System.out.println("\n");

    // To demonstrate the checked list, first
    // create a raw List reference.
    Collection rawCol;

    // Next, assign chkCol, which is a List<string> reference,
    // to the raw reference.
    rawCol = chkCol;
```

```
      // Now, add an Integer object to the list.
      // This compiles because a raw List can hold any
      // type of object (because type-safety is bypassed).
      // However, at runtime, a ClassCastException is
      // generated because the underlying list is wrapped
      // in a checked list.
      rawCol.add(new Integer(23));

      // Display the list.
      // If chkCol is NOT wrapped in a checked list, then
      // the type mismatch will not be found until this
      // loop executes.
      for(String x : chkCol)
        System.out.print(x + " ");
      System.out.println("\n");
  }
}
```

The output from the program is shown here:

```
Here is the list:
Alpha Beta Gamma

Exception in thread "main" java.lang.ClassCastException:
Attempt to insert class java.lang.Integer element into collection with
element type class java.lang.String
  at java.util.Collections$CheckedCollection.typeCheck(Collections.java:2206)
  at java.util.Collections$CheckedCollection.add(Collections.java:2240)
  at CheckedDemo.main(CheckedDemo.java:50)
```

Notice that the exception is found when the attempt is made to insert an **Integer** object into the list, which is expecting objects of type **String**.

Here is how the program works. First, a **LinkedList** called **llStr** is created that holds **String** objects. The program then creates a checked collection called **chkCol**, adds a few strings to the collection, and displays them. Next, a raw (i.e., untyped) **Collection** reference called **rawCol** is created and then **chkCol** is assigned to it. Therefore, after this step, **rawCol** refers to the checked collection **chkCol**. This step by itself is completely legal. Next, an attempt is made to add an **Integer** to **rawCol**. Normally this too would be legal (although highly suspect) because any untyped (i.e., raw) collection can hold any type of object. However, because **rawCol** refers to a checked collection, this causes a **ClassCastException** to be thrown, thus preventing **chkCol** from containing an invalid element.

If a checked collection had not been used, then the invalid element would not have caused an exception until the attempt was made to display the list after the **Integer** had been inserted. To confirm this for yourself, comment out this line:

```
Collection<String> chkCol =
    Collections.checkedCollection(llStr, String.class);
```

Next, remove the comment from this line:

```
//    Collection<String> chkCol = llStr;
```

Then, recompile and run the program. The exception occurs when the integer element is encountered by the last **for** loop, which is after it has been added to the list.

Options and Alternatives

In addition to **checkedCollection( )**, **Collections** provides several other methods that return checked views tailored for specific types of collections. They are shown here:

static <E> List<E> checkedList(List<E> col, Class<E> t)	Returns a runtime type-safe view of a **List**.
static <E> List<E> checkedSet(Set<E> col, Class<E> t)	Returns a runtime type-safe view of a **Set**.

static <E> SortedSet<E>
    checkedSortedSet(SortedSet<E> col,
        Class<E> t)
	Returns a runtime type-safe view of a **SortedSet**.

For each method, an attempt to insert an incompatible element will cause a **ClassCastException**. You should use one of these methods when you need to call methods that are specific to a **List**, **Set**, or **SortedSet**.

Collections also defines the following methods that let you obtain type-safe views of a map:

static <K, V> Map<K, V>
    checkedMap(Map<K, V> c,
        Class<K> keyT,
        Class<V> valueT)
	Returns a runtime type-safe view of a **Map**.

static <K, V> SortedMap<K, V>
    checkedSortedMap(SortedMap<K, V> c,
        Class<K> keyT,
        Class<V> valueT)
	Returns a runtime type-safe view of a **SortedMap**.

For both methods, an attempt to insert an incompatible entry will cause a **ClassCastException**.

Create a Synchronized Collection

Key Ingredients	
Classes	**Methods**
java.util.Collections	static <T> Collection<T> synchronizedCollection(Collection<T> col)

The collection classes provided by the Collections Framework are not synchronized. If you need a thread-safe collection, then you will need to use one of the **synchronized...** methods defined by **Collections**. A synchronized collection is required in those cases in which one thread will be (or, at least, might be) modifying a collection when another thread is also accessing the collection. This recipe shows how to create a synchronized collection view using **synchronizedCollection( )**, but the same basic procedure applies to the other **synchronized...** methods.

Step-by-Step

To create a synchronized view of a collection involves these steps:

1. Create the collection that will be synchronized.
2. Obtain a synchronized view of the collection by calling the **synchronizedCollection( )** method.
3. Operate on the collection through the synchronized view.

Discussion

If multiple threads will be using a collection, then it is necessary for each thread to operate on a synchronized view of that collection. If an attempt is made to use an unsynchronized collection by multiple threads, then (in addition to other errors) it is possible that a **ConcurrentModificationException** will be thrown. This can happen even when one thread only reads, but does not modify, the collection. For example, if the collection is in the process of being iterated by one thread and a second thread changes the collection, then a **ConcurrentModificationException** will occur. To avoid this, and other errors associated with non-synchronized collections, you must obtain and exclusively use a synchronized view of the collection.

To obtain a synchronized (i.e., thread-safe) view of a collection, use one of the four **synchronized...** methods defined by the **Collections** class. The version used by this recipe is **synchronizedCollection( )**. It is shown here:

static <T> Collection<T> synchronizedCollection(Collection<T> *col*)

It returns a thread-safe view of the collection passed to *col*. This view can be safely used in a multithreaded environment. However, *all access* (including read-only access) to the collection must take place through the returned reference.

Example

The following example demonstrates the use of a synchronized collection.

```
// Create and demonstrate a synchronized collection.

import java.util.*;

// Create a second thread of execution that adds
// an element to the collection that it is passed.
// Then iterate through the collection.
class MyThread implements Runnable {
  Thread t;
```

```
    Collection<String> col;

    MyThread(Collection<String> c) {
      col = c;

      t = new Thread(this, "Second Thread");
      t.start();
    }

    public void run() {

      try {
        Thread.sleep(100); // let the main thread run

        col.add("Omega"); // add another element

        // Iterate through the elements.
        synchronized(col) {
          for(String str : col) {
            System.out.println("Second thread: " + str);

            // Let the main thread run, if it can.
            Thread.sleep(500);
          }
        }

      } catch(InterruptedException exc) {
        System.out.println("Second thread interrupted.");
      }
    }
}

// Demonstrate a synchronized collection.
class SyncDemo {

  public static void main(String args[]) {

    // Create a TreeSet for strings.
    TreeSet<String> tsStr = new TreeSet<String>();

    // Create a synchronized reference and assign it to syncCol.
    Collection<String> syncCol =
        Collections.synchronizedCollection(tsStr);

    // To see the difference that a synchronized collection
    // makes, comment-out the preceding line and un-comment
    // the following line. It assigns tsStr to syncCol
    // without first wrapping it in a synchronized collection.
//    Collection<String> syncCol = tsStr;

    // Add some strings to the set.
    syncCol.add("Gamma");
    syncCol.add("Beta");
    syncCol.add("Alpha");
```

```
   // Start the second thread.
   new MyThread(syncCol);

   try {

     synchronized(syncCol) {
       for(String str : syncCol) {
         System.out.println("Main thread: " + str);

         // Let the second thread run, if it can.
         Thread.sleep(500);
       }
     }
   } catch(InterruptedException exc) {
     System.out.println("Main thread interrupted.");
   }
 }
}
```

The output produced by this program is shown here.

```
Main thread: Alpha
Main thread: Beta
Main thread: Gamma
Second thread: Alpha
Second thread: Beta
Second thread: Gamma
Second thread: Omega
```

Here is how the program works. **SyncDemo** begins by creating a **TreeSet** called **tsStr**. This set is then wrapped in a synchronized collection called **syncCol** and three elements are added to it. Next, **main( )** starts a second thread of execution, which is defined by **MyThread**. The **MyThread** constructor is passed a reference to **syncCol**. This thread begins by sleeping for a short period of time, which lets the main thread resume running. **MyThread** then adds another element to the collection and then begins iterating through the collection. After creating **MyThread**, the main thread starts iterating over the set, delaying 500 milliseconds between iterations. This delay enables the second thread to run, if it can. However, because **syncCol** is synchronized, the second thread can't run until the main thread finishes. Therefore the iteration of the elements in **main( )** finishes before **MyThread** adds another element to the set, thus avoiding a **ConcurrentModificationException**.

To prove the necessity of using a synchronized collection when multithreading, try this experiment. In the example, comment out these lines:

```
Collection<String> syncCol =
    Collections.synchronizedCollection(tsStr);
```

Then, remove the comment from this line:

```
//    Collection<String> syncCol = tsStr;
```

Now, recompile and run the program. Because **syncCol** is no longer synchronized, both the main thread and **MyThread** can access it simultaneously. This results in a **ConcurrentModificationException** when **MyThread** attempts to add an element to it.

Options and Alternatives

In addition to **synchronizedCollection( )**, **Collections** provides several other methods that return synchronized views tailored for specific types of collections. They are shown here:

static <T> List<T> synchronizedList(List<T> *col*)	Returns a thread-safe list backed by *col*.
static <T> Set<T> synchronizedSet(Set<T> *col*)	Returns a thread-safe set backed by *col*.
static <T> SortedSet<T> synchronizedSortedSet(SortedSet<T> *col*)	Returns a thread-safe sorted set backed by *col*.

Collections also supplies the following methods that return synchronized views of maps:

static <K, V> Map<K, V> synchronizedMap(Map<K, V> *map*)	Returns a thread-safe map backed by *map*.

static <K, V> SortedMap<K, V>
    synchronizedSortedMap(
        SortedMap<K, V> *map*)
	Returns a thread-safe sorted map backed by *map*.

Create an Immutable Collection

Key Ingredients	
Classes	**Methods**

java.util.Collections	static <T> Collection<T>
	    unmodifiableCollection(
	        Collection<? extends T> *col*)

Collections supplies a set of methods that create an *immutable view* of a collection. These methods begin with the name **unmodifiable**. The underlying collection cannot be changed through such a view. This is useful in cases in which you want to ensure that a collection will not be modified, such as when it is passed to third-party code.

Step-by-Step

To create an immutable view of a collection involves these steps:

1. Create a collection that will be read-only.
2. Obtain an immutable view of the collection by calling the **unmodifiableCollection( )** method.
3. Operate on the collection through the read-only view.

Discussion

To create an immutable view of a collection, use one of the **unmodifiable...** methods defined by the **Collections** class. It defines four methods that return immutable views of a collection. The one used by this recipe is **unmodifiableCollection( )**. It is shown here.

static <T> Collection<T> unmodifiableCollection(Collection<? extends T> *col*)

It returns a reference to a read-only view of the collection passed to *col*. This reference can then be passed to any code that is not allowed to modify the collection. Any attempt to modify the collection through this reference will result in an **UnsupportedOperationException**.

Example

The following example demonstrates the use of an immutable collection.

```
// Create and demonstrate an immutable collection.

import java.util.*;

class NoModDemo {

  public static void main(String args[]) {
    // Create a ArrayList for strings.
    ArrayList<Character> list = new ArrayList<Character>();

    // Add an element.
    list.add('X');

    System.out.println("Element added to list: " + list.get(0));

    // Now, create an immutable view of list.
    Collection<Character> immutableCol =
        Collections.unmodifiableCollection(list);

    // Try to add another element.
    // This won't work and will cause an exception.
    immutableCol.add('Y');
  }
}
```

The output is shown here. Notice that it throws an **UnsupportedOperationException** when an attempt is made to modify the collection.

```
Element added to list: X
Exception in thread "main" java.lang.UnsupportedOperationException
    at java.util.Collections$UnmodifiableCollection.add(Collections.java:1018)
    at NoModDemo.main(NoModDemo.java:24)
```

Options and Alternatives

In addition to **unmodifiableCollection( )**, **Collections** provides several other methods that return immutable views tailored for specific types of collections. They are shown here:

static <T> List<T> unmodifiableList(List<? extends T> *col*)	Returns an unmodifiable list backed by *col*.
static <T> Set<T> unmodifiableSet(Set<? extends T> *col*)	Returns an unmodifiable set backed by *col*.
static <T> SortedSet<T> unmodifiableSortedSet(SortedSet<T> *col*)	Returns an unmodifiable sorted set backed by *col*.

Collections also supplies the following methods that return immutable views of maps:

static <K, V> Map<K, V>
    unmodifiableMap(
        Map<? extends K, ? extends V> *map*)
	Returns an unmodifiable map backed by *map*.

static <K, V> SortedMap<K, V>
    unmodifiableSortedMap(
        SortedMap<K, ? extends V> *map*)
	Returns an unmodifiable sorted map backed by *map*.

Basic Map Techniques

Key Ingredients	
Classes and Interfaces	**Methods**
java.util.Map	void clear( ) boolean containsKey(Object *k*) boolean containsValue(Object *v*) Set<Map.Entry<K, V>> entrySet( ) V get(Object *k*) boolean isEmpty( ) Set<K> KeySet() V put(K *k*, V *v*) void putAll(Map<? extends K, ? extends V> *m*) V remove(Object *k*) int size( ) Collection<V> values( )
java.util.TreeMap	

As explained in the overview, maps are not, technically speaking, collections because they do not implement the **Collection** interface. However, maps are part of the Collections Framework. Maps store key/value pairs, and all keys must be unique. All maps implement the **Map** interface. Thus, all maps share a common functionality. For example, all maps allow you to add a key/value pair to a map or obtain a value, given its key. This recipe demonstrates this common functionality by showing how to

- Add a key/value pair to a map
- Obtain a value given a key
- Determine the size of a map
- Obtain an entry set of the map's elements
- Cycle through a map's entries using the entry set
- Obtain a collection of the keys and of the values in a map
- Remove a key/value pair from a map
- Change the value associated with a key
- Determine if a map is empty

This recipe uses **TreeMap**, which is a concrete implementation of **Map**, but only those methods defined by **Map** are used. Thus, the same general principles can be applied to any map.

Step-by-Step

To create and use a map involves these steps:

1. Create an instance of the desired map. In this recipe, **TreeMap** is used, but any other map could have been selected.
2. Perform various operations on the map by using the methods defined by **Map** as described by the following steps.
3. Add entries to the map by calling **put( )** or **putAll( )**.
4. Obtain the number of entries in a map by calling **size( )**.
5. Determine if a map contains a specific key by calling **containsKey( )**. Determine if a map contains a specific value by calling **containsValue( )**.
6. Determine if a map is empty (i.e., contains no entries) by calling **isEmpty( )**.
7. Obtain a set of the entries in the map by calling **entrySet( )**.
8. Use the entry set obtained from **entrySet( )** to cycle through the entries in the map.
9. Obtain a value given its key by calling **get( )**.
10. Obtain a set of the keys in the map by calling **keySet( )**. Obtain a set of the values by calling **values( )**.
11. Remove entries from the map by calling **remove( )**.
12. Remove all entries from the map by calling **clear( )**.

Discussion

Map is a generic interface that is defined as shown here:

interface Map<K, V>

Here, **K** defines the type of the keys in the map and **V** defines the type of the values. It is permissible for both **K** and **V** to be of the same type.

The methods defined by **Map** are shown in Table 5-8, which is in *Collections Overview* earlier in this chapter. Here is a brief description of their operation.

Objects are added to a map by calling **put( )**. Notice that **put( )** takes arguments of types **K** and **V**. This means that entries added to a map must be compatible with the type of data expected by the map. You can add the entire contents of one map to another by calling **putAll( )**. Of course, the two maps must be compatible.

You can remove an entry by using **remove( )**. To empty a map, call **clear( )**.

You can determine whether a map contains a specific key by calling **containsKey( )**. You can determine whether a map contains a specific value by calling **containsValue( )**. You can determine when a map is empty by calling **isEmpty( )**. The number of elements currently held in a map is returned by **size( )**.

As explained in the overview, maps do not implement the **Iterable** interface and, therefore, do not support iterators. However, you can still cycle through the contents of a map by first obtaining a *collection view* of the map. There are three types of collection views that are available:

- A set of the entries in the map
- A set of the keys in the map
- A collection of the values in the map

A set of the entries in the map is obtained by calling **entrySet( )**. It returns a **Set** collection that contains the entries. Each entry is held in an object of type **Map.Entry**. Given a **Map.Entry** object, you can obtain the key by calling **getKey( )**. To obtain the value, call **getValue( )**. Using the entry set, it is easy to cycle through a map, obtaining each entry in turn.

The other two collection-views let you deal with the keys and values separately. To obtain a **Set** of the keys in the map, call **keySet( )**. To obtain a **Collection** of the values, call **values( )**.

The example that follows uses a **TreeMap** to hold the map. See *Collections Overview* presented near the start of this chapter for a discussion of its constructors.

Example

The following example demonstrates the basic techniques used to create and use a map. It creates a map called **atomNums**, which links the names of elements with their atomic numbers. For example, Hydrogen has the atomic number of 1, Oxygen has the atomic number of 8, and so on.

```
// Demonstrate basic Map techniques.

import java.util.*;

class BasicMaps {
  public static void main(String args[]) {

    // Create a tree map.
    TreeMap<String, Integer> atomNums =
                    new TreeMap<String, Integer>();
```

```java
// Put entries into the map.
// Each entry consists of the name of an element
// and its atomic number. Thus, the key is the
// element's name and the value is its atomic number.
atomNums.put("Hydrogen", 1);
atomNums.put("Oxygen", 8);
atomNums.put("Iron", 26);
atomNums.put("Copper", 29);
atomNums.put("Silver", 47);
atomNums.put("Gold", 79);

System.out.println("The map contains these " +
                   atomNums.size() + " entries:");

// Get a set of the entries.
Set<Map.Entry<String, Integer>> set = atomNums.entrySet();

// Display the keys and values in the map.
for(Map.Entry<String, Integer> me : set) {
  System.out.print(me.getKey() + ", Atomic Number: ");
  System.out.println(me.getValue());
}

System.out.println();

// Add another map to atomNums.
TreeMap<String, Integer> atomNums2 =
                         new TreeMap<String, Integer>();

// Put elements into the map.
atomNums2.put("Zinc", 30);
atomNums2.put("Lead", 82);

// Insert atomNums2 into atomNums.
atomNums.putAll(atomNums2);

// Show the map after the additions.
set = atomNums.entrySet();
// Display the keys and values in the map.
System.out.println("The map now contains these " +
                   atomNums.size() + " entries:");
for(Map.Entry<String, Integer> me : set) {
  System.out.print(me.getKey() + ", Atomic Number: ");
  System.out.println(me.getValue());
}

System.out.println();

// Search for a key.
if(atomNums.containsKey("Gold"))
  System.out.println("Gold has an atomic number of " +
                     atomNums.get("Gold"));

// Search for a value.
if(atomNums.containsValue(82))
  System.out.println("The atomic number 82 is in the map.");
```

```
    System.out.println();

    // Remove an entry.
    if(atomNums.remove("Gold") != null)
      System.out.println("Gold has been removed.\n");
    else
      System.out.println("Entry not found.\n");

    // Display the key set after the removal of gold.
    Set<String> keys = atomNums.keySet();
    System.out.println("Here are the keys after removing gold:");
    for(String str : keys)
      System.out.println(str + " ");
    System.out.println();

    // Display the value set after the removal of gold.
    Collection<Integer> vals = atomNums.values();
    System.out.println("Here are the values after removing gold:");
    for(Integer n : vals)
      System.out.println(n + " ");
    System.out.println();

    // Clear the map.
    System.out.println("Clearing the map.");
    atomNums.clear();
    if(atomNums.isEmpty())
      System.out.println("The map is now empty.");
  }
}
```

The output is shown here:

```
The map contains these 6 entries:
Copper, Atomic Number: 29
Gold, Atomic Number: 79
Hydrogen, Atomic Number: 1
Iron, Atomic Number: 26
Oxygen, Atomic Number: 8
Silver, Atomic Number: 47

The map now contains these 8 entries:
Copper, Atomic Number: 29
Gold, Atomic Number: 79
Hydrogen, Atomic Number: 1
Iron, Atomic Number: 26
Lead, Atomic Number: 82
Oxygen, Atomic Number: 8
Silver, Atomic Number: 47
Zinc, Atomic Number: 30

Gold has an atomic number of 79
The atomic number 82 is in the map.

Gold has been removed.
```

```
Here are the keys after removing gold:
Copper
Hydrogen
Iron
Lead
Oxygen
Silver
Zinc

Here are the values after removing gold:
29
1
26
82
8
47
30

Clearing the map.
The map is now empty.
```

Options and Alternatives

Although **TreeMap** was used to demonstrate the basic map techniques, any map class could
have been used. For example, try substituting **HashMap** for **TreeMap** in the example. The
program will compile and run properly. The reason is, of course, because all maps implement
the **Map** interface, and only the methods defined by **Map** are used by the example.

When using a sorted map, such as **TreeMap**, you can specify a custom comparator in
the same way as you do with a sorted collection. See *Use a Comparator with a Collection*.

Convert a Properties List into a HashMap

Key Ingredients	
Classes and Interfaces	**Methods**
java.util.Properties	Object setProperty(String *k*, String *v*)
java.util.HashMap<K, V>	

Early versions of Java did not include the Collections Framework. Instead, an ad hoc group
of classes was supplied, such as **Vector**, **Properties**, and **Hashtable**. Although these classes
were adequate, they did not form a cohesive whole, and they were superceded by the
Collections Framework. However, these legacy classes are still supported by Java because
a substantial amount of code still relies on them. To help bridge the gap between the legacy
classes and the Collections Framework, the legacy classes were retrofitted for collections. For
example, **Vector** implements the **List** interface and **Hashtable** implements **Map**. This makes

it easy to convert a legacy class into a collection or map. One situation in which this is particularly useful is when working with properties that are stored in a **Properties** list.

Properties is a legacy class that stores keys and values. **Properties** is unique because each key and value is a string. **Properties** is a subclass of **Hashtable**. It was retrofitted to implement the **Map** interface. This makes it easy to convert a legacy **Properties** list into a map that is part of the Collections Framework. Because **Properties** uses a hash table for storage, it makes sense that it be converted to a **HashMap**. This recipe shows how.

Step-by-Step

To convert a **Properties** object into a **HashMap**, follow these steps:

1. Obtain a reference to the **Properties** object that you want to convert.
2. Create a **HashMap** that specifies **String** for both the keys and the values.
3. Pass the **Properties** object to the **HashMap** constructor. To do this, you must cast the **Properties** reference to **Map**.

Discussion

The easiest way to convert a **Properties** list into a **Map** is to pass the **Properties** object to the map's constructor. This works because all of the map implementations provided by the Collections Framework define a constructor that creates a map from another **Map** instance. This recipe uses a **HashMap** to store the converted **Properties** list because **Properties** uses a hash table for storage. Thus, **HashMap** provides an equivalent implementation. The following **HashMap** constructor is used to convert a **Properties** list into a map:

HashMap(Map<? extends K, ? extends V>

Of course, when passing a **Properties** object, both **K** and **V** will be **String**.

There is one issue that you need to be aware of when passing a **Properties** object to a **Map** implementation: **Properties** implements **Map<Object, Object>**. Therefore, you will need to cast the **Properties** instance to a raw **Map** reference when it is passed to the constructor for a **HashMap<String, String>** object. This will cause an unchecked conversion warning, but because **Properties** holds only **String** keys and values, the resulting **HashMap** will be correct. (Actually, in Java 5, you can cast the **Properties** reference to **Map<String, String>** to avoid the warning, but this is not allowed in Java 6.)

Because **Properties** implements **Map**, entries can be added to a **Properties** list by calling **put( )**. However, often the legacy method **setProperty( )** is used. It is shown here:

Object setProperty(String *k*, String *v*)

Here, the key is passed in *k* and the value is passed in *v*. This method is used by the following example to construct a **Properties** list.

Example

The following example shows how to convert a **Properties** list into a **HashMap**.

```
// Convert a Properties list into a map.

import java.util.*;
```

```
class PropToMap {
  public static void main(String args[]) {

    // Create a properties list.
    Properties prop =  new Properties();

    // Put entries into the properties list.
    // Each entry consists of a name and an e-mail address.
    prop.setProperty("Tom", "tom@hschildt.com");
    prop.setProperty("Ken", "ken@hschildt.com");
    prop.setProperty("Ralph", "Ralph@hschildt.com");
    prop.setProperty("Steve", "Steve@hschildt.com");

    // Create a hash map that uses strings for both
    // its keys and values.  Initialize that map
    // with the property list. Because Properties
    // was retrofitted to implement the Map interface,
    // it can be passed to the HashMap constructor.
    // However, a cast to the raw type Map is required.
    HashMap<String, String> propMap =
        new HashMap<String, String>((Map) prop);

    // Get a set of the map entries and display them.
    Set<Map.Entry<String, String>> propSet;
    propSet = propMap.entrySet();

    System.out.println("Contents of map: ");
    for(Map.Entry<String, String> me : propSet) {
      System.out.print(me.getKey() + ": ");
      System.out.println(me.getValue());
    }
  }
}
```

The output is shown here:

```
Contents of map:
Ralph: Ralph@hschildt.com
Tom: tom@hschildt.com
Ken: ken@hschildt.com
Steve: Steve@hschildt.com
```

Options and Alternatives

In cases in which you want to convert only certain entries in a **Properties** list into a map, you can iterate through the properties, manually adding those that you want to store in the map. To do this, you can obtain a collection view of the **Properties** list by calling **entrySet( )** (which is defined by the **Map** interface). It returns a **Set** that contains the properties encapsulated in **Map.Entry** objects. You can then iterate through the set as you would any other collection, selecting those items to add to the map.

Other legacy classes can be converted to collections or maps using the same general procedure demonstrated by this recipe. For example, because **Vector** has been retrofitted to implement **List**, a **Vector** instance can be passed to an **ArrayList** constructor.

6

CHAPTER

Applets and Servlets

This chapter presents several recipes based on applets and servlets. An *applet* is a small program that is dynamically delivered over the Web and run inside a browser. A *servlet* is a small program that executes on the server side of the connection. Thus, an applet expands the functionality of the browser and a servlet extends the functionality of the server. Together, they form two of the most important uses of Java. This chapter begins with an overview of both applets and servlets. It then illustrates several core techniques.

Here are the recipes in this chapter:

- Create an AWT-Based Applet Skeleton
- Create a Swing-Based Applet Skeleton
- Create a GUI and Handle Events in a Swing Applet
- Paint Directly to the Surface of an Applet
- Pass Parameters to Applets
- Use **AppletContext** to Display a Web Page
- Create a Simple Servlet Using **GenericServlet**
- Handle HTTP Requests in a Servlet
- Use a Cookie with a Servlet

NOTE *Chapters 7 and 8, which discuss multithreading and Swing, describe techniques and features that can be used in or that relate to applet programming.*

Applet Overview

Applets are small applications that are downloaded from the Internet and executed inside a browser. They are not stand-alone applications. Because Java's virtual machine is in charge of executing all Java programs, including applets, applets offer a secure way to dynamically download and execute programs over the Web.

Before continuing, an important point needs to be made: There are two varieties of applets. The first are those based directly on the **Applet** class defined by **java.applet**.

These applets use the Abstract Window Toolkit (AWT) to provide the graphic user interface (GUI), or use no GUI at all. This style of applet has been available since Java was first created.

The second type of applet is based on the Swing class **javax.swing.JApplet**. Swing applets use the Swing classes to provide the GUI. Swing offers a richer and often easier-to-use user interface than does the AWT. Thus, Swing-based applets are now the most popular. Because **JApplet** inherits **Applet**, all the features found in **Applet** are also available in **JApplet**, and the basic structures of both types of applets are largely the same. (Swing applets must, however, abide by a few additional constraints.) Because both types of applets are still used, both types are described in this chapter.

NOTE *As a general rule, if you will be creating an applet that uses GUI controls, such as push buttons, check boxes, text controls, and the like, then you will normally create a Swing-based applet. However, if your applet does not use a GUI, or if it paints directly to the surface of the applet window, then an AWT-based applet is a valid alternative.*

The Applet Class

All applets are derived (either directly or indirectly) from **java.applet.Applet**. It contains several methods that give you detailed control over the execution of an applet and that let you access other resources on the Web. They are shown in Table 6-1.

Method	Description
void destroy( )	Called by the browser just before an applet is terminated. Your applet will override this method if it needs to perform any cleanup prior to its destruction.
AccessibleContext getAccessibleContext( )	Returns the accessibility context for the invoking object.
AppletContext getAppletContext( )	Returns the context associated with the applet.
String getAppletInfo( )	Returns a string that describes the applet.
AudioClip getAudioClip(URL *url*)	Returns an **AudioClip** object that encapsulates the audio clip found at the location specified by *url*.
AudioClip getAudioClip(URL *url*, String *clipName*)	Returns an **AudioClip** object that encapsulates the audio clip found at the location specified by *url* and having the name specified by *clipName*.
URL getCodeBase( )	Returns the URL associated with the invoking applet.
URL getDocumentBase( )	Returns the URL of the HTML document that invokes the applet.
Image getImage(URL *url*)	Returns an **Image** object that encapsulates the image found at the location specified by *url*.
Image getImage(URL *url*, String *imageName*)	Returns an **Image** object that encapsulates the image found at the location specified by *url* and having the name specified by *imageName*.

TABLE 6-1 The Methods Defined by **Applet**

Method	Description
Locale getLocale( )	Returns a **Locale** object that is used by various locale-sensitive classes and methods.
String getParameter(String *paramName*)	Returns the parameter associated with *paramName*. **null** is returned if the specified parameter is not found.
String[ ] [ ] getParameterInfo( )	Returns a **String** table that describes the parameters recognized by the applet. Each entry in the table must consist of three strings that contain the name of the parameter, a description of its type and/or range, and an explanation of its purpose.
void init( )	Called when an applet begins execution. It is the first method called for any applet.
boolean isActive( )	Returns **true** if the applet has been started. It returns **false** if the applet has been stopped.
static final AudioClip newAudioClip(URL *url*)	Returns an **AudioClip** object that encapsulates the audio clip found at the location specified by *url*. This method is similar to **getAudioClip( )** except that it is static and can be executed without the need for an **Applet** object.
void play(URL *url*)	If an audio clip is found at the location specified by *url*, the clip is played.
void play(URL *url*, String *clipName*)	If an audio clip is found at the location specified by *url* with the name specified by *clipName*, the clip is played.
void resize(Dimension *dim*)	Resizes the applet according to the dimensions specified by *dim*. **Dimension** is a class packaged in **java.awt**. It contains two integer fields: **width** and **height**.
void resize(int *width*, int *height*)	Resizes the applet according to the dimensions specified by *width* and *height*.
final void setStub(AppletStub *stubObj*)	Makes *stubObj* the stub for the applet. This method is used by the runtime system and is not usually called by your applet. A *stub* is a small piece of code that provides the linkage between your applet and the browser.
void showStatus(String *str*)	Displays *str* in the status window of the browser or applet viewer. If the browser does not support a status window, then no action takes place.
void start( )	Called by the browser when an applet should start (or resume) execution. It is automatically called after **init( )** when an applet first begins.
void stop( )	Called by the browser to suspend execution of the applet. Once stopped, an applet is restarted when the browser calls **start( )**.

TABLE 6-1   The Methods Defined by **Applet** (*continued*)

Applet is tightly integrated with the AWT because it extends three key AWT classes:

Component
Container
Panel

Applet's immediate superclass is **Panel**. It defines a simple container that can hold components. **Panel** is derived from **Container**, which is the superclass for all containers. **Container** is derived from **Component**, which specifies those qualities that define an AWT-based component. These include (among many other things) the ability to display and paint a window, and to receive events. Thus, an **Applet** is both a component and a container for other components.

The **JApplet** class, which is used for Swing-based applets, is directly derived from **Applet**. In general, most Swing components are derived from **JComponent**. The only exceptions to this are the four top-level Swing containers, which include **JApplet**. Thus, **JApplet** includes all of the features available to any other AWT-based component. However, it adds support for Swing, including methods that access the various panes defined by Swing. In Swing, components are not added to a top-level container directly. Instead, they are added to the container's *content pane*, and **JApplet** handles this process. (See Chapter 8 for an overview of Swing's component architecture and its various panes.)

To use an applet, it must be specified in an HTML file. At the time of this writing, Sun recommends using the APPLET tag for this purpose, and this is the tag used by examples in this book. The applet will be executed by a Java-enabled web browser when it encounters the APPLET tag. For example, the following HTML executes an applet called **MyApplet**.

```
<applet code="MyApplet" width=200 height=60>
</applet>
```

When this tag is encountered, **MyApplet** is executed in a window that is 200 pixels wide and 60 pixels high. For convenience, each applet example in this chapter includes the HTML necessary to execute the applet in a comment near the top of its source code.

Although applets are ultimately for use inside a browser, for testing purposes, you can execute an applet within an applet viewer, such as **appletviewer**, which is supplied with the JDK. An applet viewer makes testing during development much easier and faster. To use **appletviewer** to execute an applet, specify the name of a file that contains the APPLET tag that launches the applet. Because each of the applet examples in this book contain the necessary APPLET tag in a comment, you can specify the name of the source file; **appletviewer** will find the tag and execute the applet.

Applet Architecture

All applets (whether based on **Applet** or **JApplet**) share the same general architecture and have the same life cycle. Architecturally, applets resemble window-based, GUI programs. This means that they *are not* organized like console-based programs. Execution of an applet does not begin at **main( )**. Actually, few applets even have **main( )** methods. Instead, execution of an applet is started and controlled by its life cycle methods. Output to an applet's window is not performed by **System.out.println( )** and you won't normally use a method like **readLine( )** for input. Instead, user interactions are handled by the various controls provided by AWT or Swing components, such as check boxes, lists, and buttons. It is also possible to write output directly to an applet's window, but you will use a method such as **drawString( )** rather than **println( )**.

Applets are event-driven. Here is how the process works. An applet waits until an event occurs, such as the user clicking the mouse or selecting an item from a list. The runtime system notifies the applet about the event by calling an event handler that has been provided by the applet. Once this happens, the applet must take appropriate action and then quickly return. This is a crucial point. For the most part, an applet must not enter a "mode" of operation in which it maintains control for an extended period. Instead, it must perform specific actions in response to events and then return control to the runtime system. In those situations in which your applet needs to perform a repetitive task on its own (such as displaying a scrolling message across its window), you must start an additional thread of execution.

The Applet Life Cycle

Because applets are dynamically executed under the control of a browser, **Applet** defines a set of *life cycle* methods that control an applet's execution. The life cycle methods are **init( )**, **start( )**, **stop( )**, and **destroy( )**. Default implementations for all of these methods are provided, and you do not need to override those that you do not use.

It is important to understand the order in which the life cycle methods are executed. When an applet begins, the following methods are called in this sequence:

1. init( )
2. start( )

When an applet is terminated, the next sequence of method calls takes place:

1. stop( )
2. destroy( )

Let's look more closely at these methods.

The **init( )** method is the first method to be called. In **init( )** your applet will initialize variables and perform any other startup activities. It is called only once.

The **start( )** method is called after **init( )**. It is also called to restart an applet after it has been stopped, such as when the user returns to a previously displayed web page that contains an applet. Thus, **start( )** might be called more than once during the life cycle of an applet.

When the page containing your applet is left, the **stop( )** method is called. You will use **stop( )** to suspend any child threads created by the applet and to perform any other activities required to put the applet in a safe, idle state. Remember, a call to **stop( )** does not mean that the applet should be terminated. A stopped applet might be restarted with a call to **start( )** if the user returns to the page.

The **destroy( )** method is called when the applet is no longer needed. It is used to perform any shutdown operations required of the applet.

The AppletContext, AudioClip, and AppletStub Interfaces

In addition to the **Applet** class, **java.applet** also defines three interfaces, **AppletContext**, **AppletStub**, and **AudioClip**, that provide additional support for applets. **AudioClip** specifies three methods, **play( )**, **loop( )**, and **stop( )**, that let you play an audio file. The **AppletStub** interface specifies the linkage between an applet and the browser. It is not typically used when developing applets.

The most commonly used applet interface is **AppletContext**. It encapsulates information about the applet's execution environment. It specifies several methods. The one used by this chapter is **showDocument( )**, which causes the browser to display a specified web page. The context of an applet can be obtained by calling **getAppletContext( )**, which is defined by **Applet**.

Servlet Overview

Servlets are small programs that execute on the server side of a Web connection. Just as applets extend the functionality of a Web browser, servlets extend the functionality of a Web server. They do so by providing a convenient means of generating dynamic content, such as price and availability information for products sold through an online store.

The servlet API classes and interfaces are packaged in **javax.servlet** and **javax.servlet.http**. These packages are not part of the Java API. Instead, they are standard extensions provided by Tomcat, the standard servlet development toolkit. Tomcat is an open-source product maintained by the Jakarta Project of the Apache Software Foundation. It contains the class libraries, documentation, and runtime support that you will need to create and test servlets. You can download Tomcat from **jakarta.apache.org**.

At the time of this writing, the current version of Tomcat is 6.0.10, which supports servlet specification 2.5. This is the version of Tomcat used in this book. However, you will want to check the Jakarta web site for the latest information.

NOTE *The topic of servlets is quite large, as is the servlet API. This overview provides sufficient information to use the recipes in this chapter, but the serious servlet developer will want to explore servlets in much greater detail than can be given here.*

The javax.servlet Package

The **javax.servlet** package contains several interfaces and classes that establish the framework in which servlets operate. Of these, the recipes in this chapter make direct use of only three interfaces and one class. The interfaces are

Servlet	ServletRequest	ServletResponse

Servlet defines the basic functionality that all servlets must supply. This includes the methods that control the life cycle of the servlet. **ServletRequest** encapsulates a request. It is used to obtain information linked to the request, such as its parameters and content type. **ServletResponse** encapsulates a response. It is used to send information back to the client.

Method	Description
void destroy( )	Called when the servlet is unloaded.
ServletConfig getServletConfig( )	Returns a **ServletConfig** object that contains any initialization parameters. This is the same object that is passed to **init( )**.
String getServletInfo( )	Returns a string describing the servlet.
void init(ServletConfig sc) throws ServletException	Called when the servlet is initialized. Initialization parameters for the servlet can be obtained from *sc*. An **UnavailableException** should be thrown if the servlet cannot be initialized.
void service(ServletRequest *req*, ServletResponse *res*) throws ServletException, IOException	Called to process a request from a client. The request from the client can be read from *req*. The response to the client can be written to *res*. An exception is generated if a servlet or I/O problem occurs.

TABLE 6-2   The Methods Defined by the **Servlet** Interface

The class used by this chapter is **GenericServlet**. It implements the **Servlet** interface. It also implements the **ServletConfig** interface, which encapsulates configuration information. (**ServletConfig** is not directly used by the recipes in this chapter but may be of value when developing your own servlets.)

The following sections take a closer look at these interfaces and this class.

The Servlet Interface
All servlets must implement the **Servlet** interface. Its methods are shown in Table 6-2. Pay special attention to the **init( )**, **service( )**, and **destroy( )** methods. They are the *life cycle* methods of the servlet. These are invoked by the server and govern the execution of the servlet. (The servlet life cycle is described shortly.)

The ServletRequest Interface
The **ServletRequest** interface enables a servlet to obtain information about a client request. It defines many methods. A sampling is shown in Table 6-3.

The ServletResponse Interface
The **ServletResponse** interface enables a servlet to formulate a response for a client. It defines several methods. A sampling is shown in Table 6-4.

The GenericServlet Class
The **GenericServlet** class implements most of **Servlet** and all of **ServletConfig**. Its purpose is to make it easy to create servlets. You simply extend **GenericServlet** and override only those methods required by your application. The only method that you must override is **service( )**, which is dependent on the specific needs of your application. For this reason, **service( )** is not implemented by **GenericServlet**. The implementations of **init( )** and **destroy( )** do nothing, so if your servlet requires initialization or must release resources prior to termination, it must also override one or both of these methods.

Method	Description
Object getAttribute(String *attr*)	Returns the value of the attribute named *attr*.
Enumeration getAttributeNames( )	Returns an enumeration of the attribute names associated with the request.
String getCharacterEncoding( )	Returns the character encoding of the request.
int getContentLength( )	Returns the content length. The value –1 is returned if the length is unavailable.
String getContentType( )	Returns the type of the request. A **null** value is returned if the type cannot be determined.
ServletInputStream getInputStream( ) throws IOException	Returns a **ServletInputStream** that can be used to read binary data from the request. An **IllegalStateException** is thrown if **getReader( )** has already been invoked for this request.
String getParameter(String *pName*)	Returns the value of the parameter named *pName*. Returns **null** if *pName* is not found.
Enumeration getParameterNames( )	Returns an enumeration of the parameter names for this request.
String[ ] getParameterValues (String *pName*)	Returns an array containing values associated with the parameter specified by *pName*. Returns **null** if *pName* is not found.
String getProtocol( )	Returns a description of the protocol.
BufferedReader getReader( ) throws IOException	Returns a buffered reader that can be used to read text from the request. An **IllegalStateException** is thrown if **getInputStream( )** has already been invoked for this request.
String getRemoteAddr( )	Returns the string equivalent of the client IP address.
String getRemoteHost( )	Returns the string equivalent of the client host name.
String getScheme( )	Returns the transmission scheme of the URL used for the request (for example, "http", "ftp").
String getServerName( )	Returns the name of the server.
int getServerPort( )	Returns the port number.

TABLE 6-3   A Sampling of Methods Defined by **ServletRequest**

GenericServlet adds one method of its own called **log( )** that appends a string to the server log file. Two versions are provided and shown here:

    void log(String *str*)
    void log(String *str*, Throwable *exc*)

Here, *str* is the string to be appended to the log, and *exc* is an exception that occurred.

Method	Description
String getCharacterEncoding( )	Returns the character encoding for the response.
ServletOutputStream getOutputStream( ) throws IOException	Returns a **ServletOutputStream** that can be used to write binary data to the response. An **IllegalStateException** is thrown if **getWriter( )** has already been invoked for this request.
PrintWriter getWriter( ) throws IOException	Returns a **PrintWriter** that can be used to write character data to the response. An **IllegalStateException** is thrown if **getOutputStream( )** has already been invoked for this request.
void setContentLength(int *size*)	Sets the content length for the response to *size*.
void setContentType(String *type*)	Sets the content type for the response to *type*.

TABLE 6-4   A Sampling of Methods Defined by **ServletResponse**

The Servlet Exception Classes
The **javax.servlet** package defines two exceptions. The first is **ServletException**, which indicates that a servlet problem has occurred. The second is **UnavailableException**, which extends **ServletException**. It indicates that a servlet is unavailable.

The javax.servlet.http Package
The **javax.servlet.http** package supplies interfaces and classes that make it easier to build servlets that work with HTTP requests and responses. The interfaces used in this chapter are **HttpServletRequest** and **HttpServletResponse**. **HttpServletRequest** extends **ServletRequest** and enables a servlet to read data from an HTTP request. **HttpServletResponse** extends **ServletReponse** and enables a servlet to write data to an HTTP response. The classes used in this chapter are **HttpServlet** and **Cookie**. **HttpServlet** provides methods to handle HTTP requests and responses. **Cookie** encapsulates a cookie. Each is examined in greater detail by the following sections.

The HttpServletRequest Interface
The **HttpServletRequest** interface enables a servlet to obtain information about a client request. It extends **ServletRequest** and adds methods related to HTTP requests. A sampling of its methods is shown in Table 6-5.

The HttpServletResponse Interface
The **HttpServletResponse** interface enables a servlet to formulate an HTTP response to a client. Several constants are defined. These correspond to the different status codes that can be assigned to an HTTP response. For example, **SC_OK** indicates that the HTTP request succeeded, and **SC_NOT_FOUND** indicates that the requested resource is not available. A sampling of methods of this interface is shown in Table 6-6.

Method	Description
String getAuthType( )	Returns authentication scheme.
Cookie[ ] getCookies( )	Returns an array of the cookies in this request.
String getHeader(String *hName*)	Returns the value of the header named *hName*. Returns **null** if the header is not found.
Enumeration getHeaderNames( )	Returns an enumeration of the header names.
int getIntHeader(String *hName*)	Returns the **int** equivalent of the header named *hName*. If the header is not found, −1 is returned. A **NumberFormatException** is thrown if a conversion error occurs.
String getMethod( )	Returns a string that contains the name of the HTTP method for this request.
String getPathInfo( )	Returns any path information that is located after the servlet path and before a query string of the URL.
String getPathTranslated( )	Returns any path information that is located after the servlet path and before a query string of the URL after translating it to a real path.
String getQueryString( )	Returns the query string. Returns **null** if no query string is found.
String getRemoteUser( )	Returns the name of the user who issued this request.
String getRequestedSessionId( )	Returns the ID of the session.
String getRequestURI( )	Returns the URI.
StringBuffer getRequestURL( )	Returns the URL.
String getServletPath( )	Returns that part of the URL that identifies the servlet.
HttpSession getSession( )	Returns the session for this request. If a session does not exist, one is created and then returned.
HttpSession getSession(boolean *new*)	If *new* is **true** and no session exists, creates and returns a session for this request. Otherwise, returns the existing session for this request. Returns **null** if no session exists and *new* is **false**.
boolean isRequestedSessionIdFromCookie( )	Returns **true** if a cookie contains the session ID. Otherwise, returns **false**.
boolean isRequestedSessionIdFromURL( )	Returns **true** if the URL contains the session ID. Otherwise, returns **false**.
boolean isRequestedSessionIdValid( )	Returns **true** if the requested session ID is valid in the current session context.

TABLE 6-5   A Sampling of Methods Defined by **HttpServletRequest**

Method	Description
void addCookie(Cookie *cookie*)	Adds *cookie* to the HTTP response.
boolean containsHeader(String *hName*)	Returns **true** if the HTTP response header specified by *hName* is set.
String encodeURL(String *url*)	Determines if the session ID must be encoded in the URL identified as *url*. If so, returns the modified version of *url*. Otherwise, returns *url*. All URLs generated by a servlet should be processed by this method.
String encodeRedirectURL(String *url*)	Determines if the session ID must be encoded in the URL identified as *url*. If so, returns the modified version of *url*. Otherwise, returns *url*. All URLs passed to **sendRedirect( )** should be processed by this method.
void sendError(int *c*) throws IOException	Sends the error code *c* to the client.
void sendError(int *c*, String *s*) throws IOException	Sends the error code *c* and message *s* to the client.
void sendRedirect(String *url*) throws IOException	Redirects the client to *url*.
void setHeader(String *hName*, String *value*)	Sets the header specified by *hName* with the value *value*.
void setIntHeader(String *hName*, int *value*)	Sets the header specified by *hName* with the value *value*.
void setStatus(int *code*)	Sets the status code for this response to *code*.

TABLE 6-6   A Sampling of Methods Defined by **HttpServletResponse**

The HttpServlet Class

The **HttpServlet** class extends **GenericServlet**. It is commonly used when developing servlets that receive and process HTTP requests. It defines several **do...** methods that handle various HTTP requests. For example, **doGet( )** handles a GET request. The methods added by the **HttpServlet** class are shown in Table 6-7. All of these methods are protected.

The Cookie Class

The **Cookie** class encapsulates a cookie. A *cookie* is stored on a client and is valuable for tracking user activities or saving state information. A servlet can write a cookie to a user's machine via the **addCookie( )** method of the **HttpServletResponse** interface. The data for that cookie is then included in the header of the HTTP response that is sent to the browser.

Method	Description
void doDelete(HttpServletRequest *req*, HttpServletResponse *res*) throws IOException, ServletException	Handles an HTTP DELETE.
void doGet(HttpServletRequest *req*, HttpServletResponse *res*) throws IOException, ServletException	Handles an HTTP GET.
void doOptions(HttpServletRequest *req*, HttpServletResponse *res*) throws IOException, ServletException	Handles an HTTP OPTIONS.
void doPost(HttpServletRequest *req*, HttpServletResponse *res*) throws IOException, ServletException	Handles an HTTP POST.
void doPut(HttpServletRequest *req*, HttpServletResponse *res*) throws IOException, ServletException	Handles an HTTP PUT.
void doTrace(HttpServletRequest *req*, HttpServletResponse *res*) throws IOException, ServletException	Handles an HTTP TRACE.
long getLastModified(HttpServletRequest *req*)	Returns the time (in milliseconds since midnight, January 1, 1970, GMT) when the *req* was last modified.
void service(HttpServletRequest *req*, HttpServletResponse *res*) throws IOException, ServletException	Routes a request to the appropriate **do...** method. Do not override this method.

TABLE 6-7   The Methods Defined by **HttpServlet**

The names and values of cookies are stored on the user's machine. Some of the information that is saved for each cookie is shown here:

- The name of the cookie
- The value of the cookie
- The expiration date of the cookie
- The domain and path of the cookie

The expiration date determines when this cookie is deleted from the user's machine. If an expiration date is not explicitly assigned to a cookie, it is deleted when the current browser session ends. Otherwise, the cookie is saved in a file.

The domain and path of the cookie determine when it is included in the header of an HTTP request. If the user enters a URL whose domain and path match these values, the cookie is then supplied to the web server. Otherwise, it is not.

There is one constructor for **Cookie**. It has the signature shown here:

Cookie(String *name*, String *value*)

Method	Description
Object clone( )	Returns a copy of this object.
String getComment( )	Returns the comment.
String getDomain( )	Returns the domain.
int getMaxAge( )	Returns the maximum age (in seconds).
String getName( )	Returns the name.
String getPath( )	Returns the path to which the cookie is returned.
boolean getSecure( )	Returns **true** if the cookie is secure. Otherwise, returns **false**.
String getValue( )	Returns the value.
int getVersion( )	Returns the cookie specification version used by the cookie.
void setComment(String c)	Sets the comment to c.
void setDomain(String d)	Sets the domain to d.
void setMaxAge(int period)	Sets the maximum age of the cookie to period. This is the number of seconds after which the cookie is deleted.
void setPath(String p)	Sets the path to which the cookie is sent to p.
void setSecure(boolean secure)	Sets the security flag to secure.
void setValue(String v)	Sets the value to v.
void setVersion(int v)	Sets the cookie specification version used by the cookie to v.

TABLE 6-8   The Methods Defined by **Cookie**

Here, the name and value of the cookie are supplied as arguments to the constructor. The methods of the **Cookie** class are summarized in Table 6-8.

The Servlet Life Cycle

All servlets have the same life cycle, which is governed by three methods defined by the **Servlet** interface. These are **init( )**, **service( )**, and **destroy( )**. The life cycle begins when the server invokes the **init( )** method. This occurs when the servlet is first loaded into memory. Thus, **init( )** is executed only once. It is passed a reference to a **ServletConfig** object, which is used to pass parameters to the servlet.

After the servlet has been initialized, the server invokes the **service( )** method to process a request. The servlet can read data that has been provided in the request through the **ServletRequest** parameter. It may also formulate a response for the client, using the **ServletResponse** parameter. The **service( )** method is called for each request. (For **HttpServlet**, **service( )** invokes one of the **do...** methods to handle the request.)

The servlet remains in the server's address space and is available to process any other requests received from clients until it is terminated by the server. When the servlet is no longer needed, the server can remove the servlet from its memory and release any resources used by the servlet by calling the **destroy( )** method. No calls to **service( )** will be made after **destroy( )** has been called.

Using Tomcat for Servlet Development

To create servlets, you will need access to a servlet development environment. As mentioned earlier, the one used in this chapter is Tomcat. Tomcat is an open-source product maintained by the Jakarta Project of the Apache Software Foundation. Although Tomcat is easy to use, especially if you are an experienced Web developer who is using a high-quality development tool, it is still useful to walk through the procedure. The instructions given here assume that you are using only the JDK and Tomcat. No integrated development environment or tool is assumed.

The instructions for using Tomcat presented here assume a Windows environment. In this environment, the default location for Tomcat 6.0.10 is

```
C:\apache-tomcat-6.0.10
```

This is the location assumed by the recipes in this book. If you load Tomcat in a different location, or use a different version, you will need to make appropriate changes. You may need to set the environmental variable **JAVA_HOME** to the top-level directory in which the Java Development Kit is installed. For JDK 6, the default directory is

```
C:\Program Files\Java\JDK1.6.0
```

but you will need to confirm this for your environment.

To start Tomcat, run **startup.bat** from

```
C:\apache-tomcat-6.0.10\bin\
```

When you are done testing servlets, stop Tomcat by running **shutdown.bat**.

The directory

```
C:\apache-tomcat-6.0.10\lib\
```

contains **servlet-api.jar**. This JAR file contains the classes and interfaces that are needed to build servlets. To make this file accessible, update your **CLASSPATH** environment variable so that it includes

```
C:\apache-tomcat-6.0.10\lib\servlet-api.jar
```

Alternatively, you can specify this class file when you compile the servlets. For example, the following command compiles the first servlet example:

```
javac ServletSkel.java -classpath "C:\apache-tomcat-6.0.10\lib\servlet-api.jar"
```

Once you have compiled a servlet, you must enable Tomcat to find it. This means putting it into a directory under Tomcat's **webapps** directory and entering its name into a **web.xml** file. To keep things simple, the examples in this chapter use the directory and **web.xml** file that Tomcat supplies for its own example servlets. Here is the procedure that you will follow.

First, copy the servlet's class file into the following directory:

```
C:\apache-tomcat-6.0.10\webapps\examples\WEB-INF\classes
```

Next, add the servlet's name and mapping to the **web.xml** file in the following directory:

```
C:\apache-tomcat6.0.10\webapps\examples\WEB-INF
```

For instance, assuming the first example, called **ServletSkel**, you will add the following lines in the section that defines the servlets:

```
<servlet>
  <servlet-name>ServletSkel</servlet-name>
  <servlet-class>ServletSkel</servlet-class>
</servlet>
```

Next, you will add the following lines to the section that defines the servlet mappings:

```
<servlet-mapping>
  <servlet-name>ServletSkel</servlet-name>
  <url-pattern>/servlet/ServletSkel</url-pattern>
</servlet-mapping>
```

Follow this same general procedure for all of the servlet recipes.

Once you have compiled your servlet, copied its class file to the proper directory, and updated the **web.xml** file as just described, you can test it by using your browser. For example, to test **ServletSkel**, start the browser and then enter the URL shown here:

```
http://localhost:8080/examples/servlet/ServletSkel
```

Alternatively, you may enter the URL shown here:

```
http://127.0.0.1:8080/examples/servlet/ServletSkel
```

This can be done because 127.0.0.1 is defined as the IP address of the local machine.

Create an AWT-Based Applet Skeleton

Key Ingredients	
Classes	**Methods**
java.applet.Applet	void destroy( )
	void init( )
	void start( )
	void stop( )

As explained, all applets share a common architecture and life cycle. However, there are some minor differences between the skeleton used for AWT-based applets and the one used for Swing-based applets. This recipe shows how to create an AWT-based applet skeleton. (The Swing-based version is described in the following recipe.) The skeleton can be used as the starting point for applet development.

Step-by-Step

To create an AWT-based applet skeleton, follow these steps:

1. Import **java.applet.***. Actually, for simple applets you may need to import only **java.applet.Applet**, but real applets often need other parts of the package. So, it is usually easier to just import all of **java.applet**.
2. Create a class for the applet. This class must extend **Applet**.
3. Override the four life cycle methods: **init( )**, **start( )**, **stop( )**, and **destroy( )**.

Discussion

The four life cycle methods were described in *Applet Overview* presented earlier. As explained, default implementations of these methods are provided, so it is not technically necessary to override each one. From a practical point of view, however, you will almost always override **init( )** because it is used to initialize the applet. You will also often override **start( )** and **stop( )**, especially when the applet uses multithreading. If the applet uses any resources, then it will use **destroy( )** to release those resources.

Example

The following example assembles the life cycle methods into an applet called **AppletSkel**. Although the applet does nothing, it can still be run. Notice the APPLET tag in the HTML inside the comment at the start of the program. You can use this HTML to launch the applet in your browser or **appletviewer**. Simply create an HTML file that contains the tag. Alternatively, you can pass **AppletSkel.java** directly to **appletviewer**. It will automatically find the tag and launch the applet. This "trick" will not work with a browser, however.

```
// An Applet skeleton for an AWT-Based Applet.

import java.applet.*;
/*
<applet code="AppletSkel" width=300 height=100>
</applet>
*/

public class AppletSkel extends Applet {
  // Called first.
  public void init() {
    // Initialize the applet.
  }

  // Called second, after init().  Also called whenever
  // the applet is restarted.
  public void start() {
    // Start or resume execution.
  }
```

```
  // Called when the applet is stopped.
  public void stop() {
    // Suspend execution.
  }

  // Called when the applet is terminated.  This is the
  // last method executed.
  public void destroy() {
    // Perform shutdown activities.
  }
}
```

The window produced by **AppletSkel** when run by **appletviewer** is shown here:

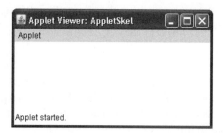

Options and Alternatives

You can use the applet skeleton as a starting point for your own AWT-based applets. Of course, you need to override only the life cycle methods that are used by your applet.

The skeleton shown in the example is suitable for use with an AWT-based applet. The following recipe shows how to create a skeleton for a Swing-based applet.

Create a Swing-Based Applet Skeleton

Key Ingredients	
Classes	**Methods**
java.swing.JApplet	void destroy( )
	void init( )
	void start( )
	void stop( )
java.swing.SwingUtilities	static void invokeAndWait(Runnable *obj*) throws InterruptedException, InvocationTargetException

Swing-based applets use the same basic skeleton and life cycle methods as does the AWT-based applet skeleton shown in the preceding recipe. However, Swing applets are derived from a different class, and they must be careful about how they interact with GUI components. This recipe shows how to create a Swing-based applet skeleton.

Step-by-Step

To create a skeleton for a Swing-based applet, follow these steps:

1. Import **javax.swing.***.
2. Create a class for the applet. For Swing applets, this class must extend **JApplet**.
3. Override the four life cycle methods: **init( )**, **start( )**, **stop( )**, and **destroy( )**.
4. Create any GUI-based components on the event-dispatching thread. To do this, use **invokeAndWait( )** defined by **SwingUtilities**.

Discussion

All Swing-based applets are derived from the **javax.swing.JApplet** class. **JApplet** is a top-level Swing container that is derived from **Applet**. Therefore, **JApplet** inherits all of **Applet**'s methods, including its life cycle methods described by the preceding recipe. The life cycle methods perform the same function in a Swing applet as they do in an AWT-based applet.

Although the skeleton does not contain any GUI-based controls, the vast majority of Swing applets will. As explained in Chapter 8 (which presents recipes that use Swing's GUI component set), all interaction with a Swing component must take place on the event-dispatching thread. In general, Swing programs are event-driven. For example, when a user interacts with a component, an event is generated. The runtime system passes an event to the application by calling an event handler defined by the application. This means that the handler is executed on the event-dispatching thread provided by Swing and not on the main thread of the application. Thus, although event handlers are defined by your program, they are called on a thread that was not created by your program.

To avoid problems (such as two different threads trying to update the same component at the same time), all Swing GUI components must be created and updated from the event-dispatching thread, not the main thread of the application. However, **init( )** *is not* executed on the event-dispatching thread. Thus, it cannot directly instantiate a GUI component. Instead, it must create a **Runnable** object that executes on the event-dispatching thread, and have this object create the GUI.

To enable the GUI code for an applet to be created on the event-dispatching thread, you must use the **invokeAndWait( )** method defined by the **SwingUtilities** class. It is shown here:

```
static void invokeAndWait(Runnable obj)
    throws InterruptedException, InvocationTargetException
```

Here, *obj* is a **Runnable** object that will have its **run( )** method called by the event-dispatching thread. The method does not return until after **obj.run( )** returns. You can use this method to call a method that constructs the GUI for your Swing applet. Therefore, the skeleton for the **init( )** method will normally be coded as shown here:

```
public void init() {
  try {
    SwingUtilities.invokeAndWait(new Runnable () {
      public void run() {
        makeGUI(); // a method that initializes the Swing components
      }
    });
  } catch(Exception exc) {
    System.out.println("Can't create because of "+ exc);
  }
}
```

Inside **run( )**, a method called **makeGUI( )** is called. This is a method that you provide that sets up and initializes the Swing components. Of course, the name **makeGUI( )** is arbitrary. You can use a different name if you like.

Example

The following example assembles the life cycle methods into an applet called **SwingAppletSkel**. It also contains the skeletal code needed to initialize a GUI. Although the applet does nothing, it can still be run.

```
// An applet skeleton for a Swing-based applet.

import javax.swing.*;
/*
<applet code="SwingAppletSkel" width=300 height=100>
</applet>
*/

public class SwingAppletSkel extends JApplet {

  // Called first.
  public void init() {
    try {
      SwingUtilities.invokeAndWait(new Runnable () {
        public void run() {
          makeGUI(); // a method that initializes the Swing components
        }
      });
    } catch(Exception exc) {
      System.out.println("Can't create because of "+ exc);
    }
  }
  // Called second, after init().  Also called whenever
  // the applet is restarted.
  public void start() {
    // Start or resume execution.
  }

  // Called when the applet is stopped.
  public void stop() {
    // Suspend execution.
  }
```

```
// Called when the applet is terminated.  This is the
// last method executed.
public void destroy() {
  // Perform shutdown activities.
}

private void makeGUI() {
  // Create and initialize GUI components here.
}
}
```

When run using **appletviewer**, it produces the same blank window as **AppletSkel**, shown in the previous recipe.

Options and Alternatives

You can use the applet skeleton as a starting point for your own Swing-based applets. Of course, you need to override only the life cycle methods that are used by your applet. However, in all cases be sure to create any GUI components on the event-dispatching thread.

If your applet will not be using a GUI, then building an AWT-based applet may be a better choice. See the preceding recipe for details.

Create a GUI and Handle Events in a Swing Applet

Key Ingredients	
Classes and Interfaces	**Methods**
java.awt.event.ActionEvent	String getActionCommand( )
java.awt.event.ActionListener	void actionPerformed(ActionEvent *ae*)
java.awt.event.ItemEvent	Object getItem( )
java.awt.event.ItemListener	void itemStateChanged(ItemEvent *ie*)
java.swing.JApplet	Component add(Component *comp*) void setLayout(LayoutManager *layout*)
javax.swing.JLabel	void setText(String *str*) String getText( )
javax.swing.JButton	void addActionListener(ActionListener *al*)
javax.swing.JCheckBox	void addItemListener(ItemListener *il*) boolean isSelected( ) void setPreferredSize(Dimension *size*) void setSelected(boolean *set*)

This recipe shows how to create a Swing applet that has a GUI and handles events. As mentioned in *Applet Overview*, most GUI-based applets will use Swing to provide the interface components, such as push buttons, labels, and text fields. This is because Swing offers a much richer component set and more flexibility than does the AWT by itself. Therefore, this is the approach used by this recipe, and by all other recipes in this chapter that create GUI-based applets.

Because all Swing components generate events (except for labels, which simply display information), an applet will also usually provide event handling. The same basic approach to handling events generated by Swing components also applies to any other types of events, such as mouse events. Therefore, the same basic event-handling techniques are applicable to both Swing-and AWT-based applets.

Be aware that the GUI shown here is very simple. GUIs and the issues surrounding them can be very complex. Furthermore, there are a variety of ways in which components can be created and events can be handled. The approach shown here is only one way. When building a GUI-based applet, you must tailor your development to match your application.

NOTE *An overview of the Swing's architecture, components, and event-handling is presented in Chapter 8, and that discussion is not repeated here. This recipe simply shows how to use these features in a Swing-based applet.*

Step-by-Step

To create an applet with a Swing-based GUI and to handle the events generated by the GUI involves the following steps:

1. Create an applet class that extends **JApplet**.
2. If necessary, set the layout manager by calling **setLayout( )**.
3. Create the components required by the applet. This recipes uses a button, three check boxes, and a label. These are instances of **JButton**, **JCheckBox**, and **JLabel**, respectively.
4. If necessary, set the preferred size of a component by calling **setPreferredSize( )**.
5. Implement event listeners for the components. This recipe uses an action listener for button events and an item listener for check box events, which are instances of **ActionListener** and **ItemListener**, respectively.
6. Add the listeners to the components. For example, add the action listener by calling **addActionListener( )** and the item listener by calling **addItemListener( )**. When an event is received, respond appropriately.
7. Add the components to the content pane of the applet.

Discussion

Today, most applets that use a GUI will be based on Swing. Swing is Java's modern GUI toolkit, and it provides a rich component set. As explained in *Create a Swing-Based Applet Skeleton*, all Swing applets must extend **JApplet**. **JApplet** extends **Applet**, adding support for Swing.

JApplet is a top-level Swing container. This means that it supports the four panes defined for top-level containers: the root pane, glass pane, layered pane, and content pane. GUI components are added to the applet's content pane, which is a **JPanel**. (For a description of these panes and other Swing essentials, see Chapter 8.)

NOTE   *It is important to understand that AWT-based applets do not have panes. For example, they do not have a content pane. The panes relate specifically to Swing.*

By default, the content pane uses border layout, but you can set the layout as needed. To do this, call **setLayout( )** on the content pane, passing in the desired layout manager. Beginning with Java 5, this is done by simply calling **setLayout( )** on the applet. The method is automatically invoked relative to the content pane. (See the historical note that follows.) The following example uses flow layout, which is encapsulated within the **FlowLayout** class. A flow layout positions the components line-by-line, top to bottom. The position of the components can change if the window is resized.

Three components are used by this recipe: **JButton**, **JCheckBox**, and **JLabel**. **JButton** creates a push button, **JCheckBox** creates a check box, and **JLabel** creates a label. These components are described in Chapter 8, but the constructors used in this recipe are shown here for convenience:

```
JButton(String str)
JCheckBox(String str)
JLabel(String str)
```

For **JButton**, *str* specifies the string that will be displayed inside the button. For **JCheckBox**, *str* specifies the string that describes the check box. For **JLabel**, *str* specifies a string that will be displayed within the label.

Sometimes you will want to set the size of a component. For example, you might want related components to line up. To set the size, call **setPreferredSize( )** on the component you want to size. Note, however, that some layout managers (such as **BorderLayout**) can override the preferred size of a component.

When a button is pressed, it generates an **ActionEvent**. In order for the applet to respond to the event, it must provide an action listener for the button. An action listener is an instance of **ActionListener**, and it is added to the button by calling **addActionListener( )** on the button. **ActionListener** defines only one method, **actionPerformed( )**. This method is called when an action event occurs, and it is passed an **ActionEvent** instance that describes the event. Inside **actionPerformed( )**, you can obtain the *action command* string associated with the button. By default, this is the string shown inside the button. You can use the action command to identify a button when an action event is received.

When a check box is checked or unchecked, it generates an **ItemEvent**. In order for the applet to respond to the event, it must provide an item listener for the check box. An item listener is an instance of **ItemListener**, and it is added to the check box by calling **addItemListener( )** on the check box. **ItemListener** defines only one method, **itemStateChanged( )**. This method is called when an item event occurs, and it is passed an **ItemEvent** instance that describes the event. Inside **itemStateChanged( )** you can obtain a reference to the check box that generated the event by calling **getItem( )**. It returns a reference to the check box that changed.

In general, event handlers can be implemented in a variety of ways. The example in this recipe uses an anonymous inner class. In this approach, each component is linked with its own event handler. The advantage of this approach is that the component that generates the event is known and does not have to be determined at runtime. Other approaches include having the applet class implement the listener interface, or using a separate class that implements the desired listener.

In order for the components to be displayed, they must be added to the content pane of the applet. Beginning with Java 5, this is done by simply calling **add( )** on the applet. The component is automatically added to the content pane of the applet. (See the historical note, next.)

Historical Note: getContentPane( )

Prior to Java 5, when adding a component to, removing a component from, or setting the layout manager for the content pane, you had to explicitly obtain a reference to the content pane by calling **getContentPane( )**. For example, in the past, to set the layout manager to **FlowLayout**, you needed to use this statement:

```
getContentPane().setLayout(new FlowLayout());
```

Beginning with Java 5, the call to **getContentPane( )** is no longer necessary because calls to **add( )**, **remove( )**, and **setLayout( )** are automatically directed to the content pane. For this reason the recipes in this book *do not* call **getContentPane( )**. However, if you want to write code that can be compiled by older versions of Java, then you will need to add calls to **getContentPane( )** where appropriate.

Example

The following example shows an applet that contains a simple Swing GUI. It has three check boxes, one button, and a label. The label displays the user's interaction with the check boxes. The button clears all three check boxes. Notice that all of the components are constructed within **makeGUI( )**, which is executed on the event-dispatching thread via **invokeAndWait( )**. As explained earlier, all program interactions with Swing components must take place on the event-dispatching, not the main, thread of the applet.

```java
// A Swing-based applet that builds a GUI and
// handles events.

import javax.swing.*;
import java.awt.*;
import java.awt.event.*;

/*
<object code="GUIApplet" width=200 height=160>
</object>
*/

public class GUIApplet extends JApplet {

  JLabel jlab;

  JCheckBox jcbSave;
  JCheckBox jcbValidate;
  JCheckBox jcbSecure;
```

```java
// Initialize the applet.
public void init() {
  try {
    SwingUtilities.invokeAndWait(new Runnable () {
      public void run() {
        makeGUI();
      }
    });
  } catch(Exception exc) {
    System.out.println("Can't create because of "+ exc);
  }
}

// Initialize the GUI.
private void makeGUI() {

  // Set the content pane's layout to flow layout.
  setLayout(new FlowLayout());

  // Note: If you are using a version of Java prior to
  // JDK 5, then you will need to use getContentPane()
  // to explicitly set the content pane's layout,
  // as shown here:
  //
  //   getContentPane().setLayout(new FlowLayout());

  // Create the label that will display selections.
  jlab = new JLabel();

  // Create three check boxes.
  jcbSave = new JCheckBox("Save data on exit");
  jcbValidate = new JCheckBox("Validate data");
  jcbSecure = new JCheckBox("Use enhanced security");

  // Make the check box dimensions uniform.
  Dimension cbSize = new Dimension(200, 20);
  jcbSave.setPreferredSize(cbSize);
  jcbValidate.setPreferredSize(cbSize);
  jcbSecure.setPreferredSize(cbSize);

  // Handle check box item events.
  ItemListener cbListener = new ItemListener() {
    public void itemStateChanged(ItemEvent ie) {
      // Get the object that generated the event.
      JCheckBox cb = (JCheckBox) ie.getItem();

      // Report if selected or cleared.
      if(cb.isSelected())
        jlab.setText(cb.getText() + " selected.");
      else
        jlab.setText(cb.getText() + " cleared.");
    }
  };
```

```
    // Add item listeners for the check boxes.
    jcbSave.addItemListener(cbListener);
    jcbValidate.addItemListener(cbListener);
    jcbSecure.addItemListener(cbListener);

    // Add a button that resets the check boxes.
    JButton jbtnReset = new JButton("Reset Options");

    // Create the action listener for the button.
    jbtnReset.addActionListener( new ActionListener() {
      public void actionPerformed(ActionEvent ae) {
        jcbSave.setSelected(false);
        jcbValidate.setSelected(false);
        jcbSecure.setSelected(false);
        jlab.setText("All check box options cleared.");
      }
    });

    // Add the label, check boxes, and button to the
    // applet's content pane.
    add(jcbSave);
    add(jcbValidate);
    add(jcbSecure);
    add(jbtnReset);
    add(jlab);

    // Note: If you are using a version of Java prior to
    // JDK 5, then you will need to use getContentPane()
    // to explicitly add components to the content pane,
    // as shown here.
    //
    //    getContentPane().add(jcbSave);
    //
    // and so on.
  }
}
```

The applet is shown here when run using **appletviewer**:

Bonus Example

The following applet creates a simple scrolling banner. It uses a timer to control the rate of scrolling. The text being scrolled is held in a **JLabel**, which is Swing's label class. Each time the timer goes off, the text is scrolled by one character position. The rate at which the timer runs determines how fast the scrolling takes place. The direction of the scroll can be reversed by clicking the Reverse button.

The timer used by the program is an instance of **Timer**, which is part of **javax.swing**. It generates action events at a regular interval until stopped. It has the following constructor:

Timer(int *period*, ActionListener *al*)

Here, *period* specifies the timing interval in terms of milliseconds and *al* is the action listener that will be notified each time the timer goes off. The timer is started by calling **start( )**. It is stopped by calling **stop( )**. **Timer** is especially useful in Swing programming because it fires an event at the end of each timing interval. Because event handlers execute on the event-dispatching thread, the event handler can update the GUI in a thread-safe manner.

The action listener associated with the timer is the part of the program that actually scrolls the text inside the label. Its **actionPerformed( )** method rotates the text left or right (depending upon whether **scrollLeft** is true or false) and then sets the text inside the label. This causes the text to scroll. Each time the Reverse button is clicked, the value of **scrollLeft** is inverted, thereby reversing the direction of the scroll.

```
// A Swing applet that scrolls text within a label and
// provides a button that reverses the direction of the scroll.

import javax.swing.*;
import java.awt.*;
import java.awt.event.*;

/*
<object code="Scroller" width=210 height=60>
</object>
*/

public class Scroller extends JApplet {

  JLabel jlab;

  String msg = " Java moves the Web! ";

  boolean scrollLeft = true;

  ActionListener scroller;

  // This timer controls scrolling. The shorter
  // its delay, the faster the scroll.
  Timer stTimer;

  // Initialize the applet.
  public void init() {
    try {
      SwingUtilities.invokeAndWait(new Runnable () {
        public void run() {
```

```
        makeGUI();
      }
    });
  } catch(Exception exc) {
    System.out.println("Can't create because of "+ exc);
  }
}

// Start the timer when the applet is started.
public void start() {
  stTimer.start();
}

// Stop the timer when the applet is stopped.
public void stop() {
  stTimer.stop();
}

// Stop the timer when the applet is destroyed.
public void destroy() {
  stTimer.stop();
}

// Initialize the timer GUI.
private void makeGUI() {

  // Use flow layout.
  setLayout(new FlowLayout());

  // Create the label that will scroll the message.
  jlab = new JLabel(msg);
  jlab.setHorizontalAlignment(SwingConstants.CENTER);

  // Create the action listener for the timer.
  scroller = new ActionListener() {
    // Each time the timer goes off, scroll the text
    // one character.
    public void actionPerformed(ActionEvent ae) {
      if(scrollLeft) {
        // Left-scroll the message one character.
        char ch = msg.charAt(0);
        msg = msg.substring(1, msg.length());
        msg += ch;
        jlab.setText(msg);
      }
      else {
        // Right-scroll the message one character.
        char ch = msg.charAt(msg.length()-1);
        msg = msg.substring(0, msg.length()-1);
        msg = ch + msg;
        jlab.setText(msg);
      }
    }
  };
```

```
  // Create the timer.  Scroll every fifth of a second.
  stTimer = new Timer(200, scroller);

  // Add a button that reverses direction of scroll.
  JButton jbtnRev = new JButton("Reverse");

  // Create the action listener for the button.
  jbtnRev.addActionListener( new ActionListener() {
    public void actionPerformed(ActionEvent ae) {
      scrollLeft = !scrollLeft;
    }
  });

  // Add the label and button to the applet's content pane.
  add(jlab);
  add(jbtnRev);
 }
}
```

The applet is shown here when run using **appletviewer**:

Options and Alternatives

Many of Swing's components generate more than one type of event. For example, in addition to firing an action event, a **JButton** will also generate a change event (which is an instance of **ChangeEvent**) when a change to the component's state occurs. For example, a change event is generated when a button is rolled over by the mouse pointer. Therefore, what events your applet needs to handle will depend both on the type of the component and the situation in which it is employed.

As mentioned, event handlers can be implemented in three basic ways: as inner classes, as part of the applet class, or by a stand-alone class. There is one advantage to having the applet class implement the necessary event handler or handlers for the application: it reduces the number of classes that need to be generated. By reducing the number of classes, download times can be decreased. Of course, when the applet class implements a listener, if two objects generate the same event (such as an action event), you must explicitly determine what object generated the event. See Chapter 8 for more information about handling events and using Swing components.

Paint Directly to the Surface of an Applet

Key Ingredients	
Classes	**Methods**
java.awt.Applet	void paint(Graphics *g*)
	void repaint( )
	void setBackground(Color *newColor*)
	void setForeground(Color *newColor*)
java.awt.Graphics	void drawString(String *msg*,
	int *x*, int *y*)
	void drawLine(int *startX*, int *startY*,
	int *endX*, int *endY*)

Although most often, interaction with the user will take place through one or more GUI components, such as buttons, scroll bars, and spin controls, it is possible to write directly to the surface of an applet's window. You might want to do this if the applet only displays text or graphics and requires no other components. This recipe shows how painting to an applet's window is accomplished.

Before continuing, three important points need to be made. First, the topic of painting in a component is very large. Java provides rich functionality in this regard, and there are many specialized techniques. This recipe shows only the basic mechanism required to paint on the surface of an applet. It does not attempt to describe all of the intricacies involved.

Second, the technique shown here is useful only in situations in which the applet uses no GUI components. In other words, aside from the output created by writing directly to the surface of the applet, the applet displays no other visual items. Trying to mix direct output to the surface of an applet with other graphic components will cause a problem because one will (or at least might) overwrite the other.

Third, although the technique shown here will work with applets derived from **JApplet**, normally when working with Swing you will want create a separate panel into which you paint output. The reason is that Swing offers more finely grained support for painting that can only be achieved by painting to a Swing component, such as **JPanel**. Therefore, the technique described here is most applicable to AWT-based applets.

NOTE *Detailed coverage of the AWT's support for painting, including graphics, fonts, and font metrics, can be found in my book* Java: The Complete Reference.

Step-by-Step

To paint to the surface of an applet involves these steps:

1. In the applet class, override the **paint( )** method specified by **Component** (and inherited by **Applet**).

2. Inside your version of **paint( )**, use one or more of the AWT-based output methods defined by the **Graphics** class. Two are used in this recipe: **drawString( )**, which outputs a text string, and **drawLine( )**, which draws a line.

3. You can set the drawing color by calling **setForeground( )**. To set the background, call **setBackground( )**.

4. To cause output to be displayed, call **repaint( )**. This will result in a call to **paint( )**.

Discussion

The **paint( )** method is defined by **Component** and is inherited by **Applet**. It is shown here:

   void paint(Graphics g)

This method is called each time that an applet must redisplay its output. This situation can occur for several reasons. For example, the window in which the applet is running can be overwritten by another window and then uncovered. Or, the applet window can be minimized and then restored. The **paint( )** method is also called when the applet begins execution. Whatever the cause, whenever the applet must redraw its output, **paint( )** is called. Therefore, **paint( )** is where you will put the code that outputs to the surface of an applet.

   The **paint( )** method has one parameter of type **java.awt.Graphics**. This parameter contains the graphics context, which describes the graphics environment in which the applet is running. This context is used by various drawing methods, such as **drawString( )**. **Graphics** also defines various methods that output to the applet's surface. Two of these methods are used by this recipe. The first is **drawString( )**, which outputs a text string. It is shown here:

   void drawString(String msg, int x, int y)

This method outputs the string passed in msg, beginning at the X,Y location specified by x and y. The string is drawn in the current foreground color. In a Java window, the upper-left corner is location 0,0. However, x and y specify the upper-left edge of the *baseline* of the characters, not their upper-left corner. Therefore, you must take this into consideration when attempting to write a string in the upper-left corner of the window.

   The second output method is **drawLine( )**, which draws a line. It is shown here:

   void drawLine(int $startX$, int $startY$, int $endX$, int $endY$)

It draws a line in the current foreground color. The line begins at $startX,startY$ and ends at $endX,endY$.

   You can set the background color by calling **setBackground( )**. You can set the drawing color by calling **setForeground( )**. These methods are specified by **Component**. They are shown here.

   void setBackground(Color $newColor$)
   void setForeground(Color $newColor$)

Here, *newColor* specifies the new color. The class **Color**, which is packaged in **java.awt**, defines the constants shown here that can be used to specify colors:

Color.black	Color.magenta
Color.blue	Color.orange
Color.cyan	Color.pink
Color.darkGray	Color.red
Color.gray	Color.white
Color.green	Color.yellow
Color.lightGray	

Uppercase versions of the constants are also defined.

As a general rule, an applet never calls **paint( )** directly. Instead, when the surface of the applet needs to be painted, it will execute a call to **repaint( )**. The **repaint( )** method is defined by the AWT. It requests that the runtime system execute **paint( )**. Thus, for another part of your applet to output to its window, simply store the output and then call **repaint( )**. This causes a call to **paint( )**, which can display the stored information. For example, if part of your applet needs to output a string, it can store this string in a **String** variable and then call **repaint( )**. Inside **paint( )**, you will output the string using **drawString( )**.

NOTE *Technically, calling **repaint( )** on heavyweight components (including **Applet** and **JApplet**) results in a call to **update( )**, which in its default implementation calls **paint( )**. Therefore, if you override **update( )**, you must make sure that **paint( )** is ultimately called.*

The **repaint( )** method has four forms. The one used by this recipe is shown here:

void repaint( )

This version causes the entire window to be repainted. Other versions of **repaint( )** let you specify a region to be repainted.

Example

The following example shows how to paint directly to the surface of an applet. It is an AWT-based applet because it uses no GUI components other than the main window of the applet. It uses **drawString( )** to write a line of text and **drawLine( )** to draw lines. Each time the mouse is clicked inside the applet, the drawing color and the message are changed. Then, **repaint( )** is called. This causes the applet to be repainted to reflect the new color and message. As an experiment, try removing the call to **repaint( )**. As you will see, the applet is not updated when the mouse is clicked. (Of course, it will be repainted if the window needs to be redrawn—because it was covered and then uncovered, for example.)

There is one other point of interest in the program. Mouse events are listened for by use of an anonymous inner class that is based on **MouseAdapter**. Java provides several adapter classes that make it easier to implement event listeners that define several methods.

The adapters provide default (empty) methods for all of the methods defined by an event. You can then simply override the methods in which you are interested. You don't have to provide empty implementations of the others. In this example, the only mouse event in which we are interested is when the left button is pressed. This event is handled by **mousePressed( )**. The other methods defined by **MouseListener** (**mouseEntered( )**, **mouseReleased( )**, and so on) are not used, so they can be handled by the empty handlers.

```java
// Paint to the surface of an applet.

import java.awt.*;
import java.awt.event.*;
import java.applet.*;

/*
<applet code="AppletPaint" width=250 height=250>
</applet>
*/

public class AppletPaint extends Applet {
  String msg = "This is black";
  int count = 0;
  Color textColor = Color.black;

  public void init() {

    // Change the drawing color each time the mouse
    // is clicked inside the applet.
    addMouseListener(new MouseAdapter() {
      public void mousePressed(MouseEvent me) {
        count++;
        if(count > 3) count = 0;

        switch(count) {
          case 0:
            textColor = Color.black;
            msg = "This is black";
            break;
          case 1:
            textColor = Color.red;
            msg = "This is red";
            break;
          case 2:
            textColor =  Color.green;
            msg = "This is green";
            break;
          case 3:
            msg = "This is blue";
            textColor = Color.blue;
            break;
        }
```

```
        // Request the window to be redrawn.
        repaint();
      }
    });
  }

  // Called when the applet's window must be restored.
  public void paint(Graphics g) {

    // Set the drawing color.
    setForeground(textColor);

    // Display a message.
    g.drawString(msg, 30, 20);

    // Draw two lines.
    g.drawLine(50, 50, 200, 200);
    g.drawLine(50, 200, 200, 50);
  }
}
```

The applet is shown here when run using **appletviewer**:

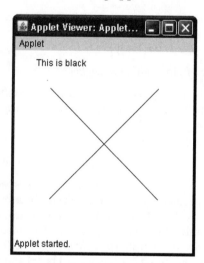

Options and Alternatives

In addition to the form used by the recipe, **repaint( )** supports three other forms. The first specifies the region that will be repainted:

void repaint(int *left*, int *top*, int *width*, int *height*)

Here, the coordinates of the upper-left corner of the region are specified by *left* and *top*, and the width and height of the region are passed in *width* and *height*. These dimensions are specified in pixels. You can save time by specifying a region to repaint. Painting is costly in terms of time. If you need to update only a small portion of the window, it is more efficient to repaint only that region.

The last two forms of **repaint( )** let you specify a maximum delay that can occur before the repainting is performed. Calling **repaint( )** is essentially a request that your applet be repainted sometime soon. However, if your system is slow or busy, repainting might not happen immediately. This can be a problem in many situations, including animation, in which a consistent update time is necessary. The following versions of **repaint( )** help solve this problem:

> void repaint(long *maxDelay*)
> void repaint(long *maxDelay*, int *x*, int *y*, int *width*, int *height*)

Here, *maxDelay* specifies the maximum number of milliseconds that can elapse before repainting is performed.

In addition to **drawString( )** and **drawLine( )**, the **Graphics** class provides many other drawing methods. For example, to draw a rectangle, use **drawRect( )**:

> void drawRect(int *top*, int *left*, int *width*, int *height*)

The upper-left corner of the rectangle is at *top,left*. The dimensions of the rectangle are specified by *width* and *height*.

To draw a circle or ellipse, use **drawOval( )**:

> void drawOval(int *top*, int *left*, int *width*, int *height*)

The ellipse is drawn within a bounding rectangle whose upper-left corner is specified by *top,left* and whose width and height are specified by *width* and *height*. To draw a circle, specify a square as the bounding rectangle.

You can draw an arc by using **drawArc( )**:

> void drawArc(int *top*, int *left*, int *width*, int *height*, int *startAngle*, int *sweepAngle*)

The arc is bounded by the rectangle whose upper-left corner is specified by *top*, *left* and whose width and height are specified by *width* and *height*. The arc is drawn from *startAngle* through the angular distance specified by *sweepAngle*. Angles are specified in degrees. Zero degrees is on the horizontal, at the three o'clock position. The arc is drawn counterclockwise if *sweepAngle* is positive, and clockwise if *sweepAngle* is negative. Therefore, to draw an arc from twelve o'clock to six o'clock, the start angle would be 90 and the sweep angle 180.

There is an alternative to using **paint( )** and **repaint( )** to handle output to a window. Output can be accomplished by obtaining a graphics context by calling **getGraphics( )** (defined by **Component**) and then using this context to output to the window. However, this option must be used with caution because you will be painting into the window in a way that neither Swing nor the AWT has control over. Thus, conflicts may (probably will) occur. It is usually better, safer, and easier to route window output through **paint( )** as illustrated by the recipe.

Pass Parameters to Applets

Key Ingredients	
Classes	**Methods**
java.applet.Applet	String getParameter(String *paramName*)

Often it is useful to pass one or more parameters to an applet. For example, parameters might be used to configure the applet or pass in information provided by the Web page designer. Whatever the purpose, it is easy to pass parameters to an applet. This recipe shows the process.

Step-by-Step

To pass a parameter to an applet involves the following steps:

1. In the APPLET tag that invokes the applet, use PARAM to specify the parameters that you want to pass to the applet.
2. Inside the applet, call **getParameter( )** to obtain the value of a parameter given its name.
3. Inside the applet, convert numeric parameters from their string representation to their binary representation.

Discussion

To pass a parameter to an applet, you must include a PARAM attribute in the APPLET tag that invokes the applet. Here is the general form:

<PARAM name=*pName* value=*pValue*>

Here, *pName* is the name of the parameter and *pValue* is its value. All parameters are passed as strings.

Inside the applet, use **getParameter( )** to obtain the parameter. It is shown here:

String getParameter(String *paramName*)

It returns the value of the parameter passed in *paramName*. If the parameter is not found, **null** is returned.

Because all parameters are passed as strings, you will need to manually convert numeric parameters into their binary format. One way to do this is to use one of the static **parse...** methods defined by the numeric type wrappers, such as **Integer** and **Double**. For example, to obtain an **int** value, use **Integer.parseInt( )**. To obtain a **double** value, use **Double.parseDouble( )**. They are shown here:

static int parseInt(String *str*) throws NumberFormatException
static int parseDouble(String *str*) throws NumberFormatException

The string passed in *str* must represent a numeric value for the desired format. A **NumberFormatException** is thrown if *str* does not contain a valid numeric string.

Example

The following example shows how to pass parameters to an applet. It uses two parameters. The first is **userName**, which holds a user's name, and the second is **accountNum**, which holds an integer account number. The comment at the top of the program shows an example APPLET tag that passes these parameters to the applet. Inside the applet, the parameters are retrieved and the account number is converted into its **int** format.

```
// A Swing-based applet that uses parameters.

import javax.swing.*;
import java.awt.*;

/*
<applet code="ParamApplet" width=300 height=60>
<param name=UserName value=George>
<param name=AccountNum value=12345>
</applet>
*/

public class ParamApplet extends JApplet {

  JLabel jlab;

  int accNum;
  String user;

  // Initialize the applet.
  public void init() {
    // Get the parameters.
    user = getParameter("UserName");
    if(user == null) user = "Unknown";

    // Numbers are passed as strings. You must convert
    // them into their binary format manually.
    try {
      accNum = Integer.parseInt(getParameter("AccountNum"));
    } catch(NumberFormatException exc) {
      accNum = -1;
    }

    try {
      SwingUtilities.invokeAndWait(new Runnable () {
        public void run() {
          makeGUI();
        }
      });
```

```
      } catch(Exception exc) {
        System.out.println("Can't create because of "+ exc);
      }
   }

   // Initialize the GUI.
   private void makeGUI() {

     // Create the label that will display the parameters
     // passed to this applet.
     jlab = new JLabel("User Name: " + user +
                      ",  Account Number: " + accNum,
                      SwingConstants.CENTER);

     // Add the label to the applet's content pane.
     add(jlab);

     // Note: If you are using a version of Java prior to
     // JDK 5, then you will need to use getContentPane()
     // to explicitly add components to the content pane,
     // as shown here.
     //
     //   getContentPane().add(jlab);
   }
}
```

The output is shown here:

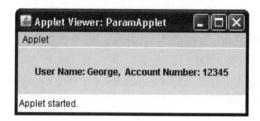

Options and Alternatives

In the example, if a parameter is not found or is invalid, then a default value is used. In some cases you will want to prompt the user to enter the missing information when the applet begins. This way, the applet can be used in cases in which the parameter values are known in advance, and when they aren't.

When passing a string that contains spaces, you can enclose that string within quotes. For example, this specifies the user's name as George Williams:

```
<param name=UserName value="George Williams">
```

Use AppletContext to Display a Web Page

Key Ingredients	
Classes and Interfaces	**Methods**
java.applet.Applet	AppletContext getAppletContext( )
java.applet.AppletContext	showDocument(URL *url*)

This recipe shows how to use an applet to display a Web page. You might use such an applet to let the user choose between various options, and then display the page that he or she selected. To do this, you will obtain the applet's **AppletContext** and then use its **showDocument( )** method to display the page.

Step-by-Step

To display a Web page from an applet, follow these steps:

1. Obtain a reference to the **AppletContext** associated with the applet by calling **getAppletContext( )**.
2. Construct a **URL** object that represents the desired page.
3. Using the **AppletContext**, call **showDocument( )**, specifying the **URL**.

Discussion

To obtain the **AppletContext** for an applet, call **getAppletContext( )** shown here:

    AppletContext getAppletContext( )

It returns a reference to the **AppletContext** associated with the invoking applet. As explained in *Applet Overview*, **AppletContext** encapsulates information about the applet's execution environment.

Construct a **URL** instance that describes the page that you want to display. **URL** defines several constructors. The one used here is

    URL(String *url*) throws MalformedURLException

Here *url* must specify a valid URL, including protocol. If it doesn't, a **MalformedURLException** is thrown.

To display the page, call **showDocument( )**, shown here, on the **AppletContext**, passing in the desired URL:

    void showDocument(URL *url*)

Here, *url* specifies the page to display.

Example

The following example shows how to display a Web page from an applet. It allows the user to choose between two Web sites, both of which are passed in as parameters. (See the preceding recipe for information on passing parameters to applets.) To display the page, the user must press the Show Page Now button. This causes **showDocument( )** to be invoked, which results in the browser navigating to the specified page.

One other point: Notice that it uses **showStatus( )**, which is defined by **Applet**, to output an error message to the browser's status window if the URL is in error. The status window can be a useful place to display feedback to the user. However, its behavior may differ between browsers.

NOTE *This example must be run inside a browser that is currently online and not by* **appletviewer***.*

```
// A Swing-based applet that uses the showDocument()
// method defined by AppletContext to display
// a web page. It takes two parameters. The first
// specifies the URL of the primary web site and the second
// specifies the URL of a secondary web site.
// The user selects which site to display by checking
// or clearing a check box. Pressing the Show Page Now
// button causes the page to be displayed.

import javax.swing.*;
import java.awt.*;
import java.awt.event.*;
import java.net.*;

/*
<applet code="ShowURL" width=220 height=100>
<param name=primarySite value=HerbSchildt.com>
<param name=secondarySite value=McGrawHill.com>
<param name=default value=0>
</applet>
*/

public class ShowURL extends JApplet {

  JLabel jlab;

  JCheckBox jcbPrimary;

  String primary;
  String secondary;

  // Initialize the applet.
  public void init() {
    primary = getParameter("primarySite");
    secondary = getParameter("secondarySite");

    try {
      SwingUtilities.invokeAndWait(new Runnable () {
        public void run() {
          makeGUI();
        }
```

```
      });
    } catch(Exception exc) {
      System.out.println("Can't create because of "+ exc);
    }
  }

  // Initialize the GUI.
  private void makeGUI() {

    // Set the content pane's layout to flow layout.
    setLayout(new FlowLayout());

    // Note: If you are using a version of Java prior to
    // JDK 5, then you will need to use getContentPane()
    // to explicitly set the content pane's layout,
    // as shown here:
    //
    //    getContentPane().setLayout(new FlowLayout());

    // Create the label that will display the target
    // web site.
    jlab = new JLabel("Transfer to " + primary);

    // Create a check box.
    jcbPrimary = new JCheckBox("Use Primary Site", true);

    // Handle check box item events.
    jcbPrimary.addItemListener(new ItemListener() {
      public void itemStateChanged(ItemEvent ie) {

        // Toggle between primary and secondary sites.
        if(jcbPrimary.isSelected())
          jlab.setText("Transfer to " + primary);
        else
          jlab.setText("Transfer to " + secondary);
      }
    });

    // Add a button that transfers to selected web site.
    JButton jbtnJump = new JButton("Show Page Now");

    // Create the action listener for the button.
    jbtnJump.addActionListener( new ActionListener() {
      public void actionPerformed(ActionEvent ae) {
        showStatus("Transferring to selected site.");

        // Transfer to the desired site.
        try {
          if(jcbPrimary.isSelected())
            getAppletContext().showDocument(
              new URL("http://www." + primary));
```

```
        else
          getAppletContext().showDocument(
            new URL("http://www." + secondary));
      } catch(MalformedURLException exc) {
        showStatus("Error in URL.");
      }
    }
  }
});

    // Add the label, check boxes, and button to the
    // applet's content pane.
    add(jcbPrimary);
    add(jlab);
    add(jbtnJump);

    // Note: If you are using a version of Java prior to
    // JDK 5, then you will need to use getContentPane()
    // to explicitly add components to the content pane,
    // as shown here.
    //
    //    getContentPane().add(jcbPrimary);
    //
    // and so on.
  }
}
```

The output as displayed in a browser is shown here:

Options and Alternatives

The version of **showDocument( )** used in the example lets the browser decide how to display the new page, but you can control this. To specify how the new page is displayed, use this form of **showDocument( )**:

  void showDocument(URL *url*, String *where*)

Here, *where* determines where the Web page is displayed. Valid arguments for *where* are "_self" (show in current frame), "_parent" (show in parent frame), "_top" (show in topmost frame), and "_blank" (show in new window). You can also specify a name, which causes the document to be shown in a window by that name. If that window does not already exist, it will be created.

Create a Simple Servlet Using GenericServlet

Key Ingredients	
Classes and Interfaces	**Methods**
javax.servlet.GenericServlet	void destroy( )
	void init(ServletConfig *sc*)
	void service(ServletRequest *srq*,
	ServletResponse *srp*)
javax.servlet.ServletResponse	PrintWriter getWriter( )
	void setContentType(String *cType*)
javax.servlet.ServletRequest	String getServerName( )

This recipe creates a simple servlet by extending **GenericServlet**. As explained in *Servlet Overview,* all servlets must implement the **Servlet** interface. **GenericServlet** makes this easy because it provides default implementations for all of the methods defined by **Servlet**, with the exception of the **service( )** method. Thus, by extending **GenericServlet**, you can create a servlet without having to implement all of the required methods yourself.

Step-by-Step

To create a servlet based on **GenericServlet**, follow these steps:

1. Create a class that extends **GenericServlet**.

2. Override the **service( )** life cycle method. **GenericServlet** provides no default implementation for **service( )** because its implementation is specific to each servlet. You may also need to override **init( )**, to initialize the servlet, and **destroy( )**, to release resources when the servlet is deactivated. Default versions of these methods are provided, however, if no initialization or termination actions are required.

3. Inside **service( )**, handle requests by returning a response. Information about the request is available through a **ServletRequest** object. The response is returned via a **ServletResponse** object. The example responds to requests by writing to the output stream linked to the response parameter. The output stream is obtained by calling **getWriter( )**. Before responding, you can set the content type by calling **setContentType( )**.

Discussion

GenericServlet provides default implementations of **ServletConfig** and most of **Servlet**. The only method that it does not implement is **service( )** because its actions are determined by the needs and functionality of your servlet. Therefore, when using **GenericServlet**, you will always provide an implementation of **service( )**. The **service( )** method is shown here:

```
void service(ServletRequest srq, ServletResponse srp)
        throws ServletException, IOException
```

The first argument is a **ServletRequest** object that enables the servlet to read data that is provided via the client request. The second argument is a **ServletResponse** object. This enables the servlet to formulate a response for the client. It throws a **ServletException** if a servlet error occurs. It throws an **IOException** if an I/O error occurs.

The **ServletRequest** and **ServletResponse** interfaces provide methods that enable you to obtain information about the request or provide a response. A sampling of these methods is shown in Tables 6-2 and 6-3 in *Servlet Overview* earlier in this chapter. The example that follows uses three of these methods. This first is **getServerName( )**. It is defined by **ServletRequest** and is shown here:

    String getServerName( )

It returns the name of the server. The other two, **getWriter( )** and **setContentType( )**, are defined by **ServletResponse**. They are shown here:

    PrintWriter getWriter( ) throws IOException
    void setContentType(String *cType*)

The **getWriter( )** method returns a reference to a stream to which a response can be written. Anything written to this stream is sent to the client as part of the response. It throws an **IOException** if an I/O error occurs while attempting to obtain the stream. The **setContentType( )** method establishes the content type (MIME type) of the response. In the example, the content type is text/html. This indicates that the browser should interpret the content as HTML.

GenericServlet provides default implementations of the other two life cycle methods, **init( )** and **destroy( )**, but you can override these as required by the needs of your application. Of course, if your servlet does not need to initialize or release any resources, then there is usually no reason to override these methods.

Example

Following is a skeletal servlet. It overrides the three life cycle methods, and it returns a response when its **service( )** method is called. This response is the same for all requests: it simply returns a message that shows what life cycle methods have been called and the name of the server. However, your own servlet will provide implementations appropriate for your application.

NOTE *For instructions on using Tomcat to run a servlet see* Using Tomcat for Servlet Development.

```
// A simple servlet.

import java.io.*;
import javax.servlet.*;

public class ServletSkel extends GenericServlet {
  String msg = "";
```

```java
  // Called once, at startup.
  public void init(ServletConfig sc) {
    msg = "Servlet initialized.";
  }

  // Called once, when the servlet is removed.
  public void destroy() {
    msg += " This won't be seen.";
  }

  // Called repeatedly to handle requests.
  public void service(ServletRequest request,
                      ServletResponse response)
                      throws ServletException, IOException {

    // Set the content type.
    response.setContentType("text/html");

    // Get a response stream.
    PrintWriter pw = response.getWriter();

    // Show that the service() method has been called
    // and display the server name.
    msg += "<br>Inside service(). Server: " + request.getServerName();
    pw.println(msg);

    pw.close();
  }
}
```

The output displayed in the browser is shown here:

```
Servlet initialized.
Inside service(). Server: localhost
```

Notice that the server name is localhost. This is because the servlet was run on the same computer as the browser. Also note that the message added by **destroy( )** is not shown. As the comments inside **destroy( )** indicate, you will not see the string added by **destroy( )** because it is the last method called when the servlet is being removed. Thus, **service( )** is not called after **destroy( )** is called.

Options and Alternatives

As explained, when extending **GenericServlet**, there is no need to override **init( )** or **destroy( )** if they are not needed. Default implementations are provided.

To create a servlet that handles various HTTP requests, such as GET or POST, it is often more convenient to extend **HttpServlet** rather than **GenericServlet**. The following recipe shows how.

Handle HTTP Requests in a Servlet

Key Ingredients	
Classes and Interfaces	**Methods**
javax.servlet.http .HttpServlet	void doGet(HttpServletRequest *hsreq*, HttpServletResponse *hsrep*)
javax.servlet.http .HttpServletRequest	String getParameter(String *paramName*)
javax.servlet.http .HttpServletResponse	PrintWriter getWriter( )

If you are creating a servlet that will be responding to HTTP requests, such as GET or POST, then you will usually want your servlet to extend **HttpServlet** rather than **GenericServlet**. The reason is that **HttpServlet** provides methods that handle the various HTTP requests. **HttpServlet** extends **GenericServlet** and is packaged in **javax.servlet.http**.

Step-by-Step

To create a servlet based on **HttpServlet**, follow these steps:

1. Create a class that extends **HttpServlet**.

2. If necessary, override the **init( )** and **destroy( )** life cycle methods. However, do not override **service( )** because it is implemented by **HttpServlet** and it automatically routes HTTP requests to the handlers defined by **HttpServlet**.

3. Override the handler or handlers needed by your servlet. The handler used in this recipe is **doGet( )**. It handles GET requests. Information about the request is available through an **HttpServletRequest** object. The response is returned via an **HttpServletResponse** object. The example responds to requests by writing to the output stream linked to the response parameter. The output stream is obtained by calling **getWriter( )**. Before responding, you can set the content type by calling **setContentType( )**.

4. You can obtain the value of a parameter associated with a request by calling **getParameter( )** on the **HttpServletRequest** object.

Discussion

HttpServlet defines several **do...** methods that handle various HTTP requests. The one used by the recipe is **doGet( )**. It handles GET requests and is shown here:

    void doGet(HttpServletRequest *hsreq*, HttpServletResponse *hsrep*)
        throws IOException, ServletException

It is called when a GET request is received. Information about the request is available through *hsreq*. To respond, use *hsrep*. An **IOException** is thrown if an I/O error occurs while handling the request. A **ServletException** is thrown if the request fails.

HttpServletRequest extends **ServletRequest** and adds support for HTTP requests. **HttpServletResponse** extends **ServletResponse** and adds support for HTTP responses.

To obtain the value of a parameter associated with the request, call **getParameter( )**. This method is inherited from **ServletRequest** and is shown here:

String getParameter(String *paramName*)

The name of the parameter is passed in *paramName*. The value (in string form) is returned. If the parameter is not found, **null** is returned.

For a description of **setContentType( )** and **getWriter( )**, see *Create a Simple Servlet Using GenericServlet*.

Example

The following example creates a servlet that uses the Pythagorean theorem to compute the length of the hypotenuse given the lengths of the two opposing sides of a right triangle. The lengths of the two sides are passed in through parameters.

NOTE *For instructions on using* Tomcat *to run a servlet see* Using Tomcat for Servlet Development.

```java
// This servlet computes the length of the hypotenuse
// given the length of the two opposing sides.
import java.io.*;
import javax.servlet.*;
import javax.servlet.http.*;

public class HypotServlet extends HttpServlet {

  public void doGet(HttpServletRequest request,
                    HttpServletResponse response)
                throws ServletException, IOException {

    // Obtain the parameters that contain the lengths
    // of the two sides.
    String side1 = request.getParameter("firstside");
    String side2 = request.getParameter("secondside");

    // Set the content type and get a stream
    // for the response.
    response.setContentType("text/html");
    PrintWriter pw = response.getWriter();

    try {
      double a, b;
      a = Double.parseDouble(side1);
      b = Double.parseDouble(side2);
      pw.println("Hypotenuse is " + Math.sqrt(a*a + b*b));
```

```
    } catch(NumberFormatException exc) {
      pw.println("Invalid Data");
    }

    pw.close();
  }
}
```

The following HTML presents a form that prompts the user for the length of the two sides and then invokes **HypotServlet** to compute and display the result. Therefore, to use the servlet, first load the following HTML into your browser and enter the length of both sides. Then, press the Compute button. This causes **HypotServlet** to be invoked. It computes the length of the hypotenuse and displays the result.

```
<html>
<body>
<left>
<form name="Form1"
  action="http://localhost:8080/examples/servlet/HypotServlet">
Compute the Hypotenuse
<br><br>
Enter length of side one:
<input type=textbox name = "firstside" size=12 value="">
<br>
Enter length of side two:
<input type=textbox name = "secondside" size=12 value="">
<br><br>
<input type=submit value="Compute">
</form>
</body>
</html>
```

The following figures show the HTML that prompts the user for the length of the sides and the result when executed within a browser.

Compute the Hypotenuse

Enter length of side one: 3

Enter length of side two: 4

Hypotenuse is 5.0

Compute

Bonus Example

Although the preceding example demonstrates an HTTP-based servlet and the use of parameters, it is possible to substantially improve it in two ways. First, there is no need to have a separate HTML file that invokes **HypotServlet**. Instead, the servlet itself can display a page that prompts the user for the length of the sides. Second, the length of the hypotenuse can be displayed on the same page, allowing the user to easily compute the length of the hypotenuse for other triangles. The following version of **HypotServlet** implements this approach.

NOTE *For instructions on using Tomcat to run a servlet see* Using Tomcat for Servlet Development.

```
// An improved version of HypotServlet.

// This version improves on the one shown in the previous
// example in two ways. First, it displays the HTML necessary
// to input the length of the sides and execute the servlet.
// Second, it displays the result on the same page.

import java.io.*;
import javax.servlet.*;
import javax.servlet.http.*;

public class HypotServlet extends HttpServlet {

  public void doGet(HttpServletRequest request,
                    HttpServletResponse response)
                       throws ServletException, IOException {

    // Obtain the parameters that contain the lengths
    // of the two sides.
    String side1 = request.getParameter("firstside");
    String side2 = request.getParameter("secondside");

    // This string will hold the computed length of
    // the hypotenuse.
    String hypot;

    // If a parameter is missing, then set
    // strings to a null string.
    if(side1 == null | side2 == null) {
      side1 = "";
      side2 = "";
      hypot = "";
    } else {
      // Compute the hypotenuse.
      try {
        double a, b, h;
        a = Double.parseDouble(side1);
        b = Double.parseDouble(side2);
        h = Math.sqrt(a*a + b*b);
        hypot = "" + h;
      } catch(NumberFormatException exc) {
        hypot = "Invalid Data";
      }
    }
```

```
        // Set the content type and get a stream
        // for the response.
        response.setContentType("text/html");
        PrintWriter pw = response.getWriter();

        // Display HTML form.
        pw.print("<html> <body> <left>" +
                "<form name=\"Form1\"" +
                "action=\"http://localhost:8080/" +
                "examples/servlet/HypotServlet\">" +
                "Compute the Hypotenuse<br><br>" +
                "Enter length of side one: " +
                "<input type=textbox name = " +
                "\"firstside\" size=12 value=\"" +
                side1 + "\">" +
                "<br>Enter length of side two: " +
                "<input type=textbox name = " +
                "\"secondside\" size=12 value=\"" +
                side2 +"\"><br><br>" +
                "<input type=submit value=\"Compute\">" +
                "</form>" +
                "Length of hypotenuse: " +
                "<input READONLY type=textbox name = " +
                "\"hypot\" size=20 value=\"" +
                hypot +"\"> </body> </html>");

    pw.close();
  }
}
```

Sample output is shown here:

Compute the Hypotenuse

Enter length of side one: 3

Enter length of side two: 4

Compute

Length of hypotenuse: 5.0

Notice how the **doGet( )** method automatically prompts the user for the lengths of the sides if they are not part of the request (as they won't be when the servlet is first executed). If either **side1** or **side2** is **null**, it means that one or both of the parameters is missing. This causes the **side1**, **side2**, and **hypot** (the result) to be set to the null string. Otherwise, the hypotenuse is computed. Then, the HTML is sent that includes the prompting and result text boxes. If **side1**, **side2**, and **hypot** are null strings, then the text boxes are empty, and the user will enter the lengths. Otherwise, the lengths and the result are displayed.

Notice one other thing: the text box that displays the result is read-only. This means that the user cannot enter a string into it.

Options and Alternatives

In addition to **doGet( )**, **HttpServlet** provides handlers for several other HTTP requests. For example, you can use **doPost( )** to handle a POST request and **doPut( )** to handle a PUT request. When creating an **HttpServlet**, override the handlers required by your application.

Use a Cookie with a Servlet

Key Ingredients	
Classes	**Methods**
javax.servlet.http.Cookie	String getName( ) String getValue( ) void setMaxAge(int *period*)
javax.servlet.http.HttpServletRequest	Cookie[ ] getCookies( )
javax.servlet.http.HttpServletResponse	void addCookie(Cookie *ck*)

Cookies are an important part of many web applications. For this reasons, servlets provide substantial support for them. For example, cookies can be created by a servlet and they can be read by a servlet. Cookies are instances of the **Cookie** class. This recipe shows how to create a cookie and then obtain its value.

Step-by-Step

To use cookies with a servlet involves these steps:

1. Create a **Cookie** object that contains the name and value that you want to give to the cookie. All names and values are represented as strings.

2. To save a cookie, call **addCookie( )** on the **HttpServletReponse** object.

3. To retrieve a cookie, first obtain an array of the cookies associated with a request by calling **getCookies( )** on the **HttpServletRequest** object. Then, search for the cookie whose name matches the one that you are looking for. Use **getName( )** to obtain the name of each cookie. Finally, obtain the value of the cookie by calling **getValue( )**.

Discussion

In a servlet, a cookie is encapsulated by the **Cookie** class. It defines one constructor, which is shown here:

Cookie(String *name*, String *value*)

Here, *name* specifies the name of the cookie and *value* specifies its value.

By default, an instance of **Cookie** is removed from the browser when the browser is terminated. However, you can persist a cookie by setting its maximum age by calling **setMaxAge( )**:

> void setMaxAge(int *period*)

The cookie will persist until *period* seconds have transpired. For example, if you want a cookie to remain for 24 hours, pass 86,400 to **setMaxAge( )**.

To add a cookie, call **addCookie( )** on the **HttpServletResponse** object. It is shown here:

> void addCookie(Cookie *ck*)

The cookie to add is passed via *ck*.

To obtain an array of the cookies associated with a request, call **getCookies( )**. It is shown here:

> Cookie[ ] getCookies( )

If there are no cookies linked to the request, **null** is returned.

Given a **Cookie**, you can obtain its name by calling **getName( )**. Its value is obtained by calling **getValue( )**. These methods are shown here:

> String getName( )
> String getValue( )

Therefore, using the array returned by **getCookies( )**, you can search for a specific cookie by name by calling **getName( )** on each cookie until a cookie with the matching name is found. Using the cookie, you can obtain its value by calling **getValue( )**.

Example

The following example illustrates cookies with servlets. It creates a servlet called **CookieServlet** that first checks for a cookie called "who". If it is found, it uses the name linked with the cookie to display a welcome message that includes the name. For example, if your name is Tom, then this message is displayed:

> Hello Tom. Nice to see you again.

However, if the cookie is not found, then you are prompted to enter a name and the "who" cookie is created, using the name. The next time the servlet is run, the cookie will be found.

As the example is written, the cookie persists for only 60 seconds, so you must rerun **CookieServlet** within that 60-second time frame to find the cookie. Furthermore, you will need to either exit and restart the browser, or use the refresh/reload browser option between executions so that the servlet will be re-run from the top.

Notice that the servlet explicitly handles two HTTP requests: POST and GET. When a GET request is received, the servlet attempts to retrieve the "who" cookie. If the cookie is not found, then the HTML is displayed that prompts the user. When a POST request is received, a new cookie is created that contains the user's name and it is added to the response by calling **addCookie( )**.

NOTE *For instructions on using Tomcat to run a servlet see* Using Tomcat for Servlet Development.

```java
// This example demonstrates the use of a cookie.
// When first executed, if it does not find a
// cookie called "who", it prompts the user
// for a name and then creates a cookie called "who"
// that contains the name. If the cookie is found,
// then the name is used to display a welcome message.

// Note: the "who" cookie is persisted for only
// 60 seconds. Therefore, you must execute
// CookieServlet twice within 60 seconds. You will
// need to restart your browser between executions
// of CookieServlet, or use Refresh/Reload.

import java.io.*;
import javax.servlet.*;
import javax.servlet.http.*;

public class CookieServlet extends HttpServlet {

  // Retrieve a cookie.
  public void doGet(HttpServletRequest request,
                    HttpServletResponse response)
                throws ServletException, IOException {

    // Initialize customer to null.
    String customer = null;

    response.setContentType("text/html");
    PrintWriter pw = response.getWriter();

    // Get cookies from header of HTTP request.
    Cookie[] cookies = request.getCookies();

    // If cookies are present, find the "who" cookie.
    // It contains the customer's name.
    if(cookies != null)
      for(int i = 0; i < cookies.length; i++) {
        if(cookies[i].getName().equals("who")) {
          customer = cookies[i].getValue();
          pw.println("Hello " + customer + "." +
                  " Nice to see you again.");
        }
      }

    // Otherwise, prompt for customer name.
    if(customer == null) {
      pw.print("<html> <body> <left>" +
              "<form name=\"Form1\"" +
              "method=\"post\" "+
```

```
                    "action=\"http://localhost:8080/" +
                    "examples/servlet/CookieServlet\">" +
                    "Please enter your name: " +
                    "<input type=textbox name = " +
                    "\"custname\" size=40 value=\"\"" +
                    "<input type=submit value=\"Submit\">" +
                    "</form> </body> </html>");
    }
    pw.close();
  }

  // Create a cookie.
  public void doPost(HttpServletRequest request,
                 HttpServletResponse response)
                   throws ServletException, IOException {

    // Get the custname parameter.
    String customer = request.getParameter("custname");

    // Create cookie called "who" that contains
    // the customer's name.
    Cookie cookie = new Cookie("who", customer);

    // Persist the cookie for 60 seconds.
    cookie.setMaxAge(60);

    // Add cookie to HTTP response.
    response.addCookie(cookie);

    response.setContentType("text/html");
    PrintWriter pw = response.getWriter();
    pw.println("Hello " + customer + ".");

    pw.close();
  }
}
```

Options and Alternatives

There are several cookie options that you might find useful. You can obtain the maximum age of a cookie by calling **getMaxAge( )**. You can associate a comment with a cookie by calling **setComment( )**. You can retrieve the comment by calling **getComment( )**. You can set the value of a cookie after it has been created by calling **setValue( )**.

Somewhat related to cookies in a conceptual sense are *sessions,* which can be used to save state information. A session is encapsulated by the **HttpSession** class, which defines methods such as **getAttribute( )** and **setAttribute( )** that can be used to set or retrieve state information. The current session can be obtained (or created) calling **getSession( )** defined by **HttpServletRequest**.

7

CHAPTER

Multithreading

A mong the defining characteristics of Java is its built-in support for multithreaded programming. This support, which has been present in Java from the start, is provided by the **Thread** class, the **Runnable** interface, several methods supplied by **Object**, and the **synchronized** keyword. Multithreading enables you to write programs that contain two or more separate paths of execution that can execute concurrently. Each path of execution is called a *thread*. Through the careful use of multithreading, you can create programs that make efficient use of system resources and maintain a responsive user interface.

Because multiple threads can interact in ways that are not always intuitive, adding a level of complexity that is not present in a single-threaded program, some programmers avoid multithreading whenever possible. However, the modern programming world is moving toward more use of multithreading, not less. Highly parallel architectures are becoming the norm. Simply put, multithreading will continue to play a critical part in many (perhaps most) real-world applications of Java.

This chapter contains several recipes that show how to create and manage threads and the multithreaded environment. It begins by describing the basic procedures needed to create a thread. It then shows key multithreading techniques, such as synchronizing threads, setting priorities, and interthread communication. It also illustrates the use of daemon threads, thread interrupts, and how to monitor the status of a thread.

Here are the recipes in this chapter:

- Create a Thread by Implementing **Runnable**
- Create a Thread by Extending **Thread**
- Use a Thread's Name and ID
- Wait for a Thread to End
- Synchronize Threads
- Communicate Between Threads
- Suspend, Resume, and Stop a Thread
- Use a Daemon Thread

- Interrupt a Thread
- Set and Obtain a Thread's Priority
- Monitor a Thread's State
- Use a Thread Group

NOTE *A relatively recent addition to the Java API are the* concurrency utilities, *which are packaged in* **java.util.concurrent** *and its subpackages. These are also commonly referred to as the* concurrent API. *Added by Java 5, the concurrent API supplies several high-level constructs that aid in the development of highly sophisticated, multithreaded programs. For example, the concurrent API supplies semaphores, countdown latches, and futures, to name a few. Although the concurrency utilities are not the focus of this chapter, they are something that will be of interest to readers who are developing thread-intensive applications.*

Multithreading Fundamentals

At its core, multithreading is a form of multitasking. There are two distinct types of multitasking: *process-based* and *thread-based.* It is important to differentiate between the two. As it relates to this discussion, a process is, in essence, a program that is executing. Thus, process-based multitasking is the feature that allows your computer to run two or more programs concurrently. For example, it is process-based multitasking that allows you to download a file at the same time you are compiling a program or sorting a database. In process-based multitasking, a program is the smallest unit of code that can be dispatched by the scheduler.

In a *thread-based* multitasking environment, the thread is the smallest unit of dispatchable code. Because a program can contain more than one thread, a single program can use multiple threads to perform two or more tasks at once. For instance, a browser can begin rendering a Web page while it is still downloading the remainder of the page. This is possible because each action is performed by a separate thread. Although Java programs make use of process-based multitasking environments, process-based multitasking is not under the direct control of Java. Multithreaded multitasking is.

All processes have at least one thread of execution, which is called the *main thread,* because it is the one that is executed when a program begins. From the main thread, you can create other threads. These other threads can also create threads, and so on.

Multithreading is important to Java for two main reasons. First, multithreading enables you to write very efficient programs because it lets you utilize the idle time that is present in most programs. Most I/O devices, whether they be network ports, disk drives, or the keyboard, are much slower than the CPU. Thus, a program will often spend a majority of its execution time waiting to send or receive information to or from a device. By using multithreading, your program can execute another task during this idle time. For example, while one part of your program is sending a file over the Internet, another part can be handling user interaction (such as mouse clicks or button presses), and still another can be buffering the next block of data to send.

The second reason that multithreading is important to Java relates to Java's event-handling model. A program (such as an applet) must respond quickly to an event and then return. An event handler must not retain control of the CPU for an extended period of time.

If it does, other events will not be handled in a timely fashion. This will make an application appear sluggish. It is also possible that an event will be missed. Therefore, if an event requires some extended action, then it must be performed by a separate thread.

A thread can be in one of several states. It can be *running*. It can be *ready to run* as soon as it gets CPU time. A running thread can be *suspended*, which is a temporary halt to its execution. It can later be *resumed*. A thread can be *blocked* when waiting for a resource. A thread can be *terminated*, in which case its execution ends and cannot be resumed.

Along with thread-based multitasking comes the need for *synchronization*, which allows the execution of threads to be coordinated in certain well-defined ways. Java has extensive, integrated support for synchronization, which is achieved through the use of a monitor, which all objects have, and the **synchronized** keyword. Thus, all objects can be synchronized.

Two or more threads can communicate with each other through methods that are defined by **Object**. These methods are **wait( )**, **notify( )**, and **notifyAll( )**. They enable one thread to wait on another. For example, if one thread is using a shared resource, then another thread must wait until the first thread has finished. The waiting thread can resume execution when the first thread notifies it that the resource is now available.

There are two basic types of threads: user and daemon. A *user thread* is the type of thread created by default. For example, the main thread is a user thread. In general, a program continues to execute as long as there is at least one active user thread. It is possible to change the status of a thread to daemon. *Daemon threads* are automatically terminated when all non-daemon threads have terminated. Thus, they are subordinate to user threads.

Threads can be part of a group. A *thread group* enables you to manage related threads collectively. For example, you can obtain an array of the threads in the group.

Java's multithreading system is built upon the **Thread** class and its companion interface, **Runnable**. **Thread** encapsulates a thread of execution. To create a new thread, your program will either implement the **Runnable** interface or extend **Thread**. Both **Runnable** and **Thread** are packaged in **java.lang**. Thus, they are automatically available to all programs.

The Runnable Interface

The **java.lang.Runnable** interface abstracts a unit of executable code. You can construct a thread on any object that implements the **Runnable** interface. Therefore, any class that you intend to run in a separate thread must implement **Runnable**.

Runnable defines only one method called **run( )**, which is declared like this:

    void run( )

Inside **run( )**, you will define the code that constitutes the new thread. It is important to understand that **run( )** can call other methods, use other classes, and declare variables just like the main thread. The only difference is that **run( )** establishes the entry point for another, concurrent thread of execution within your program. This thread will end when **run( )** returns.

Once you have created an instance of a class that implements **Runnable**, you create a thread by constructing an object of type **Thread**, passing in the **Runnable** instance. To start the thread running, you will call **start( )** on the **Thread** object, as described in the next section.

The Thread Class

The **Thread** class encapsulates a thread. It is packaged in **java.lang** and implements the **Runnable** interface. Therefore, a second way to create a thread is to extend **Thread** and override the **run( )** method. **Thread** also defines several methods that help manage threads. Here are the ones used in this chapter:

Method	Meaning
static Thread currentThread( )	Returns a reference to a **Thread** object that represents the invoking thread.
long getID( )	Returns a thread's ID.
final String getName( )	Obtains a thread's name.
final int getPriority( )	Obtains a thread's priority.
Thread.State getState( )	Returns the current state of the thread.
static boolean holdsLock(Object *obj*)	Returns **true** if the invoking thread holds the lock on *obj*.
void interrupt( )	Interrupts a thread.
static boolean interrupted( )	Returns **true** if the invoking thread has been interrupted.
final boolean isAlive( )	Determines whether a thread is still running.
final boolean isDaemon( )	Returns **true** if the invoking thread is a daemon thread.
boolean isInterrupted( )	Returns **true** if the thread on which it is called has been interrupted.
final void join( )	Waits for a thread to terminate.
void run( )	Entry point for the thread.
final void setDaemon(boolean *how*)	If *how* is true, the invoking thread is set to daemon status.
final void setName(String *thrdName*)	Sets a thread's name to *thrdName*.
final void setPriority(int *level*)	Sets a thread's priority to *level*.
static void sleep(long *milliseconds*)	Suspends a thread for a specified period of milliseconds.
void start( )	Starts a thread by calling its **run( )** method.
static void yield( )	Yields the CPU to another thread.

Pay special attention to the **start( )** method. After an instance of **Thread** has been created, call **start( )** to begin execution of the thread. The **start( )** method calls **run( )**, which is the method defined by **Runnable** that contains the code to be executed in the thread. This process is described in detail in the following recipes.

Another method of special interest is **sleep( )**. It suspends execution of a thread for a specified period of time. When a thread sleeps, another thread can execute until the sleeping thread awakes and resumes execution. Several examples in this chapter use **sleep( )** to demonstrate the effects of multiple threads.

Thread defines two sets of constructors, one for constructing a thread on a separate instance of **Runnable** and the other for constructing a thread on classes that extend **Thread**. Here are the constructors that take a separate instance of **Runnable**:

Thread(Runnable *thrdOb*)
Thread(Runnable *thrdOb*, String *thrdName*)
Thread(ThreadGroup *thrdGroup*, Runnable *thrdObj*)
Thread(ThreadGroup *thrdGroup*, Runnable *thrdObj*, String *thrdName*)

Here, *thrdObj* is a reference to an instance of a class that implements **Runnable**. This object's **run( )** method contains the code that will be executed as the new thread. The name of thread is passed in *thrdName*. If no name is specified (or the name is null), then a name is supplied automatically by the JVM. The thread group to which the thread belongs (if any) is passed via *thrdGroup*. If the thread group is not specified, then the thread group is determined by the security manager (if there is one) or is set to the same group as the invoking thread.

Here are the constructors that create a thread for classes that extend **Thread**:

Thread( )
Thread(String *thrdName*)
Thread(ThreadGroup *thrdGroup*, String *thrdName*)

The first constructor creates a thread that uses the default name and thread group, as described already. The second lets you specify the name. The third lets you specify the thread group and the name.

For both sets of constructors, the thread will be created as a user thread unless the creating thread is a daemon thread. In this case, the thread will be created as a daemon thread.

There is another **Thread** constructor that lets you specify a stack size for the thread. However, because of differences in execution environments, the API documentation states that "extreme care should be exercised in its use." Therefore, it is not used in this book.

Create a Thread by Implementing Runnable

Key Ingredients	
Classes and Interfaces	**Methods**
java.lang.Runnable	void run( )
java.lang.Thread	static void sleep(long *milliseconds*)
	void start( )

Perhaps the most common way to construct a thread is to create a class that implements **Runnable** and then construct a **Thread** using an instance of that class. If you won't be overriding any of **Thread**'s methods or extending its functionality in some way, then implementing **Runnable** is often the best approach. This recipe describes the process. The example also demonstrates **Thread.sleep( )**, which suspends execution of a thread for a specified period of time.

Step-by-Step

To create a thread by implementing **Runnable** involves these steps:

1. Create a class that implements the **Runnable** interface. Objects of this class can be used to create new threads of execution.

2. Inside the **run( )** method specified by **Runnable**, put the code that you want to execute in the thread.

3. Create an instance of the **Runnable** class.

4. Create a **Thread** object, passing in the **Runnable** instance.

5. Begin execution of the thread by calling **start( )** on the **Thread** instance.

Discussion

As explained in *Multithreading Fundamentals*, **Runnable** specifies only one method, **run( )**, which is defined like this:

    void run( )

Inside the body of this method, put the code that you want to be executed in a separate thread. The thread will continue to execute until **run( )** returns.

To actually create a thread, pass a **Runnable** instance to one of **Thread**'s constructors. The one used by this recipe is shown here:

    Thread(Runnable *thrdObj*, String *thrdName*)

Here, *thrdObj* is an instance of a class that implements **Runnable** and *thrdName* specifies the name of the thread.

To begin execution of the thread, call **start( )** on the **Thread** instance. This results in a call to **run( )** on the **Runnable** on which the thread was constructed.

The example program uses **Thread.sleep( )** to temporarily suspend execution of a thread. When a thread sleeps, another thread can execute. Thus, sleeping relinquishes the CPU for the specified period of time. The **sleep( )** method has two forms. The one used by the example is shown here:

    static void sleep(long *milliseconds*) throws InterruptedException

The number of milliseconds to suspend is specified in *milliseconds*. This method can throw an **InterruptedException**.

Example

The following example shows the steps needed to create and execute a thread. It defines a class called **MyThread** that implements **Runnable**. Inside the **main( )** method of **DemoRunnable**, an instance of **MyThread** is created and passed to a **Thread** constructor, which creates a new thread of execution. The thread is then started by calling **start( )** on the new thread.

```java
// Create a thread by implementing Runnable.

// This class implements Runnable, which means that
// it can be used to create a thread of execution.
class MyThread implements Runnable {
  int count;

  MyThread() {
    count = 0;
  }

  // Entry point of thread.
  public void run() {

    System.out.println("MyThread starting.");

    try {
      do {
        Thread.sleep(500);
        System.out.println("In MyThread, count is " + count);
        count++;
      } while(count < 5);
    }
    catch(InterruptedException exc) {
      System.out.println("MyThread interrupted.");
    }

    System.out.println("MyThread terminating.");
  }
}

class RunnableDemo {
  public static void main(String args[]) {
    System.out.println("Main thread starting.");

    // First, construct a MyThread object.
    MyThread mt = new MyThread();

    // Next, construct a thread from that object.
    Thread newThrd = new Thread(mt);

    // Finally, start execution of the thread.
    newThrd.start();

    // Give the main thread something to do.
    do {
      System.out.println("In main thread.");
      try {
        Thread.sleep(250);
      }
      catch(InterruptedException exc) {
        System.out.println("Main thread interrupted.");
      }
```

```
    } while (mt.count != 5);

    System.out.println("Main thread ending.");
  }
}
```

Sample output is shown here. (The precise output may vary, based on platform, task load, processor speed, and which version of the Java runtime system is used.)

```
Main thread starting.
In main thread.
MyThread starting.
In main thread.
In MyThread, count is 0
In main thread.
In main thread.
In MyThread, count is 1
In main thread.
In main thread.
In MyThread, count is 2
In main thread.
In main thread.
In MyThread, count is 3
In main thread.
In main thread.
In MyThread, count is 4
MyThread terminating.
Main thread ending.
```

Let's look closely at how this program works. As stated, **MyThread** implements **Runnable**. This means that an object of type **MyThread** is suitable for use as a thread and can be passed to the **Thread** constructor. Inside **MyThread**'s **run( )** method, a loop is established that counts from 0 to 4. This is the code that will be executed in a separate thread.

Inside **run( )**, notice the call to **Thread.sleep(500)**. This static method causes the thread from which it is called to suspend execution for the specified period of milliseconds, which is 500 milliseconds (one-half second) in this case. The **sleep( )** method is used to delay the execution of the loop within **run( )**. As a result, the message output by the loop is displayed only once each half second.

Inside **main( )**, the following sequence is used to create and start a thread:

```
// First, construct a MyThread object.
MyThread mt = new MyThread();

// Next, construct a thread from that object.
Thread newThrd = new Thread(mt);

// Finally, start execution of the thread.
newThrd.start();
```

First, a **Runnable** instance is created, which is a **MyThread** object in this case. Then, the **Runnable** instance is passed to the **Thread** constructor to create the thread. Finally, the thread is started by calling **start( )**. Although it is possible to write this sequence in

different or more compact ways (see *Options and Alternatives*), all threads based on a
separate **Runnable** will construct and start a thread using the same general approach.

After creating and starting **MyThread**, **main( )** enters a loop that also contains a call to
sleep( ). In this case, it sleeps for only 250 milliseconds. Therefore, the loop in **main( )** will
iterate twice for each iteration of the loop in **MyThread**, as the output confirms.

Options and Alternatives

The preceding example is designed to clearly show each step in the thread creation/
execution process. Therefore, each step is handled individually. First, a **MyThread** object is
created. Next, a **Thread** is created using this object. Finally, the thread is started by calling
start( ). However, it is possible to streamline this process by combining these three steps so
that when a **MyThread** object is created, it is automatically passed to **Thread( )**, and then
the thread is started. To do this, create the **Thread** instance within the **MyThread**
constructor, and then call **start( )** on the thread. This approach is shown here:

```
// Streamlining the creation of a thread.

// This class implements Runnable. Its constructor
// automatically creates a Thread object by passing
// this instance of MyThread to Thread. The thread
// is then started by calling start().  Therefore,
// the thread begins execution as soon as a MyThread
// object is created.
class MyThread implements Runnable {
  int count;

  MyThread() {
    count = 0;

    // Create the thread and start its execution.
    new Thread(this).start();
  }

  // Entry point of thread.
  public void run() {

    System.out.println("MyThread starting.");

    try {
      do {
        Thread.sleep(500);
        System.out.println("In MyThread, count is " + count);
        count++;
      } while(count < 5);
    }
    catch(InterruptedException exc) {
      System.out.println("MyThread interrupted.");
    }

    System.out.println("MyThread terminating.");
  }
}
```

```
class RunnableDemo {
  public static void main(String args[]) {
    System.out.println("Main thread starting.");

    // Construct and start running a MyThread object.
    MyThread mt = new MyThread();

    // Give the main thread something to do.
    do {
      System.out.println("In main thread.");
      try {
        Thread.sleep(250);
      }
      catch(InterruptedException exc) {
        System.out.println("Main thread interrupted.");
      }
    } while (mt.count != 5);

    System.out.println("Main thread ending.");
  }
}
```

This program produces the same output as the previous version.

The **sleep( )** method also has a second form, which allows you to specify the delay period in terms of milliseconds and nanoseconds. It is shown here:

static void sleep(long *milliseconds*, int *nanoseconds*)

Of course, this version of **sleep( )** is useful only if you need nanosecond precision.

Another way to create a thread is to extend **Thread**. This approach is shown in the next recipe.

Create a Thread by Extending Thread

Key Ingredients	
Classes	**Methods**
java.lang.Thread	void run( )
	static void sleep(long *milliseconds*)
	void start( )

Instead of creating a separate class that implements **Runnable**, you can extend **Thread** to create a thread. This works because **Thread** implements the **Runnable** interface. You simply override the **run( )** method, adding the code that will be executed by the thread. This recipe shows the process.

Step-by-Step

To create a thread by extending **Thread** involves these steps:

1. Create a class that extends **Thread**.
2. Override the **run( )** method, specifying the code that you want to execute in a thread.
3. Create an instance of the class that extends **Thread**.
4. Begin execution of the thread by calling **start( )** on that instance.

Discussion

When you create a thread by extending **Thread**, you must override the **run( )** method, which is specified by the **Runnable** interface. Inside **run( )**, put the code that you want executed by the thread. The thread will end when **run( )** returns.

Next, construct an object of the class that extends **Thread**. This creates a new thread. To start the thread, call **start( )**. The call to **start( )** results in the overridden **run( )** method being invoked.

Example

The following example shows how to create a thread by extending **Thread**. It is functionally equivalent to the example in the previous recipe.

```
// Create a thread by extending Thread.

// This class extends Thread. Constructing an
// instance of this class creates a thread of execution.
class MyThread extends Thread {
  int count;

  MyThread() {
    count = 0;
  }

  // Override the run( ) method.
  public void run() {

    System.out.println("MyThread starting.");

    try {
      do {
        Thread.sleep(500);
        System.out.println("In MyThread, count is " + count);
        count++;
      } while(count < 5);
    }
    catch(InterruptedException exc) {
      System.out.println("MyThread interrupted.");
    }
```

```
      System.out.println("MyThread terminating.");
    }
}

class ExtendThreadDemo {
  public static void main(String args[]) {
    System.out.println("Main thread starting.");

    // Construct a MyThread object. Because MyThread
    // extends Thread, this creates a new thread.
    MyThread mt = new MyThread();

    // Start execution of the thread.
    mt.start();

    // Give the main thread something to do.
    do {
      System.out.println("In main thread.");
      try {
        Thread.sleep(250);
      }
      catch(InterruptedException exc) {
        System.out.println("Main thread interrupted.");
      }
    } while (mt.count != 5);

    System.out.println("Main thread ending.");
  }
}
```

The output is the same as shown in the previous recipe.

Options and Alternatives

When extending **Thread**, you may want to invoke a **Thread** constructor from within the constructor of your thread class. For example, if you want to give a name to the thread, then you will need to invoke this version of **Thread**'s constructor:

Thread(String *thrdName*)

Of course, this is accomplished via a call to **super**. For example, this version of **MyThread( )** gives the thread the name "Alpha".

```
MyThread() {
  super("Alpha");
  count = 0;
}
```

See *Use a Thread's Name and ID* for information on thread names.

   Since it is possible to create a thread by implementing **Runnable** in a separate class, or by extending **Thread**, a question naturally arises: which is the better approach? Although there is no hard and fast rule to this effect, many programmers believe that classes should be extended only when they are being expanded or changed in some way. Therefore, often

Thread is extended only when there is a reason to do so (for example, if you are providing a custom implementation of **start( )**). Otherwise, it usually makes more sense to simply implement **Runnable**.

Use a Thread's Name and ID

Key Ingredients	
Classes	**Methods**
java.lang.Thread	long getId( ) final String getName( ) final void setName(String *thrdName*)

All threads have a name. This name is either created by the runtime system or specified by you when a thread is created. Although released code won't always make use of a thread's name, thread names are very helpful when developing, testing, and debugging.

Although a thread name can be used to identify a thread, doing so has two drawbacks. First, thread names are not necessarily unique. More than one thread can have the same name. Second, because thread names are strings, comparing a name involves a string comparison, which is costly in terms of time. To avoid these problems, you can use another mechanism to identify a thread. Beginning with Java 5, all threads are given a thread ID, which is a long integer value. Thread IDs are unique, and because they are integers, comparisons are very fast. Thus, you can efficiently identify a thread through its ID. This recipe shows how to use both thread names and IDs.

NOTE *Remember that thread IDs were added by Java 5. Thus, thread IDs are available only if you are using a modern version of Java.*

Step-by-Step

To use thread names and IDs involves the following steps:

1. There are two ways to give a thread a name. First, and most convenient, you can specify its name when constructing a thread by passing it to one of **Thread**'s constructors. Second, you can change a thread's name by calling **setName( )**.

2. You can obtain a thread's name by calling **getName( )**.

3. Beginning with Java 5, threads are automatically given ID numbers when they are created. These numbers cannot be set by your program, but you can obtain the ID by calling **getID( )**.

Discussion

Thread provides several constructors that let you specify a name when a thread is created. The one used by this recipe is shown here:

Thread(Runnable *thrdOb*, String *thrdName*)

Here, *thrdOb* specifies the **Runnable** that will be executed and *thrdName* specifies the name of the thread. As explained in *Multithreading Fundamentals,* if you don't explicitly give a thread a name, then one is provided by the runtime system. Thus, all threads have names. Specifying the name simply lets you use a name of your own choosing.

You can change a thread's name after it is constructed by calling **setName( )** on the **Thread** instance. It is shown here:

final void setName(String *thrdName*)

The new name is passed in *thrdName.* It is important to understand that the same thread name can be used by more than one thread. Thus, thread names are not necessarily unique. For example, you could have three active threads, each having the name "MyThread." However, often you will want to use unique names so that a thread's name identifies a specific, individual thread.

You can obtain the current name of a thread by calling **getName( )**, shown next:

final String getName( )

The name of the thread is returned.

Because thread names are not necessarily unique, you might encounter situations in which you will want to identify a thread by its ID number rather than its name. Beginning with Java 5, all threads are automatically given a unique, long integer ID when they are created. You can obtain a thread's ID by calling **getId( )**, shown here:

long getId( )

The ID is returned. Although all IDs are unique, they can be reused. For example, if a thread ends, then a new thread might be assigned the old thread's ID.

Example

The following example illustrates thread names and IDs. It creates a **Runnable** called **MyThread** whose constructor takes the name of a thread as a parameter. Within **MyThread( )**, the name is passed to **Thread( )** when a thread is constructed. Notice that **MyThread( )** automatically begins executing the new thread. Inside **run( )**, the name of the thread, its ID value, and the count are displayed within a loop. When the count equals 3, the thread name is changed to uppercase. Inside **main( )**, two new threads with the names First Thread and Second Thread are created.

```
// Use thread names and IDs.

// MyThread creates a thread that has a specified
// name. The name is uppercased after three
// iterations of the loop in run().
class MyThread implements Runnable {
```

```java
    int count;
    Thread thrd;

    MyThread(String thrdName) {
      count = 0;

      // Construct a new thread using this object
      // and the specified name.
      thrd = new Thread(this, thrdName);

      // Start execution of the thread.
      thrd.start();
    }

    // Entry point of thread.
    public void run() {

      System.out.println(thrd.getName() + " starting.");

      try {
        do {
          Thread.sleep(500);

          // Display the thread's name, ID, and count.
          System.out.println("In " + thrd.getName() +
                             " (ID: " + thrd.getId( ) + ")" +
                             ", count is " + count);
          count++;

          // Change a thread's name.
          if(count == 3) thrd.setName(thrd.getName().toUpperCase());

        } while(count < 5);
      }
      catch(InterruptedException exc) {
        System.out.println(thrd.getName() + " interrupted.");
      }

      System.out.println(thrd.getName() + " terminating.");
    }
}

class NamesAndIDsDemo {
  public static void main(String args[]) {

    System.out.println("Main thread starting.");

    // Construct and start a thread.
    MyThread mt = new MyThread("First Thread");

    // Construct and start a second thread.
    MyThread mt2 = new MyThread("Second Thread");
```

```
    // Give the main thread something to do.
    do {
      System.out.println("In main thread.");

      try {
        Thread.sleep(250);
      }
      catch(InterruptedException exc) {
        System.out.println("Main thread interrupted.");
      }

      // Wait until both threads end.
    } while (mt.count != 5 && mt2.count != 5);

    System.out.println("Main thread ending.");
  }
}
```

Sample output is shown here:

```
Main thread starting.
In main thread.
First Thread starting.
Second Thread starting.
In main thread.
In main thread.
In First Thread (ID: 7), count is 0
In Second Thread (ID: 8), count is 0
In main thread.
In main thread.
In First Thread (ID: 7), count is 1
In Second Thread (ID: 8), count is 1
In main thread.
In main thread.
In First Thread (ID: 7), count is 2
In Second Thread (ID: 8), count is 2
In main thread.
In main thread.
In FIRST THREAD (ID: 7), count is 3
In SECOND THREAD (ID: 8), count is 3
In main thread.
In main thread.
In FIRST THREAD (ID: 7), count is 4
FIRST THREAD terminating.
In SECOND THREAD (ID: 8), count is 4
SECOND THREAD terminating.
Main thread ending.
```

Options and Alternatives

You can obtain a reference to the currently executing thread by calling **currentThread( )**, shown here:

```
static Thread currentThread( )
```

This method is useful when you want to obtain information about or manage the currently executing thread. For example, you can obtain the ID for the main thread by executing this statement within **main( )**:

```
System.out.println("Main thread ID is " +
                Thread.currentThread().getId());
```

You can obtain the name of the main thread, using the same approach:

```
System.out.println("Main thread ID is " +
                Thread.currentThread().getName());
```

Wait for a Thread to End

Key Ingredients	
Classes	**Methods**
java.lang.Thread	final void join( )

When using multiple threads, it is not uncommon for one thread to wait until another thread has ended. For example, a thread might be performing a task that must run to completion before a second thread can continue execution. In other situations, you might want a thread, such as the main thread, to finish last so that it can perform various "clean-up" chores, such as releasing system resources that are no longer needed. Whatever the reason, **Thread** provides a convenient means of waiting for a thread to end: the **join( )** method. This recipe demonstrates the process.

Step-by-Step

To wait for a thread to end involves these steps:

1. Begin execution of a thread.
2. Call **join( )** on the thread. This call must be executed from within the waiting thread.
3. When **join( )** returns, the thread has ended.

Discussion

The **join( )** method waits until the thread on which it is called terminates. Its name comes from the concept of the calling thread waiting until the specified thread *joins* it. Thus, **join( )** causes the calling thread to suspend execution until the joining thread ends.

There are three forms of **join( )**. The one used by this recipe is shown here:

final void join( ) throws InterruptedException

The other two forms of **join( )** let you specify the maximum amount of time that you want the invoking thread to wait for the specified thread to terminate.

Example

The following example illustrates **join( )**. It creates a thread based on **MyThread** that counts to 5 and then ends. Inside **main( )**, **join( )** is called on this thread. Therefore, the main thread waits until the thread has ended.

```java
// Demonstrate join().

class MyThread implements Runnable {
  int count;

  MyThread() {
    count = 0;
  }

  // Count to 5.
  public void run() {

    System.out.println("MyThread starting.");

    try {
      do {
        Thread.sleep(500);
        System.out.println("In MyThread, count is " + count);
        count++;
      } while(count < 6);
    }
    catch(InterruptedException exc) {
      System.out.println("MyThread interrupted.");
    }

    System.out.println("MyThread terminating.");
  }
}

class JoinDemo {
  public static void main(String args[]) {

    System.out.println("Main thread starting.");

    // Construct a thread based on MyThread.
    Thread thrd = new Thread(new MyThread());

    // Start execution of thrd.
    thrd.start();
```

```
   // Wait until thrd ends.
   try {
     thrd.join();
   }
     catch(InterruptedException exc) {
       System.out.println("Main thread interrupted.");
   }

   System.out.println("Main thread ending.");
  }
}
```

Sample output is shown here. (Your exact output may vary.)

```
Main thread starting.
MyThread starting.
In MyThread, count is 0
In MyThread, count is 1
In MyThread, count is 2
In MyThread, count is 3
In MyThread, count is 4
In MyThread, count is 5
MyThread terminating.
Main thread ending.
```

Options and Alternatives

The version of **join( )** used in the example waits indefinitely for a thread to end. This is often what you need, but sometimes you will want to limit the amount of time that the invoking thread will wait. Remember, calling **join( )** causes the invoking thread to suspend execution. In some cases, it might be necessary for the invoking thread to resume execution even if the thread on which **join( )** is called has not terminated. To handle this possibility, **Thread** defines two additional forms of **join( )** that let you specify a maximum wait time. They are shown here:

final void join(long *milliseconds*) throws InterruptedException
final void join(long *milliseconds*, int *nanoseconds*) throws InterruptedException

For both versions, the number of milliseconds to wait is specified by *milliseconds.* The second form lets you specify nanosecond precision.

Another way to wait until a thread ends is to poll its state by calling **isAlive( )**. Although using **join( )** is almost always a better, more efficient approach, using **isAlive( )** may be appropriate in some special cases. It is shown here:

final boolean isAlive( )

The **isAlive( )** method returns **true** if the thread on which it is called is still active. It returns **false** if the thread has ended.

The trouble with using **isAlive( )** to wait for a thread to end is that the polling loop used to call **isAlive( )** continues to consume CPU cycles while waiting. In contrast, **join( )** suspends execution of the invoking thread, thus freeing CPU cycles. To fully understand the problem, consider this version of **main( )** from the previous example. It is rewritten to use **isAlive( )**.

```
// This version of main() uses isAlive() to wait for
// a thread to end. It is NOT as efficient as the version
// that uses join() and is for demonstration purposes only.
// This approach is NOT recommended for real code.
public static void main(String args[]) {

  System.out.println("Main thread starting.");

  // Construct a thread based on MyThread.
  Thread thrd = new Thread(new MyThread());

  // Start execution of thrd.
  thrd.start();

  // Wait until thrd ends.
  while(thrd.isAlive()) ;

  System.out.println("Main thread ending.");
}
```

This version of **main( )** will produce the same results as before. However, the program is no longer written as efficiently as it was from a performance point of view. The reason is that the main thread no longer suspends execution, waiting for **thrd** to end. Instead, it continues to execute, making repeated calls to **isAlive( )**. This consumes many CPU cycles unnecessarily. Therefore, in this case, using **join( )** is a much better approach.

Synchronize Threads

Key Ingredients	
Keyword	**Forms**

synchronized	synchronized *type methodName(arg-list)*{
	  // synchronized method body
	}
	synchronized(*objref*) {
	  // synchronized statements
	}

When using multiple threads, it is sometimes necessary to prevent one thread from accessing an object that is currently in use by another. This situation can occur when two or more threads need access to a shared resource that can be used by only one thread at a time. For example, when one thread is writing to a file, a second thread must be prevented from doing so at the same time. The mechanism by which access to an object by multiple threads is controlled is called *synchronization.*

Key to synchronization in Java is the concept of the *monitor.* A monitor works by implementing the concept of a *lock.* When a thread enters an object's monitor, the object is locked and no other thread can gain access to the object. When the thread exits the monitor, the object is unlocked and becomes available for use by another thread.

All objects in Java have a monitor. This feature is built into the Java language itself. Thus, all objects can be synchronized. Synchronization is supported by the keyword **synchronized** and a few well-defined methods that all objects have. Since synchronization was designed into Java from the start, it is much easier to use than you might first expect. In fact, for many programs, the synchronization of objects is almost transparent.

This recipe shows how to synchronize access to an object.

Step-by-Step

To synchronize access to an object, follow these steps:

1. You can synchronize one or more methods defined for the object by specifying the **synchronized** modifier. When a synchronized method is called, the object is locked until the method returns

2. You can synchronize specific actions on an object by using a synchronized block of code, which is created by using the **synchronized** statement. When a synchronized block is entered, the object is locked. When the synchronized block is left, the object is unlocked.

Discussion

There are two ways to synchronize access to an object. First, you can modify one or more of its methods with the **synchronized** keyword. A synchronized method has the following general form:

```
synchronized type methodName(arg-list){
    // synchronized method body
}
```

Here, *type* is the return type of the method and *methodName* is its name.

When a synchronized method is called on an object, that object's monitor is acquired by the calling thread and the object is locked. No other thread can execute a synchronized method on the object until the thread releases the lock, either by returning from the method or by calling the **wait( )** method. (For an example that uses **wait( )**, see *Communicate Between Threads.*) Once the monitor has been released, it can be acquired by another thread.

The second way to synchronize access to an object is to use a synchronized block. It has this general form:

```
synchronized(objref) {
  // synchronized statements
}
```

Here, *objref* is a reference to the object for which you want to limit access. Once a synchronized block has been entered, *obref* is locked and no other thread can acquire that lock until the block ends. Therefore, a synchronized block ensures that a call to a method on *objref* proceeds only after the current thread has acquired *objref*'s lock. A second thread desiring access to *objref* will wait until the first thread has released the lock.

The primary benefit of a synchronized block is that it lets you synchronize access to an object that is not otherwise thread-safe. In other words, using a synchronized block lets you synchronize access to an object whose methods are not synchronized. This can be quite valuable in a number of situations. For example, you might need to synchronize an object of a class for which you do not have access to the source code (such as a class supplied by a third party).

Example

The following example creates a class called **Prompter**, which simulates a very simple teleprompter that slowly displays a message, one word at a time. The message is displayed by the **display( )** method, which sleeps one or more seconds between each word. This method is synchronized, meaning that it can be used by only one object at a time.

The program creates two threads that both use the same **Prompter** instance. Without synchronization, the message displayed by one thread would be jumbled together with the message displayed by the other. However, by synchronizing **display( )**, the two messages are kept separate.

```
// Demonstrate synchronized methods.

// A very simple teleprompter that sleeps one or more seconds
// between words.
class Prompter {
  int delay; // number of seconds to delay between words

  Prompter(int d) {
    if(d <= 0) d = 1;
    delay = d;
  }

  // Because display() is synchronized, only one
  // thread at a time can use it.  This prevents
  // different messages from getting mixed up.
  synchronized void display(String msg) {

    for(int i=0; i < msg.length(); i++) {
      System.out.print(msg.charAt(i));

      if(Character.isWhitespace(msg.charAt(i))) {
        try {
```

```
            Thread.sleep(delay*1000);
          } catch(InterruptedException exc) {
            return;
          }
        }
      }
    }
    System.out.println();
  }
}

// A thread that uses a Prompter.
class UsePrompter implements Runnable {
  Prompter prompter; // the Prompter to use
  String message; // the message to display

  UsePrompter(Prompter p, String msg) {
    prompter  = p;
    message = msg;

    // Create and start running thread.
    new Thread(this).start();
  }

  // Use prompter to show the message.
  public void run() {
    prompter.display(message);
  }
}

// Demonstrate that a synchronized method prevents
// multiple threads from accessing a shared object
// at the same time.
class SyncDemo {
  public static void main(String args[]) {

    // Construct one Prompter object.
    Prompter p = new Prompter(1);

    // Construct two threads that use p. Thus, both threads
    // will attempt to use p at the same time. However, because
    // display() is synchronized, only one at a time can use p.
    UsePrompter promptA = new UsePrompter(p, "One Two Three Four");
    UsePrompter promptB = new UsePrompter(p, "Left Right Up Down");
  }
}
```

Sample output is shown here:

```
One Two Three Four
Left Right Up Down
```

As you can see, the first thread's message is displayed in its entirety before the second thread's message begins. Because **display( )** is synchronized, a thread cannot use **p** until it obtains its lock. In this case, **promptA** gains the lock first. Even though **display( )** sleeps for one second between words, the second thread, **promptB**, cannot run because the lock for **p** is already owned by **promptA**. This means that **promptA** has sole access to **display( )** until the lock is released when **display( )** returns. At this point, **promptB** gains access to the lock and its message can be displayed.

To fully appreciate the benefit of synchronization, try removing the synchronized modifier from **display( )** and then rerun the program. You will see something similar to the following, jumbled, output:

```
One Left Two Right Three Up Four
Down
```

Because **display( )** is no longer synchronized, both threads have access to **p** and the output is mixed up.

Options and Alternatives

Although using synchronized methods is often the best approach, a synchronized block provides an alternative that is useful in some cases. A synchronized block lets you synchronize an object that might not otherwise be synchronized. For example, using a synchronized block, you can synchronize access to a method that is not modified by **synchronized**. You can experiment with a synchronized block by modifying the example program. First, remove the **synchronized** modifier from **display( )**. Then substitute this version of **run( )** into **UsePrompter**:

```
public void run() {
  // Use a synchronized block to manage access to prompter.
  synchronized(prompter) {
    prompter.display(message);
  }
}
```

The synchronized block based on **prompter** synchronizes access to **display( )** even though **display( )** is no longer a synchronized method. Therefore, after making these changes, the program will still run correctly.

Communicate Between Threads

Key Ingredients	
Classes	**Methods**
java.lang.Object	final void wait( )
	final void notify( )

As demonstrated by the previous recipe, a synchronized method or block prevents asynchronous access to an object. However, they do so in an unconditional way. Once a thread has entered the object's monitor, no other thread can gain access to the same object until the first thread has exited the monitor. While this approach is quite powerful (and extremely useful), sometimes a more subtle technique is required.

To understand why, consider the following situation. A thread called T is executing inside a synchronized method and needs access to a resource called R that is temporarily unavailable. What should T do? If T enters some form of polling loop that waits for R, T ties up the object, preventing another thread from using it. This is a less than optimal solution because it partially defeats the advantages of multithreading. A better solution is to have T temporarily relinquish control of the object, allowing another thread to run. When R becomes available, T can be notified and resume execution. Such an approach relies upon some form of interthread communication in which one thread can temporarily relinquish control of an object, and then wait until it is notified that it can resume execution. Java supports interthread communication with the **wait( )** and **notify( )** methods defined by **Object**. This recipe demonstrates their use.

Step-by-Step

To communicate between threads by use of **wait( )** and **notify( )** involves these steps:

1. To cause a thread to wait until notified by some other thread, call **wait( )**.
2. To notify a waiting thread, call **notify( )**.
3. Typically, a thread uses **wait( )** to pause execution until some event has occurred or some shared resource is available. It is notified that it can continue when another thread calls **notify( )**.

Discussion

The **wait( )** and **notify( )** methods are part of all objects because they are implemented by the **Object** class. These methods can only be called from within a synchronized method. Here is how they are used. When a thread is temporarily blocked from running, it calls **wait( )**. This causes the thread to go to sleep and the monitor for that object to be released. This allows another thread to use the object. At a later point, the sleeping thread is awakened when some other thread enters the same monitor and calls **notify( )**. A call to **notify( )** resumes one waiting thread.

There are three forms of **wait( )** defined by **Object**. The one used by this recipe is shown here:

    final void wait( ) throws InterruptedException

It causes the invoking thread to release the object's monitor and wait (i.e., suspend execution) until notified by another thread. Of course, the invoking thread must have acquired a lock on the object prior to calling **wait( )**. In other words, the thread must have entered the object's monitor. Thus, **wait( )** must be called from within a synchronized method or block.

To notify a waiting thread that it can resume execution, call **notify( )**. It is shown here:

    final void notify( )

A call to **notify( )** resumes one waiting thread. Like **wait( )**, **notify( )** must also be called from within a synchronized context, which means from within a synchronized method or block. Thus, the calling thread must have entered the object's monitor and acquired its lock.

An important point needs to be made: Although **wait( )** normally waits until **notify( )** or **notifyAll( )** is called, there is a possibility that in very rare cases the waiting thread could be awakened due to a *spurious wakeup*. In this case, a waiting thread resumes without **notify( )** or **notifyAll( )** having been called. (In essence, the thread resumes for no apparent reason.) Because of this remote possibility, Sun recommends that calls to **wait( )** should take place within a loop that checks the condition on which the thread is waiting. The following example shows this technique.

Example
The following example provides a simple demonstration of **wait( )** and **notify( )**.

```
// A simple demonstration of wait() and notify().

class SyncOb {

  boolean ready = false;

  // This method waits until it receives notification
  // that the ready variable is true.
  synchronized void waitFor() {
    String thrdName = Thread.currentThread().getName();
    System.out.println(thrdName + " is entering waitFor().");

    System.out.println(thrdName +
                       " calling wait() to wait for" +
                       " notification to proceed.\n");

    try {

      // Wait for notification.
      while(!ready) wait();

    } catch(InterruptedException exc) {
      System.out.println("Interrupted.");
    }

    System.out.println(thrdName +
                       " received notification and is" +
                       " resuming execution.");
  }

  // This method sets the ready variable to true
  // and then sends a notification.
  synchronized void goAhead() {
    String thrdName = Thread.currentThread().getName();
    System.out.println("\n" + thrdName +
                       " thread calling notify() inside goAhead().\n" +
                       "This will let MyThread resume execution.\n");
```

```
      // Set ready and notify.
      ready = true;
      notify();
    }
  }

// A thread class that uses SyncOb.
class MyThread implements Runnable {
  SyncOb syncOb;

  // Construct a new thread.
  MyThread(String name, SyncOb so) {
    syncOb = so;
    new Thread(this, name).start();
  }

  // Begin execution of the thread.
  public void run() {
    syncOb.waitFor();
  }
}

class ThreadComDemo {
  public static void main(String args[]) {

    try {
      SyncOb sObj = new SyncOb();

      // Construct a thread on sObj that waits for
      // a notification.
      new MyThread("MyThread", sObj);

      // Burn some CPU time.
      for(int i=0; i < 10; i++) {
        Thread.sleep(250);
        System.out.print(".");
      }
      System.out.println();

      // The main thread will now notify sObj.
      sObj.goAhead();

      // At this point, MyThread resumes execution.

    } catch(InterruptedException exc) {
      System.out.println("Main thread interrupted.");
    }
  }
}
```

Sample output is shown here:

```
MyThread is entering waitFor().
MyThread calling wait() to wait for notification to proceed.
```

. . . .

```
main thread calling notify() inside goAhead().
This will let MyThread resume execution.
```

```
MyThread received notification and is resuming execution.
```

The program warrants a close examination. It begins by creating a class called **SyncOb** that defines one instance variable called **ready** and two synchronized methods called **waitFor( )** and **goAhead( )**. Notice that the **ready** variable is initially set to **false**. The **waitFor( )** method waits for **ready** to be **true**. It does this by executing a call to **wait( )**. This causes **waitFor( )** to pause until another thread calls **notify( )** on the same object. The second method is **goAhead( )**. It sets **ready** to **true** and then calls **notify( )**. Thus, the thread that calls **waitFor( )** will wait until another thread calls **goAhead( )**.

A key point to understand is how the **ready** variable is used in conjunction with **wait( )** to wait for notification. As explained earlier, because of the remote possibility of a spurious wakeup, Sun recommends that all calls to **wait( )** take place within a loop that tests the condition upon which the thread is waiting. In this case, the thread is waiting for **ready** to be **true**. The wait loop is coded like this:

```
while(!ready) wait();
```

Therefore, as long as **ready** is **false**, **wait( )** is called. Actually, in the vast majority of cases, **wait( )** will only be called once because no spurious wake-up will occur and the call to **wait( )** will not return until the **goAhead( )** method calls **notify( )**. However, because of the spurious wakeup issue, the loop is required.

Next, the program defines the **MyThread** class. It creates a thread that uses a **SyncOb** object. This object is stored in an instance variable called **syncOb**. **MyThread**'s **run( )** method executes a call to **waitFor( )** on **syncOb**, which results in a call to **wait( )**. Thus, **MyThread** will suspend execution until a call to **notify( )** has been executed on the same object. Inside **main( )**, a **SyncOb** object called **sObj** is instantiated. Then, a **MyThread** object is created, passing in **sObj** as the **SyncOb** object. Next, **main( )** displays ten periods (just to use some CPU time). Then, **main( )** calls **goAhead( )** on **sObj**, which is the same **SyncOb** used by the **MyThread** instance. This results in **ready** being set to **true** and **notify( )** being called. This enables **MyThread** to resume execution.

Options and Alternatives

There are two additional forms of **wait( )** that let you specify the maximum amount of time that a thread will wait to gain access to an object. They are shown here:

> final void wait(long *millis*) throws InterruptedException
> final void wait(long *millis*, int *nanos*) throws InterruptedException

The first form waits until notified or until the specified period of milliseconds has expired. The second form allows you to specify the wait period in terms of nanoseconds.

You can notify all waiting threads by calling **notifyAll( )**. It is shown here:

> final void notifyAll( )

After the call to **notifyAll( )**, one waiting thread will gain access to the monitor.

Suspend, Resume, and Stop a Thread

Key Ingredients	
Classes	**Methods**
java.lang.Thread	final void wait( )
	final void notify( )

In the early days of Java, it was very easy to suspend, resume, or stop a thread. Why? Because the **Thread** class defines methods called **suspend( )**, **resume( )**, and **stop( )** that were designed precisely for this purpose. However, a rather unexpected event occurred when Java 1.2 was released: these methods were deprecated! Therefore, they must not be used for new code and their use in old code should be eliminated. Instead of using API methods to suspend, resume, and stop a thread, you must embed these features into your thread class. Thus, each thread class will supply its own mechanism to suspend, resume, and stop, relying on **wait( )** and **notify( )**. This recipe shows one way to do this.

Before moving on, it is useful to understand why **suspend( )**, **resume( )**, and **stop( )** were deprecated. The **suspend( )** method was deprecated because its use can lead to deadlock. In fact, the Java API documentation states that **suspend( )** is "inherently deadlock-prone." To understand how, assume two threads called A and B. Also assume that A holds a lock on an object and then suspends. Further assume that B is responsible for resuming thread A. However, if B attempts to obtain the same lock before resuming A, deadlock will result because the lock is still held by A, which is suspended. Thus, the lock is not released. As a result, B waits indefinitely. The **resume( )** method is deprecated because it's used only as a counterpart of **suspend( )**.

The **stop( )** method is deprecated because, as the Java API documentation states, it is "inherently unsafe." The reason is that a call to **stop( )** causes all locks held by that thread to be released. This could result in the corruption of an object being synchronized by a lock that is released prematurely. For example, if a data structure is being updated when the thread is stopped, the lock on that object will be released, but the data will be in an incomplete or corrupted state.

Step-by-Step

One way to implement the ability to suspend and resume a thread involves these steps:

1. Create a **volatile boolean** variable called **suspended** that will indicate a suspended state of the thread. If **suspended** is true, the thread will be suspended. If it is false, the thread will resume execution.

2. Inside the thread's **run( )** method, create a **while** loop that uses **suspended** as its condition. Inside the body of the loop, call **wait( )**. In other words, while **suspended** is true, make repeated calls to **wait( )**. Therefore, when **suspended** is true, a call to **wait( )** takes place, which causes the thread to pause. When **suspended** is false, the loop exits and execution is resumed.

3. To suspend the thread, set **suspended** to **true**. To resume, set **suspended** to **false** and then call **notify( )**.

One way to implement the ability to stop a thread involves these steps:

1. Create a **volatile boolean** variable called **stopped** that indicates the stopped/running state of the thread.

2. When **stopped** is true, terminate the thread, often by simply letting the **run( )** method return. Otherwise, allow the thread to continue executing.

3. When the thread is created, set **stopped** to **false**. To stop a thread, set **stopped** to **true**.

Discussion

For a discussion of **wait( )** and **notify( )**, see *Communicate Between Threads*.

To suspend, resume, and stop execution of a thread, you can set up a loop similar to the one shown here inside the thread's **run( )** method:

```
volatile boolean suspended;
volatile boolean stopped;

// ...

// Use synchronized block to check suspended and stopped variables.
synchronized(this) {
  while(suspended) wait();
  if(stopped) break;
}
```

Here, **suspended** is an instance variable of the thread class.

To suspend the thread, you will set **suspended** to **true**. You might want to do this by creating a method for this purpose, as shown here:

```
// Suspend the thread.
synchronized void mySuspend() {
  suspended = true;
}
```

The advantage to using such a method is that you can mark **suspended** as private, which prevents it from being changed in unintended ways.

To resume a thread, set **suspended** to **false** and then call **notify( )**. Again, you might want to do this via a method, such as the one shown here:

```
// Resume the thread.
synchronized void myResume() {
  suspended = false;
  notify();
}
```

The call to **notify( )** causes the call to **wait( )** in the synchronized block to return, thus enabling the thread to resume execution.

To enable a thread to be stopped, create a variable called **stopped** that is initially false. Then, include code that checks **stopped**. If it is true, terminate the thread. Otherwise, take no action. You will often want to create a method, such as the one shown here, that sets the value of **stopped**:

```
// Stop the thread.
synchronized void myStop() {
  stopped = true;

  // The following lets a suspended thread be stopped.
  suspended = false;
  notify();
}
```

Notice that this method handles the situation in which a suspended thread is stopped. The suspended thread must be allowed to resume so that it can end.

Example

The following example puts into action the pieces just described and demonstrates one way to suspend, resume, and stop execution of a thread.

```
// Suspend, resume, and stop a thread.

// This class provides its own means of suspending,
// resuming, and stopping a thread.
class MyThread implements Runnable {
  Thread thrd;
  private volatile boolean suspended;
  private volatile boolean stopped;

  MyThread(String name) {
    thrd = new Thread(this, name);
    suspended = false;
    stopped = false;
    thrd.start();
  }

  // Run the thread.
  public void run() {

    System.out.println(thrd.getName() + " starting.");

    try {

      for(int i = 1; i < 1000; i++) {

        // Display periods.
        System.out.print(".");
        Thread.sleep(250);
```

```
        // Use synchronized block to suspend or stop.
        synchronized(this) {

          // If suspended is true, then wait until
          // notified. Then, recheck suspended.
          // The suspended variable is set to true
          // by a call to mySuspend(). It is set to
          // false by a call to myResume().
          while(suspended) wait();

          // If thread is stopped, exit the loop and
          // let the thread end. The stopped variable is
          // set to true by a call to myStop().
          if(stopped) break;
        }
      }

    } catch (InterruptedException exc) {
      System.out.println(thrd.getName() + " interrupted.");
    }
    System.out.println("\n" + thrd.getName() + " exiting.");
  }

  // Stop the thread.
  synchronized void myStop() {
    stopped = true;

    // The following lets a suspended thread be stopped.
    suspended = false;
    notify();
  }

  // Suspend the thread.
  synchronized void mySuspend() {
    suspended = true;
  }

  // Resume the thread.
  synchronized void myResume() {
    suspended = false;
    notify();
  }
}

// Demonstrate mySuspend(), myResume(), and myStop().
class ThreadControlDemo {

  public static void main(String args[]) {
    MyThread mt = new MyThread("MyThread");

    try {
      // Let mt start executing.
      Thread.sleep(3000);
```

```
      // Suspend mt.
      System.out.println("\nSuspending MyThread.");
      mt.mySuspend();
      Thread.sleep(3000);

      // Now, resume mt.
      System.out.println("\nResuming MyThread.");
      mt.myResume();
      Thread.sleep(3000);

      // Suspend and resume a second time.
      System.out.println("\nSuspending MyThread again.");
      mt.mySuspend();
      Thread.sleep(3000);

      System.out.println("\nResuming MyThread again.");
      mt.myResume();
      Thread.sleep(3000);

      // Now Stop the thread.
      System.out.println("\nStopping thread.");
      mt.myStop();
    } catch (InterruptedException e) {
      System.out.println("Main thread Interrupted");
    }
  }
}
```

The output is shown here:

```
MyThread starting.
............
Suspending MyThread.

Resuming MyThread.
............
Suspending MyThread again.

Resuming MyThread again.
............
Stopping thread.

MyThread exiting.
```

Options and Alternatives

As one would expect, there is more than one way to implement suspend, resume, and stop. One helpful alternative, which is based on an approach described by Java's API documentation, eliminates the overhead of repeatedly entering a synchronized block. This is accomplished by first checking the values of the **suspended** and **stopped** variables before the synchronized block is entered. If neither of these variables is true, then the synchronized block is skipped, thus avoiding its overhead.

```
// Check suspended and stopped before entering synchronized block.
if(suspended || stopped)
  synchronized(this) {

    // If suspended is true, then wait until
    // notified. Then, recheck suspended.
    // The suspended variable is set to true
    // by a call to mySuspend(). It is set to
    // false by a call to myResume().
    while(suspended) wait();

    // If thread is stopped, exit the loop and
    // let the thread end. The stopped variable is
    // set to true by a call to myStop().
    if(stopped) break;
}
```

A question that is commonly asked regarding suspending and stopping a thread is "If I am really careful, can't I just use the deprecated **suspend( )**, **resume( )**, and **stop( )** methods?" The answer is No! Because Sun explicitly states that they are deprecated, and because their use can cause potentialy serious problems, they cannot be used. To use them would mean, at the very least, that your code does not reflect "best practices". At worst, your code fails after it is released, causing damage to property or people.

Use a Daemon Thread

Key Ingredients	
Classes	**Methods**
java.lang.Thread	final boolean isDaemon( )
	final void setDaemon(boolean *how*)

Java supports two general types of threads: user threads and daemon threads. The difference between the two is simply this: a daemon thread will be automatically terminated when all user threads of an application have ended, but a user thread will continue to execute until its **run( )** method ends. Therefore, a daemon thread is inherently subordinate to a user thread. This is important because an application will continue to execute until all user threads have ended, but the application will not wait for daemon threads. This recipe shows how to create a daemon thread.

The principal use of a daemon thread is to provide some service that is used by one or more user threads, and typically runs in the background. Once started, the daemon thread continues to provide that service until the application ends. There is no need to manually implement some sort of termination condition to which the thread must respond. Its termination is automatic. Of course, in principle a user thread can be used anywhere you would employ a daemon thread, but then you would have to terminate the thread by hand. Therefore, in cases in which the only "termination condition" is that the thread is no longer needed, the automatic termination feature of a daemon thread is a major advantage.

Step-by-Step

To create and use a daemon thread involves these steps:

1. If a **Thread** instance is created by a daemon thread, then the new thread will automatically be a daemon thread.

2. If a **Thread** instance is created from a user thread, it will be a user thread. However, it can be changed to a daemon thread by calling **setDaemon( )**. This call must take place before the thread is started via a call to **start( )**.

3. You can determine if a thread is a daemon thread by calling **isDaemon( )**.

Discussion

When created, a **Thread** instance will be of the same type as its creating thread. Therefore, if a user thread creates a thread, then it will be a user thread by default. When a daemon thread creates a thread, the new thread is automatically a daemon thread.

To change a user thread into a daemon thread, call **setDaemon( )** shown here:

final void setDaemon(boolean *how*)

If *how* is true, the thread will set to daemon. If *how* is false, the thread will be set to user. In both cases, **setDaemon( )** must be called before the thread is started. This means that it must be called before **start( )** is invoked. If you call **setDaemon( )** on an active thread, **IllegalThreadStateException** is thrown.

You can determine if a thread is daemon or user by calling **isDaemon( )**, shown here:

final boolean isDaemon( )

It returns **true** if the invoking thread is daemon and false if it is user.

Example

Here is a simple example that illustrates a daemon thread. In the program the daemon thread executes an infinite loop that displays periods. Thus, it will continue to execute until the program ends. The main thread sleeps for ten seconds and then ends. Because the main thread was the only user thread in the program, the daemon thread is automatically terminated when the main thread ends.

```
// Demonstrate a daemon thread.

// This class creates a daemon thread.
class MyDaemon implements Runnable {
  Thread thrd;
```

```
    MyDaemon() {

      // Create the thread.
      thrd = new Thread(this);

      // Set to daemon
      thrd.setDaemon(true);

      // Start the thread.
      thrd.start();
    }

    // Entry point of thread.
    // It displays a period once a second.
    public void run() {

      try {
        for(;;) {
          System.out.print(".");
          Thread.sleep(1000);
        }
      }
      catch(InterruptedException exc) {
        System.out.println("MyDaemon interrupted.");
      }
    }
  }

class DaemonDemo {
  public static void main(String args[]) {

    // Construct and start running a MyDaemon thread.
    MyDaemon dt = new MyDaemon();

    if(dt.thrd.isDaemon())
      System.out.println("dt is a daemon thread.");

    // Keep the main thread alive for 10 seconds.
    System.out.println("Sleeping in main thread.");
    try {
        Thread.sleep(10000);
    }
    catch(InterruptedException exc) {
      System.out.println("Main thread interrupted.");
    }

    System.out.println("\nMain thread ending.");

    // At this point, the daemon thread will
    // automatically terminate.
  }
}
```

The output is shown here:

```
dt is a daemon thread.
Sleeping in main thread.
..........
Main thread ending.
```

As you can see, the daemon thread automatically ends when the application ends.

As an experiment, try commenting out the line that marks the thread as daemon, as shown here:

```
// thrd.setDaemon(true);
```

Next, recompile and execute the program. As you will see, the application no longer ends when the main thread ends, and the periods continue to be displayed. (You will need to use CTRL-C to stop the program.)

Bonus Example: A Simple Reminder Class

A good use for a background thread is a service that performs some activity at a predetermined time, waiting silently until the time arrives. One such service is a "reminder" that pops up a message at a specified time to remind you about some event, such as an appointment, meeting, or conference call. The following example creates a simple "reminder" class called **Reminder** that implements such a feature.

Reminder creates a thread that waits until a specified time in the future and then displays a message. **Reminder** is not designed as a stand-alone program. Rather, it is designed to be used as an accessory to a larger application. For this reason, it is implemented as a daemon thread. If the application using a **Reminder** instance terminates before the target time has been reached, the **Reminder** thread will be automatically terminated. It won't "hang" the application, waiting for the target time to be reached. It also means that there is no need to explicitly stop the thread when the application ends.

Reminder lets you specify the time at which to be reminded in two ways. First, you can use a delay period, which is in terms of seconds. This delay is then added to the current system time. The reminding message will be displayed after the delay has passed. This approach is good for reminders that are needed in the near future. Second, you can specify a **Calendar** object that contains the time and date at which you want to receive the reminder. This way is good for reminders that are needed in a more distant future.

```
// A simple reminder class that runs as a daemon thread.
//
// To use Reminder, pass in the message to display
// and then specify either a delay from the current
// time, or the future time that you want to have
// the reminder message displayed.
//
// If the application that creates a Reminder
// ends before the target time, then the
// Reminder thread is automatically terminated.

import java.util.*;
```

```
// A simple implementation of a "reminder" class.
// An object of this class starts a daemon thread
// that waits until the specified time. It then
// displays a message.
class Reminder implements Runnable {

  // Time and date to display reminder message.
  Calendar reminderTime;

  // Message to display.
  String message; // message to display

  // Use this constructor to display a message after
  // a specified number of seconds have elapsed.
  // This value is then added to the current time
  // to compute the desired reminder time.
  //
  // In practice, you might want to change the
  // delay to minutes rather than seconds, but
  // seconds make testing easier.
  Reminder(String msg, int delay) {

    message = msg;

    // Get the current time and date.
    reminderTime = Calendar.getInstance();

    // Add the delay to the time and date.
    reminderTime.add(Calendar.SECOND, delay);

    System.out.printf("Reminder set for %tD %1$tr\n", reminderTime);

    // Create the reminder thread.
    Thread dThrd = new Thread(this);

    // Set to daemon.
    dThrd.setDaemon(true);

    // Start execution.
    dThrd.start();
  }

  // Notify at the specified time and date.
  Reminder(String msg, Calendar cal) {

    message = msg;

    // Use the specified time and date as the
    // reminder time.
    reminderTime = cal;

    System.out.printf("Reminder set for %tD %1$tr\n", reminderTime);

    // Create the reminder.
    Thread dThrd = new Thread(this);
```

```
      // Set to daemon.
      dThrd.setDaemon(true);

      // Start execution.
      dThrd.start();
    }

    // Run the reminder.
    public void run() {

      try {

        for(;;) {
          // Get the current time and date.
          Calendar curTime = Calendar.getInstance();

          // See if it's time for the reminder.
          if(curTime.compareTo(reminderTime) >= 0) {
            System.out.println("\n" + message + "\n");
            break; // let the thread end
          }

          Thread.sleep(1000);
        }
      }
      catch(InterruptedException exc) {
        System.out.println("Reminder interrupted.");
      }
    }
}

class ReminderDemo {
  public static void main(String args[]) {
    // Get a reminder 2 seconds from now.
    Reminder mt = new Reminder("Call Harry", 2);

    // Get a reminder on April 5, 2007 at 2:30 pm.
    Reminder mt2 = new Reminder("Meet with Bill",
                  new GregorianCalendar(2007, 3, 5, 14, 30));

    // Keep the main thread alive for 20 seconds.
    for(int i=0; i < 20; i++) {
      try {
        Thread.sleep(1000);
      }
      catch(InterruptedException exc) {
        System.out.println("Main thread interrupted.");
      }
      System.out.print(".");
    }

    System.out.println("\nMain thread ending.");
  }
}
```

The output is shown here:

```
Reminder set for 04/05/07 02:29:56 PM
Reminder set for 04/05/07 02:30:00 PM
..
Call Harry


...
Meet with Bill


...............
Main thread ending.
```

Here are a few things that you might want to try. To prove the benefit of using a daemon thread to execute the reminder, try commenting out the call to **setDaemon( )** in both of **Reminder**'s constructors as shown here:

```
// dThrd.setDaemon(true);
```

Because the thread is no longer marked as daemon, it remains a user thread and the application will not end until the reminder thread has finished. Thus, the application "hangs" until the future time is reached.

For ease of testing and experimentation, the delay period used by the first **Reminder** constructor is assumed to be seconds. However, for real-world use, this delay is probably better specified in terms of minutes. You might want to try this change.

One optimization that might be applicable in some cases is to simply have the **run( )** method sleep for a period of time equal to the difference between the time at which the **Reminder** was started and the specified future time. With this approach, there is no need to keep checking the time. However, this approach will not work in situations in which the reminder is to be displayed based on the system time, which might change—for example, if the user changes time zones or if daylight saving time comes into effect.

Finally, you can try having the reminder display a pop-up window that contains the message rather than using a console-based approach. This is easily done using Swing's **JFrame** and **JLabel** classes. **JFrame** (which is a top-level Swing container) creates the standard window and **JLabel** displays the message. To try this, substitute the following version of **run( )** in the preceding program:

```java
// Display the reminder in a pop-up window.
public void run() {

  try {

    for(;;) {
      // Get the current time and date.
      Calendar curTime = Calendar.getInstance();

      // See if it's time for the reminder.
      if(curTime.compareTo(reminderTime) >= 0) {

        // Create GUI on the event-dispatching thread
        // as recommended by Sun.
```

```
              SwingUtilities.invokeLater(new Runnable() {
                public void run() {

                  // Pop up a window when the time is up.

                  // First, create a window for the message.
                  jfrm = new JFrame();

                  // Set its size. For the sake of simplicity,
                  // an arbitrary size is used here. However,
                  // you can compute an exact size to fit the
                  // message if you want.
                  jfrm.setSize(200, 50);

                  // Create a label that contains the message.
                  JLabel jlab = new JLabel(message);

                  // Add the message to the window.
                  jfrm.add(jlab);

                  // Show the window .
                  jfrm.setVisible(true);
                }
              });

              // Pause for 5 seconds.
              Thread.sleep(5000);

              // Now, remove the window.
              SwingUtilities.invokeLater(new Runnable() {
                public void run() {
                  // Remove the window from the screen.
                  jfrm.setVisible(false);

                  // Remove the window from the system.
                  jfrm.dispose();
                }
              });

              break; // let the thread end
            }

            Thread.sleep(1000);
          }
        }
        catch(InterruptedException exc) {
          System.out.println("Reminder interrupted.");
        }
      }
}
```

You will also need to **import javax.swing.*** and add the following instance variable to
the **Reminder** class:

```
JFrame jfrm;
```

As the comment before the call to **invokeLater( )** states, Sun currently recommends that all Swing GUIs be constructed and updated from the event-dispatching thread to avoid problems. Therefore, this approach is used here. (For more information about Swing and Swing recipes, see Chapter 8.)

Options and Alternatives

Even though a daemon thread is automatically terminated when the application using it ends, it is still possible for a daemon thread to terminate on its own. For example, this version of **run( )** from the first example will terminate after five iterations:

```
public void run() {

  try {
    for(int i=0; i < 5; i++) {
      System.out.print(".");
      Thread.sleep(1000);
    }
  }
  catch(InterruptedException exc) {
    System.out.println("MyDaemon interrupted.");
  }
  System.out.println("Daemon thread ending.");
}
```

Of course, in practice, if a thread has a well-defined termination point, then you won't usually mark it as a daemon. However, you might want to terminate a daemon thread in cases in which a background service is not needed because some precondition is not met. In such a case, terminating the thread removes it from the system, eliminating its impact on performance.

Interrupt a Thread

Key Ingredients	
Classes	**Methods**
java.lang.Thread	static boolean interrupted( )
	void interrupt( )

Sometimes it is useful for one thread to be able to interrupt another. For example, a thread might be waiting for a resource that is no longer available (such as a network connection that has been lost). A second thread could interrupt the first thread, possibly allowing an alternative resource to be used. Fortunately, Java makes it easy for one thread to interrupt another because the **Thread** class defines methods for this purpose. This recipe demonstrates their use.

Step-by-Step

To interrupt a thread involves these steps:

1. To interrupt a thread, call **interrupt( )** on the thread.
2. To determine if a thread is interrupted, call **interrupted( )**.

Discussion

One thread can interrupt another by calling **interrupt( )** on the **Thread** instance. It is shown here:

    void interrupt( )

The **interrupt( )** method has somewhat different effects, depending upon what the interrupted thread is doing. If the thread is not suspended, then calling **interrupt( )** results in the thread's interrupt status being set. The interrupt status can be determined by calling **interrupted( )** or **isInterrupted( )**, described shortly. If the thread is in a wait state, then three possible scenarios are possible.

The first, and the most common, situation in which a suspended thread is interrupted occurs when the thread is waiting for a call to **sleep( )**, **wait( )**, or **join( )** to return. In this case, calling **interrupted( )** results in an **InterruptedException** being sent to the interrupted thread. In the process, the thread's interrupt status is cleared.

Two other less common situations are also possible. If the thread is waiting on an instance of **InterruptableChannel**, then calling **interrupt( )** results in a **ClosedByInterruptException** and its interrupt status is set. If the thread is waiting on a **Selector**, then calling **interrupt( )** causes the interrupted state to be set and the selector returns as if a call to **wakeup( )** had taken place.

You can determine if a thread has been interrupted by calling either **interrupted( )** or **isInterrupted( )**. The method used by this recipe is **interrupted( )** and it is shown here:

    static boolean interrupted( )

It returns true if the invoking thread has been interrupted and false otherwise. In the process, the interrupted status of the thread is cleared.

Example

The following example shows how to interrupt a thread. It shows what happens when a thread is interrupted while suspended (in this case by a call to **sleep( )**) and what happens when it is interrupted while active. The key point is that when a thread is interrupted while suspended because of a call to **sleep( )**, **join( )**, or **wait( )**, it receives an **InterruptedException**. If interrupted while active, its interrupt status is set, but no **InterruptedException** is received.

```
// Interrupt a thread.

// This class handles an interrupt in two ways.
// First, if interrupted while sleeping(),
// it catches the InterruptedException that will
// be thrown.  Second, it calls interrupted()
// while active to check its interrupt status.
```

```java
// If interrupted while active, the thread
// terminates.
class MyThread implements Runnable {

  // Run the thread.
  public void run() {
    String thrdName = Thread.currentThread().getName();

    System.out.println(thrdName + " starting.");

    try {

      // First, sleep for 3 seconds. If sleep() is
      // interrupted, then an InterruptedException
      // will be received.
      Thread.sleep(3000);

      // Next, keep the thread active by displaying
      // periods. Use a time-delay loop rather than
      // sleep() to slow down the thread. This means
      // that the thread remains active.  Interrupting
      // the thread at this point does not cause an
      // an InterruptedException. Rather, its interrupted
      // status is set.
      for(int i = 1; i < 1000; i++) {
        if(Thread.interrupted()) {
          System.out.println("Thread interrupted while active.");
          break;
        }

        // Display periods.
        System.out.print(".");

        // Don't sleep at this point. Instead, burn CPU
        // time to keep thread active.
        for(long x = 0; x < 10000000; x++) ;
      }
    } catch (InterruptedException exc) {
      System.out.println(thrdName + " interrupted.");
    }
    System.out.println(thrdName + " exiting.");
  }
}

// Demonstrate thread interrupts.
class InterruptDemo {

  public static void main(String args[]) {
    MyThread mt = new MyThread();
    MyThread mt2 = new MyThread();
    Thread thrd = new Thread(mt, "MyThread #1");
    Thread thrd2 = new Thread(mt2, "MyThread #2");
```

```
try {
  // Start the thread.
  thrd.start();

  // Give thrd time to begin executing.
  Thread.sleep(1000);

  // Now, interrupt thrd when it is sleeping.
  thrd.interrupt();

  // Next, start second thread.
  thrd2.start();

  System.out.println();

  // This time, wait until thrd2 begins
  // showing periods.
  Thread.sleep(4000);

  // Now, interrupt thrd2 when it is active.
  thrd2.interrupt();

} catch (InterruptedException e) {
  System.out.println("Main thread Interrupted");
  }
 }
}
```

The output is shown here. (The exact output may vary.)

```
MyThread #1 starting.
MyThread #1 interrupted.
MyThread #1 exiting.

MyThread #2 starting.
.....Thread interrupted while active.
MyThread #2 exiting.
```

Options and Alternatives

The example program handles an interrupt that occurs while the thread is suspended differently from the way that it handles an interrupt that occurs while the thread is executing. This is often what you will want because an interrupt to **wait( )**, **sleep( )**, or **join( )** might require a different response than required when an active thread is interrupted. However, both types of interrupts can be handled in the same way in cases in which the same response is appropriate. Simply throw an **InterruptedException** if **interrupted( )** returns true. This results in the thread's **InterruptedException** handler catching the exception and processing the interrupt. To see this approach in action, substitute this **try** block into the **run( )** method of **MyThread** in the example:

```
try {

  // First, sleep for 3 seconds. If sleep() is
  // interrupted, then an InterruptedException
  // will be received.
  Thread.sleep(3000);

  // Next, keep the thread active by displaying
  // periods. Use a time-delay loop rather than
  // sleep() to slow down the display. This means
  // that the thread remains active.  Interrupting
  // the thread at this point does not cause an
  // an InterruptedException. Rather, its interrupted
  // status is set.
  for(int i = 1; i < 1000; i++) {
    if(Thread.interrupted()) {
      // Throw an exception so that both types of
      // interrupts are processed by the same handler.
      throw new InterruptedException();
    }

    // Display periods.
    System.out.print(".");

    // Burn CPU time to keep thread active.
    for(long x = 0; x < 10000000; x++) ;
  }
} catch (InterruptedException exc) {
  System.out.println(thrdName + " interrupted.");
}
```

In this version, pay special attention to this **if** statement:

```
if(Thread.interrupted()) {
  // Throw an exception so that both types of
  // interrupts are processed by the same handler.
  throw new InterruptedException();
}
```

If **interrupted( )** returns true, an **InterruptedException** object is created and thrown. This exception will be caught by the **catch** statement. This enables each type of interrupt to be handled by the same handler.

The **interrupted( )** method resets the interrupted status of the thread. If you don't want to clear the interrupted status, then you can check for an interrupt by calling **isInterrupted( )** on a **Thread** instead. It is shown here:

boolean isInterrupted( )

It returns true if the invoking thread has been interrupted and false otherwise. The thread's interrupted status is unchanged. Thus, it can be called repeatedly and will return the same result. This method is very useful in some situations because it lets a thread take a different course of action if it is interrupted while active rather than if it is running normally.

Set and Obtain a Thread's Priority

Key Ingredients	
Classes	**Methods**
java.lang.Thread	void setPriority(int *level*)
	int getPriority( )
	static void yield( )

Each thread has associated with it a priority setting. A thread's priority is used by the scheduler to decide when a thread gets to run. Therefore, in a multithreaded application, a thread's priority determines (in part) how much CPU time a thread receives relative to the other active threads. In general, low-priority threads receive little. High-priority threads receive a lot. Because a thread's priority affects the thread's access to the CPU, it has a profound impact on the execution characteristics of the thread and the way that the thread interacts with other threads. This recipe shows how to set a thread's priority and illustrates the effect that different priorities have on thread execution. It also shows how one thread can yield to another.

Before moving on to the recipe, it is necessary to clarify one point: Although a thread's priority does play an important role in determining when a thread gains access to the CPU, it is not the only factor. If a thread is blocked, such as when waiting for a resource to become available, it will suspend, allowing another thread to execute. Therefore, if a high-priority thread is waiting on some resource, a lower-priority thread will run. Furthermore, in some cases a high-priority thread may actually run less frequently than a low-priority thread. For example, consider a situation in which a high-priority thread is used to obtain data from a network. Because data transmission over a network is relatively slow compared to the speed of the CPU, the high-priority thread will spend much of its time waiting. While the high-priority thread is suspended, a lower-priority thread can execute. Of course, when data becomes available, the scheduler can preempt the low-priority thread and resume execution of the high-priority thread. Another factor that affects the scheduling of threads is the way the operating system implements multitasking, and whether the OS uses preemptive or nonpreemptive scheduling. The key point is that just because you give one thread a high priority and another a low priority, that does not necessarily mean that one thread will run faster or more often than the other. It's just that the high-priority thread has *greater potential access* to the CPU.

Step-by-Step

To set and obtain a thread's priority involves these steps:

1. To set a thread's priority, call **setPriority( )**.
2. To obtain a thread's priority, call **getPriority( )**.
3. To force a high-priority thread to yield to a lower-priority thread, call **yield( )**.

Discussion

When a thread is created, it is given the same priority as the creating thread. To change the priority, call **setPriority( )**. This is its general form:

final void setPriority(int *level*)

Here, *level* specifies the new priority setting for the calling thread. The value of *level* must be within the range **MIN_PRIORITY** and **MAX_PRIORITY**. Currently, these values are 1 and 10, respectively. The default priority is specified by the value **NORM_PRIORITY**, which is currently 5. These priorities are defined as **static final** variables within **Thread**.

You can obtain the current priority setting by calling the **getPriority( )** method of **Thread**, shown here:

final int getPriority( )

The returned value will be within the range specified by **MIN_PRIORITY** and **MAX_PRIORITY**.

You can cause a thread to yield the CPU by calling **yield( )**, shown here:

static void yield( )

By calling **yield( )**, a thread enables other threads, including lower-priority threads, to gain access to the CPU.

Example

The following example demonstrates two threads at different priorities. The threads are created as instances of the **PriThread** class. The **run( )** method contains a loop that counts the number of iterations. The loop stops when the count reaches 100,000,000 or the static variable **stop** is **true**. Initially, **stop** is set to **false**, but the first thread to finish counting sets **stop** to **true**. This causes the second thread to terminate with its next time slice. After both threads stop, the number of iterations for each loop is displayed.

```
// Demonstrate thread priorities.

class PriThread implements Runnable {
  long count;
  Thread thrd;

  static boolean stop = false;

  // Construct a new thread using the priority
  // specified by pri.
  PriThread(String name, int pri) {
    thrd = new Thread(this, name);

    // Set priority.
    thrd.setPriority(pri);

    count = 0;
    thrd.start();
  }
```

```
    // Begin execution of the thread.
    public void run() {
      do {
        count++;

        if((count % 10000) == 0) {
          if(thrd.getPriority() > Thread.NORM_PRIORITY)
            // To see the effect of yield(), remove the comment
            // from the following line and comment-out the
            // "count = count" placeholder line.
//            Thread.yield(); // yield to low-priority thread
            count = count; // do-nothing placeholder
        }

      } while(stop == false && count < 100000000);
      stop = true;

    }
}

class PriorityDemo {
  public static void main(String args[]) {
    PriThread mt2 = new PriThread("Low Priority",
                          Thread.NORM_PRIORITY-1);
    PriThread mt1 = new PriThread("High Priority",
                          Thread.NORM_PRIORITY+1);
    try {
      mt1.thrd.join();
      mt2.thrd.join();
    }
    catch(InterruptedException exc) {
      System.out.println("Main thread interrupted.");
    }

    System.out.println("\nHigh priority thread counted to " +
                      mt1.count);
    System.out.println("Low priority thread counted to " +
                      mt2.count);
  }
}
```

Here is a sample run:

```
High priority thread counted to 100000000
Low priority thread counted to 3464911
```

As you can see, the high-priority thread received the vast majority of the CPU time. Be aware that specific results will vary, depending on what version of the Java runtime system you are using, your operating system, processor speed, and task load.

To see the effect of **yield( )**, remove the comments from the call to **yield( )** in **run( )** and comment out the statement **count = count;** (which is simply a placeholder). Thus, the nested **if** statements inside **run( )** should look like this:

```
if((count % 10000) == 0) {
  if(thrd.getPriority() > Thread.NORM_PRIORITY)
    // To see the effect of yield(), remove the comment
    // from the following line and comment-out the
    // "count = count" placeholder line.
    Thread.yield(); // yield to low-priority thread
//    count = count; // do-nothing placeholder
}
```

Becaue the high-priority thread is occasionally yielding the CPU, the low-priority thread will gain more access to the CPU. Although specific results will vary, here are the results of one sample run:

```
High priority thread counted to 10850000
Low priority thread counted to 100000000
```

Notice that, because of the calls to **yield( )**, the low-priority thread actually finishes first! This graphically illustrates the fact that a thread's priority setting is only one of several factors that affect the amount of CPU access a thread receives.

Options and Alternatives

Although **yield( )** is a good way for a thread to yield the CPU, it is not the only way. For example, **sleep( )**, **wait( )**, and **join( )** all cause the invoking thread to suspend execution. In general, suspending a thread implicitly yields the CPU.

Because of the many variations that can occur in the environments in which a Java program might execute, the specific behavior of a multithreaded program experienced in one environment cannot be generalized. Therefore, when setting thread priorities, the execution characteristics of your program in one situation might not be the same in another. You should not rely on thread priorities to achieve a desired flow of execution. You should use interthread communication via **wait( )** and **notify( )**, instead. Remember: A thread's priority affects its potential access to the CPU but does not guarantee any sort of synchronization between threads.

Monitor a Thread's State

Key Ingredients	
Classes	**Methods**
java.lang.Thread	Thread.State getState( )
	final boolean isAlive( )

The **Thread** class supplies two methods that let you obtain information about the state of a thread: **isAlive( )** and **getState( )**. As explained in *Wait for a Thread to End*, **isAlive( )** returns **true** if the thread is active in the system and false if it has ended. While **isAlive( )** is useful, beginning with Java 5, you can obtain finely grained information about a thread's state, including whether it is runnable, waiting, or blocked, by using the **getState( )** method. Using both **isAlive( )** and **getState( )**, it is possible to fully monitor the state of a thread. This recipe demonstrates the process.

Step-by-Step

To obtain state information about a thread involves the following steps:

1. To determine if a thread is alive, call **isAlive( )**.
2. To obtained the state of a thread, call **getState( )**.

Discussion

When working with threads, you will often need to know whether a thread is alive, or if it has ended. To make this determination, call **isAlive( )**, shown here:

    final boolean isAlive( )

It returns **true** if the invoking thread is alive. A thread is alive if its **run( )** method has been called but has not yet returned. (A thread that has been created but not started is not yet alive.) It returns **false** if the thread has ended. The **isAlive( )** method has many uses. For example, you might use **isAlive( )** to confirm that a thread is active before waiting on a resource that is produced by that thread.

You can obtain fine-grained information about the state of a thread by calling **getState( )**, shown here:

    Thread.State getState( )

It returns a **State** object that represents the current state of the thread. **State** is an enumeration defined by **Thread** that has the following values:

State Value	Meaning
BLOCKED	The thread is blocked, which means that it is waiting for access to a **synchronized** code.
NEW	The thread has been created, but its **start( )** method has not yet been called.
RUNNABLE	The thread is either currently executing or will execute as soon as it gets access to the CPU.
TERMINATED	The thread has ended. A thread ends when its **run( )** method returns, or when the thread is stopped via a call to **stop( )**. (Note that **stop( )** is deprecated and should not be used.)
TIMED_WAITING	The thread is suspended, waiting on another thread for a specific period of time. This can occur because of a call to the timeout versions of **sleep( )**, **wait( )**, or **join( )**, for example.
WAITING	The thread is suspended, waiting on another thread. This can occur because of a call to the non-timeout versions of **wait( )** or **join( )**, for example.

Although you will not normally need to monitor the state of a thread in released code, it can be very helpful during development, debugging, and performance tuning. It can also be useful for creating custom instrumentation that monitors the status of the threads in a multithreaded application. As mentioned, **getState( )** was added by Java 5, so a modern version of Java is required to use it.

Example

The following example creates a method called **showThreadStatus( )** that uses **isAlive( )** and **getState( )** to display the status of a thread. The program illustrates **showThreadStatus( )** by creating a thread and then causing that thread to enter a variety of states. Each state is displayed.

```
// Monitor a thread's status.

class MyThread implements Runnable {
  int count;
  boolean holding;
  boolean ready;

  MyThread() {
    count = 0;
    holding = true;
    ready = false;
  }

  // Entry point of thread.
  public void run() {

    // Get the name of this thread.
    String thrdName = Thread.currentThread().getName();

    System.out.println(thrdName + " starting.");

    // Burn CPU time.
    System.out.println(thrdName + " using the CPU.");
    while(holding) ; // do nothing

    // Now, enter a wait state via a call to wait().
    System.out.println("waiting...");
    w(); // execute a call to wait() on this thread.

    // Next, enter a timed wait state via a call to sleep().
    try {
      System.out.println("Sleeping...");
      Thread.sleep(1000);
    } catch(InterruptedException exc) {
      System.out.println(thrdName + " interrupted.");
    }

    System.out.println(thrdName + " terminating.");
  }
```

```
    // Execute a call to wait().
    synchronized void w() {
      try {
        while(!ready) wait();
      } catch(InterruptedException exc) {
        System.out.println("wait() interrupted");
      }
    }

    // Execute a call to notify().
    synchronized void n() {
      ready = true;
      notify();
    }
}

class ThreadStateDemo {
    public static void main(String args[]) {

      try {

        // Construct a MyThread object.
        MyThread mt = new MyThread();
        Thread thrd = new Thread(mt, "MyThread #1");

        // Show state of newly created thread.
        System.out.println("MyThread #1 created but not yet started.");
        showThreadStatus(thrd);

        // Show state of thread that is running.
        System.out.println("Calling start() on MyThread #1.");
        thrd.start();
        Thread.sleep(50); // let MyThread #1 thread run
        showThreadStatus(thrd);

        // Show state of a thread waiting on wait().
        mt.holding = false; // let MyThread #1 call wait()
        Thread.sleep(50); // let MyThread #1 thread run
        showThreadStatus(thrd);

        // Let MyThread #1 move on by calling notify().
        // This lets MyThread #1 go to sleep.
        mt.n();
        Thread.sleep(50); // let MyThread #1 thread run

        // Now, show state of a thread sleeping.
        showThreadStatus(thrd);

        // Wait for thread to finish.
        while(thrd.isAlive()) ;
```

```
        // Show final status.
        showThreadStatus(thrd);
      }
      catch(InterruptedException exc) {
        System.out.println("Main thread interrupted.");
      }
    }

  // Show a thread's status.
  static void showThreadStatus(Thread thrd) {
    System.out.println("Status of " + thrd.getName() + ":");

    if(thrd.isAlive())
      System.out.println("  Alive");
    else
      System.out.println("  Not alive");

    System.out.println("  State is " + thrd.getState());

    System.out.println();
  }
}
```

The output is shown here:

```
MyThread #1 created but not yet started.
Status of MyThread #1:
  Not alive
  State is NEW

Calling start() on MyThread #1.
MyThread #1 starting.
MyThread #1 using the CPU.
Status of MyThread #1:
  Alive
  State is RUNNABLE

waiting...
Status of MyThread #1:
  Alive
  State is WAITING

Sleeping...
Status of MyThread #1:
  Alive
  State is TIMED_WAITING

MyThread #1 terminating.
Status of MyThread #1:
  Not alive
  State is TERMINATED
```

Bonus Example: A Real-Time Thread Monitor

Using the capabilities of **Thread**, it is possible to create a thread monitor that displays in real time the status of a thread, including its name, state, priority, and whether it is alive or dead. The monitor runs in its own thread, so it is fully independent of the thread under scrutiny. The monitor is passed a reference to the thread to monitor. It then uses a timer to update, at regular intervals, the thread's status display within a Swing-based window. The refresh rate is initially set to 100 milliseconds but can be adjusted using a spinner. Thus, the thread's status can be watched during the execution of the thread.

A thread monitor can be a very useful tool when debugging and tuning multithreaded applications because it lets you see what a thread is doing during execution. In other words, a thread monitor provides a window into the execution profile of the thread being monitored. Because changes to the thread's state can be seen in real time, it is possible to spot some types of bottlenecks, unexpected wait states, and deadlocks as they happen. Although the thread monitor shown here is quite simple, it is still useful and can easily be expanded or enhanced to better suit your own needs.

The thread monitor is defined by the **ThreadMonitor** class shown here.

```java
// A real-time thread monitor.

import javax.swing.*;
import javax.swing.event.*;
import java.awt.*;
import java.awt.event.*;

class ThreadMonitor {

  JSpinner jspSampleRate;
  JLabel jlabName;  // shows name of thread
  JLabel jlabState; // shows thread state
  JLabel jlabAlive; // shows isAlive() result
  JLabel jlabPri;   // shows priority
  JLabel jlabRate;  // label for sample rate spinner

  Thread thrd; // reference to thread being monitored

  Timer thrdTimer; // timer for updating thread status

  // Pass in the thread to be monitored.
  ThreadMonitor(Thread t) {
    // Create a new JFrame container.
    JFrame jfrm = new JFrame("Thread Monitor");

    // Specify FlowLayout manager.
    jfrm.getContentPane().setLayout(new FlowLayout());

    // Give the frame an initial size.
    jfrm.setSize(240, 160);

    // Terminate the program when the user closes the application.
    // Remove or change this if you like.
    jfrm.setDefaultCloseOperation(JFrame.EXIT_ON_CLOSE);
```

```java
// Store the thread reference.
thrd = t;

// Create an integer spinner model.
SpinnerNumberModel spm =
        new SpinnerNumberModel(100, 1, 5000, 10);

// Create a JSpinner using the model.
jspSampleRate = new JSpinner(spm);

// Set the preferred size of the spinner.
jspSampleRate.setPreferredSize(new Dimension(50, 20));

// Add change listener for the Sample Rate spinner.
jspSampleRate.addChangeListener(new ChangeListener() {
  public void stateChanged(ChangeEvent ce) {
    thrdTimer.setDelay((Integer)jspSampleRate.getValue());
  }
});

// Make and initialize the labels.
jlabName = new JLabel("Thread Name: " + thrd.getName());
jlabName.setPreferredSize(new Dimension(200, 22));
jlabState = new JLabel("Current State: " + thrd.getState());
jlabState.setPreferredSize(new Dimension(200, 22));
jlabAlive = new JLabel("Thread Alive: " + thrd.isAlive());
jlabAlive.setPreferredSize(new Dimension(200, 22));
jlabPri = new JLabel("Current Priority: " + thrd.getPriority());
jlabPri.setPreferredSize(new Dimension(200, 22));
jlabRate = new JLabel("Sample Rate: ");

// Create an action listener for the timer.
// Each time the timer goes off, update the
// monitor's display.
ActionListener timerAL = new ActionListener() {
  public void actionPerformed(ActionEvent ae) {
    updateStatus();
  }
};

// Create the refresh time using timerAL.
thrdTimer = new Timer(100, timerAL);

// Use two Boxes to hold the components.
Box vbox = Box.createVerticalBox();
vbox.add(jlabName);
vbox.add(jlabPri);
vbox.add(jlabState);
vbox.add(jlabAlive);
jfrm.add(vbox);

Box hbox = Box.createHorizontalBox();
hbox.add(jlabRate);
```

```
      hbox.add(jspSampleRate);
      jfrm.add(hbox);

      // Display the frame.
      jfrm.setVisible(true);

      // Start the timer. Each time the timer goes off
      // the monitor display is updated.
      thrdTimer.start();
    }

    // Update the information about the thread.
    void updateStatus() {
      jlabName.setText("Thread Name: " + thrd.getName());
      jlabState.setText("Current State: " + thrd.getState());
      jlabAlive.setText("Thread Alive: " + thrd.isAlive());
      jlabPri.setText("Current Priority: " + thrd.getPriority());
    }
}
```

The code is straightforward, and the comments describe each step. Here are a few highlights. When a **ThreadMonitor** is created, it must be passed a reference to the thread to be monitored. This reference is stored in the **thrd** instance variable. Next, the monitor's GUI is created. Notice that a spinner is used to set the sample rate. This is the rate at which the display is updated. This rate is initially set to 100 milliseconds, but you can change the rate during execution. The range is limited to 10 to 5,000 milliseconds, but you can expand this if you like.

The sample rate is used to set the delay period of a Swing timer, which is an instance of **javax.swing.Timer**. Each time the timer goes off, an action event is sent to all of the timer's registered action listeners. In this case, there is only one listener. It handles the timer's action event by calling **updateStatus( )**, which updates the GUI to reflect the current state of the thread.

NOTE *For information about, and recipes that use, Swing, see Chapter 8.*

You can put the thread monitor into action by substituting this version of **ThreadStateDemo** into the previous example program. (You will also need to have the program **import javax.swing.***) Instead of showing the status of a thread on the console, it shows the status in real time, in the monitor's window.

```
// This version of ThreadStateDemo uses a ThreadMonitor
// to report a thread's name, state, and priority in real time.
class ThreadStateDemo {

  public static void main(String args[]) {

    try {
```

```
      // Construct a MyThread object.
      MyThread mt = new MyThread();
      final Thread thrd = new Thread(mt, "MyThread #1");

      // Create the thread monitor. Because ThreadMonitor creates
      // a Swing GUI, ThreadMonitor must be instantiated on
      // the event dispatching thread.
      SwingUtilities.invokeLater(new Runnable() {
        public void run() {
          new ThreadMonitor(thrd);
        }
      });

      // Use sleep() here and elsewhere to slow down
      // execution in order to allow the various
      // thread states to be seen.
      Thread.sleep(3000);

      // Start the thread.
      thrd.start();

      Thread.sleep(3000);

      // Show state of a thread waiting on wait().
      mt.holding = false; // let MyThread #1 enter call wait()

      Thread.sleep(3000);

      // Change the thread's priority.
      System.out.println("Changing the thread's priority.");
      thrd.setPriority(Thread.NORM_PRIORITY-2);

      Thread.sleep(3000);

      // Change the thread's name to MyThread ALPHA.
      System.out.println("Changing name to MyThread ALPHA.");
      thrd.setName("MyThread ALPHA");
      Thread.sleep(3000);

      // Let the thread move on by calling notify().
      // This lets MyThread #1 go to sleep.
      mt.n();

      Thread.sleep(3000);

      System.out.println("Main thread ending.");
    }
    catch(InterruptedException exc) {
      System.out.println("Main thread interrupted.");
    }
  }
}
```

A sample of the monitor's window is shown here:

Here are some enhancements that you might want to try adding. First, add a spinner that lets you set the priority of the thread being monitored. Thus, in addition to displaying the thread's priority, you can set it. This feature would let you experiment with different priorities, helping you tune the thread's execution characteristics. Second, try adding buttons that suspend, resume, and stop the thread. Third, you might want to display when the thread is interrupted. Finally, you might want to indicate if the thread is a user or a daemon.

Options and Alternatives

Although not often needed, there is one other piece of thread-related information that can be useful in some cases: the lock status of an object. For example, when debugging multithreaded code, it can occasionally be useful to know if a thread holds the lock on some object. This question can be answered by calling **holdsLock( )**, shown here:

    static boolean holdsLock(Object *obj*)

The object in question is passed in *obj*. If the calling thread holds that object's lock, then **holdsLock( )** returns true. Otherwise, it returns false.

Use a Thread Group

Key Ingredients	
Classes	**Methods**
java.lang.Thread	
java.lang.ThreadGroup	int activeCount( )
	int enumerate(Thread[ ] *thrds*)
	final void interrupt( )

In a large application it is not uncommon to have several separate, but related threads of execution. In such a case, it is sometimes useful to deal with these threads collectively as a group, rather than individually. For example, consider a situation in which multiple users are accessing a database. One possible implementation is to create a separate thread for each user. This way, the database queries can easily be handled asynchronously and independently. If these threads are managed as a group, then some event that affects all of them, such as the loss of the network connection, can be easily handled by interrupting all threads in the group. To handle groups of threads Java provides the **ThreadGroup** class, which is packaged in **java.lang**. This recipe demonstrates its use.

Step-by-Step

Using a thread group involves the following steps:

1. Create a **ThreadGroup**.
2. Create each thread that will be part of the group, using one of **Thread**'s constructors that enables the thread group to be specified.
3. To obtain a list of the threads in the group, call **enumerate( )**.
4. To obtain an estimate of the number of active threads in the group, call **activeCount( )**.
5. To interrupt all threads in a group, call **interrupt( )** on the **ThreadGroup** instance.

Discussion

ThreadGroup defines two constructors. The one used by this recipe is shown here:

ThreadGroup(String *name*)

The name of the **ThreadGroup** is passed in *name*.

Threads are added to a thread group when they are created. **Thread** supplies several constructors that take a **ThreadGroup** argument. The one used by this recipe is shown here:

Thread(ThreadGroup *tg*, Runnable *thrdObj*, String *name*)

The thread will become part of the **ThreadGroup** specified by *tg*. A reference to an instance of a class that implements **Runnable** is passed in *thrdObj*. The name of the thread is passed in *thrdName*. (See *Multithreading Fundamentals* for details on the other **Thread** constructors.) You can obtain a list of all threads in a group by using this form of **enumerate( )**:

int enumerate(Thread[ ] *thrds*, boolean *all*)

It returns all threads in the invoking **ThreadGroup** in the array referred to by *thrds*. The number of threads actually stored in *thrds* is returned. Be careful, however. No error is reported if *thrds* is not large enough to hold all threads. Therefore, the length of *thrds* must be sufficient to hold all active threads to avoid trouble.

You can obtain the number of active (non-terminated) threads in the group by calling **activeCount( )**, shown here.

int activeCount( )

It returns the number of active threads in the invoking **ThreadGroup** (and in any child groups that have the invoking group as a parent). Be aware, however, that if threads are in the process of being added to the group or the process of being terminated, then the number returned might be inaccurate by the time you receive it.

You can interrupt all threads in a group by calling **interrupt( )**, shown next:

final void interrupt( )

Calling **interrupt( )** on a **ThreadGroup** instance results in **Thread's** version of **interrupt( )** being called on each thread in the group. See *Interrupt a Thread* for details.

Example

The following example demonstrates a thread group. It creates four threads, displays the active count, enumerates the threads, stops one thread, displays the updated active count, and then interrupts the remaining threads.

```
// Use a ThreadGroup.

class MyThread implements Runnable {
  private volatile boolean stopped;

  MyThread() {
    stopped = false;
  }

  // Run the thread.
  public void run() {
    String thrdName = Thread.currentThread().getName();

    System.out.println(thrdName + " starting.");

    try {

      for(int i = 1; i < 1000; i++) {
        // Display periods
        System.out.print(".");

        Thread.sleep(250);

        synchronized(this) {
          if(stopped) break;
        }
      }
    } catch (InterruptedException exc) {
      System.out.println(thrdName + " interrupted.");
    }
    System.out.println(thrdName + " exiting.");
  }

  // Stop the thread.
  synchronized void myStop() {
    stopped = true;
  }
}
```

```java
// Demonstrate thread interrupts.
class TGDemo {

  public static void main(String args[]) {
    MyThread mt = new MyThread();
    MyThread mt2 = new MyThread();
    MyThread mt3 = new MyThread();
    MyThread mt4 = new MyThread();

    // Create a thread group.
    ThreadGroup tg = new ThreadGroup("My Group");

    // Put each thread into the group.
    Thread thrd = new Thread(tg, mt, "MyThread #1");
    Thread thrd2 = new Thread(tg, mt2, "MyThread #2");
    Thread thrd3 = new Thread(tg, mt3, "MyThread #3");
    Thread thrd4 = new Thread(tg, mt4, "MyThread #4");

    // Start each thread.
    thrd.start();
    thrd2.start();
    thrd3.start();
    thrd4.start();

    try {

      // Let the other threads run for a while.
      Thread.sleep(1000);

      // Display active threads in group.
      System.out.println("\nThere are " + tg.activeCount() +
                         " threads in tg.");

      // Enumerate the threads and display their names.
      System.out.println("Here are their names: ");
      Thread thrds[] = new Thread[tg.activeCount()];
      tg.enumerate(thrds);
      for(Thread t : thrds)
        System.out.println(t.getName());

      System.out.println();

      // Stop thrd2.
      System.out.println("\nStopping My Thread #2");
      mt2.myStop();

      Thread.sleep(1000); // Let the threads run.

      System.out.println("\nThere are now " + tg.activeCount() +
                         " threads in tg.");
```

```
        // Interrupt all remaining threads.
        System.out.println("\nInterrupting all remaining " +
                           "threads in the group.");
        tg.interrupt();

    } catch (InterruptedException e) {
      System.out.println("Main thread Interrupted");
    }
  }
}
```

Sample output is shown here. (Your exact output may vary.)

```
MyThread #1 starting.
.MyThread #2 starting.
.MyThread #3 starting.
.MyThread #4 starting.
. . . . . . . . . . . .
There are 4 threads in tg.
Here are their names:
MyThread #1
MyThread #2
MyThread #3
MyThread #4


Stopping My Thread #2
.MyThread #2 exiting.
. . . . . . . . . .
There are now 3 threads in tg.

Interrupting all remaining threads in the group.
.MyThread #1 interrupted.
MyThread #1 exiting.
.MyThread #3 interrupted.
MyThread #3 exiting.
.MyThread #4 interrupted.
MyThread #4 exiting.
```

Options and Alternatives

A **ThreadGroup** can contain other thread groups. In this situation, the **ThreadGroup** that
contains the other groups is called the *parent*. A **ThreadGroup** is given a parent when it is
created. By default, the parent group is the one used by the thread that creates the
ThreadGroup. However, you can specify to which parent group a child group belongs by
using this form of the **ThreadGroup** constructor:

ThreadGroup(ThreadGroup *parent*, String *name*)

Here, *parent* is the parent of the object being created. The name of the child **ThreadGroup** is
passed in *name*.

You can obtain the parent of a **ThreadGroup** by calling **getParent( )**, shown next:

final ThreadGroup getParent( )

If the invoking **ThreadGroup** has no parent, then **null** is returned.

You can obtain a list of all threads in a group, including those in child groups, by using this form of **enumerate( )**:

int enumerate(Thread[ ] *thrds*, boolean *all*)

It obtains all threads in the invoking **ThreadGroup** and returns them in *thrds*. If *all* is true, then all threads in all child groups are also obtained. The number of threads actually stored in *thrds* is returned. Be careful, however. No error is reported if *thrds* is not large enough to hold all threads. Therefore, *thrds* should be large enough to hold all active threads.

You can obtain a list of all thread groups in a group by using this form of **enumerate( )**:

int enumerate(ThreadGroup[ ] *thrdGourps*)

It obtains all thread groups in the invoking **ThreadGroup** and returns them in *thrds*. The number of thread groups actually stored in *thrdGroups* is returned. Be careful, however. No error is reported if *thrdGroups* is not large enough to hold all thread groups. Therefore, *thrdGroups* should be large enough to hold all active threads. You can obtain a count of the groups by calling **activeGroupCount( )** on the thread group.

You can obtain a list of all thread groups in a group, including those in child groups, by using this form of **enumerate( )**:

int enumerate(ThreadGroup[ ] *thrdGroups*, boolean *all*)

It works the same as the preceding method except that when *all* is true, all thread groups in all child groups are also obtained.

8

CHAPTER

Swing

This chapter presents a series of recipes that demonstrate Swing, Java's premier GUI toolkit. Defined by a rich set of visual components and a tightly integrated, highly adaptive architecture, Swing enables the creation of sophisticated, yet streamlined user interfaces. Today's user demands a high-quality visual experience, and Swing is the framework that you will use to supply it.

Swing is a *very* large topic, and an entire book is needed to describe all of its features. Therefore, it is not possible to address all aspects of Swing in this chapter. For example, Swing allows a high level of customization and supports many advanced features that let you tailor aspects of its inner workings. Although important, these features are not used by most programmers on a daily basis, and they are not the focus of this chapter. Instead, the recipes presented here illustrate fundamental techniques and commonly used components. The recipes also answer many frequently asked "how to" questions about Swing. In essence, the goal is to show key pieces of Swing's component set in action, as they are used in day-to-day programming. Of course, you can adapt the recipes and layer on additional functionality as needed by your application.

Here are the recipes in this chapter:

- Create a Simple Swing Application
- Set the Content Pane's Layout manager
- Work with **JLabel**
- Create a Simple Push Button
- Use Icons, HTML, and Mnemonics with **JButton**
- Create a Toggle Button
- Create Check Boxes
- Create Radio Buttons
- Input Text with **JTextField**
- Work with **JList**
- Use a Scroll Bar
- Use **JScrollPane** to Handle Scrolling
- Display Data in a **JTable**

- Handle **JTable** Events
- Display Data in a **JTree**
- Create a Main Menu

NOTE *For a comprehensive introduction to Swing, see my book* Swing: A Beginner's Guide *published by McGraw-Hill, 2007. The overview that follows and many of the discussions in this chapter are adapted from that work.*

Overview of Swing

Swing did not exist in the early days of Java. Rather, it was a response to deficiencies present in Java's original GUI subsystem: the Abstract Window Toolkit (AWT). The AWT defines a basic set of components that support a usable, but limited graphical interface. One reason for the limited nature of the AWT is that it translates its various visual components into their corresponding, platform-specific equivalents, or *peers*. This means that the look and feel of an AWT component is defined by the platform, not by Java. Because the AWT components use native code resources, they are referred to as *heavyweight*.

The use of native peers led to several problems. First, because of differences between operating systems, a component might look, or even act, differently on different platforms. This potential variability threatened the overarching philosophy of Java: write once, run anywhere. Second, the look and feel of each component was fixed (because it is defined by the platform) and could not be (easily) changed. Third, the use of heavyweight components caused some frustrating restrictions. For example, a heavyweight component is always rectangular and opaque.

Not long after Java's original release, it became apparent that the limitations and restrictions present in the AWT were sufficiently serious that a better approach was needed. The solution was Swing. Introduced in 1997, Swing was included as part of the Java Foundation Classes (JFC). Swing was initially available for use with Java 1.1 as a separate library. However, beginning with Java 1.2, Swing (and the rest of the JFC) was fully integrated into Java.

Swing addresses the limitations associated with the AWT's components through the use of two key features: *lightweight components* and a *pluggable look and feel*. Although they are largely transparent to the programmer, these two features are at the foundation of Swing's design philosophy and the reason for much of its power and flexibility. Let's look at each.

With very few exceptions, Swing components are *lightweight*. This means that a component is written entirely in Java. It does not rely on platform-specific peers. Lightweight components have some important advantages, including efficiency and flexibility. For example, a lightweight component can be transparent, which enables non-rectangular shapes. Furthermore, because lightweight components do not translate into platform-specific peers, the look and feel of each component is determined by Swing, not by the underlying operating system. This means that each component will work in a consistent manner across all platforms.

Because each Swing component is rendered by Java code rather than by platform-specific peers, it is possible to separate the look and feel of a component from the logic of the component, and this is what Swing does. Separating out the look and feel provides a significant advantage: it becomes possible to change the way that a component is rendered without affecting any of its other aspects. In other words, it is possible to "plug in" a new look and feel for any given component without creating any side effects in the code that uses that component.

Java provides look and feels, such as metal and Motif, that are available to all Swing users. The metal look and feel is also called the *Java look and feel*. It is a platform-independent look and feel that is available in all Java execution environments. It is also the default look and feel. For this reason, the default Java look and feel (metal) is used by the examples in this chapter.

Swing's pluggable look and feel is made possible because Swing uses a modified version of the classic *model-view-controller* (MVC) architecture. In MVC terminology, the *model* corresponds to the state information associated with the component. For example, in the case of a check box, the model contains a field that indicates if the box is checked or unchecked. The *view* determines how the component is displayed on the screen, including any aspects of the view that are affected by the current state of the model. The *controller* determines how the component reacts to the user. For example, when the user clicks on a check box, the controller reacts by changing the model to reflect the user's choice (checked or unchecked). This then results in the view being updated. By separating a component into a model, a view, and a controller, the specific implementation of each can be changed without affecting the other two. For instance, different view implementations can render the same component in different ways without affecting the model or the controller.

Although the MVC architecture and the principles behind it are conceptually sound, the high level of separation between the view and the controller was not beneficial for Swing components. Instead, Swing uses a modified version of MVC that combines the view and the controller into a single logical entity called the *UI delegate*. For this reason, Swing's approach is called either the *model-delegate* architecture or the *separable model* architecture. Therefore, although Swing's component architecture is based on MVC, it does not use a classical implementation of it. Although the recipes in this chapter do not work directly with models or UI delegates, they are, nevertheless, present behind the scene.

One last point: Although Swing eliminates a number of the limitations present in the AWT, Swing does not replace the AWT. Rather, Swing builds upon the foundation provided by the AWT. Swing also uses the same event-handling mechanism as the AWT. Therefore, the AWT is still a crucial part of Java.

Components and Containers

A Swing GUI consists of two key items: *components* and *containers*. However, this distinction is mostly conceptual because all containers are also components. The difference between the two is found in their intended purpose. As the term is commonly used, a component is an independent visual control, such as a push button or text field. A container holds a group of components. Thus, a container is a special type of component that is designed to hold other components. Furthermore, in order for a component to be displayed, it must be held within a container. Thus, all Swing GUIs will have at least one container. Because containers are components, a container can also hold other containers. This enables Swing to define what is called a *containment hierarchy*, at the top of which must be a *top-level container*.

Components

In general, Swing components are derived from the **JComponent** class. (The only exceptions to this are the four top-level containers, described in the next section.) **JComponent** provides the functionality that is common to all components. For example, **JComponent** supports the pluggable look and feel. **JComponent** inherits the AWT classes **Container** and **Component**. Thus, a Swing component is built on and compatible with an AWT component.

All of Swing's components are represented by classes defined within the package **javax.swing**. The following table shows the class names for Swing components (including those used as containers):

JApplet	JButton	JCheckBox	JCheckBoxMenuItem
JColorChooser	JComboBox	JComponent	JDesktopPane
JDialog	JEditorPane	JFileChooser	JFormattedTextField
JFrame	JInternalFrame	JLabel	JLayeredPane
JList	JMenu	JMenuBar	JMenuItem
JOptionPane	JPanel	JPasswordField	JPopupMenu
JProgressBar	JRadioButton	JRadioButtonMenuItem	JRootPane
JScrollBar	JScrollPane	JSeparator	JSlider
JSpinner	JSplitPane	JTabbedPane	JTable
JTextArea	JTextField	JTextPane	JToggleButton
JToolBar	JToolTip	JTree	JViewport
JWindow			

Notice that all component classes begin with the letter **J**. For example, the class for a label is **JLabel**, the class for a push button is **JButton**, and the class for a check box is **JCheckBox**.

Containers

Swing defines two types of containers. The first are top-level containers: **JFrame**, **JApplet**, **JWindow**, and **JDialog**. These containers do not inherit **JComponent**. They do, however, inherit the AWT classes **Component** and **Container**. Unlike Swing's other components, which are lightweight, the top-level containers are heavyweight. This makes the top-level containers a special case in the Swing component library.

As the name implies, a top-level container must be at top of a containment hierarchy. A top-level container is not contained within any other container. Furthermore, every containment hierarchy must begin with a top-level container. The one most commonly used for applications is **JFrame**. The one used for applets is **JApplet**.

The second type of containers supported by Swing are lightweight containers. Lightweight containers *do* inherit **JComponent**. Examples of lightweight containers are **JPanel**, **JScrollPane**, and **JRootPane**. Lightweight containers are often used to collectively organize and manage groups of related components because a lightweight container can be contained within another container. Thus, you can use lightweight containers to create subgroups of related controls that are contained within an outer container.

The Top-Level Container Panes

Each top-level container defines a set of *panes*. At the top of the hierarchy is an instance of **JRootPane**. **JRootPane** is a lightweight container whose purpose is to manage the other panes. It also helps manage the optional menu bar. The panes that comprise the root pane are called the *glass pane,* the *content pane,* and the *layered pane.*

The glass pane is the top-level pane. It sits above and completely covers all other panes. The glass pane enables you to manage mouse events that affect the entire container (rather than an individual control) or to paint over any other component, for example. In most cases, you won't need to use the glass pane directly. The layered pane allows components to be given a depth value. This value determines which component overlays another. (Thus, the layered pane lets you specify a Z-order for a component, although this is not something that you will usually need to do.) The layered pane holds the content pane and the (optional) menu bar. Although the glass pane and the layered pane are integral to the operation of a top-level container and serve important purposes, much of what they provide occurs behind the scene.

The pane with which your application will interact the most is the content pane, because this is the pane to which you will add visual components. In other words, when you add a component, such as a button, to a top-level container, you will add it to the content pane. Therefore, the content pane holds the components that the user interacts with. By default, the content pane is an opaque instance of **JPanel** (which is one of Swing's lightweight containers).

Layout Manager Overview

In Java, the positioning of components within a container is controlled by a *layout manager.* Java offers several layout managers. Many are provided by the AWT (within **java.awt**), but Swing adds a few of its own in **javax.swing**. All layout managers are instances of a class that implements the **LayoutManager** interface. (Some will also implement the **LayoutManager2** interface.) Here is a list of the layout managers used in the examples in this chapter:

java.awt.FlowLayout	A simple layout that positions components left-to-right, top-to-bottom. (Positions components right-to-left for some cultural settings.)
java.awt.BorderLayout	Positions components within the center or the borders of the container. This is the default layout for a content pane.
java.awt.GridLayout	Lays out components within a grid.
javax.swing.BoxLayout	Lays out components vertically or horizontally within a box.

It is beyond the scope of this chapter to describe these layout managers in detail, but the following discussions present a brief overview. (Additional information about these layout managers is also found in the recipes.)

BorderLayout is default layout manager for the content pane. It implements a layout style that defines five locations to which a component can be added. The first is the center. The other four are the sides (i.e., borders), which are called north, south, east, and west. By default, when you add a component to the content pane, you are adding the component to the center. To add a component to one of the other regions, specify its name.

Although a border layout is useful is some situations, often another, more flexible layout manager is needed. One of the simplest is **FlowLayout**. A flow layout lays out components one row at a time, top to bottom. When one row is full, layout advances to the next row. Although this scheme gives you little control over the placement of components, it is quite simple to use. However, be aware that if you resize the frame, the position of the components will change. Because of its simplicity, flow layout is used by several of the examples.

GridLayout creates a grid of rectangular cells into which individual components are placed. The size of each cell in the grid is the same, and a component put into a cell is sized to fill the dimensions of the cell. The grid dimensions are specified when you create an instance of **GridLayout**. For example, this expression

```
new GridLayout(5, 2)
```

creates a grid that has 5 rows and 2 columns.

BoxLayout gives you an easy way to create groups of components that are organized into boxes. Usually, you won't use **BoxLayout** as the layout manager for the content pane itself. Instead, you will normally create one or more panels that use **BoxLayout**, add components to the panels, and then add the panels to the content pane. In this way, you can easily create groups of components that lay out as a unit. Although you can implement this approach manually (by using **JPanel**), Swing offers a more convenient approach. The **Box** class can be used to create a container that automatically uses **BoxLayout**. This approach is used by one of the examples.

Event Handling

Another important part of most Swing programs is event handling. Most Swing components respond to user input, and the events generated by those interactions need to be handled. For example, an event is generated when the user clicks on a button, types a key on the keyboard, or selects an item from a list. Events are also generated in ways not directly related to user input. For example, an event is generated when a timer goes off. Whatever the case, event handling is a large part of any program that uses Swing.

The event-handling mechanism used by Swing is called the *delegation event model*. Its concept is quite simple. A *source* generates an event and sends it to one or more *listeners*. In this scheme, the listener simply waits until it receives an event. Once an event arrives, the listener processes the event and then returns. The advantage of this design is that the application logic that processes events is cleanly separated from the user interface logic that generates the events. A user interface element is able to "delegate" the processing of an event to a separate piece of code. In the delegation event model, a listener must register with a source in order to receive an event notification.

Events

In the delegation model, an event is an object that describes a state change in a source. It can be generated as a consequence of a person interacting with an element in a graphical user interface or it can be generated under program control. The superclass for all events is **java.util.EventObject**. Many events are declared in **java.awt.event**. These are the events defined by the AWT. Although Swing uses these events, it also defines several of its own. These are found in **javax.swing.event**.

Event Sources

An event source is an object that generates an event. When a source generates an event, it must send that event to all registered listeners. Therefore, in order for a listener to receive an event, it must register with the source of that event. Listeners register with a source by calling an **add*Type*Listener( )** method on the event source object. Each type of event has its own registration method. Here is the general form:

public void add*Type*Listener(*Type*Listener *el*)

Here, *Type* is the name of the event and *el* is a reference to the event listener. For example, the method that registers a keyboard event listener is called **addKeyListener( )**. The method that registers a mouse motion listener is called **addMouseMotionListener( )**. When an event occurs, all registered listeners are notified.

A source must also provide a method that allows a listener to unregister an interest in a specific type of event. The general form of such a method is this:

public void remove*Type*Listener(*Type*Listener *el*)

Here, *Type* is the name of the event and *el* is a reference to the event listener. For example, to remove a keyboard listener, you would call **removeKeyListener( )**.

The methods that add or remove listeners are provided by the source that generates events. For example, the **JButton** class provides a method called **addActionListener( )** that adds an *action listener*, which handles the action event generated when the button is pressed.

Event Listeners

A listener is an object that is notified when an event occurs. It has two major requirements. First, it must have registered with one or more sources to receive notifications about a specific type of event. Second, it must implement a method to receive and process that event.

The methods that receive and process events are defined in a set of interfaces found in **java.awt.event** and **javax.swing.event**. For example, the **ActionListener** interface defines a method that receives a notification when an action, such as clicking on a button, takes place. Any object may receive and process this event if it provides an implementation of the **ActionListener** interface.

There is an important general principle that applies to event handlers: An event handler must do its job quickly and then return. It should not engage in a long operation because doing so will slow down the entire application. If a time-consuming operation is required, then a separate thread will usually be created for this purpose.

Create a Simple Swing Application

Key Ingredients	
Classes	**Methods**
javax.swing.JFrame	void setSize(int *width*, int *height*) void setDefaultCloseOperation(int *what*) Component add(Component *comp*) void setVisible(boolean *show*)
javax.swing.JLabel	
javax.swing.SwingUtilities	static void invokeLater(Runnable *obj*)

There are two types of Java programs in which Swing is typically used. The first is the applet. The creation of a Swing applet is described in Chapter 6, in the recipes *Create a Swing-Based Applet Skeleton* and *Create a GUI and Handle Events in a Swing Applet*. The second common Swing program is the desktop application. This is the type of Swing program described by this recipe.

Although Swing is easy to use, Swing programs differ from both console-based programs and from AWT-based GUI programs. For example, a Swing program uses the Swing component set to handle user interaction. Thus, I/O is not handled by **System.in** or **System.out** as it is in a console-based application, but by visual controls, such as push buttons, spinners, and scroll bars. Also, Swing has special requirements that relate to threading. This recipe shows the steps needed to create a minimal Swing application. It also introduces Swing's simplest component: **JLabel**.

Step-by-Step

To create a Swing desktop application involves the following steps:

1. Create a top-level container for the program. This will usually be an instance of **JFrame**.
2. Set the size of the frame by calling **setSize( )**.
3. Set the default close operation by calling **setDefaultCloseOperation( )**.
4. Create one or more components.
5. Add the components to the content pane of the frame by calling **add( )**.
6. Display the frame by calling **setVisible( )**.
7. In all cases, the Swing GUI must be created on the event-dispatching thread through the use of **invokeLater( )**. Thus, the preceding steps must be executed by the event-dispatching thread.

Discussion

As explained in *Overview of Swing,* the Swing classes and interfaces are packaged in **javax.swing**. Thus, any program that uses Swing must import this package.

All Swing applications must have a heavyweight container at the top of the containment hierarchy. This top-level container holds all other containers and components associated with the application. A Swing application will typically use an instance of **JFrame** as the top-level container. **JFrame** inherits the following AWT classes: **Component**, **Container**, **Window**, and **Frame**. It defines several constructors. The one used by this recipe is shown here:

JFrame(String *name*)

The title of the window is passed in *name.*

The size of the frame can be set by calling **setSize( )**, shown next:

void setSize(int *width*, int *height*)

The *width* and *height* parameters specify the width and height of the window in pixels.

By default, when a top-level window is closed (such as when the user clicks on the close box), the window is removed from the screen, but the application is not terminated. While this default behavior is useful in some situations, it is not what is needed for most applications. Instead, you will usually want the entire application to terminate when its top-level window is closed. There are a couple of ways to achieve this. The easiest way is to call **setDefaultCloseOperation( )**. Its general form is shown here:

void setDefaultCloseOperation(int *what*)

The value passed in *what* determines what happens when the window is closed. Here are the valid values:

JFrame.DISPOSE_ON_CLOSE

JFrame.EXIT_ON_CLOSE

JFrame.HIDE_ON_CLOSE

JFrame.DO_NOTHING_ON_CLOSE

These constants are declared in **WindowConstants**, which is an interface declared in **javax.swing** that is implemented by **JFrame** and defines many constants related to Swing. To cause the program to terminate when its top-level window is closed, use **EXIT_ON_CLOSE**.

You create a Swing component by instantiating one of Swing's component classes. Swing defines many component classes that support push buttons, check boxes, text fields, and so on. This recipe uses only one of those classes: **JLabel**. This is Swing's simplest component because it does not accept user input. Instead, it simply displays information, which can consist of text, an icon, or a combination of both. The label used by this recipe contains only text. **JLabel** defines several constructors. The one used here is:

JLabel(String *str*)

This creates a label that displays the string passed in *str*. (See *Work with **JLabel*** for more information on labels.)

After you have a created a component, it must be added to a container. In this case, it will be added to the application's top-level container. All top-level containers have a content pane in which components are stored. Thus, to add a component to a frame, you must add it to the frame's content pane. Beginning with Java 5, this is accomplished by calling **add( )** on the **JFrame** reference. This causes the component to be added to the content pane associated with the **JFrame**. (See the historical note that follows.) The **add( )** method has several versions. The one used by the program is shown here:

Component add(Component *comp*)

When the frame is made visible, *comp* will also be displayed. Its position will be determined by the layout manager. By default, the content pane associated with a **JFrame** uses a border layout. This version of **add( )** adds the component to the center location. Other versions of **add( )** enable you to specify one of the border regions. When a component is added to the center, its size is automatically adjusted to fit the size of the center.

To display the frame (and the components that it contains), you must call **setVisible( )**, shown here:

void setVisible(boolean *show*)

If *show* is true, the frame is displayed. If *show* is false, the frame is hidden. By default, a **JFrame** is invisible, so **setVisible(true)** must be called to display it.

There is a very important constraint that must be adhered to when using Swing. All interaction with Swing's visual components must take place through the *event-dispatching thread* rather than on the main thread of the application. This includes the initial construction of the GUI. Here's why: In general, Swing programs are event-driven. For example, when a user interacts with a component, an event is generated. An event is passed to the application by calling an event handler defined by the application. This means that the handler is executed on the event-dispatching thread provided by Swing and not on the main thread of the application. Thus, although event handlers are defined by your program, they are called on a thread that was not created by your program. To avoid problems (such as two different threads trying to update the same component at the same time), all Swing GUI components must be created and updated from the event-dispatching thread, not the main thread of the application. However, **main( )** is executed on the main thread. Thus, it cannot directly instantiate a Swing GUI. Instead, the program must create a **Runnable** object that executes on the event-dispatching thread, and have this object create the GUI.

To enable the GUI code to be created on the event-dispatching thread, you must use one of two methods that are defined by the **SwingUtilities** class. These methods are **invokeLater( )** and **invokeAndWait( )**. They are shown here:

static void invokeLater(Runnable *obj*)

static void invokeAndWait(Runnable *obj*)
    throws InterruptedException, InvocationTargetException

Here, *obj* is a **Runnable** object that will have its **run( )** method called by the event-dispatching thread. The difference between the two methods is that **invokeLater( )** returns immediately, but **invokeAndWait( )** waits until **obj.run( )** returns. You can use these methods to call a method that constructs the GUI for your Swing application, or whenever you need to modify the state of the GUI from code not executed by the event-dispatching thread. You will normally want to use **invokeLater( )**, as the following example does. However, when constructing the initial GUI for an applet, you will want to use **invokeAndWait( )**. (See *Create a Swing-Based Applet Skeleton* in Chapter 6.)

Historical Note: getContentPane( )

Prior to Java 5, when adding a component to, removing a component from, or setting the layout manager for the content pane of a top-level container, such as a **JFrame**, you had to explicitly obtain a reference to the content pane by calling **getContentPane( )**. For example, assuming a **JLabel** called **jlab** and a **JFrame** called **jfrm**, in the past, you had to use the following statement to add **jlab** to **jfrm**:

```
jfrm.getContentPane().add(jlab); // old-style
```

Beginning with Java 5, the call to **getContentPane( )** is no longer necessary because calls to **add( )**, **remove( )**, and **setLayout( )** on a **JFrame** are automatically directed to the content pane. For this reason the recipes in this book *do not* call **getContentPane( )**. However, if you want to write code that can be compiled by older versions of Java, then you will need to add calls to **getContentPane( )** where appropriate.

Example

The following program shows one way to write a Swing application. In the process it demonstrates several key features of Swing. It uses two Swing components: **JFrame** and **JLabel**. **JFrame** is the top-level container that is commonly used for Swing applications. **JLabel** is the Swing component that creates a label, which is a component that displays information. The label is Swing's simplest component because it is passive. That is, a label does not respond to user input. It just displays output. The program uses a **JFrame** container to hold an instance of **JLabel**. The label displays a short text message.

```
// A simple Swing program.

import javax.swing.*;
import java.awt.*;

class SwingDemo {

  SwingDemo() {

    // Create a new JFrame container.
    JFrame jfrm = new JFrame("A Simple Swing Application");

    // Give the frame an initial size.
    jfrm.setSize(275, 100);

    // Terminate the program when the user closes the application.
    jfrm.setDefaultCloseOperation(JFrame.EXIT_ON_CLOSE);
```

```
      // Create a text-based label.
      JLabel jlab = new JLabel(" This is a text label.");

      // Add the label to the content pane.
      jfrm.add(jlab);

      // Display the frame.
      jfrm.setVisible(true);
   }

  public static void main(String args[]) {
     // Create the frame on the event dispatching thread.
     SwingUtilities.invokeLater(new Runnable() {
       public void run() {
         new SwingDemo();
       }
     });
   }
}
```

Swing programs are compiled and run in the same way as other Java applications. Thus, to compile this program, you can use this command line:

```
javac SwingDemo.java
```

To run the program, use this command line:

```
java SwingDemo
```

When the program is run, it will produce the window shown here:

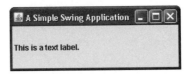

Pay special attention to these lines of code within **main( )**:

```
SwingUtilities.invokeLater(new Runnable() {
  public void run() {
    new SwingDemo();
  }
});
```

As explained, all interaction with Swing's visual components, including the initial construction of the GUI, must take place on the event-dispatching thread. Here, the **invokeLater( )** method is used to instantiate a **SwingDemo** instance on the event-dispatching thread.

Options and Alternatives

The example uses the default layout manager for the content pane of a **JFrame**, which is **BorderLayout**. It implements a layout style that defines five locations to which a component can be added. The first is the center. The other four are the sides (i.e., borders), which are called north, south, east, and west. By default, when you add a component to the content pane, you are adding the component to the center. To specify one of the other locations, use this form of **add( )**:

void add(Component *comp*, Object *loc*)

Here, *comp* is the component to add and *loc* specifies the location to which it is added. The *loc* value must be one of the following:

BorderLayout.CENTER	BorderLayout.EAST	BorderLayout.NORTH
BorderLayout.SOUTH	BorderLayout.WEST	

To see the effect of putting a component at each location, change the example program so that it creates five labels and adds one to each location, as shown here:

```
// Create five labels, one for each location in the BorderLayout.
JLabel jlabC = new JLabel("Center", SwingConstants.CENTER);
JLabel jlabW = new JLabel("West", SwingConstants.CENTER);
JLabel jlabE = new JLabel("East", SwingConstants.CENTER);
JLabel jlabN = new JLabel("North", SwingConstants.CENTER);
JLabel jlabS = new JLabel("South", SwingConstants.CENTER);

// Add the labels to the content pane, in the specified locations.
jfrm.add(jlabC);
jfrm.add(jlabE, BorderLayout.EAST);
jfrm.add(jlabW, BorderLayout.WEST);
jfrm.add(jlabN, BorderLayout.NORTH);
jfrm.add(jlabS, BorderLayout.SOUTH);
```

Notice that the labels specify a center alignment. By default, the contents of a label are left-aligned. Using center alignment makes it easier to see each **BorderLayout** location. (See *Work with JLabel* for details on alignment.) After making these changes, the window will now look like this:

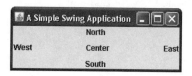

As you can see, each of the five locations is occupied by the appropriate label.

In general, **BorderLayout** is most useful when you are creating a **JFrame** that contains a centered component that has a header and/or footer component associated with it. (Often the component being centered is a group of components held within one of Swing's lightweight containers, such as **JPanel**.) You can specify a different layout manager by calling **setLayout( )**. This is illustrated by the following recipe.

A key aspect of most Swing programs is event handling. However, the preceding example program does not respond to any events because **JLabel** is a passive component. In other words, a **JLabel** does not generate any events based on user interaction. As a result, the preceding program does not include any event handlers. Most other Swing components *do* generate events. Several of these components, along with appropriate event handling, are demonstrated by the recipes in this chapter.

Set the Content Pane's Layout Manager

Key Ingredients	
Classes	**Methods**
java.awt.FlowLayout	
javax.swing.JFrame	void setLayout(LayoutManager *lm*)

By default, the content pane associated with a **JFrame** or a **JApplet** uses a border layout, which is encapsulated by the **BorderLayout** layout manager. This layout is demonstrated by the preceding recipe. Although a border layout is useful for many applications, there are times when one of the other layout managers will be more convenient. When this is the case, the layout manager can be changed by calling **setLayout( )**. This recipe shows the procedure. It also demonstrates one of the most common layout managers: **FlowLayout**.

Step-by-Step

To change the layout manager involves these steps:

1. If necessary, import **java.awt** to gain access to the desired layout manager.
2. Create an instance of the new layout manager.
3. Call **setLayout( )** on the **JFrame** or **JApplet** instance, passing in the new layout manager.

Discussion

Most general-purpose layout managers are packaged in **java.awt** or **javax.swing**. If you will be using a layout manager stored in **java.awt**, then you will need to import **java.awt** into your program. Understand that the layout managers in **java.awt** are perfectly acceptable to use with Swing. They simply predate the creation of Swing. For example, the default

BorderLayout class is packaged in **java.awt**. Swing also provides several layout managers of its own, such as **BoxLayout** and **SpringLayout**.

One of the most popular layout managers is **FlowLayout**. It is very simple to use, making it especially convenient when experimenting or when creating sample programs. For this reason it is used by several of the examples in this chapter. **FlowLayout** automatically lays out components one row at a time, top to bottom. When one row is full, layout advances to the next row. Although very easy to use, there are two drawbacks to **FlowLayout**. First, it gives you little control over the precise placement of the components. Second, resizing the frame may result in a change in the position of the components. Despite these limitations, **FlowLayout** is often appropriate for simple GUIs.

FlowLayout supplies three constructors. The one used by this recipe is shown here:

FlowLayout( )

It creates a flow layout that automatically centers components on the line and separates each component from the next with five pixels in all four directions.

To set the layout manager, call **setLayout( )**, shown here:

void setLayout(LayoutManager *lm*)

The new layout manager is passed in *lm*. Since the release of Java 5, calling **setLayout( )** on any top-level container, including **JFrame** and **JApplet**, causes the layout of the content pane to be set. Older versions of Java required that you explicitly obtain a reference to the content pane by calling **getContentPane( )** on the top-level container, but this is not required for new code. (See *Historical Note* in *Create a Simple Swing Application*.)

Example

The following example creates a Swing application that sets the layout manager of the content pane of the **JFrame** instance to flow layout. It then creates two buttons (which are instances of **JButton**) and a label, and adds them to the frame. In this example, the buttons have no effect and are for display purposes only. (See *Create a Simple Push Button* for a recipe that demonstrates buttons.)

```
// Change the Content Pane's layout manager.

import javax.swing.*;
import java.awt.*;

class ChangeLayout {

  ChangeLayout() {

    // Create a new JFrame container.
    JFrame jfrm = new JFrame("Use FlowLayout");

    // Give the frame an initial size.
    jfrm.setSize(275, 100);
```

```
    // Set the layout manager to FlowLayout.
    jfrm.setLayout(new FlowLayout());

    // Terminate the program when the user closes the application.
    jfrm.setDefaultCloseOperation(JFrame.EXIT_ON_CLOSE);

    // Create a label.
    JLabel jlab = new JLabel("A sample of flow layout.");

    // Create do-nothing buttons.
    JButton jbtnA = new JButton("Alpha");
    JButton jbtnB = new JButton("Beta");

    // Add the buttons and label to the content pane.
    jfrm.add(jbtnA);
    jfrm.add(jbtnB);
    jfrm.add(jlab);

    // Display the frame.
    jfrm.setVisible(true);
  }

  public static void main(String args[]) {
    // Create the frame on the event dispatching thread.
    SwingUtilities.invokeLater(new Runnable() {
      public void run() {
        new ChangeLayout();
      }
    });
  }
}
```

The output is shown here:

As stated, when using flow layout, the position of the components may change when the frame is resized. For example, making the frame wider causes the buttons and label to be positioned in-line, as shown here:

Options and Alternatives

By default, **FlowLayout** centers components within a line and separates each component from the next with five pixels. You can alter these defaults by using one of the following **FlowLayout** constructors:

FlowLayout(int *horizAlign*)

FlowLayout(int *horizAlign*, int *horizSep*, int *vertSep*)

The horizontal alignment of components within a line is specified by *horizAlign*. It must be one of these values:

FlowLayout.CENTER	FlowLayout.LEADING	FlowLayout.LEFT
FlowLayout.RIGHT	FlowLayout.TRAILING	

By default, the values **LEADING** and **TRAILING** are the same as **LEFT** and **RIGHT**. They will be reversed in containers whose orientation is set up for languages that read right to left, rather than left to right. The horizontal and vertical spacing between components is specified in pixels by *horizSep* and *vertSep*, respectively. To see the effect of changing the alignment and the spacing, substitute this call to **setLayout( )** into the example.

```
jfrm.setLayout(new FlowLayout(FlowLayout.RIGHT, 20, 5));
```

This right-justifies each line and uses a 20-pixel horizontal spacing.

In addition to **BorderLayout** and **FlowLayout**, Java supplies several others that are commonly used. Three that you will want to experiment with are **GridLayout**, **GridBagLayout**, and **BoxLayout**. Each is briefly described here.

GridLayout creates a grid of rectangular cells into which individual components are placed. The number of rows and columns in the grid is specified when the layout is created. The size of each cell in the grid is the same, and a component put into a cell is sized to fill the dimensions of the cell. **GridLayout** is packaged in **java.awt**.

GridBagLayout is, in essence, a collection of grids. With **GridBagLayout** you can specify the relative placement of components by specifying their positions within cells inside each grid. The key is that each component can be a different size, and each row in the grid can have a different number of columns. This scheme gives you considerable control over how components are arranged within a container. Although **GridBagLayout** requires a bit of work to set up, it is often worth the effort when creating a frame that contains several controls. **GridBagLayout** is also packaged in **java.awt**.

An alternative to **GridBagLayout** that is easier to use in some cases is **BoxLayout**. It lets you easily create a group of components that are laid out either vertically or horizontally as a unit. **BoxLayout** is not often used as the layout manager for the content pane. Rather, it is used as the layout manager for one or more panels (such as instances of **JPanel**). Components are then added to these panels, and then the panels are added to the content pane. (The easiest way to obtain a container that uses **BoxLayout** is to create a **Box**. See *Use JScrollPane to Handle Scrolling* for an example that uses **Box**.)

Although this example is a Swing application, the same basic procedure used to set the layout manager also applies to Swing applets. For example, to change the layout manager for the content pane associated with a **JApplet** container, simply call **setLayout( )** on the **JApplet** instance.

Work with JLabel

Key Ingredients	
Classes and Interfaces	**Methods**
javax.swing.border.BorderFactory	static Border createLineBorder(color *lineColor*)
javax.swing.JLabel	String getText( ) void setBorder(Border *border*) void setDisabledIcon(Icon *disIcon*) void setEnabled(boolean *state*) void setHorizontalAlignment(int *horzAlign*) void setVerticalAlignment(int *vertAlign*) void setText(String *msg*)
javax.swing.Icon	
javax.swing.ImageIcon	

JLabel creates a Swing label. It is Swing's simplest component because it does not respond to user interaction. Although **JLabel** is very easy to use, it does support many features and it allows a substantial amount of customization, making it possible to create very sophisticated labels. For example, a label's contents can be aligned horizontally and vertically, a label can use HTML, it can be disabled, and it can contain an icon. A label can also have a border. Frankly, the inherent simplicity of **JLabel** makes it easy to overlook its more subtle features. This recipe demonstrates how to create and manage various types of **JLabel**s.

Step-by-Step

To create and manage a Swing label involves these steps:

1. Create an instance of **JLabel**, specifying the text and/or icon that will be displayed within the label. You can also specify the horizontal alignment if desired.
2. To put a border around a label, call **setBorder( )**.
3. To align the contents of the label vertically, call **setVerticalAlignment( )**. To set the horizontal alignment after the label has been constructed, call **setHorizontalAlignment( )**.
4. To disable/enable a label, call **setEnabled( )**.

5. To change the text within a label, call **setText( )**. To obtain the text within a label, call **getText( )**.

6. To use HTML within a label, begin the text with **<html>**.

Discussion

JLabel defines several constructors. They are shown here:

JLabel( )
JLabel(Icon *icon*)
JLabel(String *str*)
JLabel(Icon *icon*, int *horizAlign*)
JLabel(String *str*, int *horizAlign*)
JLabel(String *str*, Icon *icon*, int *horzAlign*)

Here, *str* and *icon* are the text and icon used for the label. By default, the text and/or icon in a label is left-aligned. You can change the horizontal alignment by specifying the *horzAlign* parameter. It must be one of the following values:

SwingConstants.LEFT	SwingConstants.RIGHT
SwingConstants.CENTER	SwingConstants.LEADING
SwingConstants.TRAILING	

The **SwingConstants** interface defines several constants that relate to Swing. This interface is implemented by **JLabel** (and several other components). Thus, you can also refer to these constants through **JLabel**, such as **JLabel.RIGHT**.

Notice that icons are specified by objects of type **Icon**, which is an interface defined by Swing. The easiest way to obtain an icon is to use the **ImageIcon** class. **ImageIcon** implements **Icon** and encapsulates an image. Thus, an object of type **ImageIcon** can be passed as an argument to the **Icon** parameter of **JLabel**'s constructor. There are several ways to provide the image, including reading it from a file or downloading it from a URL. Here is the **ImageIcon** constructor used by this recipe:

ImageIcon(String *filename*)

It obtains the image in the file named *filename*.

You can put a border around a label. Borders are helpful when you want to clearly show the extents of the label. All Swing borders are instances of the **javax.swing.border.Border** interface. Although it is possible to define your own borders, you won't usually need to because Swing provides several predefined border styles, which are available through **javax.swing.BorderFactory**. This class defines several factory methods that create various types of borders, ranging from simple line borders to beveled, etched, or matte borders. You can also create a titled border, which includes a short caption embedded in the border, or an empty border, which is an invisible border. Empty borders are useful when a gap around a component is desired.

NOTE *It is possible to add a border to nearly any Swing component, but this is not usually a good idea. Most other Swing components, such as buttons, text fields, and lists, draw their own borders. Specifying another border will cause a conflict. The two exceptions to this rule are JLabel and JPanel.*

This recipe uses only one type of border: the line border. To create a line border, use the following factory method:

static Border createLineBorder(Color *lineColor*)

Here, *lineColor* specifies the color of the line used as the border. For example, to draw a black border, pass **Color.BLACK**. This method creates a line border with the default thickness.

Once you have created a border, you can assign it to a label by calling the **setBorder( )** method. It is shown here:

void setBorder(Border *border*)

Here, *border* specifies the border to use. One thing to understand is that the same border can be used for multiple components. That is, you don't need to create a new **Border** object for each label on which you will be setting the border.

Although specifying the horizontal alignment when a label is constructed is generally the easiest approach, Swing provides an alternative. You can call the **setHorizontalAlignment( )** method on the label after it has been constructed. It is shown here:

void setHorizontalAlignment(int *horzAlign*)

Here, *horzAlign* must be one of the horizontal alignment constants just described.

You can also set the vertical alignment of a label. To do so, call the **setVerticalAlignment( )** method on the label. It is shown here:

void setVerticalAlignment(int *vertAlign*)

The value passed to *vertAlign* must be one of these vertical alignment constants:

SwingConstants.TOP	SwingConstants.CENTER	SwingConstants.BOTTOM

Of course, text is centered top-to-bottom by default, so you will use **CENTER** only if you are returning the vertical alignment to its default.

There is one important thing to understand when setting a label's alignment: it won't necessarily have an effect. For example, when you use **FlowLayout**, the label will be sized to fit its contents. In this case, there is no difference between aligning to the top or bottom of the label. In general, label alignment affects only those labels that are sized larger than their contents. One way this can occur is when using a layout manager, such as **GridLayout**, that automatically adjusts the size of a label to fit an available space. It can also happen when you specify a preferred component size that is larger than that needed to hold its contents. To set the preferred size of a component, call **setPreferredSize( )**.

You can disable a label by calling **setEnabled( )**, shown here:

void setEnabled(boolean *state*)

When *state* is false, the label is disabled. To enable the label, pass true. When a label is disabled, it is shown in gray.

You can obtain or change the contents of a label at runtime. For example, to set the text, call **setText( )**. To obtain the text, call **getText( )**. They are shown here:

void setText(String *newMsg*)
String getText( )

The string passed in *newMsg* is displayed within the label, replacing the previous string.

You can use a string containing HTML as the text to be displayed by a label. To do so, begin the string with **<html>**. When this is done, the text is automatically formatted as specified by the markup. Using HTML offers one big advantage: it lets you display text that spans two or more lines.

Example

The following example illustrates several features of **JLabel**. Notice that the Change button lets you experiment with various alignment options. Each time the button is pressed, the alignment of the text within the label is changed.

```
// Demonstrate JLabel.

import javax.swing.*;
import java.awt.*;
import java.awt.event.*;
import javax.swing.border.*;

class LabelDemo {

  JLabel jlabSimple;
  JLabel jlabBorder;
  JLabel jlabIcon;
  JLabel jlabHTML;
  JLabel jlabDis;
  JLabel jlabAlign;

  JButton jbtnChange;

  int next;

  LabelDemo() {
    next = 0;

    // Create a new JFrame container.
    JFrame jfrm = new JFrame("Label Demo");
```

```
// Set the layout manager to FlowLayout.
jfrm.setLayout(new FlowLayout());

// Give the frame an initial size.
jfrm.setSize(200, 360);

// Terminate the program when the user closes the application.
jfrm.setDefaultCloseOperation(JFrame.EXIT_ON_CLOSE);

// Create a Border instance for a line border.
Border border = BorderFactory.createLineBorder(Color.BLACK);

// Create a default label that centers its text.
jlabSimple = new JLabel("A default label");

// Create a label with a border.
jlabBorder = new JLabel("This label has a border");
jlabBorder.setBorder(border);

// Create a label that includes an icon.
ImageIcon myIcon = new ImageIcon("myIcon.gif");
jlabIcon = new JLabel("Text with icon.", myIcon, JLabel.LEFT);

// Create a label that displays HTML and surround it
// with a line border.
jlabHTML = new JLabel("<html>Use HTML to create<br>" +
                      "a multiline message." +
                      "<br>One<br>Two<br>Three");
jlabHTML.setBorder(border);

// Disable a label.
jlabDis= new JLabel("This label is disabled.");
jlabDis.setEnabled(false);

// Create a label that lets you experiment with various
// alignment options. This label has a border so that
// the alignment of its contents is easy to see.
jlabAlign = new JLabel("Centered", JLabel.CENTER);
jlabAlign.setBorder(border);

// Set the preferred size for the alignment label.
jlabAlign.setPreferredSize(new Dimension(150, 100));

// Create the Change button. Pressing this button
// changes the alignment of the text within jlabAlign.
jbtnChange = new JButton("Change Alignment");

// Add an action listener for the Change button.
jbtnChange.addActionListener(new ActionListener() {
  public void actionPerformed(ActionEvent ae) {
    next++;
```

```
      if(next > 4) next = 0;
      switch(next) {
        case 0:
          jlabAlign.setText("Centered");
          jlabAlign.setHorizontalAlignment(JLabel.CENTER);
          jlabAlign.setVerticalAlignment(JLabel.CENTER);
          break;
        case 1:
          jlabAlign.setText("Top Left");
          jlabAlign.setHorizontalAlignment(JLabel.LEFT);
          jlabAlign.setVerticalAlignment(JLabel.TOP);
          break;
        case 2:
          jlabAlign.setText("Bottom Right");
          jlabAlign.setHorizontalAlignment(JLabel.RIGHT);
          jlabAlign.setVerticalAlignment(JLabel.BOTTOM);
          break;
        case 3:
          jlabAlign.setText("Top Right");
          jlabAlign.setHorizontalAlignment(JLabel.RIGHT);
          jlabAlign.setVerticalAlignment(JLabel.TOP);
          break;
        case 4:
          jlabAlign.setText("Bottom Left");
          jlabAlign.setHorizontalAlignment(JLabel.LEFT);
          jlabAlign.setVerticalAlignment(JLabel.BOTTOM);
          break;
      }
    }
  });

  // Add the components to the content pane.
  jfrm.add(jlabSimple);
  jfrm.add(jlabBorder);
  jfrm.add(jlabIcon);
  jfrm.add(jlabHTML);
  jfrm.add(jlabDis);
  jfrm.add(jlabAlign);
  jfrm.add(jbtnChange);

  // Display the frame.
  jfrm.setVisible(true);
}

public static void main(String args[]) {
  // Create the frame on the event dispatching thread.
  SwingUtilities.invokeLater(new Runnable() {
    public void run() {
      new LabelDemo();
    }
  });
}
}
```

Sample output is shown here:

Options and Alternatives

In addition to setting or obtaining the text within a label, you can obtain or set the icon by using these methods:

Icon getIcon( )
void setIcon(Icon *icon*)

Here, *icon* specifies the icon to display inside the label. Because the icon can be specified when the label is created, you will only need to use **setIcon( )** if you want to change the icon after the label has been created.

When a label is disabled, its contents are automatically shown in gray; this includes its icon. However, you can specify a separate image to use when the label is disabled by calling **setDisabledIcon( )**, shown next:

void setDisabledIcon(Icon *icon*)

Here, *icon* is the image shown when the label is disabled.

When a label contains both an icon and text, by default the icon is displayed on the left. This can be changed by calling one or both of these methods:

void setVerticalTextPosition(int *loc*)
void setHorizontalTextPosition(int *loc*)

For **setVerticalTextPosition( )**, *loc* must be one of the vertical alignment constants described earlier. For **setHorizontalTextPosition( )**, *loc* must be one of the horizontal alignment constants. For example, in the preceding program, you can put the text in **jlabIcon** above its icon, by including the following statements:

```
jlabIcon.setVerticalTextPosition(JLabel.TOP);
jlabIcon.setHorizontalTextPosition(JLabel.CENTER);
```

Sometimes a label describes the purpose or meaning of another component, such as a text field. For example, a text field that accepts a name might be preceded by a label that displays "Name." In this situation, it is also common for the label to display a keyboard mnemonic that acts as a shortcut key that will cause input focus to move to the other component. Thus, for the Name field, the mnemonic might be *N*. When a mnemonic has been specified, pressing that key in combination with the ALT key causes input focus to move to the text field. To add a mnemonic to a label involves two steps. First, you must specify the mnemonic character by calling **setDisplayedMnemonic( )**. Second, you must link the component that will receive focus with the label by calling **setLabelFor( )**. Both methods are defined by **JLabel**.

The **setDisplayedMnemonic( )** method has two versions. Here is one of them:

void setDisplayedMnemonic(char *ch*)

Here, *ch* specifies the character that will be shown as a keyboard shortcut. Typically, this means that the character is underlined. If more than one of the specified characters exist in the label text, then the first occurrence is underlined. The character passed via *ch* can be either upper- or lowercase.

After you have set the mnemonic, you must link the label with the component that will receive focus when the shortcut key is pressed. To do this, use the **setLabelFor( )** method:

void setLabelFor(Component *comp*)

Here, *comp* is a reference to the component that will get focus when the mnemonic key is pressed in conjunction with the ALT key.

Create a Simple Push Button

Key Ingredients	
Classes and Interfaces	**Methods**
java.awt.event.ActionEvent	String getActionCommand( )
java.awt.event.ActionListener	void actionPerformed(ActionEvent *ae*)
javax.swing.JButton	void addActionListener(ActionListener *al*) void setEnabled(boolean *state*) boolean isEnabled( )

Perhaps the most commonly used GUI control is the push button. A push button is an instance of **JButton**. **JButton** inherits the abstract class **AbstractButton**, which defines the functionality common to all buttons. The model used by **JButton** is **ButtonModel**.

Swing push buttons support a rich array of functionality. Here are a few examples. A **JButton** can contain text, an image, or both. The button can be enabled or disabled under program control. The icon can change dynamically based on the state of the button. For instance, the button can display one icon when the button is rolled over by the mouse and another when it is pressed or when it is disabled. Because of the importance of buttons, two recipes are used to describe them. This recipe shows how to create and manage a basic button. The following recipe shows how to add icons, use HTML, and define a default button.

Step-by-Step

To create and manage a push button involves these steps:

1. Create an instance of **JButton**.
2. Define an **ActionListener** for the button. This listener will handle button-press events in its **actionPerformed( )** method.
3. Add the **ActionListener** instance to the button by calling **addActionListener( )**.
4. One way to identify which button has generated an **ActionEvent** is to call **getActionCommand( )**. It returns the action command string associated with the button.
5. To disable or enable a button, call **setEnabled( )**.
6. To determine if a button is enabled or disabled, call **isEnabled( )**.

Discussion

To create a push button, create an instance of **JButton**. It defines several constructors. The one used here is:

JButton(String *msg*)

Here, *msg* specifies the message displayed inside the button.

When a push button is pressed, it generates an **ActionEvent**, which is packaged in **java.awt.event**. To listen for this event, you must first create an implementation of the **ActionListener** interface (also packaged in **java.awt.event**) and then register this listener with the button. After doing so, the registered listener is passed an **ActionEvent** each time the button is pressed.

The **ActionListener** interface defines only one method: **actionPerformed( )**. It is shown here:

void actionPerformed(ActionEvent *ae*)

This method is called when a button is pressed. In other words, it is the event handler for button presses.

To register an action listener for a button, use the **addActionListener( )** method provided by **JButton**. It is shown here:

void addActionListener(ActionListener *al*)

The object passed in *al* will receive event notifications. This object must be an instance of a class that implements the **ActionListener** interface as just described.

Using the **ActionEvent** object passed to **actionPerformed( )**, you can obtain several useful pieces of information relating to the button-press event. The one used by this recipe is the *action command* string associated with the button. All push buttons have an action command string associated with them. By default, this is the string displayed inside the button. The action command string is obtained by calling **getActionCommand( )** on the event object. It is declared like this:

String getActionCommand( )

When using two or more buttons within the same application, the action command string gives you an easy way to identify which button generated the event. In other words, you can use the action command string to determine which button was pressed.

You can disable or enable a button under program control by calling **setEnabled( )**. It is shown here:

void setEnabled(Boolean *state*)

If *state* is false, the button is disabled. This means that the button cannot be pressed and is shown in gray. If *state* is true, the button is enabled.

To determine the enabled/disabled state of a button, call **isEnabled( )**:

boolean isEnabled( )

It returns true if the button is enabled and false if it is disabled.

Example

The following example shows **JButton** in action. The program creates two buttons and a label. Each time a button is pressed, this fact is reported in the label. The buttons are called Alpha and Beta. Thus, "Alpha" and "Beta" are the action command strings for the buttons. These strings are used by the action listener to identify which button was pressed. Each time Alpha is pressed, the enabled/disabled state of Beta is switched.

```
// Demonstrate JButton.

import java.awt.*;
import java.awt.event.*;
import javax.swing.*;

class ButtonDemo implements ActionListener {

  JLabel jlab;

  JButton jbtnA;
  JButton jbtnB;

  ButtonDemo() {

    // Create a new JFrame container.
    JFrame jfrm = new JFrame("A Button Example");

    // Set the layout manager to FlowLayout.
    jfrm.setLayout(new FlowLayout());
```

```java
    // Give the frame an initial size.
    jfrm.setSize(220, 90);

    // Terminate the program when the user closes the application.
    jfrm.setDefaultCloseOperation(JFrame.EXIT_ON_CLOSE);

    // Create a label.
    jlab = new JLabel("Press a button.");

    // Make two buttons.
    jbtnA = new JButton("Alpha");
    jbtnB = new JButton("Beta");

    // Add action listeners.
    jbtnA.addActionListener(this);
    jbtnB.addActionListener(this);

    // Add the buttons and label to the content pane.
    jfrm.add(jbtnA);
    jfrm.add(jbtnB);
    jfrm.add(jlab);

    // Display the frame.
    jfrm.setVisible(true);
  }

  // Handle button events.
  public void actionPerformed(ActionEvent ae) {
    String ac = ae.getActionCommand();

    // See which button was pressed.
    if(ac.equals("Alpha")) {

      // Change the state of Beta each time that Alpha is pressed.
      if(jbtnB.isEnabled()) {
        jlab.setText("Alpha pressed. Beta is disabled.");
        jbtnB.setEnabled(false);
      } else {
        jlab.setText("Alpha pressed. Beta is enabled.");
        jbtnB.setEnabled(true);
      }
    } else if(ac.equals("Beta"))
      jlab.setText("Beta pressed.");
  }

  public static void main(String args[]) {
    // Create the frame on the event dispatching thread.
    SwingUtilities.invokeLater(new Runnable() {
      public void run() {
        new ButtonDemo();
      }
    });
  }
}
```

Here is sample output. The first window shows both buttons enabled. The second shows Beta disabled, which means that it is grayed-out.

Options and Alternatives

JButton supplies constructors that let you specify an icon or an icon and text within the button. You can specify additional icons that indicate when the button is rolled over, when it is disabled, and when it is pressed. You can also use HTML within the text shown within the button. These features are described by the following recipe.

You can set the text within a button after it has been created by calling **setText( )**. You can obtain the text within a button by calling **getText( )**. These methods are shown here:

```
void setText(String msg)
String getText( )
```

If the button has had its action command set explicitly, then setting the text will not affect the action command. Otherwise, changing the text changes the action command.

By default, the action command string associated with a button is the string displayed within the button. However, it is possible to set the action command to another string by calling **setActionCommand( )**, shown here:

```
void setActionCommand(String newCmd)
```

The string passed in *newCmd* becomes the action command for the button. The text in the button is unaffected. For example, this sets the action command string for **jbtnA** in the example to "My Button":

```
jbtnA.setActionCommand("My Button");
```

After making this change, the name inside the button is still Alpha, but "My Button" is the action command string. Setting the action command is especially useful when two different components use the same name. Changing the action command strings lets you tell them apart.

Another way to determine what component generated an action event (or any other type of event) is to call **getSource( )** on the event object. This method is defined by **EventObject**, which is the superclass of all event classes. It returns a reference to the object that generated the event. For example, here is another way to write the **actionPerfomed( )** method in the example program:

```
// Use getSource() to determine the source of the event.
public void actionPerformed(ActionEvent ae) {
  // See which button was pressed by calling getSource().
  if(ae.getSource() == jbtnA) {
```

```
    // Change the state of Beta each time that Alpha is pressed.
    if(jbtnB.isEnabled()) {
      jlab.setText("Alpha pressed. Beta is disabled.");
      jbtnB.setEnabled(false);
    } else {
      jlab.setText("Alpha pressed. Beta is enabled.");
      jbtnB.setEnabled(true);
    }
  } else if(ae.getSource() == jbtnB)
    jlab.setText("Beta pressed.");
}
```

Many programmers like this approach better than using the action command string because it avoids the overhead of a string comparison. Of course, it does imply that the handler has access to the original component reference. This may not always be convenient, or possible. In these cases, the following alternative may be a good choice.

In the example, the **ButtonDemo** class implemented the **ActionListener** interface, supplying the **actionPerformed( )** method. While there is nothing wrong with this, it is not the only way to handle events. Two other approaches are commonly used. First, you can implement separate listener classes. Thus, different classes could handle different events and these classes would be separate from the main class of the application. Second, you can implement listeners through the use of *anonymous inner classes.*

Anonymous inner classes are inner classes that don't have a name. Instead, an instance of the class is simply generated "on the fly" as needed. Anonymous inner classes make implementing some types of event handlers much easier. For instance, the action event handlers for **jbtnA** in the preceding example could be implemented using an anonymous inner class, as shown here:

```
jbtnA.addActionListener(new ActionListener() {
  public void actionPerformed(ActionEvent ae) {
    if(jbtnB.isEnabled()) {
      jlab.setText("Alpha pressed. Beta is disabled.");
      jbtnB.setEnabled(false);
    } else {
      jlab.setText("Alpha pressed. Beta is enabled.");
      jbtnB.setEnabled(true);
    }
  }
});
```

In this approach, an anonymous inner class is created that implements the **ActionListener** interface. Pay special attention to the syntax. The body of the inner class begins after the **{** that follows **new ActionListener( )**. Also notice that the call to **addActionListener( )** ends with a **)** and a **;** just like normal. The same basic syntax and approach is used to create an anonymous inner class for any event handler. Of course, for different events, you specify different event listeners and implement different methods.

One advantage to using an anonymous inner class is that the component that invokes the class's methods is already known. There is no need to call **getActionCommand( )**, for example, to determine what button generated the event because each implementation of **actionPerformed( )** is associated with only one button, the one that generated the event.

Here is how the preceding example program looks when reworked to use anonymous inner classes to handle button action events.

```
// Use anonymous inner classes to handle JButton
// action events. Notice that ButtonDemo no longer
// implements ActionListener.

import java.awt.*;
import java.awt.event.*;
import javax.swing.*;

class ButtonDemo {

  JLabel jlab;

  JButton jbtnA;
  JButton jbtnB;

  ButtonDemo() {

    // Create a new JFrame container.
    JFrame jfrm = new JFrame("A Button Example");

    // Set the layout manager to FlowLayout.
    jfrm.setLayout(new FlowLayout());

    // Give the frame an initial size.
    jfrm.setSize(220, 90);

    // Terminate the program when the user closes the application.
    jfrm.setDefaultCloseOperation(JFrame.EXIT_ON_CLOSE);

    // Create a label.
    jlab = new JLabel("Press a button.");

    // Make two buttons.
    jbtnA = new JButton("Alpha");
    jbtnB = new JButton("Beta");

    // Use anonymous inner classes to handle button events.
    jbtnA.addActionListener(new ActionListener() {
      public void actionPerformed(ActionEvent ae) {
        if(jbtnB.isEnabled()) {
          jlab.setText("Alpha pressed. Beta is disabled.");
          jbtnB.setEnabled(false);
        } else {
          jlab.setText("Alpha pressed. Beta is enabled.");
          jbtnB.setEnabled(true);
        }
      }
    });
```

```
    jbtnB.addActionListener(new ActionListener() {
      public void actionPerformed(ActionEvent ae) {
        jlab.setText("Beta pressed.");
      }
    });

    // Add the buttons and label to the content pane.
    jfrm.add(jbtnA);
    jfrm.add(jbtnB);
    jfrm.add(jlab);

    // Display the frame.
    jfrm.setVisible(true);
  }

  public static void main(String args[]) {
    // Create the frame on the event dispatching thread.
    SwingUtilities.invokeLater(new Runnable() {
      public void run() {
        new ButtonDemo();
      }
    });
  }
}
```

This program is functionally equivalent to the first version. The difference is that now, each button is linked with its own action event handler. There is no need for **ButtonDemo** to implement **ActionListener** or to use **getActionCommand( )** to determine which button was pressed.

One last point: You can create a two-state button by using **JToggleButton**. See *Create a Toggle Button*.

Use Icons, HTML, and Mnemonics with JButton

Key Ingredients	
Classes	**Methods**
javax.swing.JRootPane	void setDefaultButton(JButton *button*)
javax.swing.JButton	void setDisabledIcon(Icon *disabledIcon*)
	void setIcon(Icon *defIcon*)
	void setMnemonic(int *mnemKey*)
	void setPressedIcon(Icon *pressedIcon*)
	void setRolloverIcon(Icon *rolloverIcon*)

Beyond the basic functionality described by the preceding recipe, **JButton** supports many options and customizations. This recipe examines four:

- Add icons to a button
- Use HTML in a button
- Define a default button
- Add a mnemonic to a button

These features help give your application a distinctive appearance and can improve usability.

Step-by-Step

To add icons to a button, specify a default button, or use HTML in a button involves one or more of these steps:

1. To specify the default icon (which is shown when the button is enabled), pass the icon to the **JButton** constructor. You can also set the default icon by calling **setIcon( )**.
2. To specify an icon that is displayed when the button is rolled over by the mouse, call **setRolloverIcon( )**.
3. To specify an icon that is displayed when the button is disabled, call **setDisabledIcon( )**.
4. To specify an icon that is displayed when the button is pressed, call **setPressedIcon( )**.
5. To specify a mnemonic for a button, call **setMnemonic( )**.
6. To define a default button (a button that will be pressed when the user presses ENTER), call **setDefaultButton( )**.
7. To display HTML inside a button, begin the string with **<html>**.

Discussion

To create a push button that contains an icon, you will use this **JButton** constructor:

   JButton(Icon *icon*)

Here, *icon* specifies the icon used for the button. To create a push button that contains both an icon and text, use this constructor:

   JButton(String *str*, Icon *icon*)

When both text and an icon are present, the icon is on the leading edge and the text is on the trailing edge. However, you can change the relative positions of image and text. The icon specified in these constructors is the *default icon*. This is the icon that will be used for all purposes if no other icons are specified.

The default icon can also be specified or changed after it has been created by calling **setIcon( )**. It is shown here:

void setIcon(Icon *defIcon*)

The default icon is specified by *defIcon*.

JButton also allows you to specify icons that are displayed when the button is disabled, when it is pressed, and when it is rolled over by the mouse. To set these icons, you will use the following methods:

void setDisabledIcon(Icon *disabledIcon*)
void setPressedIcon(Icon *pressedIcon*)
void setRolloverIcon(Icon *rolloverIcon*)

Once the specified icon has been set, it will be displayed whenever one of the events occurs. Keep in mind, however, that the rollover icon may not be supported by all look and feels. You can determine if the rollover icon is enabled by calling **isRolloverEnabled( )**. Setting the rollover icon automatically enables the rollover icon. You can explicitly set the rollover-enabled property by calling **setRolloverEnabled(true)**.

You can define a button that will automatically be "pressed" when the user presses ENTER on the keyboard. This is called a *default button.* To create a default button, call **setDefaultButton( )** on the **JRootPane** object that holds the button. This method is shown here:

void setDefaultButton(JButton *button*)

Here, *button* is the push button that will be selected as the default button. Remember, this method is defined by **JRootPane** and, therefore, must be called on the root pane. You can obtain a reference to the root pane by calling **getRootPane( )** on the top-level container.

You can add a mnemonic to the text displayed within a button by calling **setMnemonic( )**. When this key is pressed in conjunction with the ALT key, the button will be pressed. This method is shown here:

void setMnemonic(int *mnemKey*)

Here, *mnemKey* specifies the mnemonic. It should be one of the constants defined in **java.awt.event.KeyEvent**, such as **VK_A**, **VK_X**, or **VK_S**. The **KeyEvent** class defines **VK_** constants for all the keys on the keyboard. Therefore, assuming a **JButton** called **jbtn**, you can set the keyboard mnemonic to T with this statement:

```
jtbn.setMnemonic(KeyEvent.VK_T);
```

After this statement executes, the button can be pressed by typing ALT-T.

NOTE *There is another version of* ***setMnemonic( )*** *that takes a* ***char*** *argument, but it is considered obsolete.*

You can use a string containing HTML as the text to be displayed inside a button. To do so, begin the string with **<html>**. When this is done, the text is automatically formatted as specified by the markup. This lets you create buttons that have titles that span two or more lines. But be careful—this can lead to overly large buttons, which sometimes have a disagreeable effect. One other point: when using HTML, the mnemonic associated with a button will not be displayed.

Example

The following example expands the example from the previous recipe by adding icons and mnemonics, and by setting **jbtnA** as the default button. When you try the program, you will notice that the rollover icon is displayed when the mouse passes over a button. The pressed icon will be displayed when the button is pressed. Each time you press **jbtnA**, **jbtnB** toggles between enabled and disabled. When the button is disabled, the disabled icon is displayed. When either button is pressed, the pressed icon is displayed. Notice that the mnemonics for **jbtnA** and **jbtnB** are A and B, respectively. Also notice that **jbtnA** is set as the default button. This means that it is pressed when you press ENTER.

```
// Demonstrate button icons, a default button, HTML in a button,
// and button mnemonics.

import java.awt.*;
import java.awt.event.*;
import javax.swing.*;

class CustomizeButtons {

  JLabel jlab;

  JButton jbtnA;
  JButton jbtnB;

  CustomizeButtons() {

    // Create a new JFrame container.
    JFrame jfrm = new JFrame("Customize Buttons");

    // Set the layout manager to FlowLayout.
    jfrm.setLayout(new FlowLayout());

    // Give the frame an initial size.
    jfrm.setSize(220, 90);

    // Terminate the program when the user closes the application.
    jfrm.setDefaultCloseOperation(JFrame.EXIT_ON_CLOSE);

    // Create a label.
    jlab = new JLabel("Press a button.");

    // Load the icons.
    ImageIcon iconA = new ImageIcon("IconA.gif");
    ImageIcon iconADis = new ImageIcon("IconADis.gif");
    ImageIcon iconARO = new ImageIcon("IconARO.gif");
    ImageIcon iconAP = new ImageIcon("IconAPressed.gif");
```

```
ImageIcon iconB = new ImageIcon("IconB.gif");
ImageIcon iconBDis = new ImageIcon("IconBDis.gif");
ImageIcon iconBRO = new ImageIcon("IconBRO.gif");
ImageIcon iconBP = new ImageIcon("IconBPressed.gif");

// Specify the default icon when constructing the buttons.
jbtnA = new JButton("Alpha", iconA);
jbtnB = new JButton("Beta", iconB);

// Set rollover icons.
jbtnA.setRolloverIcon(iconARO);
jbtnB.setRolloverIcon(iconBRO);

// Set pressed icons.
jbtnA.setPressedIcon(iconAP);
jbtnB.setPressedIcon(iconBP);

// Set disabled icons.
jbtnA.setDisabledIcon(iconADis);
jbtnB.setDisabledIcon(iconBDis);

// Set jbtnA as the default button.
jfrm.getRootPane().setDefaultButton(jbtnA);

// Set mnemonics for the buttons.
jbtnA.setMnemonic(KeyEvent.VK_A);
jbtnB.setMnemonic(KeyEvent.VK_B);

// Handle button events.
jbtnA.addActionListener(new ActionListener() {
  public void actionPerformed(ActionEvent ae) {
    if(jbtnB.isEnabled()) {
      jlab.setText("Alpha pressed. Beta is disabled.");
      jbtnB.setEnabled(false);
    } else {
      jlab.setText("Alpha pressed. Beta is enabled.");
      jbtnB.setEnabled(true);
    }
  }
});

jbtnB.addActionListener(new ActionListener() {
  public void actionPerformed(ActionEvent ae) {
    jlab.setText("Beta pressed.");
  }
});

// Add the buttons and label to the content pane.
jfrm.add(jbtnA);
jfrm.add(jbtnB);
jfrm.add(jlab);
```

```
      // Display the frame.
      jfrm.setVisible(true);
   }

   public static void main(String args[]) {
      // Create the frame on the event dispatching thread.
      SwingUtilities.invokeLater(new Runnable() {
         public void run() {
            new CustomizeButtons();
         }
      });
   }
}
```

Sample output is shown here, but to truly appreciate the effect of the icons, mnemonics, and the default button, you will need to run the program yourself.

Options and Alternatives

To see the effect of using HTML inside a button, change the declarations for **jbtnA** and **jbtnB**, as shown here:

```
jbtnA = new JButton("<html>Alpha<br>Press Me", iconA);
jbtnB = new JButton("<html>Beta<br>Press Me, Too!", iconB);
```

The buttons will now look as shown here:

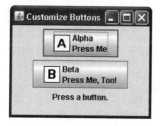

Notice that the mnemonics are no longer displayed. They will, however, still work.

You can determine if a button is the default button by calling **isDefaultButton( )**, shown here:

boolean isDefaultButton( )

You can indicate that a button should not be used as the default button by calling **setDefaultCapable( )**, shown here:

void setDefaultCapable(boolean *on*)

If *on* is true, the button can be used as a default button. If *on* is false, it should not be used as a default button. You determine if a button is default-capable by calling **isDefaultCapable( )**, shown next:

boolean isDefaultCapable( )

It returns true if the button should be used as a default button and false otherwise. As a general rule, buttons are default-capable by default, but this property can be set to false if the look and feel does not support default buttons. You should be careful when specifying a default button because it is easy for the user to press it unintentionally. The rule that I follow is simple: a default button should do no harm. If the default button will change a file, for example, then you need to have a safety check that prevents the user from accidentally overwriting the preexisting file.

The addition of the default, rollover, disabled, and pressed icons adds visual appeal to your interface. However, adding these icons will also increase download time. Therefore, you must balance their benefits against their cost.

Create a Toggle Button

Key Ingredients

Classes and Interfaces	Methods
javax.swing.event.ItemEvent	Object getItem( ) int getStateChange( )
javax.swing.event.ItemListener	void itemStateChanged(ItemEvent *ie*)
javax.swing.JToggleButton	void addItemListener(ItemListener *il*) boolean isSelected( ) void setSelected(boolean *on*)

Sometimes you will want to use a button to turn some function on or off. For example, imagine a desktop application that controls a conveyor belt. The GUI for this application could use a button called Run to turn the conveyor on and off. The first time the button is pressed, the conveyor turns on. When pressed again, the conveyor turns off. Although this type of functionality can be implemented using **JButton**, Swing offers a better option: **JToggleButton**. This recipe shows how to use it.

JToggleButton looks just like a push button, but it acts differently because it has two states: pushed and released. When you press a toggle button, it stays pressed rather than popping back up as a regular push button does. When you press the toggle button a second time, it releases (pops up). Therefore, each time a toggle button is pushed, it toggles between its two states.

Although useful in its own right, **JToggleButton** is important for another reason: it a superclass for two other Swing components that also represent two-state controls. These are **JCheckBox** and **JRadioButton**, which are described in *Create Check Boxes* and *Create Radio Buttons*. Thus, **JToggleButton** defines the basic functionality of all two-state components.

Step-by-Step

To use a toggle button involves these steps:

1. Create an instance of **JToggleButton**.

2. Register an **ItemListener** for the button and handle item events generated by the button.

3. To determine if the button is on or off, call **isSelected( )** on the **JButton** instance. If the button is pushed, this method will return true. Alternatively, call **getStateChange( )** on the **ItemEvent** instance. It returns the button's current state.

4. You can select (i.e., push) a toggle button under program control by calling **setSelected( )**.

Discussion

Toggle buttons are objects of the **JToggleButton** class. **JToggleButton** extends **AbstractButton**. (Although related to a push button, **JToggleButton** does not extend **JButton**.) **JToggleButton** defines several constructors, which allow you to specify the text and/or image that is displayed within the button. You can also set its initial state. The constructor used by this recipe is shown here:

JToggleButton(String *str*, boolean *state*)

This creates a toggle button that contains the text passed in *str*. If *state* is true, the button is initially pressed (selected). Otherwise, it is released (deselected).

JToggleButton generates an action event each time it is pressed. It also generates an item event, which is an object of type **ItemEvent**. An item event is used by those components that support the concept of selection. When a **JToggleButton** is pressed in, it is selected. When it is popped out, it is deselected. Although you can manage a toggle button by handling its action events, a toggle button is typically managed by handling its item events.

Item events are handled by implementing the **ItemListener** interface. This interface specifies only one method: **itemStateChanged( )**, which is shown here:

void itemStateChanged(ItemEvent *ie*)

The item event is received in *ie*.

To obtain a reference to the item that changed, call **getItem( )** on the **ItemEvent** object. This method is shown here:

Object getItem( )

The reference returned must be cast to the component class being handled, which in this case is **JToggleButton**. The **getItem( )** method is particularly helpful in cases in which two or more components share the same **ItemEvent** handler, because it gives you a way to identify which component generated the event.

When an item event occurs, the component will be in one of two states: selected and deselected. The **ItemEvent** class defines the following **static int** constants that represent these two states.

ItemEvent.SELECTED	ItemEvent.DESELECTED

To obtain the new state, call the **getStateChange( )** method defined by **ItemEvent**. It is shown here:

    int getStateChange( )

It returns either **ItemEvent.SELECTED** or **ItemEvent.DESELECTED**.

You can also determine the selected/deselected state of a toggle button by calling **isSelected( )**. This is often the easier approach. It is shown here:

    boolean isSelected( )

It returns true if the toggle button is pressed and false if it is released.

You can select or deselect (i.e., push or pop out) a toggle button by calling **setSelected( )**, shown here:

    void setSelected(boolean *on*)

If *on* is true, the button is pushed. If *on* is false, the button is popped out.

Example

The following example demonstrates a toggle button by showing how a toggle button could be used to control a conveyor. Notice how the item listener works. It simply calls **isSelected( )** to determine the button's state.

```
// Demonstrate a JToggleButton.

import java.awt.*;
import java.awt.event.*;
import javax.swing.*;

class TBDemo {

  JLabel jlab;
  JLabel jlab2;
  JToggleButton jtbtn;

  TBDemo() {
    // Create a new JFrame container.
    JFrame jfrm = new JFrame("Demonstrate JToggleButton");
```

```
    // Set the layout manager to FlowLayout.
    jfrm.setLayout(new FlowLayout());

    // Give the frame an initial size.
    jfrm.setSize(290, 80);

    // Terminate the program when the user closes the application.
    jfrm.setDefaultCloseOperation(JFrame.EXIT_ON_CLOSE);

    // Create a label.
    jlab = new JLabel("Conveyor Control: ");
    jlab2 = new JLabel("Conveyor Stopped");

    // Make a toggle button.
    jtbtn =  new JToggleButton("Run / Stop", false);

    // Add item listener for jtbtn.
    jtbtn.addItemListener(new ItemListener() {
      public void itemStateChanged(ItemEvent ie) {
        if(jtbtn.isSelected())
          jlab2.setText("Conveyor Running");
        else
          jlab2.setText("Conveyor Stopped");
      }

    });

    // Add toggle button and label to the content pane.
    jfrm.add(jlab);
    jfrm.add(jtbtn);
    jfrm.add(jlab2);

    // Display the frame.
    jfrm.setVisible(true);
  }

  public static void main(String args[]) {
    // Create the frame on the event dispatching thread.
    SwingUtilities.invokeLater(new Runnable() {
      public void run() {
        new TBDemo();
      }
    });
  }
}
```

Sample output is shown here:

Options and Alternatives

Like a **JButton**, a **JToggleButton** can display an icon, or a combination of icon and text. To add the default icon, you can use this form of the **JToggleButton** constructor:

JToggleButton(String *str*, Icon *icon*)

It creates a toggle button that contains the text passed in *str* and the image passed in *icon.* Also like **JButton**, it lets you specify icons that indicate when the button is pressed, released, or rolled over by the mouse. To add the other icons, use these methods: **setDisabledIcon( )**, **setPressedIcon( )**, and **setRolloverIcon( )**. Because **JToggleButton** has two states (pushed and released), it also lets you add icons that depict these two states by calling **setRolloverSelectedIcon( )** and **setSelectedIcon( )**. Keep in mind that you must supply a default icon in order for the other icons to be used. You can specify the position of the text relative to an icon by calling **setVerticalTextPosition( )** or **setHorizontalTextPosition( )**.

When using a toggle button, it is sometimes useful to display a different message when the button is pressed than when it is popped out. To do this, simply set the text each time the state of the button changes. (The text inside the button can be set by calling **setText( )**.)

You can add a mnemonic to the text displayed within a **JToggleButton** by calling **setMnemonic( )**. You can disable/enable a **JToggleButton** by calling **setEnabled( )**. These work the same for a toggle button as they do for a regular button.

Create Check Boxes

Key Ingredients	
Classes and Interfaces	**Methods**
javax.swing.JCheckBox	void addItemListener(ItemListener *il*)
	boolean isSelected( )
	void setSelected(boolean *on*)
javax.swing.event.ItemEvent	Object getItem( )
	int getStateChange( )
javax.swing.event.ItemListener	void itemStateChanged(ItemEvent *ie*)

This recipe demonstrates the check box, which is an object of type **JCheckBox**. A check box is commonly used to select an option. For example, an IDE could use check boxes to select various compiler options, such as warning levels, code optimization, and debug mode. If a box is checked, the option is selected. If the box is cleared, the option is ignored. Whatever the use, check boxes are a primary ingredient in many GUIs.

Step-by-Step

To use a check box involves these steps:

1. Create an instance of **JCheckBox**.

2. Register an **ItemListener** for the check box and handle item events generated by the check box.

3. To determine if the check box is selected, call **isSelected( )**. If the box is checked, true is returned. If the box is cleared, false is returned. Alternatively, call **getStateChange( )** on the **ItemEvent** instance. It returns the check box's current state.

4. You can select a check box under program control by calling **setSelected( )**.

Discussion

JCheckBox defines several constructors. The one used here is:

JCheckBox(String *str*)

This creates a check box that is associated with the text specified by *str*.

In Swing, a check box is a special type of two-state button. As a result, **JCheckBox** inherits **AbstractButton** and **JToggleButton**. Therefore, the same techniques that manage a toggle button also apply to a check box. See *Create a Toggle Button* for details. A brief review is given here.

When a check box is selected or deselected, an item event is generated. This is handled by **itemStateChanged( )**. Inside **itemStateChanged( )**, the **getItem( )** method can be used to obtain a reference to the **JCheckBox** object that generated the event. Next, you can call **getStateChange( )** to determine if the box was selected or cleared. If the box was selected, **ItemEvent.SELECTED** is returned. Otherwise, **ItemEvent.DESELECTED** is returned. Alternatively, you can call **isSelected( )** on the check box to determine if it is selected. You can set the state of a check box by calling **setSelected( )**.

Check boxes generate an item event whenever the state of a check box changes. Check boxes also generate action events when a selection changes, but it is often easier to use an **ItemListener** because it gives you direct access to the **getStateChange( )** method. It also gives you access to the **getItem( )** method.

Example

The following program demonstrates check boxes. It defines four check boxes that support foreign-language translation. The first check box is called Translate. It is enabled by default, but unchecked. The remaining three are called French, German, and Chinese. They are disabled by default. When the Translate check box is checked, it causes the other three check boxes to be enabled, which allows the user to select one or more languages. The selected languages are displayed in **jlabWhat**. Each time a check box is changed, the current action is displayed in **jlabChange**.

```java
// Demonstrate check boxes.

import java.awt.*;
import java.awt.event.*;
import javax.swing.*;

class CBDemo implements ItemListener {

  JLabel jlabTranslateTo;
  JLabel jlabWhat;
  JLabel jlabChange;
  JCheckBox jcbTranslate;
  JCheckBox jcbFrench;
  JCheckBox jcbGerman;
  JCheckBox jcbChinese;

  CBDemo() {
    // Create a new JFrame container.
    JFrame jfrm = new JFrame("Check Box Demo");

    // Specify a 1 column, 7 row grid layout.
    jfrm.setLayout(new GridLayout(7, 1));

    // Give the frame an initial size.
    jfrm.setSize(260, 160);

    // Terminate the program when the user closes the application.
    jfrm.setDefaultCloseOperation(JFrame.EXIT_ON_CLOSE);

    // Create labels.
    jlabTranslateTo = new JLabel("Translate To:");
    jlabChange = new JLabel("");
    jlabWhat = new JLabel("Languages selected: None");

    // Make check boxes.
    jcbTranslate = new JCheckBox("Translate");
    jcbFrench = new JCheckBox("French");
    jcbGerman = new JCheckBox("German");
    jcbChinese = new JCheckBox("Chinese");

    // Initially disable the language check boxes
    // and the Translate To and selected languages labels.
    jlabTranslateTo.setEnabled(false);
    jlabWhat.setEnabled(false);
    jcbFrench.setEnabled(false);
    jcbGerman.setEnabled(false);
    jcbChinese.setEnabled(false);

    // Add item listener for jcbTranslate.
    jcbTranslate.addItemListener(new ItemListener() {

      // Change the enabled/disabled state of
      // the language check boxes and related labels.
```

```
      // Also, report the state ofjcbTranslate.
      public void itemStateChanged(ItemEvent ie) {
        if(jcbTranslate.isSelected()) {
          jlabTranslateTo.setEnabled(true);
          jcbFrench.setEnabled(true);
          jcbGerman.setEnabled(true);
          jcbChinese.setEnabled(true);
          jlabWhat.setEnabled(true);

          jlabChange.setText("Translation enabled.");
        }
        else {
          jlabTranslateTo.setEnabled(false);
          jcbFrench.setEnabled(false);
          jcbGerman.setEnabled(false);
          jcbChinese.setEnabled(false);
          jlabWhat.setEnabled(false);

          jlabChange.setText("Translation disabled.");
        }
      }
    });

    // Changes to the language check boxes are handled
    // in common by the itemStateChanged() method
    // implemented by CBDemo.
    jcbFrench.addItemListener(this);
    jcbGerman.addItemListener(this);
    jcbChinese.addItemListener(this);

    // Add check boxes and labels to the content pane.
    jfrm.add(jcbTranslate);
    jfrm.add(jlabTranslateTo);

    jfrm.add(jcbFrench);
    jfrm.add(jcbGerman);
    jfrm.add(jcbChinese);
    jfrm.add(jlabChange);
    jfrm.add(jlabWhat);

    // Display the frame.
    jfrm.setVisible(true);
  }

  // This handles all of the language check boxes.
  public void itemStateChanged(ItemEvent ie) {
    String opts = "";

    // Obtain a reference to the check box that
    // caused the event.
    JCheckBox cb = (JCheckBox) ie.getItem();

    // Tell the user what they did.
```

```
        if(ie.getStateChange() == ItemEvent.SELECTED)
          jlabChange.setText("Selection change: " +
                              cb.getText() + " selected.");
        else
          jlabChange.setText("Selection change: " +
                              cb.getText() + " cleared.");

        // Build a string that contains all selected languages.
        if(jcbFrench.isSelected()) opts += "French ";
        if(jcbGerman.isSelected()) opts += "German ";
        if(jcbChinese.isSelected()) opts += "Chinese ";

        // Show "None" if no language is selected.
        if(opts.equals("")) opts = "None";

        // Display the currently selected options.
        jlabWhat.setText("Translate to: " + opts);
      }


  public static void main(String args[]) {
    // Create the frame on the event dispatching thread.
    SwingUtilities.invokeLater(new Runnable() {
      public void run() {
        new CBDemo();
      }
    });
  }
}
```

The output is shown here:

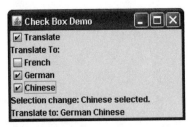

As mentioned, you can select a check box under program control by calling **setSelected( )**. To try this, add this line of code after adding the item listener for **jcbTranslate**:

```
jcbTranslate.setSelected(true);
```

This causes the Translate check box to be initially checked. It also causes an **ItemEvent** to fire. This results in the language options being enabled when the window is first displayed. (Remember, an **ItemEvent** is fired each time the check box changes, whether under program control or by the user.)

Options and Alternatives

Like all Swing buttons, check boxes offer a rich array of options and features that let you easily create a custom look. For example, you can substitute an icon that will replace the small box that holds the check mark. You can also specify both the icon and a string. Here are the **JCheckBox** constructors that support these options:

JCheckBox(Icon *icon*)
JCheckBox(String *str*, Icon *icon*)

Here, the default icon used by the check box is specified by *icon*. Typically, this icon serves as the unchecked icon. That is, it is the icon shown when the box is unchecked. Normally, when specifying this icon, you will also need to specify the checked icon.

To specify the checked icon, call **setSelectedIcon( )**, shown here:

void setSelectedIcon(Icon *icon*)

The icon passed via *icon* specifies the image to display when the check box is checked. Because the checked and unchecked icons work together as a pair, you almost always need to specify both when you are using an icon with a check box.

You can specify an initial state for the check box with these constructors:

JCheckBox(String *str*, boolean *state*)
JCheckBox(Icon *icon*, boolean *state*)
JCheckBox(String *str*, Icon *icon*, boolean *state*)

If *state* is true, the check box is initially checked. Otherwise, it is initially cleared.

You can set the alignment of the check box and the alignment of the text relative to the icon. The methods that handle this are defined by **AbstractButton** and are **setVerticalAlignment( )**, **setHorizontalAlignment( )**, **setVerticalTextPosition( )**, and **setHorizontalTextPosition( )**. You can set a mnemonic that is shown in the check box label by calling **setMnemonic( )**, which is also defined by **AbstractButton**.

Create Radio Buttons

Key Ingredients	
Classes and Interfaces	**Methods**
java.awt.event.ActionEvent	String getActionCommand( )
java.awt.event.ActionListener	void actionPerformed(ActionEvent *ae*)
javax.swing.ButtonGroup	void add(AbstractButton *button*)
javax.swing.JRadioButton	void addActionListener(ActionListener *al*)
	boolean isSelected( )
	void setSelected(boolean *on*)

This recipe shows how to create and manage radio buttons. Radio buttons are typically used to display a group of mutually exclusive buttons, in which only one button can be selected at any one time. Thus, they provide a means for the user to select just one of two or more options. For example, when buying a computer through an online store, radio buttons might be displayed to allow you to select between a laptop, handheld, or tower. Radio buttons are supported by the **JRadioButton** class, which extends **AbstractButton** and **JToggleButton**. Radio buttons are usually organized into groups, which are instances of **ButtonGroup**. As a result, this recipe explains how to use both **JRadioButton** and **ButtonGroup**.

Step-by-Step

To create and manage radio buttons involves these steps:

1. Create an instance of **ButtonGroup**.
2. Create instances of **JRadioButton**.
3. Add each **JRadioButton** instance to the **ButtonGroup** instance.
4. Register an **ActionListener** for each radio button and handle the action events generated by buttons.
5. To determine if a radio button is selected, call **isSelected( )**. If the button is selected, true is returned. Otherwise, false is returned. Remember, only one button in any given group can be selected at any one time.
6. You can select a radio button under program control by calling **setSelected( )**.

Discussion

JRadioButton provides several constructors. The two used by this recipe are shown here:

JRadioButton(String *str*)
JRadioButton(String str, boolean *state*)

Here, *str* is the label for the button. The first constructor creates a button that is cleared by default. For the second constructor, if *state* is true, the button is selected. Otherwise, it is cleared.

In order for the buttons to be mutually exclusive, they must be configured into a group. Once this is done, only one of the buttons in the group can be selected at any time. For example, if a user selects a radio button that is in a group, any previously selected button in that group is automatically deselected. Of course, each button group is separate from the next. Thus, you can have two different groups of radio buttons, each having one button selected.

A button group is created by the **ButtonGroup** class. Its default constructor is invoked for this purpose. Elements are then added to the button group via the following method:

void add(AbstractButton *ab*)

Here, *ab* is a reference to the button to be added to the group.

A **JRadioButton** generates action events, item events, and change events each time the button selection changes. Most often it is the action event that is handled, which means that you will normally implement the **ActionListener** interface. Action events and action listeners are described in detail in *Create a Simple Push Button*. As explained there, the only method defined by **ActionListener** is **actionPerformed( )**. Inside this method, you can use a number of different ways to determine which button was selected.

First, you can check the action command string associated with the action event by calling **getActionCommand( )**. By default the action command is the same as the button label, but you can set the action command to something else by calling **setActionCommand( )** on the radio button. Second, you can call **getSource( )** on the **ActionEvent** object, and check that reference against the buttons. Finally, you can simply check each radio button to find out which one is currently selected by calling **isSelected( )** on each button. Remember, each time an action event occurs, it means that the button being selected has changed, and that one and only one button will be selected.

When using radio buttons, you will normally want to initially select one of the buttons. This is done by calling **setSelected( )**.

For details on **isSelected( )** and **setSelected( )**, see *Create a Toggle Button*.

Example
The following example reworks the check box example in the previous recipe so that it uses radio buttons.

```
// Demonstrate Radio Buttons.

import java.awt.*;
import java.awt.event.*;
import javax.swing.*;

class RBDemo implements ActionListener {

  JLabel jlabTranslateTo;
  JLabel jlabWhat;
  JLabel jlabChange;
  JCheckBox jcbTranslate;

  JRadioButton jrbFrench;
  JRadioButton jrbGerman;
  JRadioButton jrbChinese;

  ButtonGroup bg;

  RBDemo() {
    // Create a new JFrame container.
    JFrame jfrm = new JFrame("Radio Button Demo");

    // Specify a 1 column, 7 row grid layout.
    jfrm.setLayout(new GridLayout(7, 1));
```

```
// Give the frame an initial size.
jfrm.setSize(260, 160);

// Terminate the program when the user closes the application.
jfrm.setDefaultCloseOperation(JFrame.EXIT_ON_CLOSE);

// Create labels.
jlabTranslateTo = new JLabel("Translate To:");
jlabChange = new JLabel("");
jlabWhat = new JLabel("Translate into French");

// Make a check box.
jcbTranslate = new JCheckBox("Translate");

// Create the button group.
bg = new ButtonGroup();

// Create the radio buttons. Select the first one.
jrbFrench = new JRadioButton("French", true);
jrbGerman = new JRadioButton("German");
jrbChinese = new JRadioButton("Chinese");

// Add the radio buttons to the group.
bg.add(jrbFrench);
bg.add(jrbGerman);
bg.add(jrbChinese);

// Initially disable the language buttons and
// the Translate To label.
jlabTranslateTo.setEnabled(false);
jlabWhat.setEnabled(false);
jrbFrench.setEnabled(false);
jrbGerman.setEnabled(false);
jrbChinese.setEnabled(false);

// Add item listener for jcbTranslate.
jcbTranslate.addItemListener(new ItemListener() {

  // Change the enabled/disabled state of
  // the language radio buttons and related labels.
  // Also, report the state of jcbTranslate.
  public void itemStateChanged(ItemEvent ie) {
    if(jcbTranslate.isSelected()) {
      jlabTranslateTo.setEnabled(true);
      jrbFrench.setEnabled(true);
      jrbGerman.setEnabled(true);
      jrbChinese.setEnabled(true);
      jlabWhat.setEnabled(true);

      jlabChange.setText("Translation enabled.");
    }
    else {
      jlabTranslateTo.setEnabled(false);
```

```
        jrbFrench.setEnabled(false);
        jrbGerman.setEnabled(false);
        jrbChinese.setEnabled(false);
        jlabWhat.setEnabled(false);

        jlabChange.setText("Translation disabled.");
      }
    }
  });

  // Changes to the language radio buttons are handled
  // in common by the actionPerformed() method
  // implemented by RBDemo.
  jrbFrench.addActionListener(this);
  jrbGerman.addActionListener(this);
  jrbChinese.addActionListener(this);

  // Add the components to the content pane.
  jfrm.add(jcbTranslate);
  jfrm.add(jlabTranslateTo);

  jfrm.add(jrbFrench);
  jfrm.add(jrbGerman);
  jfrm.add(jrbChinese);
  jfrm.add(jlabChange);
  jfrm.add(jlabWhat);

  // Display the frame.
  jfrm.setVisible(true);
}

// This handles all of the language radio buttons.
public void actionPerformed(ActionEvent ie) {

  // Only one button will be selected at any one time.
  if(jrbFrench.isSelected())
    jlabWhat.setText("Translate into French");
  else if(jrbGerman.isSelected())
    jlabWhat.setText("Translate into German");
  else
    jlabWhat.setText("Translate into Chinese");

}

public static void main(String args[]) {
  // Create the frame on the event dispatching thread.
  SwingUtilities.invokeLater(new Runnable() {
    public void run() {
      new RBDemo();
    }
  });
}
}
```

The output is shown here:

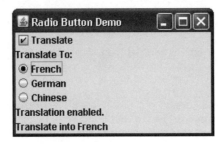

Options and Alternatives

Radio buttons support several options. A few are mentioned here. For example, you can substitute an icon that will replace the small circle that indicates selection. You can also specify both the icon and a string. Here are the **JRadioButton** constructors that support these options:

JRadioButton(Icon *icon*)
JRadioButton(String *str*, Icon *icon*)

The default icon used by the radio button is specified by *icon*. Typically, this icon serves as the deselected icon. That is, it is the icon shown when the button is not selected. Normally, when specifying this icon, you will also need to specify the selected icon.

To specify the selected icon, call **setSelectedIcon( )**, shown here:

void setSelectedIcon(Icon *icon*)

The icon passed via *icon* specifies the image to display when the radio button is selected. Because the selected and deselected icons work together as a pair, you almost always need to specify both when you are using an icon.

JRadioButton also supplies constructors that let you specify an icon and initial state, as shown here:

JRadioButton(Icon *icon*, boolean *state*)
JRadioButton(String *str*, Icon *icon*, boolean *state*)

If *state* is true, the radio button is initially selected. Otherwise, it is initially deselected.

You can set the alignment of the radio button and the alignment of the text relative to the icon. The methods that handle this are defined by **AbstractButton** and are **setVerticalAlignment( )**, **setHorizontalAlignment( )**, **setVerticalTextPosition( )**, and **setHorizontalTextPosition( )**. You can set a mnemonic that is shown in the radio button string by calling **setMnemonic( )**.

Input Text with JTextField

Key Ingredients	
Classes and Interfaces	**Methods**
java.awt.event.ActionListener	void actionPerformed(ActionEvent *ae*)
java.awt.event.ActionEvent	String getActionCommand( )
javax.swing.event.CaretListener	void caretUpdate(CaretEvent *ce*)
javax.swing.event.CaretEvent	
javax.swing.JTextField	void addActionListener(ActionListener *al*)
	void addCaretListener(CaretListener *cl*)
	void cut( )
	void copy( )
	String getSelectedText( )
	String getText( )
	void paste( )
	void setActionCommand(String *newCmd*)
	void setText(String *text*)

Swing provides extensive support for text entry, supplying several components for this purpose. This recipe looks at what is perhaps the most commonly used text component: **JTextField**. It offers a simple, yet very useful service: it enables the user to enter a single line of text. For example, you could use **JTextField** to obtain a user's name or e-mail address, a filename, or a telephone number. Despite its simplicity, there are many input situations in which **JTextField** is exactly the right component. It is an easy-to-use but effective solution to a wide variety of text input tasks.

Although **JTextField** is just one of several text components, most of the techniques that apply to it also apply to the others. Thus, much of what is presented in this recipe can be adapted for use with **JTextArea**, **JFormattedTextField**, or **JPasswordField**, for example. It is necessary to state that Swing's text components constitute a very large topic. The techniques shown in this recipe represent a typical use of one component. More sophisticated applications are possible.

Step-by-Step

To use **JTextField** to input a line of text involves these steps:

1. Create a **JTextField** instance. Make the component wide enough to handle a typical entry.

2. If desired, handle action events by registering an **ActionListener** for the text field. Action events are generated when the user presses ENTER when the text field has input focus.

3. If desired, handle caret events by registering a **CaretListener** for the text field. Caret events are generated each time the caret (also commonly referred to as the cursor) changes position.

4. To obtain the text currently displayed in the text field, call **getText( )**.

5. You can set the text by calling **setText( )**. You can use this method to reset the text, for example, if the user makes a mistake.

6. You can obtain text that has been selected by calling **getSelectedText( )**.

7. You can cut selected text by calling **cut( )**. This method removes the text and also puts the cut text into the clipboard. You can copy selected text, but not remove it, by calling **copy( )**.

8. You can copy whatever text is in the clipboard into the text field at the current caret location by calling **paste( )**.

Discussion

JTextField inherits the abstract class **javax.swing.text.JTextComponent**, which is the superclass of all text components. **JTextComponent** defines the functionality common to all of the text components, including **JTextField**. For example, the **cut( )**, **copy( )**, and **paste( )** methods are defined by **JTextComponent**. The model for **JTextField** (and all other text components) is **javax.swing.text.Document**.

    JTextField defines several constructors. The two used here are:

JTextField(int *cols*)
JTextField(int *str*, int cols)

Here, *cols* specifies the width of the text field in columns. It is important to understand that you can enter a string that is longer than the number of columns. It's just that the physical size of the text field on the screen will be *cols* columns wide. The second constructor lets you initialize the text field with the string passed in *str*.

    Pressing ENTER when a text field has focus causes an **ActionEvent** to be generated. If you want to handle this event, you must register an **ActionListener** for the text field. The **ActionListener** interface defines only one method, **actionPerformed( )**. This method is called whenever an action event is generated by the text field. For details on handling action events, see *Create a Simple Push Button*.

    A **JTextField** has an action command string associated with it. By default, the action command is the current contents of the text field. Thus, the action command string changes each time the contents of the text field change. Although this may be useful in some situations, it makes it impossible to use the action command string as a means of determining the source of an action event. If you *do* want to use the action command string to identify a text field, then you must set the action command to a fixed value of your own choosing by calling the **setActionCommand( )** method, shown here.

    void setActionCommand(String *newCmd*)

The string passed in *newCmd* becomes the new action command. The text in the text field is unaffected. Once you set the action command string, it remains the same no matter what is entered into the text field.

Each a time a text field's caret changes location, such as when you type a character, a **CaretEvent** is generated. You can listen for these events by implementing a **CaretListener**. By handling caret events, your program can respond to changes in the text field as they occur, without waiting for the user to press ENTER. **CaretListener** is packaged in **javax.swing.event**. It defines only one method, called **caretUpdate( )**, which is shown here:

    void caretUpdate(CaretEvent *ce*)

Remember, a caret event is generated each time the caret changes position. This includes changes to the caret caused by selected text, cutting or pasting, or repositioning the caret within the text. Therefore, handling caret events lets you monitor changes to the text in real time.

To obtain the string that is currently displayed in the text field, call **getText( )** on the **JTextField** instance. It is declared as shown here:

    String getText( )

You can set the text in a **JTextField** by calling **setText( )**, shown next:

    void setText(String *text*)

Here, *text* is the string that will be put into the text field.

A subset of the characters within a text field can be selected, either by the user or under program control. You can obtain the portion of the text that has been selected by calling **getSelectedText( )**, shown here:

    String getSelectedText( )

If no text has been selected, then **null** is returned.

Although the precise procedures may differ in different environments, **JTextField** automatically supports the standard cut, copy, and paste editing commands that let you move text between a text field and the clipboard. (For example, in Windows you can use CTRL-X to cut, CTRL-V to paste, and CTRL-C to copy.) You can also accomplish these actions under program control by using the methods **cut( )**, **copy( )**, and **paste( )**, shown here:

    void cut( )
    void copy( )
    void paste( )

The **cut( )** method removes any text that is selected within the text field and copies it to the clipboard. The **copy( )** method copies, but does not remove, the selected text. The **paste( )** method copies any text that may be in the clipboard to the text field. If the text field has selected text, then that text is replaced by what is in the clipboard. Otherwise, the clipboard text is inserted immediately before the current caret position.

Example

The following program demonstrates **JTextField**. It handles both the action events and caret events that are generated by the text field. Recall that an action event is generated each time the user pressed ENTER when the text field has keyboard focus. When this occurs, the current contents of the text field are obtained and displayed in a label. Each time a caret event is generated, the current contents of the text field are also obtained and displayed in a second label. Because a caret event is generated each time the caret moves (which will occur when characters are typed), the second label always contains the current contents of the text field. Finally, there is a push button called Get Text In Uppercase. When pressed, it generates an action event. The action event handler responds to the push button by obtaining the text from the text field and displaying it in uppercase.

```java
// Demonstrate JTextField.
//
// For demonstration purposes, TFDemo implements ActionListener.
// This handler is used for both the push button and for the
// text field. Notice that the action command strings for both the
// text field and the push button are explicitly set so that each
// can be recognized by the action event handler. In a real
// application, it is often easier to use anonymous inner classes
// to handle action events.

import java.awt.*;
import java.awt.event.*;
import javax.swing.*;
import javax.swing.event.*;

// Notice that TFDemo implements ActionListener.
class TFDemo implements ActionListener {

  JTextField jtf;
  JButton jbtnGetTextUpper;
  JLabel jlabPrompt;
  JLabel jlabContents;
  JLabel jlabRealTime;

  TFDemo() {

    // Create a new JFrame container.
    JFrame jfrm = new JFrame("Demonstrate a Text Field");

    // Specify FlowLayout for the layout manager.
    jfrm.setLayout(new FlowLayout());

    // Give the frame an initial size.
    jfrm.setSize(240, 140);

    // Terminate the program when the user closes the application.
    jfrm.setDefaultCloseOperation(JFrame.EXIT_ON_CLOSE);

    // Create a text field.
    jtf = new JTextField(10);

    // Set the action command for the text field.
    // This lets the text field be identified by its
    // action command string when an action event occurs.
    jtf.setActionCommand("TF");

    // Create the button.
    JButton jbtnGetTextUpper = new JButton("Get Text In Uppercase");
```

```
    // Add this instance as an action listener.
    jtf.addActionListener(this);
    jbtnGetTextUpper.addActionListener(this);

    // Add a caret listener.
    jtf.addCaretListener(new CaretListener() {
      public void caretUpdate(CaretEvent ce) {
        jlabRealTime.setText("Text in real time: " + jtf.getText());
      }
    });

    // Create the labels.
    jlabPrompt = new JLabel("Enter text: ");
    jlabContents = new JLabel("Waiting for action event.");
    jlabRealTime = new JLabel("Text in real time: ");

    // Add the components to the content pane.
    jfrm.add(jlabPrompt);
    jfrm.add(jtf);
    jfrm.add(jbtnGetTextUpper);
    jfrm.add(jlabRealTime);
    jfrm.add(jlabContents);

    // Display the frame.
    jfrm.setVisible(true);
  }

  // Handle action events for both the text field
  // and the push button.
  public void actionPerformed(ActionEvent ae) {

    if(ae.getActionCommand().equals("TF")) {
      // ENTER was pressed while focus was in the
      // text field.
      jlabContents.setText("ENTER key pressed: " +
                        jtf.getText());
    } else {
      // The Get Text in Uppercase button was pressed.
      String str = jtf.getText().toUpperCase();
      jlabContents.setText("Button pressed: " + str);
    }

  }

  public static void main(String args[]) {
    // Create the frame on the event dispatching thread.
    SwingUtilities.invokeLater(new Runnable() {
      public void run() {
        new TFDemo();
      }
    });
  }
}
```

Sample output is shown here:

Although most of the program is straightforward, a few parts warrant special attention. First, notice that the action command associated with **jtf** (the text field) is set to "TF" by the following line.

```
jtf.setActionCommand("TF");
```

After this line executes, the action command string for **jtf** will always be "TF" no matter what text it currently holds. This enables the action command string to be used to identify the text field and prevents potential conflicts with other components that generate action commands (such as the push button in this case). As explained, if the action command string were not set, then the string would be the current contents of the text field at the time the event was generated, which could lead to conflicts with the action command string associated with another component.

For the sake of demonstration, the **TFDemo** class implements **ActionListener** and this handler is used for both the push button and the text field. Because the action command string of **jtf** is explicitly set, it can be used to identify the text field. If this were not the case, then another method of determining the source of the event, such as **getSource( )**, would need to be used. Frankly, in a real application, it would normally be easier to use anonymous inner classes to handle the action events for each component separately than it would be to use a single handler. As stated, a single action event handler is used in this example for the sake of demonstration.

Bonus Example: Cut, Copy, and Paste

JTextField supports the standard clipboard actions of cut, paste, and copy. These can be utilized through standard keyboard editing commands, such as CTRL-X, CTRL-V, and CTRL-C in the Windows environment. They can also be actuated under program control, as this example illustrates.

The program displays a text field, three buttons, and two labels. The buttons are called Cut, Paste, and Copy, and they perform the functions indicated by their names. For example, if text has been selected in the text field, then pressing Cut causes the selected text to be removed and put into the clipboard. Pressing Paste causes any text in the clipboard to be copied to the text field at the current caret location. Pressing Copy copies the selected text into the clipboard but does not remove it. The two labels display the current contents of the text field and the currently selected text, if any.

```
// Cut, paste, and copy in a JTextField under program control.

import java.awt.*;
import java.awt.event.*;
import javax.swing.*;
import javax.swing.event.*;
```

```java
class CutCopyPaste {

  JLabel jlabAll;
  JLabel jlabSelected;

  JTextField jtf;

  JButton jbtnCut;
  JButton jbtnPaste;
  JButton jbtnCopy;

  public CutCopyPaste() {

    // Create a JFrame container.
    JFrame jfrm = new JFrame("Cut, Copy, and Paste");

    // Specify FlowLayout for the layout manager.
    jfrm.setLayout(new FlowLayout());

    // Give the frame an initial size.
    jfrm.setSize(230, 150);

    // Terminate the program when the user closes the application.
    jfrm.setDefaultCloseOperation(JFrame.EXIT_ON_CLOSE);

    // Create the labels.
    jlabAll = new JLabel("All text: ");
    jlabSelected = new JLabel("Selected text: ");
    jlabAll.setPreferredSize(new Dimension(200, 20));
    jlabSelected.setPreferredSize(new Dimension(200, 20));

    // Create the text field.
    jtf = new JTextField(15);

    // Create the Cut, Paste, and Copy buttons.
    jbtnCut = new JButton("Cut");
    jbtnPaste = new JButton("Paste");
    jbtnCopy = new JButton("Copy");

    // Add action listener for the Cut button.
    jbtnCut.addActionListener(new ActionListener() {
      public void actionPerformed(ActionEvent le) {
        // Cut any selected text and put it
        // in the clipboard.
        jtf.cut();
        update();
      }
    });

    // Add action listener for the Paste button.
    jbtnPaste.addActionListener(new ActionListener() {
      public void actionPerformed(ActionEvent le) {
        // Paste text from the clipboard into
        // the text field.
```

```java
      jtf.paste();
      update();
    }
  });

  // Add action listener for the Copy button.
  jbtnCopy.addActionListener(new ActionListener() {
    public void actionPerformed(ActionEvent le) {
      // Put selected text into the clipboard.
      jtf.copy();
      update();
    }
  });

  // Add a caret listener. This lets the application
  // respond in real time to changes in the text field.
  jtf.addCaretListener(new CaretListener() {
    public void caretUpdate(CaretEvent ce) {
      update();
    }
  });

  // Add the components to the content pane.
  jfrm.add(jtf);
  jfrm.add(jbtnCut);
  jfrm.add(jbtnPaste);
  jfrm.add(jbtnCopy);
  jfrm.add(jlabAll);
  jfrm.add(jlabSelected);

  // Display the frame.
  jfrm.setVisible(true);
}

// Show the complete and selected text in jtf.
private void update() {
  jlabAll.setText("All text: " + jtf.getText());

  if(jtf.getSelectedText() != null)
    jlabSelected.setText("Selected text: " +
                         jtf.getSelectedText());
  else jlabSelected.setText("Selected text: ");
}

public static void main(String args[]) {
  // Create the frame on the event dispatching thread.
  SwingUtilities.invokeLater(new Runnable() {
    public void run() {
      new CutCopyPaste();
    }
  });
}
}
}
```

Sample output is shown here:

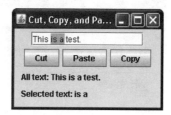

Options and Alternatives

As explained, each time the caret changes position, a caret event is generated, which causes the **caretUpdate( )** method specified by **CaretListener** to be called. This method is passed a **CaretEvent** object that encapsulates the event. **CaretEvent** defines two methods that can be useful in some text entry situations. They are shown next:

```
int getDot( )
int getMark( )
```

The **getDot( )** method returns the current location of the caret. This is called the *dot*. The **getMark( )** method returns the beginning point of a selection. This is called the *mark*. Thus, a selection is bound by the mark and the dot. If no selection has been made, then the dot and mark will be the same value.

You can position the caret under program control by calling **setCaretPosition( )** on the text field. It is shown here:

```
void setCaretPosition(int newLoc)
```

You can select a portion of text under program control by calling **moveCaretPosition( )** on the text field. It is shown next:

```
void moveCaretPosition(int newLoc)
```

The text between the original caret location and the new position is selected.

There is a very useful subclass of **JTextField** called **JFormattedTextField**. It enables you to enforce a specific format for the text that is being entered. For example, you can create formats for date, time, and numeric values. You can also create custom formats.

If you want to provide a text field into which the user enters a password, then you should use **JPasswordField**. It is designed expressly for obtaining passwords because the characters entered by the user are not echoed. Rather, a placeholder character is displayed. Also, the standard cut and copy editing functions are disabled in a **JPasswordField**.

JTextField allows only one line of text to be entered. To allow the input of multiple lines, you must employ a different text component. The easiest-to-use multiline text component is **JTextArea**. It works much like **JTextField** but allows multiple lines of text.

There are two other text components that will be of interest to some readers: **JEditorPane** and **JTextPane**. These are substantially more sophisticated controls because they support the editing of styled documents, such as those that use HTML or RTF. They can also contain images and other components.

Work with JList

Key Ingredients	
Classes and Interfaces	**Methods**
javax.swing.event. ListSelectionEvent	
javax.swing.event. ListSelectionListener	void valueChanged(ListSelectionEvent *le*)
javax.swing.JList	void addListSelectionListener(ListSelectionListener *lsl*) int getSelectedIndex( ) int[ ] getSelectedIndices( ) void setSelectionMode(int *mode*)

JList is Swing's basic list class. It supports the selection of one or more items from a list. Although often the list consists of strings, it is possible to create a list of just about any object that can be displayed. **JList** is so widely used in Swing GUIs that it is highly unlikely that you have not seen one before. This recipe shows how to create and manage one.

Step-by-Step
Using a **JList** involves these steps:

1. Create a **JList** instance.
2. If necessary, set the selection mode by calling **setSelectionMode( )**.
3. Handle list selection events by registering a **ListSelectionListener** for the list. List selection events are generated each time the user makes or changes a selection.
4. For single-selection lists, obtain the index of a selection by calling **getSelectedIndex( )**. For multiple-selection lists, obtain an array containing the indices of all selected items by calling **getSelectedIndices( )**.

Discussion
JList provides several constructors. The one used here is:

    JList(Object[ ] *items*)

This creates a **JList** that contains the items in the array specified by *items*. In this recipe, the items are instances of **String**, but you can specify other objects. **JList** uses **javax.swing.ListModel** as its data model. **javax.swing.ListSelectionModel** is the model that governs list selections.

Although a **JList** will work properly by itself, most of the time you will wrap a **JList** inside a **JScrollPane**, which is a container that automatically provides scrolling for its contents.

(See *Use JScrollPane to Handle Scrolling* for details.) Here is the **JScrollPane** constructor used by this recipe:

JScrollPane(Component *comp*)

Here, *comp* specifies the component to be scrolled, which in this case will be a **JList**. By wrapping a **JList** in a **JScrollPane**, long lists will automatically be scrollable. This simplifies GUI design. It also makes it easy to change the number of entries in a list without having to change the size of the **JList** component.

A **JList** generates a **ListSelectionEvent** when the user makes or changes a selection. This event is also generated when the user deselects an item. It is handled by implementing **ListSelectionListener**, which is packaged in **javax.swing.event**. This listener specifies only one method, called **valueChanged( )**, which is shown here.

void valueChanged(ListSelectionEvent *le*)

Here, *le* is a reference to the object that generated the event. **ListSelectionEvent** is also packaged in **javax.swing.event**. Although **ListSelectionEvent** does provide some methods of its own, normally you will obtain information about a list selection by using methods defined by **JList**.

By default, a **JList** allows the user to select multiple ranges of items within the list, but you can change this behavior by calling **setSelectionMode( )**, which is defined by **JList**. It is shown here.

void setSelectionMode(int *mode*)

Here, *mode* specifies the selection mode. It must be one of the values defined by its model, which is defined by **javax.swing.ListSelectionModel**. They are shown here:

SINGLE_SELECTION
SINGLE_INTERVAL_SELECTION
MULTIPLE_INTERVAL_SELECTION

The default, multiple-interval selection lets the user select multiple ranges of items within a list. With single-interval selection, the user can select one range of items. With single selection, the user can select only a single item. Of course, a single item can be selected in the other two modes, too. It's just that they also allow a range to be selected.

You can obtain the index of the first item selected, which will also be the index of the only selected item when using single-selection mode, by calling **getSelectedIndex( )**, shown here:

int getSelectedIndex( )

Indexing begins at zero. So, if the first item is selected, this method will return 0. If no item is selected, –1 is returned.

You can obtain an array containing all selected items by calling **getSelectedIndices( )**, shown next:

int[ ] getSelectedIndices( )

In the returned array, the indices are in order from smallest to largest. If a zero-length array is returned, it means that no items are selected.

Example

The following program demonstrates a single-selection **JList**. It presents a list of computer
languages, from which the user may select one. Each time a selection is made or changed, a
ListSelectionEvent is generated, which is handled by the **valueChanged( )** method defined
by **ListSelectionListener**. It responds by obtaining the index of the selected item and
displaying the selection.

```
// Demonstrate a single-selection JList.

import javax.swing.*;
import javax.swing.event.*;
import java.awt.*;
import java.awt.event.*;

class ListDemo {

  JList jlst;
  JLabel jlab;
  JScrollPane jscrlp;

  // Create an array of computer languages..
  String languages[] = { "Java", "Perl", "Python",
                          "C++", "Basic", "C#" };

  ListDemo() {

    // Create a new JFrame container.
    JFrame jfrm = new JFrame("Use JList");

    // Set the layout manager to FlowLayout.
    jfrm.setLayout(new FlowLayout());

    // Give the frame an initial size.
    jfrm.setSize(200, 160);

    // Terminate the program when the user closes the application.
    jfrm.setDefaultCloseOperation(JFrame.EXIT_ON_CLOSE);

    // Create a JList.
    jlst = new JList(languages);

    // Set the list selection mode to single-selection.
    jlst.setSelectionMode(ListSelectionModel.SINGLE_SELECTION);

    // Add the list to a scroll pane.
    jscrlp = new JScrollPane(jlst);

    // Set the preferred size of the scroll pane.
    jscrlp.setPreferredSize(new Dimension(100, 74));

    // Make a label that displays the selection.
    jlab = new JLabel("Choose a Language");
```

```
   // Add list selection handler.
   jlst.addListSelectionListener(new ListSelectionListener() {
      public void valueChanged(ListSelectionEvent le) {
         // Get the index of the changed item.
         int idx = jlst.getSelectedIndex();

         // Display selection, if item was selected.
         if(idx != -1)
            jlab.setText("Current selection: " + languages[idx]);
         else // Otherwise, reprompt.
            jlab.setText("Please choose a language.");
      }
   });

   // Add the list and label to the content pane.
   jfrm.add(jscrlp);
   jfrm.add(jlab);

   // Display the frame.
   jfrm.setVisible(true);
}

public static void main(String args[]) {
   // Create the frame on the event dispatching thread.
   SwingUtilities.invokeLater(new Runnable() {
      public void run() {
         new ListDemo();
      }
   });
}
}
```

The output is shown here:

Let's look closely at a few aspects of this program. First, notice the **languages** array near the top of the program. It is initialized with a list of strings that contains the names of various computer languages. Inside **ListDemo( )**, a **JList** called **jlst** is constructed using the **languages** array. This causes the list to be initialized to the strings contained in the array.

A second point of interest is the call to **setSelectionMode( )**. As explained, by default, **JList** supports multiple selections. It must be explicitly set to allow only single selections.

Next, **jlst** is wrapped inside a **JScrollPane**, and the preferred size of the scroll pane is set to 100 by 74. The **setPreferredSize( )** method sets the desired size of a component. Be aware, however, that some layout managers will ignore this request. Because the list contains only a few entries, it would have been possible in this case to avoid the use of a scroll pane. However, the use of a scroll pane lets the list be presented in a compact form. It also allows entries to be added to the list without affecting the layout of the GUI.

Options and Alternatives

Another commonly used **JList** constructor lets you specify the items in the list in the form of a **Vector**. It is shown here:

    JList(Vector<?> *items*)

The items contained in *items* will be shown in the list.

As explained, by default a **JList** allows multiple items to be selected from the list. When using multiple selection, you will need to use **getSelectedIndices( )** to obtain an array of the items selected. For example, here is the **valueChanged( )** handler from the example rewritten to support multiple selection:

```
// Handler for multiple selections.
jlst.addListSelectionListener(new ListSelectionListener() {
  public void valueChanged(ListSelectionEvent le) {
    String langs = "Current Selections: ";

    // Get the indices of the selected items.
    int indices[] = jlst.getSelectedIndices();

    // Display selection, if one or more items were selected.
    if(indices.length != 0) {
      for(int i = 0; i < indices.length; i++)
        langs += languages[indices[i]] + " ";

      jlab.setText(langs);
    }
    else // Otherwise, reprompt.
      jlab.setText("Please choose a language.");
  }
});
```

To try this handler, you must also comment out the call to **setSelectionMode( )** in the example.

You can select an item under program control by calling **setSelectedIndex( )**, shown here:

    void setSelectedIndex(int *idx*)

Here, *idx* is the index of the item to be selected. One reason you might want to use **setSelectedIndex( )** is to preselect an item when the list is first displayed. For example, try adding this line to the preceding program after **jlst** has been added to the content pane:

```
jlst.setSelectedIndex(0);
```

After making this addition, the first item in the list, which is Java, will be selected when the program starts.

If the list supports multiple selection, then you can select more than one item by calling **setSelectedIndices( )**, shown here:

    void setSelectedIndices(int[ ] *idxs*)

The array passed through *idxs* contains the indices of the items to be selected.

In a multiple-selection list, you can select a range of items by calling **setSelectionInterval( )**, shown here:

    void setSelectionInterval(int *idxStart*, int *idxStop*)

The range selected is inclusive. Thus, both *idxStart* and *idxStop,* and all items in between, will be selected.

You can select an item by value instead of by index if you call **setSelectedValue( )**:

    void setSelectedValue(Object *item*, boolean *scrollToItem*)

The item to select is passed via *item*. If *scrollToItem* is true, and the selected item is not currently in view, it is scrolled into view. For example, the statement

```
jlst.setSelectedValue("C#", true);
```

selects C# and scrolls it into view.

You can deselect all selections by calling **clearSelection( )**, shown here:

    void clearSelection( )

After this method executes, all selections are cleared.

You can determine if a selection is available by calling **isSelectionEmpty( )**, shown here:

    boolean isSelectionEmpty( )

It returns true if no selections have been made and false otherwise.

When using a list that supports multiple selection, sometimes you will want to know which item was selected first and which item was selected last. In the language of **JList**, the first item is called the *anchor*. The last item is called the *lead*. You can obtain these indices by calling **getAnchorSelectionIndex( )** and **getLeadSelectionIndex( )**, shown here:

    void getAnchorSelectionIndex( )
    void getLeadSelectionIndex( )

Both return −1 if no selection has been made.

You can set the items in a **JList** by calling **setListData( )**. It has the following two forms:

    void setListData(Object[ ] *items*)
    void setListData(Vector<?> *items*)

Here, *items* is an array or vector that contains the items that you want to be displayed in the invoking list.

A **JList** may generate several list selection events when the user is in the process of selecting or deselecting one or more items. Often you won't want to respond to selections until the user has completed the process. You can use the **getValueIsAdjusting( )** method to determine when the selection process has ended. It is shown here:

boolean getValueIsAdjusting( )

It returns true if the selection process is ongoing and false when the user stops the selection process. By using this method, you can wait until the user is done before processing selections.

In addition to those options just described, **JList** supports several others. Here are two more advanced options that might be of interest. First, instead of creating a list by specifying an array or vector of the items when the **JList** is constructed, you can first create an implementation of **ListModel**. Next, populate the model and then use it to construct a **JList**. This has two advantages: you can create custom list models, if desired, and you can alter the contents of the list at runtime by adding or removing elements from the model. The second advanced option is to create a custom cell renderer for the list. A custom cell renderer determines how each entry in the list gets drawn. It must be an object of a class that implements the **ListCellRenderer** interface.

For cases in which you want to combine an edit field with a list, use **JComboBox**.

A very useful alternative to **JList** in some cases is **JSpinner**. It creates a component that incorporates a list with a set of arrows that scroll through the list. The advantage of **JSpinner** is that it creates a very compact component that provides a convenient way for the user to select from a list of values.

Use a Scroll Bar

Key Ingredients	
Classes and Interfaces	**Methods**
java.awt.event.AdjustmentEvent	Adjustable getAdjustable( ) int getValue( ) boolean getValueIsAdjusting( )
java.awt.event.AdjustmentListener	void adjustmentValueChanged(AdjustmentEvent *ae*)
javax.swing.JScrollBar	void addAdjustmentListener(AdjustmentListener *al*) int getValue( ) boolean getValueIsAdjusting( )

A Swing scroll bar is an instance of **JScrollBar**. Despite their many options, scroll bars are surprisingly easy to program. Furthermore, often the default scroll bar provides precisely the right functionality. Scroll bars come in two basic varieties: vertical and horizontal.

Although their orientation differs, both are handled in the same way. This recipe shows the basic techniques needed to create and use a scroll bar.

Step-by-Step

To use a scroll bar involves these steps:

1. Create an instance of **JScrollBar**.
2. Add an **AdjustmentListener** to handle the events generated when the scroll bar's slider is moved.
3. Handle adjustment events by implementing **adjustmentValueChanged( )**.
4. If appropriate to your application, use **getValueIsAdjusting( )** to wait until the user has stopped moving the scroll bar.
5. Obtain the scroll bar's value by calling **getValue( )**.

Discussion

It is useful to begin by reviewing key aspects of the scroll bar. A scroll bar is actually a composite of several individual parts. At each end are arrows that you can click to change the current value of the scroll bar one unit in the direction of the arrow. The current value of the scroll bar relative to its minimum and maximum values is indicated by position of the *thumb*. The thumb can be dragged by the user to a new position. This new position then becomes the current value of the scroll bar. The scroll bar's model will then reflect this value. Clicking on the bar (which is also called the *paging area*) causes the thumb to jump in that direction by some increment that is usually larger than 1. Typically, this action translates into some form of page up and page down.

In Swing, a scroll bar is one of three related components: **JScrollBar**, **JSlider**, and **JProgressBar**. These components all share a central theme: a visual indicator that moves through a predefined range. Because of this, these components are based on the same model, which is encapsulated by the **BoundedRangeModel** interface. Although we won't need to use the model directly, it defines the basic operation of all three components.

A key aspect of **BoundedRangeModel** is that it defines four important values:

- Minimum
- Maximum
- Current
- Extent

The minimum and maximum values define the endpoints of the range over which a component based on the **BoundedRangeModel** can operate. The current value of the component will be within that range. In general, the extent represents the conceptual "width" of a sliding element that moves between the endpoints of the component. For example, in the scroll bar, the extent corresponds to the width (or "thickness") of the scroll bar's slider box.

BoundedRangeModel enforces a relationship between these four values. First, the minimum must be less than or equal to the maximum. The current value must be greater than or equal to the minimum value. The current value *plus the extent* must be less than or equal to the maximum value. Thus, if you specify a maximum value of 100 and an extent of 20, then the current value can never be larger than 80 (which is 100 – 20). You can specify an extent of 0, which enables the current value to be anywhere within the range specified by the minimum and maximum, inclusive.

JScrollBar also implements the **Adjustable** interface. This interface is defined by the AWT.

JScrollBar defines three constructors. The first creates a default scroll bar:

JScrollBar( )

This creates a vertical scroll bar that uses the default settings for the initial value, extent, minimum, and maximum. They are:

Initial value	0
Extent	10
Minimum	0
Maximum	100

The next constructor lets you specify the orientation of the scroll bar:

JScrollBar(int *VorH*)

The scroll bar is oriented as specified by *VorH*. The value of *VorH* must be either **JScrollBar.VERTICAL** or **JScrollBar.HORIZONTAL**. The default settings are used. The final constructor lets you specify both the orientation and the settings:

JScrollBar(int *VorH*, int *initialValue*, int *extent*, int *min*, int *max*)

This creates a scroll bar oriented as specified by *VorH*, with the specified initial value, extent, and minimum and maximum values.

For scroll bars, the extent specifies the size of the thumb. However, the physical size of the thumb on the screen will never drop below a certain point because it must remain large enough to be dragged. It is important to understand that the largest value that the scroll bar can have is equal to the maximum value minus the extent. Thus, by default, the value of a scroll bar can range between 0 and 90 (100 – 10).

JScrollBar generates an adjustment event whenever its slider is changed. Adjustment events are objects of type **java.awt.AdjustmentEvent**. To process an adjustment event, you will need to implement the **AdjustmentListener** interface. It defines only one method, **adjustmentValueChanged( )**, shown here:

void adjustmentValueChanged(AdjustmentEvent *ae*)

This method is called whenever a change is made to the value of the scroll bar.

You can obtain a reference to the scroll bar that generated the event by calling **getAdjustable( )** on the **AdjustmentEvent** object. It is shown here:

Adjustable getAdjustable( )

As mentioned, **JScrollBar** implements the **Adjustable** interface, and many of the properties supported by **JScrollBar** are defined by **Adjustable**. This means that you can operate directly on those properties through the reference returned by this method rather than having to use the scroll bar reference explicitly.

When the user drags the thumb to a new location or executes a series of page-up or page-down commands, then a stream of **AdjustmentEvents** will be generated. While this may be useful in some cases, in others all you care about is the final value. You can use **getValueIsAdjusting( )** to ignore events until the user completes the operation. It is shown here:

boolean getValueIsAdjusting( )

It returns true if the user is still in the process of moving the thumb. When the adjustment has ended, it returns false. Thus, you can use this method to wait until the user has stopped changing the scroll bar before you respond to the changes.

You can obtain the current value of the scroll bar by calling **getValue( )** on the **JScrollBar** instance. It is shown here:

int getValue( )

Example

The following example shows both vertical and a horizontal scroll bars in action. The program displays the values of both bars. The value of the horizontal bar is updated in real time, as the thumb is moved. The value of the vertical bar is updated only at the conclusion of each adjustment. This is accomplished through the use of the **getValueIsAdjusting( )** method.

```
// Demonstrate JScrollBar.

import java.awt.*;
import java.awt.event.*;
import javax.swing.*;
import javax.swing.event.*;

class SBDemo {

  JLabel jlabVert;
  JLabel jlabHoriz;

  JScrollBar jsbVert;
  JScrollBar jsbHoriz;

  SBDemo() {

    // Create a new JFrame container.
    JFrame jfrm = new JFrame("Demonstrate JScrollBar");

    // Set the layout manager to FlowLayout.
    jfrm.setLayout(new FlowLayout());
```

```java
      // Give the frame an initial size.
      jfrm.setSize(280, 300);

      // Terminate the program when the user closes the application.
      jfrm.setDefaultCloseOperation(JFrame.EXIT_ON_CLOSE);

      // Display the current scroll bar values.
      jlabVert = new JLabel("Value of vertical scroll bar: 0");
      jlabHoriz = new JLabel("Value of horizontal scroll bar: 50");

      // Create default vertical and horizontal scroll bar.
      jsbVert = new JScrollBar(); // vertical by default
      jsbHoriz = new JScrollBar(Adjustable.HORIZONTAL);

      // Set the preferred size for the scroll bars.
      jsbVert.setPreferredSize(new Dimension(20, 200));
      jsbHoriz.setPreferredSize(new Dimension(200, 20));

      // Set the thumb value of the horizontal scroll bar.
      jsbHoriz.setValue(50);


      // Add adjustment listeners for the scroll bars.

      // The vertical scroll bar waits until the user
      // stops changing the scroll bar's value before
      // it responds.
      jsbVert.addAdjustmentListener(new AdjustmentListener() {
        public void adjustmentValueChanged(AdjustmentEvent ae) {

          // If the scroll bar is in the process of being
          // changed, simply return.
          if(jsbVert.getValueIsAdjusting()) return;

          // Display the new value.
          jlabVert.setText("Value of vertical scroll bar: "
                      + ae.getValue());
        }
      });

      // The horizontal scroll bar handler responds to all
      // adjustment events, including those generated while
      // the scroll bar is in the process of being changed.
      jsbHoriz.addAdjustmentListener(new AdjustmentListener() {
        public void adjustmentValueChanged(AdjustmentEvent ae) {
          // Display the new value.
          jlabHoriz.setText("Value of horizontal scroll bar: "
                      + ae.getValue());
        }
      });
```

```
    // Add components to the content pane.
    jfrm.add(jsbVert);
    jfrm.add(jsbHoriz);
    jfrm.add(jlabVert);
    jfrm.add(jlabHoriz);

    // Display the frame.
    jfrm.setVisible(true);
  }

  public static void main(String args[]) {
    // Create the frame on the event dispatching thread.
    SwingUtilities.invokeLater(new Runnable() {
      public void run() {
        new SBDemo();
      }
    });
  }
}
```

The output is shown here:

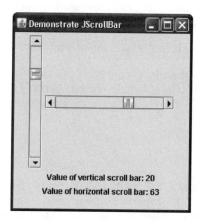

Options and Alternatives

As explained, when a scroll bar is changed, an **AdjustmentEvent** is generated.
AdjustmentEvent defines its own versions of the **getValue( )** and **getValueIsAdjusting( )**
methods. These methods may be more convenient to use in some cases than the ones
defined by **JScrollBar** because you don't have to explicitly obtain a reference to the
scroll bar.

In addition to adjustment events, a **JScrollBar** will also generate change events when its
value is changed. Change events are objects of type **javax.swing.ChangeEvent** and are
handled by implementing a **javax.swing.ChangeListener**. This listener is registered with
the scroll bar's model, which is obtained by calling **getModel( )** on the **JScrollBar** instance.

JScrollBar defines several properties that determine its behavior. First, it supports the minimum, maximum, extent, and current value properties defined by **BoundedRangeModel**. These values can be accessed by the following methods:

```
int getMinimum( )
void setMinimum(int val)

int getMaximum( )
void setMaximum(int val)

int getVisibleAmount( )
void setVisibleAmount(int val)

int getValue( )
void setValue(int val)
```

Notice that the methods that get or set the extent use the name **VisibleAmount**. This is because these methods are defined by the **Adjustable** interface (which predates Swing). However, they still set the extent property defined by **BoundedRangeModel**.

JScrollBar also defines a convenience method called **setValues( )**, which lets you set the value, visible amount (extent), minimum, and maximum values in a single call. It is shown here:

```
void setValues(int value, int visibleAmount, int min, int max)
```

In addition to dragging the thumb, a scroll bar's position can be changed by clicking on the arrows at its ends, or on the paging area of the bar. When the arrows are clicked, the scroll bar changes its position by the value contained in the *unit increment* property. Its accessors are shown here:

```
int getUnitIncrement( )
void setUnitIncrement(int val)
```

When the paging area is clicked, the position of the thumb changes by the value contained in the *block increment* property. This property can be accessed via the **getBlockIncrement( )** and **setBlockIncrement( )** methods. Here are the commonly used versions of these methods:

```
int getBlockIncrement( )
void setBlockIncrement(int val)
```

A pleasing alternative to a scroll bar in some cases is the slider, which is an instance of **JSlider**. It presents a control that allows a knob to be moved through a range. Sliders are often used to set values. For example, a slider might be used to set the volume for an audio player.

Although stand-alone scroll bars are important, there is often an alternative approach that is both easier to use and more powerful: the scroll pane. Scroll panes are instances of **JScrollPane**. A scroll pane is a specialized container that automatically provides scrolling for the component that it contains. **JScrollPane** is described by the next recipe.

Another component that can be used in place of a scroll bar in some cases is **JSpinner**. It creates a component that incorporates a list with a set of arrows that scroll through the list.

Use JScrollPane to Handle Scrolling

Key Ingredients	
Classes	**Methods**
javax.swing.JScrollPane	

JScrollPane is a specialized component that automatically handles the scrolling of another component. The component being scrolled can be either an individual component, such as a table, or a group of components contained within a lightweight container, such as a **JPanel**. Because **JScrollPane** automates scrolling, it usually eliminates the need to manage individual scroll bars. This recipe shows how to put **JScrollPane** into action.

The viewable area of a scroll pane is called the *viewport*. It is a window in which the component being scrolled is displayed. Thus, the viewport displays the visible portion of the component being scrolled. The scroll bars scroll the component through the viewport. In its default behavior, a **JScrollPane** will dynamically add or remove a scroll bar as needed. For example, if the component is taller than the viewport, a vertical scroll bar is added. If the component will completely fit within the viewport, the scroll bars are removed.

Step-by-Step

Here are the steps to follow to use a scroll pane:

1. Create the component to be scrolled.
2. Create an instance of **JScrollPane**, passing to it the object to scroll.
3. Add the scroll pane to the content pane.

Discussion

JScrollPane defines several constructors. The one used by this recipe is shown here:

    JScrollPane(Component *comp*)

The component to be scrolled is specified by *comp*. Scroll bars are automatically displayed when the content of the pane exceeds the dimensions of the viewport.

Because **JScrollPane** automates scrolling for the specified component, no other actions need be provided by your program.

Example

The following example demonstrates **JScrollPane**. To do so, it uses a scroll pane to handle two common situations. First, it uses a scroll pane to scroll the contents of a label that contains a large, multiline string. Second, it uses a scroll pane to scroll the contents of a **Box**, which is a lightweight container that uses **BoxLayout**.

```java
// Demonstrate JScrollPane.

import javax.swing.*;
import java.awt.*;

class SPDemo {

  SPDemo() {

    // Create a new JFrame container.
    JFrame jfrm = new JFrame("Use JScrollPane");

    // Set the layout manager to FlowLayout.
    jfrm.setLayout(new FlowLayout());

    // Give the frame an initial size.
    jfrm.setSize(240, 250);

    // Terminate the program when the user closes the application.
    jfrm.setDefaultCloseOperation(JFrame.EXIT_ON_CLOSE);

    // Create a long, HTML-based label.
    JLabel jlab =
      new JLabel("<html>JScrollPane provides an easy way to<br>" +
                 "handle situations in which a component is<br>" +
                 "(or might be) too large for the available<br>" +
                 "space. Wrapping the component in a scroll<br>" +
                 "pane is a convenient solution.<br><br>" +
                 "JScrollPane is especially useful for scrolling<br>" +
                 "tables, lists, images, or the contents of<br>" +
                 "lightweight containers, such as JPanel or Box.");

    // Create a scroll pane and have it scroll the label.
    JScrollPane jscrlpLabel = new JScrollPane(jlab);

    // Set the preferred size of the scroll pane that holds the label.
    jscrlpLabel.setPreferredSize(new Dimension(200, 100));


    // Next, use a scroll pane to scroll the contents of a Box.
    // A Box is a lightweight container that uses BoxLayout.

    // First, create some components that will be contained
    // within the box.
    JLabel jlabSelect = new JLabel("Select Languages");
    JCheckBox jrbEn = new JCheckBox("English");
    JCheckBox jrbFr = new JCheckBox("French");
    JCheckBox jrbGe = new JCheckBox("German");
    JCheckBox jrbCh = new JCheckBox("Chinese");
    JCheckBox jrbSp = new JCheckBox("Spanish");
```

```java
      // No event handlers are needed for this example, but
      // you can try adding some on your own, if you wish.

      // Create a Box container to hold the language choices.
      Box box = Box.createVerticalBox();

      // Add components to the box.
      box.add(jlabSelect);
      box.add(jrbEn);
      box.add(jrbFr);
      box.add(jrbGe);
      box.add(jrbCh);
      box.add(jrbSp);

      // Create a scroll pane that will hold the box.
      JScrollPane jscrlpBox = new JScrollPane(box);

      // Set the size of the scroll pane that holds the box.
      jscrlpBox.setPreferredSize(new Dimension(140, 90));

      // Add both scroll panes to the content pane.
      jfrm.add(jscrlpLabel);
      jfrm.add(jscrlpBox);

      // Display the frame.
      jfrm.setVisible(true);
  }

  public static void main(String args[]) {
    // Create the frame on the event dispatching thread.
    SwingUtilities.invokeLater(new Runnable() {
      public void run() {
        new SPDemo();
      }
    });
  }
}
```

The output is shown here:

JScrollPane is commonly used to provide scrolling for a **JList** or a **JTable**. See *Work with JList* and *Display Data in a JTable* for additional examples.

Options and Alternatives

Like most Swing components, **JScrollPane** supports many options and customizations. Perhaps the most common enhancement is the addition of headers. **JScrollPane** supports both a column header and a row header. You can use either or both. A header can consist of any type of component. This means that you are not limited to only passive labels; a header can contain active controls, such as a push button.

The easiest way to set a row header is to call **setRowHeaderView( )**, shown here:

void setRowHeaderView(Component *comp*)

Here, *comp* is the component that will be used as a header.

The easiest way to set a column header is to call **setColumnHeaderView( )**, shown next:

void setColumnHeaderView(Component *comp*)

Here, *comp* is the component that will be used as a header.

When using headers, it is sometimes useful to include a border around the viewport. This is easily accomplished by calling **setViewportBorder( )**, which is defined by **JScrollPane**. It is shown here:

void setViewportBorder(Border *border*)

Here, *border* specifies the border. Standard borders can be created by using the **BorderFactory** class.

To see the effect of headers and a border, try adding the following code to the example. It adds row and column headers to the **jscrlpBox** scroll pane and puts a border around its viewport. Insert the code immediately after **jscrlpBox** is created.

```
jscrlpBox.setColumnHeaderView(
            new JLabel("Internationalization", JLabel.CENTER));

jscrlpBox.setRowHeaderView(new JLabel("   "));

jscrlpBox.setViewportBorder(
            BorderFactory.createLineBorder(Color.BLACK));
```

Notice that the row and column headers are instances of **JLabel**; however, another type of component, such as **JButton**, could be used. Also notice that the label for the row header is simply a string containing spaces. It is used to balance the visual look of the scroll pane. After making these additions, **jscrlpBox** now looks like this:

Another popular customization is to use the corners of a **JScrollPane**. These corners are created when the scroll bars intersect with each other or with the row or column headers. These corners can contain any component, such as a label or push button. However, be aware of two issues concerning the use of these corners. First, the size of the corners depends entirely on the thickness of the scroll bars or the headers. Therefore, they are often very small. Second, the corners will be visible only if the scroll bars and headers are shown. For example, there will be a lower-right corner only if both the horizontal and vertical scroll bars are both shown. If you want to put a control in that corner, then the scroll bars will need to remain visible at all times. To do this, you will need to set the scroll bar policy, as described shortly.

To put a component into a corner, call **setCorner( )** shown here:

void setCorner(String *which*, Component *comp*)

Here, *which* specifies which corner. It must be one of the following constants defined by the **ScrollPaneConstants** interface, which is implemented by **JScrollPane**:

LOWER_LEADING_CORNER	LOWER_LEFT_CORNER
LOWER_RIGHT_CORNER	LOWER_TRAILING_CORNER
UPPER_LEADING_CORNER	UPPER_LEFT_CORNER
UPPER_RIGHT_CORNER	UPPER_TRAILING_CORNER

You can set the *scroll bar policy* used by the scroll pane. The scroll bar policy determines when the scroll bars are shown. By default, a **JScrollPane** displays a scroll bar only when it is needed. For example, if the information being scrolled is too long for the viewport, a vertical scroll bar is automatically displayed to enable the viewport to be scrolled up and down. When the information all fits within the viewport, then no scroll bars are shown. Although the default scroll bar policy is appropriate for many scroll panes, it might be a problem when the corners are used, as just described. One other point: each scroll bar has its own policy. This lets you specify a separate policy for the vertical and the horizontal scroll bar.

You can specify scroll bar policies when a **JScrollPane** is created by passing the policy using one of these constructors.

JScrollPane(int *vertSBP*, int *horizSPB*)
JScrollPane(Component *comp*, int *vertSBP*, int *horizSBP*)

Here, *vertSBP* specifies the policy for the vertical scroll bar and *horizSBP* specifies the policy for the horizontal scroll bar. The scroll bar policies are specified using constants defined by the interface **ScrollPaneConstants**. The scroll bar policies are shown here:

Constant	Policy
HORIZONTAL_SCROLLBAR_AS_NEEDED	Horizontal scroll bar shown when needed. This is the default.
HORIZONTAL_SCROLLBAR_NEVER	Horizontal scroll bar never shown.
HORIZONTAL_SCROLLBAR_ALWAYS	Horizontal scroll bar always shown.
VERTICAL_SCROLLBAR_AS_NEEDED	Vertical scroll bar shown when needed. This is the default.
VERTICAL_SCROLLBAR_NEVER	Vertical scroll bar never shown.
VERTICAL_SCROLLBAR_ALWAYS	Vertical scroll bar always shown.

You can set the scroll bar policies after a scroll pane has been created by calling these methods:

void setVerticalScrollBarPolicy(int *vertSBP*)
void setHorizontalScrollBarPolicy(int *horizSBP*)

Here, *vertSBP* and *horizSBP* specify the scroll bar policy.

Although a scroll pane is a good way to handle containers that hold more information than can be displayed at once, there is another option that you may find more appropriate in some cases: **JTabbedPane**. It manages a set of components by linking them with tabs. Selecting a tab causes the component associated with that tab to come to the forefront. Therefore, using **JTabbedPane**, you can organize information into panels of related components and then let the user choose which panel to display.

Display Data in a JTable

Key Ingredients	
Classes	**Methods**
javax.swing.JScrollPane	
javax.swing.JTable	void setCellSelectionEnabled(boolean *on*)
	void setColumnSelectionAllowed(boolean *enabled*)
	void setPreferredScrollableViewportSize(Dimension *dim*)
	void setRowSelectionAllowed(Boolean *enabled*)
	void setSelectionMode(int *mode*)

JTable creates, displays, and manages tables of information. It is arguably the single most powerful component in the Swing library. It is also one of the most challenging to use to its fullest potential because it provides very rich (and sometimes intricate) functionality. It also supports many sophisticated customizations. That said, **JTable** is also one of Swing's most important components, especially in enterprise applications, because tables are often used to display database entries. Because of the complexity of **JTable**, two recipes are used to demonstrate it. This recipe describes how to create a table that will display information in a tabular form. The following recipe shows how to handle table events.

Like the other Swing components, **JTable** is packaged inside **javax.swing**. However, many of its support classes and interfaces are found in **javax.swing.table**. A separate package is used because of the large number of interfaces and classes that are related to tables.

At its core, **JTable** is conceptually simple. It is a component that consists of one or more columns of information. At the top of each column is a heading. In addition to describing the data in a column, the heading also provides the mechanism by which the user can change the size of a column and change the location of a column within the table.

The information within the table is contained in *cells*. Each cell has associated with it a *cell renderer*, which determines how the information is displayed, and a *cell editor*, which determines how the user edits the information. **JTable** supplies default cell renderers and editors that are suitable for many applications. However, it is possible to specify your own custom renderers and editors if desired.

JTable relies on three models. The first is the table model, which is defined by the **TableModel** interface. This model defines those things related to displaying data in a two-dimensional format. The second is the table column model, which is represented by **TableColumnModel**. **JTable** is defined in terms of columns, and it is **TableColumnModel** that specifies the characteristics of a column. These two models are packaged in **javax.swing.table**. The third model is **ListSelectionModel**. It determines how items are selected. It is packaged in **javax.swing**.

Step-by-Step

To display data in a **JTable** involves these steps:

1. Create an array of the data to be displayed.

2. Create an array of the column headers.

3. Create an instance of **JTable**, specifying the data and headings.

4. In most cases, you will want to set the size of the scrollable viewport. This is done by calling **setPreferredScrollableViewportSize( )**.

5. Change the selection mode by calling **setSelectionMode( )**, if desired.

6. By default, the user can select a row. To allow column or cell selections, use **setColumnSelectionAllowed( ), setRowSelectionAllowed( )**, and/or **setCellSelectionEnabled( )**.

7. Create a **JScrollPane**, specifying the **JTable** as the component to be scrolled.

Discussion

JTable supplies several constructors. The one used by this recipe is shown here:

JTable(Object[ ] [ ] *data*, Object[ ] *headerNames*)

This constructor automatically creates a table that fits the data specified in *data* and has the header names specified by *headerNames*. The table will use the default cell renderers and editors, which are suitable for many table applications. The *data* array is two-dimensional, with the first dimension specifying the number of rows in the table and the second dimension specifying the number of elements in each row. In all cases, the length of each row must be equal to the length of *headerNames*.

JTable does not provide any scrolling capabilities. Instead, a table is normally wrapped in a **JScrollPane**. This also causes the column header to be automatically displayed. If you don't wrap a **JTable** in a **JScrollPane**, then you must explicitly display both the table and header.

When using a scroll pane to display the table, you will normally also want to set the preferred size of the table's *scrollable viewport*. The scrollable viewport defines a region within the table in which the data is displayed and scrolled. It does not include the column headers. If you don't set this size, a default size will be used, which may or may not be appropriate. Thus, it's usually best to explicitly set the scrollable viewport size. To do so, use **setPreferredScrollableViewportSize( )**, shown here:

void setPreferredScrollableViewportSize(Dimension *dim*)

Here, *dim* specifies the desired size of the scrollable area.

By default, when the user clicks on an entry in the table, the entire row is selected. Although this behavior is often what you will want, it can be changed to allow a column to be selected, or just an individual cell. These alternatives may be more appropriate than row selection for some applications.

To enable column selection involves two steps. First, enable column selection. Second, disable row selection. This process is accomplished by using both **setColumnSelectionAllowed( )** and **setRowSelectionAllowed( )**. The **setColumnSelectionAllowed( )** method is shown here:

void setColumnSelectionAllowed(boolean *enabled*)

When *enabled* is true, column selection is enabled. When it is false, column selection is disabled. The **setRowSelectionAllowed( )** method is shown next:

void setRowSelectionAllowed(booleadn *enabled*)

When *enabled* is true, row selection is enabled. When it is false, row selection is disabled. After turning on column selection and turning off row selection, clicking on the table results in a column (rather than a row) being selected.

There are two different ways to enable individual cell selection. First, you can enable both column selection and row selection. Because row selection is on by default, this means that if you simply turn on column selection, then both will be enabled. This condition causes cell selection to be turned on.

The second way to enable cell selection is to call **setCellSelectionEnabled( )**, shown here:

    void setCellSelectionEnabled(boolean *on*)

If *on* is true, then cell selection is enabled. If *on* is false, then cell selection is disabled. This method translates into calls to **setRowSelectionAllowed( )** and **setColumnSelectionAllowed( )** with *on* passed as an argument. Thus, you need to be a bit careful when using this method to turn off cell selection. It will result in both row and column selection also being turned off, which means that nothing can be selected! Thus, the best way to turn off cell selection is to turn off *either* row or column selection.

    JTable defines a *selection mode,* which determines how many items can be selected at any one time. By default, **JTable** allows the user to select multiple items. You can change this behavior by calling **setSelectionMode( )**. It is shown here:

    void setSelectionMode(int *mode*)

Here, *mode* specifies the selection mode. It must be one of the following values, which are defined by **ListSelectionModel**:

SINGLE_SELECTION	One row, column, or cell can be selected.
SINGLE_INTERVAL_SELECTION	A single range of rows, columns, or cells can be selected.
MULTIPLE_INTERVAL_SELECTION	Multiple ranges of rows, columns, or cells can be selected. This is the default.

Notice that **MULTIPLE_INTERVAL_SELECTION** is the default mode.

Example

The following example demonstrates **JTable**. It uses a table to display status information about orders for items purchased from an online store. Although the program does not handle any table events (see the following recipe for details on table events), it is still a fully functional table. For example, the widths of the columns can be adjusted and the position of the columns relative to each other can be changed. The program also includes radio buttons that let you switch between row, column, and cell selection. You can also switch between single-selection mode and multiple-selection mode by checking or clearing a check box.

```
// Demonstrate JTable.
//
// This program simply displays a table. It does not
// handle any table events. See "Handle JTable Events"
// for information on table events.

import java.awt.*;
import java.awt.event.*;
import javax.swing.*;
import javax.swing.event.*;
import javax.swing.table.*;
```

```
class TableDemo implements ActionListener {

  String[] headings = { "Name", "Customer ID",
                        "Order #", "Status" };

  Object[][] data = {
    { "Tom", new Integer(34723), "T-01023", "Shipped" },
    { "Wendy", new Integer(67263), "W-43Z88", "Shipped" },
    { "Steve", new Integer(97854), "S-98301", "Back Ordered" },
    { "Adam", new Integer(70851), "A-19287", "Pending" },
    { "Larry", new Integer(40952), "L-18567", "Shipped" },
    { "Mark", new Integer(88992), "M-22345", "Cancelled" },
    { "Terry", new Integer(67492), "T-18269", "Back Ordered" }
  };

  JTable jtabOrders;

  JRadioButton jrbRows;
  JRadioButton jrbColumns;
  JRadioButton jrbCells;

  JCheckBox jcbSingle;

  TableDemo() {

    // Create a new JFrame container.
    JFrame jfrm = new JFrame("JTable Demo");

    // Specify FlowLayout for the layout manager.
    jfrm.setLayout(new FlowLayout());

    // Give the frame an initial size.
    jfrm.setSize(460, 180);

    // Terminate the program when the user closes the application.
    jfrm.setDefaultCloseOperation(JFrame.EXIT_ON_CLOSE);

    // Create a table that displays order data.
    jtabOrders = new JTable(data, headings);

    // Wrap the table in a scroll pane.
    JScrollPane jscrlp = new JScrollPane(jtabOrders);

    // Set the scrollable viewport size.
    jtabOrders.setPreferredScrollableViewportSize(
            new Dimension(420, 62));

    // Create the radio buttons that determine
    // what type of selections are allowed.
    jrbRows = new JRadioButton("Select Rows", true);
    jrbColumns = new JRadioButton("Select Columns");
    jrbCells = new JRadioButton("Select Cells");
```

```
    // Add the radio buttons to a group.
    ButtonGroup bg = new ButtonGroup();
    bg.add(jrbRows);
    bg.add(jrbColumns);
    bg.add(jrbCells);

    // Radio button events are handled in common by the
    // actionPerformed() method implemented by TableDemo.
    jrbRows.addActionListener(this);
    jrbColumns.addActionListener(this);
    jrbCells.addActionListener(this);

    // Create the Single Selection Mode check box.
    // When checked, only single selections are allowed.
    jcbSingle = new JCheckBox("Single Selection Mode");

    // Add item listener for jcbSingle.
    jcbSingle.addItemListener(new ItemListener() {

      public void itemStateChanged(ItemEvent ie) {
        if(jcbSingle.isSelected())
          // Allow single selections.
          jtabOrders.setSelectionMode(
                    ListSelectionModel.SINGLE_SELECTION);
        else
          // Allow multiple selections.
          jtabOrders.setSelectionMode(
                    ListSelectionModel.MULTIPLE_INTERVAL_SELECTION);
      }
    });

    // Add the components to the content pane.
    jfrm.add(jscrlp);
    jfrm.add(jrbRows);
    jfrm.add(jrbColumns);
    jfrm.add(jrbCells);
    jfrm.add(jcbSingle);

    // Display the frame.
    jfrm.setVisible(true);
}

// This handles the row, column, and cell selection buttons.
public void actionPerformed(ActionEvent ie) {

  // See which button is selected.
  if(jrbRows.isSelected()) {
    // Enable row selection.
    jtabOrders.setColumnSelectionAllowed(false);
    jtabOrders.setRowSelectionAllowed(true);
  }
  else if(jrbColumns.isSelected()) {
    // Enable column selection.
```

```
        jtabOrders.setColumnSelectionAllowed(true);
        jtabOrders.setRowSelectionAllowed(false);
      }
      else {
        // Enable cell selection.
        jtabOrders.setCellSelectionEnabled(true);
      }

    }

    public static void main(String args[]) {
      // Create the frame on the event dispatching thread.
      SwingUtilities.invokeLater(new Runnable() {
        public void run() {
          new TableDemo();
        }
      });
    }
  }
```

The output is shown here:

Options and Alternatives

JTable is a very sophisticated, feature-rich component. It is far beyond the scope of this book to examine all of its options or customizations. However, a few of the more common ones are mentioned here. If you will be making extensive use of tables, then you will want to study the capabilities of this component in depth. (For information on handling table events, see the following recipe.)

If you are constructing a table from a fixed set of data that can be easily stored in an array, then the constructor used by the example is the easiest way to create a **JTable**. However, in cases in which the size of the data set is subject to change, or when its size is not easily known in advance, such as when the data is being obtained from a collection, it can be easier to use the following constructor:

JTable(Vector *data*, Vector *headerNames*)

In this case, *data* is a **Vector** of **Vector**s. Each **Vector** must contain as many elements as there are header names specified by *headerNames*. Since **Vector**s are dynamic data structures, the size of the data does not need to be known in advance.

JTable supports several *resizing modes,* which control the way that column widths are changed when the user adjusts the size of a column by dragging its header border. By default, when you change the width of a column, all subsequent columns (that is, all columns to the right of the one being changed) are adjusted in width so that the overall width of the table is unchanged. Any columns prior to the one being changed remain as-is. However, this default behavior is just one of five different resize modes from which you can select.

To change the resize mode, use the **setAutoResizeMode( )** method, shown here:

void setAutoResizeMode(int *how*)

Here, *how* must be one of five constants defined by **JTable**. They are shown here:

AUTO_RESIZE_ALL_COLUMNS	The widths of all columns are adjusted when the width of one column is changed.
AUTO_RESIZE_LAST_COLUMN	The width of only the rightmost column is adjusted when a column is changed.
AUTO_RESIZE_NEXT_COLUMN	The width of only the next column is adjusted when a column is changed.
AUTO_RESIZE_OFF	No column adjustments are made. Instead, the table width is changed. If the table is wrapped in a scroll pane and the table width is expanded beyond the bounds of the viewport, then the viewport remains the same size and a horizontal scroll bar is added that allows the table to be scrolled left and right to bring the other columns into view. When the table is first created, the columns are not necessarily sized to fill the table width. Thus, if you turn auto-resize off, you may need to specify the columns widths manually.
AUTO_RESIZE_SUBSEQUENT_COLUMNS	The widths of all columns to the right of the column being changed are adjusted. This is the default setting.

The best way to understand the effects of the various resize modes is to experiment. One other point: when you use **AUTO_RESIZE_OFF**, you must take a significant amount of manual control over the table. As a general rule, you should use this option only as a last resort. It is usually better to let **JTable** handle the resizing for you automatically.

One option that you will find very useful is **JTable**'s ability to print a table. This is accomplished by calling **print( )**. This method has several forms and was added by Java 5. Its simplest form is shown here:

boolean print( ) throws java.awt.print.PrinterException

It returns true if the table is printed and false if the user cancels the printing. This method causes the standard Print dialog to be displayed. For example, to print the **jtabOrders** table used in the example, you can use the following code sequence:

```
try {
  jtabOrders.print();
} catch (java.awt.print.PrinterException exc) { // ... }
```

Other versions of **print( )** let you specify various options, including a header and a footer.

You can control whether or not the table displays grid lines (which are the lines between cells) by calling **setShowGrid( )**. By default, the grid lines are shown. If you pass false to this method, the grid lines are not shown. Alternatively, you can control the display of the horizontal and vertical grid lines independently by calling **setShowVerticalLines( )** and **setShowHorizontalLines( )**.

Here are three other customizations that you may find of value. First, you can create your own table model, which lets you control how the data in a table is obtained. This enables you to easily handle cases in which the data is dynamically obtained or computed. Second, you can create your own cell renderers, which let you specify how the data in the table should be displayed. Third, you can define your own cell editors. A cell editor is the component invoked when the user edits the data within a cell. Thus, a cell editor determines how a cell can be edited.

Handle JTable Events

Key Ingredients	
Classes and Interfaces	**Methods**
javax.swing.event.ListSelectionEvent	
javax.swing.event.ListSelectionListener	void valueChanged(ListSelectionEvent *le*)
javax.swing.ListSelectionModel	void addListSelectionListener(ListSelectionListener *lsl*)
javax.swing.event.TableModelEvent	int getColumn( ) int getFirstRow( ) int getType( )
javax.swing.event.TableModelListener	void tableChanged(TableModelEvent *tme*)
javax.swing.JTable	TableColumnModel getColumnModel( ) int getSelectedColumn( ) int [ ] getSelectedColumns( ) int getSelectedRow( ) int [ ] getSelectedRows( ) TableModel getModel( ) ListSelectionModel getSelectionModel( )
javax.swing.table.TableModel	void addTableModelListener(TableModelListener *tml*) Object getValueAt(int *row*, int *column*)

The preceding recipe describes the basic techniques required to create a **JTable** and use it to display data. This recipe shows how to handle two important events generated by the table: **ListSelectionEvent** and **TableModelEvent**. A **ListSelectionEvent** is generated when the user selects something in the table. A **TableModelEvent** is fired when a table changes in some way. By handling these events, you can respond when the user interacts with the table. Although neither of these events is difficult to handle, both require a bit more work than you might expect because of the various models that are used by **JTable**.

Step-by-Step

Handling a **ListSelectionEvent** generated when a row is selected involves these steps:

1. Register a **ListSelectionListener** with the **ListSelectionModel** used by the table. This model is obtained by calling **getSelectionModel( )** on the **JTable**.

2. You can determine which row or rows are selected by calling **getSelectedRow( )** or **getSelectedRows( )** on the **JTable**.

Handling a **ListSelectionEvent** generated when a column is selected involves these steps:

1. Register a **ListSelectionListener** with the **ListSelectionModel** used by the table's column model. This model is obtained by first calling **getColumnModel( )** on the **JTable**, and then calling **getSelectionModel( )** on the column model reference.

2. You can determine which column or columns are selected by calling **getSelectedColumn( )** or **getSelectedColumns( )** on the **JTable**.

Handling a **TableModelEvent** generated when a table's data changes involves these steps:

1. Register a **TableModelListener** with the table's **TableModel**. A reference to the **TableModel** is obtained by calling **getModel( )** on the **JTable** instance.

2. You can determine the nature of the change by calling **getType( )** on the **TableModelEvent** instance.

3. You can determine the indices of the changed cell by calling **getFirstRow( )** and **getColumn( )** on the **TableModelEvent** instance.

4. You can obtain the value of the cell that has changed by calling **getValueAt( )** on the **TableModelEvent** instance.

Discussion

When a row, column, or cell is selected within a table, a **ListSelectionEvent** is fired. To handle this event, you must register a **ListSelectionListener**. **ListSelectionEvent** and **ListSelectionListener** are described in *Work with JList,* and that discussion is not repeated here. Recall, however, that **ListSelectionListener** specifies only one method, called **valueChanged( )**, which is shown here:

```
void valueChanged(ListSelectionEvent le)
```

Here, *le* is a reference to the object that generated the event. Although **ListSelectionEvent** does provide some methods of its own, often you will interrogate the **JTable** object or its models to determine what has occurred.

To handle row selection events, you must register a **ListSelectionListener**. This listener is *not* added to the **JTable** instance. Instead, it is added to the list selection model. You obtain a reference to this model by calling **getSelectionModel( )** on the **JTable** instance. It is shown here:

ListSelectionModel getSelectionModel( )

The **ListSelectionModel** interface defines several methods that let you determine the state of the model. Much of its functionality is directly available in **JTable**. However, there is one method defined by **ListSelectionModel** that is useful: **getValueIsAdjusting( )**. It returns true if the selection process is still taking place and false when the selection process is over. (It works just like the method by the same name used by **JList** and **JScrollBar**, described in *Work with JList* and *Use a Scroll Bar*.)

Once a **ListSelectionEvent** has been retrieved, you can determine what row has been selected by calling **getSelectedRow( )** or **getSelectedRows( )**. They are shown here:

int getSelectedRow( )
int [ ] getSelectedRows( )

The **getSelectedRow( )** method returns the index of the first row selected, which will be the only row selected if single-selection mode is being used. If no row has been selected, then –1 is returned. When multiple selection is enabled (which it is by default), then call **getSelectedRows( )** to obtain a list of the indices of all selected rows. If no rows are selected, the array returned will have a length of zero. If only one row is selected, then the array will be exactly one element long. Thus, you can use **getSelectedRows( )** even when you are using a single-selection mode.

To handle column selection events, you must also register a **ListSelectionListener**. However, this listener is *not* registered with the list selection model provided by **JTable**. Instead, it must be registered with the list selection model used by the table's column model. (The model for each column is specified by its implementation of **TableColumnModel**.) You obtain a reference to this model by calling **getColumnModel( )** on the **JTable** instance. It is shown here:

TableColumnModel getColumnModel( )

Using the reference returned, you can obtain a reference to the **ListSelectionModel** used by the columns. Therefore, assuming a **JTable** called **jtable**, you will use a statement like this to obtain the list selection model for a column:

```
ListSelectionModel colSelMod = jtable.getColumnModel().getSelectionModel();
```

Once a **ListSelectionEvent** has been received, you can determine what column has been selected by calling **getSelectedColumn( )** or **getSelectedColumns( )** on the **JTable**. They are shown here:

int getSelectedColumn( )
int [ ] getSelectedColumns( )

The **getSelectedColumn( )** method returns the index of the first column selected, which will be the only column selected if single-selection mode is being used. If no column has been selected, then –1 is returned. When multiple selection is enabled (which it is by default), then call **getSelectedColumns( )** to obtain a list of the indices of all selected columns. If no columns are selected, the array returned will have a length of zero. If only one column is selected, then the array will be exactly one element long. Thus, you can use **getSelectedColumns( )** even when you are using a single-selection mode. One fact to keep firmly in mind is that the indices returned by these methods are relative to the view (in other words, the column positions displayed on the screen). Because the columns can be repositioned by the user, these indices might differ from that of the table model, which is fixed.

To handle cell selection, register listeners for both row and column selection events. Then, determine which cell was selected by obtaining both the row and the column index.

You can listen for changes to the table's data (such as when the user changes the value of a cell) by registering a **TableModelListener** with the table model. The table model is obtained by calling **getModel( )** on the **JTable** instance. It is shown here:

TableModel getModel( )

TableModel defines the **addTableModelListener( )** method, which you use to add a listener for **TableModelEvents**. It is shown here:

void addTableModelListener(TableModelListener *tml*)

TableModelListener defines only one method, **tableChanged( )**. It is shown next:

void tableChanged(TableModelEvent *tme*)

This method is called whenever the table model changes, which includes changes to the data, changes to the headers, and insertions or deletions of columns.

TableModelEvent defines the methods shown here:

Method	Description
int getColumn( )	Returns the zero-based index of the column in which the event occurred. A return value of **TableModelEvent.ALL_COLUMNS** means that all columns within the selected row were affected.
int getFirstRow( )	Returns the zero-based index of the first row in which the event occurred. If the header changed, the return value is **TableModelEvent.HEADER_ROW**.
int getLastRow( )	Returns the zero-based index of the last row in which the event occurred.
int getType( )	Returns a value that indicates what type of change occurred. It will be one of these values: **TableModelEvent.DELETE**, **TableModelEvent.INSERT**, or **TableModelEvent.UPDATE**.

The methods **getFirstRow( )**, **getLastRow( )**, and **getColumn( )** return the index of the row (or rows) and column that have been changed. This same information can be obtained by calling methods defined by **JTable** (as previously described), but sometimes it is more convenient to obtain it from the event object. However, you need to be careful because **getColumn( )** returns the column index as maintained by the table model. If the user rearranges the columns, then it will differ from the column index returned by a method such as **JTable**'s **getSelectedColumn( )**, which reflects the position of the columns in the current view. Therefore, don't mix the two indices.

Also notice **getType( )**. It returns a value that indicates what type of change has taken place. The possible return values, defined by **TableModelEvent**, are shown here:

DELETE	A row or column has been removed.
INSERT	A row or column has been added.
UPDATE	Cell data has changed.

Often, if cell data has been changed, your application will need to update the underlying data source to reflect this change. Thus, if your table allows cell editing, watching for **UPDATE** table model events is especially important.

When data inside a cell changes, you can obtain the new value by calling **getValueAt( )** on the model instance. It is shown here:

Object getValueAt(int *row*, int *column*)

Here, *row* and *column* specify the coordinates of the cell that changed.

Example

The following example shows the steps needed to handle list selection and table model events. Each time you select a new row, column, or cell (depending upon which selection option is chosen), the indices of the selected item are displayed. If you change the contents of a cell, then the updated contents are displayed along with the indices of the cell that changed.

```java
// Handle selection and model change events for a JTable.

import java.awt.*;
import java.awt.event.*;
import javax.swing.*;
import javax.swing.event.*;
import javax.swing.table.*;

class TableEventDemo implements ActionListener, ListSelectionListener {

  String[] headings = { "Name", "Customer ID",
                        "Order #", "Status" };

  Object[][] data = {
    { "Tom", new Integer(34723), "T-01023", "Shipped" },
    { "Wendy", new Integer(67263), "W-43Z88", "Shipped" },
    { "Steve", new Integer(97854), "S-98301", "Back Ordered" },
    { "Adam", new Integer(70851), "A-19287", "Pending" },
    { "Larry", new Integer(40952), "L-18567", "Shipped" },
    { "Mark", new Integer(88992), "M-22345", "Cancelled" },
    { "Terry", new Integer(67492), "T-18269", "Back Ordered" }
  };

  JTable jtabOrders;
```

```
JRadioButton jrbRows;
JRadioButton jrbColumns;
JRadioButton jrbCells;

JCheckBox jcbSingle;

JLabel jlab;
JLabel jlab2;

TableModel tm;

TableEventDemo() {

  // Create a new JFrame container.
  JFrame jfrm = new JFrame("JTable Event Demo");

  // Specify FlowLayout for the layout manager.
  jfrm.setLayout(new FlowLayout());

  // Give the frame an initial size.
  jfrm.setSize(460, 220);

  // Terminate the program when the user closes the application.
  jfrm.setDefaultCloseOperation(JFrame.EXIT_ON_CLOSE);

  // Create a label that will display a selection.
  jlab = new JLabel();
  jlab.setPreferredSize(new Dimension(400, 20));

  // Create a label that will display changes to a cell.
  jlab2 = new JLabel();
  jlab2.setPreferredSize(new Dimension(400, 20));

  // Create a table that displays order data.
  jtabOrders = new JTable(data, headings);

  // Wrap the table in a scroll pane.
  JScrollPane jscrlp = new JScrollPane(jtabOrders);

  // Set the scrollable viewport size.
  jtabOrders.setPreferredScrollableViewportSize(
              new Dimension(420, 62));

  // Get the list selection model for rows.
  ListSelectionModel rowSelMod = jtabOrders.getSelectionModel();

  // Get the list selection model for columns.
  ListSelectionModel colSelMod =
      jtabOrders.getColumnModel().getSelectionModel();

  // Listen for selection events.
  rowSelMod.addListSelectionListener(this);
  colSelMod.addListSelectionListener(this);
```

```java
// Get the table model.
tm = jtabOrders.getModel();

// Add a table model listener. This listens for
// changes to a cell's data.
tm.addTableModelListener(new TableModelListener() {

  public void tableChanged(TableModelEvent tme) {
    // If a cell's data changed, report it.
    if(tme.getType() == TableModelEvent.UPDATE) {
      jlab2.setText("Cell " + tme.getFirstRow() + ", " +
                    tme.getColumn() + " changed." +
                    " The new value: " +
                    tm.getValueAt(tme.getFirstRow(),
                                  tme.getColumn())));
    }
  }
});


// Create the radio buttons that determine
// what type of selections are allowed.
jrbRows = new JRadioButton("Select Rows", true);
jrbColumns = new JRadioButton("Select Columns");
jrbCells = new JRadioButton("Select Cells");

// Add the radio buttons to a group.
ButtonGroup bg = new ButtonGroup();
bg.add(jrbRows);
bg.add(jrbColumns);
bg.add(jrbCells);

// Radio button events are handled in common by the
// actionPerformed() method implemented by TableEventDemo.
jrbRows.addActionListener(this);
jrbColumns.addActionListener(this);
jrbCells.addActionListener(this);

// Create the Single Selection Mode check box.
// When checked, only single selections are allowed.
jcbSingle = new JCheckBox("Single Selection Mode");

// Add item listener for jcbSingle.
jcbSingle.addItemListener(new ItemListener() {

  public void itemStateChanged(ItemEvent ie) {
    if(jcbSingle.isSelected())
      // Allow single selections.
      jtabOrders.setSelectionMode(
                  ListSelectionModel.SINGLE_SELECTION);
    else
      // Return to the default selection mode, which
      // allows multiple interval selections.
```

```
          jtabOrders.setSelectionMode(
              ListSelectionModel.MULTIPLE_INTERVAL_SELECTION);
      }
    });

    // Add the components to the content pane.
    jfrm.add(jscrlp);
    jfrm.add(jrbRows);
    jfrm.add(jrbColumns);
    jfrm.add(jrbCells);
    jfrm.add(jcbSingle);

    jfrm.add(jlab);
    jfrm.add(jlab2);

    // Display the frame.
    jfrm.setVisible(true);
  }

  // This handles the row, column, and cell selection buttons.
  public void actionPerformed(ActionEvent ie) {

    // See which button is selected.
    if(jrbRows.isSelected()) {
      // Enable row selection.
      jtabOrders.setColumnSelectionAllowed(false);
      jtabOrders.setRowSelectionAllowed(true);
    }
    else if(jrbColumns.isSelected()) {
      // Enable column selection.
      jtabOrders.setColumnSelectionAllowed(true);
      jtabOrders.setRowSelectionAllowed(false);
    }
    else {
      // Enable cell selection.
      jtabOrders.setCellSelectionEnabled(true);
      jcbSingle.setSelected(true);
      jtabOrders.setSelectionMode(
                ListSelectionModel.SINGLE_SELECTION);
    }

  }

  // Handle selection events by displaying the indices
  // of the selected elements. All indices are relative
  // to the view. (See Options and Alternatives for
  // details on converting view indices to model indices.)
  public void valueChanged(ListSelectionEvent le) {
    String str;

    // Determine what has been selected.
    if(jrbRows.isSelected()) {
```

```
      str = "Selected Row(s): ";

      // Get a list of all selected rows.
      int[] rows = jtabOrders.getSelectedRows();

      // Create a string that contains the indices of the selected rows.
      for(int i=0; i < rows.length; i++)
        str += rows[i] + " ";

    } else if(jrbColumns.isSelected()) {

      str = "Selected Column(s): ";

      // Get a list of all selected columns.
      int[] cols = jtabOrders.getSelectedColumns();

      // Create a string that contains the indices of the selected columns.
      for(int i=0; i < cols.length; i++)
        str += cols[i] + " ";

    } else {
      str = "Selected Cell: (View Relative) " +
            jtabOrders.getSelectedRow() + ", " +
            jtabOrders.getSelectedColumn();
    }

    // Display the indices.
    jlab.setText(str);
  }

  public static void main(String args[]) {
    // Create the frame on the event dispatching thread.
    SwingUtilities.invokeLater(new Runnable() {
      public void run() {
        new TableEventDemo();
      }
    });
  }
}
```

The output is shown here:

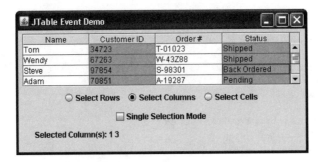

Options and Alternatives

Because the order of the columns displayed on the screen can change, such as when the user drags a column to a new location, the column index returned by methods such as **getSelectedColumn( )** or **getSelectedColumns( )** may differ from the index used by the model. This may be an issue in cases in which you want to use the index to access the data in the model. To handle this situation, **JTable** supplies the **convertColumnIndexToModel( )** method. It is shown here:

    int convertColumnIndexToModel(int *viewIdx*)

It returns the model index of the column that corresponds to the view index passed in *viewIdx*. You can also perform the reverse operation, converting a model column index into a view index, by calling **convertColumnIndexToView( )**. It is shown here:

    int convertColumnIndexToView(int *modelIdx*)

It returns the view index of the column that corresponds to the model index passed in *modelIdx*.

    For example, in the preceding example, you can display the model indexes rather than the view indexes of the selected columns by substituting this sequence in the portion of the **valueChanged( )** method that displays column selections:

```
// Create a string that contains the model-relative indices of the selected columns.
for(int i=0; i < cols.length; i++)
  str += jtabOrders.convertColumnIndexToModel(cols[i]) + " ";
```

    Begining with Java 6 it is easy to allow the user to sort the data in a table based on the entries in a column. Sorting results in a rearrangement of the rows, which can result in the index of any given row in the view being different than its index in the model. Because of this, Java 6 added the methods **convertRowIndexToModel( )** and **convertRowIndexToView( )**. They work like their column-oriented counterparts.

    To enable the user to sort data, you must set the row sorter by calling **setRowSorter( )**. This method was added by Java 6 and is shown here:

    void setRowSorter(RowSorter<? extends TableModel> *rowSorter*)

The row sorter is specified by *rowSorter*, which is an instance of the **RowSorter** class. For the sorting of rows in a **JTable**, this can be an instance of **javax.swing.table.TableRowSorter**. For example, to enable sorting for the **jtabOrders** table used by the example, add this line:

```
jtabOrders.setRowSorter(new TableRowSorter<TableModel>(tm));
```

After making this change, the rows can be sorted by column entries by simply clicking on the desired column heading.

    You can set the data in a cell under program control by calling **setValueAt( )** on the table model. It is shown here:

    void setValueAt(Object *val*, int *row*, int *column*)

It sets the value of the cell located at *row* and *column* to the *val*. For both methods, the values of *row* and *column* are relative to the model, not the view.

Display Data in a JTree

Key Ingredients	
Classes and Interfaces	**Methods**

javax.swing.JTree	void addTreeExpansionListener(
	            TreeExpansionListener *tel*)
	void addTreeSelectionListener(
	            TreeSelectionListener *tsl*)
	TreeModel getModel( )
	TreeSelectionModel
	            getSelectionModel( )
	void setEditable(boolean *on*)

javax.swing.tree.DefaultMutableTreeNode	void add(MutableTreeNode *child*)
javax.swing.tree.TreeModel	void addTreeModelListener(TreeModelListener *tml*)
javax.swing.tree.TreeExpansionEvent	TreePath getPath( )

javax.swing.tree.TreeExpansionListener	void treeCollapsed(
	            TreeExpansionEvent *tee*)
	void treeExpanded(
	            TreeExpansionEvent *tee*)

javax.swing.tree.TreeModelEvent	Object[ ] getChildren( ) TreePath getTreePath( )

javax.swing.tree.TreeModelListener	void treeNodesChanged(
	            TreeModelEvent *tme*)
	void treeStructureChanged(
	            TreeModelEvent *tme*)
	void treeNodesInserted(
	            TreeModelEvent *tme*)
	void treeNodesRemoved(
	            TreeModelEvent *tme*)

javax.swing.tree.TreePath	Object getLastPathComponent( ) Object[ ] getPath( )
javax.swing.tree.TreeSelectionEvent	TreePath getPath( )
javax.swing.tree.TreeSelectionListener	void valueChanged(TreeSelectionEvent *tse*)
javax.swing.tree.TreeSelectionModel	void setSelectionMode(int *how*)

JTree presents a hierarchical view of data in a tree-like format. This makes a **JTree** best suited for displaying data that can be ordered into categories and subcategories. For example, a tree is commonly used to display the contents of a file system. In this case, the individual files are subordinate to the directory that contains them, which itself might be subordinate to another, higher-level directory. In the tree, branches can be expanded or collapsed on demand, by the user. This allows the tree to present hierarchical data in a compact, yet expandable form.

JTree is packaged inside **javax.swing**, but many of its support classes and interfaces are found in **javax.swing.tree**. A separate package is used because a large number of interfaces and classes are related to trees. **JTree** supports many customizations and options—far more than can be described in this recipe. Fortunately, the defaults provided by **JTree** are sufficient for a large number of applications. Frankly, given the sophistication of **JTree**, it is surprisingly easy to work with.

JTree supports a conceptually simple, tree-based data structure. A tree begins with a single *root node* that indicates the start of the tree. Under the root are one or more *child nodes*. There are two types of child nodes: *leaf nodes* (also called *terminal nodes*), which have no children, and *branch nodes*, which form the root nodes of *subtrees*. A subtree is simply a tree that is part of a larger tree. The sequence of nodes that leads from the root to a specific node is called a *path*.

Each node has associated with it a *cell renderer,* which determines how the information is displayed, and a *cell editor,* which determines how the user edits the information. **JTree** supplies default cell renderers and editors that are suitable for many (perhaps most) applications. As you would expect, it is possible to specify your own custom renderers and editors if desired.

JTree does not provide any scrolling capabilities of its own, but you will almost always need to provide them. As one soon finds out when working with **JTree**, it takes only a small amount to data to produce a tree that is quite large when fully expanded. Instead of trying to create a **JTree** large enough to hold a fully expanded tree (which won't even be possible in many cases), it is better to wrap a **JTree** in a **JScrollPane**. This lets the user scroll through the tree, bringing the portion of interest into view.

JTree relies on two models: **TreeModel** and **TreeSelectionModel**. The **TreeModel** interface defines those things related to displaying data in a tree format. Swing provides a default implementation of this model called **DefaultTreeModel**. Both **TreeModel** and **DefaultTreeModel** are packaged in **javax.swing.tree**. The **TreeSelectionModel** interface determines how items are selected. It is also packaged in **javax.swing.tree**.

JTree can generate a variety of events, but three relate directly to trees: **TreeSelectionEvent**, **TreeExpansionEvent**, and **TreeModelEvent**. These events are generated when an item in the tree is selected, when the tree is expanded or collapsed, and when the data in the tree changes, respectively. They are packaged in **javax.swing.event**.

Each node in a tree is an instance of the **TreeNode** interface. Thus, a **JTree** is a collection of **TreeNode** objects. The **MutableTreeNode** interface extends **TreeNode** and defines the behavior of nodes that are mutable (i.e., that can be changed). Swing provides a default implementation of **MutableTreeNode** called **DefaultMutableTreeNode**. This class is appropriate for a wide variety of tree nodes, and it is used for creating the nodes in this recipe.

Step-by-Step

To display data in a **JTree** involves these steps:

1. Create the nodes that will be displayed. This recipes uses nodes of type **DefaultMutableTreeNode**.

2. Create the desired tree hierarchy by adding one node to another. Make one of the nodes the root.

3. Create an instance of **JTree**, passing in the root node.

4. When the user selects an item in the tree, a **TreeSelectionEvent** is generated. To listen for this event, register a **TreeSelectionListener** with the **JTree**.

5. When the tree is expanded or collapsed, a **TreeExpansionEvent** is generated. To listen for this event, register a **TreeExpansionListener** with the **JTree**.

6. When the data or structure of the tree changes, a **TreeModelEvent** is generated. To listen for this event, register a **TreeModelListener** with the tree's model. To obtain a reference to the model, call **getModel( )** on the **JTree** instance. Using the event object, you can obtain information about the path that changed.

7. You can change the selection mode by calling **setSelectionMode( )** on the tree selection model. (The tree selection model is obtained by calling **getSelectionModel( )** on the **JTree** instance.)

8. You can allow a tree node to be edited by calling **setEditable( )** on the **JTree** instance.

Discussion

JTree defines many constructors. The one used by this recipe is shown here:

JTree(TreeNode *tn*)

This constructs a tree that has *tn* as its root.

A **JTree** holds a collection of objects that represent the tree. These objects must be instances of the **TreeNode** interface. It declares methods that encapsulate information about a tree node. For example, it is possible to obtain a reference to the parent node or an enumeration of the child nodes. You can also determine if a node is a leaf. The **MutableTreeNode** interface extends **TreeNode**. It defines a node that can have its data changed, or have child nodes added or removed. Swing provides a default implementation of **MutableTreeNode** called **DefaultMutableTreeNode**. This is the class that is used by this recipe to construct nodes for the tree.

DefaultMutableTreeNode defines three constructors. The one used by this recipe is

DefaultMutableTreeNode(Object *obj*)

Here, *obj* is the object to be enclosed in this tree node. In order to create a hierarchy of tree nodes, one node is added to another. This is accomplished by calling the **add( )** method of **DefaultMutableTreeNode**. It is shown here:

void add(MutableTreeNode *child*)

Here, *child* is a mutable tree node that will be added as a child of the invoking node. Thus, to build a tree, you will create a root node and then add subordinate nodes to it.

To listen for a **TreeSelectionEvent**, you must implement the **TreeSelectionListener** interface and register the listener with the **JTree** instance. **TreeSelectionListener** defines the following method:

    void valueChanged(TreeSelectionEvent *tse*)

Here, *tse* is the selection event.

TreeSelectionEvent defines several methods. One of particular interest is **getPath( )** because it is used by this recipe. It is shown here:

    TreePath getPath( )

The path that leads to the selection is returned as a **TreePath** object.

TreePath is a class packaged in **javax.swing.tree**. It encapsulates a path that leads from the root of the tree to the node selected. **TreePath** defines several methods. Two are of special interest:

    Object[ ] getPath( )
    Object getLastPathComponent( )

The **getPath( )** method returns an array of objects that represent all nodes in the path. The **getLastPathComponent( )** returns a reference to the last node in the path.

To listen for a **TreeExpansionEvent**, you must implement the **TreeExpansionListener** interface and register the listener with the **JTree** instance. **TreeExpansionListener** defines the following two methods:

    void treeCollapsed(TreeExpansionEvent *tee*)
    void treeExpanded(TreeExpansionEvent *tee*)

Here, *tee* is the tree expansion event. The first method is called when a subtree is hidden, and the second method is called when a subtree becomes visible. As a point of interest, **JTree** allows you to listen for two types of tree expansion notifications. First, you can be notified *just before* an expansion event by registering a **TreeWillExpandListener**. Second, you can be notified after the expansion event by registering a **TreeExpansionListener**. Usually, you will register a **TreeExpansionListener**, as this recipe does, but Swing gives you the choice.

TreeExpansionEvent defines only one method, **getPath( )**, which is shown here.

    TreePath getPath( )

This method returns a **TreePath** object that contains the path to the node that was or will be expanded or collaspsed.

To listen for a **TreeModelEvent**, you must implement the **TreeModelListener** interface and register the listener with the tree model. **TreeModelListener** defines the following methods:

    void treeNodesChanged(TreeModelEvent *tme*)
    void treeStructureChanged(TreeModelEvent *tme*)
    void treeNodesInserted(TreeModelEvent *tme*)
    void treeNodesRemoved(TreeModelEvent *tme*)

Here, *tme* is the tree model event. The names imply the type of model event that has occurred. Of these, only **treeNodesChanged( )** is used by this recipe.

TreeModelEvent defines several methods. Two are used by this recipe. The first is shown here:

TreePath getTreePath( )

This method returns the path to the parent of the node at which point the change occurred. The second is

Object[ ] getChildren( )

This method returns an array that contains references to the node(s) that changed. This node (or nodes) will be child nodes of the last node in the path returned by **getTreePath( )**. If the returned value is **null**, then it is the root node that changed. Otherwise, the changed node or nodes are returned in an array. In the example that follows, only one node can change at a time, so a reference to the changed node is found at the first location in the returned array.

As mentioned, a tree model listener must be registered with the tree model, not with the **JTree** instance. The tree model is obtained by calling **getModel( )** on the **JTree** instance. It is shown here:

TreeModel getModel( )

The default **TreeModel** is **DefaultTreeModel**. This is the model that is used if you don't specify a model of your own.

JTree supports three selection modes, which are defined by **TreeSelectionModel**. They are shown here:

CONTIGUOUS_TREE_SELECTION
DISCONTIGUOUS_TREE_SELECTION
SINGLE_TREE_SELECTION

By default, trees support discontiguous selection. You can change the selection mode by calling **setSelectionMode( )** on the tree selection model, passing in the new node. The model is obtained by calling **getSelectionModel( )** on the **JTree** instance. Both methods are shown here:

TreeSelectionModel getSelectionModel( )
void setSelectionMode(int *how*)

Here, *how* must be one of the values just mentioned.

By default, a tree is not editable. That is, the contents of its nodes cannot be edited by the user. To enable editing, call **setEditable( )**, shown here:

void setEditable(boolean *on*)

To enable editing, pass true to *on*.

Example

The following example demonstrates **JTree**. It creates a small tree that shows the derivation of several Swing components. In this example, the node that represents **JComponent** is the root. Subtrees representing buttons and text components are then added.

```
// Demonstrate JTree.

import java.awt.*;
import javax.swing.*;
import javax.swing.event.*;
import javax.swing.tree.*;

class TreeDemo {

  JLabel jlab;

  TreeDemo() {
    // Create a new JFrame container.
    JFrame jfrm = new JFrame("JTree Demo");

    // Specify FlowLayout for the layout manager.
    jfrm.setLayout(new FlowLayout());

    // Give the frame an initial size.
    jfrm.setSize(260, 240);

    // Terminate the program when the user closes the application.
    jfrm.setDefaultCloseOperation(JFrame.EXIT_ON_CLOSE);

    // Create a label that will display the tree selection
    // and set its size.
    jlab = new JLabel();
    jlab.setPreferredSize(new Dimension(230, 50));

    // Create a tree that shows the relationship of several
    // Swing classes.

    // First, create the root node of the tree.
    DefaultMutableTreeNode root =
                 new DefaultMutableTreeNode("JComponent");

    // Next, create two subtrees.  One begins with
    // AbstractButton and the other with JTextComponent.

    // Create the root of the AbstractButton subtree.
    DefaultMutableTreeNode absBtnNode =
                 new DefaultMutableTreeNode("AbstractButton");
    root.add(absBtnNode); // add the AbstractButton node to the tree.

    // The AbstractButton subtree has two nodes:
    // JButton and JToggleButton. Under JToggleButton
    // are JCheckBox and JRadioButton. These nodes
    // are created by the following statements.
```

```
// Create the nodes under AbstractButton.
DefaultMutableTreeNode jbtnNode =
                new DefaultMutableTreeNode("JButton");
absBtnNode.add(jbtnNode); // add JButton to AbstractButton

DefaultMutableTreeNode jtoggleNode =
                new DefaultMutableTreeNode("JToggleButton");
absBtnNode.add(jtoggleNode); // add JToggleButton to AbstractButton

// Add a subtree under JToggleButton.
jtoggleNode.add(new DefaultMutableTreeNode("JCheckBox"));
jtoggleNode.add(new DefaultMutableTreeNode("JRadioButton"));

// Now, create a JTextComponent subtree.
DefaultMutableTreeNode jtxtCompNode =
                new DefaultMutableTreeNode("JTextComponent");
root.add(jtxtCompNode); // add JTextComponent to the root

// Populate the JTextComponent subtree.
DefaultMutableTreeNode jtxtFieldNode =
                new DefaultMutableTreeNode("JTextField");
jtxtCompNode.add(jtxtFieldNode);
jtxtCompNode.add(new DefaultMutableTreeNode("JTextArea"));
jtxtCompNode.add(new DefaultMutableTreeNode("JEditorPane"));

// Create a subtree under JTextField.
jtxtFieldNode.add(new DefaultMutableTreeNode("JFormattedTextField"));
jtxtFieldNode.add(new DefaultMutableTreeNode("JPasswordField"));

// Now, create a JTree that uses the structure
// defined by the preceding statements.
JTree jtree = new JTree(root);

// Allow the tree to be edited so that model
// events can be generated.
jtree.setEditable(true);

// Set the tree selection mode to single-selection.
TreeSelectionModel tsm = jtree.getSelectionModel();
tsm.setSelectionMode(TreeSelectionModel.SINGLE_TREE_SELECTION);

// Wrap the tree in a scroll pane.
JScrollPane jscrlp = new JScrollPane(jtree);

// Set the preferred size of the scroll pane.
jscrlp.setPreferredSize(new Dimension(160, 140));

// Listen for tree expansion events.
jtree.addTreeExpansionListener(new TreeExpansionListener() {
  public void treeExpanded(TreeExpansionEvent tee) {
    // Get the path to the expansion point.
    TreePath tp = tee.getPath();
```

```
      // Display the node.
      jlab.setText("Expansion: " +
                   tp.getLastPathComponent());
    }

    public void treeCollapsed(TreeExpansionEvent tee) {
      // Get the path to the expansion point.
      TreePath tp = tee.getPath();

      // Display the node.
      jlab.setText("Collapse: " +
                   tp.getLastPathComponent());
    }
  });

  // Listen for tree selection events.
  jtree.addTreeSelectionListener(new TreeSelectionListener() {
    public void valueChanged(TreeSelectionEvent tse) {
      // Get the path to the selection.
      TreePath tp = tse.getPath();

      // Display the selected node.
      jlab.setText("Selection event: " +
                   tp.getLastPathComponent());
    }
  });

  // Listen for tree model events. Notice that the
  // listener is registered with the tree model.
  jtree.getModel().addTreeModelListener(new TreeModelListener() {
    public void treeNodesChanged(TreeModelEvent tme) {

      // Get the path to the parent of the node that changed.
      TreePath tp = tme.getTreePath();

      // Get the children of the parent of the node that changed.
      Object[] children = tme.getChildren();

      DefaultMutableTreeNode changedNode;

      if(children != null)
        changedNode = (DefaultMutableTreeNode) children[0];
      else
        changedNode = (DefaultMutableTreeNode) tp.getLastPathComponent();


      // Display the path.
      jlab.setText("<html>Model change path: " + tp + "<br>" +
                   "New data: " + changedNode.getUserObject());

    }
```

```
      // Empty implementations of the remaining TreeModelEvent
      // methods. Implement these if your application
      // needs to handle these actions.
      public void treeNodesInserted(TreeModelEvent tme) {}
      public void treeNodesRemoved(TreeModelEvent tme) {}
      public void treeStructureChanged(TreeModelEvent tme) {}
    });

    // Add the tree and label to the content pane.
    jfrm.add(jscrlp);
    jfrm.add(jlab);

    // Display the frame.
    jfrm.setVisible(true);
  }

  public static void main(String args[]) {
    // Create the frame on the event dispatching thread.
    SwingUtilities.invokeLater(new Runnable() {
      public void run() {
        new TreeDemo();
      }
    });
  }
}
```

The output is shown here:

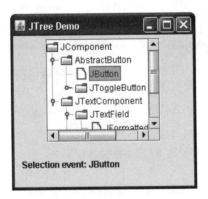

Options and Alternatives

Like **JTable**, **JTree** is a very sophisticated control that supports many options and allows a substantial amount of customization—so much so that it is not possible to discussion them all. However, a few of the more popular ones are mentioned here.

You can cause a node to become visible (that is, to be brought into view) by calling **makeVisible( )** on the **JTree** instance. It is shown here:

    void makeVisible(TreePath *pathToNode*)

The path to the desired node is specified by *pathToNode*. For example, if you add this line to the preceding program immediately after **jtree** is declared, then the **JTextField** node will be visible when the tree is first displayed:

```
jtree.makeVisible(new TreePath(jtxtFieldNode.getPath()));
```

In general, a common use for **makeVisible( )** is to cause a node to be displayed when the tree is first displayed. For example, if a tree is used to present help information, then the requested help topic is made visible in the tree.

Depending on the look and feel, the root node may or may not have *handles* associated with it. (A handle is a small icon that indicates whether a branch is expanded or collapsed.) You can turn on or off the root handles by calling **setShowsRootHandles( )**, shown here:

void setShowsRootHandles(boolean *on*)

If *on* is true, the root handles are shown. Otherwise, they are not shown.

You can modify the contents of a tree by using one or more of the methods provided by **DefaultMutableTreeNode**. For example, you can change the contents of a node by calling **setUserObject( )**, shown here:

void setUserObject(Object *obj*)

Here, *obj* becomes the new object associated with the invoking node. You can remove a node by calling **remove( )** on the parent node. One form is shown here:

void remove(MutableTreeNode *node*)

Here, *node* must be a child of the invoking node.

You can determine if a node is a leaf by calling **isLeaf( )** on the node. It is shown here:

boolean isLeaf( )

It returns true if the invoking node is a terminal node (one without any child nodes). It returns false otherwise.

You can determine if a node is the root by calling **isRoot( )** on the node. It is shown here:

boolean isRoot( )

It returns true if the invoking node is the root. It returns false otherwise.

DefaultMutableTreeNode also defines this set of methods that perform various traversals of the nodes:

Enumeration breadthFirstEnumeration( )
Enumeration depthFirstEnumeration( )
Enumeration postorderEnumeration( )
Enumeration preorderEnumeration( )

Each returns the specified enumeration. Beginning at the root, a breadth-first traversal visits all nodes on the same level before advancing to the next level. A depth-first traversal (which is the same as a postorder traversal) first visits the leaves and then the root of each subtree. A preorder traversal visits the root followed by the leaves of each subtree.

You can also define custom cell renderers and editors for a tree. These give you control over how the items in the tree are displayed and how they are edited. When working with trees, you will want to explore not just **JTree**, but **TreeNode**, **DefaultMutableTreeNode**, and **TreePath**, along with **TreeModel** and **TreeSelectionModel**, to take full advantage of the customizations and options available.

Create a Main Menu

Key Ingredients	
Classes and Interfaces	**Methods**
java.awt.event.ActionEvent	String getActionCommand( )
java.awt.event.ActionListener	void actionPerformed(ActionEvent *ae*)
javax.swing.JFrame	void setJMenuBar(JMenuBar *mb*)
javax.swing.JMenu	JMenuItem add(JMenuItem *item*) void addSeparator( )
javax.swing.JMenuBar	JMenu add(JMenu *menu*)
javax.swing.JMenuItem	

Swing supports an extensive subsystem dedicated to menus. For example, you can create a main menu, a popup menu, and a toolbar. You can also add keyboard accelerators, mnemonics, and images, and you can use radio button and check box style menu items. Frankly, an entire book could be dedicated to Swing's menu subsystem. Thus, it is not possible to detail it here. However, this recipe shows how to create one of the most important menus: the main menu. Many of the techniques described here are also applicable to other types of menus.

As most readers will know, the main menu of an application is displayed in the menu bar of the main frame of the application. It is typically displayed across the top of the frame, and it is the menu that defines all (or nearly all) of the functionality of an application. For example, the main menu will include items such as File, Edit, and Help.

Swing defines several menu-related classes. The ones used by this recipe are shown here:

JMenuBar	An object that holds the top-level menu for the application.
JMenu	A standard menu. A menu consists of one or more **JMenuItem**s.
JMenuItem	An object that populates menus.

These classes work together to form the main menu of an application. **JMenuBar** is, loosely speaking, a container for menus. A **JMenuBar** instance holds one or more instances of **JMenu**. Each **JMenu** object defines a menu. That is, each **JMenu** object contains one or more selectable items. The items displayed by a **JMenu** are objects of **JMenuItem**. Thus, a **JMenuItem** defines a selection that can be chosen by the user.

Another key point is that **JMenuItem** is a superclass of **JMenu**. This allows the creation of submenus, which are, essentially, menus within menus. To create a submenu, you first create and populate a **JMenu** object and then add it to another **JMenu** object.

Swing's menuing system also relies on two important interfaces: **SingleSelectionModel** and **MenuElement**. **SingleSelectionModel** determines the actions of a component that contains multiple elements, but from which one and only one element can be selected at any one time. This model is used by **JMenuBar**. There is a default implementation called **DefaultSingleSelectionModel**. The **MenuElement** interface defines the nature of a menu item. In general, you will not need to interact with these interfaces directly unless you are customizing the menu system.

Step-by-Step

To create and use a main menu bar involves the following steps:

1. Create an instance of **JMenuBar**.
2. Create an instance of **JMenu** for each top-level menu in the bar.
3. Create instances of **JMenuItem** that represent the items in the menus.
4. Add instances of **JMenuItem** to a **JMenu** instance by calling **add( )** on the **JMenu**. If desired, separate one item from the next by calling **addSeparator( )** on the **JMenu** instance.
5. Repeat Steps 2 through 4 until all top-level menus have been created.
6. Add each **JMenu** instance to the menu bar by calling **add( )** on the **JMenuBar** instance.
7. Add the menu bar to the frame by calling **setJMenuBar( )** on the **JFrame** instance.
8. An **ActionEvent** is generated each time the user selects an item from a menu. To handle these events, register an action listener for each menu item.

Discussion

JMenuBar is essentially a container for menus. Like all components, it inherits **JComponent** (which inherits **Container** and **Component**). It has only one constructor, which is the default constructor. Therefore, initially the menu bar will be empty and you will need to populate it with menus prior to use. Each application has one and only one menu bar.

JMenuBar defines several methods, but often you will only need to use one: **add( )**. The **add( )** method adds a **JMenu** to the menu bar. It is shown here:

JMenu add(JMenu *menu*)

Here, *menu* is a **JMenu** instance that is added to the menu bar. A reference to the menu is returned. Menus are positioned in the bar from left to right, in the order in which they added.

JMenu encapsulates a menu, which is populated with **JMenuItem**s. It is derived from **JMenuItem**. This means that one **JMenu** can be a selection in another **JMenu**. This enables one menu to be a submenu of another. **JMenu** defines several constructors. The one used here is

JMenu(String *name*)

It creates a menu that has the title specified by *name*.

To add an item to the menu, use the **add( )** method. It has several forms. The one used by this recipe is shown here:

JMenuItem add(JMenuItem *item*)

Here, *item* is the menu item to add. It is added to the end of the menu.

You can add a separator (an object of type **JSeparator**) to a menu by calling **addSeparator( )**, shown here:

void addSeparator( )

The separator is added onto the end of the menu. By default, a separator is a horizontal bar.

JMenuItem encapsulates an element in a menu. This element can be either a selection linked to some program action, such as Save or Close, or it can cause a submenu to be displayed. **JMenuItem** defines several constructors. The one used by this recipe is shown here:

JMenuItem(String *name*)

It creates a menu item with the name specified by *name*.

One key point is that **JMenuItem** extends **AbstractButton**. Recall that **AbstractButton** is also the superclass of all Swing button components, such as **JButton**. Thus, although they look different, all menu items are, essentially, buttons. For example, selecting a menu item generates an action event in the same way that pressing a button does.

Once a menu bar has been created and populated, it is added to a **JFrame** by calling **setJMenuBar( )** on the **JFrame** instance. (Menu bars *are not* added to the content pane.) The **setJMenuBar( )** method is shown here:

void setJMenuBar(JMenuBar *mb*)

Here, *mb* is a reference to the menu bar. The menu bar will be displayed in a position determined by the look and feel. Usually, this is at the top of the window.

When a menu item is selected, an action event is generated. The **ActionEvent** generated by a menu item is similar to that generated by a **JButton**. For details on handling action events, see *Create a Simple Push Button.* The action command string associated with that action event will, by default, be the name of the selection. (The action command string can be obtained by calling **getActionCommand( )** on the action event object.) Thus, you can determine which item was selected by examining the action command string. Of course, you can also recognize the source of an event by calling **getSource( )** on the event object. You can also use a separate anonymous inner class to handle each menu item's action events. Be aware, however, that menu systems tend to get quite large. Using a separate class to handle events for each menu item can cause a large number of classes to be created, which can lead to runtime inefficiencies.

Example

Here is a program that creates a simple menu bar that contains three menus. The first is a standard File menu that contains Open, Close, Save, and Exit selections. The second menu is called Options and it contains two submenus called Language and Target. The third menu is called Help and it has one item: About. When a menu item is selected, the name of the selection is displayed in a label in the content pane.

```java
// Create a main menu.

import java.awt.*;
import java.awt.event.*;
import javax.swing.*;

class MakeMainMenu implements ActionListener {

  JLabel jlab;

  MakeMainMenu() {

    // Create a new JFrame container.
    JFrame jfrm = new JFrame("Menu Demo");

    // Specify FlowLayout for the layout manager.
    jfrm.setLayout(new FlowLayout());

    // Give the frame an initial size.
    jfrm.setSize(220, 200);

    // Terminate the program when the user closes the application.
    jfrm.setDefaultCloseOperation(JFrame.EXIT_ON_CLOSE);

    // Create a label that will display the menu selection.
    jlab = new JLabel();

    // Create the menu bar.
    JMenuBar jmb = new JMenuBar();

    // Create the File menu.
    JMenu jmFile = new JMenu("File");
    JMenuItem jmiOpen = new JMenuItem("Open");
    JMenuItem jmiClose = new JMenuItem("Close");
    JMenuItem jmiSave = new JMenuItem("Save");
    JMenuItem jmiExit = new JMenuItem("Exit");
    jmFile.add(jmiOpen);
    jmFile.add(jmiClose);
    jmFile.add(jmiSave);
    jmFile.addSeparator();
    jmFile.add(jmiExit);
    jmb.add(jmFile);

    // Create the Options menu.
    JMenu jmOptions = new JMenu("Options");
```

```
    // Create the Language submenu.
    JMenu jmLanguage = new JMenu("Language");
    JMenuItem jmiJava = new JMenuItem("Java");
    JMenuItem jmiCpp = new JMenuItem("C++");
    JMenuItem jmiCsharp = new JMenuItem("C#");
    jmLanguage.add(jmiJava);
    jmLanguage.add(jmiCpp);
    jmLanguage.add(jmiCsharp);
    jmOptions.add(jmLanguage);

    // Create the Target submenu.
    JMenu jmTarget = new JMenu("Target");
    JMenuItem jmiDebug = new JMenuItem("Debugging");
    JMenuItem jmiDeploy = new JMenuItem("Deployment");
    jmTarget.add(jmiDebug);
    jmTarget.add(jmiDeploy);
    jmOptions.add(jmTarget);

    // Finally, add the entire Options menu to the menu bar.
    jmb.add(jmOptions);

    // Create the Help menu.
    JMenu jmHelp = new JMenu("Help");
    JMenuItem jmiAbout = new JMenuItem("About");
    jmHelp.add(jmiAbout);
    jmb.add(jmHelp);

    // Add action listeners for the menu items.
    // Use one handler for all menu events.
    jmiOpen.addActionListener(this);
    jmiClose.addActionListener(this);
    jmiSave.addActionListener(this);
    jmiExit.addActionListener(this);
    jmiJava.addActionListener(this);
    jmiCpp.addActionListener(this);
    jmiCsharp.addActionListener(this);
    jmiDebug.addActionListener(this);
    jmiDeploy.addActionListener(this);
    jmiAbout.addActionListener(this);

    // Add the label to the content pane.
    jfrm.add(jlab);

    // Add the menu bar to the frame.
    jfrm.setJMenuBar(jmb);

    // Display the frame.
    jfrm.setVisible(true);
  }

  // Handle menu item action events.
  public void actionPerformed(ActionEvent ae) {
```

```
      // Get the action command from the menu selection.
      String comStr = ae.getActionCommand();

      // If user chooses Exit, then exit the program.
      if(comStr.equals("Exit")) System.exit(0);

      // Otherwise, display the selection.
      jlab.setText(comStr + " Selected");
    }

  public static void main(String args[]) {
    // Create the frame on the event dispatching thread.
    SwingUtilities.invokeLater(new Runnable() {
      public void run() {
        new MakeMainMenu();
      }
    });
  }
}
```

Sample output is shown here:

Options and Alternatives

As stated at the start of this recipe, the subject of menus is very large. They support many options, have many variations, and offer many opportunities for customization. It is far beyond the scope of this recipe to discuss them all. However, a few of the more commonly used options are mentioned here.

In addition to "standard" menu items, you can also include check boxes and radio buttons in a menu. A check box menu item is created by **JCheckBoxMenuItem**. A radio button menu item is created by **JRadioButtonMenuItem**. Both of these classes extend **JMenuItem**.

JToolBar creates a stand-alone component that is related to the menu. It is often used to provide fast access to functionality contained within the menus of the application. For example, a tool bar might provide fast access to the formatting commands supported by a word processor.

As described earlier, by default when you add a **JMenuItem** to a **JMenu**, it is added to the end of the menu. However, by using the following version of **add( )** you can add a menu item to a menu at a specific location:

Component add(Component *menuItem*, int *idx*)

Here, *menuItem* is added at the index specified by *idx*. Indexing begins at 0. For example, in the preceding program, the following statement makes Deployment the first entry in the Target menu:

```
jmTarget.add(jmiDeploy, 0);
```

Although *menuItem* is declared as a **Component**, you will typically add **JMenuItem**s to a menu. (This version of **add( )** is inherited from **Component**. As mentioned at the start of this chapter, all Swing components inherit **JComponent**, which inherits **Component**.)

In some cases you might want to remove a menu item that is no longer needed. You can do this by calling **remove( )** on the **JMenu** instance. It has these two forms:

  void remove(JMenuItem *menuItem*)
  void remove(int *idx*)

Here, *menuItem* is a reference to the menu item to remove and *idx* is the index of the menu to remove. Indexing begins at 0.

JMenuBar also supports versions of **add( )** and **remove( )** that let you add a **JMenu** object to the bar at a specific index or remove an instance of **JMenu** from the bar.

Sometimes it is useful to know how many items are in the menu bar. To obtain a count of the items in the main menu bar, call **getMenuCount( )** on the **JMenuBar** instance. It is shown here:

  int getMenuCount( )

It returns the number of elements contained within the menu bar.

You can determine how many items are in a **JMenu** by calling **getMenuComponentCount( )**, shown here:

  int getMenuComponentCount( )

The count is returned. You can retrieve an array of the items in the menu by calling **getMenuComponents( )** on the **JMenu** instance. It is shown next:

  Component[ ] getMenuComponents( )

An array containing the components is returned.

Because menu items inherit **AbstractButton**, you have access to the functionality provided by **AbstractButton**. For example, you can enable/disable a menu item by calling **setEnabled( )**, shown here:

  void setEnabled(boolean *enable*)

If *enable* is true, the menu item is enabled. If *enable* is false, the item is disabled and cannot be selected.

The main menu is not the only kind of menu that you can create. You can also create stand-alone, popup menus. These are menus that do not descend from a menu bar. Rather, they are activated independently, usually by right-clicking the mouse. Popup menus are instances of **JPopupMenu**.

CHAPTER 9

Potpourri

One of the problems with writing a programming cookbook is finding an appropriate stopping point. There is a nearly unlimited universe of topics to choose from, any number of which could merit inclusion. It's difficult to find where to draw the line. Of course, all books must end. Thus, a stopping point, whether easily found or not, is always required. This book is, of course, no exception.

In this, the final chapter of the book, I have chosen to conclude with an assortment of recipes that span a variety of topics. These recipes represent techniques that I wanted covered in the book, but for which a complete chapter was, for one reason or another, not possible. The recipes do, however, meet the requirements that I set forth when I began this book: they answer a frequently asked question and are applicable to a wide range of programmers. Furthermore, they all describe key concepts that you can easily adapt and enhance.

Here are the recipes contained in this chapter:

- Access a Resource via an HTTP Connection
- Use a Semaphore
- Return a Value from a Thread
- Use Reflection to Obtain Information about a Class at Runtime
- Use Reflection to Dynamically Create an Object and Call Methods
- Create a Custom Exception Class
- Schedule a Task for Future Execution

Access a Resource via an HTTP Connection

Key Ingredients	
Classes	**Methods**
java.net.HttpURLConnection	String getRequestMethod( )
	int getResponseCode( )
	String getResponseMessage( )
java.net.URL	URLConnection openConnection( )
java.net.URLConnection	int getContentLength( )
	String getContentType( )
	long getDate( )
	long getExpiration( )
	Map<String, List<String>> getHeaderFields( )
	long getLastModified( )
	InputStream getInputStream( )

Java was designed for the Internet. As a result, it contains extensive support for networking. Although most Java programmers are familiar with these capabilities, no Java cookbook would be complete without a recipe that uses the Internet. This recipe shows how to handle one of the most basic, yet important network tasks: accessing a resource at a specified URL.

Java supplies two classes that are pivotal in network programming: **URLConnection** and **HttpURLConnection**. **URLConnection** encapsulates the basic functionality of any URL connection. **HttpURLConnection** extends **URLConnection** for HTTP-based connections. This recipe uses **HttpURLConnection**. However, much of the functionality is inherited from **URLConnection** and is applicable to all types of URL-based connections. Both classes are packaged in **java.net**.

Step-by-Step

To access a resource through an HTTP-based connection involves these steps:

1. Create a **URL** object that represents the URL at which the resource is located.

2. Open the connection to the URL by calling **openConnection( )** on the **URL** object created in Step 1.

3. Cast the reference returned by **openConnection( )** to **HttpURLConnection**. Of course, the URL must specify an HTTP address.

4. If necessary, obtain the content type of the resource by calling **getContentType( )** on the **HttpURLConnection** object.

5. If necessary, obtain the length of the content by calling **getContentLength( )** on the **HttpURLConnection** object.

6. Open an input stream to the resource by calling **getInputStream( )** on the **HttpURLConnection** object. You can download the resource by reading from this stream.

To obtain information about a connection, follow these steps:

1. Create an **HttpURLConnection** as described by the first three steps just given. You can obtain information about this connection as described by the following steps.

2. Obtain the date contained in the date header field by calling **getDate( )**.

3. Obtain the expiration time and date by calling **getExpiration( )**.

4. Obtain a map of the header fields by calling **getHeaderFields( )**.

Given a reference to the **HttpURLConnection**, you can obtain information about an HTTP request or response by following these steps:

1. To obtain the request method, call **getRequestMethod( )**.

2. To obtain the response code, call **getResponseCode( )**.

3. To get the response message, call **getResponseMessage( )**.

Discussion

In Java, a URL is encapsulated by the **URL** class. It defines several constructors. The one used here is

URL(String *url*) throws MalformedURLException

Here, *url* is a string that specifies a valid URL, such as **http://HerbSchildt.com**. Notice that a **MalformedURLException** is thrown if the format or protocol of *url* is invalid.

Both **URLConnection** and **HttpURLConnection** are abstract classes. A reference to a concrete implementation is obtained by calling the **openConnection( )** method defined by **URL**. One version is shown here:

URLConnection openConnection( ) throws IOException

If the **URL** specifies an HTTP connection, then a reference to an **HttpURLConnection** is returned and you can cast the return value to **HttpURLConnection**.

You can obtain the content type of the resource by calling **getContentType( )** on the connection. It is shown here:

String getContentType( )

It returns the value associated with the **content-type** header field. It returns null if the content type is unavailable.

You can obtain the length of the content by calling **getContentLength( )** on the connection shown here:

int getContentLength( )

It returns the value associated with the **content-length** header field. This is the size in bytes of the content or −1 if the length is unavailable.

You can obtain an **InputStream** linked to the resource by calling **getInputStream( )**, shown next:

InputStream getInputStream( ) throws IOException

Using the stream returned by this method, you can read the content of the resource.

You can obtain a map that contains all of the header fields and values by calling **getHeaderFields( )**. It is shown here:

Map<String, List<String>> getHeaderFields( )

As the declaration shows, both the fields and the values are strings.

When obtaining the value of a standard header field, it is often easier to use one of the convenience methods provided by **URLConnection**. For example, you can obtain the value of the **date** header field by calling **getDate( )**. You can obtain the value of the **expires** header field by calling **getExpiration( )**. You can obtain the value of the **last-modified** field by calling **getLastModified( )**. They are shown here:

long getDate( )

long getExpiration( )

long getLastModified( )

In each case, the value returned indicates the time and date in terms of milliseconds since January 1, 1970, GMT. If a value is not present, zero is returned.

When using an **HttpURLConnection** (which is the case in this recipe), you can obtain information about the request and response by calling **getRequestMethod( )**, **getResponseCode( )**, and **getResponseMessage( )** on the **HttpURLConnection** object. They are shown here:

String getRequestMethod( )

int getResponseCode( ) throws IOException

String getResponseMessage( ) throws IOException

Each returns the indicated information. If no response code is available, **getResponseCode( )** returns –1. If no response message is available, **getResponseMessage( )** returns null. Notice that **getResponseCode( )** and **getResponseMessage( )** throw an **IOException** if the connection fails.

Example

The following example puts into action the preceding discussions. It first opens a connection to **http://HerbSchildt.com** (you can use another URL if you like) and then displays the information associated with it. Finally, it displays the content.

```
// Demonstrate HttpURLConnection.

import java.net.*;
import java.io.*;
import java.util.*;
```

```java
class HttpConDemo
{
  public static void main(String args[]) {

    URL url;
    HttpURLConnection httpCon;

    try {

      // Create a URL.
      url = new URL("http://www.herbschildt.com");

      // Open an HTTP connection using url.
      httpCon = (HttpURLConnection) url.openConnection();

    } catch(MalformedURLException exc) {
      System.out.println("Invalid URL.");
      return;
    } catch(IOException exc) {
      System.out.println("Error opening connection.");
      return;
    }

    // Display information about the resource,
    // beginning with the date.
    long date = httpCon.getDate();
    if(date == 0)
      System.out.println("No date information.");
    else
      System.out.println("Date: " + new Date(date));

    // Show the expiration date.
    date = httpCon.getExpiration();
    if(date == 0)
      System.out.println("No expiration information.");
    else
      System.out.println("Expires: " + new Date(date));

    // Show the last-modified date.
    date = httpCon.getLastModified();
    if(date == 0)
      System.out.println("No last-modified information.");
    else
      System.out.println("Last-Modified: " + new Date(date));

    // Show the content type.
    System.out.println("Content-Type: " + httpCon.getContentType());

    // Show the content length.
    int len = httpCon.getContentLength();
    if(len == -1)
      System.out.println("Content length unavailable.");
    else
      System.out.println("Content-Length: " + len);
```

```java
// Display request method.
System.out.println("Request method is " +
                    httpCon.getRequestMethod());

try {
  // Display response code.
  System.out.println("Response code is " +
                      httpCon.getResponseCode());

  // Display response message.
  System.out.println("Response Message is " +
                      httpCon.getResponseMessage());
} catch(IOException exc) {
  System.out.println("Cannot obtain response info " +
                      "because the connection failed.");
  return;
}

// Display header fields.
Map<String, List<String>> hdrs = httpCon.getHeaderFields();
Set<String> hdrKeys = hdrs.keySet();

System.out.println("\nHere is the header info:");

// Display the header.
for(String k : hdrKeys)
  System.out.println("Key: " + k +
                      "  Value: " + hdrs.get(k));

// Download and display the content. This will be
// displayed as text. It is not rendered as HTML.
if(len != 0) {
  InputStream inStrm;

  try {
    // Open a stream to the content.
    inStrm = httpCon.getInputStream();
  } catch(IOException exc) {
    System.out.println("Can't open input stream. " + exc);
    return;
  }

  System.out.println("\nContent at " + url);

  try {
    int ch;

    // Display the content.
    while(((ch = inStrm.read()) != -1))
      System.out.print((char) ch);

  } catch(IOException exc) {
    System.out.println("Error reading content. " + exc);
  }
```

```
      try {
        inStrm.close();
      } catch(IOException exc) {
        System.out.println("Error closing stream. " + exc);
      }
    } else
      System.out.println("No content available.");
  }
}
```

Sample output is shown here. (Of course, the output you see will vary over time, or if you use a different URL.)

```
Date: Fri Jun 01 10:02:45 GMT-06:00 2007
No expiration information.
Last-Modified: Thu Mar 22 11:51:07 GMT-06:00 2007
Content-Type: text/html
Content-Length: 9635
Request method is GET
Response code is 200
Response Message is OK

Here is the header info:
Key: Content-Length  Value: [9635]
Key: Connection  Value: [Keep-Alive]
Key: ETag  Value: ["afae1c-25a3-4602c20b"]
Key: Date  Value: [Fri, 01 Jun 2007 16:02:45 GMT]
Key: Keep-Alive  Value: [timeout=5, max=100]
Key: Accept-Ranges  Value: [bytes]
Key: Server  Value: [Apache/1.3.37]
Key: Content-Type  Value: [text/html]
Key: Last-Modified  Value: [Thu, 22 Mar 2007 17:51:07 GMT]
Key: null  Value: [HTTP/1.1 200 OK]

Content at http://www.herbschildt.com

<html>

<head>
<meta http-equiv="Content-Type" content="text/html; charset=windows-1252">
<meta http-equiv="Content-Language" content="en-us">
<title>Herb Schildt Home</title>
.
.
.
```

Options and Alternatives

Java's support of networking is quite extensive, and it is not possible to discuss all of its options in a single recipe. However, here are a few things that you may find of interest when using **URLConnection** and **HttpURLConnection**.

In addition to **getHeaderFields( )**, which returns all header fields and values, **HttpURLConnection** gives you the ability to obtain the value of a specific header field by calling **getHeaderField( )**. It has two forms. The one defined by **URLConnection** is shown here:

String getHeaderField(String *fieldName*)

The name of the field (i.e., its key) is specified by *fieldName.* The value is returned. If the field does not exist, null is returned.

The second form of **getHeaderField( )**, which is defined by **HttpURLConnection**, lets you obtain the value associated with a specific header field by specifying its index. This version is shown here:

String getHeaderField(int *idx*)

The index of the field is passed in *idx.* The value is returned. Null is returned if *idx* specifies a non-existent field.

You can obtain a header field key (i.e., the name of the field) by calling **getHeaderFieldKey( )** on an **HttpURLConnection** object. It is shown here:

String getHeaderFieldKey(int *idx*)

The index of the field is passed in *idx.* The key is returned. Null is returned if *idx* specifies a non-existent field.

In general, header values are returned in their string form. However, you can obtain the value of header field as an integer by using **getHeaderFieldInt( )**, shown next:

int getHeaderFieldInt(String *fieldName*, int *defaultVal*)

Here, the name of the field is passed in *fieldName* and a default value is passed in *defaultVal.* If the value of the specified field is a string that contains an integer, then the **int** equivalent of the string is returned. Otherwise, *defaultVal* is returned.

You can obtain an **OutputStream** that can be used to write to the invoking **URLConnection**. This is done by calling **getOutputStream( )**, shown here:

OutputStream getOutputStream( ) throws IOException

It returns an output stream to the connection. If the stream cannot be obtained, an **IOException** is thrown.

Use a Semaphore

Key Ingredients	
Classes	**Methods**
java.util.concurrent.Semaphore	void acquire( )
	void release( )

Beginning with version 5, Java has included expanded support for concurrent programming called the *concurrency utilities.* This is a set of classes and interfaces packaged in **java.util.concurrent** and two subpackages, **java.util.concurrent.atomic** and **java.util.concurrent.locks**. Commonly referred to as the *concurrent API,* the concurrency utilities supplement Java's built-in support for multithreaded programming by supplying several well-known, high-level features, such as semaphores and locks. These features are of particular value when creating programs that make intensive use of multiple threads whose actions must be coordinated.

This chapter presents two recipes that use the concurrent API. This recipe shows how to use a semaphore, which is an object of type **Semaphore**. The following recipe shows how to use the **Callable** and **Future** interfaces to asynchronously compute and return a value. Although much of the concurrent API is best suited for specialized situations, these two features are more generally applicable. They also show the power available in the concurrent API.

The semaphore will be familiar to most readers. It is the classic device that is used to manage access to a resource shared by multiple threads. A semaphore controls access through the use of a counter. If the counter is greater than zero, then access is allowed. If it is zero, then access is denied. What the counter is counting are *permits* that allow access to the shared resource.

In general, here is how a semaphore is used. When a thread wants access to a shared resource, it tries to acquire a permit from the semaphore that controls access to the resource. If the semaphore's count is greater than zero, the permit is granted and the semaphore's count is decremented. Otherwise, if the semaphore's count is already zero when the thread tries to acquire the permit, the thread will be blocked until a permit can be granted. When the thread no longer needs access to the shared resource, it releases the permit, which causes the semaphore's count to be incremented. If there is another thread waiting for a permit, then that thread will acquire a permit at that time. This mechanism is implemented by the **Semaphore** class, which is packaged in **java.util.concurrent**.

NOTE *It is important to emphasize that the concurrency utilities add to, not replace, Java's original approach to multithreading and synchronization that has been in place from the start. As all Java programmers know, threads are created from classes that implement **Runnable**, synchronization is available through the use of the **synchronized** keyword, and interthread communication is handled by **wait( )** and **notify( )**, defined by **Object**. Java's original approach is both elegant and efficient, and it is still the mechanism that should be employed for many Java programs. The main purpose of the concurrency utilities is to provide off-the-shelf solutions to some fairly challenging threading situations. They also supply implementations of several classic synchronization objects, such as the semaphore described in this recipe, which are familiar to many programmers.*

Step-by-Step

To use a semaphore to control access to a shared resource involves these steps:

1. Create a **Semaphore** instance, specifying the number of permits available. For a mutex semaphore, specify one permit.

2. Before a thread accesses the shared resource, it must acquire a permit by calling **acquire( )** on the semaphore.

3. When the thread is finished with the shared resource, it must release the permit by calling **release( )** on the semaphore.

Discussion

Semaphore has two constructors. The one used by the recipe is shown here:

Semaphore(int *num*, boolean *how*)

Here, *num* specifies the initial permit count. Thus, *num* specifies the number of threads that can access a shared resource at any one time. If *num* is one, then only one thread can access the resource at any one time. (In this case, a mutex semaphore is created.) If *how* is true, waiting threads are granted a permit in the order in which they requested access. This is called *fairness*, and it is what you will typically want to be the case when synchronizing access to a shared resource. Fairness prevents the same thread from immediately reacquiring the semaphore and effectively locking out another thread, for example. If *how* is false, then the "first in line" rule is not enforced.

To acquire a permit, call the **acquire( )** method. The form used by this recipe is shown here:

void acquire( ) throws InterruptedException

This form acquires one permit. If the permit cannot be granted at the time of the call, then the invoking thread suspends until the permit is available.

To release a permit, call **release( )**. The form used by this recipe is shown next:

void release( )

The first form releases one permit.

Here is how you use a semaphore to control access to a resource. When a thread wants to use the resource, it must first call **acquire( )** before accessing the resource. If a permit is not available, then the calling thread will block until another thread releases a permit. When the thread is done with the resource, it must call **release( )**. Failure to call **release( )** causes the resource to remain unavailable to other threads. Therefore, you must not forget this important step.

Example

The following example illustrates the use of a semaphore. It creates a class called **SyncOutput**, which creates a thread that writes to a file called **Log.dat**. It uses a semaphore to synchronize output. The constructor is passed a reference to a semaphore that will be used to synchronize access, a reference to an open **FileWriter**, and a message to output. It then outputs the message, one character at a time, sleeping for ten milliseconds between characters. The program creates two instances of **SyncOutput** that both use the same semaphore and that both write to the same file. Without the use of the semaphore, the output from the two threads both writing to the same file would produce jumbled output. (The call to **sleep( )** between each character would normally allow the other thread to run; thus the output of the two threads would be mixed together.) Because of the semaphore, the output of the two threads is kept separate.

```
// Demonstrate a semaphore
//
// In this example, the shared resource is a file,
// such as a log file that is used to record program
```

```java
// events. A semaphore is used to prevent two threads
// from writing to the file at the same time. Without
// the use of the semaphore, the output of one thread
// would be mixed with the other. The semaphore
// synchronizes access and prevents this.

import java.util.concurrent.*;
import java.io.*;

class SemDemo {

  public static void main(String args[]) {

    // Create a semaphore that allows only one permit.
    Semaphore sem = new Semaphore(1, true);

    FileWriter fw;

    try {

      // Open the output file.
      fw = new FileWriter("Log.dat");

    } catch(IOException exc) {
      System.out.println("Error Opening Log File");
      return ;
    }

    // Create two threads, with each using the semaphore
    // to control access to the file, which is a
    // shared resource.
    Thread thrdA = new Thread(new SyncOutput(sem, fw,
                            "Transfer Complete"));
    Thread thrdB = new Thread(new SyncOutput(sem, fw,
                            "Connection Lost!"));

    thrdA.start();
    thrdB.start();

    // Wait for the threads to end.
    try {
      thrdA.join();
      thrdB.join();

      fw.close();
    } catch(InterruptedException exc) {
      System.out.println("Interrupted");
    } catch(IOException exc) {
      System.out.println("Error Closing File");
    }
  }
}
```

```
// A thread that synchronizes the writing of
// a message to a file. This class could be used
// to write output to a log file, for example.
class SyncOutput implements Runnable {
  Semaphore sem;
  String msg;
  FileWriter fw;

  // Pass this class the semaphore used for synchronization,
  // a FileWriter to write to, and the message to write.
  SyncOutput(Semaphore s, FileWriter f, String m) {
    sem = s;
    msg = m;
    fw = f;
  }

  public void run() {

    try {
      // First, get a permit.
      sem.acquire();

      // Now, write to the file, one character at a time.
      // Notice that sleep( ) is called after each character
      // is output. This would normally allow another thread
      // to run, which would produce jumbled output. However,
      // since only one thread at a time can acquire the
      // semaphore, only one thread a time can output to
      // the file. Thus, the outputs are kept separate.
      // To confirm the importance of the semaphore, try
      // commenting out the calls to acquire() and release().
      // As you will see, the outputs are mixed together.

      for(int i=0; i < msg.length(); i++) {

        // Write messages to the file, one character at a time.
        fw.write(msg.charAt(i));

        // Allow another thread to run, if possible.
        Thread.sleep(10);
      }
      fw.write("\n");
    } catch(IOException exc) {
      System.out.println("Error Writing File");
    } catch (InterruptedException exc) {
      System.out.println(exc);
    }

    // Release the permit.
    sem.release();
  }
}
```

The contents of **Log.dat** are shown here:

```
Transfer Complete
Connection Lost!
```

To understand the importance of the semaphore for producing the correct output, try commenting out the call to **acquire( )** and then re-run the program. The file **Log.dat** will now contain this jumbled output:

```
TCroannnsefcetri oCno mLpolsett!e
```

Options and Alternatives

The second **Semaphore** constructor is shown here:

Semaphore(int *num*)

It creates a semaphore with *num* permits and does not guarantee fairness. Thus, a thread might reacquire a semaphore that it has just released even though another thread has been waiting for it. Usually, you will want to specify fairness by using the constructor described earlier.

There is a second form of **acquire( )** that lets you obtain more than one permit. It is shown here:

void acquire(int *num*) throws InterruptedException

The number of permits to obtain is passed in *num*.

There is a second form of **release( )**, shown next, that lets you free more than one permit:

void release(int *num*)

It releases the number of permits specified by *num*.

You can determine the number of permits currently available for a semaphore by calling **availablePermits( )**, shown here:

int availablePermits( )

It returns the number of unallocated permits that the semaphore currently has.

You can attempt to acquire a permit without blocking if there is no permit available by calling **tryAcquire( )**. Here are two of its forms:

boolean tryAcquire( )

boolean tryAcquire(int *num*)

The first form attempts to acquire one permit. The second attempts to acquire *num* permits. If possible, it acquires the permit(s) and returns true. If the permit(s) cannot be acquired, it returns false. Other forms are available that let you specify a time-out period.

You can acquire all remaining permits by calling **drainPermits( )**:

int drainPermits( )

After the call, the semaphore will have no available permits until one is released. This method is useful for situations in which a resource that can normally be used by multiple threads needs to be temporarily restricted to a single thread, or when a resource needs to be temporarily taken out of service.

Semaphore is one of four *synchronizers* provided by the concurrent API. The others are **CountDownLatch**, **CyclicBarrier**, and **Exchanger**. A **CountDownLatch** waits until a specified number of events have occurred. A **CyclicBarrier** enables a group of threads to wait at a predefined execution point. An **Exchanger** exchanges data between two threads. These synchronization objects offer alternatives to **Semaphore** that solve some otherwise challenging situations.

Return a Value from a Thread

Key Ingredients	
Classes and Interfaces	**Methods**
java.util.concurrent.Callable<V>	V call( )
java.util.concurrent.Executors	static ExecutorService newFixedThreadPool(int *num*)
java.util.concurrent.ExecutorService	<T> Future<T> submit(Callable<T> *task*) void shutdown( )
java.util.concurrent.Future<V>	V get( )

As explained by the preceding recipe, beginning with Java 5, a subsystem called the *concurrency utilities* has been included in the Java API. Also called the *concurrent API,* this collection of interfaces and classes provides various features that streamline the solutions to certain thread synchronization problems. The concurrent API is packaged in **java.util.concurrent** and two subpackages, **java.util.concurrent.atomic** and **java.util.concurrent.locks**.

One of the most innovative features of the concurrent API is the ability for a thread to return a value. This feature enables a thread to asynchronously compute a value and return the result. This is a powerful mechanism because it facilitates the coding of many types of numerical computations in which partial results are computed simultaneously. It can also be used to run a thread that returns a status code that indicates success or failure.

Two interfaces are used to create a thread that returns a value: **Callable** and **Future**. **Callable** represents a thread that returns a value. An application can use **Callable** objects to compute results that are then returned to the invoking thread. **Future** contains a value that is returned by a thread after it executes. Its name comes from the fact that its value is defined "in the future," when the thread terminates.

To execute a **Callable** thread, you must use another part of the concurrent API, called an *executor.* An executor initiates and controls the execution of threads. Executors are based on the **Executor** interface. **ExecutorService** extends **Executor**, providing support for threads that return values. Various concrete implementations of **ExecutorService** are provided by factory methods in the **Executors** class. This recipe uses a fixed thread pool executor, but other types of executors are available.

Step-by-Step

To return a value from a thread involves these steps:

1. Create a class that implements the **Callable** interface. This interface defines only one method, **call( )**. The value returned by **call( )** becomes the value returned by the thread.

2. Obtain an **ExecutorService** by using one of the factory methods defined by the **Executors** class. The executor will be used to execute an instance of the **Callable** created in Step 1.

3. Create an instance of **Future** that will receive the value returned by the **Callable** after it has returned.

4. Execute the **Callable** by passing it to the **submit( )** method defined by the **ExecutorService**. The value returned by **submit( )** is assigned to the **Future**.

5. Obtain the value returned by the thread by calling **get( )** on the **Future** returned by **submit( )**.

6. When you are done with the **ExecutorService**, terminate it by calling **shutdown( )**.

Discussion

Callable is a generic interface that is defined like this:

interface Callable<V>

Here, **V** indicates the type of data returned by the task. **Callable** defines only one method, **call( )**, which is shown here:

V call( ) throws Exception

Inside **call( )**, you define the task that you want performed. After that task completes, you return the result. If the result cannot be computed, **call( )** must throw an exception.

A **Callable** task is executed by an instance of **ExecutorService**. An **ExecutorService** is obtained by calling one of the factory methods defined by the **Executors** class. The one used by this recipe is **newFixedThreadPool( )**, shown here:

static ExecutorService newFixedThreadPool(int *num*)

This creates an executor service that uses a pool of threads to execute tasks. The number of threads in the pool is fixed. However, a thread can be reused. In other words, when a thread completes a task, it can be used for another. Reusing threads is more efficient than creating many separate threads.

Given an executor service, a **Callable** task is executed by calling the executor's **submit( )** method. There are three forms of **submit( )**, but only one is used to execute a **Callable**. It is shown here:

<T> Future<T> submit(Callable<T> *task*)

Here, *task* is the **Callable** object that will be executed in its own thread. The result is returned through an object of type **Future**.

Future is a generic interface that represents the value that will be returned by a **Callable** object. Because this value is obtained at some future time, the name **Future** is appropriate. **Future** is defined like this:

interface Future<V>

Here, **V** specifies the type of the result.

To obtain the returned value, you will call **Future**'s **get( )** method, which has two forms. The one used by this recipe is shown here:

V get( ) throws InterruptedException, ExecutionException

This method will wait for the result indefinitely. Thus, it will not return until the result is available.

When you are done with the **ExecutorService**, you should terminate it by calling **shutdown( )** on it. This method is shown here:

void shutdown( )

This method allows all threads currently under the control of the invoking **ExecutorService** to complete and then stops the executor service. After the call to **shutdown( )** no new threads can be executed.

Example

The following program shows how to return a value from a thread. It creates three **Callable** threads. The first averages an array of doubles. The second computes the factorial of an integer. The third writes a string to a file and returns true if successful and false otherwise. All three actions occur concurrently because each runs in its own thread.

```
// Return a value from a thread.
//
// This program creates three Callable threads.
// The first averages an array of doubles. The
// second computes the factorial of an integer.
// The third writes a string to a file. It returns
// true if successful and false otherwise.

import java.util.concurrent.*;
import java.io.*;

class ThrdRetValDemo {
  public static void main(String args[]) {
    ExecutorService es = Executors.newFixedThreadPool(3);
```

```
    // Create three Futures that will receive values
    // computed asynchronously.
    Future<Double> f;
    Future<Integer> f2;
    Future<Boolean> f3;

    Double nums[] = { 1.0, 2.2, 3.5, 7.25 };

    // Start all three threads running.
    f = es.submit(new Avg(nums));
    f2 = es.submit(new Factorial(4));
    f3 = es.submit(new writeFile("test.dat", "This is a test."));

    // Wait for the results.
    try {
      System.out.println(f.get());
      System.out.println(f2.get());
      System.out.println(f3.get());
    } catch (InterruptedException exc) {
      System.out.println(exc);
    }
    catch (ExecutionException exc) {
      System.out.println(exc);
    }

    // Stop the executor service.
    es.shutdown();
  }
}

// Following are three Callable threads.

// Return the average of an array of double values.
class Avg implements Callable<Double> {
  Double[] data;

  Avg(Double[] d) { data = d; }

  public Double call() {
    double sum = 0;

    for(int i = 0; i < data.length; i++) {
      sum += data[i];
    }
    return sum/data.length;
  }
}

// Write a string to a file. Return true if
// successful and false otherwise.
class writeFile implements Callable<Boolean> {

  String fname;
  String msg;
```

```
    writeFile(String n, String info) {
      fname = n;
      msg = info;
    }

    public Boolean call() {
      FileWriter fw = null;
      boolean result = true;

      try {
        fw = new FileWriter(fname);
        fw.write(msg);
      } catch(IOException exc) {
        // Return false if the file cannot be
        // opened or written.
        result = false;
      }

      try {
        if(fw != null) fw.close();
      } catch(IOException exc) {
        // Return false if the file can't be closed.
        result = false;
      }

      return result;
    }
  }

// Compute the factorial of a number and return
// the result.
class Factorial implements Callable<Integer> {
  int num;

  Factorial(int v) { num = v; }

  public Integer call() {
    int fact = 1;

    for(int i = 2; i <= num; i++) {
      fact *= i;
    }

    return fact;
  }
}
```

The output is shown here:

```
3.4875
24
true
```

Options and Alternatives

There is a second form of **get( )** that is defined by **Future** that lets you specify how long to wait for a result. It is shown here.

V get(long *wait*, TimeUnit *tu*)
    throws InterruptedException, ExecutionException, TimeoutException

The period of time to wait is passed in *wait*. The units of *wait* are passed in *tu*, which is an object of the **java.util.concurrent.TimeUnit** enumeration.

Java 6 added the interface **RunnableFuture**, which extends **Future**. It also extends **Runnable**. Thus, a **RunnableFuture** can be used when a **Runnable** is needed.

Use Reflection to Obtain Information about a Class at Runtime

Key Ingredients	
Classes	**Methods**
java.lang.Class<T>	static Class<?> forName(String *name*)
	Constructor<?>[ ] getDeclaredConstructors( )
	Field[ ] getDeclaredFields( )
	Method[ ] getDeclaredMethods( )
java.lang.reflect.Constructor<T>	
java.lang.reflect.Field	
java.lang.reflect.Method	

Reflection is the feature that enables information about a class to be obtained at runtime by a program. The name *reflection* comes from the fact that a class returns (i.e., reflects) its capabilities when queried. For example, using reflection you can obtain information about the methods and constructors supported by a class. Reflection is useful for a number of different reasons, but it is especially important when working with software components, such as JavaBeans, because it allows you to analyze the capabilities of a component at runtime. It also makes it possible to invoke methods and constructors that are discovered via reflection. This makes reflection one of Java's most powerful subsystems. Support for the reflection API is packaged in **java.lang.reflect**. It is also encapsulated within **java.lang.Class**.

This recipe shows how to use reflection to obtain information about three aspects of a class: its methods, constructors, and fields.

Step-by-Step

To obtain information about a class's methods, fields, and constructors at runtime involves the following steps:

1. Obtain a **Class** object that represents the class in question. There are various ways to do this. The approach used by this recipe is to call **forName( )**, which is a static method defined by **Class**.

2. One way to obtain information about a class's constructors is to call **getDeclaredConstructors( )** on the **Class** object.

3. One way to obtain information about a class's methods is to call **getDeclaredMethods( )** on the **Class** object.

4. One way to obtain information about a class's fields is to call **getDeclaredFields( )** on the **Class** object.

Discussion

The first step when using reflection is to obtain a **Class** object that represents the class in question. One way to obtain this object is to call the static method **forName( )**. This method is defined by **java.lang.Class** and returns a **Class** object given the name of the class. It is shown here:

static Class<set> forName(String *name*) throws ClassNotFoundException

The name of the class (which must be fully qualified with its package name) is specified by *name*. A **Class** object representing the class is returned. If the class is not found, a **ClassNotFoundException** is thrown. Given a **Class** object, you can obtain information about the class that it represents.

NOTE   *You can also use forName( ) to obtain a Class object that represents an interface and reflection can be used to obtain information about that interface at runtime. The same basic techniques apply. However, the focus of this recipe is on obtaining information about a class.*

To obtain an array that describes the constructors defined by the class, call **getDeclaredConstructors( )** on the **Class** object. It is shown here:

Constructor<?>[ ] getDeclaredConstructors( ) throws SecurityException

It returns an array of **Constructor** objects that encapsulate information about each constructor defined by the class. This also includes the default constructor. (Be aware that if you call **getDeclaredConstructors( )** on a **Class** object that represents an interface, array, primitive type, or void, a zero-length array is returned.)

To obtain an array that describes the methods of the class, call **getDeclaredMethods( )**, shown here:

Method[ ] getDeclaredMethods( ) throws SecurityException

It returns an array of **Method** objects that encapsulate information about each method defined by the class. If there are no methods, a zero-length array is returned.

To obtain an array that describes the fields of the class, call **getDeclaredFields( )**, shown here:

Field[ ] getDeclaredFields( ) throws SecurityException

It returns an array of **Field** objects that encapsulate information about each field declared by the class. If the class has no fields, a zero-length array is returned.

The **Constructor, Method,** and **Field** classes are packaged in **java.lang.reflect,** and they encapsulate information about a constructor, method, and field, respectively. An easy way to display this information is to call the **toString( )** method defined by each of these classes. (Recall that **toString( )** is called automatically when you output to the console via **println( )**, for example). This is the approach used by this recipe.

Example

The following program illustrates the basic mechanism used to obtain information about a class at runtime through the use of reflection. It creates a class called **MyClass** and then uses reflection to display information about its constructors, methods, and fields.

```
// Demonstrate reflection basics.

import java.lang.reflect.*;

// The members of this class will be reflected.
class MyClass {
  private int count;

  MyClass(int c) {
    count = c;
  }

  MyClass() {
    count = 0;
  }

  void setCount(int c) {
    count = c;
  }

  int getCount() {
    return count;
  }

  void showcount() {
    System.out.println("count is " + count);
  }
}

class ReflectionDemo {
  public static void main(String args[]) {
    try {
      // Get a Class object that represents MyClass.
```

```
      Class c = Class.forName("MyClass");

      System.out.println("Reflecting MyClass\n");

      // Obtain and display information about
      // the constructors, methods, and fields
      // declared by MyClass.

      System.out.println("Constructors:");
      Constructor constructors[] = c.getDeclaredConstructors();
      for(Constructor cons : constructors)
        System.out.println("  " + cons);

      System.out.println("\nMethods:");
      Method methods[] = c.getDeclaredMethods();
      for(Method meth : methods)
        System.out.println("  " + meth);

      System.out.println("\nFields:");
      Field fields[] = c.getDeclaredFields();
      for(Field fld : fields)
        System.out.println("  " + fld);

    }
    catch(Exception exc) {
      // Handle all exceptions with a single catch. In a real
      // application, you may want to handle the various
      // exceptions individually.
      System.out.println(exc);
    }
  }
}
```

The output is shown here:

```
Reflecting MyClass

Constructors:
 MyClass()
 MyClass(int)

Methods:
 void MyClass.setCount(int)
 int MyClass.getCount()
 void MyClass.showcount()

Fields:
 private int MyClass.count
```

Bonus Example: A Reflection Utility

The preceding example shows how to use reflection to display the capabilities of a specific class, but it is simple to generalize the procedure. Because of the streamlined design of the reflection API, information can easily be obtained about any class. This example shows one approach. It creates a short utility program called **ShowClass** that displays the constructors, methods, and fields declared by the class (or interface) specified on the command line. (Of course, an interface won't have any constructors.) Therefore, the utility lets you see the members of any class or interface. This can be helpful when debugging, or for exploring the capabilities of components for which no source code or documentation is available. Here is the program:

```
// A simple, yet effective reflection utility that shows
// the constructors, methods, and fields for a class or
// interface specified on the command line.

import java.lang.reflect.*;

class ShowClass {
  public static void main(String args[]) {
    try {
      // Get a Class object for the specified class or interface.
      Class c = Class.forName(args[0]);

      System.out.println("Reflecting " + args[0] + "\n");

      // Obtain and display information about the constructors,
      // methods, and fields.

      System.out.println("Constructors:");
      Constructor constructors[] = c.getDeclaredConstructors();
      for(Constructor cons : constructors)
        System.out.println("  " + cons);

      System.out.println("\nMethods:");
      Method methods[] = c.getDeclaredMethods();
      for(Method meth : methods)
        System.out.println("  " + meth);

      System.out.println("\nFields:");
      Field fields[] = c.getDeclaredFields();
      for(Field fld : fields)
        System.out.println("  " + fld);

    } catch(ArrayIndexOutOfBoundsException exc) {
      System.out.println("Usage: ShowClass <classname>");
    } catch(Exception exc2) {
      // Handle all other exceptions. You can add more
      // sophisticated exception handling if you like.
      System.out.println(exc2);
    }
  }
}
```

To use the program, specify the fully qualified name of the class or interface on the command line. For example, to see the members of **java.lang.Object**, use this command line:

```
C>java ShowClass java.lang.Object
```

Remember, the name must be fully qualified with its package name.

Options and Alternatives

In addition to the use of **forName( )**, there are various other ways to obtain a **Class** object. For example, given an object of the class, you can use **getClass( )**, which is defined by **Object**. It returns a **Class** object that represents the class type of the invoking object. Another way to obtain a class object is to use a class literal. For example, here is another way to obtain a **Class** object that represents **MyClass**:

```
MyClass.class
```

Of course, this approach requires that you know the name of the class at compile time. The **forName( )** method lets you specify the name of the class at runtime, which can be important in some situations.

As explained, the **getDeclaredMethods( )** and **getDeclaredFields( )** methods return information about the methods and fields actually declared by a class or interface. If you want to obtain information about all methods and fields, including those specified by superclasses, then you will need to use the **getMethods( )** and **getFields( )** methods defined by **Class**. These return information about all public methods and fields that are members of the class.

Class provides many additional features. Here are some examples. You can obtain information about a specific constructor, method, or field by calling **getConstructor( )**, **getMethod( )**, or **getField( )**. The **getDeclaredConstructor( )**, **getDeclaredMethod( )**, and **getDeclaredField( )** methods are also provided. You can obtain information about the annotations (if any) that are associated with a class by calling **getAnnotations( )**, **getDeclaredAnnotations( )**, or **getAnnotation( )**. Frankly, it is worth the time and effort needed to fully explore **Class**. It contains many useful capabilities.

A key feature of Java's reflection API is the ability to create an instance of an object at runtime and call methods on it. This aspect of reflection is demonstrated by the following recipe.

Use Reflection to Dynamically Create an Object and Call Methods

Key Ingredients	
Classes	**Methods**
java.lang.Class<T>	Constructor<T> getConstructor(Class<?> ... *params*)
	Method getMethod(String *methName*, Class<T> ... *params*)
java.lang.reflect.Constructor<T>	Class<?>[ ] getParameterTypes( )
	T newInstance(Object ... *arglist*)
java.lang.reflect.Method	Class<?>[ ] getParameterTypes( )
	Class<?> getReturnType( )
	Object invoke(Object *obj*, Object ... *arglist*)

An important aspect of reflection is its ability to instantiate objects and execute methods dynamically, at runtime. For example, you can use reflection to query the capabilities of a class and then create an object of that class and execute methods on it. This is a powerful capability because it enables you to write programs that use classes that are not necessarily present at compile time. It is, of course, also useful when using components, such as JavaBeans. This recipe shows the basic procedure needed to discover the capabilities of a class, create an instance of the class, and then call methods on that instance.

Step-by-Step

To create an object and invoke methods on it at runtime using reflection involves these steps:

1. Obtain a **Class** object that represents the class you want to use.

2. Obtain a list of the constructors supported by the class by calling **getDeclaredConstructors( )** on the **Class** object. It returns an array of type **Constructor**, with each element representing one form of the constructor.

3. You can determine how many and what type of parameters a constructor has by calling **getParameterTypes( )** on a **Constructor** object.

4. Using the list of constructors obtained in Step 2 and the parameter type information obtained in Step 3, create an instance of the class by calling **newInstance( )** on one of the **Constructor** objects.

5. Obtain a list of the methods supported by the class by calling **getDeclaredMethods( )** on the **Class** object. It returns an array of type **Method**, with each element representing one specific method.

6. You can determine how many and what type of parameters a method has by calling **getParameterTypes( )** on a **Method** object.

7. You can determine the return type of a method by calling **getReturnType( )** on a **Method** object.

8. Using the list of methods obtained in Step 5, the parameter type information obtained in Step 6, and the return type obtained in Step 7, call the desired method by calling **invoke( )** on the **Method** object.

Discussion

The general procedure needed to obtain a **Class** object that represents a class, and to obtain a list of constructors and methods for the class, is given in *Use Reflection to Obtain Information about a Class at Runtime*. That information is not repeated here. However, recall that **getDeclaredConstructors( )** returns an array of type **Constructor** (which represents the constructors declared by the class) and **getDeclaredMethods( )** returns an array of type **Method** (which represents the methods declared by the class).

After calling **getDeclaredConstructors( )**, you can determine what type and how many parameters a constructor has by calling **getParameterTypes( )** on a **Constructor** object. It is shown here:

```
Class<?>[ ] getParameterTypes( )
```

It returns an array of **Class** objects that represent the types of the constructor's parameters. The number of parameters is equal to the length of the array. If the constructor has no parameters, then a zero-length array is returned.

To dynamically create an instance of a class, use the **newInstance( )** method defined by **Constructor**. It is shown here:

> T newInstance(Object ... *arglist*)
>   throws IllegalAccessException, IllegalArgumentException,
>   InstantiationException, InvocationTargetException

This method calls the constructor whose parameter list matches the type and number of the arguments passed via *arglist*. It returns an object of type **T**, which will be the class that is represented by the **Class** object from which the **Constructor** instance was obtained.

After calling **getDeclaredMethods( )**, you can determine what type and how many parameters a method has by calling **getParameterTypes( )** on a **Method** object. It is shown here:

> Class<?>[ ] getParameterTypes( )

It returns an array of **Class** objects that represent the types of the method's parameters. The number of parameters is equal to the length of the array. If the method has no parameters, then a zero-length array is returned.

You can obtain a method's return type by calling **getReturnType( )** on a **Method** object. It is shown next:

> Class<?> getReturnType( )

It returns a **Class** object that describes the return type of the method.

To call one of the methods obtained from **getDeclaredMethods( )**, call **invoke( )** on the **Method** object that represents the method that you want to execute. The **invoke( )** method is shown here:

> Object invoke(Object *obj*, Object ... *arglist*)
>   throws IllegalAccessException, IllegalArgumentException,
>   InvocationTargetException

The method whose argument list matches the type and number of that specified is executed. The object returned by **invoke( )** contains the return value of the method.

Example

The following example shows how to use reflection to dynamically create an object and execute methods on it. Notice how class literals are used to determine at runtime the type of a parameter or return value.

```
// Use reflection to dynamically discover the
// capabilities of a class. Then, instantiate
// an object of that class and call methods on it.

import java.lang.reflect.*;
```

```java
// The members of this class will be reflected.
class MyClass {
  private int count;

  MyClass(int c) {
    System.out.println("Executing MyClass(int)." +
                       " Argument is " + c);
    count = c;
  }

  MyClass() {
    System.out.println("Executing MyClass().");
    count = 0;
  }

  void setCount(int c) {
    System.out.println("Executing setCount(int)." +
                       " Argument is " + c);
    count = c;
  }

  int getCount() {
    System.out.println("Executing getCount()." +
                       " Return value is " + count);
    return count;
  }

  void showcount() {
    System.out.println("Executing showCount().");
    System.out.println("count is " + count);
  }
}

class UseReflection {
  public static void main(String args[]) {
    try {

      // Get a Class object that represents MyClass.
      Class c = Class.forName("MyClass");

      System.out.println("Use Reflection to execute MyClass " +
                         "constructors and methods.\n");

      System.out.println("Create an instance of MyClass.");

      // Find a MyClass constructor that takes one int argument.
      Constructor constructors[] = c.getDeclaredConstructors();
      Object obj = null;
      for(Constructor cons : constructors) {
        Class[] params = cons.getParameterTypes();
        if(params.length == 1 && params[0] == int.class) {
          obj = cons.newInstance(10);
          break;
        }
      }
```

```
      // Make sure that an object was instantiated.
      if(obj == null) {
        System.out.println("Can't Create MyClass object.");
        return;
      }

      // Execute all methods declared by MyClass.
      System.out.println("\nExecute all MyClass methods.");

      // Get an array of all the methods.
      Method methods[] = c.getDeclaredMethods();

      for(Method meth : methods) {
        // Get the parameter type list for each method.
        Class[] params = meth.getParameterTypes();

        // Execute methods based on parameters and return
        // values.
        if(params.length == 1 && params[0] == int.class)
          // If a method takes one int parameter, then
          // execute it by passing an argument of 99.
          meth.invoke(obj, 99);
        else if(params.length == 0) {
          if(meth.getReturnType() == int.class) {
            // Execute a method that returns an int
            // and that has no parameters.
            Object retval =  meth.invoke(obj);
            System.out.println("Method returns: " + (Integer)retval);
          } else if(meth.getReturnType() == void.class)
            // Execute a void method that has no parameters.
            meth.invoke(obj);
        }
      }

    }
    catch(Exception exc) {
      // Handle all exceptions with a single catch. In a real
      // application, you may want to handle the various
      // exceptions individually.
      System.out.println(exc);
    }
  }
}
```

The output is shown here:

```
Use Reflection to execute MyClass constructors and methods.

Create an instance of MyClass.
Executing MyClass(int). Argument is 10
```

```
Execute all MyClass methods.
Executing setCount(int). Argument is 99
Executing getCount(). Return value is 99
Method returns: 99
Executing showCount().
count is 99
```

Options and Alternatives

In addition to instantiating objects and calling methods, you can get or set the value of a field by using various methods defined by **Field**. For example, after obtaining a **Field** object that represents a field (which can be done by calling a method such as **getDeclaredField( )** on the **Class** object that represents the class), you can get the value of an **int** field by calling **getInt( )** or set the value of a **double** field by calling **setDouble( )**. You can determine the type of a field by calling **getType( )** on the **Field** object.

You can obtain information about an annotation that is associated with an element, such as a class, constructor, method, and so on, by first obtaining an **Annotation** object that represents each annotation associated with the element. This is done by calling a method such as **getAnnotations( )** on the object that represents the element. This method is available in these (and other) classes: **Class**, **Constructor**, **Method**, and **Field**.

There are many other methods available in the **Constructor**, **Method**, and **Field** classes that give you access to additional details. For example, all define the **getName( )** method, which returns the name of the method or field. (Of course, for **Constructor**, **getName( )** returns the name of the class.) All also define the **getModifiers( )** method, which returns the modifiers, such as **private**, **static**, and so on, applied to the element. If you will be making significant use of reflection, then you will want to carefully study these methods and interfaces (and the others) declared in **java.lang.reflect**.

Create a Custom Exception Class

Key Ingredients	
Classes	**Methods**
java.lang.Exception	String toString( )

Although it is quite easy to create a custom exception class (and most experienced Java programmers know how to do this), it is still a topic that generates a number of "how to" questions. Therefore, it seemed that this cookbook would not be complete without a recipe that shows how to accomplish this important task.

As most readers know, Java relies on exceptions to report runtime errors. For example, if a file cannot be opened, a **FileNotFoundException** is thrown. Java's use of exceptions represents the modern way in which programming languages handle runtime errors. In contrast, older languages, such as C, rely on return values. In this approach, a method returns a special value, typically referred to as an *error code,* when an error has occurred. Otherwise, if successful, the method returns a valid result. There is, of course, a fundamental problem with this approach; it makes the return value represent two separate, unrelated things: a valid result or an error code. This is an inherently confusing and error-prone situation. Your program must always explicitly look for the error code to avoid accidentally operating on it as if it were a valid result. Unfortunately, such checks can be forgotten. While in theory these problems are not difficult, in practice they have been the cause of a lot of trouble. The use of exceptions avoids the problem. A return value always represents a valid result (never an error), and there is no possibility of overlooking an error code. If an error occurs, an exception is thrown. Therefore, exceptions offer a superior way to report error conditions.

Given the benefit of exceptions, you should use them to report error conditions in classes that you create. This way, errors generated by your code are handled in the same way as errors generated by the Java API and you avoid the need to return special error codes. This recipe shows how to accomplish this.

NOTE *It is important not to confuse failure with error. For example, **String** defines the method **indexOf( )**, of which one version returns the index at which a substring is found within a string. This method returns –1 if the substring is not found. In other words, it returns –1 on failure. Thus, –1 is a valid return value that does not represent an error. It simply indicates that the string is not contained within the invoking string. This is a perfectly good use for the return value.*

Step-by-Step

To create a custom exception class involves these steps:

1. Extend **Exception** to create a class that represents an error that can occur in your code.
2. If desired, override one or more of the methods supplied by **Exception**.
3. When an error represented by the exception occurs, throw an instance of your exception class.

Discussion

Exception is the exception class that forms the top of an exception hierarchy that represents errors that should normally be caught and handled by your program. For example, **Exception** is a superclass of **IOException**. It is also the superclass for exceptions that you create. Like all exception classes, **Exception** is a subclass of **Throwable**. It does not add any methods of its own. However, your custom exception class is free to do so.

Exception defines the following constructors:

Exception( )
Exception(String *msg*)

Exception(Throwable *causeExc*)
Exception(String *msg*, Throwable *causeExc*)

The first form creates an exception that has no description. The second form lets you specify a description of the exception. The next two forms let you specify a cause. Causes support *chained exceptions,* which were added by Java 1.4. This feature lets you associate another exception with an exception. The second exception describes the cause of the first.

When creating your own exception class, you can override any of the methods provided by **Exception** (which are inherited from **Throwable**), but you don't have to. The methods defined by **Throwable** are shown here:

Method	Description
Throwable fillInStackTrace( )	Returns a **Throwable** object that contains a completed stack trace. This object can be rethrown.
Throwable getCause( )	Returns the exception that underlies the current exception. If there is no underlying exception, **null** is returned.
String getLocalizedMessage( )	Returns a localized description of the exception.
String getMessage( )	Returns a description of the exception.
StackTraceElement[ ] getStackTrace( )	Returns an array that contains the stack trace, one element at a time, as an array of **StackTraceElement**. The method at the top of the stack is the last method called before the exception was thrown. This method is found in the first element of the array. The **StackTraceElement** class gives your program access to information about each element in the trace, such as its method name.
Throwable initCause(Throwable *causeExc*)	Associates *causeExc* with the invoking exception as a cause of the invoking exception. Returns a reference to the exception.
void printStackTrace( )	Displays the stack trace.
void printStackTrace(PrintStream *stream*)	Sends the stack trace to the specified stream.
void printStackTrace(PrintWriter *stream*)	Sends the stack trace to the specified stream.
void setStackTrace(StackTraceElement *elements*[ ])	Sets the stack trace to the elements passed in *elements*. This method is for specialized applications, not normal use.
String toString( )	Returns a string that contains a description of the exception. This method is called by **println( )** when outputting a **Throwable** object, for example.

In many cases, your exception class does not need to override any of these methods or create any additional functionality. Rather, it is its existence in the type system that lets you use it for an exception.

As a general rule, a custom exception should be carefully designed to represent precisely one type of error that can occur in your code. Therefore, when the exception is thrown, it means one and only one thing. For this reason, it is usually best to avoid creating a single class that you use for all types of errors.

Example

The following example creates a simple custom exception called **ArraySizeMismatchException** that is used to report when there is a mismatch between the length of two arrays. It is used by the **absCompare( )** method, which compares the absolute values of the elements of two integer arrays. This method returns true if the arrays compare equal and false otherwise. It throws an **ArraySizeMismatchException** if the two arrays differ in length. This means that **absCompare( )** returns false *only* if the absolute values of elements in the two arrays differ, not if the arrays differ in length. Notice that **ArraySizeMismatchException** overrides **toString( )** to provide a custom report of the exception.

```
// This program creates a simple custom exception type.
// It is used by the absCompare() method to report when
// the two arrays being compared are not the same length.

// A custom exception class.
class ArraySizeMismatchException extends Exception {
  private int sizeA;
  private int sizeB;

  ArraySizeMismatchException(int a, int b) {
    sizeA = a;
    sizeB = b;
  }

  // Override toString() to provide a custom response.
  public String toString() {
    return "\nArray Size Mismatch!\n" +
           "First array is " + sizeA + " elements long.\n" +
           "Second array is " + sizeB + " elements long. ";
  }
}

class CustomExceptionDemo {

  // Compare the absolute values of two arrays.
  // This method requires that the arrays be the
  // same length. Therefore, a return value of false
  // means that the arrays differed in the absolute
  // value of their elements and not just in their length.
  static boolean absCompare(int[] nums, int[] nums2)
    throws ArraySizeMismatchException {

    // If the arrays are not the same size, throw an exception.
    if(nums.length != nums2.length)
      throw new ArraySizeMismatchException(nums.length,
                                           nums2.length);
```

```
    // Determine if the absolute values of the arrays
    // are equal.
    for(int i=0; i < nums.length; i++)
      if(Math.abs(nums[i]) != Math.abs(nums2[i]))
        return false;

    return true;
  }

  public static void main(String args[]) {
    int alpha[] = { 1, 2, 3, 4 };
    int beta[] = { 1, -2, 3, -4 };
    int gamma[] = { 1, 2, 3, 4, 5};

    try {
      if(absCompare(alpha, beta))
        System.out.println("The absolute values contained " +
                           "in alpha and beta compare equal.");

      if(absCompare(alpha, gamma))
        System.out.println("The absolute values contained " +
                           "in alpha and gamma compare equal.");

    } catch (ArraySizeMismatchException exc) {
      System.out.println(exc);
    }
  }
}
```

The output is shown here:

```
The absolute values contained in alpha and beta compare equal.

Array Size Mismatch!
First array is 4 elements long.
Second array is 5 elements long.
```

Options and Alternatives

As the preceding example shows, not much effort is required to create a simple exception class. Of course, you can layer on more functionality as required by your application. For example, you can implement all four of the constructors supported by **Exception**. Doing so lets you specify a message and/or cause that supports chained exceptions. Here is such an implementation applied to **ArraySizeMismatchException** from the example:

```
// An expanded version of ArraySizeMismatchException.
class ArraySizeMismatchException extends Exception {
  private int sizeA;
  private int sizeB;

  ArraySizeMismatchException(int a, int b) {
    sizeA = a;
    sizeB = b;
  }
```

```
ArraySizeMismatchException(String msg, int a, int b) {
  super(msg);
  sizeA = a;
  sizeB = b;
}

ArraySizeMismatchException(String msg, Throwable cause,
                          int a, int b) {
  super(msg, cause);
  sizeA = a;
  sizeB = b;
}

ArraySizeMismatchException(Throwable cause, int a, int b) {
  super(cause);
  sizeA = a;
  sizeB = b;
}

// Override toString() to provide a custom response.
public String toString() {
  return "\nArray Size Mismatch!\n" +
         "First array is " + sizeA + " elements long.\n" +
         "Second array is " + sizeB + " elements long. ";
}
}
```

If you will be creating many custom exception classes for an application, then you may want to consider using a class hierarchy in which you create an abstract class at the top and then specific subclasses for each error. This way, in situations in which it is appropriate, you can catch all exceptions that your code generates using a single **catch** statement that catches the top-level class.

Schedule a Task for Future Execution

Key Ingredients	
Classes	**Methods**
java.util.Timer	void cancel( )
	void schedule(TimerTask *TTask*, long *wait*, long *repeat*)
java.util.TimerTask	void run( )

In **java.util** are two classes that serve a very useful purpose: they let you schedule a task for future execution. The classes are **Timer** and **TimerTask**. They work together, with **TimerTask** defining the task to execute and **Timer** providing the scheduling. Once started, the task waits in the background until the specified execution time arrives. At that point, the task is executed. It is also possible to schedule a task for repeated execution. This recipe shows how to put **Timer** and **TimerTask** into action.

NOTE *In javax.swing, Swing also defines a class called* **Timer**. *It serves a different purpose than does* **java.util.Timer**, *and it is important not to confuse the two. For recipes that use Swing, see Chapter 8. For general-purpose recipes that use multithreading, see Chapter 7.*

Step-by-Step

To schedule a task for future execution involves these steps:

1. Create a class that encapsulates the task to be scheduled by extending **TimerTask**.
2. Create an instance of the **TimerTask**.
3. Create a **Timer** instance that will be used to schedule the task.
4. Schedule the task by calling **schedule( )** on the **Timer** instance. You can schedule either a single or repeated execution of the task.
5. Stop the **Timer** by calling **cancel( )**.

Discussion

To create a task that can be executed by **Timer**, you must create an instance of **TimerTask**. **TimerTask** is an abstract class that implements the **Runnable** interface. You will extend it to create the class that encapsulates your task. **TimerTask** defines three methods, but the only one used by this recipe is **run( )**, which is specified by the **Runnable** interface. It is shown here:

    abstract void run( )

Notice that **run( )** is abstract. This means that it must be overridden by the extending class. In **run( )** you will put the code that constitutes the task to be executed.

To schedule a task for future execution, you must first create an instance of **Timer** and then call **schedule( )** on that object. There are several versions of **schedule( )**. The one used by this recipe is shown here:

    void schedule(TimerTask *TTask*, long *wait*, long *repeat*)

The task to schedule is passed in *TTask*. This must be an instance of the **TimerTask** class that you created, as just described. The number of milliseconds to wait before the task is executed is passed in *wait*. When the delay period expires, the **run( )** method of *TTask* is executed. The number of milliseconds to wait between repetitions is passed in *repeat*.

You can stop a **Timer** by calling **cancel( )**, shown next:

    void cancel( )

Once stopped, a timer cannot be restarted. If any task is currently executing, it will be allowed to finish.

Example

The following example shows **Timer** and **TimerTask** in action. It creates a class called **AutoBkUp** that automatically copies a file every two seconds. Of course, this short period is for demonstration purposes only. A longer period is probably more useful. Notice the field **success**. This field is initially set to false. If the copy operation succeeds, then **success** is set to true. Otherwise, it is set to false. You can obtain the success or failure status of the last backup by calling the accessor method **isSuccessful( )**. It returns the value of **success**.

```java
// Schedule a task by using Timer and TimerTask.

import java.util.*;
import java.io.*;

// This class automatically backs up a file
// whenever its run() method is executed.
class AutoBkUp extends TimerTask {
  private String bkupName;
  private String fName;
  private boolean success;

  AutoBkUp(String fn, String bk) {
    fName = fn;
    bkupName = bk;
    success = false;
  }

  // Create a backup copy of a file.
  // If an IO error occurs, this method sets the
  // "success" variable to false, attempts to close
  // open files, and resets the streams to null.
  // It then tries again on the next repetition.
  // However, in some applications, it might be
  // better to terminate the scheduler on failure.
  public void run() {
    FileInputStream fin = null;
    FileOutputStream fout = null;
    int len;
    byte b[] = new byte[1024];

    try {

      // Open the files.
      fin = new FileInputStream(fName);
      fout = new FileOutputStream(bkupName);

      // Copy the file.
      for(;;) {
        len = fin.read(b);
        if(len == -1) break;
        else fout.write(b, 0, len);
      }
      success = true;
```

```
    } catch(IOException exc) {
      success = false;
    }

    // Close the files. If either close fails,
    // indicate failure.
    if(fin != null) {
      try {
        fin.close();
      } catch(IOException exc) {
        success = false;
      }
    }

    if(fout != null) {
      try {
        fout.close();
      } catch(IOException exc) {
        success = false;
      }
    }

    // Reset the stream variables to null to be
    // ready for the next backup.
    fout = null;
    fin = null;
  }

  boolean isSuccessful() {
    return success;
  }
}

class SchedTaskDemo {
  public static void main(String args[]) {

    // Create TimerTask and Timer.
    AutoBkUp bkupTask = new AutoBkUp("MyData.dat", "MyData.bak");
    Timer bkTimer = new Timer();

    // Schedule backup for every 2 seconds.
    bkTimer.schedule(bkupTask, 2000, 2000);

    // Let autobackup run for a few seconds. Periodically
    // check for the success or failure of the backup.
    for(int i = 0; i < 5; i++) {
      try {
        Thread.sleep(2100);
      } catch (InterruptedException exc) {}
      if(bkupTask.isSuccessful())
        System.out.println("Last backup was successful.");
```

```
        else
          System.out.println("Last backup attempt failed.");
      }

    bkTimer.cancel();
  }
}
```

Options and Alternatives

There are several other forms of **schedule( )** defined by **Timer**. For example, you can schedule a task that executes only once by using this form:

> void schedule(TimerTask *TTask*, long *wait*)

Here, *TTask* is the task scheduled for execution after the number of milliseconds passed in *wait* has elapsed.

Timer also gives you the ability to schedule a task by specifying a **Date** at which to execute the task with these two forms of **schedule( )**:

> void schedule(TimerTask *TTask*, Date *targetTime*)

> void schedule(TimerTask *TTask*, Date *targetTime*, long *repeat*)

In both cases, *TTask* is scheduled for execution at the time specified by *targetTime*. In the second form, the task is then executed repeatedly at the interval passed in *repeat*, which is specified in milliseconds.

The versions of **schedule( )** that repeat the task apply the delay period to the time at which the task actually executed. Because of variations caused by task load and the execution of higher-priority tasks, it is possible that the delay might be longer than requested. If you need to execute a task at fixed intervals based on the original execution time, use the **scheduleAtFixedRate( )** method, instead.

In addition to **run( )**, **TimerTask** defines the following two methods:

boolean cancel( )	Terminates the task. Returns **true** if an execution of the task is prevented. Otherwise, returns **false**.
long scheduledExecutionTime( )	Returns the time at which the task was scheduled to have last executed.

These methods may be helpful in some applications.

Timer and **TimerTask** are not the only way to create a scheduled task. For example, it is possible to manually create a task that would be executed at a specific time using the **Thread** class. Of course, **Timer** and **TimerTask** are easier to use. When working with Swing, the **javax.swing.Timer** provides another option. It generates an action event each time it goes off.

Index

A

Abstract Window Toolkit (AWT). *See* AWT (Abstract Window Toolkit)
AbstractButton class, 383, 397, 400, 405, 406, 410, 468, 472
AbstractCollection class, 173, 177
AbstractList class, 173, 174
AbstractMap class, 183, 184, 185
AbstractQueue class, 173, 176
AbstractSequentialList class, 173, 174
AbstractSet class, 173, 175, 176, 178
accept( ), 91, 94
acquire( ), 481, 482, 485
Action command, 262, 384, 385, 387, 407, 412
    explicitly setting the, 387, 407, 412
Action events,
    and JButtons (push buttons), 262, 384, 385, 387–390
    and JCheckBoxes, 401
    and JRadioButtons, 406, 407
    and JTextFields, 411, 412, 413
    and JToggleButtons, 397
    and Swing menus, 467, 468
Action listener, 261, 262
ActionEvent class, 262, 384, 385, 412, 467
ActionListener interface, 262, 365, 384, 388, 390, 406, 407, 411, 412
actionPerformed( ), 262, 384, 385, 387–388, 407, 412
activeCount( ), 354–355
activeGroupCount( ), 358
Adapter classes, 271–272
add( ), 165, 167, 170, 187, 192, 196, 206, 214, 215, 217, 263, 366, 368, 369, 371, 458–459, 467, 468, 471–472
addActionListener( ), 261, 262, 384, 388
addAll( ), 165, 167, 187
addCookie( ), 251, 290, 291
addFirst( ), 171, 172
addItemListener( ), 261, 262
addKeyListener( ), 365
addLast( ), 171, 172
addMouseMotionListener( ), 365
addSeparator( ), 467, 468
addTableModelListener( ), 449
add*Type*Listener( ), 365

Adjustable interface, 428, 429
Adjustment events, 428, 429, 431
AdjustmentEvent class, 428, 429, 431
AdjustmentListener interface, 427, 428
adjustmentValueChanged( ), 427, 428
Alder32 class, 99
Algorithms (Collections class), 163, 185
allOf( ), 178
Annotation class, 501
Anonymous inner classes for event handling, using, 262–263, 388–390, 468
Apache Software Foundation, 246, 254
append( ), 55, 72, 76
Appendable interface, 72, 76, 118, 120
Applet class, 241, 242–244, 256, 258, 261, 269, 270, 279
    methods defined by, table of, 242–243
APPLET tag, 244, 256, 275
Applet(s)
    architecture, 244–245
    AWT-based versus Swing-based, 242
    definition of, 241
    display a Web page using an, 278–281
    event handling in Swing-based, 261, 262–263, 266, 268
    executing, 244
    layout manager for a Swing, setting the, 376
    life cycle, 244, 245
    overview, 241–246
    painting directly to the surface of an, 269–274
    parameters to an, passing, 275–277
    skeleton, creating AWT-based, 255–257
    skeleton, creating Swing-based, 257–260
    Swing, creating a GUI and handling events in a, 260–268
    with a scrolling banner, creating an, 266–268
AppletContext interface, 246
    to display a Web page, using the, 278–281
AppletStub interface, 246
appletviewer, 244, 256
Argument index, 123
Array, dynamic, 173–174, 192
Array of strings
    reverse-sorting an, 14–17
    ignore case differences when sorting an, 18–21

ArrayDeque class, 173, 177–178, 214–218
ArrayList class, 163, 173–174, 186, 187, 190, 191–195, 240
Arrays class, 14
AudioClip interface, 246
Autoboxing/unboxing, 163
availablePermits( ), 485
AWT (Abstract Window Toolkit), 242, 244, 245
    components, limitations of, 360
    creating an applet skeleton based on the, 255–257
    Swing's relationship to the, 361

B

binarySearch( ) algorithm, 221–223
Block of code, synchronized, 315, 316, 317, 319, 320
    to suspend, resume, and stop a thread, using a, 324–328
Border interface, 377
BorderFactory class, 377, 436
BorderLayout class, 262, 363, 364, 371, 372, 373
Borders
    JScrollpane viewport, 436
    Swing GUI component, 377–378
Boundary matchers, regular expression, 11
BoundedRangeModel, 427–428, 432
Box class, 364, 375, 434
BoxLayout, 363, 364, 373, 375, 434
breadthFirstEnumeration( ), 465
BufferedInputStream class, 51, 53, 62, 66, 68, 100
BufferedOutputStream class, 53, 65, 66, 68
BufferedReader class, 51, 56, 72, 76, 77, 79
BufferedWriter class, 56, 75, 76, 76, 77, 79
Button(s), 261
    default, 391, 392, 393–396
    group, 406
    menus as, 468
    radio, 405–410
    toggle (two-state), 390, 396–400, 401
    See also Push button(s)
ButtonGroup class, 406
ButtonModel interface, 383

C

Calendar class, 134, 137
call( ), 487
Callable interface, 481, 486, 487, 488
cancel( ), 507, 510
canExecute( ), 86
canRead( ), 84
canWrite( ), 84
Caret events, 412, 413–414, 419
CaretEvent class, 413, 419
CaretListener interface, 412, 413, 419
caretUpdate( ), 413
Cell, 439
    selection, handling, 449

Cell editor
    for a table, 439, 440, 446
    for a tree, 457, 466
Cell renderer, 439, 440, 446, 457, 466
    for a list, custom, 426
Change events
    and JButtons, 268
    and JRadioButtons, 407
    and JScrollBars, 431
ChangeEvent class, 268, 431
ChangeListener interface, 431
Character classes, regular expression, 9–10
charAt( ), 7
CharBuffer class, 69
CharSequence interface, 33
Check boxes, 261, 262
    creating, 400–405
    and menus, 471
    See also JCheckBox class
checkedCollection( ), 224–227
CheckedInputStream class, 99
checkedList( ), 227
checkedMap( ), 227
CheckedOutputStream class, 99
checkedSet( ), 227
checkedSortedMap( ), 227
checkedSortedSet( ), 227
Checksums, 99
ChoiceFormat class, 154
Class class, 492, 496, 497, 498, 501
Class, using reflection to obtain information about a, 491–496
ClassCastException, 165, 166, 168, 170, 171, 180, 181, 202, 206, 224, 225, 227
ClassNotFoundException, 112, 492
clear( ), 165, 179, 187, 234, 235
clearSelection( ), 425
Clipboard actions and text fields, 413, 416–419
close( ), 52, 54, 55, 56, 59, 60, 63, 66, 69, 72, 73, 77, 107, 112, 119
Closeable interface, 55, 56, 59, 63, 66, 69, 72, 76, 80, 95, 101, 118
CloseByInterruptException, 337
closeEntry( ), 100, 101
Collator, 21
Collection
    checked, creating a, 224–227
    comparator to order a, using a, 204, 205–209
    immutable, creating an, 231–233
    iterating a, 209–213
    sorted, using Comparable to store objects in a, 201–204
    synchronized (thread-safe), creating a, 227–231
    techniques, basic, 186–191
Collection interface, 162, 164–166, 167, 170, 178, 186, 187, 191, 196, 211, 215, 234
    methods defined by, table of, 165–166
Collections class, 163, 209, 218, 221, 222
    algorithms, 163, 185

checked... methods, 224, 227
synchronized... methods, 228, 231
unmodifiable... methods, 232, 233
Collections Framework, 161
   algorithms, 163, 185
   autoboxing/unboxing and the, 163
   collection classes, 173–178
   collection interfaces, 164–173
   for-each style for loop and the, 163–164
   generics and the, 163, 224
   and maps, 178. *See also* Map(s)
   overview, 162–178
   recipes using the, 186–240
Color class, 271
Comparable interface, 15, 221
   and sorted collections, 201–204, 205
Comparator
   creating a case-insensitive, 18–29
   to order a collection, using a, 204, 205–209
   reverse, using compare( ) to create a, 14–16
   using reverseOrder( ) to obtain a reverse, 209
Comparator interface, 14–15, 164
   with a collection, 205–209
comparator( ), 168, 177, 180
compare( ), 15, 16, 19, 205, 206
     ensuring full internationalization support
      when using, 21
compareTo( ), 7, 15–16, 17, 202–204, 205
compareToIgnoreCase( ), 7, 17, 19, 21, 204
compile( ) factory method of Pattern, 33, 34, 36
Component class, 244, 269, 270, 274, 362,
   367, 467, 472
Component(s), Swing GUI, 244, 245,
   258–259, 260, 361–362
   borders, 377–378
   class names for, list of, 362
   creating an applet containing, 260–268
   and the event-dispatching thread, 368, 369
   lightweight versus heavyweight, 360
   text, 411, 412, 419
Concurrency utilities, 296, 481, 486
Concurrent API, 296, 481, 486
ConcurrentModificationException, 228
Console
   using Formatter to write directly
     to the, 140–142, 143
   using printf( ) to write to the, 142, 143–144
Constructor class, 493, 497, 498, 501
Container class, 244, 362, 367, 467
Container(s), Swing
   definition of, 361
   lightweight versus heavyweight, 362–363
   panes. *See* Panes
   top-level, 361, 362, 363, 367
Containment hierarchy, 361, 362, 367
contains( ), 6, 22, 24, 165, 187
containsAll( ), 165, 187
containsKey( ), 179, 234, 235
containsValue( ), 179, 234, 235

Content pane, 244, 261, 262, 263, 363, 368
   and BoxLayout, 375
   layout manager of the, setting the, 372–376
contentEquals( ), 7
convertColumnIndexToModel( ), 455
convertColumnIndexToView( ), 455
convertRowIndexToModel( ), 455
convertRowIndexToView( ), 455
Cookie class, 251–253, 290
   methods defined by, table of, 253
Cookies, 251–253
copy( ), 412, 413
CountDownLatch class, 486
CRC32 class, 99
createLineBorder( ), 378
Currency values, using NumberFormat to
   format, 156–157
currentThread( ), 298, 310–311
Cursor, 412
cut( ), 412, 413
CyclicBarrier class, 486

D

Daemon thread, 297, 328–336
DataInput interface, 54, 55, 80, 81, 111
DataOutput interface, 54, 55, 80, 81, 110
DataInputStream class, 53, 96
DataOutputStream class, 53, 95, 96
Date class, 134, 137, 147, 148, 151, 152, 510
DateFormat class, 117, 123, 137
   formatting time and date using, 147–150
DecimalFormat class, 117, 123, 154, 156
   formatting numeric values with patterns
     using the, 158–160
   formatting symbols, table of, 158
DefaultMutableTreeNode, 457, 458, 465, 466
DefaultSingleSelectionModel, 467
DefaultTreeModel, 457, 460
Deflater class, 57, 95, 96
DeflaterOutputStream class, 85, 96, 99, 101
Delegation event model, 364–365
delete( ), 89
depthFirstEnumeration( ), 465–466
Deque interface, 164, 171–173, 174, 177, 191, 195
   capacity-restricted implementations of the,
     172, 215
   create a queue or stack using the, 214–218
   methods defined by, table of, 171–172
Deques, 171–173
   capacity-restricted, 172, 215
descendingIterator( ), 171, 172
destroy( ), 242, 245, 247, 253, 256, 258, 282,
   283, 284, 285
Dictionary class, 162
Directory
   creating a, 89
   deleting an empty, 89
   obtaining a list of files within a, 90–94

doGet( ), 251, 252, 285–286
doPost( ), 290
doPut( ), 290
Double.parseDouble( ), 275–276
drainPermits( ), 485–486
drawArc( ), 274
drawLine( ), 270
drawOval( ), 274
drawRect( ), 274
drawString( ), 245, 270, 271

E

Edit field, combining a list with an, 426
end( ), 34
endsWith( ), 6, 22
ensureCapacity( ), 174, 192
entries( ), 105, 106
entrySet( ), 179, 182, 234, 235, 240
enumerate( ), 354, 358
EnumMap class, 183, 185
EnumSet class, 173, 178, 187, 190–191
EOFException, 115
equals( ), 15, 165, 166, 167, 179, 183, 202–204, 206
Error handling
    creating a custom exception class for, 501–506
    error code and, 502
    tips for, 57–58
Error versus failure, 502
Event
    definition of, 365
    listeners, 364, 365
    sources, 364, 365
Event handling
    and action commands, 262, 384, 385,
        387, 407, 412
    and action events. See Action events
    and adapter classes, 271–272
    and adjustment events, 428, 429, 431
    and anonymous inner classes, 262–263,
        388–390, 468
    and caret events, 412, 413–414, 419
    and change events. See Change events
    and item events. See Item events
    and list selection events. See List
        selection events
    and mouse events, 271–272
    and multithreading, 296–297
    in Swing, 364–365
    in Swing applets, 261, 262–263, 266, 268
    and table model events, 447, 449–450
    and tree events, 458, 459–460
EventObject class, 365, 387
Exception class, 502–503, 505
    methods inherited from Throwable,
        table of, 503
Exception(s)
    chained, 503, 505
    class, creating a custom, 501–506

Exchanger class, 486
Execution, scheduling a task for future, 506–510
Executor, 487
    fixed thread pool, using a, 487–491
Executor interface, 487
Executors class, 487
ExecutorService interface, 487, 488
exists( ), 84, 87, 90
Externalizable interface, 115

F

Failure versus error, 502
Field class, 493, 501
Field, using reflection to get or set the value of a, 501
File attributes
    obtaining, 83–86
    setting, 86–89
File class, 54, 62, 64, 65, 72, 75, 83, 84, 86, 87,
    89, 90, 91, 94
File(s)
    compressed, 57, 95–99
    delete, 89
    Formatter to write directly to a, using, 140–142
    handling, overview of, 50–58
    in a directory, obtaining a list of, 90–94
    I/O, buffer byte-based, 65–68
    I/O, buffer character-based, 75–79
    pointer, 81
    printf( ) to write formatted output to a,
        using, 143, 144
    random access to, 53–54, 55, 80–83
    read bytes from a, 59–62
    read characters from a, 62, 69–72
    rename, 89
    serializing objects in a, 110–115
    write bytes to a, 62–65
    write characters to a, 72–75
File, ZIP
    creating a, 100–105
    decompressing a, 105–110
FileDescriptor, 62, 64, 72, 75
FileFilter interface, 55, 56, 90, 91, 94
FileInputStream class, 51, 53, 59, 61, 72, 100
FilenameFilter interface, 55, 56, 94
FileNotFoundException, 57, 59, 63, 65, 69, 80, 501
FileOutputStream class, 51, 53, 63, 64–65,
    75, 101, 141, 144
FileReader class, 51, 53, 62, 69, 71, 72, 76, 79
FileWriter class, 51, 53, 72, 73, 75, 76, 79, 144
FilterInputStream class, 53, 66, 95
FilterOutputStream class, 53, 66, 95
find( ), 33, 36, 37, 40
findWithinHorizon( ), 48
first( ), 168, 196
FlowLayout, 262, 363, 364, 372, 373, 375, 378
    drawbacks of, 373
flush( ), 52, 55, 56, 119
Flushable interface, 55, 56, 63, 66, 72, 76, 95, 101, 118

For-each style for loop, 163–164, 165, 187, 191, 195, 213
Format class, 147, 154
Format flags, 122
Format specifiers, 119–123
    minimum field-width specifier and.
        See Minimum field-width specifier
    precision specifiers and, 121–122, 124
    table of, 121
format( ), 119–120, 124, 127, 130, 131, 134, 138, 140, 141, 143, 144, 147, 148, 151, 152, 154, 155, 156, 157, 158, 159
    argument index with, using an, 123
    PrintStream version of, 146
    PrintWriter version of, 147
Formatter class, 117
    left-justify output using, 131–133
    locale specification using, 138–140
    methods defined by, table of, 119
    numeric formatting techniques
        using, 124–126, 160
    overview, 118–123
    streams with the, using, 140–142
    time and date formatting using, 133–137, 153
    vertically align numeric data using, 126–131
FormatterClosedException, 119
forName( ), 492, 496
Frame class, 367
Future interface, 481, 486, 487, 488, 491

— G —

Generics and collections, 163, 224
GenericServlet class, 247–248, 251, 285
    to create a simple servlet, using the, 282–284
GET request, 251
    handling a, 284, 285–286
get( ), 166, 167, 179, 192, 221, 222, 234, 487, 488, 491
getActionCommand( ), 384, 385, 388, 390, 407, 468
getAdjustable( ), 428–429
getAnchorSelectionIndex( ), 425
getAnnotation( ), 496
getAnnotations( ), 496, 501
getAppletContext( ), 242, 246, 278, 279
getAttribute( ), 293
getBlockIncrement( ), 432
getChildren( ), 460
getClass( ), 496
getColumn( ), 447, 449
getColumnModel( ), 447, 448
getConstructor( ), 496
getContentLength( ), 474, 475
getContentPane( ), 263, 369, 373
getContentType( ), 474, 475
getCompressedSize( ), 101, 102, 106, 107
getCookies( ), 250, 290, 291
getCurrencyInstance( ), 156, 157
getDate( ), 475, 476
getDateInstance( ), 147, 148, 149, 150

getDeclaredAnnotations( ), 496
getDeclaredConstructor( ), 496
getDeclaredConstructors( ), 492, 496, 497
getDeclaredField( ), 496, 501
getDeclaredFields( ), 492, 493, 496
getDeclaredMethod( ), 496
getDeclaredMethods( ), 492, 496, 497, 498
getDefaultFractionDigits( ), 496
getDot( ), 419
getEntry( ), 110
getExpiration( ), 475, 476
getField( ), 496
getFields( ), 496
getFirstRow( ), 447, 449
getGraphics( ), 274
getHeaderField( ), 480
getHeaderFieldInt( ), 480
getHeaderFieldKey( ), 480
getHeaderFields( ), 475, 476
getIcon( ), 382
getID( ), 298, 307, 308
getInputStream( ), 106, 107, 475, 476
getInstance( ) factory method
    of Calendar, 134
    of Collator, 21
    of NumberFormat, 154, 156
getInt( ), 501
getItem( ), 262, 397–398, 401
getKey( ), 183, 235
getLastModified( ), 476
getLastPathComponent( ), 459
getLastRow( ), 449
getLeadSelectionIndex( ), 425
getMark( ), 419
getMaxAge( ), 253, 293
getMaximum( ), 432
getMenuComponentCount( ), 472
getMenuComponents( ), 472
getMenuCount( ), 472
getMethod( ), 496
getMethods( ), 496
getMinimum( ), 432
getModel( ), 431, 447, 449, 460
getModifiers( ), 501
getName( ), 90, 91, 105, 106, 253, 290, 291, 298, 307, 308, 501
getParameter( ), 275, 285, 286
getParameterTypes( ), 497–498
getParent( ), 358
getPath( ), 459
getPriority( ), 298, 341, 342
getRequestMethod( ), 475, 476
getResponseCode( ), 475, 476
getResponseMessage( ), 475, 476
getReturnType( ), 497, 498
getRootPane( ), 392
getSelectedColumn( ), 447, 448–449, 455
getSelectedColumns( ), 447, 448–449, 455
getSelectedIndex( ), 420, 421

getSelectedIndices( ), 420, 421, 424
getSelectedRow( ), 447, 448
getSelectedRows( ), 447, 448
getSelectedText( ), 412, 413
getSelectionModel( ), 447, 448, 460
getServerName( ), 248, 283
getSession( ), 250, 293
getSize( ), 100–101, 102, 106, 107
getSource( ), 387–388, 407, 468
getState( ), 298, 345, 346
getStateChange( ), 397, 398, 401
getSymbol( ), 140
getText( ), 377, 379, 387, 412, 413
getTime( ), 105, 137
getTimeInMillis( ), 137
getTimeInstance( ), 148, 149
getTreePath( ), 460
getType( ), 447, 449, 450, 501
getUnitIncrement( ), 432
getValue( ), 183, 235, 253, 290, 291, 427, 429, 431, 432
getValueAt( ), 447, 450
getValueIsAdjusting( ), 426, 427, 429, 431, 448
getVisibleAmount( ), 432
getWriter( ), 249, 282, 283, 285, 286
Glass pane, 262, 363
Graphic user interface (GUI). *See* GUI
    (Graphic User Interface)
Graphics class, 270, 274
GregorianCalendar class, 137
GridBagLayout, 375
GridLayout, 363, 364, 375, 378
group( ), 33, 36, 37
GUI (Graphic user interface), 242
    components and Swing, 258–259, 260–268,
       360–361
GZIP
    files, 95, 96
    format, 57, 99, 100
GZIPInputStream class, 99, 100
GZIPOutputStream class, 99, 100

H

Hash code, 175
Hash table, 175
    and Properties, 239
hashCode( ), 165, 179, 183
Hashing, 175
HashMap class, 28, 183, 184, 185, 238
    converting a Properties list into an instance
      of the, 238–240
HashSet class, 163, 173, 175, 176, 196–198
HashTable class, 162, 238, 239
hasNext( ), 210
hasPrevious( ), 210, 211
Header fields, 475, 476
higher( ), 169, 196
holdsLock( ), 298, 353
<html>, 379, 391, 392

HTML
    file for applets, 244, 256
    in a label, using, 379
    and mnemonics, 393, 395
    and push buttons, 391, 392–393, 395
HTTP connection, accessing a resource
    via an, 474–480
HTTP requests
    in a servlet, handling, 284, 285–290
    and responses, obtaining information about,
      475, 476
HttpServlet class, 251, 253, 285, 290
    do... methods, 251, 253
    methods defined by, table of, 252
HttpServletRequest interface, 249, 285, 286, 290, 293
    a sampling of methods defined by,
      table of, 250
HttpServletResponse interface, 249, 251, 285,
    286, 290, 291
    a sampling of methods defined by,
      table of, 251
HttpSession class, 293
HttpUrlConnection class to access a resource,
    using an, 474–480

I

Icon interface, 377
Icons and Swing
    check boxes, 405
    labels, 382
    push buttons, 391–392, 393–395, 396
    radio buttons, 410
    toggle buttons, 400
IdentityHashMap class, 183
IllegalArgumentException, 165, 166, 168,
    170, 171, 180, 181
IllegalFormatException, 120, 130, 144
IllegalStateException, 33, 34, 165, 170, 171,
    172, 210, 215
IllegalThreadStateException, 329
ImageIcon class, 377
indexOf( ), 6, 22, 25, 32, 167, 192
IndexOutOfBoundsException, 211
Inflater class, 57, 95, 96
InflaterInputStream class, 95, 96, 99
init( ), 243, 245, 247, 253, 256, 258–259, 282,
    283, 284, 285
InputStream class, 51, 53, 55, 57, 59, 66, 80,
    95, 96, 111, 476
    methods defined by, table of, 52
InputStreamReader class, 53, 69
insert( ), 8
Integer.parseInt( ), 275–276
Interface, using reflection to obtain information
    about an, 495–496
Internet and Java, 474
interrupt( ), 298, 337, 354, 355
InterruptableChannel, 337

interrupted( ), 298, 337, 339, 340
InterruptedException, 300, 337, 339, 340
InvalidClassException, 111
invoke( ), 497, 498
invokeAndWait( ), 258–259, 263, 368–369
invokeLater( ), 366, 368–369, 370
I/O
     buffering file, 65–68, 75–79
     channel-based, 50
     error handling, 57–58
     file, overview of, 50–58
     interfaces, 55–57
     streams. *See* Stream(s)
     Swing, 366
     See also File(s)
IOException, 57, 58, 59, 60, 63, 66, 68, 69, 73, 75,
     77, 79, 81, 101, 102, 106, 111, 112, 115, 283,
     286, 480, 502
ioException( ), 119
isAlive( ), 298, 313–314, 345, 346
isDaemon( ), 298, 329
isDefaultButton( ), 395
isDefaultCapable( ), 396
isDirectory( ), 84, 90
     and Windows paths, 105
isEmpty( ), 165, 179, 187, 214, 215, 218, 234, 235
isEnabled( ), 384, 385
isFile( ), 84
isHidden( ), 84
isInterrupted( ), 298, 337, 340
isLeaf( ), 465
isRolloverEnabled( ), 392
isRoot( ), 465
isSelected( ), 397, 398, 401, 406, 407
isSelectionEmpty( ), 425
isSuccessful( ), 508
Item events
     and JCheckBoxes, 262, 401
     and JRadioButtons, 407
     and JToggleButtons, 397–398
Item listener, 261, 262
ItemEvent class, 262, 397, 398, 401, 404
ItemListener interface, 262, 397, 401
itemStateChanged( ), 262, 397, 401
Iterable interface, 163–164, 165, 178, 191,
     211, 213, 235
Iterator interface, 163, 164, 210–213
iterator( ), 165, 210, 211
Iterators, 163, 186, 191, 195, 209–213

━━ **J** ━━

Jakarta Project, 246, 254
jakarta.apache.org, 246
JApplet class, 242, 244, 258, 261, 262, 269, 362,
     372, 373, 375
Java Foundation Classes (JFC), 360
Java: A Beginner's Guide, 4
Java: The Complete Reference, 4, 50, 162, 269
java.applet package, 241, 246, 256

java.awt package, 271, 363, 372, 375
java.awt.event, 365, 384
java.awt.event.KeyEvent, 392
java.awt.Graphics, 270
java.io package, 49, 50, 51, 55, 110
java.lang, 6, 8, 69, 72, 76, 220, 297, 298, 354
java.lang.Class, 491, 492
java.lang.reflect package, 491, 493, 501
java.lang.Runnable. *See* Runnable interface
java.net package, 474
java.nio package, 50, 72
java.text package, 123, 147
java.text.CollationKey, 21
java.text.Collator, 21
java.text.DateFormat. *See* DateFormat class
java.text.DecimalFormat. *See* DecimalFormat class
java.text.NumberFormat. *See* NumberFormat class
java.text.SimpleDateFormat. *See*
     SimpleDateFormat class
java.util package, 14, 118, 134, 138, 162, 173, 183, 191,
     196, 205, 221, 507
java.util.Arrays.sort( ), 14, 16, 19
java.util.concurrent package, 162, 296, 486
java.util.concurrent.atomic package, 480, 486
java.util.concurrent.locks package, 480, 486
java.util.concurrent.TimeUnit enumeration, 491
java.util.Currency, 140
java.util.Date. *See* Date class
java.util.EventObject, 365
java.util.Formatter. *See* Formatter class
java.util.regex, 5, 8
java.util.Stack, 162, 191, 214
java.util.zip package, 49, 51, 57, 95, 100
JavaBeans, 491, 497
javax.servlet package, 246–249
javax.servlet.http package, 246, 249–253, 285
javax.swing package, 258, 266, 362, 363, 366,
     372, 439, 457
javax.swing.border.Border interface, 377
javax.swing.BorderFactory, 377
javax.swing.ChangeEvent, 431
javax.swing.ChangeListener, 431
javax.swing.event package, 365, 413, 421, 457
javax.swing.JApplet, 242, 258
javax.swing.ListModel, 420
javax.swing.ListSelectionModel, 420, 421
javax.swing.table package, 439
javax.swing.table.TableRowSorter, 455
javax.swing.text.Document, 412
javax.swing.text.JTextComponent, 412
javax.swing.tree package, 457, 459
JButton class, 261, 262, 268, 373, 397
     action events, 262, 384, 385, 387–390
     change events, 268
     to create a simple push button,
          using the, 383–390
     using icons, HTML, and mnemonics
          with, 390–396
     See also Push button(s)

JCheckBox class, 261, 262, 397
    action events, 401
    to create a check box, using the, 400–405
    item events, 262, 401
JCheckBoxMenuItem class, 471
JComboBox class, 426
JComponent class, 244, 362, 467, 472
JEditorPane, 419
JFC (Java Foundation Classes), 360
JFormattedTextField, 411, 419
JFrame container, 334, 362, 366, 367, 368, 369, 371,
    372, 373, 467, 468
JLabel, 261, 262, 266, 334, 366, 367, 369, 372
    working with, 376–383
    See also Label(s), Swing
JList class
    and scroll panes, 436
    working with, 420–426
JMenu class, 466–467, 468, 471, 472
JMenuBar class, 466–467, 472
JMenuItem class, 466–467, 468, 471
join( ), 298, 311–313, 314, 337, 339, 344, 345
JPanel class, 262, 269, 362, 363, 364, 375, 378
JPasswordField, 411, 419
JPopupMenu class, 472
JProgressBar, 427
JRadioButton class, 397
    action events, 406, 407
    change events, 407
    to create radio buttons, using the, 405–410
    item events, 407
    See also Radio buttons
JRadioButtonMenuItem class, 471
JRootPane container, 362, 363, 392
JScrollBar class
    adjustment events, 431
    change events, 431
    to create a scroll bar, using the, 427–432
    properties, 432
    See also Scroll bar(s)
JScrollPane container, 362
    corners, 437
    to handle scrolling, using, 433–438
    headers, 436
    to scroll the contents of a JList,
      using, 420–421, 432
    viewport, 433, 436
    wrapping a JTable in a, 439, 440
    wrapping a JTree in a, 457
JSeparator class, 468
JSlider class, 427, 432
JSpinner class, 426, 432
JTabbedPane container, 438
JTable
    to display data in a table, using, 438–446
    events, handling, 446–455
    using JScrollPane with, 436, 439, 440
    resizing modes, 445
    using Vector to create a dynamic, 444
    See also Table, Swing

JTextArea class, 411, 419
JTextComponent class, 412
JTextField class
    action events, 411, 412, 413
    caret events, 412, 413–414, 419
    inputting text with, 411–419
JTextPane, 419
JToggleButton class, 390, 401, 406
    action events, 397
    to create a toggle button, using the, 396–400
    item events, 397–398
JToolBar class, 471
JTree
    display data in a, 456–466
    using JScrollPane with, 457
    See also Tree, Swing

K

Key/value pairs
    from a string, retrieving, 28–32
    and maps, 258, 234
KeyEvent class, 392
keySet( ), 179, 234, 235

L

Label(s), Swing
    alignment, setting, 371, 378
    icons and, 382
    mnemonic to a, adding a, 383
    See also JLabel component
last( ), 168, 196
lastIndexOf( ), 6, 22, 167, 192
lastModified( ), 84
Layered pane, 262, 363
Layout manager
    content pane, setting the, 372–376
    overview, 363–364
LayoutManager interface, 363
LayoutManager2 interface, 363
Left justification using Formatter, 131–133
length( ), 7, 81, 84
LinkedHashMap class, 183, 184–185
LinkedHashSet class, 173, 175–176, 196, 201
LinkedList class, 161, 163, 173, 174–175, 191–195, 213,
    214, 216
List interface, 164, 166–167, 173, 174, 191–195, 196,
    210, 211, 213, 218, 219, 221, 227, 238, 240
    methods defined by, table of, 167
List selection events
    and JList, 420, 421
    and JTable, 447–449
list( ), 94
List(s)
    doubly-linked, 174, 175
    into a HashMap, converting a
      Properties, 238–240
    reverse, rotate, and shuffle a, 218–220
    sort and search a, 221–223

Swing, 420–426
thread-safe (synchronized), 231
unmodifiable, 233
working with, 191–195
ListCellRenderer interface, 426
listFiles( ), 90, 91, 94
ListIterator interface, 164, 210–213
listIterator( ), 167, 210, 211
ListModel, 426
ListSelectionEvent class, 421, 422, 447
ListSelectionListener interface, 420, 421, 422, 447, 448
ListSelectionModel, 439, 441, 447, 448
Locale class, 138–139, 149, 153, 156, 157
predefined locales, list of, 139
Lock, 315, 319, 320
and deadlock, 323
premature release of a, 323
status, determining the, 353
log( ), 248
long, 134, 137
Long class, 134, 137
Look and feel, 360–361
loop( ), 246
lower( ), 169, 196

M

main( )
and applets, 244
and Swing GUIs, 368
makeVisible( ), 464–465
MalformedURLException, 278, 475
Map interface, 28, 178, 183, 184, 185, 227, 234, 238, 239, 240
methods defined by, table of, 179
Map, sorted
and Comparable, 202, 204
comparator with a, using a, 209
thread-safe (synchronized), 231
type-safe (checked), 227
unmodifiable, 233
Map(s), 163, 178–184
algorithms, 185
classes, 183–185
collection-view of, 163, 178, 235
interfaces, 178–183
techniques, basic, 233–238
thread-safe (synchronized), 231
type-safe view of a, obtaining a, 227
unmodifiable, 233
Map.Entry interface, 178, 182–183, 235, 240
methods defined by, table of, 183
mark( ), 52, 54, 68, 79
Matcher class, 8, 28
to match and extract substrings, using the, 32–34
to tokenize a string, using the, 36–48
matcher( ) factory method of Matcher, 33
matches( ), 7, 8, 22–23, 24, 93

Menu(s), Swing, 466
events, handling, 467, 468
main, creating a, 466, 472
popup, 472
MenuElement interface, 467
Metal look and feel, 361
Method
reflection to call a, using, 496–501
synchronized, 315, 316–317, 319, 320
Method class, 493, 497, 498, 501
Minimum field-width specifier, 121, 126, 127, 131
and left-justifying output, 131–133
mkdir( ), 89
mkdirs( ), 89
Mnemonics
and check boxes, 405
and HTML, 393, 395
to a label, adding keyboard, 383
and push buttons, 391, 392, 393–395
and radio buttons, 410
and toggle buttons, 400
Model-delegate architecture, 361
Model-view-controller (MVC) architecture, 361
Monitor, 315, 319, 320, 322
Mouse events, 271–272
MouseAdapter class, 271
mouseEntered( ), 272
MouseListener interface, 272
mousePressed( ), 272
mouseReleased( ), 272
moveCaretPosition( ), 419
Multitasking, process-based versus thread-based, 296
Multithreaded programming, 295–358
fundamentals, 296–299
and semaphores, 480–486
and threads. *See* Thread
MutableTreeNode, 457, 458
MVC (Model-view-controller) architecture, 361

N

NavigableMap interface, 178, 180–182, 183, 184
methods defined by, table of, 181–182
NavigableSet interface, 164, 168–169, 176, 196–198
methods defined by, table of, 169
Networking and Java, 474, 479
newFixedThreadPool( ), 487
newInstance( ), 497, 498
next( ), 210, 213
NIO, 50, 72
NoSuchElementException, 168, 170, 171, 173, 180, 210, 211, 215, 218
notify( ), 297, 319–320, 322, 323, 324, 344, 481
notifyAll( ), 297, 320, 322
NotSerializableException, 111
NullPointerException, 115, 165, 166, 168, 170, 171, 180, 181

NumberFormat class, 117, 123, 158, 159
    format currency values using the, 156–157
    format numeric values using the, 153–156, 160
NumberFormatException, 276
Numeric values
    using Formatter to format, 124–126
    using NumberFormat to format, 153–156
    with patterns using DecimalFormat,
        formatting, 158–160
    vertically align, 126–131

O

Object class, 130, 295, 297, 319, 481, 496
Object, using reflection to dynamically create an,
    496–501
ObjectInput interface, 55, 57, 111
ObjectInputStream class, 110, 111, 112
ObjectOutput interface, 55, 57, 110
ObjectOutputStream class, 110–111, 112
Objects, serialize, 110–115
ObjectStreamConstants interface, 111
offer( ), 170, 206
offerFirst( ), 171, 172, 217
offerLast( ), 171, 172, 217
openConnection( ), 474, 475
out( ), 119, 120
OutputStream class, 51, 53, 55, 57, 63, 66, 80, 95, 96,
    101, 110, 118, 141, 142, 480
    methods defined by, table of, 52
OutputStreamWriter class, 53, 72

P

Paging area, 427
paint( ), 269, 270, 271, 274
Panel class, 244
Panes, 262, 363
    content. *See* Content pane
    scroll. *See* Scroll panes
PARAM, 275
Parameters to an applet, passing, 275–277
parse... methods, 275
paste( ), 412, 413
Pattern class, 8, 28
    to match and extract substrings,
        using the, 32–34
    to tokenize a string, using the, 36–48
PatternSyntaxException, 8, 23, 24, 25, 26, 28, 33
peek( ), 170, 218
Peers, 360
play( ), 246
Pluggable look and feel, 360–361, 362
poll( ), 170, 177, 206, 217, 218
pollFirst( ), 172, 173
pollLast( ), 172, 173
pop( ), 171, 172, 173, 215, 217, 218
POST requests, handling, 284, 285, 290
postorderEnumeration( ), 465–466
Precision specifier, 121–122, 124

preorderEnumeration( ), 465–466
previous( ), 210, 211, 213
print( ), 141, 445
printf( ), 117, 150
    to create a time stamp, using, 145–146
    to display formatted data, using, 142, 143–147
println( ), 120, 141, 144, 244, 245, 493
PrintStream class, 117, 118, 141, 143, 144
    printf( ) method of the, 143–144
PrintWriter class, 117, 118, 143, 144
    printf( ) method of the, 144
PriorityQueue class, 173, 176–177, 202, 205, 206–209
Properties class, 28, 162, 238–240
    object into a HashMap, converting a, 238–240
Push button(s), 262
    creating a simple, 383–390
    default, 391, 392, 393–396
    and icons, 391–392, 393–395, 396
    and mnemonics, 391, 392, 393–395
    setting and obtaining text within a, 387
push( ), 171, 172, 214, 215, 217, 218
PUT request, 290
put( ), 179, 234, 235, 239
putAll( ), 179, 234, 235
putNextEntry( ), 100, 101

Q

Quantifiers, regular expression, 10–11
Queue interface, 164, 170, 171, 173, 176, 214
    methods defined by, table of, 170
Queue, using Deque to create a first-in, first-out
    (FIFO), 171, 214–218

R

Radio buttons
    creating, 405–410
    and menus, 471
    See also JRadioButton class
Random class, 220
Random number generator, 220
RandomAccess interface, 164, 174, 191
RandomAccessFile class, 53–54, 55, 80, 81, 83
range( ), 178
Raw type, 224, 226
read( ), 52, 54, 55, 59, 61–62, 66, 69, 71–72,
    76–77, 80, 81, 96
Readable interface, 69, 72, 76
readDouble( ), 96, 97
Reader class, 51, 69, 76
    methods defined by, table of, 54
readExternal( ), 115
readInt( ), 55, 80, 97
readLine( ), 79, 244
readObject( ), 111, 112
Reflection, 491
    to dynamically create an object and call
        methods, using, 496–501
    to get or set the value of a field, using, 501

to obtain information about a class at runtime, using, 491–496
to obtain information about an interface, using, 492, 495–496
utility program, 494–495
region( ), 48
regionEnd( ), 48
regionMatches( ), 7, 17, 24
regionStart( ), 48
Regular expression API, 5, 8
to match and extract substrings, using the, 32–34
to tokenize a string, using the, 36–48
Regular expression(s), 5, 8–13
boundary matchers, 11
character classes, 9–10
and file filtering, 91, 93–94
flag sequences, 13
groups, 12–13
and the OR (|) operator, 11–12
quantifiers, 10–11
to search for or replace substrings, using, 22–24, 25
to split strings, 25–28
wildcard character, 10
release( ), 481, 482
Remote Method Invocation (RMI), 110
remove( ), 165, 167, 170, 179, 187, 192, 210, 214, 215, 217, 218, 234, 235, 263, 369, 465, 472
removeAll( ), 165, 187
removeFirst( ), 172, 173
removeKeyListener( ), 365
remove*Type*Listener( ), 365
renameTo( ), 89
repaint( ), 270, 271, 273–274
replace( ), 7, 22
replaceAll( ), 7, 22, 23
replaceFirst( ), 7, 25
reset( ), 52, 54, 68, 79
resume( ), 323, 328
retainAll( ), 166, 187
reverse( ) algorithm, 218–220
reverseOrder( ) algorithm, 209
Root pane, 262, 392
rotate( ) algorithm, 218–220
Row selection events, 448
RowSorter class, 455
run( ), 258–259, 297, 298, 299, 300, 302, 304, 305, 323, 324, 328, 336, 345, 368, 507, 510
Runnable interface, 258, 295, 297, 298, 299, 304, 308, 354, 368, 481, 491, 507
implementing, 299–304, 306–307
RunnableFuture interface, 491

S

Scanner class, 36, 47, 48
schedule( ), 507, 510
scheduleAtFixedRate( ), 510
scheduledExecutionTime( ), 510

Scroll bar(s), 426–432
using JScrollPane to automate handling of, 433
policy, 437–438
thumb, 427, 428, 429
See also JScrollBar
Scroll panes, 432, 433–438
and scroll bars, 433
See also JScrollPane
ScrollPaneConstants interface, 437, 438
SecurityException, 57–58
seek( ), 54, 80, 81
Semaphore
fairness, 482, 485
permits, 481, 482, 485–486
using a, 480–486
Semaphore class, 481, 485, 486
Separable model architecture, 361
Serializable interface, 111
Serialization, 110
service( ), 247, 252, 253, 282–283, 285
Servlet interface, 246, 247, 253, 282
methods defined by, table of, 247
servlet-api.jar, 254
Servlet(s)
cookie with, use a, 290–293
definition of, 241
development, using Tomcat for, 246, 254–255
exception classes, 249
GenericServlet to create a simple, using, 282–284
HTTP requests in a, handling, 285–290
life cycle, 253
overview, 246–255
ServletConfig interface, 247, 253, 282
ServletException, 249, 283, 286
ServletRequest interface, 246, 247, 282, 283, 286
a sampling of methods defined by, table of, 248
ServletResponse interface, 246, 247, 253, 282, 283, 286
a sampling of methods defined by, table of, 249
Sessions, 293
Set interface, 162–163, 164, 167, 168, 173, 175, 178, 182, 196–201, 227, 235
Set, sorted
checked (type-safe), 227
synchronized (thread-safe), 231
unmodifiable, 233
set( ), 137, 166, 167, 192, 213
Set(s)
checked (type-safe), 227
synchronized (thread-safe), 231
unmodifiable, 233
working with, 195–201
setActionCommand( ), 387, 407, 412
set Attribute( ), 293
setAutoResizeMode( ), 445
setBackground( ), 270–271
setBlockIncrement( ), 432

setBorder( ), 376, 378
setCaretPosition( ), 419
setCellSelectionEnabled( ), 439, 441
setCharAt( ), 8
setColumnHeaderView( ), 436
setColumnSelectionAllowed( ), 439, 440, 441
setComment( ), 253, 273
setContentType( ), 249, 282, 283, 285, 286
setCorner( ), 437
setDaemon( ), 298, 329
setDefaultButton( ), 391, 392
setDefaultCapable( ), 395–396
setDefaultCloseOperation( ), 366, 367
setDisabledIcon( ), 382, 391, 392, 400
setDisplayedMnemonic( ), 383
setDouble( ), 501
setEditable( ), 456, 460
setEnabled( ), 376, 379, 384, 385, 400, 472
setExecutable( ), 89
setForeground( ), 270–271
setGroupingUsed( ), 154, 155
setHorizontalAlignment( ), 376, 378, 405, 410
setHorizontalScrollBarPolicy( ), 438
setHorizontalTextPosition( ), 382, 400, 405, 410
setIcon( ), 382, 391, 392
setJMenuBar( ), 468
setLabelFor( ), 383
setLastModified( ), 87
setLayout( ), 261, 262, 263, 369, 372, 373, 375
setListData( ), 425
setMaxAge( ), 253, 291
setMaximum( ), 432
setMaximumFractionDigits( ), 154–155
setMinimum( ), 432
setMinimumFractionDigits( ), 154–155
setMnemonic( ), 391, 392, 400, 405, 410
setName( ), 105, 298, 307, 308
setPreferredScrollableViewportSize( ), 439, 440
setPreferredSize( ), 261, 262, 378, 423
setPressedIcon( ), 391, 392, 400
setPriority( ), 298, 341, 342
setProperty( ), 239
setReadable( ), 89
setReadOnly( ), 87
setRolloverIcon( ), 391, 392, 400
setRolloverSelectedIcon( ), 400
setRowHeaderView( ), 436
setRowSelectionAllowed( ), 439, 440, 441
setRowSorter( ), 455
setSelected( ), 397, 401, 404, 406, 407
setSelectedIcon( ), 400, 405, 410
setSelectedIndex( ), 424
setSelectedIndices( ), 425
setSelectedValue( ), 425
setSelectionInterval( ), 425
setSelectionMode( ), 420, 421, 423, 424,
    439, 441, 460
setShowGrid( ), 446
setShowHorizontalLines( ), 446

setShowsRootHandles( ), 465
setShowVerticalLines( ), 446
setSize( ), 366, 367
setStrength( ), 21
setText( ), 377, 379, 387, 400, 412, 413
setTime( ), 105
setUnitIncrement( ), 432
setUserObject( ), 465
setValue( ), 253, 293, 432
setValueAt( ), 455
setValues( ), 432
setVerticalAlignment( ), 376, 378, 405, 410
setVerticalScrollBarPolicy( ), 438
setVerticalTextPosition( ), 382, 400, 405, 410
setViewportBorder( ), 436
setVisible( ), 366, 368
setVisibleAmount( ), 432
setWritable( ), 87
showDocument( ), 246, 278, 281
showStatus( ), 243, 279
shuffle( ) algorithm, 218–220
shutdown( ), 487, 488
SimpleDateFormat class, 117, 123, 137, 147, 150
    formatting symbols, table of, 151
    formatting time and date with patterns
        using the, 150–153
SingleSelectionModel, 467
size( ), 166, 179, 234, 235
sleep( ), 298, 300, 302, 303, 304, 337, 339, 344, 345
sort( ), 14, 16, 19
sort( ) algorithm, 221–223
SortedMap interface, 178, 180, 181, 202, 227
    methods defined by, table of, 180
SortedSet interface, 164, 168, 173, 196–198,
    202–203, 206, 227
    methods defined by, table of, 168
split( ), 7, 8
    to retrieve key/value pairs from a string,
        using, 28–32
    to split a string into pieces, using, 25–28
    to tokenize a string, using, 35, 36, 47
SpringLayout, 373
Stack class, 162, 191, 214
Stack(s)
    Deque to create a, using, 171, 214–218
    last-in, first-out (LIFO), 171, 214
StackTraceElement class, 503
start( ), 34, 243, 245, 256, 258, 297, 298, 300, 302, 303,
    305, 307, 329, 345
startsWith( ), 6, 22
State enumeration, 345
stop( ), 243, 245, 246, 256, 258
    deprecated Thread version of, 323, 328, 345
Stream(s)
    classes, byte, 51, 52–53
    classes, character, 51, 53, 54, 56
    compressed file, 57, 95
    definition of, 50
    with Formatter, using, 140–142
StreamTokenizer class, 36, 47

String class, 5, 6–7, 93, 94
    methods defined by, 6–7
String(s)
    array of. *See* Array of strings
    immutable, 6
    in Java, 6
    key/value pairs from, retrieving, 28–32
    literal, 6
    sorting, 14–21
    splitting, 25–28
    tokenizing. *See* Tokenizing a string
    See also Substring
StringBuffer class, 7–8
StringBuilder class, 8, 118, 120, 140
StringTokenizer class, 36, 47
submit( ), 487, 488
substring( ), 7, 25, 32
Substring(s)
    case-insensitive replacement of a, 22–25
    case-insensitive search for a, 22–25
    regular expression API to match and extract a,
        using the, 32–34
    searching for, 22
suspend( ), 323, 328
Swing
    applets, 242, 244, 257–260, 376
    AWT's relationship to, 361
    desktop application, creating
        a simple, 366–372
    event-driven nature of, 258, 368
    and GUI components. *See* Component(s),
        Swing GUI
    I/O, 366
    overview of, 360–361
    painting and, 269
Swing: A Beginner's Guide, 360
SwingConstants interface, 377
SwingUtilities class, 258, 368
Synchronization, 297, 315–318
    and semaphores, 481–486
    and thread priorities, 344
synchronized, 295, 297, 315, 318, 481
synchronizedCollection( ), 228–231
synchronizedList( ), 231
synchronizedMap( ), 231
synchronizedSet( ), 231
synchronizedSortedMap( ), 231
synchronizedSortedSet( ), 231
Synchronizers, 486
System.out( ), 141, 143, 144, 366

T

Table model events, 447, 449–450
Table, Swing
    column model, 439
    model, 439, 446
    printing a, 445
    sorting data in a, 455
    See also JTable

tableChanged( ), 449
TableColumnModel interface, 439, 448
TableModel interface, 439, 449
TableModelEvent class, 447, 449
TableModelListener interface, 447, 449
Task, scheduling the future execution of a, 506–510
Text field. *See* JTextField
Thread class, 295, 297, 298–299, 329, 336, 337,
    345, 354, 355
    create a thread by extending the, 304–307
    to create a task to be executed at a specific
        time, using the, 510
Thread, states of a
    monitoring the, 344–353
    possible, 297
Thread(s)
    communicate between, 318–322
    create a, extend Thread to, 304–307
    create a, implement Runnable to, 299–304
    definition of, 295, 296
    to end, waiting for a, 311–314
    event-dispatching, 258, 260, 266, 336,
        366, 368, 369
    group, 297, 353–358
    interrupting a, 336–340
    main, 296, 297, 368
    monitor, creating a, 349–353
    names and IDs, using, 307–311
    priority of a, setting and
        obtaining the, 341–344
    returning a value from a, 486–491
    spurious wakeup of a, 320, 322
    suspend, resume, and stop a, 323–328
    synchronizing, 314–318, 481
    user, 297, 328, 329
Thread.sleep( ), 300
ThreadGroup class, 354, 355, 357–358
Throwable class, 502
    methods defined by, table of, 503
Thumb, scroll bar, 427, 428, 429
Time and date, formatting
    using DateFormat, 147–150
    using Formatter, 133–137
    with patterns using SimpleDateFormat,
        150–153
Time stamp, using printf( ) to create a, 145–146
Timer class (java.util version) to schedule a task for
    future execution, using the, 507–510
Timer class (javax.swing version), 266, 510
TimerTask class to schedule a task for future
    execution, using the, 507–510
toArray( ), 166, 187
Toggle (two-state) buttons, 390, 396–400, 401
Token, definition of a, 35
Tokenizing a string, 28, 32
    based on delimiters, 35, 36, 47–48
    based on patterns by using the regular
        expression API, 36–48
toLowerCase( ), 7

Tomcat, 246
    how to use, 254–255
Tool bar, 471
toString( ), 119, 120, 493, 503, 504
toUpperCase( ), 7
Tree, Swing
    nodes, 457, 458–459, 460, 464–466
    selection modes, 460
    See also JTree
treeCollapsed( ), 459
treeExpanded( ), 459
TreeExpansionEvent class, 457, 458, 459
TreeExpansionListener interface, 458, 459
TreeMap class, 183, 184, 204, 209, 234, 235–238
TreeModel, 457, 466
TreeModelEvent class, 457, 459, 460
TreeModelListener interface, 459
TreeNode interface, 457, 458, 466
treeNodesChanged( ), 459–460
ttreeNodesInserted( ), 459–460
treeNodesRemoved( ), 459–460
TreePath, 459, 466
TreeSelectionEvent class, 457, 458, 459
TreeSelectionListener interface, 458, 459
TreeSelectionModel, 457, 460, 466
TreeSet class, 173, 176, 196–201, 202, 205, 221
    versus sorted lists, 223
treeStructureChanged( ), 459–460
TreeWillExpandListener, 459
trim( ), 7, 29
trimToSize( ), 174, 192, 195
try block for error handling, 57, 58
tryAcquire( ), 485
Type safety
    and checked collections. 224
    and generics, 163, 224

U

UI delegate, 361
UnavailableException, 249
Unicode, uppercase and lowercase in, 18
unmodifiableCollection( ), 231–233
unmodifiableList( ), 233
unmodifiableMap( ), 233
unmodifiableSet( ), 233
unmodifiableSortedMap( ), 233
unmodifiableSortedSet( ), 233
UnsupportedOperationException, 164, 165,
    166, 180, 210, 232
update( ), 271
URI class, 86
URL, accessing a resource at a specified, 474–480

URL class, 278, 474, 475
URLConnection class, 474, 476, 479, 480
usePattern( ), 37, 40
User thread, 297

V

valueChanged( ), 421, 422, 424, 447–448, 455, 459
values( ), 179, 234, 235
Vector class, 162, 191, 238, 240, 424, 444
Viewport
    scroll pane, 433, 436
    in a table, scrollable, 440
Virtual machine, 241

W

wait( ), 297, 315, 319, 322, 323, 337, 339,
    344, 345, 481
wakeup( ), 337
WeakHashMap class, 183
Web
    browser and applets, 241, 244, 246
    server and servlets, 241, 246
web.xml file, 254, 255
webapps directory, 254
Whitespace, removing leading and trailing, 29
Window class, 367
WindowConstants interface, 367
write( ), 52, 55, 63, 64, 66, 72, 73, 74, 77, 80,
    81, 95, 96, 101
writeDouble( ), 55, 80, 96, 97
writeExternal( ), 115
writeInt( ), 96, 97
writeObject( ), 110–111
Writer class, 51, 72, 73, 76, 77
    methods defined by, table of, 55

Y

yield( ), 298, 341, 342, 344

Z

ZIP files, 95, 96
    creating, 100–105
    compressing, 105–110
ZIP format, 57, 99, 100
ZipEntry class, 100, 101, 102, 105, 106
ZipException, 57, 101, 102, 106, 110
ZipFile class, 105, 106, 107, 109–110
ZipInputStream class, 99, 105
ZipOutputStream class, 100, 101, 102
ZLIB compression library, 57, 95